Literary Devices

"All Writers Should Know!"

Edited by Paul F. Kisak

Contents

Chapter 1

List of narrative techniques

A **narrative technique** (also known, more narrowly for literary fictional narratives, as a **literary technique**, **literary device**, or **fictional device**) is any of several specific methods the creator of a narrative uses to convey what they want[*][1] —in other words, a strategy used in the making of a narrative to relay information to the audience and, particularly, to "develop" the narrative, usually in order to make it more complete, complicated, or interesting. Literary techniques are distinguished from literary elements, which exist inherently in works of writing.

1.1 Narrative techniques pertaining to setting

1.2 Narrative techniques pertaining to plots

1.3 Narrative techniques pertaining to perspective

1.4 Narrative techniques pertaining to style

See also: Figure of speech

1.5 Narrative techniques pertaining to theme

1.6 Narrative techniques pertaining to character

1.7 Notes

[1] Orehovec, Barbara (2003). *Revisiting the Reading Workshop: A Complete Guide to Organizing and Managing an Effective Reading Workshop That Builds Independent, Strategic Readers* (illustrated ed.). Scholastic Inc. p. 89. ISBN 0439444047.

[2] http://beyondthemargins.com/2010/05/do-you-defamiliarize-2/

[3] Fiske, Robert Hartwell (1 November 2011). *Robert Hartwell Fiske's Dictionary of Unendurable English: A Compendium of Mistakes in Grammar, Usage, and Spelling with commentary on lexicographers and linguists.* Scribner. p. 71. ISBN 978-1-4516-5134-8.

[4] Abrams, Meyer Howard; Harpham, Geoffrey Galt (2009). *A Glossary of Literary Terms*. Cengage Learning. p. 24. ISBN 978-1-4130-3390-8.

[5] High School Analogies

[6] Graham Allen (2 June 2004). *Roland Barthes*. Routledge. p. 29. ISBN 1-134-50341-5.

[7] Heath, Peter (May 1994), "Reviewed work(s): *Story-Telling Techniques in the Arabian Nights* by David Pinault", *International Journal of Middle East Studies* (Cambridge University Press) **26** (2): 358–360, doi:10.1017/s0020743800060633

[8] Heath (1994) p.360

Chapter 2

Backstory

This article is about the literary device. For "back-stories" of consumer goods, see Back-story (production).

A **backstory**, **background story**, **back-story** or **background** is a set of events invented for a plot, presented as preceding and leading up to that plot. It is a literary device of a narrative history all chronologically earlier than the narrative of primary interest.

It is the history of characters and other elements that underlie the situation existing at the main narrative's start. Even a purely historical work selectively reveals backstory to the audience.[1][2]

2.1 Usage

As a literary device backstory is often employed to lend depth or believability to the main story. The usefulness of having a dramatic revelation was recognized by Aristotle, in *Poetics*.

Backstories are usually revealed, partially or in full, chronologically or otherwise, as the main narrative unfolds. However, a story creator may also create portions of a backstory or even an entire backstory that is solely for their own use.[3]

Backstory may be revealed by various means, including flashbacks, dialogue, direct narration, summary, recollection, and exposition. The original Star Wars movie and its first two sequels are examples of a work with a preconceived backstory, which was later released as the "prequel" second set of three movies.

2.2 Recollection

Recollection is the fiction-writing mode whereby a character calls something to mind, or remembers it. A character's memory plays a role for conveying backstory, as it allows a fiction-writer to bring forth information from earlier in the story or from before the beginning of the story. Although recollection is not widely recognized as a distinct fiction-writing mode, recollection is commonly used by authors of fiction.

For example, Orson Scott Card observes that "If it's a memory the character could have called to mind at any point, having her think about it just in time to make a key decision may seem like an implausible coincidence . . . ." Furthermore, "If the memory is going to prompt a present decision, then the memory in turn must have been prompted by a recent event." [4]

2.3   Shared universe

In a shared universe more than one author may shape the same backstory. The later creation of a backstory that conflicts with a previously written main story may require the adjustment device known as retroactive continuity, informally known as "retcon".

2.4   See also

- Prequel
- Racconto
- Characterization
- Origin story

2.5   References

[1] Backstory at Merriam Webster online

[2] Backstory at Dictionary.com

[3] Backstory: The Importance of What Isn't Told

[4] Card, Orson Scott (1988), "Character & Viewpoint", p. 113. Cincinnati, OH: Writer's Digest Books. ISBN 0-89879-307-6.

Chapter 3

Cliffhanger

For other uses, see Cliffhanger (disambiguation).
"To be continued" redirects here. For other uses, see To Be Continued (disambiguation).

A **cliffhanger** or **cliffhanger ending** is a plot device in fiction which features a main character in a precarious or difficult dilemma, or confronted with a shocking revelation at the end of an episode of serialized fiction. A cliffhanger is hoped to ensure the audience will return to see how the characters resolve the dilemma.

Some serials end with the caveat "To Be Continued..." or "The End?" In movie serials and television series the following episode sometimes begins with a recap sequence (e.g., "Previously on *L. A. Law*").

3.1   History

An early example of a cliffhanger is found in Homer's epic poem the *Odyssey*. At the end of Book 4, The Suitors, the villains are setting an ambush for Telemachus, Odysseus' son; the story then moves on to Odysseus' own adventures, and much of the narrative passes before readers can learn Telemachus' fate.

A cliffhanger is a central theme and framing device of the collection of stories known as the *One Thousand and One Nights*, wherein the queen Scheherazade, who is facing a morning execution on the orders of her husband, King Shahryar, devises the solution of telling him a story but leaving it at a cliffhanger, thus forcing the king to postpone her execution to hear the rest of the tale. At the time, newspapers published novels in a serial format with one chapter appearing every month. To ensure continued interest in the story, many authors employed different techniques.

Wilkie Collins is famous for saying about the technique: "Make 'em cry, make 'em laugh, make 'em wait – exactly in that order." He is famous for the Sensation Novel, which relied heavily upon the cliffhanger. Examples of his endings include: "The next witnesses called were witnesses concerned with the question that now followed--the obscure and terrible question: Who Poisoned Her?" (*The Law and the Lady*) "Why are we to stop her, sir? What has she done?" "Done! She has escaped from my Asylum. Don't forget; a woman in white. Drive on." (*The Woman in White*) "You can marry me privately today," she answered. "Listen--and I will tell you how!" (*Man and Wife*)"

This anticipation and conversation-inducing authorial technique would often be very contrived as the only purpose was to maintain interest in the monthly serial. Therefore, these were regularly removed from the plot when the serial was published as a full novel. The cliff-hanger migrated to film and is best known from the popular silent film series *The Perils of Pauline* (1914), shown in weekly installments and featuring Pearl White as the title character, a perpetual damsel in distress who was menaced by assorted villains, with each installment ending with her placed in a situation that looked sure to result in her imminent death – to escape at the beginning of the next installment only to get into fresh danger at its end. Specifically, an episode filmed around the New Jersey Palisades ended with her literally left hanging over a cliff and seemingly about to fall.*[1] A history of the cliffhanger and important stages of serial narration was written by Vincent Fröhlich in German.

3.2 Serial media

Cliffhangers were especially popular in 1920s and 1930s serials when movie theaters filled the cultural niche now primarily occupied by television. Cliffhangers are often used in television series, especially soap operas that end each episode on a cliffhanger. Prior to the early 1980s, season-ending cliffhangers were rare on U.S. television. The first such season-ender on U.S. TV was in the comedy send-up of soap operas *Soap* in 1978. Several Australian soap operas, which went off air over summer, such as *Number 96*, *The Restless Years*, and *Prisoner*, ended each year with major and much publicized catastrophe, such as a character being shot in the final seconds of the year's closing episode.

Cliffhangers were rare on American television before 1980, as television networks preferred the flexibility of airing episodes in any order. The phenomenal success of the 1980 "Who shot J. R.?" third season-ending cliffhanger of *Dallas*, and the "Who Done It" fourth-season episode that finally solved the mystery, contributed to the cliffhanger becoming a common storytelling device on television.*[2] Another notable cliffhanger was the "Moldavian Massacre" on *Dynasty* in 1985, which fueled speculation throughout the summer months regarding who lived or died when almost all the characters attended a wedding in the country of Moldavia, only to have revolutionaries topple the government and machine-gun the entire wedding party.

On British TV, cliffhangers had been used regularly since the 1960s (and, to lesser extent 70s and 80s), such as in the hit BBC1 science fiction show *Doctor Who*.

The two main ways for cliffhangers to keep readers/viewers coming back is to either involve characters in a suspenseful, possibly life-threatening situation, or to feature a sudden shocking revelation. The 2003 Season Finale of *Home and Away* features an example of both a shock cliffhanger (in the revelation that Angie Russell was Tasha Andrews' mother) and a suspense cliffhanger (the Sutherland family trapped in a mine shaft).

Cliffhangers are also used to leave open the possibility of a character being killed off due to the actor not continuing to play the role.

Cliffhangers are also sometimes deliberately inserted by writers who are uncertain whether a new series or season will be commissioned, in the hope that viewers will demand to know how the situation is resolved. Such was the case with the second season of *Twin Peaks*, which ended in a cliffhanger similar to the first season with a high degree of uncertainty about the fate of the protagonist, but the cliffhanger could not save the show from being canceled, resulting in the unresolved ending. Another notable example of this case was the *Sledge Hammer!* season 1 episode "The Spa Who Loved Me", which ended with the city destroyed by a nuclear explosion followed by this caption: "To Be Continued...Next Season?" A second season was eventually signed, but instead of explaining the fate of the characters following the explosion, the season 2 opener took place five years prior to the incident. The cliffhanger has become a genre staple (especially in comics, due to the multi-part storylines becoming the norm instead of self-contained stories). To such a degree, in fact, that series writers no longer feel they have to be immediately resolved, or even referenced, when the next episode is shown---for example, the last episode of the second series of Graham Linehan's *The IT Crowd* ended with a substantial cliffhanger that was not addressed until the third episode of series three,*[3] variously because the writer didn't feel it was "a strong enough opener," *[4] or simply "couldn't be bothered." *[5] The heavily serialized television drama *True Blood* has become notorious for cliffhangers. Not only do the seasons conclude with cliffhangers, but almost every episode finishes at a cliffhanger directly after or during a highly dramatic moment.*[6]

Commercial breaks can be a nuisance to script writers because some sort of incompleteness or minor cliffhanger should be provided before each to stop the viewer from changing channels during the commercial break. Sometimes a series ends with an unintended cliffhanger caused by a very abrupt ending without a satisfactory dénouement, but merely assuming that the viewer will assume that everything sorted itself out.

Sometimes a movie, book, or season of a television show will end with the defeat of the main villain before a second, evidently more powerful villain makes a brief appearance (becoming the villain of the next film). A good example of this is the anime version of *Viewtiful Joe*, which ends with Captain Blue being defeated and returned to normal, and then a large space craft approaching Earth. Pixar's *The Incredibles* spoofed this convention by having a new villain, The Underminer, burst into view from underground at the very end of the movie. The 2009 computer-animated film *Astro Boy* ended with an octopus-like alien hovering over the city and Astro flying to confront it. In 2012, Fox TV series *Glee* gave way to a cliffhanger with its winter finale episode "On My Way" where Quinn Fabray (played by Dianna Agron) is involved in a car accident after responding to a text message while driving.*[7]

3.3 See also

- Back to back film production
- Zeigarnik effect

3.4 References

[1] Verdon, Joan (03/05/2012). "A hike back in time to era of silent film". *The Record*. p. L-6. Check date values in: |date= (help)

[2] Meisler, Andy (1995-05-07). "TELEVISION; When J. R. Was Shot The Cliffhanger Was Born". *The New York Times*. Retrieved June 14, 2012.

[3] "The IT Crowd: Tramps Like Us". Noise to Signal. Retrieved 2012-11-21.

[4] "···and we like tramps! « Why, That\'s Delightful!". Whythatsdelightful.wordpress.com. Retrieved 2012-11-21.

[5] Ben Falk (2007-08-24). "One of the IT Crowd | Manchester Evening News - menmedia.co.uk". Manchester Evening News. Retrieved 2012-11-21.

[6] "'True Blood' Finale Sets Up More Cliffhangers". Buddytv.com. 2009-09-14. Retrieved 2012-11-21.

[7] "'Glee's' winter finale ends in cliffhanger". *CNN*. February 22, 2012.

3.5 Books

- Vincent Fröhlich: Der Cliffhanger und die serielle Narration. Bielefeld: Transcript Verlag, 2015. ISBN 978-3837629767.

3.6 External links

- Word Detective
- Mid-Atlantic Nostalgia Convention Cliffhanger Film Showings

*Poster of the 1914 "Perils of Pauline", which popularized the term **cliffhanger** in the medium of film.*

Chapter 4

Deus ex machina

For other uses, see Deus ex machina (disambiguation).

Deus ex machina (Latin: [ˈdeʊs ɛks ˈmaː.kʰɪ.na]: /ˈdeɪ.əs ɛks ˈmɑːkiːnə/ or /ˈdiːəs ɛks ˈmækinə/;[1] plural: *dei ex machina*) is a calque from Greek ἀπὸ μηχανῆς θεός *(apò mēkhanês theós)*, meaning "god from the machine".[2] The term has evolved to mean a plot device whereby a seemingly unsolvable problem is suddenly and abruptly resolved by the contrived and unexpected intervention of some new event, character, ability or object. Depending on how it is done, it can be intended to move the story forward when the writer has "painted himself into a corner" and sees no other way out, to surprise the audience, to bring the tale to a happy ending, or as a comedic device.

4.1   Origin of the expression

The term was coined from the conventions of Greek tragedy, where a machine is used to bring actors playing gods onto the stage. The machine could be either a crane (*mechane*) used to lower actors from above or a riser that brought actors up through a trapdoor. Preparation to pick up the actors was done behind the *skene*. The idea was introduced by Aeschylus and was used often to resolve the conflict and conclude the drama. Although the device is associated most with Greek tragedy, it also appeared in comedies.[3]

4.1.1   Ancient examples

Aeschylus used the device in his *Eumenides*, but it was with Euripides that it became an established stage machine. More than half of Euripides' extant tragedies employ a *deus ex machina* in their resolution, and some critics claim that Euripides, not Aeschylus, invented it.[4] A frequently cited example is Euripides' *Medea*, in which the *deus ex machina*, a dragon-drawn chariot sent by the sun god, is used to convey his granddaughter Medea, who has just committed murder and infanticide, away from her husband Jason to the safety and civilization of Athens. In *Alcestis*, the eponymous heroine agrees to give up her own life in order to spare the life of her husband, Admetus. At the end, Heracles shows up and seizes Alcestis from Death, restoring her to life and to Admetus.

Aristophanes' play *Thesmophoriazusae* parodies Euripides' frequent use of the crane by making Euripides himself a character in the play and bringing him on stage by way of the *mechane*.

The effect of the device on Greek audiences was a direct and immediate emotional response. Audiences would have a feeling of wonder and astonishment at the appearance of the gods, which would often add to the moral effect of the drama.[5]

4.1.2   Modern theatrical examples

Shakespeare used the device in *As You Like It*, *Pericles, Prince of Tyre*, *Cymbeline* and *The Winter's Tale*.[6] It was also

Deus ex machina *in classical theatre: Euripides'* Medea, *performed in 2009 in Syracuse, Italy.*

used in John Gay's *The Beggar's Opera* where the author uses a character to break the action and rewrite the ending as a reprieve of the hanging of MacHeath. Both in Shakespeare's and Gay's plays the *deus ex machina* happens with breaking the dramatic illusion often in the form of an episodic narrator exposing the play itself and laying bare the author. This is different from the use of the *deus ex machina* in the ancient examples with the ending coming from a participant in the action in the form of a god. It is natural for the gods to be considered participants and not outside sources because of their privileged position and power. It is these attributes that allow the Greek gods to believably wrap up and solve the series of events.[7]

During the politically turbulent 17th and 18th centuries, the *deus ex machina* was sometimes used to make a controversial thesis more palatable to the powers of the day. For example, in the final scene of Molière's *Tartuffe* the heroes are saved from a terrible fate by an agent of the compassionate, all-seeing king —the same king that held Molière's career and livelihood in his hands.[8]

4.2 Plot device

Aristotle was the first to use *deus ex machina* as a term to describe the technique as a device to resolve the plot of tragedies.[3] It is generally deemed undesirable in writing and often implies a lack of creativity on the part of the author. The reasons for this are that it does not pay due regard to the story's internal logic (although it is sometimes deliberately used to do this) and is often so unlikely that it challenges suspension of disbelief, allowing the author to conclude the story with an unlikely, though perhaps more palatable, ending.[9]

4.2.1 Examples

In the novel *Lord of the Flies* the rescue of the savage children by a passing navy officer (which author William Golding called a "gimmick") is viewed by some critics as a *deus ex machina*. The abrupt ending conveys to the audience the terrible fate which would have afflicted the children (in particular Ralph) if the officer had not arrived at that moment.[10]

J. R. R. Tolkien coined the term *eucatastrophe* to refer to a sudden turn of events that ensures the protagonist does not meet some impending fate. He also referred to the Great Eagles that appear in several places in *The Hobbit* and *The Lord of the Rings* as "a dangerous 'machine'." [11] Some critics have argued that eucatastrophe, and in particular the eagles, exemplify *deus ex machina*. For example, they save Frodo and Sam from certain death on Mount Doom in *The Return of the King*.[12][13] Others contend that the two concepts are not the same, and that eucatastrophe is not merely a convenience, but is an established part of a fictive world in which hope ultimately prevails.[14]

Deus ex machina was also used by Charles Dickens in *Oliver Twist*, when in the very peak of climax, Rose Maylie turns out to be the long-lost sister of Agnes, and therefore Oliver's aunt and she marries her long-time sweetheart Harry, allowing Oliver to live happily with his saviour, Mr. Brownlow.[15]

4.3 Criticism

The *deus ex machina* device has many criticisms attached to it, mainly referring to it as inartistic, too convenient, and overly simplistic. On the other hand, champions of the device say that it opens up ideological and artistic possibilities.[16]

4.3.1 Ancient criticism

Antiphanes was one of the device's earliest critics. Antiphanes believed that the use of the "deus ex machina" was a sign that the playwright was unable to properly manage the complications of his plot.

> when they don't know what to say
> and have completely given up on the play
> just like a finger they lift the machine

and the spectators are satisfied.[*][17]

Another critical reference to the device can be found in Plato's dialogue *Cratylus*, 425d, though it is made in the context of an argument unrelated to drama.

Aristotle criticized the device in his *Poetics*, where he argued that the resolution of a plot must arise internally, following from previous action of the play:[*][18]

> In the characters too, exactly as in the structure of the incidents, [the poet] ought always to seek what is either necessary or probable, so that it is either necessary or probable that a person of such-and-such a sort say or do things of the same sort, and it is either necessary or probable that this [incident] happen after that one. It is obvious that the solutions of plots too should come about as a result of the plot itself, and not from a contrivance, as in the *Medea* and in the passage about sailing home in the *Iliad*. A contrivance must be used for matters outside the drama —either previous events which are beyond human knowledge, or later ones that need to be foretold or announced. For we grant that the gods can see everything. There should be nothing improbable in the incidents; otherwise, it should be outside the tragedy, e.g., that in Sophocles' *Oedipus*.
> —*Poetics*, (1454a33–1454b9)

Aristotle praised Euripides, however, for generally ending his plays with bad fortune, which he viewed as correct in tragedy, and somewhat excused the intervention of a deity by suggesting that "astonishment" should be sought in tragic drama:[*][19]

> Irrationalities should be referred to what people say: that is one solution, and also sometimes that it is not irrational, since it is probable that improbable things will happen.

Such a device was referred to by Horace in his *Ars Poetica* (lines 191–2), where he instructs poets that they should never resort to a "god from the machine" to resolve their plots "unless a difficulty worthy of a god's unraveling should happen" [*nec deus intersit, nisi dignus uindice nodus inciderit; nec quarta loqui persona laboret*].[*][20]

4.3.2   Modern criticism

Following Aristotle, Renaissance critics continued to view the *deus ex machina* as an inept plot device, although it continued to be employed by Renaissance dramatists.

Towards the end of the 19th century, Friedrich Nietzsche criticized Euripides for making tragedy an optimistic genre via use of the device, and was highly skeptical of the "Greek cheerfulness", prompting what he viewed as the plays' "blissful delight in life".[*][21] The *deus ex machina* as Nietzsche saw it was symptomatic of Socratic culture, which valued knowledge over Dionysiac music and ultimately caused the death of tragedy:[*][22]

> But the new non-Dionysiac spirit is most clearly apparent in the *endings* of the new dramas. At the end of the old tragedies there was a sense of metaphysical conciliation without which it is impossible to imagine our taking delight in tragedy; perhaps the conciliatory tones from another world echo most purely in *Oedipus at Colonus*. Now, once tragedy had lost the genius of music, tragedy in the strictest sense was dead: for where was that metaphysical consolation now to be found? Hence an earthly resolution for tragic dissonance was sought; the hero, having been adequately tormented by fate, won his well-earned reward in a stately marriage and tokens of divine honour. The hero had become a gladiator, granted freedom once he had been satisfactorily flayed and scarred. Metaphysical consolation had been ousted by the *deus ex machina*.
> —Friedrich Nietzsche

Nietzsche argued that the *deus ex machina* creates a false sense of consolation that ought not to be sought in phenomena.[*][23] His denigration of the plot device has prevailed in critical opinion.

In Arthur Woollgar Verrall's publication, *Euripides the Rationalist* (1895), he surveyed and recorded other late 19th century responses to the device. He recorded that some of the critical responses to the term referred to it as 'burlesque', 'coup de théâtre', and 'catastrophe'. Verrall notes that critics have a dismissive response to authors who deploy the device in their writings. He comes to the conclusion that critics feel that the *deus ex machina* is evidence of the author's attempt to ruin the whole of his work and prevent anyone from putting any importance on his work.[*][17]

However, other scholars have looked at Euripides' use of *deus ex machina* and described its use as an integral part of the plot designed for a specific purpose. Often Euripides' plays would begin with gods, so it is argued that it would be natural for the gods to finish the action. The conflict throughout Euripides' plays would be caused by the meddling of the gods and therefore would make sense to both the playwright and the audience of the time that the gods would resolve all conflict that they began.[*][24] Half of Euripides' eighteen extant plays end with the use of *deus ex machina*, therefore it was not simply a device to relieve the playwright of the embarrassment of a confusing plot ending. This device enabled him to bring about a natural and more dignified dramatic and tragic ending.[*][25]

Other champions of the device believe that it can be a spectacular agent of subversion. It can be used to undercut generic conventions and challenge cultural assumptions and the privileged role of tragedy as a literary/theatrical model.[*][16]

Some 20th-century revisionist criticism suggests that *deus ex machina* cannot be viewed in these simplified terms, and contends that the device allows mortals to "probe" their relationship with the divine.[*][26] Rush Rehm in particular cites examples of Greek tragedy in which the *deus ex machina* serves to complicate the lives and attitudes of characters confronted by the deity while simultaneously bringing the drama home to its audience.[*][26] Sometimes, the unlikeliness of the *deus ex machina* plot device is employed deliberately. For example, comic effect is created in a scene in *Monty Python's Life of Brian* when Brian, who lives in Judea at the time of Christ, is saved from a high fall by a passing alien space ship.[*][27]

4.4 Notes

[1] *Random House Dictionary*

[2] One of the earliest occurrences of the phrase is in fragment 227 of Menander: ἀπὸ μηχανῆς θεὸς [ἡμιν] ἐπεφάνης "You are by your epiphany a veritable god from the machine", as quoted in *The Woman Possessed with a Divinity*, as translated in *Menander: The Principal Fragments* (1921) by Francis Greenleaf Allinson.

[3] Chondros, Thomas G.; Milidonis, Kypros; Vitzilaios, George; Vaitsis, John (September 2013). ""Deus-Ex-Machina" reconstruction in the Athens theater of Dionysus". *Mechanism and Machine Theory* **67**: 172–191. doi:10.1016/j.mechmachtheory.2013.04.010.

[4] Rehm (1992, 72) and Walton (1984, 51).

[5] Cunningham, Maurice P. (July 1954). "Medea ΑΠΟ ΜΗΧΑΝΗΣ". *Classical Philology* **19** (3): 151–160.

[6] Rehm (1992, 70).

[7] Dunn, Francis M (1996). *Tragedy's End : Closure and Innovation in Euripidean Drama: Closure and Innovation in Euripidean Drama*. New York, New York: Oxford University Press.

[8] "Tartuffe: Novel Guide". 2003. Retrieved November 2, 2011.

[9] Dr. L. Kip Wheeler. "Literary Terms and Definitions: D". Retrieved 2008-07-26.

[10] Friedman, Lawrence S. (2008). "Grief, grief, grief: *Lord of the Flies*". In Bloom, Harold. *William Golding's Lord of the Flies*. Infobase Publishing. pp. 67–68.

[11] J. R. R. Tolkien, letter 210 as quoted here

[12] *Tolkien's Art: A Mythology for England* by Jane Chance (2001), p. 179

[13] The Greenwood Encyclopedia of Science Fiction and Fantasy: Themes, Works, and Wonders, Volume 1, p. 195

[14] Mallinson, Jeffrey (2011). "Eucatastrophe". In Mazur, Eric Michael. *Encyclopedia of Religion and Film*. ABC-CLIO. p. 175.

[15] Abrams, MH, ed. (1993). *A Glossary of Literary Terms*. Harcourt Brace & Company, USA. pp. 44–45. Retrieved 2013-12-31.

[16] Breton, Rob (Summer 2005). "Ghosts in the Machina: Plotting in Chartist and Working-Class Fiction". *Victorian Studies* **47** (4): 557–575. doi:10.1353/vic.2006.0003.

[17] Handley, Miriam. "Shaw's response to the deus ex machina: From The Quintessence of Ibsenism to Heartbreak House". January Conference 1999 THEATRE : ANCIENT & MODERN.

[18] Janko (1987, 20)

[19] *Poetics* 11.5, Penguin (1996, 45).

[20] *Ars Poetica* by Horace

[21] Nietzsche (2003, 85).

[22] Nietzsche (2003, 84–86).

[23] Nietzsche (2003, 80).

[24] Abel, D. Herbert (December 1954). "Euripides' Deus ex Machina: Fault or Excellence". *The Classical Journal* **50** (3): 127–130.

[25] Flickinger, Roy Caston (1926). *The Greek Theatre and its Drama*. Chicago, Illinois: The University of Chicago Press.

[26] Rehm (1992, 71).

[27] James Berardinelli, James. "Review: Life of Brian". Reelviews Movie Reviews. 2003

4.5 References

- Bushnell, Rebecca ed. 2005. *A Companion to Tragedy*. Malden, MA and Oxford: Blackwell Publishing. ISBN 1-4051-0735-9.

- Heath, Malcolm, trans. 1996. *Poetics*. By Aristotle. Penguin: London. ISBN 978-0-14-044636-4.

- Janko, Richard, trans. 1987. *Poetics with Tractatus Coislinianus, Reconstruction of Poetics II and the Fragments of the On Poets*. By Aristotle. Cambridge: Hackett. ISBN 0-87220-033-7.

- Mastronarde, Donald, 1990. *Actors on High: The Skene roof, the Crane and the Gods in Attic Drama*. Classical Antiquity, Vol 9, October 1990, pp 247–294. University of California.

- Rehm, Rush, 1992. *Greek Tragic Theatre*. Routledge, London. ISBN 0-415-04831-1.

- Tanner, Michael ed. 2003. *The Birth of Tragedy*. By Nietzsche, Friedrich. Penguin: London. ISBN 978-0-14-043339-5.

- Taplin, Oliver, 1978. *Greek Tragedy in Action*. Methuen, London. ISBN 0-416-71700-4.

- Walton, J Michael, trans. 2000. *Euripides: Medea*. Methuen, London. ISBN 0-413-75280-1.

4.6 External links

- The dictionary definition of deus ex machina at Wiktionary

- "Deus ex Machina". *New International Encyclopedia*. 1905.

Chapter 5

Eucatastrophe

The prince arrives to break the spell which has kept Sleeping Beauty and her kingdom asleep for 100 years. A classic and well-known use of eucatastrophe. Illustration by Gustave Doré

Eucatastrophe is a term coined by J. R. R. Tolkien which refers to the sudden turn of events at the end of a story which ensures that the protagonist does not meet some terrible, impending, and very plausible doom.[*][1] Tolkien formed the word by affixing the Greek prefix *eu*, meaning *good*, to *catastrophe*, the word traditionally used in classically inspired literary criticism to refer to the "unraveling" or conclusion of a drama's plot. For Tolkien, the term appears to have had a thematic meaning that went beyond its literal etymological meaning in terms of form. In his definition as outlined in his 1947 essay "On Fairy-Stories",[2] eucatastrophe is a fundamental part of his conception of mythopoeia. Though Tolkien's interest is in myth, it is also connected to the gospel; Tolkien calls the Incarnation the eucatastrophe of "human history" and the Resurrection the eucatastrophe of the Incarnation.[3]

Eucatastrophe has been labelled as a form of deus ex machina, due to both sharing an impossible problem being suddenly resolved.[4][5] However, differences between the two have also been noted, such as its inherent connection to an optimistic view on the unfolding of events in the narrative of the world.[6] Eucatastrophe can also occur without the use of a deus ex machina.[7]

5.1   Examples in Tolkien's work

The climax of The Lord of The Rings, *as portrayed by Ted Nasmith.*

Eucatastrophe has been observed in the climax of *The Lord of the Rings*. Though victory seems assured for Sauron, the One Ring is permanently destroyed as a result of Gollum's attack on Frodo at Mount Doom.[8]

Another example of eucatastrophe is the recurring role of the eagles as unexpected rescuers throughout Tolkien's writing. Tolkien described Bilbo's "'eucatastrophic' emotion" at the eagles appearance in *The Hobbit* as one of the key moments of the book.[9]

5.2 See also

- Happy ending
- Peripeteia

5.3 References

5.3.1 Inline citations

[1] Mazur 2011, p. 174

[2] Tolkien 1990, pp. 109–161

[3] Tolkien 1990, p. 156

[4] Westfahl, Gary (2005). *The Greenwood Encyclopedia of Science Fiction and Fantasy: Themes, Works, and Wonders* **1**. Greenwood Publishing Group. p. 195. ISBN 978-0-313-32951-7.

[5] Hart, Trevor (2013). *Between the Image and the Word*. Ashgate Publishing, Ltd. ISBN 978-1-4724-1370-3. Retrieved 7 September 2014.

[6] Mazur 2011, p. 175

[7] Magill, Frank (1983). *Survey of modern fantasy literature* (First ed.). Salem Press. p. 2065. ISBN 978-0893564506. Retrieved 8 September 2014.

[8] Solopova, Elizabeth (2009), *Languages, Myths and History: An Introduction to the Linguistic and Literary Background of J.R.R. Tolkien's Fiction*, New York City: North Landing Books, p. 29, ISBN 0-9816607-1-1

[9] Carpenter, Humphrey, ed. (1981), *The Letters of J. R. R. Tolkien*, Boston: Houghton Mifflin, Letter No. 89, ISBN 0-395-31555-7

5.3.2 General references

- Mazur, Eric Michael, ed. (2011). *Encyclopedia of Religion and Film*. ABC-CLIO. ISBN 0313013985.

- Tolkien, J.R.R. (1990). *The Monsters and the Critics and Other Essays*. London: HarperCollinsPublishers. ISBN 0-261-10263-X.

Chapter 6

Flashback (narrative)

This article is about the type of scene in narratives. For other uses, see Flashback (disambiguation).

A **flashback** is an interjected scene that takes the narrative back in time from the current point in the story.[1] Flashbacks are often used to recount events that happened before the story's primary sequence of events to fill in crucial backstory.[2] In the opposite direction, a flashforward (or prolepsis) reveals events that will occur in the future.[3] Both flashback and flashforward are used to create suspense in a story, develop a character, or add structure to the narrative. In literature, **internal analepsis** is a flashback to an earlier point in the narrative; **external analepsis** is a flashback to a time before the narrative started.[4]

In movies and television, several camera techniques and special effects have evolved to alert the viewer that the action shown is a flashback or flashforward; for example, the edges of the picture may be deliberately blurred, photography may be jarring or choppy, or unusual coloration or sepia tone, or monochrome when most of the story is in full color, may be used.

6.1 Notable examples

6.1.1 Literature

An early example of analepsis is in the *Ramayana* and *Mahabharata*, where the main story is narrated through a frame story set at a later time. Another ancient example occurs in the *Odyssey*, in which the main action is told in flashback by Odysseus to a listener.

Another early use of this device in a murder mystery was in "The Three Apples", an *Arabian Nights* tale. The story begins with the discovery of a young woman's dead body. After the murderer later reveals himself, he narrates his reasons for the murder in a series of flashbacks leading up to the discovery of her dead body at the beginning of the story.[5] Flashbacks are also employed in several other *Arabian Nights* tales such as "Sinbad the Sailor" and "The City of Brass".

Analepsis was used extensively by author Ford Madox Ford, and by poet, author, historian and mythologist Robert Graves.

The 1927 book *The Bridge of San Luis Rey* by Thornton Wilder is the progenitor of the modern disaster epic in literature and film-making, where a single disaster intertwines the victims, whose lives are then explored by means of flashbacks of events leading up to the disaster.

Analepsis is also used in *Night* by Elie Wiesel.

If flashbacks are extensive and in chronological order, one can say that these form the present of the story, while the rest of the story consists of flash forwards. If flashbacks are presented in non-chronological order, the time at which the story takes place can be ambiguous: An example of such an occurrence is in *Slaughterhouse-Five* where the narrative jumps back and forth in time, so there is no actual present time line.

The *Harry Potter* series employs a magical device called a Pensieve, which changes the nature of flashbacks from a mere narrative device to an event directly experienced by the characters, which are thus able to provide commentary.*[6]

Os Lusíadas is a story about voyage of Vasco da Gama to India and back. The narration starts when they were arriving Africa but it quickly flashes back to the beginning of the story which is when they were leaving Portugal.*[7]*[8]

6.1.2 Film

The creator of the flashback technique in cinema was D.W. Griffith.

Flashbacks were first employed during the sound era in Rouben Mamoulian's 1931 film *City Streets*, but were rare until about 1939 when, in William Wyler's *Wuthering Heights* as in Emily Brontë's original novel, the housekeeper Ellen narrates the main story to overnight visitor Mr. Lockwood, who has witnessed Heathcliff's frantic pursuit of what is apparently a ghost. More famously, also in 1939, Marcel Carne's movie *Le jour se lève* is told almost entirely through flashback: the story starts with the murder of a man in a hotel. While the murderer, played by Jean Gabin, is surrounded by the police, several flashbacks tell the story of why he killed the man at the beginning of the movie.

One of the most famous examples of non-chronological flashback is in the Orson Welles' film *Citizen Kane* (1941). The protagonist, Charles Foster Kane, dies at the beginning, uttering the word *Rosebud*. The remainder of the film is framed by a reporter's interviewing Kane's friends and associates, in a futile effort to discover what the word meant to Kane. As the interviews proceed, pieces of Kane's life unfold in flashback, but not always chronologically. Welles' use of such unconventional flashbacks was thought to have been influenced by William K. Howard's *The Power and the Glory*, written by Preston Sturges and released in 1933.

Though usually used to clarify plot or backstory, flashbacks can also act as an unreliable narrator. Alfred Hitchcock's *Stage Fright* from 1950 notoriously featured a flashback that did not tell the truth but dramatized a lie from a witness. The multiple and contradictory staged reconstructions of a crime in Errol Morris's 1988 documentary *The Thin Blue Line* are presented as flashbacks based on divergent testimony. Akira Kurosawa's 1950 *Rashomon* does this in the most celebrated fictional use of contested multiple testimonies.

Sometimes a flashback is inserted into a film even though there was none in the original source from which the film was adapted. The 1956 film version of Rodgers and Hammerstein's stage musical *Carousel* used a flashback device which somewhat takes the impact away from a very dramatic plot development later in the film. This was done because the plot of *Carousel* was then considered unusually strong for a film musical. In film version of *Camelot* (1967), according to Alan Jay Lerner, a flashback was added not to soften the blow of a later plot development but because the stage show had been criticized for shifting too abruptly in tone from near-comedy to tragedy.

A good example of both flashback and flashforward is the first scene of *La jetée* (1962). As we learn a few minutes later, what we are seeing in that scene is a flashback to the past, since the present of the film's diegesis is a time directly following World War III. However, as we learn at the very end of the film, that scene also doubles as a prolepsis, since the dying man the boy is seeing is, in fact, himself. In other words, he is proleptically seeing his own death. We thus have an analepsis and prolepsis in the very same scene.

Occasionally, a story may contain a flashback within a flashback, with the earliest known example appearing in Jacques Feyder's *L'Atlantide*. In John Ford's *The Man Who Shot Liberty Valance* (1962), the main action of the film is told in flashback, with the scene of Liberty Valance's murder occurring as a flashback within that flashback. Other examples that contains flashbacks within flashbacks are the 1968 Japanese film *Lone Wolf Isazo*[9] and 2004's *The Phantom of the Opera*, where almost the entire film (set in 1870) is told as a flashback from 1919 (in black-and-white) and contains other flashbacks; for example, Madame Giry rescuing the Phantom from a freak show. An extremely convoluted story may contain flashbacks within flashbacks within flashbacks, as in *Six Degrees of Separation*, *Passage to Marseille*, and *The Locket*. This technique is a hallmark of Kannada movie director Upendra whose futuristic flick *Super* (2010) is set in 2030 and contains multiple flashbacks ranging from 2010 to 2015 depicting a utopian India.

Satyajit Ray experimented with flashbacks in *The Adversary* (1972), pioneering the technique of photo-negative flashbacks.*[10]

6.1.3   Television

The television series *Kung Fu*, *Psych*, *How I Met Your Mother*, *Grounded for Life* and *I Didn't Do It* use flashbacks in every episode. Flashbacks were also a predominant feature of the television show *Lost*. The television sitcom *The Odd Couple* made use of flashbacks when certain episodes dealt with Felix (Tony Randall) and Oscar's (Jack Klugman) earlier lives. In one of those episodes, Murray the Cop (Al Molinaro) even says, "Hey! This is just like a flashback scene in a movie. You know when the screen gets all wavy..." The series *Murder, She Wrote* also used flashbacks every week, revealing the culprit's actions. Lead character Jessica Fletcher would then explain how the victim died and why.

6.2   See also

- 1916 in film

6.3   References

[1] Pavis, Shantz (1998). *Dictionary of the Theatre: Terms, Concepts, and Analysis.* University of Toronto Press. p. 151. ISBN 0802081630.

[2] Kenny (2004). *Teaching Tv Production in a Digital World: Integrating Media Literacy.* Libraries Unltd Incorporated. p. 163. ISBN 1591581990.

[3] http://www.thefreedictionary.com/flash-forward

[4] Jung (2010). *Narrating Violence in Post-9/11 Action Cinema: Terrorist Narratives, Cinematic Narration, and Referentiality.* VS Verlag für Sozialwissenschaften. p. 67. ISBN 3531926020.

[5] Pinault, David (1992), *Story-Telling Techniques in the Arabian Nights*, Brill Publishers, p. 94, ISBN 90-04-09530-6

[6] Pensieve Flashback @ TV Tropes wiki

[7] Os Lusíadas

[8] The physical book itself

[9] "The Lone Stalker A.K.A. Lone Wolf Isazo". Japan Society. Retrieved 2011-03-16.

[10] Nick Pinkerton (14 April 2009). "First Light: Satyajit Ray From the Apu Trilogy to the Calcutta Trilogy". *The Village Voice.* Retrieved 2009-07-09.

- Pattison, Darcy. Writing Flashbacks. When and why to include a flashback and tips on writing a flashback.

Chapter 7

Flashforward

This article is about the narrative device. For other uses, see Flashforward (disambiguation).

A **flashforward** (also spelled **flash-forward**; also called a **prolepsis**) is a scene that takes the narrative forward in time from the current point of the story in literature, film, television and other media.*[1] Flashforwards are often used to represent events expected, projected, or imagined to occur in the future. They may also reveal significant parts of the story that have not yet occurred, but soon will in greater detail. It is primarily a postmodern narrative device. In the opposite direction, a flashback (or analepsis) reveals events that have occurred in the past.

7.1 Examples in literature

An early example of prolepsis which predates the postmodern period is Charles Dickens' novel *A Christmas Carol*, in which the protagonist Ebenezer Scrooge is taken forward through time to visit his funeral. The subsequent events of the story imply that this future will be averted by this foreknowlege.

Terry Brooks' *Word & Void* series features a protagonist who, when he sleeps, moves forwards and backwards through time to before and after a great cataclysm. This is both analepsis and prolepsis.

Muriel Spark makes extensive use of prolepsis in her novel *The Prime of Miss Jean Brodie*.

7.2 Examples in television

Every season of *Damages* makes an extensive use of flashforwards, revealing the outcome of the season to the viewer. The whole season then revolves around discovering the circumstances that led to this outcome. For instance, the first season starts with a flashforward of the protagonist, Ellen Parsons, running in the streets of New York, covered in blood. 6 months earlier, she was only a naive young woman who had just become a lawyer in the firm of a powerful attorney, Patty Hewes. What led Ellen to the situation presented in the flashforwards is revealed little by little throughout the season. Furthermore, the series is known for its misleading use of flashforwards, which are often examples of the red herring device.

After making extensive use of flashbacks, the TV series *Lost* used flashforwards throughout the show's later seasons (the first use of this was in the third season finale; what appeared to be a flashback was revealed at the end to be a flashforward). Another episode featured what appeared to be flashforwards involving Jin and his wife Sun, showing Jin to have safely returned home and awaiting the birth of his baby, but in the end, it was revealed that Jin's flashes were flashbacks and Sun's were flashforwards. In season four, most of the episodes contained flashforwards, although flashbacks were still used.

The series finale of *Star Trek: Voyager*, "Endgame", uses a flashforward at the start to depict a future in which the U.S.S.

Voyager has returned home by conventional methods, prompting the ship's captain to go back in time with more advanced technology to get her crew home sooner.

The U.S. sci-fi TV series *FlashForward*, which revolves around the entire planet losing consciousness for 137 seconds, during which almost everyone experiences a glimpse of events 6 months in the future.*[2]

British soap opera *Hollyoaks* flashed forward six months in May 2010 for a special episode.*[3]

The last episode of *Six Feet Under* has an extensive flashforward depicting the deaths of all the central characters as they unfold.

Breaking Bad uses flashforwards throughout its second season showing a mystery regarding debris and corpses in Walter White's house and neighborhood, revealed to be the result of two planes crashing overhead. The first half of the fifth season begins with a flashforward one year into the future where White is fifty-two years old, and the second half begins with a continuation of the story, where White returns to his abandoned home. The plot of these flashforwards is resumed in the series finale.

7.3   Examples in film

Midway through the film *They Shoot Horses, Don't They?*, there is an abrupt flashforward when Robert, the character played by Michael Sarrazin, is seen being thrust into a jail cell by a police officer, even though he has done nothing to provoke such treatment. The audience is notified, later in the story, that Sarrazin's character would have indeed made choices that warrant his arrest.

7.4   See also

- Foreshadowing

- Literary technique

- Self-fulfilling prophecy

7.5   References

[1] http://www.thefreedictionary.com/flash-forward

[2] http://www.imdb.com/title/tt1441135

[3] Green, Kris (15 December 2009). "Hollyoaks to air flashforward episode" . Digital Spy. Retrieved 2009-12-15.

7.6   External links

- The dictionary definition of flashforward at Wiktionary

Chapter 8

Foreshadowing

Foreshadowing or **guessing ahead** is a literary device by which an author hints what is to come.[*][1] It is used to avoid disappointment. It is also sometimes used to arouse the reader.[*][2][*][3]

A hint that is designed to mislead the audience is referred to as a *red herring*. A similar device is the flashforward (also known as prolepsis). However, foreshadowing only hints at a possible outcome within the confinement of a narrative. A flashforward is a scene that takes the narrative forward in time from the current point of the story in literature, film, television, and other media.[*][4][*][5] Foreshadowing is sometimes employed through characters explicitly predicting the future.[*][6]

By analogy to foreshadowing, the literary critic Gary Morson described its opposite, **sideshadowing**.[*][7] Found notably in the epic novels of Leo Tolstoy and Fyodor Dostoyevsky, it is the practice of including scenes that turn out to have no relevance to the plot. This, according to Morson, increases the verisimilitude of the fiction because the audience knows that in real life, unlike in novels, most events are in fact inconsequential. This "sense of structurelessness" invites the audience to "interpret and question the events that actually do come to pass".[*][8]

8.1   See also

- Chekhov's gun

8.2   References

[1] Mogensen (2009). *Along Literary Lines*. Gyldendal. p. 55. ISBN 8702056178.

[2] Author's Craft - "Narrative Elements - Foreshadowing" Retrieved 2013-07-18

[3] Nicola Onyett (30 November 2012). *Philip Allan Literature Guide (for A-Level): A Streetcar Named Desire*. Hodder Education. p. 50. ISBN 978-1-4441-5376-7. Retrieved 18 July 2013.

[4] Ulrike Spierling; Nicolas Szilas (3 December 2008). *Interactive Storytelling: First Joint International Conference on Interactive Digital Storytelling, ICIDS 2008 Erfurt, Germany, November 26-29, 2008, Proceedings*. Springer. p. 156. ISBN 978-3-540-89424-7.

[5] flash-forward - definition of flash-forward by the Free Online Dictionary, Thesaurus and Encyclopedia

[6] Philip Martin, *The Writer's Guide to Fantasy Literature: From Dragon's Lair to Hero's Quest*, p 146, ISBN 0-87116-195-8

[7] Morson, Gary Saul (Autumn 1998). "Sideshadowing and Tempics". *New Literary History* **29** (4): 599–624.

[8] Calixto, Joshua (3 August 2015). "LET'S TALK ABOUT ROSA VAR ATTRE, THE IMPOSSIBLE ROMANCE OF THE WITCHER 3". *Kill Screen*. Retrieved 3 August 2015.

In this Arthur Rackham illustration, the Rhinemaidens warn Siegfried of a curse, foreshadowing the disasters of Götterdämmerung.

Chapter 9

Frame story

A **frame story** (also known as a **frame tale** or **frame narrative**) is a literary technique that sometimes serves as a companion piece to a story within a story, whereby an introductory or main narrative is presented, at least in part, for the purpose of setting the stage either for a more emphasized second narrative or for a set of shorter stories. The frame story leads readers from a first story into another, smaller one (or several ones) within it.

9.1   Origins

Among earliest known frame stories are those preserved on the ancient Egyptian Papyrus Westcar. Other early examples are from first millennium BCE ancient India, when the Sanskrit epics *Mahabharata*, *Ramayana*, Vishnu Sarma's *Panchatantra*, Syntipas's *The Seven Wise Masters*, and the fable collections *Hitopadesha* and *Vikram and The Vampire* were written.[*][1] This form gradually spread west through the centuries and became popular, giving rise to such classic frame tale collections as the *One Thousand and One Nights (Arabian Nights)*, *The Decameron*, and *Canterbury Tales*. This format had flexibility in that various narrators could retain the stories they liked or understood, while dropping ones they didn't and adding new ones they heard from other places. This occurred particularly with *One Thousand and One Nights*, where different versions over the centuries have included different stories.

The use of a frame story in which a single narrative is set in the context of the telling of a story is also a technique with a long history, dating back at least to the beginning section of the *Odyssey*, in which the narrator Odysseus tells of his wandering in the court of King Alcinous.

9.2   A set of stories

This literary device acts as a convenient conceit for the organization of a set of smaller narratives which are either of the devising of the author, or taken from a previous stock of popular tales slightly altered by the author for the purpose of the longer narrative. Sometimes a story within the main narrative can be used to sum up or encapsulate some aspect of the framing story, in which case it is referred to in literary criticism by the French term *mise en abyme*.

A typical example of the frame story is *One Thousand and One Nights*, in which the character Scheherazade narrates a set of fairy tales to the Sultan Shahriyar over many nights. Many of Scheherazade's tales are also frame stories, such as *Tale of Sindbad the Seaman and Sindbad the Landsman*, a collection of adventures related by Sindbad the Seaman to Sindbad the Landsman.

An extensive use of this device is Ovid's *Metamorphoses* where the stories nest several deep, to allow the inclusion of many different tales in one work. Emily Brontë's *Wuthering Heights* uses this literary device to tell the story of Heathcliff and Catherine, along with the subplots. Her sister Anne also uses this device in her epistolary novel *The Tenant of Wildfell Hall*. The main heroine's diary is framed by the narrator's story and letters.

Mary Shelley's novel *Frankenstein* is another good example of a book with multiple framed narratives. In the book, Robert Walton writes letters to his sister describing the story told to him by Victor Frankenstein; Frankenstein's story contains the creature's story; the creature's story even briefly contains the story of a family he had been living among.

Frame stories have also appeared in media forms, such as comic books. Neil Gaiman's comic book series *The Sandman* featured a story arc called *Worlds End* which consisted of Frame Stories, and sometimes even featured stories within stories within stories.

Frame stories are often organized as a gathering of people in one place for the exchange of stories. Each character tells his or her tale, and the frame tale progresses in that manner. Historically famous frame stories include Chaucer's *Canterbury Tales*, about a group of pilgrims who tell stories on their journey to Canterbury; and Boccaccio's *Decameron* about a group of young aristocrats escaping the Black Death to the countryside and spending the time telling stories.

The Return of Rip Van Winkle, painting by John Quidor, 1849

Sometimes only one storyteller exists, and in this case there might be different levels of distance between the reader and author. In this mode, the frame tale can become more fuzzy. In the case of Washington Irving's *Sketch Book*, which contains "The Legend of Sleepy Hollow" and "Rip Van Winkle" among others, the conceit is that the author of the book is not Irving, but a certain gentleman named Crayon. Here the frame includes both the world of the imagined Crayon, his stories, and the possible reader who is assumed to play along and "know" who Crayon is.

Donald Westlake's short story "No Story" is a parody of frame stories, in which a series of narrators start to tell stories, each of which contains a narrator who starts to tell a story, culminating in a narrator who announces that there will be no story. Essentially, it is a frame story without a story to be framed.

9.3 Single story

When there is a single story, the frame story is used for other purposes – chiefly to position the reader's attitude toward the tale. One common one is to draw attention to the narrator's unreliability. By explicitly making the narrator a character within the frame story, the writer distances himself from the narrator; he may also characterize the narrator to cast doubt on his truthfulness. In P. G. Wodehouse's stories of Mr Mulliner, Mulliner is made a fisherman in order to cast doubt on the outrageous stories he tells. The movie *Amadeus* is framed as a story an old Antonio Salieri tells to a young priest, because the movie is based more on stories Salieri told about Mozart than on historical fact.

Another use is a form of procatalepsis, where the writer puts the readers' possible reactions to the story in the characters listening to it. In *The Princess Bride* the frame of a grandfather reading the story to his reluctant grandson puts the cynical reaction a viewer might have to the romantic fairytale into the story in the grandson's persona, and helps defuse it. This is the use when the frame tells a story that lacks a strong narrative hook in its opening; the narrator can engage the reader's interest by telling the story to answer the curiosity of his listeners, or by warning them that the story began in an ordinary seeming way, but they must follow it to understand later actions, thereby identifying the reader's wondering whether the story is worth reading to the listeners'. Such an approach was used by Edith Wharton in her novella Ethan Frome, in which a nameless narrator hears from many characters in the town of Starkfield about the main character Ethan's story.

A specialized form of the frame is a dream vision, where the narrator claims to have gone to sleep, dreamed the events of the story, and then awoken to tell the tale. In medieval Europe, this was a common device, used to indicate that the events included are fictional; Geoffrey Chaucer used it in *The Book of the Duchess*, *The House of Fame*, *Parlement of Foules*, and *The Legend of Good Women* (the last also containing a multi-story frame story within the dream). In modern usage, it is sometimes used in works of fantasy as a means toward suspension of disbelief about the marvels depicted in the story. J.R.R. Tolkien, in his essay "On Fairy-Stories" complained of such devices as unwillingness to treat the genre seriously. Lewis Carroll's *Alice* stories (*Alice's Adventures in Wonderland* and *Through the Looking-Glass*) includes such a frame, but unlike most usages, the stories themselves use dream-like logic and sequences; most dream frames frame stories that appear exactly as if occurring in real life. The writer John Bunyan used a dream device in the Christian allegory Pilgrim's Progress and its sequel, explaining that they were dreams he had while he was in prison and felt God wanted him to write down. This worked because it made what might have been seen as a fantasy something more realistic and meaningful to other who believed as he did.

Still, even when the story proceeds realistically, the dream frame casts doubt on the events. In the book, *The Wonderful Wizard of Oz*, the events really occur; the dream frame added for the movie detracts from the validity of the fantasy.*[2]

9.4 Use of frame stories

As with all literary conceits, the frame tale has many variations, some clearly within the confines of the conceit, some on the border, and some pushing the boundaries of understanding. The main goal of a frame tale is as a conceit which can adequately collect otherwise disparate tales. It has been mostly replaced, in modern literature, by the short story collection or anthology absent of any authorial conceita and other rhetorical devices.

To be a frame narrative, the story must act primarily as an occasion for the telling of other stories. If the framing narrative has primary or equal interest, then it is not usually a frame narrative. For example, Odysseus narrates much of the *Odyssey* to the Phaeacians, but, even though this recollection forms a great part of the poem, the events after and before the interpolated recollection are of greater interest than the memory.

Another notable example that plays with frame narrative is the 1994 film *Forrest Gump*. Most of the film is narrated by Forrest to various companions on the park bench. However, in the last fifth or so of the film, Forrest gets up and leaves the bench, and we follow him as he meets with Jenny and her son. This final segment suddenly has no narrator unlike the rest of the film that came before it, but is instead told through Forrest and Jenny's dialogues.

This approach is also demonstrated in the 2008 film *Slumdog Millionaire* (adapted from the 2005 novel *Q & A*), about a poor street kid Jamal coming close to winning *Kaun Banega Crorepati* (the Indian version of *Who Wants to Be a Millionaire?*) and then being suspected of cheating. Most of the story is narrated at a police station by Jamal, who narrates how he knew the answers to the questions as the show is played back on video. The show itself then serves as another framing device, as Jamal sees flashbacks of his past as each question is asked. The last portion of the film then unfolds without any narrator.

Joseph Conrad's *Heart of Darkness* demonstrates a narrator telling a story, while the protagonist is quoted so as to give the framed appearance that he is telling the story. The narrator provides the transition to the one speaking the story.

A famous literary example is Emily Brontë's *Wuthering Heights*, whereby we learn events through a visitor to the house of the title, who in turn has been told these events by the housekeeper of the Linton family. None of the main characters ever directly narrates.

Another example is David Mitchell's 2004 novel Cloud Atlas, which is a frame story inside a frame story inside a frame story – and so on. There are six stories in all, each framed inside the other, forming a chiastic structure to a semi-catharistic tale spanning centuries of narrative.

Frame stories are found in many role-playing video games, such as the early *Dragon Quest IV*, released in 1990. This literary device can also be sparingly used to achieve secondary ends. For instance, the *Shining Force* series of role playing games use narrators within frame stories to implement things like starting, saving and exiting the game without breaking the fourth wall entirely, or rather by constructing a second fourth wall to shield the player from having to suspend his/her disbelief as much. A similar approach was used in the open world video game *Mafia: The City of Lost Heaven*, where the game's missions are presented as a series of flashbacks narrated by Tommy Angelo, as he confesses his involvement with an American Mafia family. Another example of frame stories in video games is the game Catherine. Catherine's first scene is a frame story.

In the game *Bastion*, the Kid's actions are narrated by one of the other characters, Rucks, as he tells the Kid's story to another character while the Kid is in the final area. Because Rucks never learns about the Kid's actions explicitly, the narration is mostly anecdotal and primarily serves to fill in background information about each level; however, it also serves to keep the fourth wall intact, as player deaths are portrayed as jokes on the narrator's part. After the player's actions catch up to the story, the narration switches to a more speculative tone, as Rucks no longer knows what the player is doing.

9.5   Notes

[1] Witzel, Michael E. J. (1987). "On the origin of the literary device of the 'Frame Story' in Old Indian literature". In Falk, H. *Hinduismus und Buddhismus, Festschrift für U. Schneider*. Freiburg. pp. 380–414. ISBN 3-925270-01-9.

[2] Jones, Steven Swann (1995). *The Fairy Tale: The Magic Mirror of Imagination*. New York: Twayne Publishers. p. 94. ISBN 0-8057-0950-9.

Chapter 10

MacGuffin

In fiction, a **MacGuffin** (sometimes **McGuffin** or **maguffin**) is a plot device in the form of some goal, desired object, or other motivator that the protagonist pursues, often with little or no narrative explanation. The specific nature of a MacGuffin is typically unimportant to the overall plot. The most common type of MacGuffin is an object, place, or person; other, more abstract types include money, victory, glory, survival, power, love, or some unexplained driving force.

The MacGuffin technique is common in films, especially thrillers. Usually the MacGuffin is the central focus of the film in the first act, and thereafter declines in importance. It may re-appear at the climax of the story, but sometimes is actually forgotten by the end of the story. Multiple MacGuffins are sometimes derisively identified as **plot coupons**.*[1]*[2]

10.1 History and use

Objects that serve as MacGuffins are familiar in narrative fiction, providing both the title and the motive for the intrigue in Dashiell Hammet's novel and the 1941 film based upon it, *The Maltese Falcon*, to cite but one well known example drawn from American popular culture. The name "MacGuffin" appears to originate in 20th-century filmmaking, and was popularized by Alfred Hitchcock in the 1930s, but the concept pre-dates the term. The World War I–era actress Pearl White used *weenie* to identify whatever object (a roll of film, a rare coin, expensive diamonds, etc.) that impelled the heroes, and often the villains as well, to pursue each other through the convoluted plots of *The Perils of Pauline* and the other silent film serials in which she starred.*[3]

10.1.1 Alfred Hitchcock

The director and producer Alfred Hitchcock popularized the term "MacGuffin" ("a plot device that motivates the characters and advances the story") and the technique, with his 1935 film *The 39 Steps*, an early example of the concept.*[4]*[5] Hitchcock explained the term "MacGuffin" in a 1939 lecture at Columbia University:

> It might be a Scottish name, taken from a story about two men on a train. One man says, "What's that package up there in the baggage rack?" And the other answers, "Oh, that's a MacGuffin". The first one asks, "What's a MacGuffin?" "Well," the other man says, "it's an apparatus for trapping lions in the Scottish Highlands." The first man says, "But there are no lions in the Scottish Highlands," and the other one answers, "Well then, that's no MacGuffin!" So you see that a MacGuffin is actually nothing at all.

Interviewed in 1966 by François Truffaut, Hitchcock illustrated the term "MacGuffin" with the same story.*[6]*[7] He also related this anecdote in a television interview for Richard Schickel's documentary *The Men Who Made the Movies*, and in an interview with Dick Cavett. According to author Ken Mogg, screenwriter Angus MacPhail, a friend of Hitchcock, may have originally coined the term.*[8]

10.1.2   George Lucas

On the commentary soundtrack to the 2004 DVD release of *Star Wars*, writer and director George Lucas describes R2-D2 as "the main driving force of the movie ⋯what you say in the movie business is the MacGuffin ⋯the object of everybody's search".*[9] In TV interviews, Hitchcock defined a MacGuffin as the object around which the plot revolves, but as to what that object *specifically* is, he declared, "the audience don't care".*[10] Lucas, on the other hand, believes that the MacGuffin should be powerful and that "the audience should care about it almost as much as the duelling heroes and villains on-screen".*[11]

10.1.3   Yves Lavandier

For filmmaker and drama writing theorist Yves Lavandier, in the strictly Hitchcockian sense, a MacGuffin is a secret that motivates the villains.*[12] *North by Northwest* 's supposed MacGuffin is nothing that motivates the protagonist; Roger Thornhill's objective is to extricate himself from the predicament that the mistaken identity has created, and what matters to Vandamm and the CIA is of little importance to Thornhill. A similar lack of motivating power applies to the alleged MacGuffins of *The Lady Vanishes*, *The 39 Steps*, and *Foreign Correspondent*. In a broader sense, says Lavandier, a MacGuffin denotes any justification for the external conflictual premises of a work.*[13]

10.1.4   Broader use

Some dictionary definitions are even more vague and generalized. For example, Princeton's *WordNet* defines a MacGuffin as simply "a plot element that catches the viewers' attention or drives the plot of a work of fiction", which could refer to nearly anything at all in a story, given that audience-member attention is not reliably predictable.*[14]

10.2   Examples

Examples in film include: the meaning of "rosebud" in *Citizen Kane* (1941),*[15] the priceless statue in *The Maltese Falcon* (1941), the NOC list in *Mission: Impossible* (1996) or the Rabbit's Foot in *Mission: Impossible III* (2006),*[16]*[17] the briefcases in *Pulp Fiction* and several Coen brothers films, the Heart of the Ocean necklace in *Titanic*,*[18] and the mineral unobtainium in *Avatar* (2009).*[19]

Examples in television include the Rambaldi device in *Alias*, the orb in *The Adventures of Brisco County, Jr.*, and Krieger Waves in the *Star Trek: The Next Generation* episode "A Matter of Perspective".*[20]*[21]*[22]*[23] Carl Macek created protoculture as a MacGuffin to unite the storylines of the three separate anime that composed *Robotech*,*[24] while the Hellmouth in *Buffy the Vampire Slayer* has been described as a kind of topological MacGuffin - "a shortcut, in lieu of scientific explanation" as Joss Whedon put it.*[25]

Examples in literature include the television set in Wu Ming's novel *54*, and the container in William Gibson's *Spook Country*.*[26]*[27]*[28]

In the popular online game *The Kingdom of Loathing* *[29] the player's character must eventually complete a long and convoluted quest named *player name and The Quest for the Holy MacGuffin*.*[30] It involves going to several locations while following clues from your father's diary and collecting various items. Eventually it ends in a boss battle and the MacGuffin is returned to the council. The game never reveals what exactly it is or how it will aid in saving the kingdom.

In discussing the mixed critical reception of *Indiana Jones and the Kingdom of the Crystal Skull*, where the crystal skull in the film was seen as an unsatisfying MacGuffin, Steven Spielberg said, "I sympathize with people who didn't like the MacGuffin because I never liked the MacGuffin".*[31]

10.3   See also

- Alien space bats

- Big Dumb Object

- Chekhov's gun

- Deus Ex Machina

- *The Double McGuffin*

- The Sampo

- Stanley Elkin

- Red herring

10.4 References

[1] Lowe, Nick (July 1986). "The Well-Tempered Plot Device". *Ansible* (Berkshire, England) (46). ISSN 0265-9816. Retrieved January 2, 2014.

[2] Sterling, Bruce (June 18, 2009). "Turkey City Lexicon – A Primer for SF Workshops". Science Fiction and Fantasy Writers of America. Retrieved January 2, 2014.

[3] Lahue, Kalton C. (1968). *Bound and Gagged: The Story of the Silent Serials*. Oak Tree Pubs. ISBN 978-0-498-06762-4.

[4] Marshall Deutelbaum; Leland A. Poague (2009). *A Hitchcock reader*. John Wiley and Sons. p. 114.

[5] Digou, Mike (October 2003). "Hitchcock's Macguffin In The Works Of David Mamet". *Literature Film Quarterly* **31** (4): 270–275.

[6] François Truffaut, Alfred Hitchcock (1967). *Hitchcock*. Helen G. Scott.

[7] "Framing Hitchcock: Selected essays from the Hitchcock annual" publisher - Wayne State University Press Detroit, pages 47–48 https://books.google.com/books?id=P2ydVge4IiIC&pg=PA47
Hitchcock's term the "MacGuffin" helped him to assert that his films were in fact not what they on the surface seemed to be about. As he explained to Truffaut in the previous note.

[8] Ken Mogg (May 12, 2006). "Frequently asked questions on Hitchcock". *Labyrinth.net.au/~{}muffin/*. Retrieved January 2, 2014.

[9] *Star Wars* (1977) Region 2 DVD release (2004). Audio commentary, 00:14:44 – 00:15:00.

[10] "The 39 Steps – Film (Movie) Plot and Review". Filmreference.com. Retrieved January 2, 2014.

[11] "Keys to the Kingdom". *Vanity Fair*. February 2008. Retrieved January 2, 2014.

[12] "Excerpts from Yves Lavandier's Writing Drama". *Clown-enfant.com*. Retrieved January 2, 2014.

[13] "Yves Lavandier's Writing Drama". *Clown-enfant.com*. Retrieved 2014-01-02.

[14] *MacGuffin*, Princeton University, WordNet 3.0

[15] "Greatest Films: Citizen Kane (1941)". *Filmsite.org*. Retrieved January 2, 2014.

[16] Andrew Sarris (May 14, 2006). "What the MacGuffin? Abrams Loses Way in Mission". *The New York Observer*. Archived from the original on November 6, 2007.

[17] "Our mission, which we accepted, was to watch the Mission: Impossible films". *A.V. Club*.

[18] Corliss, Richard (April 4, 2012). "TIME's Titanic 3D Review". *Time*. Retrieved January 2, 2014.

[19] David Bax (February 9, 2010). "The Quietus List of Macguffins". *Thequietus.com*. Retrieved January 2, 2014.

[20] Mark Englehart (ed.). "Editorial Review of "Alias – The Complete First Season"". *Amazon.com*. ASIN B00005JLF1. Retrieved January 2, 2014.

[21] "Review of *The Adventures of Brisco County, Jr.*". *DVDVerdict.com*. 2006. Retrieved January 2, 2014.

[22] *A Matter of Perspective* (1990) Region 1 DVD release (2002). Season 3, Disk 4.

[23] "The Incredible But True Story of Krieger Waves". DaveKrieger.net. November 5, 2005. Retrieved January 2, 2014.

[24] Yang, Jeff (June 28, 2011). "The 'Robotech' master". *The San Francisco Chronicle*. Retrieved January 2, 2014.

[25] Anne Billson, *Buffy the Vampire Slayer* (2005) p. 65

[26] Boyd Tonkin (June 24, 2005). "A Week in Books: An ingenious comedy-thriller, packed with clever gags". The Independent. Retrieved January 2, 2014.

[27] David Isaacson (July 11, 2005). "*54 By Wu Ming* reviewed by David Isaacson". The Independent. Retrieved January 2, 2014.

[28] Drew Taylor (October 3, 2007). "William Gibson goes cyber-spying? Who's the spy, and who is being spied on?". The Hartford Advocate. Archived from the original on February 4, 2009. Hitch said a MacGuffin was an object—a briefcase, a Maltese falcon—that drives the plot forward without you ever having to know what it is.

[29] "The Kingdom of Loathing".

[30] "The Quest for the Holy MacGuffin at KOL Koldfront".

[31] "Steven Spielberg admits he had reservations about 'Indiana Jones 4,' but still defends worst scene in 'Indiana Jones 4'". *Entertainment Weekly*. October 26, 2011. Retrieved January 2, 2014.

10.5   External links

- MacGuffin at TV Tropes

- A.Word.A.Day —McGuffin, from Wordsmith.org

- FAQs Page of the Hitchcock Scholars/'MacGuffin' website at Labyrinth.net.au/~{}muffin/

Chapter 11

In medias res

For other uses, see In Medias Res (disambiguation).

A tale beginning *in medias res* (Classical Latin: [ɪn mɛdiaːs reːs], lit. "into the middle things") opens in the midst of action. (cf. *ab ovo*, *ab initio*).[1] Often, exposition is bypassed and filled in gradually, either through dialogue, flashbacks or description of past events. For example, Hamlet begins after the death of Hamlet's father. Characters make reference to King Hamlet's death without the plot's first establishment of said fact. Since the play focuses on Hamlet and the revenge itself more so than the motivation, Shakespeare utilizes *in medias res* to bypass superfluous exposition.

In medias res often, though not always, entails subsequent use of flashback and nonlinear narrative for exposition of earlier events in order to fill in the backstory. For example, in Homer's *Odyssey*, we first learn about Odysseus' journey when he is held captive on Calypso's island. We then find out, in Books IX through XII, that the greater part of Odysseus' journey precedes that moment in the narrative. On the other hand, Homer's *Iliad* has relatively few flashbacks, although it opens in the thick of the Trojan War.

11.1 First use of the phrase

The Roman lyric poet and satirist Horace (65–8 BC) first used the terms *ab ovo* ("from the egg") and *in medias res* ("into the middle of things") in his *Ars poetica* ("Poetic Arts", c. 13 BC), wherein lines 147–149 describe the ideal epic poet:[2]

> Nor does he begin the Trojan War *from the egg*,
> but always he hurries to the action, and snatches the listener *into the middle of things*. . . .

The "egg" reference is to the mythological origin of the Trojan War in the birth of Helen and Clytemnestra from the double egg laid by Leda following her rape, as a metamorphosed swan, by Zeus.

11.2 Literary history

Likely original to the oral tradition, the narrative technique of beginning a story *in medias res* is a stylistic convention of epic poetry, the exemplar in Western literature being the *Iliad* (9th century BC) and the *Odyssey* (9th century BC), by Homer.[3] Likewise, the technique features in the Indian *Mahābhārata* (c. 8th century BC – c. 4th century AD); the Portuguese *The Lusiads* (1572); the Spanish *Cantar de Mio Cid* (c. 14th century); the German *Nibelungenlied* (12th century); and the stories "Sinbad the Sailor" and "The Three Apples" from the *One Thousand and One Nights* (c. 9th century).[4]

The Classical-era poet Virgil (Publius Vergilius Maro, 70–19 BC) continued this literary narrative technique in the *Aeneid*, which is part of the Greek literary tradition of imitating Homer,[3] *in medias res* narration further continued in early modern poetry with *Jerusalem Delivered* (1581), by Torquato Tasso, *Paradise Lost* (1667), by John Milton, and generally in Modernist literature.[5]

Modern novelists known to extensively employ *in medias res* in conjunction with flashbacks include William Faulkner and Toni Morrison. Well-known films that employ it include *Raging Bull* and *City of God*.[6]

Occasionally adaptations of source material may employ *in medias res* while the original version did not. For example, the film adaptation of the stage musical *Camelot* employed *in medias res* while the original Broadway version did not (although revivals of the musical have). Stanley Kubrick's 1962 film adaptation of *Lolita* begins *in medias res* although the novel does not. Herman Wouk's stage adaptation of his own novel *The Caine Mutiny* begins *in medias res* as it opens with the court-martial that occupies the final section of the novel, telling the earlier part of the story through flashbacks in court-room testimony.

11.3   Cinematic history

It is typical for film noir to begin *in medias res*; for example, a private detective will enter the plot already in progress.[7] *Crossfire* (1947) opens with the murder of Joseph Samuels. As the police investigate the crime, the story behind the murder is told via flashbacks.[8] *Dead Reckoning* (1947) opens with Humphrey Bogart as Rip Murdock on the run and attempting to hide in a Catholic church. Inside, the backstory is told in flashback as Murdock explains his situation to a priest.[8]

The technique continues to be used in modern crime thrillers such as *Grievous Bodily Harm* (1988),[9] *The Usual Suspects* (1995),[10] and *Kill Bill Volume 2* (2004).[11] and action thrillers such as *Firestarter* (1984),[12] and many James Bond films.[10][13]

Many war films, such as *The Thin Red Line* (1998), also begin *in medias res*, with the protagonists already actively in combat and no prior domestic scenes leading up to the film's events.[14]

The technique is not limited these specific genres, and has been used in other types of films, including drama. It has also been used in such diverse films as *Through a Glass Darkly* (1961),[15] *8½* (1963),[15] and *Dr. Strangelove* (1964).[15]

In television and movies, the technique of having a pre-credits sequence in which some of the story takes place prior to any credits is called a cold open.[16] Many television shows in the 1960s had a pre-credits 'teaser' which hooked the audience to keep their attention. It is often accompanied by *in medias res* writing. Beginning mainly with the James Bond films, many action films have a prologue pre-credits action sequence unrelated to the main storyline of the film - however, after the opening credits the main storyline of the film gets started with traditional exposition. About half the James Bond films open this way.

11.4   What *in medias res* is not

11.4.1   Not a story with a prequel

In medias res should not be confused with a self-contained story that later has a prequel, although either a prequel or the techniques accompanying *in medias res*, such as flashback or exposition, may help to explain the original story's context and background. For example, much of the background of *Lord of the Rings* is later filled in Tolkien's *The Silmarillion*, but this would not make *Rings* an example of *in medias res* writing.

Some stories like this *do* begin *in medias res* but that is not what makes them so. *Star Wars IV: A New Hope* has been described as *in medias res*: what makes this so is that it opens in the middle of a chase and battle scene explained by a prose prologue, not because it has subsequent prequels. [17][18] *The Iliad* and *The Odyssey* begin *in medias res*. Both are parts of a longer epic cycle, but that is not what makes them *in medias res*.

11.4.2 Not necessarily a story with a frame narrative

Similarly, the existence of a "frame story" which gives structure to the main story told in flashback does not necessarily constitute *in medias res*, although they may coexist. The film version of *Amadeus* is framed as a story that Antonio Salieri tells in his old age to a young priest. This would not constitute an example of *in medias res*.

Although *Wuthering Heights* opens with a frame story, it can be regarded as an example of *in medias res* as there is an encounter with a ghost and a dead character's diary prior to the launch of the backstory narrative.*[19] The same can be said of Mary Shelley's *Frankenstein*.*[20]

11.5 See also

- Reverse chronology
- Flashback
- Flashforward
- Cold open

11.6 References

[1] "In medias res". *Encyclopædia Britannica*. Retrieved July 31, 2013.

[2] Horace. *Ars poetica* (in Latin). nec **gemino** bellum Troianum orditur **ab ovo**; / semper ad eventum festinat et **in medias res** / [...] auditorem rapit

[3] Murray, Christopher John (2004). *Encyclopedia of the Romantic Era, 1760-1850*. Taylor & Francis. p. 319. ISBN 1-57958-422-5

[4] Pinault, David (1992). *Story-Telling Techniques in the Arabian Nights*. Brill Publishers. pp. 86–94. ISBN 90-04-09530-6.

[5] Forman, Carol (1984). *Dante Alighieri's Divine Comedy: The Inferno*. Barron's Educational Series. p. 24. ISBN 0-7641-9107-1

[6] What is the term, In Medias Res?

[7] Knight, Deborah (2007). Conard, Mark T.; Porfirio, Robert, eds. *The Philosophy of Film Noir*. University Press of Kentucky. p. 208. ISBN 978-0-8131-9181-2.

[8] Mayer, Geoff; McDonnell, Brian (2007). *Encyclopedia of Film Noir*. ABC-CLIO. pp. 146, 161. ISBN 978-0-313-33306-4.

[9] McFarlane, Brian; Mayer, Geoff (1992). *New Australian Cinema*. Cambridge University Press. p. 100. ISBN 978-0-521-38768-2.

[10] Murfin, Ross C.; Ray, Supryia M. (2009). *The Bedford Glossary of Critical and Literary Terms*. Bedford/St. Martins. p. 245. ISBN 978-0-230-22330-1.

[11] Chan, Kenneth (2009). *Remade in Hollywood*. Hong Kong University Press. p. 147. ISBN 978-962-209-056-9.

[12] Muir, John Kenneth (2007). *Horror Films of the 1980s*. McFarland. pp. 135, 389. ISBN 978-0-7864-2821-2.

[13] Donnelly, Kevin J. (2001). *Film Music*. Edinburgh University Press. p. 36. ISBN 978-0-7486-1288-8.

[14] Glassmeyer, Danielle (2009). "Ridley Scott's Epics: Gender of Violence". In Detora, Lisa M. *Heroes of Film, Comics and American Culture*. McFarland. pp. 297–8. ISBN 978-0-7864-3827-3.

[15] Miller, William Charles (1980). *Screenwriting for Narrative Film and Television*. Hastingshouse/Daytrips. p. 66. ISBN 978-0-8038-6773-4.

[16] *Writing Television Sitcoms - Evan S. Smith - Google Boeken*. Books.google.se. Retrieved 2013-01-03.

[17] In Medias Res: How to Protect Media and Mixed Media

[18] Brooker, Will (2009). *Star Wars*. British Film Institute/MacMillan. p. 20. ISBN 978-1-8445-7277-9.

[19] Logan, Peter Melville; Susan Hegeman; Efraín Kristal (2011). *The Encyclopedia of the Novel, Volume 1*. John Wiley and Sons. p. 812. ISBN 978-1-4051-6184-8.

[20] Murray, E.B. (2011). *Shelley's Contribution to Mary's* Frankenstein/ *Bulletin of the Keats-Shelley Memorial, Rome, Issues 23-30*. Keats-Shelley Memorial Association. p. 50.

11.7   External links

- The dictionary definition of in medias res at Wiktionary

Chapter 12

Narrative hook

A **narrative hook** (or hook) is a literary technique in the opening of a story that "hooks" the reader's attention so that he or she will keep on reading. The "opening" may consist of several paragraphs for a short story, or several pages for a novel, but ideally it is the opening sentence.[1] [2]

12.1 Examples

One of the most common forms is dramatic action, which engages the reader into wondering what the consequences of the action will be. This particular form has been recommended from the earliest days, stemming from Aristotle

The use of action as the hook, and the advice to so use it, is so widespread as to sometimes lead to the use of the term to mean an action opening, but other things can be used for narrative hooks, such mysterious settings, or engaging characters, or even a thematic statement, as with Jane Austen's opening line, "It is a truth universally acknowledged, that a single man in possession of a good fortune, must be in want of a wife." (*Pride and Prejudice*)

12.1.1 *In medias res*

In medias res is where the relating of a story begins at the midpoint, rather than at the beginning.[3] This form of story telling might be used as a narrative hook. Narrative hooks often play an important role in suspense thrillers and mystery fiction.[4] An example of both these occurrences is *One Thousand and One Nights*, in which a tale, "The Three Apples," begins with the discovery of a young woman's dead body, thus keeping the reader interested in "whodunit." [5][6]

12.2 See also

- Cold open
- Headline
- Lead paragraph

12.3 References

[1] Myers, Jack; Wukasch, Don Charles (2009). *Dictionary of poetic terms* (New ed. ed.). Denton, Tex.: University of North Texas Press. p. 244. ISBN 978-1-57441-166-9. Retrieved 25 July 2011.

[2] Lyon, Elizabeth (2008). *Manuscript makeover: revision techniques no fiction writer can afford to ignore*. Penguin. ISBN 978-0-399-53395-2. Retrieved 25 July 2011.

[3] Clifford, Tim (1 January 2013). *The Middle School Writing Toolkit: Differentiated Instruction Across the Content Areas*. Maupin House Publishing, Inc. p. 63. ISBN 978-0-929895-75-8. Retrieved 29 July 2013.

[4] Treat, America (1982). *Mystery Writer's Handbook*. Writer's Digest Books. p. 111. ISBN 0898790808.

[5] Pinault, David (1992), *Story-Telling Techniques in the Arabian Nights*, Brill Publishers, pp. 86–97, ISBN 90-04-09530-6

[6] Marzolph, Ulrich (2006), *The Arabian Nights Reader*, Wayne State University Press, pp. 240–2, ISBN 0-8143-3259-5

Chapter 13

Rakugo

"ochi" redirects here. For other uses, see ochi (disambiguation).

Rakugo (落語, literally "fallen words") is a form of Japanese verbal entertainment. The lone storyteller (落語家 *rakugoka*) sits on stage, called *Kōza* (高座). Using only a paper fan (扇子 *sensu*) and a small cloth (手拭 *tenugui*) as props, and without standing up from the seiza sitting position, the rakugo artist depicts a long and complicated comical story. The story always involves the dialogue of two or more characters, the difference between the characters depicted only through change in pitch, tone, and a slight turn of the head.

13.1   Lexical background

Rakugo was originally known as *karukuchi* (軽口).*[1] The oldest appearance of the kanji which refers specifically to this type of performance dates back to 1787, but at the time the characters themselves (落し噺) were normally read as *otoshibanashi* (falling discourse).

In the middle of the Meiji period (1868–1912) the expression *rakugo* first started being used, and it came into common usage only in the Shōwa period (1926–1989).

13.2   Description

The speaker is in the middle of the audience, and his purpose is to stimulate the general hilarity with tone and limited, yet specific body gestures. The monologue always ends with a narrative stunt known as **ochi** (落ち, lit. "fall") or *sage* (下げ, lit. "lowering"), consisting of a sudden interruption of the wordplay flow. Twelve kinds of ochi are codified and recognized, with more complex variations having evolved through time from the more basic forms.*[2]

Early rakugo has developed into various styles, including the **shibaibanashi** (芝居噺, theatre discourses), the **ongyokubanashi** (音曲噺, musical discourses), the **kaidanbanashi** (see kaidan (怪談噺, ghost discourses)), and **ninjōbanashi** (人情噺, sentimental discourses). In many of these forms the *ochi*, which is essential to the original rakugo, is absent.

Rakugo has been described as "a sitcom with one person playing all the parts" by Noriko Watanabe, assistant professor in the Department of Modern Languages and Comparative Literature at Baruch College.*[3]

13.3   History

Rakugo was invented by Buddhist monks in the 9th and 10th century to make their sermons more interesting and its written tradition can be traced back to the story collection *Uji Shūi Monogatari* (1213–18). Gradually the form turned

Rakugoka at Sanma Festival

from humorous narrative into monologue, probably upon the request of the daimyō, feudal lords, seeking people skilled enough to entertain them with various kinds of storytelling.

During the Edo period (1603–1867), thanks to the emergence of the merchant class of the chonin, the rakugo spread to the lower classes. Many groups of performers were formed, and collections of texts were finally printed. During the 17th century the actors were known as *hanashika* (found written as 噺家, 咄家, or 話家; lit. "storyteller"), corresponding to the modern term, *rakugoka* (落語家, lit. "person of the falling word").

Before the advent of modern rakugo there were the **kobanashi** (小噺): short comical vignettes ending with an ochi, popular between the 17th and the 19th century. These were enacted in small public venues, or in the streets, and printed and sold as pamphlets. The origin of kobanashi is to be found in the *Kinō wa kyō no monogatari* (*Yesterday Stories Told Today*, ca. 1620), the work of an unknown author collecting approximately 230 stories describing the common class.

13.4   Important contributors

Many artists contributed to the development of rakugo. Some were simply performers, but many also composed original works.

Among the more famous rakugoka of the Tokugawa Era were performers like Anrakuan Sakuden (1554–1642), the author of the *Seisuishō* (*Laughter to Chase Away Sleep*, 1628), a collection of more than 1,000 stories. In Edo (today's Tokyo) there also lived Shikano Buzaemon (1649–99) who wrote the *Shikano Buzaemon kudenbanashi* (*Oral Instruction Discourses of Shikano Buzaemon*) and the *Shika no makifude* (*The Deer's Brush*, 1686), a work containing 39 stories, eleven of which are about the kabuki milieu. Tatekawa Enba (1743–1822) was author of the *Rakugo rokugi* (*The Six*

Shinjuku suehirotei is a famous vaudeville theater in Tokyo which hosts rakugo events.

Meanings of Rakugo).

Kyoto was the home of Tsuyu no Gorobei (1643–1703), whose works are included in the *Karakuchi tsuyu ga hanashi* (*One-liners: Morning Dew Stories*, date of composition unknown), containing many word games, episodes from the lives of famous literary authors, and plays on the different dialects from the Tokyo, Osaka, and Kyoto areas.

Of a similar structure is the *Karakuchi gozen otoko* (*One-liners: An Important Storyteller*, date of publication unknown) in which are collected the stories of Yonezawa Hikohachi, who lived in Ōsaka towards the end of the 17th century. An example from Yonezawa Hikohachi's collection:

> A man faints in a bathing tub. In the great confusion following, a doctor arrives who takes his pulse and calmly gives the instructions: "Pull the plug and let the water out." Once the water has flowed completely out of the tub he says: "Fine. Now put a lid on it and carry the guy to the cemetery."

For the poor man is already dead. The joke becomes clearer when one notes that a Japanese traditional bathing tub is shaped like a coffin.

13.4.1 Current performers

Current rakugo artists include Tatekawa Danshi, Tachibanaya Enzō, Katsura Bunshi (6th), Tachibanaya Takezō, Tatekawa Shinosuke and Hayashiya Shōzō (9th). Furthermore, many people regarded as more mainstream comedians originally trained as rakugoka apprentices, even adopting stage names given them by their masters. Some examples include Akashiya

Asakusa Engei Hall is another famous vaudeville theater in Tokyo which hosts rakugo events.

Sanma, Shōfukutei Tsurube, and Shōfukutei Shōhei.*[4] Another famous rakugo performer, Katsura Shijaku, is known outside Japan for his performances of rakugo in English.

13.5   Titles

- *Jugemu*

- *The Cat's Plate* (Neko no Sara)

- Yamamura, Kōji, *Mt. Head* (a traditional rakugo tale adapted to film). Nominated for the "Best Animated Short" Oscar in 2003.

- Shibahama

- Pacific Saury of Meguro (Meguro no Sanma)

- I Hate Manju (Manjuu kowai)

- Botan Dōrō

13.6   List of rakugoka

13.6.1 Edo (Tokyo)

- Kairakutei Black I (Henry Black)

- Hayashiya Sanpei I

- Hayashiya Shōzō IX

- Kokontei Shinchō

- Tatekawa Danshi

- Tachibanaya Enzō

- Reireisya Bafū

- Kokontei Shinshō

- San'yūtei Enchō

- 5th San'yūtei Enraku

- 6th San'yūtei Enraku (formerly San'yūtei Rakutarō)

- Katsura Utamaru

- San'yūtei Koyūza

- San'yūtei Kōraku

- Hayashiya Kikuō (formerly Hayashiya Kikuzō I)

- Syunpūtei Shōta

- Hayashiya Konpei

- Hayashiya Taihei

- Reireisya Suzumaru (Yamada Takao)

- Syunpūtei Koasa

- Syunpūtei Ryūshō

- Yanagiya Kosan

- Sanshōtei Yumenosuke

- Katsura Yonesuke

- Ryūtei Chiraku

- Yanagiya Kosanji

- Tatekawa Shinosuke

- Tachibanaya Takezō

13.6.2   Kamigata (Ōsaka)

- Hayashiya Somemaru IV

- Katsura Bunshi V

- Katsura Bunshi VI (formerly Katsura Sanshi)

- Katsura Beichō

- Katsura Bunchin

- Shōfukutei Nikaku

- Tsukitei Kachō

- Katsura Harudanji

- Tsukitei Happō

- Shōfukutei Matsunosuke

- Shōfukutei Shōkaku

- Katsura Shijaku II

- Shōfukutei Tsurube

- Katsura Sunshine

- Tsukitei Hōsei (formerly Yamasaki Hōsei)

13.7   See also

Media related to Rakugo at Wikimedia Commons

- Joshiraku

- Stand-up comedy

- Manzai

- Kyōgen

- Xiangsheng

13.8   References

[1] *Rakugo*, Big Serving, retrieved 11 May 2007.

[2] Rakugo: universal laughter by Tim Ryan Retrieved 11 May 2007

[3] Rakugo related interview from Baruch College Retrieved 11 May 2007

[4] Rakugo Performers Retrieved 11 May 2007

13.9 External links

- English-Rakugo web site

- YouTube Rakugo examples

- Rakugo video (in English) SFGTV San Francisco

- Bilingual Kamigata (Osaka) Rakugo web site

- Katsura Sunshine's essay concerning the difference between Kamigata(Osaka) rakugo and Edo(Tokyo) rakugo

- Learning Japanese Language and Culture through Rakugo Appreciation

Chapter 14

Plot twist

A **plot twist** is a radical change in the expected direction or outcome of the plot of a novel, film, television series, comic, video game, or other work of narrative.*[1] It is a common practice in narration used to keep the interest of an audience, usually surprising them with a revelation. Some "twists" are foreshadowed.

When a plot twist happens near the end of a story, especially if it changes one's view of the preceding events, it is known as a *surprise ending*.*[2] Sometimes people use a plot twist to describe a sudden change of a situation in real life. It is often assumed that revealing the existence of a plot twist spoils a film or book, since the majority of the film/book generally builds up to the plot twist; however, at least one study suggests otherwise.*[3]

A method used to undermine the expectations of the audience is the false protagonist. It involves presenting a character at the start of the film as the main character, but then disposing of this character, usually killing them – a device known as a red herring.

14.1 Early example

An early example of the murder mystery genre*[4] with multiple twists*[5] was the *Arabian Nights* tale "The Three Apples". It begins with a fisherman discovering a locked chest. The first twist occurs when the chest is broken open and a dead body is found inside. The initial search for the murderer fails, and a twist occurs when two men appear, separately claiming to be the murderer. A complex chain of events finally reveal the murderer to be the investigator's own slave.

14.2 Surprise ending

A surprise ending is a plot twist occurring near or at the conclusion of a story: an unexpected conclusion to a work of fiction that causes the audience to reevaluate the narrative or characters.*[2]

14.2.1 Mechanics of the twist ending

Anagnorisis

Anagnorisis, or discovery, is the protagonist's sudden recognition of their own or another character's true identity or nature.*[6] Through this technique, previously unforeseen character information is revealed. A notable example of anagnorisis occurs in *Oedipus Rex*: Oedipus kills his father and marries his mother in ignorance, learning the truth only toward the climax of the play.*[7] The earliest use of this device as a twist ending in a murder mystery was in "The Three Apples", a medieval *Arabian Nights* tale, where the protagonist Ja'far ibn Yahya discovers by chance a key item towards the end of the story that reveals the culprit behind the murder to be his own slave all along.*[8]*[9]

In M. Night Shyamalan's 1999 film *The Sixth Sense*, a main character who believes he is alive, helping a boy to communicate with dead people, discovers that he is really dead. Similarly, another film to use it is the 2001 film *The Others,* in which a mother is convinced that her house is being haunted; at the end of the film, she learns that she and her children are really the ghosts. In the episode of *The Twilight Zone* titled "Five Characters in Search of an Exit", the protagonists discover at the climax, that they were discarded toys in a donation bin. Another example is in *Fight Club*, when Edward Norton's character realizes that Tyler Durden (Brad Pitt) is his own multiple personality. A mental patient in the psychological thriller film *The Ward* reveals that the three persons she's talking to are all actually herself. Sometimes the audience may discover that the true identity of a character is in fact unknown, as in *Layer Cake* or the eponymous assassins in *V for Vendetta* and *The Day of the Jackal*.

Flashback

Flashback, or analepsis, is a sudden, vivid reversion to a past event.*[6] It is used to surprise the reader with previously unknown information that provides the answer to a mystery, places a character in a different light, or reveals the reason for a previously inexplicable action. The Alfred Hitchcock film *Marnie* employed this type of surprise ending. Sometimes this is combined with the above category, as the flashback may reveal the true identity of one of the characters, or that the protagonist is related to one of the villain's past victims, as Sergio Leone did with Charles Bronson's character in "Once Upon a Time in the West" or Frederick Forsyth's "The Odessa File". The TV series *Boardwalk Empire* and manga (twice made into a movie) *Old Boy* uses similar twists.

Unreliable narrator

An unreliable narrator twists the ending by revealing, almost always at the end of the narrative, that the narrator has manipulated or fabricated the preceding story, thus forcing the reader to question their prior assumptions about the text.*[6] This motif is often used within noir fiction and films, notably in the film *The Usual Suspects*. An unreliable narrator motif was employed by Agatha Christie in *The Murder of Roger Ackroyd*, a novel that generated much controversy due to critics' contention that it was unfair to trick the reader in such a manipulative manner.*[10] Another example of unreliable narration is a character who has been revealed to be insane and thus causes the audience to question the previous narrative; notable examples of this are in the Terry Gilliam film *Brazil*, Chuck Palahniuk's *Fight Club* (and David Fincher's film adaptation), Gene Wolfe's novel *Book of the New Sun*, the second episode of Alfred Hitchcock Presents, *Premonition*, Iain Pears's "An Instance of the Fingerpost", *Shutter Island*, and 'The Hitchhiker' from *More Horowitz Horror* by Anthony Horowitz.

Peripeteia

Peripeteia is a sudden reversal of the protagonist's fortune, whether for good or ill, that emerges naturally from the character's circumstances.*[11] Unlike the *deus ex machina* device, peripeteia must be logical within the frame of the story. An example of a reversal for ill would be Agamemnon's sudden murder at the hands of his wife Clytemnestra in Aeschylus' *The Oresteia* or the inescapable situation Kate Hudson's character finds herself in at the end of *The Skeleton Key*. This type of ending was a common twist ending utilised by *The Twilight Zone*, most effectively in the episode "Time Enough at Last" where Burgess Meredith's character is robbed of all his hope by a simple but devastating accident with his glasses. A positive reversal of fortune would be Nicholas Van Orton's suicide attempt after mistakenly believing himself to have accidentally killed his brother, only to land safely in the midst of his own birthday party, in the film *The Game*.

Deus ex machina

Deus ex machina is a Latin term meaning "god out of the machine." It refers to an unexpected, artificial or improbable character, device or event introduced suddenly in a work of fiction to resolve a situation or untangle a plot.*[12] In Ancient Greek theater, the "deus ex machina" ('ἀπὸ μηχανῆς θεός') was the character of a Greek god literally brought onto the stage via a crane (μηχανῆς—*mechanes*), after which a seemingly insoluble problem is brought to a satisfactory resolution by the god's will. In its modern, figurative sense, the "deus ex machina" brings about an ending to a narrative through unexpected (generally happy) resolution to what appears to be a problem that cannot be overcome (see Mel Brooks' *History of the World, Part I*). This device is often used to end a bleak story on a more positive note.

Poetic justice

Poetic justice is a literary device in which virtue is ultimately rewarded or vice punished in such a way that the reward or punishment has a logical connection to the deed.*[12] In modern literature, this device is often used to create an ironic twist of fate in which the villain gets caught up in his/her own trap. For example, in C. S. Lewis' *The Horse and His Boy*, Prince Rabadash climbs upon a mounting block during the battle in Archenland. Upon jumping down while shouting "The bolt of Tash falls from above," his hauberk catches on a hook and leaves him hanging there, humiliated and trapped. Another example of poetic justice can be found in John Boyne's *The Boy in the Striped Pyjamas*, in which a concentration camp commander's son is mistakenly caught up with inmates rounded up for gassing, or in Chris Van Allsburg's picture book, *The Sweetest Fig*, where a cold-hearted dentist is cruel to his dog and ends up getting his comeuppance.

Chekhov's gun

Chekhov's gun refers to a situation in which a character or plot element is introduced early in the narrative.*[13] Often the usefulness of the item is not immediately apparent until it suddenly attains pivotal significance. A similar mechanism is the "plant", a preparatory device that repeats throughout the story. During the resolution, the true significance of the plant is revealed.

Red herring

A red herring is a false clue intended to lead investigators toward an incorrect solution.*[14] This device usually appears in detective novels and mystery fiction. The red herring is a type of misdirection, a device intended to distract the protagonist, and by extension the reader, away from the correct answer or from the site of pertinent clues or action. The Indian murder mystery film *Gupt: The Hidden Truth* cast many veteran actors who had usually played villainous roles in previous Indian films as red herrings in this film to deceive the audience into suspecting them. In the bestselling novel *The Da Vinci Code*, the misdeeds of a key character named "Bishop Aringarosa" draw attention away from the true master villain ("Aringarosa" literally translates as "red herring"). Agatha Christie's classic *And Then There Were None* is another famous example, and includes the term as well in a murder ploy where the intended victims are made to guess that one of them will be killed through an act of treachery. A red herring can also be used as a form of false foreshadowing.

In medias res

In medias res (Latin for "into the middle of things") is a literary technique in which narrative proceeds from the middle of the story rather than its beginning.*[15] Information such as characterization, setting, and motive is revealed through a series of flashbacks. This technique creates a twist when the cause for the inciting incident is not revealed until the climax. This technique is used within the film *The Prestige* in which the opening scenes show one of the main characters drowning and the other being imprisoned. Subsequent scenes reveal the events leading up to these situations through a series of flashbacks. In *Monsters*, a similar beginning proves to be a flashforward as it is the linear conclusion of the events that then follow; this is not apparent until the end. *In medias res* is often used to provide a narrative hook.

Non-linear narrative

A non-linear narrative works by revealing plot and character in non-chronological order.*[16] This technique requires the reader to attempt to piece together the timeline in order to fully understand the story. A twist ending can occur as the result of information that is held until the climax and which places characters or events in a different perspective. Some of the earliest known uses of non-linear story telling occur in *The Odyssey*, a work that is largely told in flashback via the narrator Odysseus. The nonlinear approach has been used in works such as the films *Mulholland Drive*, *Sin City*,

Premonition, Pulp Fiction, Memento, the television show *Lost* (especially in many episodes in the later seasons), and the book *Catch-22.*[17][18]

Reverse chronology

Reverse chronology works by revealing the plot in reverse order, i.e., from final event to initial event.[19] Unlike chronological storylines, which progress through causes before reaching a final effect, reverse chronological storylines reveal the final effect before tracing the causes leading up to it; therefore, the initial cause represents a "twist ending." Examples employing this technique include the films *Irréversible, Memento* and *5x2*, the play *Betrayal* by Harold Pinter, and Martin Amis' *Time's Arrow*.

14.3   References

[1] Ralph Stuart Singleton; James A. Conrad; Janna Wong Healy (1 August 2000). *Filmmaker's dictionary*. Lone Eagle Pub. Co. p. 229. ISBN 978-1-58065-022-9. Retrieved 27 July 2013.

[2] Judith Kay; Rosemary Gelshenen (26 February 2001). *Discovering Fiction Student's Book 2: A Reader of American Short Stories*. Cambridge University Press. p. 65. ISBN 978-0-521-00351-3. Retrieved 27 July 2013.

[3] Jonah Lehrer, Spoilers Don't Spoil Anything, *Wired Science Blogs*

[4] Marzolph, Ulrich (2006). *The Arabian Nights Reader*. Wayne State University Press. pp. 240–2. ISBN 0-8143-3259-5

[5] Pinault, David (1992). *Story-Telling Techniques in the Arabian Nights*. Brill Publishers. pp. 93, 95, 97. ISBN 90-04-09530-6

[6] Chris Baldick (2008). *The Oxford Dictionary of Literary Terms*. Oxford University Press. p. 12. ISBN 978-0-19-920827-2. Retrieved 23 July 2013.

[7] John MacFarlane, "Aristotle's Definition of Anagnorisis." *American Journal of Philology* - Volume 121, Number 3 (Whole Number 483), Fall 2000, pp. 367-383.

[8] Pinault, David (1992). *Story-Telling Techniques in the Arabian Nights*. Brill Publishers. pp. 95–6. ISBN 90-04-09530-6.

[9] Marzolph, Ulrich (2006). *The Arabian Nights Reader*. Wayne State University Press. pp. 241–2. ISBN 0-8143-3259-5.

[10] "The ubiquitous unreliable narrator". My.en.com. 1996-03-26. Retrieved 2012-12-10.

[11] Michael Payne; Jessica Rae Barbera (31 March 2010). *A Dictionary of Cultural and Critical Theory*. John Wiley & Sons. p. 689. ISBN 978-1-4443-2346-7. Retrieved 23 July 2013.

[12] Joseph Twadell Shipley (1964). *Dictionary of World Literature: Criticism, Forms, Techniques*. Taylor & Francis. p. 156. GGKEY:GL0NUL09LL7. Retrieved 23 July 2013.

[13] Gregory Bergman; Josh Lambert (18 December 2010). *Geektionary: From Anime to Zettabyte, An A to Z Guide to All Things Geek*. Adams Media. p. 201. ISBN 978-1-4405-1188-2. Retrieved 23 July 2013.

[14] Linus Asong (2012). *Detective Fiction and the African Scene: From the Whodunit? to the Whydunit?*. African Books Collective. p. 31. ISBN 978-9956-727-02-5. Retrieved 23 July 2013.

[15] Tim Clifford (1 January 2013). *The Middle School Writing Toolkit: Differentiated Instruction Across the Content Areas*. Maupin House Publishing, Inc. p. 63. ISBN 978-0-929895-75-8. Retrieved 23 July 2013.

[16] Josef Steiff (2011). *Sherlock Holmes and Philosophy: The Footprints of a Gigantic Mind*. Open Court. p. 96. ISBN 978-0-8126-9731-5. Retrieved 23 July 2013.

[17] Adrienne Redd, Nonlinear films and the anticausality of Mulholland Dr., *Prose Toad Literary Blog*

[18] "Plots Inc. Productions". Plotsinc.com. Retrieved 2012-12-10.

[19] John Edward Philips (2006). *Writing African History*. University Rochester Press. p. 507. ISBN 978-1-58046-256-3. Retrieved 23 July 2013.

14.4   See also

- List of plot twists

- Climax (narrative)

- Literary technique

- MacGuffin

- Peripeteia

Chapter 15

Poetic justice

For other uses, see Poetic justice (disambiguation).

Poetic justice is a literary device in which ultimately virtue is rewarded and vice punished. In modern literature it is often accompanied by an ironic twist of fate related to the character's own conduct.[*][1]

15.1 Origin of the term

English drama critic Thomas Rymer coined the phrase in *The Tragedies of the Last Age Considere'd* (1678) to describe how a work should inspire proper moral behaviour in its audience by illustrating the triumph of good over evil. The demand for poetic justice is consistent in Classical authorities and shows up in Horace, Plutarch, and Quintillian, so Rymer's phrasing is a reflection of a commonplace. Philip Sidney, in *Defense of Poetry,* argued that poetic justice was, in fact, the reason that fiction should be allowed in a civilized nation.

15.2 History of the notion

Notably, poetic justice does not merely require that vice be punished and virtue rewarded, but also that logic triumph. If, for example, a character is dominated by greed for most of a romance or drama; he cannot become generous. The action of a play, poem, or fiction must obey the rules of logic as well as morality. During the late 17th century, critics pursuing a neo-classical standard would criticize William Shakespeare in favor of Ben Jonson precisely on the grounds that Shakespeare's characters change during the course of the play. (See Shakespeare's reputation for more on the Shakespeare/Jonson dichotomy.) When Restoration comedy, in particular, flouted poetic justice by rewarding libertines and punishing dull-witted moralists, there was a backlash in favor of drama, in particular, of more strict moral correspondence.

15.3 Examples

15.3.1 Literature

- "For 'tis the sport to have the engineer / Hoist with his own petard." (Shakespeare, *Hamlet* (III.iv.226).)

- The story of eesh and the justice that he brought upon himself after taunting and terrorizing a Northern Virginia community for several years.

- The story of Esther includes two instances of poetic justice, both involving Haman. Ultimately, Haman is executed on the gallows that he had prepared for Esther's cousin Mordecai.

It Shoots Further Than He Dreams *by John F. Knott, March 1918*

- Dante's *Divine Comedy* reads like a compendium of examples of poetic justice.

- The self-fulfilling prophecy can be considered an early example of poetic justice. One example of this is the ancient Sanskrit story of Krishna, where King Kamsa is told in a prophecy that a child of his sister Devaki would kill him. In order to prevent it, he imprisons both Devaki and her husband Vasudeva, allowing them to live only if they hand over their children as soon as they are born. He murders nearly all of them one by one, but the eighth child, Krishna, is saved and raised by a cowherd couple, Nanda and Yasoda. After growing up and returning to his kingdom, Krishna eventually kills Kamsa. In other words, Kamsa's cruelty in order to prevent his death is what led to him being killed.

15.3.2 Television and film

- "The Shawshank Redemption"

- In the South Park episode "Chicken Lover", Kyle declares, "It's poetic justice" after Officer Barbrady gets his job back as Police Officer once he learns to read. It's poetic justice in that he learned to read because of the Booktastic Bus driver, who was making love to the town's chickens in a plot to force Barbrady to learn how to read. Barbrady's newfound literacy then allowed him to catch the very same chicken-lover in the act.

- The Wile E. Coyote and Road Runner cartoons feature repeated instances of poetic justice, as Wile E. Coyote always sets traps for Road Runner, only to end up in the traps himself.

- Poetic justice is referred to in *The Simpsons* episode "Boy Scoutz N the Hood." When Bart returns home from a Junior Campers meeting Homer asks "How was jerk practice, boy? Did they teach you how to sing to trees and build crappy furniture out of useless wooden logs?" The chair that Homer is sitting on then breaks and he declares "D'oh! Stupid poetic justice."

- In the film *Batman Returns*, The Penguin informs his traitorous cohort Max Shreck, that he will be killed in a pool of the toxic byproducts from his "clean" textile plant. The Penguin goes on to wonder if this is tragic irony or poetic justice.

- In the film *Indiana Jones and the Last Crusade*, Indy's love interest Dr. Elsa Schneider is a Nazi agent. After this revelation, she tries fooling Indy and others saying, "I believe in the grail, not the swastika." Yet, she continues working with the Nazis and Walter Donovan. She tricks Donovan into drinking from the false grail and he dies a horrible death. In the end, poetic justice comes in the form of her death. She tries stealing the grail and triggers an earthquake. Indy grabs her hand before she falls into a bottomless pit. Yet, her greed overcomes her and she reaches for the grail again, causing Indy to lose his grip on her. Indy's father, Henry Jones Sr., sums her death up, saying, "Elsa never really believed in the grail. She thought she found a prize."

- Disney films, most specifically animated films, often use poetic justice as an ending device (examples include *The Lion King*, *Aladdin*, and *The Great Mouse Detective*, among many others), with the hero being rewarded, and the villain being punished in ironic and, occasionally, fatal ways.

- In the film, *Sweeney Todd: The Demon Barber of Fleet Street*, as well as in the short story and the musical, the titular character, Sweeney Todd, kills his customers with a razor blade. In a twist of the story, at the end, having assassinated the Judge and the Beadle, Todd is killed by Toby, a boy he kept with Mrs. Lovett, with his own razor blade, while Mrs. Lovett, who bakes the dead customers into meat pies, is thrown into her own oven to bake to death by Todd.

- In the film *Back to the Future Part II*, when Marty McFly is on the roof top of Biff's Casino & Hotel, Biff issues a nod to poetic justice before admitting to killing Marty's father, George McFly, with the same gun he intends to kill Marty with.

- Some caper films end with poetic justice, when a criminal gang's takings of a well planned heist are lost in a manner that is usually not quite their own fault, in complete opposition to the perfect execution of the crime itself. A striking example are the last minutes of *Mélodie en sous-sol* or the original versions of *Ocean's Eleven* and *The Italian Job*.

- In the television series *Avatar: The Last Airbender*, several characters find poetic justice. This is most noticeable in the episode "The Southern Raiders", in which a Fire Nation soldier who killed Katara and Sokka's mother lives with his own mother in retirement, who is angry and constantly berating and talking down to him. The man killed Katara's mother, believing she was the last waterbender of the Southern Water Tribe, when she really lied to protect Katara.

- In the film *Cruel Intentions*, Kathryn, who has been holding up an image of purity, innocence, and popularity while actually being manipulative, deceitful, and two-faced, is exposed at the end of the film due to the diary of her stepbrother Sebastian, who had just recently died.

- In the film *The Killing*, after a very carefully planned—and at first successful robbery—a series of unexpected side events (an unfaithful and greedy wife, a too weak suitcase...) results in most of the gang killed, and the money scattered by the wind at the airport. This causes the mastermind to be arrested just when he was about to flee the country.

- In *The X-Files* episode "Darkness Falls," Mulder theorizes that a group of missing loggers are victims of attacks by extinct insects released from dormancy when the loggers cut down a 700-year-old tree. An environmental activist named Doug Spinney, who previously exposed the cut-down tree as one deliberately marked to be protected, then remarks, "That would be rather poetic justice, don't you think? Unleashing the very thing that would end up killing them?"

- In a scene in *The Birdcage*, it is revealed that a senator who co-founded a morality-obsessed coalition has been found dead with an underage prostitute.

- Many episodes of *The Twilight Zone* feature poetic justice, usually due to an ironic twist.

- In Marvel's The Avengers, the Hulk smashing Loki falls under poetic justice, as throughout the movie he continuously refers to him as a "mindless beast" and a "dull creature" while simultaneously believing in his own divinity.

- In Untraceable, Owen Reilly murdered his victims on camera and display it on the internet; however, his death was caught on camera and being shown all over the internet, it became poetic justice.

15.4   References

[1] Manuela Gertz (July 2010). *Poetic Justice in William Faulkner's Absalom Absalom*. GRIN Verlag. p. 4–. ISBN 978-3-640-66116-9. Retrieved 20 May 2013.

15.5   See also

- Karma

- unintended consequences

Chapter 16

Causal loop

For the cause and effect diagram, see Causal loop diagram.
For the science fiction plot device, see time loop.

A **causal loop**[1] is a paradox of time travel that occurs when a later (future) event is the cause of an earlier (past) event, through some sort of time travel. The past event is then partly or entirely the cause of the future event, which is the past event's cause. Since a causal loop has no independent origin, it is also called a **bootstrap paradox** or an **ontological paradox**.

16.1 Bootstrap paradox

The term "bootstrap paradox" refers to the expression "pulling yourself up by your bootstraps"; the use of the term for the time-travel paradox was popularized by Robert A. Heinlein's story *By His Bootstraps*. It is a paradox in the sense that an independent origin of the events that caused each other cannot be determined, they simply exist by themselves,[1] thus they may be said to have been predestined to occur. Predestination does not necessarily involve a metaphysical power, and could be the result of other "infallible foreknowledge" mechanisms.[2] The predestination paradox allows time travel to be self-consistent, similar to the Novikov self-consistency principle.

16.1.1 Bootstrap paradox in fiction

The bootstrap paradox has been used in fictional stories and films.[3] The concept is named from the Robert Heinlein story "By His Bootstraps",[3] which is considered the "ultimate time travel paradox tale" of its time.[4] In the 1980 romance film *Somewhere in Time*, based on Richard Matheson's 1975 novel *Bid Time Return*, an elderly woman gives a young man a pocket watch in 1972. He travels back in time to 1912 and gives the pocket watch to her, which she carries with her until 1972 when she meets the young man and gives the watch to him.[5] The movie *Time Lapse* is built entirely around the concept of bootstrap paradox.[6] Don D'Amassa states that "The greatest difficulty in creating a story of this type is not so much the plotting of the various times loops, but to render them in such a way that the reader can follow the logic." [4]

16.2 Self-fulfilling prophecy

A self-fulfilling prophecy may be a form of causality loop, only when the prophecy can be said to be *truly* known to occur, since only then events in the future will be causing effects in the past.[2] Otherwise, it would be a simple case of events in the past causing events in the future. A notable fictional example of a self-fulfilling prophecy occurs in classical play *Oedipus Rex*, in which Oedipus becomes the king of Thebes, whilst in the process unwittingly fulfills a prophecy that he would kill his father and marry his mother. The prophecy itself serves as the impetus for his actions, and thus it is self-fulfilling.*[7]*[8]

16.3   See also

16.4   References

[1] Nicholas J.J. Smith (2013). "Time Travel". *Stanford Encyclopedia of Philosophy*. Retrieved June 13, 2015.

[2] Craig (1987). "Divine Foreknowledge and Newcomb's Paradox". *Philosophia* **17** (3): 331–350. doi:10.1007/BF02455055.

[3] Klosterman, Chuck (2009-10-20). *Eating the Dinosaur*. Simon and Schuster. p. 60. ISBN 9781439168486. Retrieved 2 February 2013.

[4] D'Ammassa, Don (2005). *Encyclopedia Of Science Fiction*. Infobase Publishing. p. 67. ISBN 9780816059249. Retrieved 3 February 2013.

[5] Everett, Allen; Roman, Thomas (2011-12-15). *Time Travel and Warp Drives: A Scientific Guide to Shortcuts through Time and Space*. University of Chicago Press. p. 138. ISBN 9780226224985. Retrieved 3 February 2013.

[6] http://www.astronomytrek.com/time-lapse-2014-explained/

[7] E.R. Dodds, *Greece & Rome*, 2nd Ser., Vol. 13, No. 1 (Apr., 1966), pp. 37–49

[8] Popper, Karl (1976). *Unended Quest: An Intellectual Autobiography*. LaSalle, Illinois: Open Court. ISBN 978-0-87548-343-6. OCLC 2927208.

Chapter 17

Quibble (plot device)

In terms of fiction, a **quibble** is a plot device, used to fulfill the exact verbal conditions of an agreement in order to avoid the intended meaning. Typically quibbles are used in legal bargains and, in fantasy, magically enforced ones.*[1]

In one of the best known examples, William Shakespeare used a quibble in *The Merchant of Venice*. Portia saves Antonio in a court of law by pointing out that the agreement called for a pound of flesh, but no blood, and therefore Shylock can collect only if he sheds no blood.

17.1   Examples

A pact with the Devil commonly contains clauses that allow the devil to quibble over what he grants, and equally commonly, the maker of the pact finds a quibble to escape the bargain.*[1]

In Norse mythology, Loki, having bet his head with Brokk and lost, forbids Brokk to take any part of his neck, saying he had not bet it; Brokk is able only to sew his lips shut.*[1]

The Savoy Operas by Gilbert and Sullivan frequently feature quibbles; W. S. Gilbert had read law and had practiced briefly as a barrister, and regarded the minor technicalities of the law that typically gave rise to quibbles to be highly characteristic of the legalistic Victorian British society satirized in his works. For instance, in *The Pirates of Penzance*, Frederick's terms of indenture bind him to the pirates until his twenty-first birthday; the pirates point out that he was born on February 29 (a leap year) and will not have his twenty-first birthday until he is eighty-four, and so compel him to rejoin them.

When the hero of the Child ballad *The Lord of Lorn and the False Steward* is forced to trade places with an impostor and swear never to reveal the truth to anyone, he tells his story to a horse while he knows that the heroine is eavesdropping. In the similar fairy tale *The Goose Girl*, the princess pours out her story to an iron stove, but not knowing that the king is listening.*[2]

In Piers Anthony's fantasy world Xanth, the law requires that the king be a Magician, thereby excluding a Sorceress from ruling. But when in *Night Mare* one Magician after another falls to an invasion's hostile magic and it appears that no more Magicians exist to take the throne, the last Magician king observes that although the law states that only a Magician can be king, a Sorceress is technically a female Magician and thus eligible to rule. Consequently, several sorceresses successively take the throne to fight the invasion.

Quibbles are the theme of *The Twilight Zone* episode "The Man in the Bottle". A genie freed from a bottle grants a couple four wishes, warning that every wish has consequences. One of the man's wishes is to be in a position of great power, the leader of a modern and powerful country who cannot be voted out of office. The genie turns him into Adolf Hitler during his final days in World War II.

In the *Star Trek: Deep Space Nine* episode "The Circle", Captain Sisko is ordered to evacuate the titular station against his better judgment. However, he notices that his superiors did not specify the extent of the evacuation, so he orders a complete evacuation of all their equipment, which will take far longer and necessitate some officers staying on the station in the face of an impending siege, giving them a chance to fight back. Likewise, "The Way of the Warrior", Sisko is forbidden to tell the Cardassians about an imminent invasion of their empire by the Klingons. However, if the Klingons take Cardassia, the Federation and Bajor will be put at risk, so he calls in the station's resident Cardassian tailor/spy to measure him for a suit while he discusses the imminent invasion with his senior officers.

In *The Shadow Thieves*, by Anne Ursu, Hades, attempting to banish the traitorous Philonecron, uses the words "You may never set foot in the Kingdom of the Dead again." Philonecron later gets around Hades's binding proclamation by having servants carry him into the Underworld.

In the 2002 film Spider-Man, Peter Parker faces professional wrestler Bonesaw McGraw after seeing a newspaper advertisement specifying "$3000 for 3 minutes in the ring." Though Parker wins the match in two minutes, the promotion's crooked promoter only pays him $100 citing that since Parker did not last three minutes in the ring, Parker did not fulfil the required conditions and was therefore unable to receive the full $3000.

17.2   Prophecies and spells

See also: Foreshadowing

When Croesus consulted the Pythia, he was told that going to war with Cyrus the Great would destroy a great empire. Croesus assumed that the seer meant that the Persian Empire would be destroyed and Croesus would triumph. He proceeded to attack the Persians, believing victory was assured. In the end, however, the Persians were victorious, and the empire destroyed was not Cyrus's but Croesus's.

In Shakespeare's *Macbeth*, Macbeth believes that he is invincible because the Three Witches give him the prophecy that "none of woman born shall harm [him]." In the final battle of the play, Macduff is able to kill Macbeth, because Macduff reveals that he was "from his mother's womb untimely ripp'd" *[1] —born via a Caesarean section. In a second prophecy, Macbeth is told that he has nothing to fear until Great Birnam Wood comes to Dunsinane Hill. He feels safe since he knows that forests cannot move, but is overcome when the English army, shielded with boughs cut from Birnam Wood, advances on his stronghold at Dunsinane.

In *The Lord of the Rings*, the Elf Glorfindel's prophecy states that "not by the hand of man will the Witch-king of Angmar fall." The Witch-king is slain by Éowyn, a woman, during the battle of the Pelennor Fields. She is aided by Merry, a hobbit*[1] who distracted him by stabbing him with a Numenorean blade, as the Ring Wraiths are harmed by such swords.

In *Ruddigore*, the baronets are cursed to die if they do not commit a horrible crime every day, but failing to commit such a crime is committing suicide, a horrible crime (a realization that brings them all back to life).

In Terry Pratchett's *Moving Pictures*, a book is said to inflict terrible fates on any man opening it, but causes only mild annoyance to the Librarian, who is in fact an orangutan.*[1]

In *The Return of Jafar*, the sequel to Disney's film *Aladdin*, the main villain Jafar, after becoming a genie, is unable to use his powers to directly kill living beings. However, he is able to use his powers to create situations that *could* kill or harm his enemies, including possibly torture as Jafar darkly suggests, "you would be surprised what you can live through."

Jack Sparrow (from the *Pirates of the Caribbean* movies) promised to be Davy Jones' slave for 100 years in exchange for receiving the Black Pearl (a ship) and being made captain of that ship, for thirteen years. When Jones reminds Sparrow of his debt, Jack argues that he wasn't captain during those thirteen years, for a mutiny quickly occurred and he was abandoned on an island by his crew. To that, Davy Jones replies that regardless of this, he still owes him his soul, for he has been introducing himself as *Captain* Jack Sparrow during those thirteen years (and indeed, it is a running gag in the movies that each time he is called "Jack Sparrow", Jack will correct the other by saying "*Captain* Jack Sparrow").

In Death Note, the Shinigami Ryuk warns the protagonist Kira Yagami to "Don't think that a human who's used the Death Note can go to heaven or hell".*[3] At the end of the series it is revealed that there's no heaven or hell and that all humans, no matter what they did in life, are equal in death.*[4] When a human dies, the human goes to "Mu" (Nothingness),*[5] or rather ceases to exist. What Ryuk tried to say to Light at the beginning of the series was that not even a human who's used the Death Note can go to heaven or hell, like all other humans, when that human dies, it will cease to exist.

17.3   References

[1] John Grant and John Clute, *The Encyclopedia of Fantasy*, "Quibbles" p 796 ISBN 0-312-19869-8

[2] Maria Tatar, *The Annotated Brothers Grimm*, p 320 W. W. Norton & company, London, New York, 2003 ISBN 0-393-05848-4

[3] *Death Note* chapter 1, page 24

[4] *Death Note* chapter 107, page 15

[5] *Death Note* chapter 107, pages 18–19

Chapter 18

Red herring

This article is about the idiom and the logical fallacy. For the type of preserved food, see kipper. For other uses, see Red herring (disambiguation).

A **red herring** is something that misleads or distracts from a relevant or important issue.[1] It may be either a logical fallacy or a literary device that leads readers or audiences towards a false conclusion. A red herring might be intentionally used, such as in mystery fiction or as part of a rhetorical strategies (e.g. in politics), or it could be inadvertently used during argumentation.

The origin of the expression is not known. Conventional wisdom has long supposed it to be the use of a kipper (a strong-smelling smoked fish) to train hounds to follow a scent, or to divert them from the correct route when hunting; however, modern linguistic research suggests that the term was probably invented in 1807 by English polemicist William Cobbett, referring to one occasion on which he had supposedly used a kipper to divert hounds from chasing a hare, and was never an actual practice of hunters. The phrase was later borrowed to provide a formal name for the logical fallacy and literary device.

18.1   Logical fallacy

As an informal fallacy, the red herring falls into a broad class of relevance fallacies. Unlike the straw man, which is premised on a distortion of the other party's position,[2] the red herring is a seemingly plausible, though ultimately irrelevant, diversionary tactic.[3] According to the *Oxford English Dictionary*, a red herring may be intentional, or unintentional; it does not necessarily mean a conscious intent to mislead.[1]

The expression is mainly used to assert that an argument is not relevant to the issue being discussed. For example, *"I think that we should make the academic requirements stricter for students. I recommend that you support this because we are in a budget crisis and we do not want our salaries affected."* The second sentence, though used to support the first sentence, does not address that topic.

18.2   Intentional device

In fiction and non-fiction a red herring may be intentionally used by the writer to plant a false clue that leads readers or audiences towards a false conclusion.[4][5][6] For example, the character of Bishop Aringarosa in Dan Brown's *The Da Vinci Code* is presented for most of the novel as if he is at the centre of the church's conspiracies, but is later revealed to have been innocently duped by the true antagonist of the story. The character's name is a loose Italian translation of "red herring" (*aringa rossa*; *rosa* actually meaning *pink*, or rosy).[7]

A red herring is often used in legal studies and exam problems to mislead and distract students from reaching a correct conclusion about a legal issue, allegedly as a device that tests students' comprehension of underlying law and their ability to properly discern material factual circumstances.*[8]

18.3 History of the idiom

Herrings kippered by smoking and salting until they turn reddish-brown, i.e. a "red herring". Prior to refrigeration kipper was known for being strongly pungent. In 1807, William Cobbett wrote how he used red herrings to lay a false trail, while training hunting dogs— an apocryphal story that was probably the origin of the idiom.

In a literal sense, there is no such fish as a "red herring"; it refers to a particularly strong kipper, a fish (typically a herring) that has been strongly cured in brine and/or heavily smoked. This process makes the fish particularly pungent smelling and, with strong enough brine, turns its flesh reddish.*[9] In its literal sense as a strongly cured kipper, the term can be dated to the mid-13th century, in the poem *The Treatise* by Walter of Bibbesworth: "He eteþ no ffyssh But heryng red." *[10]

Until very recently,*[9] the figurative sense of "red herring" was thought to originate from a supposed technique of training young scent hounds.*[9] There are variations of the story, but according to one version, the pungent red herring would be dragged along a trail until a puppy learned to follow the scent.*[11] Later, when the dog was being trained to follow the faint odour of a fox or a badger, the trainer would drag a red herring (whose strong scent confuses the animal) perpendicular to the animal's trail to confuse the dog.*[12] The dog eventually learned to follow the original scent rather than the stronger scent. An alternate etymology points to escaping convicts who used the pungent fish to throw off hounds in pursuit.*[13]

According to etymologist Michael Quinion, the idiom likely originates from an article published 14 February 1807 by radical journalist William Cobbett in his polemical *Political Register*.*[9]*[14] In a critique of the English press, which had mistakenly reported Napoleon's defeat, Cobbett recounted that he had once used a red herring to deflect hounds in pursuit of a hare, adding "It was a mere transitory effect of the political red-herring; for, on the Saturday, the scent became as cold as a stone." *[9] Quinion concludes: "This story, and [Cobbett's] extended repetition of it in 1833, was enough to get the figurative sense of *red herring* into the minds of his readers, unfortunately also with the false idea that it came from some real practice of huntsmen." *[9]

18.3.1   Real-world usage

Although Cobbett most famously mentioned it, he was not the first to consider red herring for scenting hounds; an earlier reference occurs in the pamphlet "Nashe's Lenten Stuffe," published in 1599 by the Elizabethan writer Thomas Nashe, in which he says "Next, to draw on hounds to a scent, to a red herring skin there is nothing comparable." *[15] The *Oxford English Dictionary* makes no connection with Nashe's quote and the figurative meaning of red herring, only in the sense of a hunting practice.*[1]

The use of herring to throw off pursuing scent hounds was tested on Episode 148 of the series *MythBusters*.*[16] Although the hound used in the test stopped to eat the fish and lost the fugitive's scent temporarily, he eventually backtracked and located his target, resulting in the myth being classified as "Busted".*[17]

18.4   See also

- List of Red herring fallacies
- Chekhov's gun
- Chewbacca defense
- Decoy
- False flag
- *Five Red Herrings*
- Foreshadowing
- Garden path
- Ignoratio elenchi
- Judgmental language
- MacGuffin
- Plot twist
- Red herring prospectus
- Sidetrack
- Snipe hunt (a fool's errand or wild goose chase)
- *Twelve Red Herrings*

18.5   References

[1] *Oxford English Dictionary*. red herring, n. Third edition, September 2009; online version December 2011. http://www.oed.com/view/Entry/160314; accessed 18 December 2011. An entry for this word was first included in New English Dictionary, 1904.

[2] Patrick J. Hurley (2011). *A Concise Introduction to Logic*. Cengage Learning. pp. 131–133. ISBN 978-0-8400-3417-5.

[3] Christopher W. Tindale (2007). *Fallacies and Argument Appraisal*. Cambridge University Press. pp. 28–33. ISBN 978-0-521-84208-2.

[4] Nozar Niazi (2010). *How To Study Literature: Stylistic And Pragmatic Approaches*. PHI Learning Pvt. Ltd. p. 142. ISBN 9788120340619. Retrieved 2013-03-02.

[5] Bernard Marie Dupriez (1991). *Dictionary of Literary Devices: Gradus, A-Z*. Translated by Albert W. Halsall. University of Toronto Press. p. 322. ISBN 9780802068033. Retrieved 2013-03-02.

[6] Lewis Turco (1999). *The Book of Literary Terms: The Genres of Fiction, Drama, Nonfiction, Literary Criticism and Scholarship*. UPNE. p. 143. ISBN 9780874519556. Retrieved 2013-03-02.

[7] Michael Lieb, Emma Mason, Jonathan Roberts (2011). *The Oxford Handbook of the Reception History of the Bible*. Oxford University Press. p. 370. ISBN 9780199670390.

[8] Sheppard, [editor] Steve (2005). *The history of legal education in the United States : commentaries and primary sources* (2nd print. ed.). Clark, N.J.: Lawbook Exchange. ISBN 1584776900.

[9] Quinion, Michael (2002–2008). "The Lure of the Red Herring" . *World Wide Words*. Retrieved November 10, 2010.

[10] Bibbesworth, Walter de (c. 1250) *Femina* Trinity College, Cambridge MS B.14.40. 27. Anglo-Norman On-Line Hub, 2005. ISBN 9780955212406.

[11] Thomas Nashe, *Nashes Lenten Stuffe* (1599): "Next, to draw on hounds to a sent, to a redde herring skinne there is nothing comparable." (Since Nashe makes this statement not in a serious reference to hunting but as an aside in a humorous pamphlet, the professed aim of which is to extol the wonderful virtues of red herrings, it need not be evidence of actual practice. In the same paragraph he makes other unlikely claims, such as that the fish dried and powdered is a prophylactic for kidney or gallstones.)

[12] Currall, J.E.P; Moss, M.S.; Stuart, S.A.J. (2008). "Authenticity: a red herring?". *Journal of Applied Logic* **6** (4): 534–544. doi:10.1016/j.jal.2008.09.004. ISSN 1570-8683.

[13] Hendrickson, R. (2000). The facts on file encyclopedia of word and phrase origins. United States: Checkmark.

[14] "...we used, in order to draw oft' the harriers from the trail of a hare that we had set down as our own private property, get to her haunt early in the morning, and drag a red-herring, tied to a string, four or five miles over hedges and ditches..." For the full original story by Cobbett, see "Continental War" on pg. 231-33 of *Political Register*, February 14, 1807. In *Cobbett's political register, Volume XI, 1807* at Internet Archive

[15] Nashe, Thomas (1599) *Praise of the Red Herring* In: William Oldys and John Malham (Eds) *The Harleian miscellany* Volume 2, Printed for R. Dutton, 1809. Page 331.

[16] *MythBusters: Season 9, Episode 1 - Hair of the Dog* at the Internet Movie Database

[17] Episode 148: Hair of the Dog, Mythbustersresults.com

Chapter 19

Self-fulfilling prophecy

A **self-fulfilling prophecy** is a prediction that directly or indirectly causes itself to become true, by the very terms of the prophecy itself, due to positive feedback between belief and behavior. Although examples of such prophecies can be found in literature as far back as ancient Greece and ancient India, it is 20th-century sociologist Robert K. Merton who is credited with coining the expression "self-fulfilling prophecy" and formalizing its structure and consequences. In his 1948 article *Self-Fulfilling Prophecy*, Merton defines it in the following terms:

> The self-fulfilling prophecy is, in the beginning, a *false* definition of the situation evoking a new behavior which makes the original false conception come *true*. This specious validity of the self-fulfilling prophecy perpetuates a reign of error. For the prophet will cite the actual course of events as proof that he was right from the very beginning.*[1]

In other words, a positive or negative prophecy, strongly held belief, or delusion—declared as truth when it is actually false—may sufficiently influence people so that their reactions ultimately fulfill the once-false prophecy.

Self-fulfilling prophecy are effects in *behavioral confirmation effect*, in which behavior, influenced by expectations, causes those expectations to come true.*[2] It is complementary to the self-defeating prophecy.

19.1   History of the concept

Merton's concept of the *self-fulfilling prophecy* stems from the Thomas theorem, which states that "If men define situations as real, they are real in their consequences." *[3] According to Thomas, people react not only to the situations they are in, but also, and often primarily, to the way they perceive the situations and to the meaning they assign to these perceptions. Therefore, their behaviour is determined in part by their perception and the meaning they ascribe to the situations they are in, rather than by the situations themselves. Once people convince themselves that a situation really has a certain meaning, regardless of whether it actually does, they will take very real actions in consequence.

Merton took the concept a step further and applied it to recent social phenomena. In his book *Social Theory and Social Structure*, he conceives of a bank run at the fictional Last National Bank, over which Cartwright Millingville presides. It is a typical bank, and Millingville has run it honestly and quite properly. As a result, like all banks, it has some liquid assets (cash), but most of its assets are invested in various ventures. Then one day, a large number of customers come to the bank at once—the exact reason is never made clear. Customers, seeing so many others at the bank, begin to worry. False rumours spread that something is wrong with the bank and more customers rush to the bank to try to get some of their money out while they still can. The number of customers at the bank increases, as does their annoyance and excitement, which in turn fuels the false rumours of the bank's insolvency and upcoming bankruptcy, causing more customers to come and try to withdraw their money. At the beginning of the day—the last one for Millingville's bank—the bank was not insolvent. But the rumour of insolvency caused a sudden demand of withdrawal of too many customers, which could not be answered, causing the bank to become insolvent and declare bankruptcy. Merton concludes this example with the following analysis:

The parable tells us that public definitions of a situation (prophecies or predictions) become an integral part of the situation and thus affect subsequent developments. This is peculiar to human affairs. It is not found in the world of nature, untouched by human hands. Predictions of the return of Halley's comet do not influence its orbit. But the rumoured insolvency of Millingville's bank did affect the actual outcome. The prophecy of collapse led to its own fulfilment.*[4]

Merton concluded that the only way to break the cycle of self-fulfilling prophecy is by redefining the propositions on which its false assumptions are originally based.

In economic "expectations models" of inflation, peoples' expectations of future inflation lead them to spend more today and demand higher nominal interest rates for any savings, since they expect that prices will be rising. This demand for higher nominal interest rates and increased spending in the present, in turn, create inflationary pressure and can cause inflation even if the expectations of future inflation are unfounded. The expectations theory of inflation played a large role in Paul Volcker's actions during his tenure as the Chairman of the Federal Reserve in combating the "stagflation" of the 1970s.

Philosopher Karl Popper called the self-fulfilling prophecy the *Oedipus effect*:

> One of the ideas I had discussed in *The Poverty of Historicism* was the influence of a prediction upon the event predicted. I had called this the "Oedipus effect", because the oracle played a most important role in the sequence of events which led to the fulfilment of its prophecy. ···For a time I thought that the existence of the Oedipus effect distinguished the social from the natural sciences. But in biology, too—even in molecular biology—expectations often play a role in bringing about what has been expected.*[5]

An early precursor of the concept appears in Edward Gibbon's Decline and Fall of the Roman Empire: "During many ages, the prediction, as it is usual, contributed to its own accomplishment" (chapter I, part II).

19.1.1 Applications

Examples abound in studies of cognitive dissonance theory and the related self-perception theory; people will often change their attitudes to come into line with what they profess publicly.

In the United States the concept was broadly and consistently applied in the field of public education reform, following the "War on Poverty". Theodore Brameld noted: "In simplest terms, education already projects and thereby reinforces whatever habits of personal and cultural life are considered to be acceptable and dominant." *[6] The effects of teacher attitudes, beliefs and values, affecting their expectations have been tested repeatedly.*[7]

The phenomenon of the "inevitability of war" is a self-fulfilling prophecy that has received considerable study.*[8]

The idea is similar to that discussed by the philosopher William James as The Will to Believe. But James viewed it positively, as the self-validation of a belief. Just as, in Merton's example, the belief that a bank is insolvent may help create the fact, so too on the positive side, confidence in the bank's prospects may help brighten them. A more Jamesian example: a swain, convinced that the fair maiden *must* love him, may prove more effective in his wooing than he would had his initial prophecy been defeatist.

There is extensive evidence of "Interpersonal Expectation Effects" where the seemingly private expectations of individuals can predict the outcome of the world around them. The mechanisms by which this occurs are also reasonably well understood: it is simply that our own expectations change our behaviour in ways we may not notice and correct. In the case of the "Interpersonal Expectation Effects", others pick up on non-verbal behaviour which affects their attitudes. A famous example includes a study where teachers were told arbitrarily that random students were "going to blossom". Oddly, those random students actually ended the year with significantly greater improvements.*[9]

Other specific examples discussed in psychology include:

- 'Clever Hans' effect

- Observer-expectancy effect

- Hawthorne effect

- Placebo effect

- Pygmalion effect

- Stereotype threat

19.2   Sports

In Canadian hockey, junior league players are selected based on skill, motor coordination, physical maturity, and other individual merit criteria. However, psychologist Robert Barnsley showed that in any elite group of hockey players, 40% are born between January and March, versus the approximately 25% as would be predicted by statistics. The explanation is that in Canada, the eligibility cutoff for age-class hockey is January 1, and the players who are born in the first months of the year are older by 9–12 months, which at the preadolescent age of selection (nine or ten) manifests into an important physical advantage. The selected players are exposed to higher levels of coaching, play more games, and have better teammates. These factors make them actually become the best players, fulfilling the prophecy, while the real selection criterion was age.*[10] The same relative age effect has been noticed in Belgian soccer after 1997, when the start of the selection year was changed from August 1 to January 1.*[11]

19.3   Stereotype

This specific form of self-fulfilling prophecy is very common as it can take on many forms. This type would imply that the expectancy for a party to act a certain way based on race, religion, gender and much more, would eventually lead to said party imitating the stereotype.*[12]

19.4   Literature, media, and the arts

In literature, self-fulfilling prophecies are often used as plot devices. They have been used in stories for millennia, but have gained a lot of popularity recently in the science fiction genre. They are typically used ironically, with the prophesied events coming to pass due to the actions of one trying to prevent the prophecy (a recent example would be the life of Anakin Skywalker, the fictional Jedi-turned-Sith Lord in George Lucas' *Star Wars* saga). They are also sometimes used as comic relief.

19.4.1   Classical

Many myths, legends and fairy tales make use of this motif as a central element of narratives that are designed to illustrate inexorable fate, fundamental to the Hellenic world-view.*[13] In a common motif, a child, whether newborn or not yet conceived, is prophesied to cause something that those in power do not want to happen. This may be the death of the powerful person; in more light-hearted versions, it is often the marriage of a poor or lower-class child to his own. The events come about, nevertheless, as a result of the actions taken to prevent them: frequently child abandonment sets the chain of events in motion.

Greek

The best known example from Greek legend is that of Oedipus. Warned that his child would one day kill him, Laius abandoned his newborn son Oedipus to die, but Oedipus was found and raised by others, and thus in ignorance of his true origins. When he grew up, Oedipus was warned that he would kill his father and marry his mother. Believing his foster parents were his real parents, he left his home and travelled to Greece, eventually reaching the city where his biological parents lived. There, he got into a fight with a stranger, his real father, killed him and married his widow, Oedipus' real mother.

Although the legend of Perseus opens with the prophecy that he will kill his grandfather Acrisius, and his abandonment with his mother Danaë, the prophecy is only self-fulfilling in some variants. In some, he accidentally spears his grandfather at a competition—an act that could have happened regardless of Acrisius' response to the prophecy. In other variants, his presence at the games is explained by his hearing of the prophecy, so that his attempt to evade it does cause the prophecy to be fulfilled. In still others, Acrisius is one of the wedding guests when Polydectes tried to force Danaë to marry him, and when Perseus turns them to stone with the Gorgon's head; as Polydectes fell in love with Danaë because Acrisius abandoned her at sea, and Perseus killed the Gorgon as a consequence of Polydectes' attempt to get rid of Danaë's son so that he could marry her, the prophecy fulfilled itself in these variants.

Greek historiography provides a famous variant: when the Lydian king Croesus asked the Delphic Oracle if he should invade Persia, the response came that if he did, he would destroy a great kingdom. Assuming this meant he would succeed, he attacked—but the kingdom he destroyed was his own.*[14] In such an example, the prophecy prompts someone to action because he is led to expect a favorable result; but he achieves another, disastrous result which nonetheless fulfills the prophecy.

People do not necessarily have to unsuccessfully avoid a prophecy in order for the prophecy to be self-fulfilling. For example, when it was predicted that Zeus would overthrow his father, Cronos, and usurp his throne as King of the Gods, he actively waged war against him in a direct attempt to fulfill this prophecy. This makes the prophecy a self-fulfilling one because it was the prophecy itself that gave Zeus the inspiration to do it in the first place.

Roman

The story of Romulus and Remus is another example. According to legend, a man overthrew his brother, the king. He then ordered that his two nephews, Romulus and Remus, be drowned, fearing that they would someday kill him like he did to his brother. The boys were placed in a basket and thrown in the Tiber River. A wolf found the babies and she raised them. Later, a shepherd found the twins and named them Romulus and Remus. As teenagers, they found out who they were. They killed their uncle, fulfilling the prophecy.

Arabic

A variation of the self-fulfilling prophecy is the self-fulfilling dream, which dates back to medieval Arabic literature. Several tales in the *One Thousand and One Nights*, also known as the *Arabian Nights*, use this device to foreshadow what is going to happen, as a special form of literary prolepsis. A notable example is "The Ruined Man Who Became Rich Again Through a Dream", in which a man is told in his dream to leave his native city of Baghdad and travel to Cairo, where he will discover the whereabouts of some hidden treasure. The man travels there and experiences misfortune after losing belief in the prophecy, ending up in jail, where he tells his dream to a police officer. The officer mocks the idea of foreboding dreams and tells the protagonist that he himself had a dream about a house with a courtyard and fountain in Baghdad where treasure is buried under the fountain. The man recognizes the place as his own house and, after he is released from jail, he returns home and digs up the treasure. In other words, the foreboding dream not only predicted the future, but the dream was the cause of its prediction coming true. A variant of this story later appears in English folklore as the "Pedlar of Swaffham".*[15]

Another variation of the self-fulfilling prophecy can be seen in "The Tale of Attaf", where Harun al-Rashid consults his library (the House of Wisdom), reads a random book, "falls to laughing and weeping and dismisses the faithful *vizier*" Ja'far ibn Yahya from sight. Ja'far, "disturbed and upset flees Baghdad and plunges into a series of adventures in Damascus, involving Attaf and the woman whom Attaf eventually marries." After returning to Baghdad, Ja'far reads the same book that caused Harun to laugh and weep, and discovers that it describes his own adventures with Attaf. In other words, it was Harun's reading of the book that provoked the adventures described in the book to take place. This is an early example of reverse causality.*[16] In the 12th century, this tale was translated into Latin by Petrus Alphonsi and included in his *Disciplina Clericalis*. In the 14th century, a version of this tale also appears in the *Gesta Romanorum* and

Giovanni Boccaccio's *The Decameron.*[17]

Indian

Self-fulfilling prophecies appear in classical Sanskrit literature. In the story of Krishna in the Indian epic *Mahabharata*, the ruler of the Mathura kingdom, Kansa, afraid of a prophecy that predicted his death at the hands of his sister Devaki's son, had her cast into prison where he planned to kill all of her children at birth. After killing the first six children, and Devaki's apparent miscarriage of the seventh, Krishna (the eighth son) took birth. As his life was in danger he was smuggled out to be raised by his foster parents Yashoda and Nanda in the village of Gokula. Years later, Kansa learned about the child's escape and kept sending various demons to put an end to him. The demons were defeated at the hands of Krishna and his brother Balarama. Krishna as a young man returned to Mathura to overthrow his uncle, and Kansa was eventually killed by his nephew Krishna. It was due to Kansa's attempts to prevent the prophecy that led to it coming true, thus fulfilling the prophecy.

Russian

Oleg of Novgorod was a Varangian prince who ruled of the Rus people during the early tenth century. As old East Slavic chronicles say it was prophesied by the pagan priests that Oleg would take death from his stallion. To avoid this he sent the horse away. Many years later he asked where his horse was, and was told it had died. He asked to see the remains and was taken to the place where the bones lay. When he touched the horse's skull with his boot a snake slithered from the skull and bit him. Oleg died, thus fulfilling the prophecy. In the Primary Chronicle, Oleg is known as the Prophet, ironically referring to the circumstances of his death. The story was romanticized by Alexander Pushkin in his celebrated ballad "The Song of the Wise Oleg". In Scandinavian tradition*s, this legend lived on in the saga of Orvar-Odd.*

European fairy tales

Many fairy tales, such as *The Devil With the Three Golden Hairs*, *The Fish and the Ring*, *The Story of Three Wonderful Beggars*, or *The King Who Would Be Stronger Than Fate*, revolve about a prophecy that a poor boy will marry a rich girl (or, less frequently, a poor girl a rich boy).*[18] This is story type 930 in the Aarne–Thompson classification scheme. The girl's father's efforts to prevent it are the reason why the boy ends up marrying her.

Another fairy tale occurs with older children. In *The Language of the Birds*, a father forces his son to tell him what the birds say: that the father would be the son's servant. In *The Ram*, the father forces his daughter to tell him her dream: that her father would hold an ewer for her to wash her hands in. In all such tales, the father takes the child's response as evidence of ill-will and drives the child off; this allows the child to change so that the father will not recognize his own offspring later and so offer to act as the child's servant.

In some variants of *Sleeping Beauty*, such as *Sun, Moon, and Talia*, the sleep is not brought about by a curse, but a prophecy that she will be endangered by flax (or hemp) results in the royal order to remove all the flax or hemp from the castle, resulting in her ignorance of the danger and her curiosity.

Shakespeare

Shakespeare's *Macbeth* is another classic example of a self-fulfilling prophecy. The three witches give Macbeth a prophecy that Macbeth will eventually become king, but afterwards, the offspring of his best friend will rule instead of his own. Macbeth tries to make the first half true while trying to keep his bloodline on the throne instead of his friend's. Spurred by the prophecy, he kills the king and his friend, something he, arguably, never would have done before. In the end, the evil actions he committed to avoid his succession by another's bloodline get him killed in a revolution.

The later prophecy by the first apparition of the witches that Macbeth should "Beware Macduff" is also a self-fulfilling prophecy. If Macbeth had not been told this, then he might not have regarded Macduff as a threat. Therefore he would not have killed Macduff's family, and Macduff would not have sought revenge and killed Macbeth.

19.4.2 Modern

Similar to Oedipus above, a more modern example would be Darth Vader in the *Star Wars* films, or Lord Voldemort in the Harry Potter franchise- each attempted to take steps to prevent action against them which had been predicted could cause their downfall, but instead *created* the conditions leading to it. Another, less well-known, modern example occurred with the character John Mitchell on BBC Three's *Being Human*.

New Thought

The law of attraction is a typical example of self-fulfilling prophecy. It is the name given to the belief that "like attracts like" and that by focusing on positive or negative thoughts, one can bring about positive or negative results.[19][20] According to this law, all things are created first by imagination, which leads to thoughts, then to words and actions. The thoughts, words and actions held in mind affect someone's intentions which makes the expected result happen. Although there are some cases where positive or negative attitudes can produce corresponding results (principally the placebo and nocebo effects), there is no scientific basis to the law of attraction.[21]

19.5 See also

- Bad trip
- Clash of Civilizations
- Cognitive behavioral therapy
- Coordination game
- Copycat effect
- Deus ex machina
- Eschatology
- Expectation (epistemic)
- Factoid
- Fake it till you make it
- Fatalism
- Golem effect
- Mamihlapinatapai
- Martti Olavi Siirala
- Moore's law
- Nocebo
- Placebo
- Predestination paradox
- Pygmalion effect
- Reflexivity (social theory)
- Subject-expectancy effect

- Selection bias

- Self-defeating prophecy

- Self-licking ice cream cone

- Self-validating reduction

- Stereotype threat

- Sunspots (economics)

- Wishful thinking

19.6   Notes

[1] Merton, Robert K. (1948), "The Self Fulfilling Prophecy", *Antioch Review* **8** (2 (Summer)): 195, doi:10.2307/4609267, ISSN 0003-5769, retrieved May 4, 2014

[2] Darley, John M.; Gross, Paget H. (2000), "A Hypothesis-Confirming Bias in Labelling Effects", in Stangor, Charles, *Stereotypes and prejudice: essential readings*, Psychology Press, p. 212, ISBN 978-0-86377-589-5, OCLC 42823720

[3] Thomas, W. I. (1928). *The Child in America: Behavior Problems and Programs*. New York: Alfred A. Knopf. p. 572.

[4] Merton, Robert K (1968). *Social Theory and Social Structure*. New York: Free Press. p. 477. ISBN 978-0-02-921130-4. OCLC 253949.

[5] Popper, Karl (1976). *Unended Quest: An Intellectual Autobiography*. LaSalle, Illinois: Open Court. ISBN 978-0-87548-343-6. OCLC 2927208.

[6] Brameld, T. (1972). "Education as self-fulfilling prophecy". *Phi Beta Kappa* **54** (1): 8–11, 58–61 [p. 9]. Quoted by Wilkins (1976), p. 176.

[7] Wilkins, William E. (1976). "The Concept of a Self-Fulfilling Prophecy". *Sociology of Education* **49** (2): 175–183. doi:10.2307/2112523. ISSN 0038-0407. JSTOR 2112523.

[8] Allport, G. (1950). "The role of expectancy". In Cantril, H. *The Tensions That Cause Wars*. Urbana: University of Illinois. pp. 43–78.

[9] Rosenthal, Robert (2003). "Covert communication in laboratories, classrooms, and the truly real world" (PDF). *Current Directions in Psychological Science* (Blackwell) **12** (5): 151–154. doi:10.1111/1467-8721.t01-1-01250. Retrieved 4 May 2014.

[10] Gladwell, Malcolm (2008). "1 – The Matthew Effect". *Outliers*. Little, Brown and Company. pp. 20–25. ISBN 978-0-316-01792-3. Lay summary.

[11] Helsen, WF; Starkes, JL; Van Winckel, J (2000-11-01). "Effect of a change in selection year on success in male soccer players". *American journal of human biology : the official journal of the Human Biology Council* **12** (6): 729–735. doi:10.1002/1520-6300(200011/12)12:6<729::AID-AJHB2>3.0.CO;2-7. PMID 11534065.

[12] Carlson, N. R. (19992000). Personality. Psychology: the science of behaviour (Canandian ed., p. 492). Scarborough, Ont.: Allyn and Bacon Canada.

[13] See Nemesis, Moirai, Erinyes. "Very often the bases for false definitions and consequent self-fulfilling prophecies are deeply rooted in the individual or group norms and are subsequently difficult to change". (Wilkins 1976:177).

[14] Herodotus *Histories* 1.88

[15] Irwin, Robert (2003). *The Arabian Nights: A Companion*. Tauris Parke Paperbacks. pp. 193–4. ISBN 1-86064-983-1.

[16] Irwin, Robert (2003). *The Arabian Nights: A Companion*. Tauris Parke Paperbacks. p. 199. ISBN 1-86064-983-1.

[17] Ulrich Marzolph, Richard van Leeuwen, Hassan Wassouf (2004). *The Arabian Nights Encyclopedia*. ABC-CLIO. p. 109. ISBN 1-57607-204-5.

[18] Stith Thompson, *The Folktale*, p 139, University of California Press, Berkeley Los Angeles London, 1977

[19] Whittaker, S. Secret attraction, *The Montreal Gazette*, May 12, 2007.

[20] Redden, Guy, *Magic Happens: A New Age Metaphysical Mystery Tour*, Journal of Australian Studies: 101

[21] Carroll, Robert Todd (12 September). "law of attraction". *The Skeptic's Dictionary*. Retrieved 7 September 2012. Check date values in: |date= (help)

19.7 Further reading

- Dorothy L. Sayers, "Oedipus Simplex: Freedom and Fate in Folklore and Fiction"

Oedipus in the arms of Phorbas.

Romulus and Remus feeding from a wolf.

Krishna playing his flute with Radha.

Chapter 20

Story within a story

A **story within a story** is a literary device in which one character within a narrative himself narrates.[*][1] *Mise en abyme* is the French term for a similar literary device (also referring to the practice in heraldry of placing the image of a small shield on a larger shield). A story within a story can be used in all types of narration: novels, short stories, plays, television programs, films, poems, songs, and philosophical essays.

20.1 Types of nested story

20.1.1 Story within a story

The inner stories are told either simply to entertain or more usually to act as an example to the other characters. In either case the story often has symbolic and psychological significance for the characters in the outer story. There is often some parallel between the two stories, and the fiction of the inner story is used to reveal the truth in the outer story.

The literary device of stories within a story dates back to a device known as a frame story, when the outer story does not have much matter, and most of the bulk of the work consists of one or more complete stories told by one or more storytellers. This concept can be found in ancient Indian literature, such as the epics *Mahabharata* and *Ramayana*, Vishnu Sarma's *Panchatantra*, Syntipas' *Seven Wise Masters*, the *Hitopadesha*, and *Vikram and the Vampire*. Another early example of stories within a story can be found in the *One Thousand and One Nights* (*Arabian Nights*), which can be traced back to Arabic, Persian, and Indian storytelling traditions. Homer's Odyssey too makes use of this device; Odysseus' adventures at sea are all narrated by Odysseus to the court of king Alcinous in Scheria. Other shorter tales, many of them false, account for much of the Odyssey.

Often the stories within a story are used to satirize views, not only in the outer story but also in the real world. *The Itchy & Scratchy Show* from *The Simpsons* and *Terrance & Phillip* from *South Park* both comment on the levels of violence and acceptable behaviour in the media and allow criticism of the outer cartoon to be addressed in the cartoon itself.

Stories-within-a-story may disclose the background of characters or events, tell of myths and legends that influence the plot, or even seem to be extraneous diversions from the plot. In his 1895 historical novel *Pharaoh*, Bolesław Prus introduces a number of stories-within-the-story, ranging in length from vignette to full-blown story, many of them drawn from ancient Egyptian texts, that further the plot, illuminate characters, and even inspire the fashioning of individual characters.

The provenance of the story is sometimes explained internally, as in *The Lord of the Rings* by J. R. R. Tolkien, which depicts the Red Book of Westmarch (a story-internal version of the book itself) as a history compiled by several of the characters. The subtitles of *The Hobbit* (*There and Back Again*) is depicted as part of a rejected title of this book-within-a-book, and *The Lord of the Rings* is a part of the final title.[*][2]

When a story is told within another, rather than being told as part of the plot, it allows the author to play on the reader's perceptions of the characters—the motives and the reliability of the storyteller are automatically in question. In Chaucer's

The Canterbury Tales, the characters tell tales suited to their personalities and tell them in ways that highlight their personalities. The noble knight tells a noble story, the boring character tells a very dull tale and the rude miller tells a smutty tale.

In some cases, the story within a story is involved in the action of the plot of the outer story. An example is "The Mad Trist" in Edgar Allan Poe's *The Fall of the House of Usher*, where through somewhat mystical means the narrator's reading of the story-within-a-story influences the reality of the story he has been telling, so that what happens in "the Mad Trist" begins happening in "The Fall of the House of Usher". Also, in *Don Quixote* by Cervantes, there are many stories within the story that influence the hero's actions (there are others that even the author himself admits are purely digressive).

An inner story is often independent so that it can either be skipped over or read separately, although many subtle connections may be lost. A commonly anthologised story is *The Grand Inquisitor* by Dostoevsky from his long psychological novel *The Brothers Karamazov* and is told by one brother to another to explain, in part, his view on religion and morality. It also, in a succinct way, dramatizes many of Dostoevsky's interior conflicts.

Sometimes, the inner story serves as an outlet for discarded ideas that the author deemed to be of too much merit to leave out completely, something that is somewhat analogous to the inclusion of deleted scenes with DVD releases of films.

> An example of this is the chapter *The Town Ho's Story* in Herman Melville's novel *Moby-Dick*; that chapter tells a fully formed story of an exciting mutiny and contains many plot ideas that Melville had conceived during the early stages of writing Moby Dick, ideas originally intended to be used later on in the novel, but as writing progressed these plot ideas eventually proved impossible to fit around the characters that Melville went on to create and develop. Instead of discarding these ideas altogether, Melville instead weaved them into a coherent short story and had the character Ishmael demonstrate his eloquence and intelligence by telling the story to his impressed friends.

> Arthur Ransome uses the device to let his young characters in the *Swallows and Amazons series* of children's books, plotted in the recognisable everyday world, take part in fantastic adventures of piracy in distant lands: two books from the twelve: *Peter Duck* and *Missee Lee* (and some would include *Great Northern?* as a third) are adventures supposedly made up by the characters.*[3]

With the rise of literary modernism, writers experimented with ways in which multiple narratives might nest imperfectly within each other. A particularly ingenious example of nested narratives is James Merrill's 1974 modernist poem "Lost in Translation".

Other prime examples of experimental modernist literature that incorporate multiple narratives into one story are various novels written by American author Kurt Vonnegut. Vonnegut includes the recurring character Kilgore Trout in many of his novels. Trout acts as the mysterious science fiction writer who enhances the moral of the novel through plot descriptions of his stories. Books such as *Breakfast of Champions* and *God Bless You, Mr. Rosewater* are sprinkled with these plot descriptions.

Robert A. Heinlein's later books (*The Number of the Beast*, *The Cat Who Walks Through Walls* and *To Sail Beyond the Sunset*) propose the idea that every real universe is a fiction in another Universe. This hypothesis enables many writer who are characters in the books to interact with their own creations.

The Amory Wars, the story told through the music of Coheed and Cambria, tells a story for the first two albums but reveals that the story is being actively written by a character called the Writer in the third. During the album, the Writer delves into his own story and kills one of the characters, much to the dismay of the main character.

Several *Star Trek* tales are stories or events within stories, such as Gene Roddenberry's novelization of *Star Trek: The Motion Picture*, J. A. Lawrence's *Mudd's Angels*, John M. Ford's *The Final Reflection*, Margaret Wander Bonanno's *Strangers from the Sky* (which adopts the conceit that it is book from the future by an author called Gen Jaramet-Sauner), and J.R. Rasmussen's "Research" in the anthology *Star Trek: Strange New Worlds II*. Steven Barnes's novelization of "Far Beyond the Stars" partners with Greg Cox's *The Eugenics Wars: The Rise and Fall of Khan Noonien Singh* (Volume Two) to tell us that the story "Far Beyond the Stars" —and, by extension, all of *Star Trek* itself —is the creation of 1950s writer Benny Russell.

The *Quantum Leap* novel *Knights Of The Morningstar* also features a character who writes a book by that name.

The Crying of Lot 49 by Thomas Pynchon has several characters seeing a play called 'The Courier's Tragedy' by the fictitious Jacobean playwright Richard Wharfinger. The events of the play broadly mirror those of the novel and give the main character, Oedipa, a greater context with which to consider her predicament; the play concerns a feud between two rival mail distribution companies, which appears to be on-going to the present day, and in which, if this is the case, Oedipa has found herself involved. As in *Hamlet*, the director makes changes to the original script; in this instance, a couplet that was added, possibly by religious zealots intent on giving the play extra moral gravity, are said only on the night that Oedipa sees the play. From what Pynchon tells us, this is the only mention in the play of Thurn and Taxis' rivals' name - Trystero - and it is the seed for the conspiracy that unfurls.

A variant of this device is a flashback within a flashback, which was notably used by the Japanese film *Rashomon* (1950), based on the Japanese novel *In a Grove* (1921). The story unfolds in flashback as the four witnesses in the story—the bandit, the murdered samurai, his wife, and the nameless woodcutter—recount the events of one afternoon in a grove. But it is also a flashback within a flashback, because the accounts of the witnesses are being retold by a woodcutter and a priest to a ribald commoner as they wait out a rainstorm in a ruined gatehouse.

In Matthew Stover's novel *Shatterpoint*, the protagonist Mace Windu narrates the story within his journal, while the main story is being told from third person limited.

20.1.2 Subsequent layers

Some stories may include within themselves a story within a story, or even more than two layers.

This literary device also dates back to ancient Sanskrit literature. In Vishnu Sarma's *Panchatantra*, an inter-woven series of colorful animal tales are told with one narrative opening within another, sometimes three or four layers deep, and then unexpectedly snapping shut in irregular rhythms to sustain attention. In Ugrasrava's epic *Mahabharata*, the Kurukshetra War is narrated by a character in Vyasa's *Jaya*, which itself is narrated by a character in Vaisampayana's *Bharata*, which itself is narrated by a character in Ugrasrava's *Mahabharata*.

The structure of The Symposium and Phaedo, attributed to Plato, is of a story within a story within a story.

Another early example is the *One Thousand and One Nights* (*Arabian Nights*), where the general story is narrated by an unknown narrator, and in this narration the stories are told by Scheherazade. In many of Scheherazade's narrations there are also stories narrated, and even in some of these, there are some other stories.*[4] An example of this includes the "Sinbad the Sailor" story narrated by Scheherazade. Within the story itself, the protagonist Sinbad the Sailor narrates the stories of his seven voyages to Sinbad the Porter. Another example is "The Three Apples", a murder mystery narrated by Scheherazade. Within the story itself, after the murderer reveals himself, he narrates his reasons for the murder as a flashback of events leading up to the murder. Within this flashback, an unreliable narrator tells a story to mislead the would-be murderer, who later discovers that he was misled after another character narrates the truth to him.*[5] As the story concludes, the "Tale of Núr al-Dín Alí and his Son" is narrated within it. In yet another tale Scheherazade narrates, "The Fisherman and the Jinni", the "Tale of the Wazir and the Sage Duban" is narrated within it, and within that there are three more tales narrated.

Jan Potocki's *The Manuscript Found in Saragossa* (1797-1805) has extremely rich interlocking structure with stories-within-stories reaching several levels of depth.

Plays such as *I Hate Hamlet* or movies such as *A Midwinter's Tale* are about a production of *Hamlet*, which in turn includes a production of *The Murder of Gonzago* (or *The Mouse-trap*), so we have a story (*The Murder of Gonzago*) within a story (*Hamlet*) within a story (*A Midwinter's Tale*).

At least one line in the C. S. Lewis book *The Last Battle* implies that Lewis learned of Narnia's events - and thus wrote the Narnia books - after the Railway Accident in 1949, when Susan told him the stories in the belief that she was relating mere childhood make-believe. Further still, *The Silver Chair* states that a Narnian author wrote a book called *The Horse and His Boy* after the events related in the novel.

Mary Shelley's *Frankenstein* at one point features the narration of an Arctic explorer, who records the narration of Victor Frankenstein, who recounts the narration of his creation, who narrates the story of a cabin dwelling family he secretly observes.

Margaret Atwood's novel *The Blind Assassin* also uses this technique. The novel's expository narration is interspersed with excerpts from a novel written by one of the main characters; the novel-within-a-novel itself contains a science fiction story written by one of *that* novel's characters.

Stanisław Lem's *Tale of the Three Storytelling Machines of King Genius* from *The Cyberiad* has several levels of storytelling. Interestingly, all levels tell stories of the same person, *Trurl*.

House of Leaves, the tale of a man who finds a manuscript telling the story of a documentary that may or may not have ever existed, contains multiple layers of plot. The book even includes footnotes and letters that tell their own stories only vaguely related to the events in the main narrative of the book, and even includes footnotes for fake books. In addition, the fact that portions of the book were released through the internet and purported to be true added an even higher level to the cult following surrounding this book.

The Simpsons parodied this structure with numerous 'layers' of sub-stories in the Season 17 episode "The Seemingly Never-Ending Story".

Neil Gaiman's influential graphic novel series *The Sandman* includes several examples of this device. *Worlds' End*, volume 8 of the series, contains several instances of multiple storytelling levels, including *Cerements* (issue #55) where one of the inmost levels actually corresponds to one of the outer levels, turning the story-within-a-story structure into an infinite regression.

In the beginning of the music video for the Michael Jackson song "Thriller", the heroine is terrorized by her monster boyfriend in what turns out to be a movie within a dream.

Roald Dahl's story *The Wonderful Story of Henry Sugar* is about a rich bachelor who finds an essay written by someone who learnt to "see" playing cards from the reverse side. The full text of this essay is included in the story, and itself includes a lengthy sub-story told as a true experience by one of the essay's protagonists, Imhrat Khan.

The music video for the Björk song "Bachelorette" features a musical that is about, in part, the creation of that musical. A mini-theater and small audience appear on stage to watch the musical-within-a-musical, and at some point, within that second musical a yet-smaller theater and audience appear.

Episode 14 of the anime series *Martian Successor Nadesico* causes a rather confusing link between the world of the show itself and that of *Gekigangar III*, a popular anime that exists within its universe and that many characters are fans of; the episode is essentially a clip show, but has several newly animated segments based on Gekigangar that involves the characters of that show watching Nadesico (many of them being big fans of it themselves). The episode ends with the crew of the Nadesico watching the very same episode of Gekigangar, causing a bizarre paradox of sorts.

Since *Nadesico*, other anime series have featured shows-within-a-show; the most famous examples are *Densha Otoko*, which had the series *Getsumento Heiki Mina* and *Genshiken*, which had *Kujibiki Unbalance*. Both sub-shows have since become actual series in their own right, though three episodes of *Kujibiki Unbalance* were created as OVAs to coincide with the release of *Genshiken*. The episodes were styled as if they were part of a serial, though they were actually one-offs. There is also a *Kujibiki Unbalance* manga, being translated and published by Del Rey/Tanoshimi.

Jostein Gaarder's books often feature this device. Examples are *The Solitaire Mystery*, where the protagonist receives a small book from a baker, in which the baker tells the story of a sailor who tells the story of another sailor, and *Sophie's World* about a girl who is actually a character in a book that is being read by Hilde, a girl in another dimension. Later on in the book Sophie questions this idea, and realizes that Hilde too could be a character in a story that in turn is being read by another.

The popular graphic novel Watchmen features a story within a story called Tales of the Black Freighter, which details that man's insanity comes from fear of losing something. The story parallels that of one of the characters in the main story, hinting at his actions. The panels of the *Tales...* comic are drawn grainy and with dulled colors, to give it a pulp feel, while in the film adaptation the story is presented as a cartoon within the movie.

Daniel Handler's introduction in Lemony Snicket's *Unauthorized Autobiography* continually introduces a new story about a page into the previous one, thus creating a confusing and inconsequential (but not incorrect or self-contradictory) storyline that is never finished, always dealing with the questions he is asked but never answering them. He drops a hint in one of the layers that this is simply a technique to distract the reader from the fact that he never answers these questions.

Best New Horror, a short story from the book *20th Century Ghosts*, has the main character reading a horror tale called Button Boy.

Catheryne Valente's duology, "The Orphan's Tales" featured strong influences from 1001 Arabian Nights, with stories nestled within stories - sometimes up to more than seven layers.

20.1.3 Play within a play

This dramatic device was probably first used by Thomas Kyd in *The Spanish Tragedy* around 1587, where the play is presented before an audience of two of the characters, who comment upon the action.[6][7] From references in other contemporary works, Kyd is also assumed to have been the writer of an early, lost version of *Hamlet* (the so-called *Ur-Hamlet*), with a play-within-a-play interlude.[8]

In Francis Beaumont's *Knight of the Burning Pestle* (ca. 1608) a supposed common citizen from the audience, actually a "planted" actor, condemns the play that has just started and "persuades" the players to present something about a shopkeeper. The citizen's "apprentice" then acts, pretending to extemporise, in the rest of the play. This is a satirical tilt at Beaumont's playwright contemporaries and their current fashion for offering plays about London life.[9]

William Shakespeare used this device in many of his plays, including *A Midsummer Night's Dream, Love's Labours Lost*, and *Hamlet*. In *Hamlet* the prince, Hamlet himself, asks some strolling players to perform the *Murder of Gonzago*. The action and characters in *The Murder* mirror the murder of Hamlet's father in the main action, and Prince Hamlet writes additional material to emphasize this. Hamlet wishes to provoke the murderer, his uncle, and sums this up by saying "the play's the thing wherein I'll catch the conscience of the king." Hamlet calls this new play *The Mouse-trap* (a title that Agatha Christie later took for the long-running play *The Mousetrap*). In the Hamlet-based film *Rosencrantz & Guildenstern Are Dead* the players even feature a third-level puppet theatre version within their play. Almost the whole of *The Taming of the Shrew* is a play-within-a-play, presented to convince Christopher Sly, a drunken tinker, that he is a nobleman watching a private performance, but the device has no relevance to the plot (unless Katharina's subservience to her "lord" in the last scene is intended to strengthen the deception against the tinker[10]) and is often dropped in modern productions. *Pericles* draws in part on the 14th century *Confessio Amantis* (itself a frame story) by John Gower and Shakespeare has the ghost of Gower "assume man's infirmities" to introduce his work to the contemporary audience and comment on the action of the play.[11]

In Anton Chekhov's *The Seagull* there are specific allusions to *Hamlet*: in the first act a son stages a play to impress his mother, a professional actress, and her new lover; the mother responds by comparing her son to Hamlet. Later he tries to come between them, as Hamlet had done with his mother and her new husband. The tragic developments in the plot follow in part from the scorn the mother shows for her son's play.[12]

The opera *Pagliacci* is about a troupe of actors who perform a play about marital infidelity that mirrors their own lives, and composer Richard Rodney Bennett and playwright-librettist Beverley Cross's *The Mines of Sulphur* features a ghostly troupe of actors who perform a play about murder that similarly mirrors the lives of their hosts, from whom they depart, leaving them with the plague as nemesis. And John Adams' *Nixon in China* (1985-7) features a surreal version of Madam Mao's *Red Detachment of Women* to extraordinary effect, illuminating the ascendence of human values over the disillusionment of high politics in the meeting.

In Bertolt Brecht's *The Caucasian Chalk Circle,* a play is staged as a parable to villagers in the Soviet Union to justify the re-allocation of their farmland: the tale describes how a child is awarded to a servant-girl rather than its natural mother, an aristocrat, as the woman most likely to care for it well. This kind of play-within-a-play, which appears at the beginning of the main play and acts as a 'frame' for it, is called an 'induction'. Brecht's one-act play *The Elephant Calf* (1926) is a play-within-a-play performed in the foyer of the theatre during his *Man Equals Man*.

In Jean Giraudoux's play Ondine, all of act two is a series of scenes within scenes, sometimes two levels deep. This increases the dramatic tension and also makes more poignant the inevitable failure of the relationship between the mortal Hans and water sprite Ondine.

The Two-Character Play by Tennessee Williams has a concurrent double plot with the convention of a play within a play. Felice and Clare are siblings and are both actor/producers touring 'The Two-Character Play.' They have supposedly been abandoned by their crew and have been left to put on the play by themselves. The characters in the play are also brother and sister and are also named Clare and Felice.

The Mysteries, a modern reworking of the mediaeval mystery plays, remains faithful to its roots by having the modern actors play the sincere, naïve tradesmen and women as they take part in the original performances.[13]

The musical *Kiss Me, Kate* is about the production of a fictitious musical, *The Taming of the Shrew,* based on the Shakespeare play of the same name, and features several scenes from it. Alternatively, a play might be about the production of a play, and include the performance of all or part of the play, as in *Noises Off, A Chorus of Disapproval, Lilies* or *The Producers.*

In most stagings of the musical *Cats,* which include the song "Growltiger's Last Stand" —a recollection of an old play by Gus the Theatre Cat —the character of Lady Griddlebone sings "The Ballad of Billy McCaw" . (However, many productions of the show omit "Growltiger's Last Stand" , and "The Ballad of Billy McCaw" has at times been replaced with a mock aria, so this metastory isn't always seen.) Depending on the production, there is another musical scene called The Awful Battle of the Pekes and the Pollices where the Jellicles put on a show for their leader. In *Lestat: The Musical,* there are three play within a plays. First, when Lestat visits his childhood friend, Nicolas, who works in a theater, where he discovers his love for theater; and two more when the Theater of the Vampires perform. One is used as a plot mechanism to explain the vampire god, Marius, which sparks an interest in Lestat to find him.

A play within a play also occurs in the musical *The King and I,* where Princess Tuptim and the royal dancers give a performance of *Small House of Uncle Thomas* (or *Uncle Tom's Cabin*) to their English guests. The play mirrors Tuptim's situation, as she wishes to run away from slavery to be with her lover, Lun Tha.

In stagings of Dina Rubina's play *Always the Same Dream,* the story is about staging a school play based on a poem by Pushkin.

20.1.4 Play within a film

Director Charlie Kaufman uses this concept often in his films. It can be seen most in the 2008 film *Synecdoche, New York.* The main character Caden Cotard is a skilled director of plays and he receives a grant to make a remarkable theater piece. He ends up creating a carbon copy of the outside world. The 2001 film *Moulin Rouge!* features a fictitious musical within a film, called "Spectacular Spectacular" , which itself may have been based on an ancient Sanskrit play, *The Little Clay Cart.* The 1942 Ernst Lubitsch comedy *To Be or Not to Be* confuses the audience in the opening scenes with a play about Adolf Hitler appearing to be taking place within the actual plot of the film. Thereafter, the acting company players serve as the protagonists of the film and frequently use acting/costumes to deceive various characters in the film. *Hamlet* also serves as an important throughline in the film, as suggested by the title. Laurence Olivier sets the opening scene of his 1944 film of *Henry V* in the tiring room of the old Globe Theatre as the actors prepare for their roles on stage. The early part of the film follows the actors in these "stage" performances and only later does the action almost imperceptibly expand to the full realism of the Battle of Agincourt. By way of increasingly more artificial sets (based on mediaeval paintings) the film finally returns to The Globe.

The main plot device in *Repo! The Genetic Opera* is an opera which is going to be held the night of the events of the movie. All of the principal characters of the film play a role in the opera, though the audience watching the opera is unaware that some of the events portrayed are more than drama. At the film *To Be or Not to Be,* the play "The Naughty Nazis" is forbidden for the Gestapo at the beginning of the film. In *Diary of a Wimpy Kid,* the middle-schoolers put on a play of *The Wizard of Oz.*

20.1.5 Film within a film

TV Tropes maintains a list of movies that feature this plot device.*[14] *Singin' in the Rain* is listed as the earliest known example.

The François Truffaut film *Day for Night* is about the making of a fictitious movie called *Meet Pamela* (*Je vous présente Pamela*) and shows the interactions of the actors as they are making this movie about a woman who falls for her husband's father. The story of *Pamela* involves lust, betrayal, death, sorrow, and change, events that are mirrored in the experiences of the actors portrayed in *Day for Night.*

In *12 Angry Men,* a juror is asked what films he saw in the preceding few days, in order to demonstrate the fallibility of peoples memory. The juror identifies "The Scarlet Circle" and "The Remarkable Mrs Bainbridge" (which another juror corrects to be "The Amazing Mrs Bainbridge"). "The Scarlet Circle" is a Whodunit written by Patrick Quentin, but is yet to be adapted into a film.

The script to Karel Reisz's movie *The French Lieutenant's Woman* (1980), written by Harold Pinter, is a film-within-a-film adaptation of John Fowles's book. In addition to the Victorian love story of the book, Pinter creates a present-day background story that shows a love affair between the main actors.

In Buster Keaton's *Sherlock, Jr.*, Keaton's protagonist actually enters into a film while it is playing in a cinema.

The 2002 Pedro Almodóvar film *Talk to Her* (*Hable con ella*) has the chief character Benigno tell a story called *The Shrinking Lover* to Alicia, a long-term comatose patient whom Benigno, a male nurse, is assigned to care for. The film presents *The Shrinking Lover* in the form of a black-and-white silent melodrama. To prove his love to a scientist girlfriend, the *The Shrinking Lover* protagonist drinks a potion that makes him progressively smaller. The resulting seven-minute scene, which is readily intelligible and enjoyable as a stand-alone short subject, is considerably more overtly comic than the rest of *Talk to Her*—the protagonist climbs giant breasts as if they were rock formations and even ventures his way inside a (compared to him) gigantic vagina. Critics have noted that *The Shrinking Lover* essentially is a sex metaphor. Later in *Talk to Her,* the comatose Alicia is discovered to be pregnant and Benigno is sentenced to jail for rape. *The Shrinking Lover* was named Best Scene of 2002 in the *Skandies*, an annual survey of online cinephiles and critics invited each year by critic Mike D'Angelo.

In the 2006 Tarsem film *The Fall*, an injured silent-movie stuntman tells heroic fantasy stories to a little girl with a broken arm to pass time in the hospital, which the film visualizes and presents with the stuntman's voice becoming voiceover narration. The fantasy tale bleeds back into and comments on the film's "present-tense" story. There are often incongruities based on the fact that the stuntman is an American and the girl Persian—the stuntman's voiceover refers to "Indians," "a squaw" and "a teepee," but the visuals show a Bollywood-style devi and a Taj Mahal-like castle.

The 1973 film adaptation[*][15] of Peter Nichols's 1969 play,[*][16] *The National Health* features a send-up of a typical American hospital soap-opera being shown on a television situated in an underfunded, unmistakably British NHS hospital.

Mel Brooks's 1974 comedy *Blazing Saddles* leaves its Western setting when the climactic fight scene breaks out, revealing the setting to have been a set in the Warner Bros. studio lot; the fight spills out onto an adjacent musical set, then into the studio canteen, and finally onto the streets. The two protagonists arrive at Grauman's Chinese Theater, which is showing the "premiere" of *Blazing Saddles*; they enter the cinema to watch the conclusion of their own film.

The concept of a film within a television series is employed in the Macross universe. *The Super Dimension Fortress Macross: Do You Remember Love?* (1984) was originally intended as an alternative theatrical re-telling of the television series *The Super Dimension Fortress Macross* (1982), but was later "retconned" into the Macross canon as a popular movie within the television series *Macross 7* (1994).

In the latter two films of the *Scream* horror trilogy, a film-within-a-film format is used when the events of the first film spawn their own horror trilogy within the films themselves. In *Scream 2*, characters get killed while watching a film version of the events in the first *Scream* film, while in *Scream 3* the actors playing the trilogy's characters end up getting killed, much in the same way as the characters they are playing on screen. In the latest *Scream* movie, *Scream 4*, in the opening sequence, two characters are watching Stab 7 before they get killed. Also, the characters of Stab 7 are watching Stab 6. There's also a party in which all seven Stab movies were going to be shown. References are also made to Stab 5 involving time travel as a plot device.

Austin Powers in Goldmember begins with an action film opening, which turns out to be a sequence being filmed by Steven Spielberg. Near the ending, the events of the film itself are revealed to be a movie being enjoyed by the characters. Parts of director Spike Jonze's *Adaptation.* follows a fictionalized version of screenwriter Charlie Kaufman as he struggles to adapt a book into a script, while the movie features scenes about the making of *Being John Malkovich*, previously written by Kaufman and directed by Jonze.

Tropic Thunder (2008) is a comedy film revolving around a group of prima donna actors making a Vietnam War film (itself also named "Tropic Thunder") when their fed-up writer and director decide to abandon them in the middle of the jungle, forcing them to fight their way out.

The first episode of the anime series *The Melancholy Of Haruhi Suzumiya* consists almost entirely of a poorly made film that the protagonists created, complete with Kyon's typical, sarcastic commentary.

The television shows *30 Rock, Studio 60 on the Sunset Strip, Sonny with a Chance & Kappa Mikey* feature a sketch show within the TV show.

Chuck Jones's 1953 cartoon *Duck Amuck* shows Daffy Duck trapped in a cartoon that an unseen animator repeatedly manipulates. At the end, it is revealed that the whole cartoon was being controlled by Bugs Bunny. In 2007, this sequence was parodied on *Drawn Together* ("Nipple Ring-Ring Goes to Foster Care").

All feature-length films by Jörg Buttgereit except *Schramm* feature a film within the film. In *Nekromantik*, the protagonist goes to the cinema to see the fictional slasher film *Vera*. In *Der Todesking* one of the character watches a video of the fictional Nazi exploitation film *Vera - Todesengel der Gestapo* and in *Nekromantik 2*, the characters go to see a movie called *Mon dejeuner avec Vera* which is a parody of Louis Malle's *My Dinner with André*.

The Irish television series *Father Ted* features a television show, *Father Ben*, which has characters and storylines almost identical to that of Father Ted.

Quentin Tarantino's *Inglourious Basterds* depicts a Nazi propaganda film called *Nation's Pride*, which glorifies a soldier in the German army. *Nation's Pride* is directed by Eli Roth.

Joe Dante's *Matinee* depicts *Mant*, an early-'60s sci-fi/horror movie about a man who turns into an ant. In one scene, the protagonists see a Disney-style family movie called *The Shook-Up Shopping Cart*.

20.1.6   Video game within a video game

Main article: Minigame

In many video games, for instance the *GTA* series, mini-games exist that are non-plot oriented, and optional to the completion of the game. *Grand Theft Auto: San Andreas* features several arcade-like games, including 'Invaders from Uranus' (A *Space Invaders* parody). *Grand Theft Auto IV* has another arcade game called 'Cub3d'. Also, while not "playable" video games within video games, the main games in the *Pokémon* series generally include a television and game console in the player character's room. The specific type of console portrayed depends on which one was most recently released by Nintendo when the specific game was released, e.g. a Wii in *Pokémon Black* and *White* versions. The Nintendo 64 video game *Donkey Kong 64* also had this system, at one part of the game when playing as Donkey Kong, the player can play the original *Donkey Kong* game.

Pokémon Channel for the Nintendo GameCube included an emulation of the Pokémon mini system, along with several games. Some *Pokémon* mini games were obtainable in-game.

In the *Shenmue* series of games there are several instances of games within the main game. In the first installment, the player is able to play a Sega Saturn inside the Hazuki Residence and there are several Sega arcade games playable in different locations. In *Shenmue 2*, playable arcade machines featuring other Sega titles are scattered throughout the game world. In *Final Fantasy VII* there are several video-games that can be played in an arcade in the Gold Saucer theme park, consisting of a beat-em-up, a snowboarding game, an RPG and a submarine game. In *Animal Crossing*, the player can acquire individual NES emulations through various means and place them within their house, where they are playable in their entirety. When placed in the house, the games take the form of a Nintendo Entertainment System.

It is implied in *Assassin's Creed Rogue* and *Assassin's Creed Unity* (and directly stated in *Assassin's Creed IV: Black Flag*) that a player is controlling an employee of Abstergo Entertainment, who looks inside the memories of Desmond Miles.

In *Ratchet & Clank: Up Your Arsenal*, Ratchet must play a "vid-comic" of Captain Qwark to understand the unfolding of subsequent events.

20.1.7   TV Show within a video game

In the Remedy video game title *Max Payne* players can chance upon a number of ongoing television shows when activating or happening upon various television sets within the game environs, depending on where / when they are within the unfolding game narrative will dictate which episode of what show is found. Among them are *Lords & Ladies*, *Captain Baseball Bat Boy*, *Dick Justice* and the pinnacle television serial *Address Unknown* -heavily inspired by David Lynch style film narrative, particularly *Twin Peaks*, Address Unknown sometimes prophesies events or character motives yet to occur in the Max Payne narrative.

20.2   Deeply nested fiction

There are several cases where an author has nested his fiction more deeply than just two layers.

The earliest examples are in Ugrasrava's epic *Mahabharata* and Vishnu Sarma's *Panchatantra*. Some of the stories narrated in the *Panchatantra* often had stories within them. In the epic *Mahabharata*, the Kurukshetra War is narrated by a character in Krishna Dwaipayana Vyasa's *Jaya*, which itself is narrated by a character in Vaisampayana's *Bharata*, which itself is narrated by a character in Ugrasrava's *Mahabharata*.

Another early example is *The Book of One Thousand and One Nights*, where the general story is narrated by an unknown narrator, and in this narration the stories are told by Scheherazade. In most of Scheherazade's narrations there are also stories narrated, and even in some of these, there are some other stories.

In Douglas Hofstadter's *Gödel, Escher, Bach*, there is a narrative between Achilles and the Tortoise (characters borrowed from Lewis Carroll, who in turn borrowed them from Zeno), and within this story they find a book entitled "Provocative Adventures of Achilles and the Tortoise Taking Place in Sundry Spots of the Globe", which they begin to read, the Tortoise taking the part of the Tortoise, and Achilles taking the part of Achilles. Within this narrative, which itself is somewhat self-referential, the two characters find a book entitled "Provocative Adventures of Achilles and the Tortoise Taking Place in Sundry Spots of the Globe", which they begin to read, the Tortoise taking the part of Achilles, and Achilles taking the part of the Tortoise.

In *The Sandman* by Neil Gaiman, the necropolis apprentice Petrefax tells a story that includes a storytelling session about Destruction telling a story. It is later shown that this - along with all the other stories in World's End - are being related to a bar girl by one of the characters present at Petrefax's original storytelling session.

In Sue Townsend's *Adrian Mole: The Wilderness Years*, Adrian writes a book entitled *Lo! The Flat Hills Of My Homeland*, in which the main character, Jake Westmorland, writes a book called *Sparg of Kronk*, whose eponymous character, Sparg, writes a book with no language.

In Philip K. Dick's novel *The Man in the High Castle*, each character comes into interaction with a book called *The Grasshopper Lies Heavy*, which was written by the Man in the High Castle. As Dick's novel details a world in which the Axis Powers of World War II had succeeded in dominating the known world, the novel within the novel details an alternative to this history in which the Allies overcome the Axis and bring stability to the world - a victory which itself is quite different from our history.

In Red Orc's Rage by Philip J. Farmer a doubly recursive method is used to interwine its fictional layers. This novel is part of a science-fiction series, the World of Tiers. Farmer collaborated in the writing of this novel with an American psychiatrist, Dr. A. James Giannini. Dr. Giannini had previously used the World of Tiers series in treating patients in group therapy. During these therapeutic sessions, the content and process of the text and novelist was discussed rather than the lives of the patients. In this way subconscious defenses could be circumvented. Farmer took the real life case-studies and melded these with adventures of his characters in the series.*[17]

In Charles Maturin's classic novel Melmoth the Wanderer, the use of vast stories-within-stories creates a sense of dream-like quality in the reader.

In Rabih Alameddine's novel The Hakawati, or The Storyteller, the protagonist describes coming home to the funeral of his father, one of a long line of tradition Arabic storytellers. Throughout the narrative, the author becomes hakawati (an Arabic word for a teller of traditional tales) himself, weaving the tale of the story of his own life and that of his family with folkloric versions of tales from Qur'an, the Old Testament, Ovid, and One Thousand and One Nights. Both the tales he tells of his family (going back to his grandfather) and the emebedded folk tales, themselves embed other tales, often 2 or more layers deep.

20.3   From story within a story to separate story

Occasionally a story within a story becomes such a popular element that the producer(s) decide to develop it autonomonously (completing it if in the real world it is incomplete) as a separate and distinct work. This is an example of a "spin-off".

In the fictional world of the *Toy Story* movies, Buzz Lightyear is an animated toy action figure, which was based on a fictitious cartoon series, *Buzz Lightyear of Star Command*, which did not exist in the real world except for snippets seen within *Toy Story*. *Buzz Lightyear of Star Command* was later produced in full in the real world, perhaps prompted by people who thought that the brief showing of *Buzz Lightyear of Star Command* in *Toy Story* was an embedded real-world advertisement.

Another notable example is the relationship between *Genshiken*, a manga series about popular culture, and *Kujibiki Unbalance*, a series in the *Genshiken* universe, which has spawned merchandise of its own, and is being remade into a series on its own.

On other occasions such spin-offs may be produced as a way of providing additional information on the fictional world for fans. A well-known example of this comes in the *Harry Potter* series of J. K. Rowling, where three such supplemental books have been produced, with the profits going to charity. *Fantastic Beasts and Where to Find Them* is a textbook used by the main character, and *Quidditch Through the Ages* is a book from the library at his school. *The Tales of Beedle the Bard* provides an additional layer of fiction, the 'tales' being instructional stories told to children in the characters' world.

Perhaps the most unusual example of this was the fictitious author Kilgore Trout, who appears in the works of Kurt Vonnegut. In the world of those stories, Kilgore Trout has written a novel called *Venus on the Half-Shell*. In 1975, real-world author Philip José Farmer wrote a science-fiction novel called *Venus on the Half-Shell*, which he published under the name Kilgore Trout.

The movie *Adaptation.* was presented as if it had been written by Charlie Kaufman and his fictitious brother Donald Kaufman. Both "brothers" were nominated for an Oscar that year.

Sometimes such spin-offs are produced against the original creator's wishes. One example is that the *Calvin & Hobbes* comic strip (written by Bill Waterson) includes in its scenario a children's book *Hamster Huey & The Gooey Kablooie*, and Bill Waterson stated in *The Calvin and Hobbes Tenth Anniversary Book* that he believed that *Hamster Huey & The Gooey Kablooie* should remain an undefined story, left to the reader's imagination; but someone not associated with the strip published *Hamster Huey & The Gooey Kablooie* in the real world.

At least one complete Captain Proton story has been written in the real world: *Captain Proton: Defender of the Earth*, a text story, by Dean Wesley Smith, who presumed that in the *Star Trek* universe, the holonovel *Captain Proton* was adapted from a supposed 1930's comic; and he set out to write and publish that comic in the real world, but as a text story. (Other fan fiction described as Captain Proton stories are *Star Trek: Voyager* stories whose action happens partly in Voyager's holodeck where the Captain Proton program is running.)

20.4   Examples of stories within stories

- *Mahābhārata*

- *Panchatantra*

- *One Thousand and One Nights*

- *A Midsummer Night's Dream*

- *Hamlet*

- *Love's Labour's Lost*

20.5   Fictional artists

Like S. Morgenstern, Peter Schikele's P.D.Q. Bach can be considered a "fictional artist", who supposedly created the works actually created by the artist's own creator. P.D.Q.'s life thus becomes something of a "frame story" (albeit indirectly) for such works as his opera *The Abduction of Figaro*.

Mystery author Ellery Queen can also be considered a "fictional artist" of sorts, though the proverbial line between his "true-life" and "fictional" exploits are generally very blurred.

In this case the "frame story"—that is, the fictional creator's life—can be considered metafictional, since each story (or other work) supposedly created by that character adds a little to his or her own (fictional) story.

Sometimes a song or a poem or an image in a fiction work, which was actually composed by the author, is attributed by the author to one of his characters, for example the song "Namarie" in *The Lord of the Rings* by J. R. R. Tolkien, which Tolkien attributes to the character Galadriel.

20.6 Frame stories

Main article: Frame story

An early phenomenon related to the "story within a story" is the "framing device" or "frame story", where a supplemental story is used to help tell the main story. In the supplemental story, or "frame", one or more characters tell the main story to one or more other characters.

The earliest examples of "frame stories" and "stories within stories" were in ancient Indian literature, such as the *Mahabharata, Ramayana, Fables of Bidpai, Hitopadesha* and *Vikram and the Vampire*. Both *The Golden Ass* by Apuleius and *Metamorphoses* by Ovid extend the depths of framing to several degrees. Another early example is the famous *Arabian Nights*, in which Sheherazade narrates stories within stories, and even within some of these, more stories are narrated. Chaucer's *The Canterbury Tales* is also a frame story.

A well-known modern example of this is *The Princess Bride*, both the book and the movie. In the movie, a grandfather is reading the story of "The Princess Bride" to his grandson. In the book, a more detailed frame story has a father editing a (nonexistent) much longer work for his son, creating his own "Good Parts Version" (as the book called it) by leaving out all the parts that would bore a young boy. Both the book and the movie assert that the central story is from a book called "The Princess Bride" by a nonexistent author named S. Morgenstern.

Sometimes a frame story exists in the same setting as the main story. On the television series *The Young Indiana Jones Chronicles*, each episode was framed as though it were being told by Indy when he was older (usually acted by George Hall, but once by Harrison Ford).

The 2013 film *The Great Gatsby* was framed as if the character Nick Carraway is telling the story to another character.

20.7 See also

- Metafiction

- List of fictional plays

- List of fictional books

- List of fictional musicals

- List of fictional television shows

- Frame story

- Parable

20.8 References

[1] Herman, David; Jahn, Manfred; Ryan, Marie-Laure (13 May 2013). *Routledge Encyclopedia of Narrative Theory*. Routledge. p. 134. ISBN 978-1-134-45840-0. Retrieved 30 July 2013.

[2] Tolkien, J. R. R. (1955), *The Return of the King*, *The Lord of the Rings*, Boston: Houghton Mifflin (published 1987), "The Grey Havens", ISBN 0-395-08256-0

[3] Hardyment, Christina (1988). *Arthur Ransome and Captain Flint's Trunk*. London: Jonathan Cape. ISBN 0-224-02590-2.

[4] Burton, Richard (September 2003). *The Book of the Thousand Nights and a Night, Volume 1*. Project Gutenberg.

[5] Pinault, David (1992). *Story-Telling Techniques in the Arabian Nights*. Brill Publishers. p. 94. ISBN 90-04-09530-6.

[6] Bevington, David (ed.) (1996). *The Spanish Tragedy, Revels Student Edition*. Manchester, England: Manchester University Press. p. 5. ISBN 0-7190-4344-1. Andrea and Revenge... 'sit and see' ...the play proper is staged for them; in this sense, *The Spanish Tragedy* is itself a play within a play.

[7] Erne, Lukas (2001). *Beyond The Spanish tragedy: a study of the works of Thomas Kyd*. Manchester, England: Manchester University Press. p. 96. ISBN 0-7190-6093-1. the first play-within-a-play

[8] Barton, Anne (1980). *The New Penguin Shakespeare Hamlet*. Harmondsworth, England: Penguin Books. p. 15. ISBN 0-14-070734-4.

[9] Gurr, Andrew (1968). "Critical introduction". *The Knight of the Burning Pestle*. Edinburgh: Oliver and Boyd. pp. 2–6. ISBN 0050015710.

[10] Aspinall, Dana (2001). "The play and the critics". *The Taming of the Shrew*. London: Routledge. p. 19. ISBN 978-0-8153-3515-3.

[11] Buchanan, Judith (2001). *Shakespeare—Four late plays*. Ware, England: Wordsworth Editions. pp. 5–8. ISBN 1-84022-104-6.

[12] Pearce, Richard (1993). "Chekhov into English: the case of 'The Seagull'". In Miles, Patrick. *Chekhov on the British stage*. Cambridge, England: Cambridge University Press. p. 220. A dominant motif in the play is the recurrent Hamlet theme

[13] Normington, Katie (October 2007). *Modern mysteries: contemporary productions of medieval English cycle dramas*. Melton, Suffolk, England: Boydell and Brewer. p. 86. ISBN 978-1-84384-128-9.

[14] http://tvtropes.org/pmwiki/pmwiki.php/ShowWithinAShow/Live-ActionFilms

[15] The National Health (film)

[16] The National Health (play)

[17] Giannini, A. J. (2001). "Use of fiction in therapy". *Psychiatric Times* **18** (7): 56–57.

Chapter 21

Ticking time bomb scenario

The **ticking time bomb scenario** is a thought experiment that has been used in the ethics debate over whether torture can ever be justified. As a thought experiment, there is no need that the scenario be plausible, it need only serve to highlight ethical considerations. The scenario can be formulated as follows:

> Suppose that a person with knowledge of an imminent terrorist attack, that will kill many people, is in the hands of the authorities and that he will disclose the information needed to prevent the attack only if he is tortured. Should he be tortured?*[1]

The scenario can be better understood through the arguments of those who respond to it; the consequentialist argument is that nations, even those that legally disallow torture, can justify its use if they have a terrorist in custody who possesses critical knowledge, such as the location of a time bomb or a weapon of mass destruction that will soon explode and cause great loss of life. Opponents to the argument usually begin by exposing certain assumptions that tend to be hidden by initial presentations of the scenario and tend to obscure the true costs of permitting torture in "real-life" scenarios—e.g., the assumption that the person is in fact a terrorist, whereas in real life there usually remains uncertainty about whether the person is in fact a terrorist and that he has useful information*[2]—and rely on legal, philosophical/moral, and empirical grounds to reaffirm the need for the absolute prohibition of torture. There is also uncertainty about the effectiveness of torture, and much opposition to torture is based on the fact it is not effective rather than any moral issue.

21.1 Background

The concept was first introduced during the 1960s in the novel *Les Centurions* by Jean Lartéguy which is set during the First Indochina War. The version in the novel has the following conditions:*[3]

1. The evidence in support of the contention that he has the relevant information would satisfy the requirements of evidence for convicting him of an offence.

2. There are reasonable grounds for believing that he is likely to tell the truth if severe torture is threatened, and, if necessary, applied to him.

3. There are reasonable grounds for believing that no other means would have the effect of compelling him to tell the truth.

4. There are grounds for believing that if the information is obtained quickly, there is a good chance of defusing the bomb before it goes off.

5. There are reasonable grounds for believing that the likely damage to be caused by the bomb will include death of many citizens, the maiming of others, including the infliction of much more severe pain on others with much more lasting effect than will be the effect of the infliction of torture on the person who has been captured;

6. There are reasonable grounds for believing that the torturing will not have consequences which would be worse than the damage likely to result from the bomb going off.

According to Darius Rejali, a professor of political science at Reed College, the possibility of sudden, massive destruction of innocent life provided French liberals with a more acceptable justification for committing torture.*[4]

21.2 Views in favor of accepting torture in emergencies

Alan Dershowitz, a prominent American defense attorney, surprised some observers by giving limited support to the idea that torture could be justified. He argued that human nature can lead to unregulated abuse "off the books" . Therefore, it would be better if there were a regulated procedure through which an interrogator could request a "torture warrant" and that requiring a warrant would establish a paper trail of accountability. Torturers, and those who authorize torture, could be held to account for excesses. Dershowitz's suggested torture warrants, similar to search warrants and phone tap warrants, would spell out the limits on the techniques that interrogators may use, and the extent to which they may abridge a suspect's rights.

In September 2002, when reviewing Alan Dershowitz's book, *Why Terrorism Works: Understanding the Threat, Responding to the Challenge*, Richard Posner, legal scholar and judge of the United States Court of Appeals for the Seventh Circuit, wrote in *The New Republic*, "If torture is the only means of obtaining the information necessary to prevent the detonation of a nuclear bomb in Times Square, torture should be used--and will be used--to obtain the information.... No one who doubts that this is the case should be in a position of responsibility." *[5]

21.2.1 Views in favor of torturing the relatives of suspects

In February 2010 Bruce Anderson wrote a column for *The Independent*, arguing that the British government would have not just the right, but the duty, to torture if there was a ticking bomb, and that they should torture the relatives of suspects if they believed that doing so would yield information that would avert a terrorist attack: "It came, in the form of a devilish intellectual challenge. 'Let's take your hypothesis a bit further. We have captured a terrorist, but he is a hardened character. We cannot be certain that he will crack in time. We have also captured his wife and children'. After much agonising, I have come to the conclusion that there is only one answer to Sydney's question. Torture the wife and children." *[6]

21.3 Views rejecting torture under all circumstances

Some human rights organizations, professional and academic experts, and military and intelligence leaders have absolutely rejected the idea that torture is ever legal or acceptable, even in a so-called ticking bomb situation.*[1]*[4] They have expressed grave concern about the way the dramatic force and artificially simple moral answers the ticking bomb thought-experiment seems to offer, have manipulated and distorted the legal and moral perceptions, reasoning and judgment of both the general population and military and law enforcement officials. They reject the proposition, implicit or explicit, that certain acts of torture are justifiable, even desirable. They believe that simplistic responses to the scenario may lead well-intentioned societies down a slippery slope to legalized and systematic torture. They point out that no evidence of any real-life situation meeting all the criteria to constitute a pure ticking bomb scenario has ever been presented to the public, and that such a situation is highly unlikely.*[lower-alpha 1]

As well, torture can be criticized as a poor vehicle for discovering truth, as people experiencing torture, once broken, are liable to make anything up in order to stop the pain and can become unable to tell the difference between fact and fiction under intense psychological pressure. Additionally, since the terrorist presumably knows that the timer is ticking, he has an excellent reason to lie and give false information under torture in order to misdirect his interrogators; merely giving a convincing answer which the investigators will waste time checking out makes it more likely that the bomb will go off, and of course once the bomb has gone off not only has the terrorist won, but there is also no further point in torturing him, except perhaps as revenge.

Others point out that the ticking-bomb torture proponents adopt an extremely short-term view, which impoverishes their consequentialism. Using torture—or even declaring that one is prepared to accept its use—makes other groups of people much more likely to use torture themselves in the long run. The consequence is likely to be a long-term increase in violence. This long-term effect is so serious that the person making the torture decision cannot possibly (according to this argument) make a reasonable estimate of its results. Thus the decision-maker has no grounds for certainty that the value of the lives saved from the ticking bomb will outweigh the value of the lives lost because of the subsequent disorder. He or she cannot arrive at a successful accounting of consequences.

This anti-torture argument, in fact, works by positing that human knowledge has intrinsic limits. An analogous argument holds that human decision-makers are fundamentally prone in certain situations to believe that their judgment is better than it is, and that, to be ethical, they must pre-commit themselves to a particular course of action in those situations. Knowing that, under stress, they will never be able to accurately assess the likely success of torture in obtaining information needed to prevent an attack, humans thus pre-commit to not torture. In general, this family of arguments faults the "ticking-bomb" scenario for implicitly including an incorrect presumption that the decision-maker can know in advance the outcome of torture, either in the short run (likelihood that it will prevent an attack) or the long run (likelihood that it will not set off a general increase in human violence).

Joe Navarro, one of the FBI's top experts in questioning techniques, told The New Yorker:

> Only a psychopath can torture and be unaffected. You don't want people like that in your organization. They are untrustworthy, and tend to have grotesque other problems.[4][7][8]

The United Nations Convention against Torture and Other Cruel, Inhuman or Degrading Treatment or Punishment, which was adopted on December 10, 1984, and entered into force on June 26, 1987, explicitly states in Article 2.2 that:

> No exceptional circumstances whatsoever, whether a state of war or a threat of war, internal political instability or any other public emergency, may be invoked as a justification of torture.[9]

21.3.1 Implausibility

Critics of the thought experiment scenario maintain that it is essentially implausible, based on simultaneous presence of numerous unlikely factors. This is particularly acute in fictional exploration of the scenario.[2]

For example, in perhaps the most common variants on the scenario, one must assume that torturers know, with a reasonable degree of certainty that some form of deadly attack is imminent, but lack a crucial component of that plan, such as its precise location. They must also have in their custody someone who they are reasonably certain has said information and would talk under torture or threat of torture. They must then be able to accurately distinguish between true and false information which the subject may supply under torture. They must then be able to use this information to form a plan of response which is effective at stopping the planned attack. All of this must occur within a limited time frame allowed by the "ticking bomb".

21.4 Effect of fiction

Works of fiction, such as the television series *24*, often rely on ticking time bomb scenarios for dramatic effect. According to the Parents Television Council, given that each season represents a 24-hour period, Jack Bauer encounters someone who needs torturing to reveal a ticking bomb on average 12 times per day.[10]

Michael Chertoff, the Secretary of Homeland Security under the George W. Bush administration, declared that *24* "reflects real life", John Yoo, the former Justice Department lawyer who produced the torture memos cited Bauer in support while Supreme Court Justice Antonin Scalia went further, "Jack Bauer saved Los Angeles... He saved hundreds of thousands of lives. Are you going to convict Jack Bauer?".[10] One of the shows' creators stated:

> Most terrorism experts will tell you that the 'ticking time bomb' situation never occurs in real life, or very rarely. But on our show it happens every week.[4]

The show uses the same techniques that are used by the U.S. against terrorist suspects during the War on Terror. U.S. Army Brigadier General Patrick Finnegan, the dean of the United States Military Academy at West Point, and others, objected to the central theme of the show—that the letter of American law must be sacrificed for the country's security —as it had an adverse effect on the training of actual American soldiers by advocating unethical and illegal behavior. As Finnegan said:

> The kids see it, and say, 'If torture is wrong, what about "24"?'

He continued,

> The disturbing thing is that although torture may cause Jack Bauer some angst, it is always the patriotic thing to do.*[4]

The "ticking time bomb scenario" is subject of the drama *The Dershowitz Protocol* by Canadian author Robert Fothergill. In that play, the American government has established a protocol of "intensified interrogation" for terrorist suspects which requires participation of the FBI, CIA and the Department of Justice. The drama deals with the psychological pressure and the tense triangle of competences under the overriding importance that each participant has to negotiate the actions with his conscience.

21.5   See also

- Ethical arguments regarding torture

- Psychology of torture

- Principle of double effect

- Trolley problem

21.5.1   In fiction

- *Dirty Harry*

- *The Siege*

- *24*

- *Unthinkable*

- *Call of Duty: Black Ops*

21.6   Notes

[1] Interviewed on *Face the Nation* in May 2009, former Vice President Dick Cheney cited CIA memos that gave two examples supporting the use of enhanced interrogation techniques in a ticking bomb scenario, claiming that the interrogation of Abu Zubaydah prevented a plot to detonate a *dirty bomb* in Washington DC and similarly that information forced from Khalid Sheikh Mohammed prevented an attack on Los Angeles. These claims were later repeated in August 2009 during a FOX news interview and are still cited as valid examples. However, in 2008, the claims made in the 2007 CIA memos were investigated by the Department of Justice's Office of Professional Responsibility and heavily criticized. The Department of Justice report, released in February 2009, stated that Zubaydah had supplied the information before he was tortured and that no further credible information had been obtained from the torture itself. In the case of Mohammed, the attack on Los Angeles had already been exposed before his capture and his admissions under torture were little more than white noise given to end it.

21.7 References

[1] Defusing the Ticking Bomb Scenario: Why we must say No to torture, Always, Association for the Prevention of Torture, September 2007

[2] Spino, Joseph; Dellarosa Cummins, Denise (August 2014). "The Ticking Time Bomb: When the Use of Torture Is and Is Not Endorsed". *Review of Philosophy and Psychology* **5**: 543–563.

[3] Twining, WL; Twining, PE (1973). "Bentham on torture". *N. Ir. LQ* **24**: 305.

[4] Mayer, Jane (February 12, 2007). "Whatever it takes. The politics of the man behind "24."". *The New Yorker*. Retrieved 2009-09-28.

[5] "Review-a-Day - Why Terrorism Works Understanding The by Alan M Dershowitz, reviewed by The New Republic Online - Powell's Books". *powells.com*.

[6] We not only have a right to use torture. We have a duty, Bruce Anderson, *The Independent*, 16 February 2010

[7] "The Politics Of TV Torture Shown On '24' - Shame On You For Your Lies, Joel Surnow" by Nikki Finke, *LA Weekly*, February 9, 2007

[8] "US Military Tells Jack Bauer: Cut Out the Torture Scenes ... or Else!" by Andrew Buncombe, *The Independent*, February 13, 2007

[9] "A/RES/39/46. Convention against Torture and Other Cruel, Inhuman or Degrading Treatment or Punishment". *un.org*.

[10] Lithwick, Dahlia (July 26, 2008). "The Fiction Behind Torture Policy". *Newsweek*.

21.8 External links

- Allhoff, Fritz, "A Defense of Torture: Separation of Cases, Ticking Time-bombs and Moral Justification"(pdf) International Journal of Applied Philosophy, Fall 2005
- Allhoff, Fritz, Terrorism, Ticking Time-Bombs, and Torture (Chicago: University of Chicago Press, 2012)
- Dershowitz: Torture could be justified, *CNN*, March 4, 2003
- Want to Torture? Get a Warrant, , *San Francisco Chronicle*, January 22, 2002
- U.S.: Reject Torture as Policy Option: Torture Debate Spotlights Importance of Global Ban, *Human Rights Watch*, November 2, 2005
- The Prison Puzzle, *New York Times* republished by the *International Herald Tribune*, November 3, 2005
- Defusing the Ticking Bomb Scenario: Why we must say No to torture, always., Association for the Prevention of Torture, September 2007
- Slavoj Žižek Are we in a war? Do we have an enemy? (May 2002)
- Slavoj Žižek The depraved heroes of 24 are the Himmlers of Hollywood (January 2006)
- Uwe Steinhoff Torture —The Case for Dirty Harry and against Alan Dershowitz (August 2006)
- FringeNYC Previews: The Dershowitz Protocol

Chapter 22

Unreliable narrator

An **unreliable narrator** is a narrator, whether in literature, film, or theatre, whose credibility has been seriously compromised.[*][1] The term was coined in 1961 by Wayne C. Booth in *The Rhetoric of Fiction*.[*][1][*][2] While unreliable narrators are almost by definition first-person narrators, arguments have been made for the existence of unreliable second- and third-person narrators, especially within the context of film and television.

Sometimes the narrator's unreliability is made immediately evident. For instance, a story may open with the narrator making a plainly false or delusional claim or admitting to being severely mentally ill, or the story itself may have a frame in which the narrator appears as a character, with clues to the character's unreliability. A more dramatic use of the device delays the revelation until near the story's end. This twist ending forces readers to reconsider their point of view and experience of the story. In some cases the narrator's unreliability is never fully revealed but only hinted at, leaving readers to wonder how much the narrator should be trusted and how the story should be interpreted.

22.1 Overview

22.1.1 Classification

Attempts have been made at a classification of unreliable narrators. William Riggan analysed in his study discernible types of unreliable narrators, focusing on the first-person narrator as this is the most common kind of unreliable narration.[*][3] Adapted from his findings is the following list:

- The Pícaro: a narrator who is characterized by exaggeration and bragging, the first example probably being the soldier in Plautus's comedy *Miles Gloriosus*.

  Examples in modern literature are *Moll Flanders*, *Simplicius Simplicissimus* or *Felix Krull*.

- The Madman: A narrator who is either only experiencing mental defense mechanisms, such as (post-traumatic) dissociation and self-alienation, or severe mental illness, such as schizophrenia or paranoia.

  Examples include Franz Kafka's self-alienating narrators, Noir fiction and Hardboiled fiction's "tough" (cynical) narrator who unreliably describes his own emotions, Barbara Covett in *Notes on a Scandal*, and Patrick Bateman in *American Psycho*.

- The Clown: A narrator who does not take narrations seriously and consciously plays with conventions, truth, and the reader's expectations.

  Examples of the type include Tristram Shandy and Bras Cubas.

Illustration by Gustave Doré for Baron Munchausen: tall tales, such as those of the Baron, often feature unreliable narrators.

- The Naïf: A narrator whose perception is immature or limited through their point of view.

    Examples of naïves include Huckleberry Finn, Holden Caulfield, and Forrest Gump

- The Liar: A mature narrator of sound cognition who deliberately misrepresents himself, often to obscure his unseemly or discreditable past conduct.

    John Dowell in Ford Madox Ford's *The Good Soldier* exemplifies this kind of narrator.

This typology is surely not exhaustive and cannot claim to cover the whole spectrum of unreliable narration in its entirety or even only the first-person narrator. Further research in this area has been called for.*[4]

It also still remains a matter of debate whether and how a non-first-person narrator can be unreliable, though the deliberate restriction of information to the audience—for example in the three interweaving plays in Alan Ayckbourn's *The Norman Conquests*, each of which shows the action taking place only in one of three locations during the course of a weekend—can provide instances of unreliable *narrative*, even if not necessarily of an unreliable *narrator*.

22.1.2 Definitions and theoretical approaches

Wayne C. Booth was the earliest who formulated a reader-centered approach to unreliable narration and distinguished between a reliable and unreliable narrator on the grounds of whether the narrator's speech violates or conforms with general norms and values. He writes, "I have called a narrator *reliable* when he speaks for or acts in accordance with the norms of the work (which is to say the implied author's norms), *unreliable* when he does not." *[2] Peter J. Rabinowitz criticized Booth's definition for relying too much on the extradiegetic facts such as norms and ethics, which must necessarily be tainted by personal opinion. He consequently modified the approach to unreliable narration.

> There are unreliable narrators (c.f. Booth). An unreliable narrator however, is not simply a narrator who 'does not tell the truth' – what fictional narrator ever tells the literal truth? Rather an unreliable narrator is one who tells lies, conceals information, misjudges with respect to the narrative audience – that is, one whose statements are untrue not by the standards of the real world or of the authorial audience but by the standards of his own narrative audience. [···] In other words, all fictional narrators are false in that they are imitations. But some are imitations who tell the truth, some of people who lie.*[5]

Rabinowitz' main focus is the status of fictional discourse in opposition to factuality. He debates the issues of truth in fiction, bringing forward four types of audience who serve as receptors of any given literary work:

1. "Actual audience" (= the flesh-and-blood people who read the book)

2. "Authorial audience" (= hypothetical audience to whom the author addresses his text)

3. "Narrative audience" (= imitation audience which also possesses particular knowledge)

4. "Ideal narrative audience" (= uncritical audience who accepts what the author is saying)

Rabinowitz suggests that "In the proper reading of a novel, then, events which are portrayed must be treated as both 'true' and 'untrue' at the same time. Although there are many ways to understand this duality, I propose to analyze the four audiences which it generates." *[6] Similarly, Tamar Yacobi has proposed a model of five criteria ('integrating mechanisms') which determine if a narrator is unreliable.*[7] Instead of relying on the device of the implied author and a text-centered analysis of unreliable narration, Ansgar Nünning gives evidence that narrative unreliability can be reconceptualized in the context of frame theory and of readers' cognitive strategies.

> [···] to determine a narrator's unreliability one need not rely merely on intuitive judgments. It is neither the reader's intuitions nor the implied author's norms and values that provide the clue to a narrator's unreliability, but a broad range of definable signals. These include both textual data and the reader's preexisting

conceptual knowledge of the world. In sum whether a narrator is called unreliable or not does not depend on the distance between the norms and values of the narrator and those of the implied author but between the distance that separates the narrator's view of the world from the reader's world-model and standards of normality.*[8]

Unreliable Narration in this view becomes purely a reader's strategy of making sense of a text, i.e. of reconciling discrepancies in the narrator's account (cf. signals of unreliable narration). Nünning thus effectively eliminates the reliance on value judgments and moral codes which are always tainted by personal outlook and taste. Greta Olson recently debated both Nünning's and Booth's models, revealing discrepancies in their respective views.

> [···] Booth's text-immanent model of narrator unreliability has been criticized by Ansgar Nünning for disregarding the reader's role in the perception of reliability and for relying on the insufficiently defined concept of the implied author. Nünning updates Booth's work with a cognitive theory of unreliability that rests on the reader's values and her sense that a discrepancy exists between the narrator's statements and perceptions and other information given by the text.

and offers "[···] an update of Booth's model by making his implicit differentiation between fallible and untrustworthy narrators explicit." Olson then argues "[···] that these two types of narrators elicit different responses in readers and are best described using scales for fallibility and untrustworthiness." *[9] She proffers that all fictional texts that employ the device of unreliability can best be considered along a spectrum of fallibility that begins with trustworthiness and ends with unreliability. This model allows for all shades of grey in between the poles of trustworthiness and unreliability. It is consequently up to each individual reader to determine the credibility of a narrator in a fictional text.

22.1.3 Signals of unreliable narration

Whichever definition of unreliability one follows, there are a number of signs that constitute or at least hint at a narrator's unreliability. Nünning has suggested to divide these signals into three broad categories.*[10]

- Intratextual signs such as the narrator contradicting himself, having gaps in memory, or lying to other characters

- Extratextual signs such as contradicting the reader's general world knowledge or impossibilities (within the parameters of logic)

- Reader's Literary Competence. This includes the reader's knowledge about literary types (e.g. stock characters that reappear over centuries), knowledge about literary genres and its conventions or stylistic devices

22.2 Notable examples

22.2.1 Historical occurrences

One of the earliest uses of unreliability in literature is in *The Frogs* by Aristophanes. After the God Dionysus claims to have sunk 12 or 13 enemy ships with Cleisthenes (son of Sibyrtius), his slave Xanthias says "Then I woke up." A more well-known version is in Plautus' comedy *Miles Gloriosus* (3rd–2nd centuries BC), which features a soldier who constantly embellishes his accomplishments while his slave Artotrogus, in asides, claims the stories are untrue and he is only backing them up to get fed. The literary device of the "unreliable narrator" was used in several medieval fictional Arabic tales of the *One Thousand and One Nights*, also known as the *Arabian Nights*.*[11] In one tale, "The Seven Viziers", a courtesan accuses a king's son of having assaulted her, when in reality she had failed to seduce him (inspired by the Biblical/Qur'anic story of Joseph/Yusuf. Seven viziers attempt to save his life by narrating seven stories to prove the unreliability of the courtesan, and the courtesan responds by narrating a story to prove the unreliability of the viziers.*[12] The unreliable narrator device is also used to generate suspense in another *Arabian Nights* tale, "The Three Apples", an early murder mystery. At one point of the story, two men claim to be the murderer, one of whom is revealed to be lying. At another point in the story, in a flashback showing the reasons for the murder, it is revealed that an unreliable narrator convinced the man of his wife's infidelity, thus leading to her murder.*[13]

Another early example of unreliable narration is Geoffrey Chaucer's *The Canterbury Tales*. In "The Merchant's Tale" for example, the narrator, being unhappy in his marriage, allows his bias to slant much of his tale. In *The Wife of Bath*, the Wife often makes inaccurate quotations and incorrectly remembers stories.

22.2.2 Novels

A controversial example of an unreliable narrator occurs in Agatha Christie's novel *The Murder of Roger Ackroyd*, where the narrator hides essential truths in the text (mainly through evasion, omission, and obfuscation) without ever overtly lying. Many readers at the time felt that the plot twist at the climax of the novel was nevertheless unfair. Christie used the concept again in her 1967 novel *Endless Night*. Similar unreliable narrators often appear in detective novels and thrillers, where even a first-person narrator might hide essential information and deliberately mislead the reader in order to preserve the surprise ending. In some cases, the narrator describes himself or herself as doing things which seem questionable or discreditable, only to reveal in the end that such actions were not what they seemed (e.g. Alistair MacLean's "The Golden Rendezvous" and John Grisham's "The Racketeer").

Many novels are narrated by children, whose inexperience can impair their judgment and make them unreliable. In *Adventures of Huckleberry Finn* (1884), Huck's innocence leads him to make overly charitable judgments about the characters in the novel.

Ken Kesey's two most famous novels feature unreliable narrators. "Chief" Bromden in *One Flew Over the Cuckoo's Nest* suffers from schizophrenia, and his telling of the events often includes things such as people growing or shrinking, walls oozing with slime, or the orderlies kidnapping and "curing" Santa Claus. Narration in *Sometimes a Great Notion* switches between several of the main characters, whose bias tends to switch the reader's sympathies from one person to another, especially in the rivalry between main character Leland and Hank Stamper. Many of Susan Howatch's novels similarly use this technique; each chapter is narrated by a different character, and only after reading chapters by each of the narrators does the reader realize each of the narrators has biases and "blind spots" that cause him or her to perceive shared experiences differently.

Humbert Humbert, the main character and narrator of Vladimir Nabokov's *Lolita*, often tells the story in such a way as to justify his hebephilic fixation on young girls, in particular his sexual relationship with his 12-year-old stepdaughter. Similarly, the narrator of A. M. Homes' *The End of Alice* deliberately withholds the full story of the crime that put him in prison—the rape and subsequent murder of a young girl—until the end of the novel.

In some instances, unreliable narration can bring about the fantastic in works of fiction. In Kingsley Amis' *The Green Man*, for example, the unreliability of the narrator Maurice Allington destabilizes the boundaries between reality and the fantastic. The same applies to Nigel Williams's *Witchcraft*.*[14] *An Instance of the Fingerpost* by Iain Pears also employs several points of view from narrators whose accounts are found to be unreliable and in conflict with each other.*[15]

Mike Engleby, the narrator of Sebastian Faulks' *Engleby*, leads the reader to believe a version of events of his life that is shown to be increasingly at odds with reality.*[16]

Zeno Cosini, the narrator of Italo Svevo's *Zeno's Conscience*, is a typical example of unreliable narrator: in fact the novel is presented as a diary of Zeno himself, who unintentionally distorts the facts to justify his faults. His psychiatrist, who publishes the diary, claims in the introduction that it's a mix of truths and lies.*[17]

Pi Patel, the narrator of Yann Martel's *Life of Pi*, published in 2001, is another example of an unreliable narrator. After spending many days adrift at sea, he describes several fanciful events and tells his rescuers that his lifeboat was shared by a zebra, an orangutan, a hyena (which killed the zebra and orangutan) and a Bengal Tiger (which killed the hyena). When they question his story, he provides an alternate, darker, but more believable recounting of events, in which a sailor and his mother are murdered by a cannibalistic ship's cook, who Pi then kills and eats to survive. The rescuers notice the parallels between the people and the animals, with the zebra representing the sailor, the orangutan representing Pi's mother, the hyena representing the cook, and the tiger representing Pi himself. When Pi points out that neither story is provable and that neither story changes the outcome (the ship has sunk, and his family has died), the rescuers choose to believe the story featuring the animals, because it is a better story.

22.2.3 Films

One of the earliest examples of the use of an unreliable narrator in film is the German expressionist film *The Cabinet of Dr. Caligari*, from 1920.[*][18] In this film, an epilogue to the main story is a twist ending revealing that Francis, through whose eyes we see the action, is a patient in an insane asylum, and the flashback which forms the majority of the film is simply his mental delusion.

The 1945 film noir *Detour* is told from the perspective of an unreliable protagonist who may be trying to justify his actions.[*][19]

In *Possessed* (1947), Joan Crawford plays a woman who is taken to a psychiatric hospital in a state of shock. She gradually tells the story of how she came to be there to her doctors, which is related to the audience in flashbacks, some of which are later revealed to be hallucinations or distorted by paranoia.[*][20]

In *Rashômon* (1950), a Japanese crime drama film directed by Akira Kurosawa, adapted from "In a Grove" (1921), uses multiple narrators to tell the story of the death of a samurai. Each of the witnesses describe the same basic events but differ wildly in the details, alternately claiming that the samurai died by accident, suicide, or murder. The term "Rashômon effect" is used to describe how different witnesses are able to produce contradictory accounts of the same event, though each version is presented with equal sincerity and each is plausible when considered independently of the others. The film does not select the "authentic" narrator from the differing accounts: at its conclusion, all versions remain equally plausible and equally suspect.

The 1950 Alfred Hitchcock film *Stage Fright* (1950) uses the device of unreliable narration by presenting the aftermath of a murder in a flashback, as told by the murderer. The details of the flashback provide an explanation which helps convince the innocent main protagonist of the film to help the murderer, believing him innocent.[*][21]

In the movie version of *Forrest Gump* (1994), the title character narrates his life story, and in the process naïvely refers to Apple Computer as a "fruit company" while also assuming that sustaining a "million dollar wound" meant that one would get paid for it. He also states that Jenny's dad treated her well because "he was always kissing and touching her and her sisters." [*][22]

The 1995 film *The Usual Suspects* reveals that the narrator had been deceiving another character, and hence the audience, by inventing stories and characters from whole cloth. The character is seen as a weak, humble, and quiet criminal but it is later found by the audience that he is the fabled crime boss Keyser Soze.[*][23][*][24]

In the 1999 film *Fight Club*, it is revealed that the narrator suffers from dissociative identity disorder and that some events were fabricated, which means only one of the two main protagonists actually exists, as the other is in the narrator's mind.[*][25]

In the 2001 film *A Beautiful Mind*, it is eventually revealed that the narrator is suffering from paranoid schizophrenia, and many of the events he witnessed occurred only in his own mind.[*][26]

In the 2002 film *Hero*, the protagonist is identified as an unreliable narrator by the antagonist, who responds by constructing his own alternate version of the false story. In the last part of the film, the protagonist tells the real story, which explains his presence in the current situation.

In the 2013 film *The Lone Ranger* the narrator, *Tonto* (Johnny Depp), is identified quickly as potentially unreliable by a child attending a 1930s carnival sideshow during extensive questioning about the events leading to the origin of the Wild West character the child emulates. The child is wearing the costume identified with the fictional Western hero of radio, comics, films, and television. The events related by the narrator vaguely follow an alternative version of character development that occurred during its radio dramas and the beginning of its television series, but with novel disclosures of graphic details that occur as a series of flashbacks portraying the elderly Tonto's memories of the events.[*][27] Along with the child, the audience is left to make their own judgments about the memories of Tonto.

22.2.4 Television

As a framing device on the sitcom *How I Met Your Mother*, the main character Ted Mosby, in the year 2030, recounts to his son and daughter the events that led him to meeting their mother. Show creator Craig Thomas explicitly said in an 2008 interview that the narrator, "Future Ted" (voiced by Bob Saget), is unreliable.[*][28]

In the 2014 Showtime series, *The Affair*, the storyline is set to two independent and overlapping re-tellings of the events surrounding the affair, neither of which are shown to be completely accurate.*[29]

The 2015 USA Network series Mr. Robot features an unreliable narrator as the main character and also a plot-device.

The Fox Network series "Married with Children" implicitly presented its story from the perspective of Al Bundy as an unreliable narrator, in order to create a parody of conventional domestic situation comedies, featuring a wildly dysfunctional family.

22.2.5   Comics

In Alan Moore and Brian Bolland's *Batman: The Killing Joke*, the Joker, who is the villain of the story, reflects on the pitiful life that transformed him into a psychotic murderer. Although the Joker's version of the story is not implausible given overall Joker storylines in the Batman comics, the Joker admits at the end of *The Killing Joke* that he is uncertain if it is true.*[30]

22.3   Notable works featuring unreliable narrators

22.3.1   Literature

- Martin Amis's *Time's Arrow**[31]

- Augusto Roa Bastos's *I, the Supreme*

- Emily Brontë's *Wuthering Heights**[32]

- Peter Carey's *Illywhacker**[33]

- Angela Carter's *Wise Children**[34]

- Geoffrey Chaucer's *The Canterbury Tales*

- Wilkie Collins's *The Moonstone**[35]

- The works of Bret Easton Ellis, most prominently *American Psycho**[36]

- William Faulkner's *The Sound and the Fury**[1]

- F. Scott Fitzgerald's *The Great Gatsby*

- Ford Madox Ford's *The Good Soldier**[37]

- Charlotte Perkins Gilman's *The Yellow Wallpaper**[38]

- Günter Grass's *The Tin Drum*

- Kazuo Ishiguro's *When We Were Orphans**[39]

- Henry James's *The Turn of the Screw**[40]

- James Lasdun's *The Horned Man**[41]

- Anita Loos's *Gentlemen Prefer Blondes**[42]

- Vladimir Nabokov's *Pale Fire**[43] and *Lolita*

- Mordecai Richler's *Barney's Version**[44]*[45]*[46]

- J. D. Salinger's *The Catcher in the Rye**[47]

- The works of Gene Wolfe, most prominently *The Book of the New Sun* and *The Fifth Head of Cerberus*[48]

- Salman Rushdie's *Midnight's Children*[49]

- William Thackeray's *The Luck of Barry Lyndon*

- Chuck Palahniuk's works, most notably *Fight Club*

- Gillian Flynn's *Gone Girl*

22.3.2 Film

- *Amarcord* (1973), directed by Federico Fellini*[50]

- *Big Fish* (2003), directed by Tim Burton*[51]

- *The Cabinet of Dr. Caligari* (1920), directed by Robert Wiene*[52]

- *Fight Club* (1999), directed by David Fincher*[53]

- *Forrest Gump* (1994), directed by Robert Zemeckis*[54]

- *Hero* (2002), directed by Zhang Yimou*[55]

- *Memento* (2000), directed by Christopher Nolan

- *Rashomon* (1950), directed by Akira Kurosawa*[56]

- *Laura* (1944), directed by Otto Preminger*[57]

22.4 References

[1] Frey, James N. (1931). *How to Write a Damn Good Novel, II: Advanced Techniques for Dramatic Storytelling* (1st ed.). New York: St. Martin's Press. p. 107. ISBN 0-312-10478-2. Retrieved 20 April 2013.

[2] Booth, Wayne C. (1961). *The Rhetoric of Fiction*. Univ. of Chicago Press. pp. 158–159.

[3] Riggan, William (1981). *Pícaros, Madmen, Naïfs, and Clowns: The Unreliable First-person Narrator*. Univ. of Oklahoma Press: Norman. ISBN 0806117141.

[4] Nünning, Ansgar: "But Why Will You say That I Am mad?" On the Theory, History and Signals of Unreliable Narration in British Fiction, in *Arbeiten aus Anglistik und Amerikanistik* 22/1 (1997), pp 1 –105.

[5] Rabinowitz, Peter J.: *Truth in Fiction: A Reexamination of Audiences*. In: *Critical Inquiry*. Nr. 1, 1977, S. 121–141.

[6] Rabinowitz, Peter J.: *Truth in Fiction: A Reexamination of Audiences*. In: *Critical Inquiry*. Nr. 1, 1977, S. 121–141.

[7] Online Living Handbook of Narratology at the Wayback Machine (archived January 16, 2013)

[8] Nünning, Ansgar: *But why will you say that I am mad?: On the Theory, History, and Signals of Unreliable Narration in British Fiction*. In: *Arbeiten zu Anglistik und Amerikanistik*. Nr. 22, 1997, S. 83–105.

[9] Olson, Greta: *Reconsidering Unreliability: Fallible and Untrustworthy Narrators*. In: *Narrative*. Nr. 11, 2003, S. 93–109.

[10] Nünning, Ansgar (ed.): *Unreliable Narration*: Studien zur Theorie und Praxis unglaubwürdigen Erzählens in der englischsprachigen Erzählliteratur, Wissenschaftlicher Verlag: Trier (1998).

[11] Irwin, Robert (2003). *The Arabian Nights: A Companion*. Tauris Parke Paperbacks. p. 227. ISBN 1-86064-983-1.

[12] Pinault, David (1992). *Story-telling Techniques in the Arabian Nights*. Brill Publishers. p. 59. ISBN 90-04-09530-6. Retrieved 20 April 2013.

[13] Pinault, David (1992). *Story-Telling Techniques in the Arabian Nights*. Brill Publishers. pp. 93–97. ISBN 90-04-09530-6. Retrieved 20 April 2013.

[14] Martin Horstkotte. "Unreliable Narration and the Fantastic in Kingsley Amis's *The Green Man* and Nigel Williams's *Witchcraft*". *Extrapolation* 48,1 (2007): 137–151.

[15] "THE MYSTERY READER reviews: An Instance of the Fingerpost by Iain Pears". Themysteryreader.com. Retrieved 13 November 2011.

[16] Roberts, Michèle (18 May 2007). "Engleby, by Sebastian Faulks. Sad lad, or mad lad?". *The Independent* (London). Archived from the original on 2011-03-18. Retrieved 21 March 2009.

[17] Wood, James (3 January 2002). "Mixed Feelings". *London Review of Books* **24** (1): 17–20. ISSN 0260-9592. Retrieved 21 April 2013.

[18] M/C Reviews. "Film Studies: "Don't Believe His Lies", by Volker Ferenz". Reviews.media-culture.org.au. Retrieved 2014-01-28.

[19] Ferdinand, Marilyn (December 2006). "Detour (1945)". *ferdyonfilms.com*. Retrieved 21 April 2013.

[20] "Possessed movie review". A Life at the Movies. 20 June 2010.

[21] "Flashbacks in Hitchcock's movies". alfred-hitchcock-films.net. Retrieved 26 March 2013.

[22] Winning, Josh. "50 Unreliable Movie Narrators". Future Publishing Limited. Retrieved 10 February 2014.

[23] Schwartz, Ronald (2005). *Neo-Noir: The New Film Noir Style from Psycho to Collateral*. Scarecrow Press. p. 71. ISBN 978-0-8108-5676-9.

[24] Lehman, David (2000). *The Perfect Murder: A Study in Detection* (2nd ed.). University of Michigan Press. pp. 221–222. ISBN 978-0-472-08585-9. [H]e has improvised, spontaneously and with reckless abandon, a coherent, convincing, but false-bottomed narrative to beguile us and deceive his interrogator.

[25] Hewitt, John (21 November 2005). "John Hewitt's Writing Tips: Explaining the Unreliable Narrator". Retrieved 20 April 2013.

[26] Hansen, Per Krogh. "Unreliable Narration in Cinema". University of Southern Denmark. ...[In] the second part of the film a large part of what we hitherto have considered part of the objective perspective (persons, actions, places) are exposed as being mental constructions and projections made by the protagonist...We have not only seen the events from his perspective, but we have seen what he thinks happens.

[27] Lovece, Frank (July 2, 2013). "Film Review: *The Lone Ranger*". *Film Journal International*. Retrieved July 3, 2013.

[28] Ghosh, Korbi. "'How I Met Your Mother's' Craig Thomas on Ted & Barney's Breakup, Eriksen Babies and The Future of Robarn". *Zap2It.com*. Tribune Media Services, LLC. Retrieved 27 April 2014.

[29] "'The Affair' is this fall's most compelling puzzle".

[30] Leverenz, David (1995). "The Last Real Man in America: From Natty Bumppo to Batman". In Hutner, Gordon. *The American Literary History Reader*. New York: Oxford University Press. p. 276. ISBN 0-19-509504-9. Retrieved 21 April 2013.

[31] Kakutani, Michiko (22 October 1991). "Time Runs Backward To Point Up a Moral". *The New York Times*.

[32] Hafley, James (1958). "*The Villain in* Wuthering Heights". p. 17. Archived from the original (PDF) on 2012-05-18. Retrieved 3 June 2010.

[33] Asthana, Anushka (23 January 2010). "Parrot and Olivier in America by Peter Carey". *The Times* (London).

[34] "Comedy Is Tragedy That Happens to Other People". *The New York Times*. 19 January 1992.

[35] "Historicizing unreliable narration: unreliability and cultural". Encyclopedia.com. Archived from the original on 2012-03-24. Retrieved 13 November 2011.

[36] Webster, Sarah (2006). "When Writer Becomes Celebrity". *Oxonian Review of Books* **5** (2). Retrieved 21 April 2013.

[37] Ford, Ford Madox (2003). Womack, Kenneth; Baker, William, eds. *The Good Soldier: A Tale of Passion*. Peterborough, Ont.: Broadview Press. ISBN 9781551113814. Retrieved 21 April 2013.

[38] "The Yellow Wallpaper : Gilman's Techniques for Portraying Oppression of Women". *articlemyriad.com*. Retrieved 15 February 2015.}

[39] Mudge, Alden (September 2000). "Ishiguro takes a literary approach to the detective novel". *http://bookpage.com". Retrieved 20 April 2013.*

[40] Helal, Kathleen, ed. *The Turn of the Screw and Other Short Works*. Enriched Classics. Simon and Schuster, 2007.

[41] "DarkEcho Review: The Horned Man by James Lasdun". Darkecho.com. 3 May 2003. Retrieved 13 November 2011.

[42] Landay, Lori (1998). *Madcaps, Screwballs, and Con Women The Female Trickster in American Culture*. University of Pennsylvania Press. p. 200. ISBN 978-0-8122-1651-6. Retrieved 20 April 2013.

[43] "Dowling on Pale Fire". Rci.rutgers.edu. Retrieved 13 November 2011.

[44] Shapiro, James (21 December 1997). "The Way He Was – or Was He?". *nytimes.com* (New York Times). Retrieved 21 April 2013.

[45] *Newsday*: "'Barney's Version' of a Colorful Life"

[46] *The Globe and Mail*: "Barney's Version: Barney as an Everymensch"

[47] "Henry Sutton, Top 10 Unreliable Narrators". *The Guardian*. 17 February 2010. Retrieved 15 April 2012.

[48] "Interview with Gene Wolfe Conducted by Lawrence Person". Home.roadrunner.com. Retrieved 13 November 2011.

[49] "Salman Rushdie, 'Errata' or Unreliable Narration in Midnight's Children".

[50] Dawson, Tom (24 August 2004). "Amarcord (1973)". *bbc.co.uk*. BBC. Retrieved 21 April 2013.

[51] Lance Goldenberg, "There's Something Fishy About Father", *Creative Loafing Tampa*, 8 January 2004.

[52] Ferenz, Volker (November 2005). "FIGHT CLUBS, AMERICAN PSYCHOS AND MEMENTOS: The scope of unreliable narration in film". *New Review of Film and Television Studies* (Taylor & Francis) **3** (2): 133–159. doi:10.1080/17400300500213461. ISSN 1740-0309. Retrieved 21 April 2013.

[53] Church, David, "Remaining Men Together: Fight Club and the (Un)pleasures of Unreliable Narration", *Offscreen*, Vol. 10, No. 5 (31 May 2006). Retrieved 14 April 2009.

[54] Healy, Sue. "I, Me, Mine". WordPress.com. Retrieved 10 February 2014.

[55] "HERO". *Montrealfilmjournal.com*. Montreal Film Journal. 26 March 2003. Retrieved 13 November 2011.

[56] Tatara, Paul. "Rashomon". *tcm.com*. Retrieved 21 April 2013.

[57] "Film Freak Central". *filmfreakcentral.net*.

22.5 Further reading

- Smith, M. W. (1991). *Understanding Unreliable Narrators*. Urbana, IL: National Council of Teachers of English.

- Shan, Den: "Unreliability", in Peter Hühn (ed.): The Living Handbook of Narratology, Hamburg: Hamburg University Press. (Online at the Wayback Machine (archived January 16, 2013). Retrieved 11 May 2012)

22.6 External links

- Henry Sutton's top 10 unreliable narrators

Chapter 23

Author surrogate

As a literary technique, an **author surrogate** is a fictional character based on the author.[*][1] On occasion, authors insert themselves under their own name into their works, typically for humorous or surrealistic effect.

23.1 Usage

23.1.1 Examples

British writer David Hume used the author-surrogate 'Philo' in the *Dialogues Concerning Natural Religion*. Michael Crichton used his character Ian Malcolm to express views on catastrophic system failure in his novel *Jurassic Park*.

23.1.2 Fan fiction

Main article: Mary Sue

Author surrogacy is a frequently observed phenomenon in hobbyist and amateur writing, so much so that fan fiction critics have evolved the term Mary Sue to refer to an idealized author surrogate.[*][2] The term 'Mary Sue' is thought to evoke the cliché of the adolescent author who uses writing as a vehicle for the indulgence of self-idealization rather than entertaining others. For male author surrogates, similar names such as 'Marty Stu' or 'Gary Stu' are occasionally used.[*][3][*][4]

23.2 Other uses

The expression has also been used in a different sense, meaning the *principal author* of a multi-author document.

23.3 See also

- Audience surrogate

- Autobiographical novel

- Self-insertion

- Mary Sue

23.4 Notes

[1] Pandey, Ashish (2005). *Academic Dictionary Of Fiction*. Isha Books. p. 18. ISBN 8182052629.

[2] Segall (2008). *Fan Fiction Writing: New Work Based on Favorite Fiction*. Rosen Pub. p. 26. ISBN 1404213562.

[3] Luc Reid (4 September 2006). *Talk the Talk: The Slang of 65 American Subcultures*. Writer's Digest Books. p. 300. ISBN 978-1-59963-375-6. Retrieved 30 July 2013.

[4] Steven Harper (18 February 2011). *Writing the Paranormal Novel: Techniques and Exercises for Weaving Supernatural Elements Into Your Story*. Writer's Digest Books. p. 76. ISBN 978-1-59963-301-5. Retrieved 30 July 2013.

Chapter 24

Fourth wall

For the technique known as "breaking the fourth wall", see Meta-reference.
The **fourth wall** is the imaginary "wall" at the front of the stage in a traditional three-walled box set in a proscenium

In a box set, such as this one used in a 1904 Moscow Art Theatre production of Anton Chekhov's The Cherry Orchard, *three walls are provided by on-stage scenery while the invisible fourth wall is provided by the proscenium arch.*

theatre, through which the audience sees the action in the world of the play.[1][2] The concept is usually attributed to the philosopher, critic and dramatist Denis Diderot.[3] The term itself was used by Molière.[4] The fourth wall illusion is often associated with naturalist theatre of the mid 19th-century, and especially with the innovations of the French director André Antoine.[4]

The restrictions of the fourth wall were challenged in 20th-century theatre.[3] Speaking directly to, otherwise acknowledging or doing something to the audience through this imaginary wall – or, in film and television, through a camera – is known as "breaking the fourth wall". As it is a penetration of a boundary normally set up or assumed by works of fiction, this is considered a metafictional technique.[1][5] In literature and video games, it occurs when a character acknowledges the reader or player.[6]

Breaking the fourth wall should not be confused with the aside or the soliloquy, dramatic devices often used by playwrights where the character on stage is delivering an inner monologue, giving the audience insight into their thoughts.[7]

24.1 Convention of modern theatre

The presence of the fourth wall is an established convention of modern realistic theatre, which has led some artists to draw direct attention to it for dramatic or comedic effect when a boundary is "broken", for example by an actor onstage speaking to the audience directly.[1][5] It is common in children's theatre where, for example, a character might ask the children for help, as when Peter Pan appeals to the audience to clap for Tinkerbell. One play that uses the fourth wall extensively for comedic effect is *The Complete Works of William Shakespeare (Abridged)*.[8]

The acceptance of the transparency of the fourth wall is part of the suspension of disbelief between a fictional work and an audience, allowing them to enjoy the fiction as if they were observing real events.[2] Critic Vincent Canby described it in 1987 as "that invisible scrim that forever separates the audience from the stage".[9]

24.2 Outside theatre

The metaphor of the fourth wall has been used by the actor Sir Ian McKellen with regard to the work of the painter L. S. Lowry:

> Lowry ... stood across the road from his subjects and observed. Often enough there are a number of individuals in a crowd peering back at him. They invite us momentarily into their world, like characters on a stage sometimes do, breaking the fourth-wall illusion.[10]

McKellen justifies this application of the theatre term to Lowry's art by explaining that "Lowry's mid-air viewpoint is like a view from the dress circle", looking down as if to a stage. And, McKellen argues, Lowry "often marks the limits of the street scene with curbstones or a pavement that feel like the edge of the stage where the footlights illuminate the action." [10]

The metaphor of the fourth wall has been applied by literary critic David Barnett to *The Harvard Lampoon*'s parody of *The Lord of the Rings* when a character breaks the conventions of storytelling by referring to the text itself. The character Frodo observes "it was going to be a long epic", which in Barnett's view "breaks the 'fourth wall'".[11]

Woody Allen broke the fourth wall several times in his movie *Annie Hall*, as he explained, "because I felt many of the people in the audience had the same feelings and the same problems. I wanted to talk to them directly and confront them." [12]

On television, breaking the fourth wall is rare, though it has been done throughout the history of the medium. George Burns did it numerous times on the 1950s sitcom he starred in with his real-life wife Gracie Allen.[13] *It's Garry Shandling's Show* and *Mrs Brown's Boys* both have their title character walking between sets mid-scene, and the latter occasionally shows characters retaking fluffed lines.[14] Another television character who regularly breaks the fourth wall is Francis Urquhart in the British TV drama series *House of Cards*, *To Play the King* and *The Final Cut*. Urquhart addresses the audience several times during each episode, giving the viewer comments on his own actions on the show.[15] The same technique is also used in the American adaptation of *House of Cards*.[16]

The convention of breaking the fourth wall is often seen on mockumentary sitcoms, including *The Office*. Mockumentary shows which break the fourth wall poke fun at the documentary genre with the intention of increasing the satiric tone of the show. Characters in *The Office* directly speak to the audience during interview sequences. Characters are removed from the rest of the group to speak and reflect on their experiences. When this occurs, the rules of impersonal documentary are shattered. The person behind the camera, the interviewer, is also referenced when the characters gaze and speak straight to the camera. The interviewer, however, is only indirectly spoken to and remains hidden. The technique of breaking the fourth wall which is seen in shows with complex genres, serves to heighten the comedic tone of the show while also proving that the camera itself is far from a passive onlooker.[17]

In literature, writers often break the fourth wall of a story by having their narrator or characters address the reader either in footnotes or other literary devices, thus having the novel itself recognize what it is (a story).[*][6]

24.3   Fifth wall

The term "fifth wall" is often used by analogy with the "fourth wall" for a metaphorical barrier in engagement with a medium. It has been used as an extension of the fourth wall concept to refer to the "invisible wall between critics or readers and theatre practitioners." [*][18] This conception led to a series of workshops at the Globe Theatre in 2004 designed to help break the fifth wall.[*][19] The term has also been used to refer to "that semi-porous membrane that stands between individual audience members during a shared experience." [*][20] In media, the television set has been described metaphorically as a fifth wall because of how it allows a person to see beyond the traditional four walls of a room.[*][21][*][22] In shadow theatre the term "fifth wall" has been used to describe the screen onto which images are projected.[*][23]

24.4   **References**

[1]   Bell, Elizabeth S. (2008). *Theories of Performance.* Sage. p. 203. ISBN 978-1-4129-2637-9.

[2]   Wallis, Mick; Shepherd, Simon (1998). *Studying plays.* Arnold. p. 214. ISBN 0-340-73156-7.

[3]   Cuddon, J. A. (2012). *Dictionary of Literary Terms and Literary Theory.* John Wiley & Sons. ISBN 978-1-118-32600-8.

[4]   Mangan, Michael (2013). *The Drama, Theatre and Performance Companion.* Palgrave Macmillan. p. 172. ISBN 978-1-137-01552-5.

[5]   Abelman, Robert (1998). *Reaching a critical mass: a critical analysis of television entertainment.* L. Erlbaum Associates. pp. 8–11. ISBN 0-8058-2199-6.

[6]   "Breaking The Fourth Wall: Literature." . Retrieved 2015-08-19.

[7]   "Aside" . Longman Dictionary of Contemporary English. Retrieved 17 May 2015.

[8]   "Study Guide: The Complete Works of William Shakespeare (Abridged)" (PDF). Retrieved 17 May 2015.

[9]   Canby, Vincent (June 28, 1987), "Film view: sex can spoil the scene" , *New York Times*: A.17, retrieved July 3, 2007

[10]   "Sir Ian McKellen: My lifelong passion for LS Lowry" . *The Telegraph.* 21 April 2011.

[11]   Barnett, David (8 February 2011). "After Tolkien, get Bored of the Rings" . The Guardian. Retrieved 23 October 2012.

[12]   Björkman, Stig (1995) [1993]. *Woody Allen on Woody Allen.* London: Faber and Faber. p. 77. ISBN 0-571-17335-7.

[13]   "The George Burns and Gracie Allen Show Cast" . TVGuide.com. Retrieved 2015-04-09.

[14]   Dessau, Bruce (1 March 2011). "Mrs Brown's Boys: mainstream comedy for the middle-aged" . *The Guardian.*

[15]   Cartmell, Deborah (2007). *The Cambridge Companion to Literature on Screen.* Cambridge University Press. p. 244. ISBN 0521614864.

[16]   Macaulay, Scott (24 April 2013). "Breaking the Fourth Wall Supercut" . Filmmaker. Retrieved 5 July 2013.

[17]   Savorelli, Antonio. Beyond Sitcom: New Directions in American Television Comedy. North Carolina: McFarland, 2010. ISBN 978-0-7864-5992-6

[18]   Hunte, Lynette; Lichtenfels, Peter (2005), *Shakespeare, Language, and the Stage,* London: Arden Shakespeare, p. 1, ISBN 1-904271-49-9

[19]   Knowles, Richard Paul (2006), "Shakespeare, Language and the Stage, The Fifth Wall: Approaches to Shakespeare from Criticism, Performance and Theatre Studies (review)", *Shakespeare Quarterly* **57** (2): 235–237, doi:10.1353/shq.2006.0060

[20] Davenport, G.; Agamanolis, S.; Barry, B.; Bradley, B. & Brooks, K. (2000), "Synergistic storyscapes and constructionist cinematic sharing", *IBM Systems Journal*

[21] Newcomb, Horace (2004), *Encyclopedia of Television* (2nd ed.), New York: Fitzroy Dearborn, ISBN 1-57958-394-6

[22] Koepnick, Lutz P. (2007), *Framing Attention: Windows on Modern German Culture*, Baltimore: Johns Hopkins University Press, ISBN 0-8018-8489-6

[23] Kent, Lynne (2005), *Breaking the Fifth Wall: Enquiry into Contemporary Shadow Theatre*, Queensland University of Technology Creative Industries Faculty

24.5 External links

- List of films that break the fourth wall on the Art and Popular Culture Encyclopedia

Chapter 25

Defamiliarization

Defamiliarization or **ostranenie** (остранение) is the artistic technique of presenting to audiences common things in an unfamiliar or strange way in order to enhance perception of the familiar. A central concept in 20th-century art and theory, ranging over movements including Dada, postmodernism, epic theatre, and science fiction, it is also used as a tactic by recent movements such as culture jamming.

25.1 History

Defamiliarization of that which is or has become familiar or taken for granted, hence automatically perceived, is the basic function of all devices. And with defamiliarization come both the slowing down and the increased difficulty (impeding) of the process of reading and comprehending and an awareness of the artistic procedures (devices) causing them. (Margolin 2005)

The term "defamiliarization" was first coined in 1917 by Viktor Shklovsky in his essay "Art as Device" (alternate translation: "Art as Technique") (Crawford 209). Shklovsky invented the term as a means to "distinguish poetic from practical language on the basis of the former's perceptibility" (Crawford 209). Essentially, he is stating that poetic language is fundamentally different than the language that we use every day because it is more difficult to understand: "Poetic speech is framed speech. Prose is ordinary speech – economical, easy, proper, the goddess of prose [dea prosae] is a goddess of the accurate, facile type, of the "direct" expression of a child" (Shklovsky 20). This difference is the key to the creation of art and the prevention of "over-automatization," which causes an individual to "function as though by formula" (Shklovsky 16). This distinction between artistic language and everyday language, for Shklovsky, applies to all artistic forms:

The purpose of art is to impart the sensation of things as they are perceived and not as they are known. The technique of art is to make objects 'unfamiliar,' to make forms difficult to increase the difficulty and length of perception because the process of perception is an aesthetic end in itself and must be prolonged. (Shklovsky 16)

Thus, defamiliarization serves as a means to force individuals to recognize artistic language:

In studying poetic speech in its phonetic and lexical structure as well as in its characteristic distribution of words and in the characteristic thought structures compounded from the words, we find everywhere the artistic trademark – that is, we find material obviously created to remove the automatism of perception; the author's purpose is to create the vision which results from that deautomatized perception. A work is created "artistically" so that its perception is impeded and the greatest possible effect is produced through the slowness of the perception. (Shklovsky 19)

This technique is meant to be especially useful in distinguishing poetry from prose, for, as Aristotle said, "poetic language must appear strange and wonderful" (Shklovsky 19).

25.1.1 Defamiliarization in Russian literature

To illustrate what he means by defamiliarization, Shklovsky uses examples from Tolstoy, whom he cites as using the technique throughout his works: "The narrator of 'Kholstomer,' for example, is a horse, and it is the horse's point of view (rather than a person's) that makes the content of the story seem unfamiliar" (Shklovsky 16). As a Russian Formalist, many of Shklovsky's examples use Russian authors and Russian dialects: "And currently Maxim Gorky is changing his diction from the old literary language to the new literary colloquialism of Leskov. Ordinary speech and literary language have thereby changed places (see the work of Vyacheslav Ivanov and many others)" (Shklovsky 19-20).

Defamiliarization also includes the use of foreign languages within a work. At the time that Shklovsky was writing, there was a change in the use of language in both literature and everyday spoken Russian. As Shklovsky puts it: "Russian literary language, which was originally foreign to Russia, has so permeated the language of the people that it has blended with their conversation. On the other hand, literature has now begun to show a tendency towards the use of dialects and/or barbarisms" (Shklovsky 19).

25.1.2 Defamiliarization and différance

Shklovsky's defamiliarization can also be compared to Jacques Derrida's concept of différance:

> What Shklovskij wants to show is that the operation of defamiliarization and its consequent perception in the literary system is like the winding of a watch (the introduction of energy into a physical system): both "originate" difference, change, value, motion, presence. Considered against the general and functional background of Derridian différance, what Shklovskij calls "perception" can be considered a matrix for production of difference. (Crawford 212)

Since the term différance refers to the dual meanings of the French word difference to mean both "to differ" and "to defer," defamiliarization draws attention to the use of common language in such a way as to alter one's perception of an easily understandable object or concept. The use of defamiliarization both differs and defers, since the use of the technique alters one's perception of a concept (to defer), and forces one to think about the concept in different, often more complex, terms (to differ).

> Shklovskij's formulations negate or cancel out the existence/possibility of "real' perception: variously, by (1) the familiar Formalist denial of a link between literature and life, connoting their status as non-communicating vessels, (2) always, as if compulsively, referring to a real experience in terms of empty, dead, and automatized repetition and recognition, and (3) implicitly locating real perception at an unspecifiable temporally anterior and spatially other place, at a mythic "first time" of naïve experience, the loss of which to automatization is to be restored by aesthetic perceptual fullness. (Crawford 218)

25.2 Usage

The technique appears in English Romantic poetry, particularly in the poetry of Wordsworth, and was defined in the following way by Samuel Taylor Coleridge, in his *Biographia Literaria*: "To carry on the feelings of childhood into the powers of manhood; to combine the child's sense of wonder and novelty with the appearances which every day for perhaps forty years had rendered familiar [. . .] this is the character and privilege of genius."

In more recent times, it has been associated with the poet and playwright Bertolt Brecht, whose Verfremdungseffekt ("enstrangement effect") was a potent element of his approach to theater. Brecht, in turn, has been highly influential for artists and filmmakers including Jean-Luc Godard and Yvonne Rainer.

25.3 See also

- Verfremdungseffekt

- Problematization

25.4   References

- Crawford, Lawrence. Viktor Shklovskij: Différance in Defamiliarization. Comparative Literature 36 (1984): 209-19. JSTOR. 24 February 2008.

- Margolin, Uri. Russian Formalism . The Johns Hopkins Guide to Literary Theory and Criticism. Ed. Michael Groden, Martin Kreiswirth, and Imre Szeman. Baltimore, Maryland: The Johns Hopkins University Press, 1994.

- Shklovskij, Viktor. "Art as Technique" . Literary Theory: An Anthology. Ed. Julie Rivkin and Michael Ryan. Malden: Blackwell Publishing Ltd, 1998.

- Basil Lvov, The Twists and Turns of Defamiliarization.

- Min Tian, The Poetics of Difference and Displacement: Twentieth-Century Chinese-Western Intercultural Theatre. Hong Kong: Hong Kong University Press, 2008.

- Ostranenie Magazine

Chapter 26

First-person narrative

A **first-person narrative** is a story from the **first-person perspective**: the viewpoint of a character writing or speaking directly about themselves. In films, videos, or video games, a first-person perspective may also mean that the narrative is shot or presented as if directly coming from a character's in-body point of view, portraying exactly what the character sees or experiences.

The narrators of written works explicitly refer to themselves using variations of "I" (the first-person singular pronoun) and/or "we" (the first-person plural pronoun), typically as well as other characters. This allows the reader or audience to see the point of view (including opinions, thoughts, and feelings) only of the narrator, and no other characters. In some stories, first-person narrators may refer to information they have heard from the other characters, in order to try to deliver a larger point of view. Other stories may switch from one narrator to another, allowing the reader or audience to experience the thoughts and feelings of more than one character or character plural.

26.1 Forms

First-person narratives can appear in several forms; interior monologue, as in Fyodor Dostoevsky's *Notes from Underground*; dramatic monologue, as in Albert Camus' *The Fall*; or explicitly, as in Mark Twain's *Adventures of Huckleberry Finn*.

26.2 Point of view device

Since the narrator is within the story, he or she may not have knowledge of all the events. For this reason, first-person narrative is often used for detective fiction, so that the reader and narrator uncover the case together. One traditional approach in this form of fiction is for the main detective's principal assistant, the "Watson", to be the narrator: this derives from the character of Dr Watson in Sir Arthur Conan Doyle's Sherlock Holmes stories.

In the first-person-plural point of view, narrators tell the story using "we". That is, no individual speaker is identified; the narrator is a member of a group that acts as a unit. The first-person-plural point of view occurs rarely but can be used effectively, sometimes as a means to increase the concentration on the character or characters the story is about. Examples include:

- William Faulkner's short story "A Rose for Emily" (Faulkner was an avid experimenter in using unusual points of view; see also his *Spotted Horses*, told in third person plural).

- Frank B. Gilbreth and Ernestine Gilbreth Carey's memoir *Cheaper by the Dozen*.

- Theodore Sturgeon's short story "Crate."

- Frederik Pohl's *Man Plus.*

- Jeffrey Eugenides's *The Virgin Suicides.*

- Karen Joy Fowler's *The Jane Austen Book Club.*

- Joshua Ferris's *Then We Came to the End.*

First-person narrators can also be multiple, as in Ryūnosuke Akutagawa's *In a Grove* (the source for the movie *Rashomon*) and Faulkner's novel *The Sound and the Fury.* Each of these sources provides different accounts of the same event, from the point of view of various first-person narrators.

The first-person narrator may be the principal character or one who closely observes the principal character (see Emily Brontë's *Wuthering Heights* or F. Scott Fitzgerald's *The Great Gatsby*, each narrated by a minor character). These can be distinguished as "first person major" or "first person minor" points of view.

26.3 Styles

First-person narratives can tend towards a stream of consciousness and Interior monologue, as in Marcel Proust's *In Search of Lost Time.* The whole of the narrative can itself be presented as a false document, such as a diary, in which the narrator makes explicit reference to the fact that he is writing or telling a story. This is the case in Bram Stoker's *Dracula.* As a story unfolds, narrators may be aware that they are telling a story and of their reasons for telling it. The audience that they believe they are addressing can vary. In some cases, a frame story presents the narrator as a character in an outside story who begins to tell his own story, as in Mary Shelley's *Frankenstein.*

First-person narrators are often unreliable narrators since a narrator might be impaired (such as Benjy in Faulkner's *The Sound and the Fury*), lie (as in *The Quiet American* by Graham Greene, or *The Book of the New Sun* series by Gene Wolfe), or manipulate his or her own memories intentionally or not (as in *The Remains of the Day* by Kazuo Ishiguro, or in Ken Kesey's *One Flew Over the Cuckoo's Nest*). Henry James discusses his concerns about "the romantic privilege of the 'first person'" in his preface to *The Ambassadors*, calling it "the darkest abyss of romance." *[1]*[2]

One example of a multi-level narrative structure is Joseph Conrad's novella *Heart of Darkness*, which has a double framework: an unidentified "I" (first person singular) narrator relates a boating trip during which another character, Marlow, uses first person to tell a story that comprises the majority of the work. Within this nested story, it is mentioned that another character, Kurtz, told Marlow a lengthy story; however, its content is not revealed to readers. Thus, there is an "I" narrator introducing a storyteller as "he" (Marlow), who talks about himself as "I" and introduces another storyteller as "he" (Kurtz), who in turn presumably told his story from the perspective of "I" .

26.4 See also

- Narrative mode
- Second-person narrative

26.5 References

Notes

[1] Goetz, William R. (1986). *Henry James and the Darkest Abyss of Romance.* Baton Rouge: Louisiana State University Press. ISBN 0-8071-1259-3.

[2] *The Ambassadors* (p. 11) on Project Gutenberg Accessed 17 March 2007

Further reading

- (French) Françoise Barguillet, *Le Roman au XVIII**e siècle*, Paris: PUF Littératures, 1981, ISBN 2-13-036855-7 ;

- (French) Émile Benveniste, *Problèmes de linguistique générale*, Paris: Gallimard, 1966, ISBN 2-07-029338-6 ;

- (French) Belinda Cannone, *Narrations de la vie intérieure*, Paris: Klincksieck, 1998, ISBN 2-911285-15-8 ;

- (French) René Démoris, *Le Roman à la première personne : du classicisme aux lumières*, Paris: A. Colin, 1975, ISBN 2-600-00525-0 ;

- (French) Pierre Deshaies, *Le Paysan parvenu comme roman à la première personne*, [s.l. : s.n.], 1975 ;

- (French) Béatrice Didier, *La Voix de Marianne. Essai sur Marivaux*, Paris: Corti, 1987, ISBN 2-7143-0229-7 ;

- (French) Philippe Forest, *Le Roman, le je*, Nantes: Pleins feux, 2001, ISBN 2-912567-83-1 ;

- R. A. Francis, *The Abbé Prévost's first-person narrators*, Oxford: Voltaire Foundation, 1993, ISBN 0-7294-0448-X ;

- (French) Jean-Luc Jaccard, *Manon Lescaut. Le Personage-romancier*, Paris: Nizet, 1975, ISBN 2-7078-0450-9 ;

- (French) Annick Jugan, *Les Variations du récit dans* La Vie de Marianne *de Marivaux*, Paris: Klincksieck, 1978, ISBN 2-252-02088-1 ;

- Marie-Paule Laden, *Self-Imitation in the Eighteenth-Century Novel*, Princeton, N. J.: Princeton University Press, 1987, ISBN 0-691-06705-8 ;

- (French) Georges May, *Le Dilemme du roman au XVIII**e siècle, 1715-1761*, New Haven: Yale University Press, 1963 ;

- (French) Ulla Musarra-Schrøder, *Le Roman-mémories moderne : pour une typologie du récit à la première personne, précédé d'un modèle narratologique et d'une étude du roman-mémoires traditionnel de Daniel Defoe à Gottfried Keller*, Amsterdam: APA, Holland University Press, 1981, ISBN 90-302-1236-5 ;

- (French) Vivienne Mylne, *The Eighteenth-Century French Novel, Techniques of illusion*, Cambridge: Cambridge University Press, 1965, ISBN 0-521-23864-1 ;

- (French) Valérie Raoul, *Le Journal fictif dans le roman français*, Paris: Presses universitaires de France, 1999, ISBN 2-13-049632-6 ;

- (French) Michael Riffaterre, *Essais de stylistique structurale*, Paris: Flammarion, 1992, ISBN 2-08-210168-1 ;

- (French) Jean Rousset, *Forme et signification*, Paris: Corti, 1962, ISBN 2-7143-0356-0 ;

- (French) Jean Rousset, *Narcisse romancier : essai sur la première personne dans le roman*, Paris: J. Corti, 1986, ISBN 2-7143-0139-8 ;

- English Showalter, Jr., *The Evolution of the French Novel (1641–1782)*, Princeton, N. J. : Princeton University Press, 1972, ISBN 0-691-06229-3 ;

- Philip R. Stewart, *Imitation and Illusion in the French Memoir-Novel, 1700-1750. The Art of Make-Believe*, New Haven & London: Yale University Press, 1969, ISBN 0-300-01149-0 ;

- (French) Jean Sgard, *L' Abbé Prévost : Labyrinthes de la mémoire*, Paris: PUF, 1986, ISBN 2-13-039282-2 ;

- (French) Loïc Thommeret, *La Mémoire créatrice. Essai sur l'écriture de soi au XVIII**e siècle*, Paris: L'Harmattan, 2006, ISBN 978-2-296-00826-7 ;

- Martin Turnell, *The Rise of the French novel*, New York: New Directions, 1978, ISBN 0-241-10181-6 ;

- Ira O. Wade, *The Structure and Form of the French Enlightenment*, Princeton, N. J.: Princeton University Press, 1977, ISBN 0-691-05256-5 ;

- Ian Watt, *The Rise of the Novel*, Berkeley & Los Angeles: University of California Press, 1965, ISBN 0-520-01317-4 ;

- Arnold L. Weinstein, *Fictions of the self, 1550-1800*, Princeton, N.J. : Princeton University Press, 1981, ISBN 0-691-06448-2 ;

- (French) Agnes Jane Whitfield, *La Problématique de la narration dans le roman québécois à la première personne depuis 1960*, Ottawa: The National Library of Canada, 1983, ISBN 0-315-08327-1.

Chapter 27

Magic realism

Not to be confused with science fantasy.

Magical realism, magic realism, or **marvelous realism** is literature, painting, and film that, while encompassing a range of subtly different concepts, share in common an acceptance of magic in the rational world. It is also sometimes called **fabulism,** in reference to the conventions of fables, myths, and allegory. Of the four terms, *Magical realism* is the most commonly used and refers to literature in particular[1]:1–5 that portrays magical or unreal elements as a natural part in an otherwise realistic or mundane environment.

The terms are broadly descriptive rather than critically rigorous. Matthew Strecher defines magic realism as "what happens when a highly detailed, realistic setting is invaded by something too strange to believe." [2] Many writers are categorized as "magical realists," which confuses what the term really means and how wide its definition is.[3] Magical realism is often associated with Latin American literature, particularly authors including Gabriel García Márquez and Isabel Allende. In English literature, its chief exponents include Salman Rushdie and Alice Hoffman.

27.1   Etymology

While the term *magical realism* first appeared in 1955,[1]:16 the term *Magischer Realismus,* translated as *magic realism,* was first used by German art critic Franz Roh in 1925[4] to refer to a painterly style also known as Neue Sachlichkeit (the New Objectivity),[5] an alternative to expressionism championed by fellow German museum director Gustav Hartlaub.[1]:9–11[6] Roh identified magic realism's accurate detail, smooth photographic clarity, and portrayal of the 'magical' nature of the rational world. It reflects the uncanniness of people and our modern technological environment.[1]:9–10 Roh believed that magic realism was related to, but distinct from, surrealism, due to magic realism's focus on the material object and the actual existence of things in the world, as opposed to surrealism's more cerebral, psychological and subconscious reality.[1]:12 Magic realism was later used to describe the uncanny realism by American painters such as Ivan Albright, Paul Cadmus, George Tooker and other artists during the 1940s and 1950s. However, in contrast with its use in literature, magic realist art does not often include overtly fantastic or magical content, but rather looks at the mundane through a hyper-realistic and often mysterious lens.[7]

German magic realist paintings influenced the Italian writer Massimo Bontempelli, who has been called the first to apply magic realism to writing, aiming to capture the fantastic, mysterious nature of reality. In 1926 he founded the magic realist magazine *900.Novecento,* and his writings influenced Belgian magic realist writers Johan Daisne and Hubert Lampo.[1]:13–14

Roh's magic realism also influenced writers in Hispanic America, where it was translated as *realismo mágico* in 1927. Venezuelan writer Arturo Uslar-Pietri, who had known Bontempelli, wrote influential magic realist short stories in the 1930s and 40s that focused on the mystery and reality of how we live.[1]:14–15 Luis Leal attests that Pietri seemed to have been the first to adopt the term *realismo mágico* in Hispanic America in 1948.[8] French-Russian Cuban writer Alejo Carpentier, who rejected Roh's magic realism as tiresome pretension, developed his related concept *lo real maravilloso,* or *marvelous realism,* in 1949.[1]:14 Maggie Ann Bowers writes that marvelous realist literature and art expresses "the seemingly opposed perspectives of a pragmatic, practical and tangible approach to reality and an acceptance of magic and superstition" within an environment of differing cultures.[1]:2–3

The term *magical realism,* as opposed to *magic realism,* first emerged in the 1955 essay "Magical Realism in Spanish American Fiction" by critic Angel Flores to refer to writing that combines aspects of magic realism and marvelous realism. While Flores named Jorge Luis Borges as the first magical realist, he failed to acknowledge either Carpentier or Pietri for bringing Roh's magic realism to Latin America. Borges is often seen as a predecessor of magical realists, with only Flores considering him a true magical realist.[1]:16–18

After Flores's essay, there was a resurgence of interest in marvelous realism, which, after the Cuban revolution of 1959, led to the term *magical realism* being applied to a new type of literature known for matter-of-fact portrayal of magical events.[1]:18

27.2   Literature

27.2.1   Characteristics

The extent to which the characteristics below apply to a given magic realist text varies. Every text is different and employs a smattering of the qualities listed here. However, they accurately portray what one might expect from a magic realist text.

Fantastical elements

Magical realism portrays fantastical events in an otherwise realistic tone. It brings fables, folk tales, and myths into contemporary social relevance. Fantasy traits given to characters, such as levitation, telepathy, and telekinesis, help to encompass modern political realities that can be phantasmagorical.[9]

Real-world setting

The existence of fantasy elements in the real world provides the basis for magical realism. Writers do not invent new worlds but reveal the magical in this world, as was done by Gabriel García Márquez who wrote the seminal work of the style, *One Hundred Years of Solitude.*[10] In the binary world of magical realism, the supernatural realm blends with the natural, familiar world.[11]

Authorial reticence

Authorial reticence is the "deliberate withholding of information and explanations about the disconcerting fictitious world".[12] The narrator is indifferent, a characteristic enhanced by this absence of explanation of fantastic events; the story proceeds with "logical precision" as if nothing extraordinary took place.[13][14] Magical events are presented as ordinary occurrences; therefore, the reader accepts the marvelous as normal and common.[15] Explaining the supernatural world or presenting it as extraordinary would immediately reduce its legitimacy relative to the natural world. The reader would consequently disregard the supernatural as false testimony.

Plenitude

In his essay "The Baroque and the Marvelous Real", Cuban writer Alejo Carpentier defined the baroque by a lack of emptiness, a departure from structure or rules, and an "extraordinary" abundance (plenitude) of disorienting detail (citing Mondrian as its opposite). From this angle, Carpentier views the baroque as a layering of elements, which translates easily into the post-colonial or transcultural Latin American atmosphere that he emphasizes in *The Kingdom of this World.*[16] "America, a continent of symbiosis, mutations... mestizaje, engenders the baroque," [17] made explicit by elaborate

Aztec temples and associative Nahuatl poetry. These mixing ethnicities grow together with the American baroque; the space in between is where the "marvelous real" is seen. Marvelous: not meaning beautiful and pleasant, but extraordinary, strange, and excellent. Such a complex system of layering—encompassed in the Latin American "boom" novel, such as *One Hundred Years of Solitude*—aims towards "translating the scope of America" .*[18]

Hybridity

Magical realism plot lines characteristically employ hybrid multiple planes of reality that take place in "inharmonious arenas of such opposites as urban and rural, and Western and indigenous" .*[19]*[20] For example, as seen in Julio Cortázar's "La noche boca arriba", an individual experiences two realistic situations simultaneously in the same place but during two different time periods, centuries apart.*[21]

His dreamlike state connects these two realities; this small bit of magic makes these multiple planes of reality possible.*[22] Overall, they establish "a more deep and true reality than conventional realist techniques would illustrate" .*[19]*[23]

Metafiction

Main article: Metafiction

This trait centers on the reader's role in literature. With its multiple realities and specific reference to the reader's world, it explores the impact fiction has on reality, reality on fiction and the reader's role in between; as such, it is well suited for drawing attention to social or political criticism. Furthermore, it is the tool paramount in the execution of a related and major magic realist phenomenon: textualization. This term defines two conditions—first, where a fictitious reader enters the story within a story while reading it, making us self-conscious of our status as readers—and secondly, where the textual world enters into the reader's (our) world. Good sense would negate this process but 'magic' is the flexible convention that allows it.*[24]

Heightened awareness of mystery

Something that most critics agree on is this major theme. Magic realist literature tends to read at an intensified level. Taking *One Hundred Years of Solitude*, the reader must let go of preexisting ties to conventional exposition, plot advancement, linear time structure, scientific reason, etc., to strive for a state of heightened awareness of life's connectedness or hidden meanings. Luis Leal articulates this feeling as "to seize the mystery that breathes behind things" ,*[25] and supports the claim by saying a writer must heighten his senses to the point of "estado limite" (translated as "limit state" or "extreme") in order to realize all levels of reality, most importantly that of mystery.*[26]

Political critique

Magic realism contains an "implicit criticism of society, particularly the elite" .*[27] Especially with regard to Latin America, the style breaks from the inarguable discourse of "privileged centers of literature" .*[28] This is a mode primarily about and for "ex-centrics": the geographically, socially and economically marginalized. Therefore, magic realism's 'alternative world' works to correct the reality of established viewpoints (like realism, naturalism, modernism). Magic realist texts, under this logic, are subversive texts, revolutionary against socially dominant forces. Alternatively, the socially dominant may implement magical realism to disassociate themselves from their "power discourse".*[29] Theo D'haen calls this change in perspective "decentering."

27.2.2 Origins

Literary magic realism originated in Latin America. Writers often traveled between their home country and European cultural hubs, such as Paris or Berlin, and were influenced by the art movement of the time.*[30]*[31] Cuban writer Alejo

Carpentier and Venezuelan Arturo Uslar-Pietri, for example, were strongly influenced by European artistic movements, such as Surrealism, during their stays in Paris in the 1920s and 1930s.*[1] One major event that linked painterly and literary magic realisms was the translation and publication of Franz Roh's book into Spanish by Spain's *Revista de Occidente* in 1927, headed by major literary figure José Ortega y Gasset. "Within a year, Magic Realism was being applied to the prose of European authors in the literary circles of Buenos Aires." *[32] Jorge Luis Borges inspired and encouraged other Latin American writers in the development of magical realism - particularly with his first magical realist publication, *Historia universal de la infamia* in 1935.*[33] Between 1940 and 1950, magical realism in Latin America reached its peak, with prominent writers appearing mainly in Argentina.*[34]

The theoretical implications of visual art's magic realism greatly influenced European and Latin American literature. Italian Massimo Bontempelli, for instance, claimed that literature could be a means to create a collective consciousness by "opening new mythical and magical perspectives on reality", and used his writings to inspire an Italian nation governed by Fascism.*[1] Pietri was closely associated with Roh's form of magic realism and knew Bontempelli in Paris. Rather than follow Carpentier's developing versions of "the (Latin) American marvelous real," Uslar-Pietri's writings emphasize "the mystery of human living amongst the reality of life". He believed magic realism was "a continuation of the **vanguardia** [or Avant-garde] modernist experimental writings of Latin America" .*[1]

27.2.3   Major topics in criticism

Ambiguities in definition

The Mexican critic Luis Leal summed up the difficulty of defining magical realism by writing, "If you can explain it, then it's not magical realism." *[35] He offers his own definition by writing, "Without thinking of the concept of magical realism, each writer gives expression to a reality he observes in the people. To me, magical realism is an attitude on the part of the characters in the novel toward the world," or toward nature.

Leal and Irene Guenther both quote Arturo Uslar-Pietri, who described "man as a mystery surrounded by realistic facts. A poetic prediction or a poetic denial of reality. What for lack of another name could be called a magical realism." *[36] It is worth noting that Pietri, in presenting his term for this literary tendency, always kept its definition open by means of a language more lyrical and evocative than strictly critical, as in this 1948 statement. When academic critics attempted to define magical realism with scholarly exactitude, they discovered that it was more powerful than precise. Critics, frustrated by their inability to pin down the term's meaning, have urged its complete abandonment. Yet in Pietri's vague, ample usage, magical realism was wildly successful in summarizing for many readers their perception of much Latin American fiction; this fact suggests that the term has its uses, so long as it is not expected to function with the precision expected of technical, scholarly terminology."

Western and native worldviews   The critical perspective towards magical realism as a conflict between reality and abnormality stems from the Western reader's disassociation with mythology, a root of magical realism more easily understood by non-Western cultures.*[30] Western confusion regarding magical realism is due to the "conception of the real" created in a magical realist text: rather than explain reality using natural or physical laws, as in typical Western texts, magical realist texts create a reality "in which the relation between incidents, characters, and setting could not be based upon or justified by their status within the physical world or their normal acceptance by bourgeois mentality" .*[37]

Guatemalan author William Spindler's article, "Magic realism: a typology" ,*[38] suggests that there are three kinds of magic realism, which however are by no means incompatible: European 'metaphysical' magic realism, with its sense of estrangement and the uncanny, exemplified by Kafka's fiction; 'ontological' magical realism, characterized by 'matter-of-factness' in relating 'inexplicable' events; and 'anthropological' magical realism, where a Native worldview is set side by side with the Western rational worldview.*[39] Spindler's typology of magic realism has been criticized as "an act of categorization which seeks to define Magic Realism as a culturally specific project, by identifying for his readers those (non-modern) societies where myth and magic persist and where Magic Realism might be expected to occur. There are objections to this analysis. Western rationalism models may not actually describe Western modes of thinking and it is possible to conceive of instances where both orders of knowledge are simultaneously possible." *[40]

Lo real maravilloso

Alejo Carpentier originated the term *lo real maravilloso* (roughly the "marvelous real") in the prologue to his novel *The Kingdom of this World* (1949); however, some debate whether he is truly a magical realist writer, or simply a precursor and source of inspiration. Maggie Bowers claims he is widely acknowledged as the originator of Latin American magical realism (as both a novelist and critic);*[1] she describes Carpentier's conception as a kind of heightened reality where elements of the miraculous can appear while seeming natural and unforced. She suggests that by disassociating himself and his writings from Roh's painterly magic realism, Carpentier aimed to show how—by virtue of Latin America's varied history, geography, demography, politics, myths, and beliefs—improbable and marvelous things are made possible.*[1] Furthermore, Carpentier's meaning is that Latin America is a land filled with marvels, and that "writing about this land automatically produces a literature of marvelous reality".*[41]

"The marvelous" may be easily confused with magical realism, as both modes introduce supernatural events without surprising the implied author. In both, these magical events are expected and accepted as everyday occurrences. However, the marvelous world is a unidimensional world. The implied author believes that anything can happen here, as the entire world is filled with supernatural beings and situations to begin with. Fairy tales are a good example of marvelous literature. The important idea in defining the marvelous is that readers understand that this fictional world is different from the world where they live. The "marvelous" one-dimensional world differs from the *bidimensional* world of magical realism, as in the latter, the supernatural realm blends with the natural, familiar world (arriving at the combination of *two* layers of reality: bidimensional).*[11] While some use the terms magical realism and lo real maravilloso interchangeably, the key difference lies in the focus.*[42]

Critic Luis Leal attests that Carpentier was an originating pillar of the magical realist style by implicitly referring to the latter's critical works, writing that "The existence of the marvelous real is what started magical realist literature, which some critics claim is *the* truly American literature." *[43] It can consequently be drawn that Carpentier's "lo real maravilloso" is especially distinct from *magical realism* by the fact that the former applies specifically to *America*.*[44] On that note, Lee A. Daniel categorizes critics of Carpentier into three groups: those that don't consider him a magical realist whatsoever (Ángel Flores), those that call him "a mágicorealista writer with no mention of his "lo real maravilloso" (Gómez Gil, Jean Franco, Carlos Fuentes)," and those that use the two terms interchangeably (Fernando Alegría, Luis Leal, Emir Rodriguez Monegal).*[45]

Latin American exclusivity

Criticism that Latin America is the birthplace and cornerstone of all things magic realist is quite common. Ángel Flores does not deny that magical realism is an international commodity but articulates that it has a Hispanic birthplace, writing that, "Magical realism is a continuation of the romantic realist tradition of Spanish language literature and its European counterparts." *[46] Flores is not alone on this front; there is argument between those who see magical realism as a Latin American invention and those who see it as the global product of a postmodern world.*[47] Irene Guenther concludes, "Conjecture aside, it is in Latin America that [magic realism] was primarily seized by literary criticism and was, through translation and literary appropriation, transformed." *[48] Magic realism has taken on an internationalization: dozens of non-Hispanic writers are categorized as such, and many believe that it truly *is* an international commodity.*[49]

Postmodernism

Taking into account that, theoretically, magical realism was born in the 20th century, some have argued that connecting it to postmodernism is a logical next step. To further connect the two concepts, there are descriptive commonalities between the two that Belgian critic Theo D'haen addresses in his essay, "Magical Realism and Postmodernism". While authors such as Günter Grass, Thomas Bernhard, Peter Handke, Italo Calvino, John Fowles, Angela Carter, John Banville, Michel Tournier, Giannina Braschi, Willem Brakman and Louis Ferron might be widely considered postmodernist, they can "just as easily be categorized...magic realist".*[50] A list has been compiled of characteristics one might typically attribute to postmodernism, but which also could describe literary magic realism: "self-reflexiveness, metafiction, eclecticism, redundancy, multiplicity, discontinuity, intertextuality, parody, the dissolution of character and narrative instance, the erasure of boundaries, and the destabilization of the reader." *[51] To further connect the two, magical realism and postmodernism share the themes of post-colonial discourse, in which jumps in time and focus cannot really be explained with scientific but rather with magical reasoning; textualization (of the reader); and metafiction [more detail: under Themes and Qualities].

Concerning attitude toward audience, the two have, some argue, a lot in common. Magical realist works do not seek to primarily satisfy a popular audience, but instead, a sophisticated audience that must be attuned to noticing textual "subtleties" .*[52] While the postmodern writer condemns escapist literature (like fantasy, crime, ghost fiction), he/she is inextricably related to it concerning readership. There are two modes in postmodern literature: one, commercially successful pop fiction, and the other, philosophy, better suited to intellectuals. A singular reading of the first mode will render a distorted or reductive understanding of the text. The fictitious reader—such as Aureliano from *100 Years of Solitude*—is the hostage used to express the writer's anxiety on this issue of who is reading the work and to what ends, and of how the writer is forever reliant upon the needs and desires of readers (the market).*[53] The magic realist writer with difficulty must reach a balance between saleability and intellectual integrity. Wendy Faris, talking about magic realism as a contemporary phenomenon that leaves modernism for postmodernism, says, "Magic realist fictions do seem more youthful and popular than their modernist predecessors, in that they often (though not always) cater with unidirectional story lines to our basic desire to hear what happens next. Thus they may be more clearly designed for the entertainment of readers." *[54]

27.2.4   Comparison with related genres

When attempting to define what something *is*, it is often helpful to define what something is *not*. It is also important to note that many literary critics attempt to classify novels and literary works in only one genre, such as "romantic" or "naturalist" , not always taking into account that many works fall into multiple categories.*[55] Much discussion is cited from Maggie Ann Bowers' book *Magic(al) Realism*, wherein she attempts to delimit the terms magic and magical realism by examining the relationships with other genres such as realism, surrealism, fantastic literature, science fiction and its African version, the Animist Realism.

Realism

Realism is an attempt to create a depiction of actual life; a novel does not simply rely on what it presents but *how* it presents it. In this way, a realist narrative acts as framework by which the reader constructs a world using the raw materials of life. Understanding both realism and magical realism within the realm of a narrative mode is key to understanding both terms. Magical realism "relies upon the presentation of real, imagined or magical elements as if they were real. It relies upon realism, but only so that it can stretch what is acceptable as real to its limits" .*[56]

As a simple point of comparison, Roh's differentiation between expressionism and post-expressionism as described in *German Art in the 20th Century,* may be applied to magic realism and realism. Realism pertains to the terms "history" , "mimetic" , "familiarization" , "empiricism/logic" , "narration" , "closure-ridden/reductive naturalism" , and "rationalization/cause and effect" .*[57] On the other hand, magic realism encompasses the terms "myth/legend," "fantastic/supplementation," "defamiliarization," "mysticism/magic," "meta-narration," "open-ended/expansive romanticism," and "imagination/negative capability." *[58]

Surrealism

Surrealism is often confused with magical realism as they both explore illogical or non-realist aspects of humanity and existence. There is a strong historical connection between Franz Roh's concept of magic realism and surrealism, as well as the resulting influence on Carpentier's marvelous reality; however, important differences remain. Surrealism "is most distanced from magical realism [in that] the aspects that it explores are associated not with material reality but with the imagination and the mind, and in particular it attempts to express the 'inner life' and psychology of humans through art." It seeks to express the sub-conscious, unconscious, the repressed and inexpressible. Magical realism, on the other hand, rarely presents the extraordinary in the form of a dream or a *psychological experience.* "To do so," Bowers writes, "takes the magic of recognizable material reality and places it into the little understood world of the imagination. The ordinariness of magical realism's magic relies on its accepted and unquestioned position in tangible and *material reality.*" *[59]

Imaginary Realism

Imaginary Realism is a term first coined by Dutch painter Carel Willink as a pendant of magic realism. Where magic realism uses fantastical and unreal elements, imaginary realism strictly uses realistic elements in an imagined scene. As such, the classic painters with their biblical and mythological scenes, can be qualified as 'imaginary realists'. With the increasing availability of photo editing software, also art photographers like Karl Hammer and others create artistic works in this genre.

Fabulism

Fabulism traditionally refers to fables, parables, and myths, and is sometimes used in contemporary contexts for authors whose work falls within or relates to Magical Realism. Italo Calvino is an example of a writer in the genre who uses the term *fabulist*.

Fantasy

Prominent English-language fantasy writers have said that "magic realism" is only another name for fantasy fiction. Gene Wolfe said, "magic realism is fantasy written by people who speak Spanish",[60] and Terry Pratchett said magic realism "is like a polite way of saying you write fantasy".[61]

However, Amaryll Beatrice Chanady distinguishes magical realist literature from fantasy literature ("the fantastic") based on differences between three shared dimensions: the use of antinomy (the simultaneous presence of two conflicting codes), the inclusion of events that cannot be integrated into a logical framework, and the use of authorial reticence. In fantasy, the presence of the supernatural code is perceived as problematic, something that draws special attention—where in magical realism, the presence of the supernatural is accepted. In fantasy, while authorial reticence creates a disturbing effect on the reader, it works to *integrate the supernatural* into the natural framework in magical realism. This integration is made possible in magical realism as the author presents the supernatural as being equally valid to the natural. There is no hierarchy between the two codes.[62] The ghost of Melquíades in Márquez's *One Hundred Years of Solitude* or the baby ghost in Toni Morrison's *Beloved* who visit or haunt the inhabitants of their previous residence are both presented by the narrator as ordinary occurrences; the reader, therefore, accepts the marvelous as normal and common.[15]

To Dr. Clark Zlotchew, the differentiating factor between the fantastic and magical realism is that in fantastic literature, such as Kafka's story "The Metamorphosis", there is a hesitation experienced by the protagonist, implied author or reader in deciding whether to attribute natural or supernatural causes to an unsettling event, or between rational or irrational explanations.[63] Fantastic literature has also been defined as a piece of narrative in which there is a constant faltering between belief and non-belief in the supernatural or extraordinary event.

In Leal's view, writers of fantasy literature, such as Borges, can create "new worlds, perhaps new planets. By contrast, writers like García Márquez, who use magical realism, don't create new worlds, but suggest the magical in our world."[10] In magical realism, the supernatural realm blends with the natural, familiar world. This twofold world of magical realism differs from the onefold world that can be found in fairy-tale and fantasy literature.[11]

Animist realism

The Animist realism is a new term for conceptualize the African literature that has been written based on the strong presence of the imaginary ancestor, the traditional religion and especially the animism of African cultures.

The term was used by Pepetela (1989)[64] and Henry Garuba (2003)[65] to be a new conception of magic realism in African literature.

Science fiction

While science fiction and magical realism both bend the notion of what is real, toy with human imagination, and are forms of (often fantastical) fiction, they differ greatly. Bower's cites Aldous Huxley's *Brave New World* as a novel that exemplifies the science fiction novel's requirement of a "rational, physical explanation for any unusual occurrences". Huxley portrays a world where the population is highly controlled with mood enhancing drugs, which are controlled by the government. In this world, there is no link between copulation and reproduction. Humans are produced in giant test tubes, where chemical alterations during gestation determine their fates. Bowers argues that, "The science fiction narrative's distinct difference from magical realism is that it is set in a world different from any known reality and its realism resides in the fact that we can recognize it as a possibility for our future. Unlike magical realism, it does not have a realistic setting that is recognizable in relation to any past or present reality." *[66]

27.2.5 Major authors and works

Although critics and writers debate which authors or works fall within the magical realism genre, the following authors represent the narrative mode. Within the Latin American world, the most iconic of magical realist writers are Jorge Luis Borges and Nobel Laureate Gabriel García Márquez, whose novel *One Hundred Years of Solitude* was an instant worldwide success.

García Márquez confessed: "My most important problem was destroying the line of demarcation that separates what seems real from what seems fantastic." *[67] Isabel Allende was the first Latin American woman writer recognized outside the continent. Her most well-known novel, *The House of the Spirits*, is arguably similar to García Márquez's style of magical realist writing.*[1]*:43 Another notable novelist is Laura Esquivel, whose *Like Water for Chocolate* tells the story of the domestic life of women living on the margins of their families and society. The novel's protagonist, Tita, is kept from happiness and marriage by her mother. "Her unrequited love and ostracism from the family lead her to harness her extraordinary powers of imbuing her emotions to the food she makes. In turn, people who eat her food enact her emotions for her. For example, after eating a wedding cake Tita made while suffering from a forbidden love, the guests all suffer from a wave of longing. The Mexican Juan Rulfo pioneered the exposition through a non-linear structure with his short novel Pedro Páramo that tells the story of Comala both as a lively town in times of the eponymous Pedro Páramo and as a ghost town through the eyes of his son Juan Preciado who returns to Comala to fulfil a promise to her dead mother.

In the English-speaking world, major authors include British Indian writer Salman Rushdie, African American novelists Toni Morrison and Gloria Naylor, Latinos, as Ana Castillo, Rudolfo Anaya, Daniel Olivas, and Helena Maria Viramontes, Native American authors Louise Erdrich and Sherman Alexie; English author Louis de Bernières and English feminist writer Angela Carter. Perhaps the best known is Rushdie, whose "language form of magical realism straddles both the surrealist tradition of magic realism as it developed in Europe and the mythic tradition of magical realism as it developed in Latin America" .*[1] Morrison's most notable work, *Beloved*, tells the story of a mother who, haunted by the ghost of her child, learns to cope with memories of her traumatic childhood as an abused slave and the burden of nurturing children into a harsh and brutal society.*[1]

In Norway, the writers Erik Fosnes Hansen, Jan Kjærstad as well as the young novelist, Rune Salvesen, have marked themselves as premier writers of magical realism, something which has been seen as very un-Norwegian.

For a detailed list of authors and works considered magical realist please see Magic realism novels.

27.3 Visual art

27.3.1 Historical development

The painterly style began evolving as early as the first decade of the 20th century,*[68] but 1925 was when *magischer realismus* and *neue sachlichkeit* were officially recognized as major trends. This was the year that Franz Roh published his book on the subject, *Nach Expressionismus: Magischer Realismus: Probleme der neuesten europäischen Malerei* (translated as *After Expressionism: Magical Realism: Problems of the Newest European Painting*) and Gustav Hartlaub curated the seminal exhibition on the theme, entitled simply *Neue Sachlichkeit* (translated as *New Objectivity*), at the Kunsthalle Mannheim in Mannheim, Germany.*[69] Irene Guenthe refers most frequently to the New Objectivity, rather than magical realism; which is attributed to that New objectivity is practical based, referential (to real practicing artists), while the magical realism is theoretical or critic's rhetoric. Eventually under Massimo Bontempelli guidance, the term *magic* *realism* was fully embraced by the German as well as in Italian practicing communities.*[70]

New Objectivity saw an utter rejection of the preceding impressionist and expressionist movements, and Hartlaub curated his exhibition under the guideline: only those, "who have remained true or have returned to a positive, palpable reality," *[71] in order to reveal the truth of the times," *[72] would be included. The style was roughly divided into two subcategories: conservative, (neo-) classicist painting, and generally left-wing, politically motivated Verists.*[72] The following quote by Hartlaub distinguishes the two, though mostly with reference to Germany; however, one might apply the logic to all relevant European countries. "In the new art, he saw" *[72]

> a right, a left wing. One, conservative towards Classicism, taking roots in timelessness, wanting to sanctify again the healthy, physically plastic in pure drawing after nature...after so much eccentricity and chaos [a reference to the repercussions of World War I]... The other, the left, glaringly contemporary, far less artistically faithful, rather born of the negation of art, seeking to expose the chaos, the true face of our time, with an addiction to primitive fact-finding and nervous baring of the self... There is nothing left but to affirm it [the new art], especially since it seems strong enough to raise new artistic willpower.*[73]

Both sides were seen all over Europe during the 1920s and 1930s, ranging from the Netherlands to Austria, France to Russia, with Germany and Italy as centers of growth.*[74] Indeed, Italian Giorgio de Chirico, producing works in the late 1910s under the style *arte metafisica* (translated as *Metaphysical art*), is seen as a precursor and as having an "influence...greater than any other painter on the artists of New Objectivity".*[75]*[76]

Further afield, American painters were later (in the 1940s and 1950s, mostly) coined magical realists; a link between these artists and the Neue Sachlichkeit of the 1920s was explicitly made in the New York Museum of Modern Art exhibition, tellingly titled "American Realists and Magic Realists." *[77] French magical realist Pierre Roy, who worked and showed successfully in the US, is cited as having "helped spread Franz Roh's formulations" to the United States.*[78]

27.3.2 Magic realism that excludes the overtly fantastic

When art critic Franz Roh applied the term *magic realism* to visual art in 1925, he was designating a style of visual art that brings extreme realism to the depiction of mundane subject matter, revealing an "interior" mystery, rather than imposing external, overtly magical features onto this everyday reality. Roh explains,

> We are offered a new style that is thoroughly of this world that celebrates the mundane. This new world of objects is still alien to the current idea of Realism. It employs various techniques that endow all things with a deeper meaning and reveal mysteries that always threaten the secure tranquility of simple and ingenuous things.... it is a question of representing before our eyes, in an intuitive way, the fact, the interior figure, of the exterior world.*[79]

In painting, magical realism is a term often interchanged with post-expressionism, as Ríos also shows, for the very title of Roh's 1925 essay was "Magical Realism:Post-Expressionism".*[79] Indeed, as Dr. Lois Parkinson Zamora of the University of Houston writes, "Roh, in his 1925 essay, described a group of painters whom we now categorize generally as Post-Expressionists."

Roh used this term to describe painting that signaled a return to realism after expressionism's extravagances, which sought to redesign objects to reveal the spirits of those objects. Magical realism, according to Roh, instead faithfully portrays the exterior of an object, and in doing so the spirit, or magic, of the object reveals itself. One could relate this exterior magic all the way back to the 15th century. Flemish painter Van Eyck (1395–1441) highlights the complexity of a natural landscape by creating illusions of continuous and unseen areas that recede into the background, leaving it to the viewer's imagination to fill in those gaps in the image: for instance, in a rolling landscape with river and hills. The magic is contained in the viewer's interpretation of those mysterious unseen or hidden parts of the image.*[80]

Other important aspects of magical realist painting, according to Roh, include:

- A return to ordinary subjects as opposed to fantastical ones.

- A juxtaposition of forward movement with a sense of distance, as opposed to Expressionism's tendency to fore-shorten the subject.

- A use of miniature details even in expansive paintings, such as large landscapes.

The pictorial ideals of Roh's original magic realism attracted new generations of artists through the latter years of the 20th century and beyond. In a 1991 *New York Times* review, critic Vivien Raynor remarked that "John Stuart Ingle proves that Magic Realism lives" in his "virtuoso" still life watercolors.*[81] Ingle's approach, as described in his own words, reflects the early inspiration of the magic realism movement as described by Roh; that is, the aim is not to add magical elements to a realistic painting, but to pursue a radically faithful rendering of reality; the "magic" effect on the viewer comes from the intensity of that effort: "I don't want to make arbitrary changes in what I see to paint the picture, I want to paint what is given. The whole idea is to take something that's given and explore that reality as intensely as I can." *[82]*[83]

27.3.3   Later development: magic realism that incorporates the fantastic

While Ingle represents a "magic realism" that harks back to Roh's ideas, the term "magic realism" in mid-20th century visual art tends to refer to work that incorporates overtly fantastic elements, somewhat in the manner of its literary counterpart.

Occupying an intermediate place in this line of development, the work of several European and American painters whose most important work dates from the 1930s through to the 1950s, including Bettina Shaw-Lawrence, Paul Cadmus, Ivan Albright, Philip Evergood, George Tooker, Ricco, even Andrew Wyeth, is designated as "magic realist". This work departs sharply from Roh's definition, in that it (according to artcyclopedia.com) "is anchored in everyday reality, but has overtones of fantasy or wonder".*[84] In the work of Cadmus, for example, the surreal atmosphere is sometimes achieved via stylized distortions or exaggerations that are not realistic.

Recent "magic realism" has gone beyond mere "overtones" of the fantastic or surreal to depict a frankly magical reality, with an increasingly tenuous anchoring in "everyday reality". Artists associated with this kind of magic realism include Marcela Donoso*[85]*[86]*[87]*[88]*[89] and Gregory Gillespie.*[90]*[91]*[92]

Artists such as Peter Doig, Richard T. Scott and Will Teather have become associated with the term in the early 21st century.

27.3.4   Painters

- Felice Casorati

- John Rogers Cox

- Antonio Donghi

- Marcela Donoso

- Gian Paolo Dulbecco

- Jared French

- Edward Hopper

- Gayane Khachaturian

- Ricco

- Carel Willink

- Frida Kahlo

- Colleen Browning

- Eyvind Earle

- Rob Gonsalves

27.4 Film

Magical realism is not an officially recognized film genre, but characteristics of magic realism present in literature can also be found in many films with fantasy elements. These characteristics may be presented matter-of-factly and occur without explanation.*[93] Many films have magical realist narrative and events that contrast between real and magical elements, or different modes of production. This device explores the reality of what exists.*[1]*:109–11 Fredrick Jameson, "On Magic Realism in Film" advances a hypothesis that magical realism in film is a formal mode that is constitutionally depended on a type of historical raw material in which disjunction is structurally present.*[94] *Like Water for Chocolate* begins and ends with the first person narrative to establishing the magical realism storytelling frame. Telling a story from a child point of view, the historical gaps and holes perspective, and with cinematic color heightening the presence, are magical realist tools in films.*[95] Other films that convey elements of magic realism are *Amélie, The Green Mile, Beasts of the Southern Wild, Undertow, Birdman, The Mistress of Spices,* and a number of films by Woody Allen, including *Alice, The Purple Rose of Cairo, Midnight in Paris and To Rome With Love.* The animated films of Hayao Miyazaki often utilize magic realism. Some of the films of Emir Kusturica also contain elements of magical realism, the most famous of which is *Time of the Gypsies.*

27.5 New media

In electronic literature, early author Michael Joyce's *Afternoon, a story* deploys the ambiguity and dubious narrator characteristic of high modernism, along with some suspense and romance elements, in a story whose meaning could change dramatically depending on the path taken through its lexias on each reading. More recently, Pamela Sacred perpetuated the genre through *La Voie de l'ange*, a continuation of *The Diary of Anne Frank* written in French by a fictional character from her *Venetian Cell* hypertext saga.

27.6 See also

- List of genres

With reference to literature

- Category:Magic realism novels

- Fantasy / Low fantasy

- Latin American Boom

- Hallucinatory realism

- Hysterical realism

- McOndo

- Southern Gothic

With reference to visual art

- Fantastic realism

- Metaphysical art

- New Objectivity

With reference to both

- Metarealism

- Postmodernism

- Romantic realism

- Surrealism

27.7   References

[1] Bowers, Maggie Ann (November 4, 2004). *Magic(al) Realism*. New York: Routledge. ISBN 978-0-415-26854-7.

[2] Matthew C. Strecher, Magical Realism and the Search for Identity in the Fiction of Murakami Haruki, Journal of Japanese Studies, Volume 25, Number 2 (Summer 1999), pp. 263-298, at 267.

[3] Guenther, Irene, "Magic Realism in the Weimar Republic" tackles German roots of the term, and how art is related to literature

[4] Slemon, Stephen. *Magic realism as post-colonial discourse*. In: Canadian Literature #116 (Spring 1988),pp. 9-24, p. 9

[5] Franz Roh: Nach-Expressionismus. Magischer Realismus. Probleme der neuesten europäischen Malerei. Klinkhardt & Biermann, Leipzig 1925.

[6] Guenther, Irene, "Magic Realism in the Weimar Republic" from *MR: Theory, History, Community*, pp. 33

[7] Guenther, Irene, "Magic Realism in the Weimar Republic" from *MR: Theory, History, Community*

[8] Leal, Luis, "Magical Realism in Spanish America" from *MR: Theory, History, Community*, pp. 120.

[9] The Concise Oxford Dictionary of Literary Terms, 3rd ed., 2008

[10] García, *Leal*, p. 89.

[11] Zlotchew, Dr. Clark. *Varieties of Magical Realism*. New Jersey: Academic Press ENE, 2007. p. 15

[12] Chanady, Amaryll Beatrice. Magical Realism and the Fantastic: Resolved versus Unresolved Antinomy. New York: Garland Publishing Inc., 1985. pg. 16

[13] Flores, Angel. "Magical Realism in Spanish American Fiction." Hispania 38.2 (1955): 187-192. Web. <http://www.jstor.org/stable/335812>.

[14] Chanady, Amaryll Beatrice. Magical Realism and the Fantastic: Resolved versus Unresolved Antinomy. New York: Garland Publishing Inc., 1995. pg. 30

[15] Bowers, Maggie A. *Magic(al) Realism*, pp. 25-27. New York: Routledge, 2004. Print.

[16] Carpentier, Alejo, *El Reino de este Mundo*

[17] Carpentier, Alejo, "The baroque and the marvelous real" from *MR: Theory History, Community*

[18] Carpentier, Alejo, "The baroque and the marvelous real" from *Magical Realism: Theory, History, Community*, pp.107

[19] "Post Colonial Studies at Emory" . 1998. Retrieved June 18, 2009.

[20] Daniel, Lee A. "Realismo Magico: True Realism with a Pinch of Magic." The South Central Bulletin. 42.4 (1982): 129-130. Web. <http://www.jstor.org/stable/3188273>.

[21] Daniel, Lee A. "Realismo Magico: True Realism with a Pinch of Magic." The South Central Bulletin. 42.4 (1982): 129-130. Web. <http://www.jstor.org/stable/3188273>.

[22] Daniel, Lee A. "Realismo Magico: True Realism with a Pinch of Magic." The South Central Bulletin. 42.4 (1982): 129-130. Web. <http://www.jstor.org/stable/3188273>.

[23] Daniel, Lee A. "Realismo Magico: True Realism with a Pinch of Magic." The South Central Bulletin. 42.4 (1982): 129-130. Web. <http://www.jstor.org/stable/3188273>.

[24] Thiem, Jon, "The Textualization of the Reader in Magical Realist Fiction" from *MR: Theory, History, Community*

[25] Leal, Luis, "Magical Realism in Spanish American Literature," from *MR: Theory, History, Community*

[26] Carpentier, Alejo, "On the Marvelous Real in America", the Introduction to his novel, *The Kingdom of this World*

[27] "Twentieth-Century Spanish American Literature". University of Texas Press. 194. Retrieved June 18, 2009.

[28] D'haen, Theo, "Magical realism and postmodernism: decentering privileged centers" from *MR: Theory, History, Community*

[29] D'haen, Theo, "Magical realism and postmodernism: decentering privileged centers" from *MR: Theory, History, Community*, pp. 195

[30] Faris, Wendy B. and Lois Parkinson Zamora, Introduction to *Magical Realism: Theory, History, Community*, pp. 3-4

[31] Carpentier, Alejo: "The Baroque and the Marvelous Real (1975)" from *MR: Theory, History, Community*

[32] Guenther, Irene, "Magic realism in the Weimar Republic" from MR: Theory, History, Community, pp. 61, wherein Guenther further backs up this statement

[33] Flores, Angel. "Magical Realism in Spanish American Fiction." Hispania 38.2 (1955): 187-192. Web. <http://www.jstor.org/stable/335812>.

[34] Flores, Angel. "Magical Realism in Spanish American Fiction." Hispania 38.2 (1955): 187-192. Web. <http://www.jstor.org/stable/335812>.

[35] García, *Leal*, p. 127–128

[36] Pietri, Arturo Uslar, *Letras y hombres de Venezuela*. Mexico City, Fondo de Cultura Economica: 1949. pp. 161-61

[37] Angel Flores, qtd. in Simpkins, Scott (1988), "Magical Strategies: The Supplement of Realism", *Twentieth Century Literature* **34** (2): 140–154, doi:10.2307/441074, p. 142

[38] Spindler, W. 'Magic realism: a typology', Forum for Modern Language Studies. (1993) Vol. xxxix No. 1

[39] http://www.dspace.cam.ac.uk/bitstream/1810/225960/3/French,%20M.,%20Jackson,%20S.%20Jokisuu,%20E.%20(2010)%20'Diverse%20Engagement%20-%20Drawing%20in%20the%20Margins'{}%20online%20edition-3.pdf

[40] Liam Connell, "Discarding Magic Realism: Modernism, Anthropology, and Critical Practice," in ARIEL, Vol. 29, No. 2, April, 1998, pp. 95-110.

[41] Zlotchew, Dr. Clark. *Varieties of Magical Realism*. New Jersey: Academic Press ENE, 2007.

[42] Zlotchew, Dr. Clark. *Varieties of Magical Realism*. New Jersey: Academic Press ENE, 2007. p. 11

[43] Leal, Luis, "Magical Realism in Spanish America" from *MR: Theory, History, Community*, pp. 122

[44] Juan Barroso VIII, Daniel, Lee A. "Realismo Magico: True Realism with a Pinch of Magic." The South Central Bulletin. 42.4 (1982): 129-130. Web. <http://www.jstor.org/stable/3188273>.

[45] Daniel, Lee A. "Realismo Magico: True Realism with a Pinch of Magic." The South Central Bulletin. 42.4 (1982): 129-130. Web. <http://www.jstor.org/stable/3188273>.

[46] Flores, Angel, "Magical Realism in Spanish America" from *MR: Theory, History, Community*

[47] Faris, Wendy B. and Lois Parkinson Zamora, Introduction to *MR: Theory, History, Community*

[48] Guenther, Irene, "Magic Realism in the Weimar Republic" from *MR: Theory, History, Community*, pp. 61

[49] Faris, Wendy B. and Lois Parkinson Zamora, Introduction to MR: Theory, History, Community, pp. 4 and 8

[50] D'haen, Theo L., "Magical realism and postmodernism" from MR: Theory, History, Community, pp. 193

[51] D'haen, Theo L., "Magical realism and postmodernism" from MR: Theory, History, Community, pp. 192-3 [D'haen references many texts that attest to these qualities]

[52] Flores, Angel. "Magical Realism in Spanish American Fiction." Hispania 38.2 (1955): 187-192. Web. <http://www.jstor.org/stable/335812>.

[53] Thiem, Jon, "The textualization of the reader in magical realist fiction" from MR: Theory, History, Community

[54] Wendy Faris, "Scheherezade's Children: Magical Realism and Postmodern Fiction," from MR: Theory, History, Community, pp. 163

[55] Flores, Angel. "Magical Realism in Spanish American Fiction." Hispania 38.2 (1955): 187-192. Web. <http://www.jstor.org/stable/335812>.

[56] Bowers, Maggie A. Magic(al) Realism, pp. 22. New York: Routledge, 2004. Print.

[57] Simpkins, Scott. "Magical Strategies: The Supplement of Realism." Twentieth Century Literature 34.2 (1988): 140-154. Web. <http://www.jstor.org/stable/441074>.

[58] Simpkins, Scott. "Magical Strategies: The Supplement of Realism." Twentieth Century Literature 34.2 (1988): 140-154. Web. <http://www.jstor.org/stable/441074>.

[59] Bowers, Maggie A. Magic(al) Realism, pp. 22-24. New York: Routledge, 2004. Print.

[60] Wolfe, Gene; Baber, Brendan. "Gene Wolfe Interview". In Wright, Peter. Shadows of the New Sun: Wolfe on Writing/Writers on Wolfe. Retrieved 2009-01-20.

[61] "Terry Pratchett by Linda Richards". januarymagazine.com. 2002. Retrieved February 17, 2008.

[62] Chanady, Amaryll Beatrice, Magical realism and the fantastic: Resolved versus unresolved antinomy. New York: Garland Publishing Inc., 1985. pp. 30-31

[63] Zlotchew, Dr. Clark. Varieties of Magical Realism. New Jersey: Academic Press ENE, 2007. p. 14

[64] PEPETELA (1989). Lueji, o nascimento de um império. Porto, Portugal: União dos Escritores Angolanos.

[65] GARUBA, Harry (2003).Explorations in Animist Materialism: Notes on Reading/Writing African Literature, Culture, and Society. Public Culture

[66] Bowers, Maggie A. Magic(al) Realism, pp. 29-30. New York: Routledge, 2004. Print.

[67] Interview in Revista Primera Plana - Año V Buenos Aires, 20–26 June 1967 Nº 234, pages 52-55. I have not been able to get my hands on the original material but it is quoted in as "Mi problema más importante era destruir la línea de demarcación que separa lo que parece real de lo que parece fantástico. Porque en el mundo que trataba de evocar esa barrera no existía. Pero necesitaba un tono convincente, que por su propio prestigio volviera verosímiles las cosas que menos lo parecían, y que lo hicieran sin perturbar la unidad del relato" and this agrees well (minor textual variants) with the other quotations I have found in : "El problema más importante era destruir la línea de demarcación que separa lo que parece real de lo que parece fantástico porque en el mundo que trataba de evocar, esa barrera no existía. Pero necesitaba un tono inocente, que por su prestigio volviera verosímiles las cosas que menos lo parecían, y que lo hiciera sin perturbar la unidad del relato. También el lenguaje era una dificultad de fondo, pues la verdad no parece verdad simplemente porque lo sea, sino por la forma en que se diga." Other quotations on the Internet can be found in and . All of these quotations reinforce the rough English translation of the first sentence given in the main text of this article. For those who wish to seek the original interview, the front cover and table of contents are reproduced at

[68] "Austrian Alfred Kubin spent a lifetime wrestling with the uncanny,...[and] in 1909 [he] published Die andere Seite (The Other Side), a novel illustrated with fifty-two drawings. In it, Kubin set out to explore the 'other side' of the visible world— the corruption, the evil, the rot, as well as the power and mystery. The border between reality and dream remains consistently nebulous... in certain ways an important precursor [to Magic Realism],...[he] exerted significant influence on subsequent German and Austrian literature." Guenther, Irene, "Magic realism in the Weimar Republic" from MR: Theory, History, Community, pp. 57.

[69] Guenther, Irene, "Magic Realism in the Weimar Republic" from *MR: Theory, History, Community, pp. 41*

[70] Guenther, Irene, "Magic Realism in the Weimar Republic" from MR: Theory, History, Community, pp. 60

[71] Hartlaub, Gustav, "Werbendes Rundschreiben"

[72] Guenther, Irene, "Magic realism in the Weimar Republic" from *MR: Theory, History, Community*, pp. 41

[73] Westheim, Paul, "Ein neuer Naturalismus?? Eine Rundfrage des Kunstblatts" in *Das Kunstblatt* 9 (1922)

[74] Guenther, Irene, "Magic realism in the Weimar Republic" from *MR: Theory, History, Community*, pp. 41-45

[75] Guenther, Irene, "Magic realism in the Weimar Republic" from *MR: Theory, History, Community*, pp. 38

[76] Further, see Wieland Schmied, "*Neue Sachlichkeit* and German Realism of the Twenties" in Louise Lincoln, ed., *German Realism of the Twenties: The Artist as Social Critic*. Minneapolis: Minneapolis Institute of Arts, 1980, pp.42

[77] Dorothy C. Miller and Alfred Barr, eds., *American Realists and Magic Realists*. New York: Museum of Modern Art, 1943

[78] Guenther, Irene, "Magic realism in the Weimar Republic" from *MR: Theory, History, Community*, pp. 45

[79]

[80] Crawford, Katherine. "Recognizing Van Eyck: Magical Realism in Landscape Painting." Philadelphia Museum of Art Bulletin. 91. 386/387 (1998): 7-23. Web. http://www.jstor.org/stable/3795460

[81] Raynor, Vivien (1991-05-19). "ART; The Skill of the Watercolorist". *The New York Times*. Retrieved 2010-05-12.

[82]

[83]

[84]

[85] Elga Perez-Laborde:"Marcela Donoso," *jornal do Brasilia*, 10/10/1999

[86] Elga Perez-Laborde:"Prologo," *Iconografía de Mitos y Leyendas, Marcela Donoso*, ISBN 978-956-291-592-2. 12/2002

[87] "with an impressive chromatic delivery, images come immersed in such a magic realism full of symbols," *El Mercurio - Chile*, 06/22/1998

[88] Dr. Antonio Fernandez, Director of the Art Museum of Universidad de Concepción:"I was impressed by her original iconographic creativity, that in a way very close to magic realism, achieves to emphasize with precision the subjects specific to each folkloric tradition, local or regional," Chile, 29/12/1997

[89] http://www.marceladonoso.cl

[90] Johnson, Ken (2000-09-22). "ART IN REVIEW; Gregory Gillespie". *The New York Times*. Retrieved 2010-05-12.

[91]

[92] Johnson, Ken (2003-05-23). "ART IN REVIEW; James Valerio". *The New York Times*. Retrieved 2010-05-12.

[93] Hurd, Mary (November 30, 2006). *Women directors and their films*. Praeger. p. 73. ISBN 978-0-275-98578-3.

[94] Zamora, Lois Parkinson; Faris, Wendy B (November 30, 1995). *Magical Realism: Theory, History, Community*. Duke University Press Books. p. 426. ISBN 978-0-8223-1640-4.

[95] Hegerfeld, Anne (January 13, 2005). *Lies that Tell the Truth: Magic Realism Seen through Contemporary Fiction from Britain (Costerus NS 155)*. Rodopi. p. 147. ISBN 978-90-420-1974-4.

27.8   External links

- The Essence of Magic Realism - Critical Study of the origins and development of Magic Realism in art.

- Ten Dreams Galleries - A comprehensive discussion of the historical development of Magic Realism in painting

- The Magic Realism Time Capsule

- Video montage of George Tooker's "The Subway," which recreates the mood via pictorial editing and sound on YouTube

Plaque of Gabriel García Márquez, Paris

Love Song *1914, Museum of Modern Art*

Alexander Kanoldt, Still Life II *1922*

Paul Cadmus, The Fleet's In! *1934*

Chapter 28

Narration

Narration is the use of—or the particularly chosen methodology or process (also called the **narrative mode**) of using—a written or spoken commentary to convey a story to an audience.[*][1] Narration encompasses a set of techniques through which the creator of the story presents their story, including:

- **Narrative point of view**: the perspective (or type of personal or non-personal "lens") through which a story is communicated

- **Narrative voice**: the format (or type of presentational form) through which a story is communicated

- **Narrative time**: the placement of the story's time-frame in the past, the present, or the future

A **narrator** is a personal character or a non-personal voice that the creator of the story develops to deliver information to the audience, particularly about the plot. The narrator may be a voice devised by the author as an anonymous, non-personal, or stand-alone entity; as the author her/himself as a character; or as some other fictional or non-fictional character appearing and participating within their own story. The narrator is considered *participant* if he/she is a character within the story, and *non-participant* if he/she is an implied character or an omniscient or semi-omniscient being or voice that merely relates the story to the audience without being involved in the actual events. Some stories have multiple narrators to illustrate the story-lines of various characters at the same, similar, or different times, thus allowing a more complex, non-singular point of view.

Narration encompasses not only *who* tells the story, but also *how* the story is told (for example, by using stream of consciousness or unreliable narration). In traditional literary narratives (such as novels, short stories, and memoirs), narration is a required story element; in other types of (chiefly non-literary) narratives, such as plays, television shows, video games, and films, narration is merely optional.

28.1 Narrative point of view

Narrative point of view or narrative perspective describes the position of the narrator (the character of the storyteller) in relation to the story being told.[*][2] It has been compared to a camera:

> When you are reading a scene in a book and when you are writing a scene, you follow the character almost like a camera on the character's shoulder or in the character's head. You are looking at the character performing a specific set of actions or important actions in vivid detail.
> —Jenna Blum in *The Author at Work*, 2013[*][3]

28.1.1 First-person

Main article: First-person narrative

In a **first-person narrative,** the story is revealed through a narrator who is also a character within the story, so that the narrator reveals the plot by referring to this viewpoint character with forms of "I" or, when plural, "we". Often, the first-person narrative is used as a way to directly convey the deeply internal, otherwise unspoken thoughts of the narrator. Frequently, the narrator is the protagonist, whose inner thoughts are expressed to the audience/reader, even if not to any of the other characters. This character can be further developed through individual narrative style. First-person narrations may be told like third-person (or omniscient) ones, in the guise of a person directly undergoing the events in the story without being aware of conveying that experience to readers; alternatively, the narrator may be conscious of telling the story to a given audience, perhaps at a given place and time, for a given reason. A conscious narrator, as a human participant of past events, is an imperfect witness by definition, unable to fully see and comprehend events in their entirety as they unfurl, not necessarily objective in their inner thoughts or sharing them fully, and furthermore may be pursuing some hidden agenda. Other forms include temporary first-person narration as a story within a story, wherein a narrator or character observing the telling of a story by another is reproduced in full, temporarily and without interruption shifting narration to the speaker. The first-person narrator can also be the focal character.

The first-person narrator is always a character within his/her own story (whether the protagonist or not). This viewpoint character takes action, makes judgments and expresses opinions, thereby not always allowing the audience to comprehend the other characters' thoughts, feelings, or perceptions as much as the narrator's own. We become aware of the events and characters of the story through the narrator's views and knowledge.[*][4]

In some cases, the narrator gives and withholds information based on their own experience. It is an important task for the reader to determine as much as possible about the character of the narrator in order to decide what "really" happens. *Example:*

> I could picture it. I have a habit of imagining the conversations between my friends. We went out to the
> Cafe Napolitain to have an aperitif and watch the evening crowd on the Boulevard.
> —Ernest Hemingway as the protagonist Jake Barnes, *The Sun Also Rises*

Some stories are told in first person *plural* ("we"). Examples are the short stories *Twenty-Six Men and a Girl* by Maxim Gorky and *A Rose for Emily* by William Faulkner, *The Treatment of Bibi Haldar* by Jhumpa Lahiri, *The Virgin Suicides* by Jeffrey Eugenides, *During the Reign of the Queen of Persia* by Joan Chase, *Our Kind* by Kate Walbert, *I, Robot* by Isaac Asimov, *We Didn't* by Stuart Dybek, and *Then We Came to the End* by Joshua Ferris.[*][5]

The narrator can be the protagonist (e.g., Gulliver in *Gulliver's Travels*), someone very close to him who is privy to his thoughts and actions (Dr. Watson in *Sherlock Holmes*), or an ancillary character who has little to do with the action of the story (such as Nick Carraway in *The Great Gatsby*). Narrators can report others' narratives at one or more removes. These are called 'frame narrators': examples are Mr. Lockwood, the narrator in *Wuthering Heights* by Emily Brontë; and the unnamed narrator in *Heart of Darkness* by Joseph Conrad. Skilled writers choose to skew narratives, in keeping with the narrator's character, to an arbitrary degree, from ever so slight to extreme. For example, the aforementioned Mr. Lockwood is quite naive, of which fact he appears unaware, simultaneously rather pompous, and re-counting a combination of stories, experiences, and servants' gossip. As such, his character is an unintentionally very unreliable narrator, and serves mainly to mystify, confuse, and ultimately leave the events of Wuthering Heights open to a great range of interpretations.

Other types of narrating characters may greatly affect what the reader sees of events and how, intentionally or unintentionally, in any number of ways. Character weaknesses and faults, such as tardiness, cowardice, or vice, may leave the narrator unintentionally absent or unreliable for certain key events. Specific events may further be colored or obscured by a narrator's background, since non-omniscient characters must by definition be laypersons and foreigners to some circles, and limitations such as poor eyesight and illiteracy may also leave important blanks. Unstable or malevolent narrators can also lie to the reader.

In autobiographical fiction, the first person narrator is the character of the author (with varying degrees of historical accuracy). The narrator is still distinct from the author and must behave like any other character and any other first person narrator. Examples of this kind of narrator include Jim Carroll in *The Basketball Diaries* and Kurt Vonnegut Jr. in *Timequake* (in this case, the first-person narrator is also the author). In some cases, the narrator is writing a book — "the book in your hands" —and therefore he has most of the powers and knowledge of the author. Examples include *The Name of the Rose* by Umberto Eco, and *The Curious Incident of the Dog in the Night-Time* by Mark Haddon.

A rare form of first person is the first person omniscient, in which the narrator is a character in the story, but also knows the thoughts and feelings of all the other characters. It can seem like third person omniscient at times. A reasonable explanation fitting the mechanics of the story's world is generally provided or inferred, unless its glaring absence is a major plot point. Two notable examples are *The Book Thief* by Markus Zusak, where the narrator is Death, and *The Lovely Bones* by Alice Sebold, where a young girl, having been killed, observes, from some post-mortem, extracorporeal viewpoint, her family struggling to cope with her disappearance. Typically, however, the narrator restricts the events relayed in the narrative to those that could reasonably be known. Novice writers may make the mistake of allowing elements of omniscience into a first-person narrative unintentionally and at random, forgetting the inherent human limitations of a witness or participant of the events.

28.1.2   Second-person

Main article: Second-person narrative

The **second-person narrative mode**, in which the narrator refers to him- or herself as 'you' in a way that suggests alienation from the events described, or emotional/ironic distance, is less common in fiction, though it's often used in the short fiction of Lorrie Moore and Junot Diaz.

Perhaps the most prominent example of this mode in contemporary literature is Jay McInerney's *Bright Lights, Big City*. In this novel, the second-person narrator is observing his own out-of-control life, unable to cope with the trauma he keeps hidden from readers for most of the book, the death of his mother:

> You are not the kind of guy who would be at a place like this at this time of the morning. But here you are, and you cannot say the terrain is entirely unfamiliar, although the details are fuzzy. You are at a nightclub talking to a girl with a shaved head. The club is either Heartbreak or the Lizard Lounge. All might become clear if you could just slip into the bathroom and do a little more Bolivian Marching Powder. Then again, it might not. A small voice inside you insists that this epidemic lack of clarity is a result of too much of that already.
> —Jay McInerney, *Bright Lights, Big City*

The use of "you" as an addressee (as in poetry and song) is employed in the "Choose Your Own Adventure" and "Fighting Fantasy" series of books that were popular in the 1980s.

28.1.3   Third-person

Third-person narration provides the greatest flexibility to the author and thus is the most commonly used narrative mode in literature. In the **third-person narrative mode**, each and every character is referred to by the narrator as "he", "she", "it", or "they", but never as "I" or "we" (first-person), or "you" (second-person). In third-person narrative, it is clear that the narrator is an unspecified entity or uninvolved person who conveys the story and is not a character of any kind within the story.*[6]

If the narrator of the story is not present, or is present but is not the protagonist, and the story told is about someone else and is not the narrator's own story, the story is narrated by **He/She** perspective.*[7]

The third-person modes are usually categorized along two axes. The first is the subjectivity/objectivity axis, with "subjective" narration describing one or more character's feelings and thoughts, and "objective" narration not describing the feelings or thoughts of any characters. The second axis is the omniscient/limited axis, a distinction that refers to the knowledge available to the narrator. An omniscient narrator has knowledge of all times, people, places, and events, including all characters' thoughts; a limited narrator, in contrast, may know absolutely everything about a single character and every piece of knowledge in that character's mind, but the narrator's knowledge is "limited" to that character—that is, the narrator cannot describe things unknown to the focal character.

28.1.4 Alternating person

While the general rule is for novels to adopt a single approach to point of view throughout the novel's entirety, it is not mandatory to conform to this rule. Many stories, especially in literature, alternate between the third person limited and third person omniscient. In this case, an author will move back and forth between a more omniscient third-person narrator to a more personal third-person limited narrator. The Harry Potter series is told in "third person limited" (in which the reader is "limited" to the thoughts of some particular character) for much of the seven novels, but deviates to omniscient in that it switches the limited view to other characters from time to time, rather than only the protagonist. However, like the *A Song of Ice and Fire* series and the books by George R. R. Martin, a switch of viewpoint is done only at chapter boundaries. The Home and the World, written in 1916 by Rabindranath Tagore, is another example of a book switching among just three characters at chapter boundaries. In The Heroes of Olympus series the point of view changes between characters at intervals. *Alias Grace* switches viewpoint as well as perspective; one character's viewpoint is told from first person limited while the other's is told from third person limited. Omniscient point of view is also referred to as alternating point of view, because the story sometimes alternates between characters. Often, a narrator using the first person will try to be more objective by also employing the third person for important action scenes, especially those in which they are not directly involved or in scenes where they are not present to have viewed the events in firsthand. This mode is found in the novel *The Poisonwood Bible*.

Epistolary novels, which were common in the early years of the novel, generally consist of a series of letters written by different characters, and necessarily switching when the writer changes; the classic books *Frankenstein* by Mary Shelley, *Dracula* by Abraham "Bram" Stoker and *The Strange Case of Dr. Jekyll and Mr. Hyde* take this approach. Sometimes, however, they may all be letters from one character, such as C. S. Lewis' *The Screwtape Letters* and Helen Fielding's *Bridget Jones's Diary*. Robert Louis Stevenson's *Treasure Island* switches between third and first person, as do Charles Dickens's *Bleak House* and Vladimir Nabokov's *The Gift*. Many of William Faulkner's novels take on a series of first-person viewpoints. E.L. Konigsburg's novella *The View from Saturday* uses flashbacks to alternate between third- person and first-person perspectives throughout the book, as does Edith Wharton's novel *Ethan Frome*. *After the First Death*, by Robert Cormier, a novel about a fictional school bus hijacking in the late 1970s, also switches from first- to third-person narrative using different characters. The novel *The Death of Artemio Cruz*, by Mexican writer Carlos Fuentes, switches between the three persons from one chapter to the next, even though all refer to the same protagonist. The novel *Dreaming in Cuban*, by Cristina García alternates between third-person, limited and first-person perspectives, depending on the generation of the speaker: the grandchildren recount events in first-person viewpoints while the parents and grandparent are shown in the third-person, limited perspective.

28.2 Narrative voice

The **narrative voice** describes how the story is conveyed: for example, by "viewing" a character's thought processes, reading a letter written for someone, retelling a character's experiences, etc.

28.2.1 Stream-of-consciousness voice

Main article: Stream of consciousness (narrative mode)

A **stream of consciousness** gives the (typically first-person) narrator's perspective by attempting to replicate the thought processes—as opposed to simply the actions and spoken words—of the narrative character. Often, interior monologues and inner desires or motivations, as well as pieces of incomplete thoughts, are expressed to the audience but not necessarily to other characters. Examples include the multiple narrators' feelings in William Faulkner's *The Sound and the Fury* and *As I Lay Dying*, the character Offred's often fragmented thoughts in Margaret Atwood's *The Handmaid's Tale*, and the development of the narrator's nightmarish experience in Queen's hit song "Bohemian Rhapsody." Irish writer James Joyce exemplifies this style in his novel *Ulysses*.

28.2.2   Character voice

One of the most common narrative voices, used especially with first- and third-person viewpoints, is the character voice, in which a conscious "person" (in most cases, a living human being) is presented as the narrator. In this situation, the narrator is no longer an unspecified entity; rather, the narrator is a more relatable, realistic character who may or may not be involved in the actions of the story and who may or may not take a biased approach in the storytelling. If the character is directly involved in the plot, this narrator is also called the viewpoint character. The viewpoint character is not necessarily the focal character: examples of supporting viewpoint characters include Doctor Watson, Scout in *To Kill a Mockingbird*, and Nick Carraway of *The Great Gatsby*.

Unreliable voice

Main article: Unreliable narrator

Under the character voice is the **unreliable narrative voice**, which involves the use of a dubious or untrustworthy narrator. This mode may be employed to give the audience a deliberate sense of disbelief in the story or a level of suspicion or mystery as to what information is meant to be true and what is to be false. This lack of reliability is often developed by the author to demonstrate that the narrator is in some state of psychosis. The narrator of Poe's "The Tell-Tale Heart," for example, is significantly biased, unknowledgeable, ignorant, childish, or is perhaps purposefully trying to deceive the audience. Unreliable narrators are usually first-person narrators; however, when a third-person narrator is considered unreliable for any reason, their viewpoint may be termed "third-person, subjective".

Examples include Nelly Dean in *Wuthering Heights*, "Chief" Bromden in *One Flew Over the Cuckoo's Nest*,[8] Holden Caulfield in the novel *The Catcher In The Rye*, Dr. James Sheppard in *The Murder of Roger Ackroyd*, Stark in *Only Forward*, both John Shade and Charles Kinbote in the novel *Pale Fire* and John Dowell in the novel *The Good Soldier*.

A naive narrator is one who is so ignorant and inexperienced that they actually expose the faults and issues of their world. This is used particularly in satire, whereby the user can draw more inferences about the narrator's environment than the narrator. Child narrators can also fall under this category.

28.2.3   Epistolary voice

Main article: Epistolary novel

The **epistolary narrative voice** uses a (usually fictional) series of letters and other documents to convey the plot of the story. Although epistolary works can be considered multiple-person narratives, they also can be classified separately, as they arguably have no narrator at all—just an author who has gathered the documents together in one place. One famous example is Mary Shelley's *Frankenstein,* which is a story written in a sequence of letters. Another is Bram Stoker's *Dracula,* which tells the story in a series of diary entries, letters and newspaper clippings. *Les Liaisons dangereuses (Dangerous Liaisons),* by Pierre Choderlos de Laclos, is again made up of the correspondence between the main characters, most notably the Marquise de Merteuil and the Vicomte de Valmont. Langston Hughes does the same thing in a shorter form in his story "Passing", which consists of a young man's letter to his mother.

28.2.4   Third-person voices

The third-person narrative voices are narrative-voice techniques employed solely under the category of the third-person view.

Third-person, subjective

The **third-person subjective** is when the narrator conveys the thoughts, feelings, opinions, etc. of one or more characters. If there is just one character, it can be termed **third-person limited**, in which the reader is "limited" to the thoughts of some particular character (often the protagonist) as in the first-person mode, except still giving personal descriptions using "he", "she", "it", and "they", but not "I". This is almost always the main character (e.g., Gabriel in Joyce's *The Dead*, Nathaniel Hawthorne's *Young Goodman Brown*, or Santiago in Hemingway's *The Old Man and the Sea*). Certain third-person omniscient modes are also classifiable as "third person, subjective" modes that switch between the thoughts, feelings, etc. of all the characters.

This style, in both its limited and omniscient variants, became the most popular narrative perspective during the 20th century. In contrast to the broad, sweeping perspectives seen in many 19th-century novels, third-person subjective is sometimes called the "over the shoulder" perspective; the narrator only describes events perceived and information known by a character. At its narrowest and most subjective scope, the story reads as though the viewpoint character were narrating it; dramatically this is very similar to the first person, in that it allows in-depth revelation of the protagonist's personality, but it uses third-person grammar. Some writers will shift perspective from one viewpoint character to another, such as in George R. R. Martin's *A Song of Ice and Fire*.

The focal character, protagonist, antagonist, or some other character's thoughts are revealed through the narrator. The reader learns the events of the narrative through the perceptions of the chosen character.

Third-person, objective

The **third-person objective** employs a narrator who tells a story without describing any character's thoughts, opinions, or feelings; instead, it gives an objective, unbiased point of view. Often the narrator is self-dehumanized in order to make the narrative more neutral. This type of narrative mode, outside of fiction, is often employed by newspaper articles, biographical documents, and scientific journals. This narrative mode can be described as a "fly-on-the-wall" or "camera lens" approach that can only record the observable actions but does not interpret these actions or relay what thoughts are going through the minds of the characters. Works of fiction that use this style emphasize characters acting out their feelings observably. Internal thoughts, if expressed, are given voice through an aside or soliloquy. While this approach does not allow the author to reveal the unexpressed thoughts and feelings of the characters, it does allow the author to reveal information that not all or any of the characters may be aware of. A typical example of this so-called *camera-eye perspective* is *Hills Like White Elephants* by Ernest Hemingway.

The third-person objective is preferred in most pieces that are deliberately trying to take a neutral or unbiased view, like in many newspaper articles. It is also called the **third-person dramatic** because the narrator, like the audience of a drama, is neutral and ineffective toward the progression of the plot—merely an uninvolved onlooker. It was also used around the mid-20th century by French novelists writing in the *nouveau roman* tradition.

Third-person, omniscient

Historically, the **third-person omniscient** perspective has been the most commonly used; it is seen in countless classic novels, including works by Jane Austen, Leo Tolstoy, and George Eliot. A story in this narrative mode is presented by a narrator with an overarching point of view, seeing and knowing everything that happens within the world of the story, including what each of the characters is thinking and feeling.[*][9] It sometimes even takes a subjective approach. One advantage of omniscience is that this mode enhances the sense of objective reliability (i.e. truthfulness) of the plot. The third-person omniscient narrator is the least capable of being unreliable—although the omniscient narrator can have its own personality, offering judgments and opinions on the behavior of the characters.

In addition to reinforcing the sense of the narrator as reliable (and thus of the story as true), the main advantage of this mode is that it is eminently suited to telling huge, sweeping, epic stories, and/or complicated stories involving numerous characters. The disadvantage of this mode is the increased distance between the audience and the story, and the fact that —when used in conjunction with a sweeping, epic "cast-of-thousands" story—characterization tends to be limited, thus reducing the reader's ability to identify with or sympathize with the characters. A classic example of both the advantages and disadvantages of this mode is J. R. R. Tolkien's *The Lord of the Rings*.

Some writers and literary critics make the distinction between the third-person omniscient and the **universal omniscient**, the difference being that in the universal omniscient, the narrator reveals information that the characters do not have. Usually, the universal omniscient reinforces the idea of the narrator being unconnected to the events of the story.

28.3   Narrative time

The **narrative tense** or **narrative time** determines the grammatical tense of the story; whether in the past, present, or future.

28.3.1   Past tense

The most common in literature and story-telling in the English, Chinese, (Modern and Ancient) Greek, Italian, and Portuguese languages; the events of the plot are depicted as occurring sometime before the current moment or the time at which the narrative was constructed or expressed to an audience. (e.g. "They drove happily. They had found their way and were preparing to celebrate.").

28.3.2   Present tense

The events of the plot are depicted as occurring now—at the current moment—in real time. (e.g. "They drive happily. They find their way and now prepare to celebrate.") In English, this tense, known as the "historical present", is more common in spontaneous conversational narratives than in written literature. A recent example of this is the *Hunger Games* trilogy by Suzanne Collins.

28.3.3   Future tense

Extremely rare in literature, this tense portrays the events of the plot as occurring some time in the future. Often, these upcoming events are described such that the narrator has foreknowledge (or supposed foreknowledge) of the future. Some future-tense stories have a prophetic tone. (e.g. "They will drive happily. They will find their way and will prepare to celebrate.")

28.4   Other narrative modes

28.4.1   Fiction-writing mode

Narration has more than one meaning. In its broadest sense, narration encompasses all forms of story-telling, fictional or not: personal anecdotes, "true crime", and historical narratives all fit here, along with many other non-fiction forms. More narrowly, however, term narration refers to all written fiction. In its most restricted sense, narration is the fiction-writing mode whereby the narrator communicates directly to the reader.

Along with exposition, argumentation, and description, narration (broadly defined) is one of four rhetorical modes of discourse. In the context of rhetorical modes, the purpose of narration is to tell a story or to narrate an event or series of events. Narrative may exist in a variety of forms: biographies, anecdotes, short stories, or novels. In this context, all written fiction may be viewed as narration.

Narrowly defined, narration is the fiction-writing mode whereby the narrator is communicating directly to the reader. But if the broad definition of narration includes all written fiction, and the narrow definition is limited merely to that which is directly communicated to the reader, then what comprises the rest of written fiction? The remainder of written fiction would be in the form of any of the other fiction-writing modes. Narration, as a fiction-writing mode, is a matter for discussion among fiction writers and writing coaches.

The ability to use the different points of view is one measure of a person's writing skill. The writing mark schemes used for National Curriculum assessments in England reflect this: they encourage the awarding of marks for the use of viewpoint as part of a wider judgment.

28.4.2 Other types and uses

In literature, *person* is used to describe the viewpoint from which the narrative is presented. Although second-person perspectives are occasionally used, the most commonly encountered are first and third person. *Third person omniscient* specifies a viewpoint in which readers are provided with information not available to characters within the story; without this qualifier, readers may or may not have such information.

In movies and video games first- and third-person describe camera viewpoints. The first-person is from a character's own perspective, and the third-person is the more familiar, "general" camera showing a scene. A so-called second-person may also be used to show a main character from a secondary character's perspective.

For example, in a horror film, the first-person perspective of an antagonist could become a second-person perspective on a potential victim's actions. A third-person shot of the two characters could be used to show the narrowing distance between them.

In video games, a first-person perspective is used most often in the first-person shooter genre, such as in *Doom*, or in simulations (racing games, flight simulation games, and such). Third-person perspectives on characters are typically used in all other games. Since the arrival of 3D computer graphics in games it is often possible for the player to switch between first- and third-person perspectives at will; this is usually done to improve spatial awareness, but can also improve the accuracy of weapons use in generally third-person games such as the *Metal Gear Solid* franchise.

Text-based interactive fiction conventionally has descriptions written in the second person (though exceptions exist), telling the character what they are seeing and doing, such as Zork. This practice is also encountered occasionally in text-based segments of graphical games, such as those from Spiderweb Software which make ample use of second person flavor text in pop up text boxes with character and location descriptions. Charles Stross's novel Halting State was written in second person as an allusion to this style.*[10]*[11]

28.5 See also

- Opening narration

- Narrative structure

28.6 References

Notes

[1] Hühn, Peter; Sommer, Roy (2012). "Narration in Poetry and Drama". *The Living Handbook of Narratology*. Interdisciplinary Center for Narratology, University of Hamburg.

[2] James McCracken, ed. (2011). *The Oxford English Dictionary* (Online ed.). Oxford University Press. Retrieved October 16, 2011.

[3] Jenna Blum, 2013, *The Modern Scholar* published by Recorded Books, *The Author at Work: The Art of Writing Fiction*, Disk 1, Tracks 14-15, ISBN 978-1-4703-8437-1, "...like a camera on the character's shoulder..."

[4] Ranjbar Vahid. *The Narrator*, Iran:Baqney. 2011

[5] Miller, Laura (April 18, 2004). "We the Characters". nytimes.com. Retrieved 2007-02-25.

[6] Paul Ricoeur (15 September 1990). *Time and Narrative*. University of Chicago Press. pp. 89–. ISBN 978-0-226-71334-2.

[7] Ranjbar Vahid. *The Narrator*, Iran:Baqney 2011

[8] Jill Walker Rettberg. "trusting kids with unreliable narrators".

[9] Herman, David; Jahn, Manfred; Ryan (2005), *Routledge Encyclopedia of Narrative Theory*, Taylor & Francis, p. 442, ISBN 978-0-415-28259-8

[10] "Halting State, Review". *Publishers Weekly*. 1 October 2007.

[11] Charles Stross. "And another thing".

Further reading

- Rasley, Alicia (2008). *The Power of Point of View: Make Your Story Come to Life* (1st ed.). Cincinnati, Ohio: Writer's Digest Books. ISBN 1599633558.

- Card, Orson Scott (1988). *Characters and Viewpoint* (1st ed.). Cincinnati, Ohio: Writer's Digest Books. ISBN 0898793076.

- Fludernik, Monika (1996). *Towards a "Natural" Narratology*. London: Routledge.

- Genette, Gérard. *Narrative Discourse. An Essay in Method*. Transl. by Jane Lewin. Oxford: Blackwell 1980 (Translation of *Discours du récit*).

- Mailman, Joshua B. (2009). "An Imagined Drama of Competitive Opposition in Carter's Scrivo in Vento (with Notes on Narrative, Symmetry, Quantitative Flux, and Heraclitus)". *Music Analysis, v.28, 2-3*. Wiley.

- Mailman, Joshua B. (2013) "Agency, Determinism, Focal Time Frames, and Processive Minimalist Music," in *Music and Narrative since 1900*. Edited by Michael L. Klein and Nicholas Reyland. Musical Meaning and Interpretation series. Bloomington: Indiana University Press.

- Stanzel, Franz Karl. *A theory of Narrative*. Transl. by Charlotte Goedsche. Cambridge: CUP 1984 (Transl. of *Theorie des Erzählens*).

- Ranjbar Vahid. (2011) *The Narrator*, Iran:Baqney

28.7   External links

- The Narration

Chapter 29

Stream of consciousness (narrative mode)

For other uses, see Stream of consciousness (disambiguation).
This article is about the literary device. For the prewriting technique, see Free writing.

In literary criticism, **stream of consciousness** is a narrative mode, or device, that seeks "to depict the multitudinous thoughts and feelings which pass through the mind. Another term for it is 'interior monologue'." *[1] The term was coined by William James in 1890 in his *The Principles of Psychology*, and in 1918 May Sinclair first applied the term stream of consciousness, in a literary context, when discussing Dorothy Richardson's novels.

29.1   Definition

Stream of consciousness is a narrative device that attempts to give the written equivalent of the character's thought processes, either in a loose interior monologue (see below), or in connection to his or her actions. Stream-of-consciousness writing is usually regarded as a special form of interior monologue and is characterized by associative leaps in thought and lack of some or all punctuation.*[2] Stream of consciousness and interior monologue are distinguished from dramatic monologue and soliloquy, where the speaker is addressing an audience or a third person, which are chiefly used in poetry or drama. In stream of consciousness the speaker's thought processes are more often depicted as overheard in the mind (or addressed to oneself); it is primarily a fictional device.

The term "Stream of Consciousness" was coined by philosopher and psychologist William James in *The Principles of Psychology* (1890):

> consciousness, then, does not appear to itself as chopped up in bits ... it is nothing joined; it flows. A 'river' or a 'stream' are the metaphors by which it is most naturally described. *In talking of it hereafter, let's call it the stream of thought, consciousness, or subjective life.* *[3]

In the following example of stream of consciousness from James Joyce's *Ulysses*, Molly seeks sleep:

> a quarter after what an unearthly hour I suppose theyre just getting up in China now combing out their pigtails for the day well soon have the nuns ringing the angelus theyve nobody coming in to spoil their sleep except an odd priest or two for his night office the alarmlock next door at cockshout clattering the brains out of itself let me see if I can doze off 1 2 3 4 5 what kind of flowers are those they invented like the stars the wallpaper in Lombard street was much nicer the apron he gave me was like that something only I only wore it twice better lower this lamp and try again so that I can get up early *[4]

Cover of James Joyce's Ulysses *(first edition, 1922), considered a prime example of stream of consciousness writing styles.*

29.2 Interior monologue

While many sources use the terms stream of consciousness and interior monologue as synonyms, the *Oxford Dictionary of Literary Terms* suggests, that "they can also be distinguished psychologically and literarily. In a psychological sense, stream of consciousness is the subject-matter, while interior monologue is the technique for presenting it" . And for literature, "while an interior monologue always presents a character's thoughts 'directly', without the apparent intervention of a summarizing and selecting narrator, it does not necessarily mingle them with impressions and perceptions, nor does it necessarily violate the norms of grammar, or logic- but the stream-of-consciousness technique also does one or both of these things." *[5] Similarly the *Encyclopædia Britannica Online*, while agreeing that these terms are "often used interchangeably," suggests, that "while an interior monologue may mirror all the half thoughts, impressions, and associations that impinge upon the character's consciousness, it may also be restricted to an organized presentation of that character's rational thoughts" .*[6]

29.3 Progress and use of the technique

29.3.1 The beginnings to 1922

While the use of the narrative technique of stream of consciousness is usually associated with modernist novelists in the first part of the twentieth-century, a number of precursors have been suggested, including Laurence Sterne's psychological novel *Tristram Shandy* (1757).*[7] In the nineteenth-century it has been suggested that Edgar Allan Poe's short story "The Tell-Tale Heart" (1843) foreshadows this literary technique.*[8] The short story "An Occurrence at Owl Creek Bridge" (1890) by another American author, Ambrose Bierce, also shows instances of abandoning strict linear time in favor of the internal consciousness of its protagonist.*[9] Because of his renunciation of chronology in favor of free association, Édouard Dujardin's *Les Lauriers sont coupés* (1887) is also an important precursor. Indeed, the possibility of a direct influence is evoqued by James Joyce and Virginia Woolf and having "picked up a copy of Dujardin's novel [...] in Paris in 1903" .*[10] There are also those who point to Anton Chekhov's short stories and plays (1881-1904)*[11] and Knut Hamsun's *Hunger* (1890), and *Mysteries* (1892) as offering glimpses of the use of stream of consciousness as a narrative technique at the end of the nineteenth-century.*[12] Henry James has also been suggested as a significant precursor, in a work as early as *Portrait of a Lady* (1881).*[13]

However, it has been suggested that Arthur Schnitzler (1862-1931), in his short story "'Leutnant Gustl" ("None but the Brave" , 1900), was in fact the first to make full use of the stream of consciousness technique.*[14]

But it is only in the twentieth-century that this technique is fully developed by modernists. Marcel Proust is often presented as an early example of a writer using the stream of consciousness technique in his novel sequence *À la recherche du temps perdu* (1913–1927) (*In Search of Lost Time*), but Robert Humphrey comments, that Proust "is concerned only with the reminiscent aspect of consciousness"and, that he "was deliberately recapturing the past for the purpose of communicating; hence he did not write a stream-of consciousness novel" .*[15] The term was first applied in a literary context in *The Egoist*, April 1918, by May Sinclair, in relation to the early volumes of Dorothy Richardson's novel sequence *Pilgrimage*.

Another early example is the use of interior monologue by T. S. Eliot in his poem "The Love Song of J. Alfred Prufrock" (1915), a work probably influenced by the narrative poetry of Robert Browning, including "Soliloquy of the Spanish Cloister" .*[16]

29.3.2 1922 to the 21st century

Possibly the most famous use of the technique came in 1922 with the publication of James Joyce's *Ulysses*. Prominent uses in the years that followed include Italo Svevo in *La coscienza di Zeno* (1923),*[17] Virginia Woolf in *Mrs Dalloway* (1925) and *To the Lighthouse* (1927) and William Faulkner in *The Sound and the Fury* (1929).*[18] Though Randell Stevenson suggests, that "interior monologue, rather than stream of consciousness, is the appropriate term for the style in which [subjective experience] is recorded, both in *The Waves* and in Woolf's writing generally.*[19]

Samuel Beckett, a friend of James Joyce, uses interior monologue in novels like *Molloy* (1951), *Malone meurt* (1951; *Malone Dies*) and *L'innommable* (1953: *The Unnamable*). and the short story From an Abandoned Work (1957).*[20]

The technique continued to be used into the 1970s in a novel such as Robert Anton Wilson/Robert Shea collaborative *Illuminatus!* (1975), with regard to which *The Fortean Times* warns readers, to "[b]e prepared for streams of consciousness in which not only identity but time and space no longer confine the narrative" .*[21]

With regard to Salman Rushdie one critic comments, that "[a]ll Rushdie's novels follow an Indian/Islamic storytelling style, a stream-of-consciousness narrative told by a loquacious young Indian man" .*[22]

Other writers who use this narrative device include Sylvia Plath in *The Bell Jar* (1963),*[23] Irvine Welsh in *Trainspotting* (1993),*[24] and Terry McMillan in her novel *How Stella Got Her Groove Back.*[25]

29.3.3   *Stream of consciousness* literature in the 21st century

Stream of consciousness continues to appear in contemporary literature. Dave Eggers, author of *A Heartbreaking Work of Staggering Genius* (2000), according to one reviewer, "talks much as he writes - a forceful stream of consciousness, thoughts sprouting in all directions" .*[26] Novelist John Banville describes Roberto Bolaño's novel *Amulet*, as written in "a fevered stream of consciousness" .*[27] The first decade brought further exploration, including Jonathan Safran Foer's *Everything is Illuminated* (2002) and many of the short stories of American author Brendan Connell.*[28]*[29]

29.4   See also

- Stream of consciousness (psychology)

- Free writing

- Free indirect speech

- Internal monologue

- Modernist literature

29.5   Notes

[1] J. A. Cuddon, *A Dictionary of Literary Terms*. (Harmondsworth, Penguin Books,1984), p.660-1).

[2] For example, both Beckett and Joyce omitted full stops and paragraph breaks, but while Joyce also omitted apostrophes, Beckett left them in.

[3] (I, pp.239-43) quoted in Randall Stevenson, *Modernist Fiction: An Introduction*. (Lexington, Kentucky: University of Kentucky, 1992), p.39.

[4] Joyce p. 642 (Bodley Head edition (1960), p. 930).

[5] ed. Chris Baldick, Oxford: Oxford U.P., 2009, p.212.

[6] "interior monologue." *Encyclopædia Britannica*. *Encyclopædia Britannica Online*. Encyclopædia Britannica Inc., 2012. Web. 24 Sep. 2012. <http://www.britannica.com/EBchecked/topic/290310/interior-monologue>.

[7] J. A. Cuddon, *A Dictionary of Literary Terms*. (Harmondsworth: Penguin, 1984), p. 661

[8] <http://www.britannica.com/EBchecked/topic/1785800/The-Tell-Tale-Heart>.

[9] Khanom, Afruza. "Silence as Literary Device in Ambrose Bierce's 'The Occurrence at Owl Creek Bridge.' *Teaching American Literature: A Journal of Theory and Practice*. Spring 6.1 (2013): 45-52. Print.

[10] Randell StevensonJ *Modernist Fiction*. Lexington: University of Kentucky, 1992, p.227 fn 14; J. A. Cuddon, *A Dictionary of Literary Terms*, p. 661.

[11] James Wood, "Ramblings" . *London Review of Books*. Vol.22, no. 11, 1 June 2000, pp. 36-7.

[12] James Wood. "Addicted to Unpredictability." November 26, 1998. *London Review of Books*. November 8, 2008 <http://www.lrb.co.uk/v20/n23/wood02_.html>

[13] M. H. Abrams, *A Glossary of Literary Terms*. New York: Harcourt Brace, 1999), p. 299.

[14] <http://www.britannica.com/EBchecked/topic/133295/stream-of-consciousness>

[15] *Stream of Consciousness in the Modern Novel* (Berkeley & Los Angeles: University of California, 1954), p. 4.

[16] William Harmon & C. Holman, *A Handbook to Literature* (7th edition). (Upper Saddle River: Prentice Hall, 1996), p.272.

[17] [untitled review], Beno Weiss, *Italica*,Vol. 67, No. 3 (Autumn, 1990), p. 395.

[18] *Oxford Dictionary of Literary Terms*, p.212.

[19] *Modernist Fiction*. Lexington: University of Kentucky, 1992, p.55; *Oxford Dictionary of Literary Terms*, p.212.

[20] Karine Germoni, "'From Joyce to Beckett: The Beckettian Dramatic Interior Monologue'". *Journal of Beckett Studies*,;Spring2004, Vol. 13 Issue 2.

[21] *The Fortean Times*, issue 17 (August 1976), pp.26–27.

[22] John C. Hawley, *Encyclopedia Of Postcolonial Studies* (Westport: Greenwood, 2001), p. 384.

[23] *American Literature*, Vol. 65, No. 2, Jun., 1993, p.381.

[24] Sarah Keating, "Tales from the Other Side of the Track" . *Irish Times* 3 May, 2012.

[25] Paulette Richards, *Terry McMillan: A Critical Companion*. Page 140.

[26] "The agony and the irony" , Stephanie Merritt. *The Observer*, Sunday 14 May 2000.

[27] "Amulet by Roberto Bolaño" , John Banville. *The Guardian*, Saturday 12 September 2009.

[28] "A nine-year-old and 9/11" , Tim Adams *The Observer*, Sunday 29 May 2005

[29] Brendan Connell, *The Life of Polycrates and Other Stories for Antiquated Children*. Chomu Press, 2010.

29.6 References

- Cohn, Dorrit. *Transparent Minds: Narrative Modes for Presenting Consciousness in Fiction*, 1978.

- Joyce, James. *Ulysses*, 1922; rpt. Harmondsworth: Penguin, 1986.

- Friedman, Melvin. *Stream of Consciousness: A Study in Literary Method*, 1955.

- Humphrey, Robert. *Stream of Consciousness in the Modern Novel*, 1954.

- Randell, Stevenson. *Modernist Fiction: An Introduction*. Lexington: University of Kentucky, 1992.

- Sachs, Oliver. "In the River of Consciousness." *New York Review of Books*, 15 January 2004.

- Shaffer, E.S. (1984). *Comparative Criticism, Volume 4*. Cambridge: Cambridge University Press. p. 119. Retrieved 12 Jan 2011.

- Tumanov, Vladimir. *Mind Reading: Unframed Direct Interior Monologue in European Fiction*. Amsterdam: Editions Rodopi, 1997. Googlebooks.

Chapter 30

Allegory

For allegories in category theory, see Allegory (category theory).
Not to be confused with Allegation.

As a literary device, an *allegory* in its most general sense is an extended metaphor. **Allegory** has been used widely throughout history in all forms of art, largely because it can readily illustrate complex ideas and concepts in ways that are comprehensible or striking to its viewers, readers, or listeners.

Writers or speakers typically use allegories as literary devices or as rhetorical devices that convey hidden meanings through symbolic figures, actions, imagery, and/or events, which together create the moral, spiritual, or political meaning the author wishes to convey.*[1]

One of the best-known examples of allegory, Plato's Allegory of the Cave, forms a part of his larger work *The Republic*. In this allegory, Plato describes a group of people who have lived chained in a cave all of their lives, facing a blank wall (514a-b). The people watch shadows projected on the wall by things passing in front of a fire behind them and begin to ascribe forms to these shadows, using language to identify their world (514c-515a). According to the allegory, the shadows are as close as the prisoners get to viewing reality, until one of them finds his way into the outside world where he sees the actual objects that produced the shadows. He tries to tell the people in the cave of his discovery, but they do not believe him and vehemently resist his efforts to free them so they can see for themselves (516e-518a). This allegory is, on a basic level, about a philosopher who upon finding greater knowledge outside the cave of human understanding, seeks to share it as is his duty, and the foolishness of those who would ignore him because they think themselves educated enough.*[2]

30.1 Etymology

First attested in English in 1382, the word *allegory* comes from Latin *allegoria*, the latinisation of the Greek ἀλληγορία (*allegoria*), "veiled language, figurative," *[3] which in turn comes from both ἄλλος (*allos*), "another, different" *[4] and ἀγορεύω (*agoreuo*), "to harangue, to speak in the assembly" *[5] which originate from ἀγορά (*agora*), "assembly" .*[6]

30.2 Types

Northrop Frye discussed what he termed a "continuum of allegory", a spectrum that ranges from what he termed the "naive allegory" of *The Faerie Queene*, to the more private allegories of modern paradox literature.*[7] In this perspective, the characters in a "naive" allegory are not fully three-dimensional, for each aspect of their individual personalities and the events that befall them embodies some moral quality or other abstraction; the allegory has been selected first, and the details merely flesh it out.

Many ancient religions are based on astrological allegories, that is, allegories of the movement of the sun and the moon

Allegory of Music *by Filippino Lippi (between 1475 and 1500): The "Allegory of Music" is a popular theme in painting. Lippi uses symbols popular during the High Renaissance, many of which refer to Greek mythology.*

as seen from the Earth. Examples include the cult of Horus/Isis.

30.3   Classical allegory

In classical literature two of the best-known allegories are the Cave in Plato's *Republic* (Book VII) and the story of the stomach and its members in the speech of Menenius Agrippa (Livy ii. 32). In Late Antiquity Martianus Capella organized all the information a fifth-century upper-class male needed to know into an allegory of the wedding of Mercury and *Philologia,* with the seven liberal arts the young man needed to know as guests.[8]

Other early allegories are found in the Hebrew Bible, such as the extended metaphor in Psalm 80 of the Vine and its impressive spread and growth, representing Israel's conquest and peopling of the Promised Land.[9] Also allegorical is Ezekiel 16 and 17, wherein the capture of that same vine by the mighty Eagle represents Israel's exile to Rome.[10]

30.4   Medieval allegory

Main article: Allegory in the Middle Ages

Allegory has an ability to freeze the temporality of a story, while infusing it with a spiritual context. Medieval thinking accepted allegory as having a *reality* underlying any rhetorical or fictional uses. The allegory was as true as the facts of surface appearances. Thus, the Papal Bull *Unam Sanctam* (1302) presents themes of the unity of Christendom with the pope as its head in which the allegorical details of the metaphors are adduced as facts on which is based a demonstration with the vocabulary of logic: "*Therefore* of this one and only Church there is one body and one head—not two heads as if it were a monster... If, then, the Greeks or others say that they were not committed to the care of Peter and his successors, they *necessarily* confess that they are not of the sheep of Christ." This text also demonstrates the frequent use of allegory in religious texts during the Medieval Period, following the tradition and example of the Bible.

In the late 15th century, the enigmatic *Hypnerotomachia*, with its elaborate woodcut illustrations, shows the influence of themed pageants and masques on contemporary allegorical representation, as humanist dialectic conveyed them.

The denial of medieval allegory as found in the 11th-century works of Hugh of St Victor and Edward Topsell's *Historie of Foure-footed Beastes* (London, 1607, 1653) and its replacement in the study of nature with methods of categorization and mathematics by such figures as naturalist John Ray and the astronomer Galileo is thought to mark the beginnings of early modern science.[12]

30.5   Modern allegory

Since meaningful stories are nearly always applicable to larger issues, allegories may be read into many stories which the author may not have recognized. This is allegoresis, or the act of reading a story as an allegory. For instance, many people have suggested that *The Lord of the Rings* is an allegory for the World Wars, although Tolkien has dismissed this. Other examples of allegory in popular culture that may or may not have been intended include the works of Bertolt Brecht, and even some works of science fiction and fantasy, such as *The Chronicles of Narnia* by C.S. Lewis and *A Kingdom Far and Clear: The Complete Swan Lake Trilogy* by Mark Helprin.

30.6   Poetry and fiction

It is important to note that while allegoresis may make discovery of allegory in any work, not every resonant work of modern fiction is allegorical, and some are clearly not intended to be viewed this way. According to Henry Littlefield's 1964 article, L. Frank Baum's *The Wonderful Wizard of Oz*, may be readily understood as a plot-driven fantasy narrative in an extended fable with talking animals and broadly sketched characters, intended to discuss the politics of the time.[13] Yet, George MacDonald emphasized in 1893 that, "A fairy tale is not an allegory," in direct reference to *The Wonderful Wizard of Oz*.[14] J.R.R. Tolkien's The Lord of the Rings is another example of a well-known work sometimes perceived as allegorical, yet as the author himself once stated, "...I cordially dislike allegory in all of its manifestations and I have always done so since I grew old and wary enough to detect its presence." [15] While this does not mean his works may not be treated as having allegorical themes, especially when reinterpreted through postmodern sensibilities, it at least suggests that none were conscious in his writings. This further reinforces the idea of forced allegoresis, as allegory is often a matter of interpretation and only sometimes of original artistic intention.

Like allegorical stories, allegorical poetry has two meanings – a literal meaning and a symbolic meaning. Some unique specimens of allegory in poetry can be found in the following works:

- Edmund Spenser – *The Faerie Queene*: The several knights in the poem actually stand for several virtues.

- John Bunyan – *The Pilgrim's Progress*: The journey of the protagonists Christian and Evangelist symbolises the ascension of the soul from earth to Heaven.

- Nathaniel Hawthorne – *Young Goodman Brown*: The Devil's Staff symbolises defiance of God. The characters' names, such as *Goodman* and *Faith*, ironically serve as paradox in the conclusion of the story.

- George Orwell – *Animal Farm*: The pigs stand for political figures of the Russian Revolution.

- László Krasznahorkai - *The Melancholy of Resistance* and the film *Werckmeister Harmonies*: It uses a circus to describe an occupying dysfunctional government.

- Edgar Allan Poe – *The Masque of the Red Death*: The story can be read as an allegory how no one can evade death.*[16]

30.6.1   Art

Some elaborate and successful specimens of allegory are to be found in the following works, arranged in approximate chronological order:

- Ambrogio Lorenzetti – *Allegoria del Buono e Cattivo Governo e loro Effetti in Città e Campagna* (c. 1338–1339)

- Sandro Botticelli – *Primavera* (c. 1482)

- Albrecht Dürer – *Melencolia I* (1514)

- Bronzino – *Venus, Cupid, Folly and Time* (c. 1545)

- The English School's – *"Allegory of Queen Elizabeth"* (c. 1610)

- Artemisia Gentileschi – *Allegory of Inclination* (c. 1620), *An Allegory of Peace and the Arts under the English Crown* (1638); *Self-Portrait as the Allegory of Painting* (c. 1638–39)

- The *Feast of Herod with the Beheading of St John the Baptist* by Bartholomeus Strobel is also an allegory of Europe in the time of the Thirty Years War, with portraits of many leading political and military figures.

- Jan Vermeer – *Allegory of Painting* (c. 1666)

- Marcel Duchamp – *The Bride Stripped Bare by Her Bachelors, Even* (1912-1923)

- Graydon Parrish – *The Cycle of Terror and Tragedy* (2006)

- Many statues of Lady Justice: "Such visual representations have raised the question why so many allegories in the history of art, pertaining occupations once reserved for men only, are of female sex." *[17]

- Damien Hirst – *Verity (sculpture)* (2012)

- Albrecht Dürer, *Melencolia I* (1514): Unused tools, an hourglass, an empty scale surround a melancholic woman, other esoteric and exoteric symbols point to her alleged mental state.

- Bronzino, *Venus, Cupid, Folly and Time* (c. 1545): The deities of love are surrounded by allegories of Time (a bald, man with angry eyes), Folly (the young woman-demon on the right, possibly also so old woman on the left).

- Titian, *Allegory of Prudence* (c. 1565–1570): The three human heads symbolise past, present and future, the characterisation of which is furthered by the triple-headed beast (wolf, lion, dog), girded by the body of a big snake.

- The English School's *Allegory of Queen Elizabeth* (c. 1610), with Father Time at her right and Death looking over her left shoulder. Two cherubs are removing the weighty crown from her tired head.

- Artemisia Gentileschi, *Self-Portrait as the Allegory of Painting* (c. 1638–39)

- Jan Vermeer, *The Art of Painting* (c. 1666): Painting is shown as related to history and politics, the young woman being Clio, the muse of history, and other symbols for the political and religious division of the Netherlands appearing.

- Jan van Kessel, *Allegory of Hearing* (17th century): Diverse sources of sound, especially instruments serve as allegorical symbols.

30.6.2   Video games

See also: Video games as an art form

As video games have become more widely accepted as a medium for artistic expression, allegorical representations have grown more commonplace.

- In Rockstar games third-person crime shooter, *L.A Noire* (2011), the fictional protagonist is required to solve the Quarter-Moon Murders by means of Percy B. Shelley allegories left by the murderer who committed the infamous Black Dahlia Murder.

- The 2012 game *Journey* invokes multiple allegories, such as the our personal life journey, and the Hero's Journey.

30.7   See also

- Allegorical interpretation of the Bible

- Allegory in the Middle Ages

- Allegory in Renaissance literature

- Allegorical sculpture

- Cultural depictions of Philip II of Spain

- Diwan (poetry)

- Parable

- Semiotics

- Theagenes of Rhegium

30.8   References

[1]

[2] [Elliott, R. K. (1967). "Socrates and Plato's Cave" . Kant-Studien 58 (2): 138.]

[3] ἀλληγορία, Henry George Liddell, Robert Scott, *A Greek-English Lexicon*, on Perseus Digital Library

[4] ἄλλος, Henry George Liddell, Robert Scott, *A Greek-English Lexicon*, on Perseus Digital Library

[5] ἀγορεύω, Henry George Liddell, Robert Scott, *A Greek-English Lexicon*, on Perseus Digital Library

[6] ἀγορά, Henry George Liddell, Robert Scott, *A Greek-English Lexicon*, on Perseus Digital Library

[7] [Frye, Northrop. Anatomy of Criticism. Princeton, NJ: Princeton UP, 1957. Print.]

[8] [Capella, Martianus, William Harris. Stahl, Richard Johnson, and E. L. Burge. The Marriage of Philology and Mercury. New York: Columbia UP, 1977. Print.]

[9] Kennedy, George A. (1999). *Classical Rhetoric and Its Christian and Secular Tradition from Ancient to Modern Times* (Second ed.). UNC Press. p. 142. ISBN 0-8078-4769-0. Retrieved 2009-08-07.

[10] Jones, Alexander, ed. (1968). *The Jerusalem Bible* (Reader's ed.). Doubleday & Company. pp. 1186, 1189. ISBN 0-385-01156-3.

[11] "portrait-of-a-lady-called-elizabeth-lady-tanfield". www.artfund.org. Retrieved 2015.

[12] Peter Harrison, *The Bible, Protestantism, and the rise of natural science*, Cambridge University Press, ISBN 0-521-59196-1, pages 1 to 10 ("Introduction")

[13] [Littlefield, Henry (1964). "The Wizard of Oz: Parable on Populism". American Quarterly 16 (1): 47–58. doi:10.2307/2710826.]

[14] Lyman Frank Baum (2000). *The Annotated Wizard of Oz: The Wonderful Wizard of Oz*. Norton. p. 101. ISBN 978-0-393-04992-3.

[15] Janice M. Bogstad; Philip E. Kaveny (9 August 2011). *Picturing Tolkien: Essays on Peter Jackson's The Lord of the Rings Film Trilogy*. McFarland. p. 189. ISBN 978-0-7864-8473-7.

[16] [Roppolo, Joseph Patrick. "Meaning and 'The Masque of the Red Death'", collected in Poe: A Collection of Critical Essays, edited by Robert Regan. Englewood Cliffs, NJ: Prentice-Hall, Inc., 1967. p. 137]

[17] Cäcilia Rentmeister: The Muses, Banned From Their Occupations: Why Are There So Many Allegories Female? English summary from Kvinnovetenskaplig Tidskrift, Nr.4. 1981, Lund, Sweden as PDF. Retrieved 10.July 2011 Original Version in German: *Berufsverbot für die Musen. Warum sind so viele Allegorien weiblich?* In: Ästhetik und Kommunikation, Nr. 25/1976, S. 92–112. Langfassung in: Frauen und Wissenschaft. Beiträge zur Berliner Sommeruniversität für Frauen, Juli 1976, Berlin 1977, S.258–297. With illustrations. Full Texts Online: Cäcilia (Cillie) Rentmeister: publications

30.8.1 Further reading

- Frye, Northrop (1957) *Anatomy of Criticism.*

- Foucault, Michel (1966) *The Order of Things.*

30.9 External links

- *Dictionary of the History of Ideas*: Allegory in Literary history

- *Electronic Antiquity*, Richard Levis, "Allegory and the *Eclogues*" Roman definitions of *allegoria* and interpreting Vergil's *Eclogues*.

Salvator Rosa: Allegory of Fortune, *representing Fortuna, the Goddess of luck, with the horn of plenty*

Allegory of Arithmetic, *by Laurent de La Hyre, c. 1650*

Chapter 31

Alliteration

Alliteration is a stylistic literary device identified by the repeated sound of the first consonant in a series of multiple words, or the repetition of the same sounds or of the same kinds of sounds at the beginning of words or in stressed syllables of a phrase.[1] "Alliteration" comes from the Latin word "litera", meaning "letters of the alphabet", and the first known use of the word to refer to a literary device occurred around 1624.[2] Alliteration narrowly refers to the repetition of a consonant in any syllables that, according to the poem's meter, are stressed,[3][4][5] as in James Thomson's verse "Come···dragging the **l**azy **l**anguid **L**ine along". Another example is, "Peter Piper Picked a Peck of Pickled Peppers".[6]

Consonance (ex: As the wi**nd** will be**nd**) is another 'phonetic agreement' akin to alliteration. It refers to the repetition of consonant sounds. Alliteration is a special case of consonance where the repeated consonant sound is at the stressed syllable.[7] Alliteration may also include the use of different consonants with similar properties[8] such as alliterating *z* with *s*, as does the author of Sir Gawain and the Green Knight, or as Anglo-Saxon (Old English) poets would alliterate hard/fricative *g* with soft *g* (the latter exemplified in some courses as the letter yogh - ȝ - pronounced like the *y* in yarrow or the *j* in Jotunheim); this is known as *license*.

There is one specialised form of alliteration called *Symmetrical Alliteration*. That is, alliteration containing parallelism.[9] In this case, the phrase must have a pair of outside end words both starting with the same sound, and pairs of outside words also starting with matching sounds as one moves progressively closer to the centre. For example, "rust brown blazers rule", "purely and fundamentally for analytical purposes" or "fluoro colour co-ordination forever". Symmetrical alliteration is similar to palindromes in its use of symmetry.

31.1 Literature

- The Raven by Edgar Allan Poe has many examples of alliteration including the following line: "And the silken sad uncertain rustling of each purple curtain".

- Samuel Taylor Coleridge's Rime of the Ancient Mariner has the following lines of alliteration: "For the sky and the sea, and the sea and the sky." and "the furrow followed free..."

- Robert Frost's poem *Acquainted with the Night* has the following line of alliteration: "I have stood still and stopped the sound of feet".

- In Walter Abish's novel *Alphabetical Africa* (1974) the first chapter consists solely of words beginning with "A". Chapter two also permits words beginning with "B" and so on, until at chapter 26, Abish allows himself to use words beginning with any letter at all. For the next 25 chapters, he reverses the process.

31.1.1 Rhyme

- In "Thank-You for the Thistle" by Dorie Thurston, poetically written with alliteration in a story form: "Great Aunt Nellie and Brent Bernard who watch with wild wonder at the wide window as the beautiful birds begin to bite into the bountiful birdseed".

- In the nursery rhyme *Three Grey Geese* by Mother Goose, use of alliteration can be found in the following lines : "*Three grey geese in a green field grazing. Grey were the geese and green was the grazing.*"

- The tongue-twister rhyme *Betty Botter* by Carolyn Wells is an example of alliterative composition : "Betty Botter bought some butter, but she said, this butter's bitter; if I put it in my batter, it will make my batter bitter, but a bit of better butter will make my bitter batter better..."

- Another commonly recited tongue-twister rhyme illustrating alliteration is "Peter Piper". - "Peter Piper picked a peck of pickled peppers. If Peter Piper picked a peck of pickled peppers, where's the peck of pickled peppers Peter Piper picked?".

31.1.2 Historical use

Alliteration is used in the alliterative verse of Old English, Old Norse, Old High German, Old Saxon, and Old Irish. It was an important ingredient of the Sanskrit shlokas.[12][13] Alliteration was used in Old English given names.[14] This is evidenced by the unbroken series of 9th century kings of Wessex named Æthelwulf, Æthelbald, Æthelberht, and Æthelred. These were followed in the 10th century by their direct descendants Æthelstan and Æthelred II, who ruled as kings of England.[15] The Anglo-Saxon saints Tancred, Torhtred and Tova provide a similar example, among siblings.[16]

31.1.3 Poetry

In relation to English poetry, poets can call attention to certain words in a line of poetry by using alliteration. They can also use alliteration to create a pleasant, rhythmic effect. In the following poetic lines, notice how alliteration is used to emphasize words and to create rhythm:

"Give me the splendid silent sun with all his beams full-dazzling!' Walt Whitman, "Give Me the Splendid Silent Sun"

"They all gazed and gazed upon this green stranger,/because everyone wondered what it could mean/ that a rider and his horse could be such a color-/ green as grass, and greener it seemed/ than green enamel glowing bright against gold". (232-236) *Sir Gawain and the Green Knight*, translated by Bernard O'Donoghue

"Some papers like writers, some like wrappers. Are you a writer or a wrapper?" Carl Sandburg, "Paper I"

Alliteration can also add to the mood of a poem. If a poet repeat soft, melodious sounds, a calm or dignified mood can result. If harsh, hard sound are repeated, on the other hand, the mood can become tense or excited. In this poem, alliteration of the s, l, and f sound adds to a hushed, peaceful mood:

"Softer be they than slippered sleep the lean lithe deer the fleet flown deer." E. E. Cummings "All in green went my love riding" [17]

31.2 Rhetoric

The term "alliteration" has many potential uses in the various spheres of public speaking and rhetoric as far as persuasion is concerned. Additionally the use of alliteration can be considered an artistic constraint that is used by the Rhetor in a rhetorical situation. An artistic constraint is one that the Rhetor creates out of his or her own need to sway the audience to feel some type of urgency, or perhaps even lack of urgency, in regards to a rhetorical situation being presented.[18] Such examples of Alliteration as an artistic constraint can be seen when it is used to create an emotional effect on the audience. For example: H or E sounds can sooth where as a P or a B sound can be percussive and attention grabbing. S sounds can imply danger or make the audience feel as if they are being deceived[19] Alliteration also serves as a linguistic rhetorical device more commonly used in persuasive public speaking. Rhetoric is broadly defined as the "Art of Persuasion", which has from earliest times been concerned with specific techniques for effective communication.[20] Alliteration serves to "intensify any attitude being signified" .[20] Its significance as a rhetorical device is that it adds a textural complexity to a speech, making it more engaging, moving, and memorable. The use of alliteration[21] in a speech captivates a person's auditory senses that assists in creating a mood for the speaker. The use of a repeating sound or letter forces an audience's attention because of their distinct and noticeable nature. The auditory senses, hearing and listening, seem to perk up and pay attention with the constant sounds of alliteration. It also evokes emotion which is key in persuading an audience. The idea of pathos solidifies that playing to a person's emotions is key in persuading them and connecting them to the argument that is being made. For example, the use of a "H" sound can produce a feeling of calmness.[22] Other sounds can create feelings of happiness, discord, or anger, depending on the context of the alliteration. These feelings become memorable to a listener, which have been created by alliteration.

The most common example of this is in John F. Kennedy's Inaugural Address, where he uses alliteration twenty-one times throughout his speech. The last paragraph of his speech is given as an example here.

"Finally, whether you are citizens of America or citizens of the world, ask of us here the same high standards of strength and sacrifice (ALLITERATION) which we ask of you. With a good conscience our only sure reward, with history the final judge of our deeds, let us go forth to lead the land we love (ALLITERATION), asking His blessing and His help, but knowing that here on earth God's work must truly be our own." –JFK[23]

Other examples of alliteration in some famous speeches:

- "I have a dream that my four little children will one day live in a nation where they will not be judged by the color of their skin but by the content of their character." —Martin Luther King, Jr.[24]

- "We, the people, declare today that the most evident of truths —that all of us are created equal —is the star that guides us still; just as it guided our forebears through Seneca Falls, and Selma, and Stonewall; just as it guided all those men and women, sung and unsung, who left footprints along this great Mall, to hear a preacher say that we cannot walk alone; to hear a King proclaim that our individual freedom is inextricably bound to the freedom of every soul on Earth" . —Barack Obama.[25]

- "And our nation itself is testimony to the love our veterans have had for it and for us. All for which America stands is safe today because brave men and women have been ready to face the fire at freedom's front." —Ronald Reagan, Vietnam Veterans Memorial Address.[26]

- "Four score and seven years ago our fathers brought forth on this continent a new nation, conceived in liberty, and dedicated to the proposition that all men are created equal" . —Abraham Lincoln, Gettysburg Address.

31.3 Pop culture

Alliteration is most commonly used in modern music but is also seen in magazine article titles, advertisements, business names, comic strips, television shows, video games and in the dialogue and naming of cartoon characters.[27]

An example would be Tupac Shakur's "If I Die 2Nite" off his *Me Against The World* release.

31.4 See also

- Anadiplosis

- Assonance

- Consonance

- Onomatopoeia

- Parachesis

- Tautogram

- Tongue twister

31.5   References

[1]   "Definition of Alliteration, Literary Devices". Retrieved 2013-09-27.

[2]   "Alliteration, Merriam-Webster". Retrieved 2014-09-26.

[3]   "Alliteration, University of Tennessee Knoxville". Retrieved 2013-09-10.

[4]   "Definition of Alliteration, Literary Devices". Retrieved 2013-09-10.

[5]   "Definition of Alliteration, Bcs.bedfordstmartins.com". Retrieved 2013-09-10.

[6]   James Thomson. *The Castle of Indolence*. ISBN 0-19-812759-6.

[7]   "alliteration". *TheFreeDictionary.com*.

[8]   Stoll, E. E. (May 1940). "Poetic Alliteration". *Modern Language Notes* **55** (5): 388.

[9]   Paul Fussell (15 May 2013). *The Great War and Modern Memory*. Oxford University Press. p. 98. ISBN 978-0-19-997197-8. Retrieved 24 September 2013.

[10]   Wren, Gayden (2006). *A Most Ingenious Paradox: The Art of Gilbert and Sullivan*. Oxford University Press. p. 168. ISBN 9780195301724. Retrieved 26 October 2014.

[11]   *The Mikado* libretto, p. 16, Oliver Ditson Company

[12]   Langer, Kenneth, "Some Suggestive Uses of Alliteration in Sanskrit Court Poetry", *Journal of the American Oriental Society* Vol. 98, No. 4 (Oct. - Dec., 1978), pp. 438–45.

[13]   K.N. Jha, Figurative Poetry In Sanskrit Literature, 1975, ISBN 978-8120826694

[14]   Gelling, M., *Signposts to the Past* (2nd edition), Phillimore, 1988, pp. 163–4.

[15]   Old English "Æthel" translates to modern English "noble". For further examples of alliterative Anglo-Saxon royal names, including the use of only alliterative first letters, see e.g. Yorke, B., *Kings and Kingdoms of Early Anglo-Saxon England*, Seaby, 1990, Table 13 (p. 104; Mercia, names beginning with "C", "M", and "P"), and pp. 142–3 (Wessex, names beginning with "C"). For discussion of the origins and purposes of Anglo-Saxon "king lists" (or "regnal lists"), see e.g. Dumville, D.N., 'Kingship, Genealogies and Regnal Lists', in Sawyer, P.H. & Wood, I.N. (eds.), *Early Medieval Kingship*, University of Leeds, 1977.

[16]   Rollason, D.W., "Lists of Saints' resting-places in Anglo-Saxon England", in *Anglo-Saxon England 7*, 1978, p. 91.

[17]   Techniques Writers Use

[18]   Bitzer, Lloyd (1968). "The Rhetorical Situation". Philosophy and Rhetoric.

[19]   "Literary Devices, Author's Craft". Retrieved 2014-09-26.

[20]   Lanham, Richard (1991). *A Handlist of Rhetorical Terms*. Los Angeles: University of California Press. p. 131. ISBN 978-0-520-27368-9.

[21]   "Alliteration". Alliteration. N.p., n.d. Web. 22 Oct. 2013.

[22]   "Pathos." Pathos. N.p., n.d. Web. 22 Oct. 2013.

[23]   "What made JFK's Inaugural Address so effective?".

[24]   "I Have A Dream Speech Analysis Lesson Plan".

[25]   "Obama's Alliteration".

[26]   "Rhetorical Figures in Sound: Alliteration". *americanrhetoric.com*.

[27]   Coard, Robert L. "Wide-Ranging Alliteration." *Peabody Journal of Education*, Vol. 37, No. 1. (July 1959) pp. 30–32.

31.6 External links

- A collection of Dutch alliterations and related material (with sound files)

- Examples of alliteration in poetry

Gilbert and Sullivan's comic opera The Mikado *is the source of a well known example of alliterative lyrics:*[10]
"To sit in solemn silence in a dull, dark dock,
In a pestilential prison, with a lifelong lock,
Awaiting the sensation of a short, sharp shock,
From a cheap and chippy chopper on a big black block!"[11]

Chapter 32

Amplification (rhetoric)

Amplification comes from the Greek word auxesis.[*][1]*Merriam-Webster* defines amplification as follows: "the particulars by which a statement is expanded." [*][2] Specifically when a sentence is too abrupt, amplification is then used as a way to expand upon any details.[*][3] It can also be used to enhance the reader's attention on stuff that could be missed.[*][4] Furthermore, amplification refers to a rhetorical device used to add features to a statement.

In rhetoric, **amplification** refers to the act and means of extending thoughts or statements:

- to increase rhetorical effect,

- to add importance,

- to make the most of a thought or circumstance,

- to add an exaggeration,

- or to change the arrangement of words or clauses in a sequence to increase force.

Amplification may refer to exaggeration or to stylistic vices such as figures of excess or superfluity (e.g., hyperbole).

Amplification involves identifying parts of a text by means of a process of division; each part of the text may be subjected to amplification. Amplification is thus a set of strategies which, taken together, constitute Inventio, one of the five classical canons of rhetoric.

As a means of developing multiple forms of expression for a thought, amplification "names an important point of intersection where figures of speech and figures of thought coalesce." [*][5]

In his book, *A Handbook of Rhetorical Devices*, author Robert Harris explains in depth, "Amplification involves repeating a word or expression while adding more detail to it, in order to emphasize what might otherwise be passed over. In other words, amplification allows you to call attention to, emphasize, and expand a word or idea to make sure the reader realizes its important or centrality in the discussion." Harris provides examples of amplification: "In my hunger after ten days of rigorous dieting I saw visions of ice cream--mountains of creamy, luscious ice cream, dripping with gooey syrup and calories." [*][6] This example illustrates the rhetorical use of amplification to motivate readers to recognize the significance of this sentence, not just ignore it.

According to the Princeton Encyclopedia of Poetry and Poetics, the word amplification is one of the "special" topics used in epideictic poetry or ceremonial discourse, usually for praise, but it has been used to refer to both the expansion and the diminution of an idea or an argument.[*][7] The use of the word needs to be defined precisely and used with care.[*][7] The Princeton Encyclopedia also states that, "limits become clear only when a text signals by some other means (semantic: change of subject; syntactic: end of stanza/poem; pragmatic; change of voice, person, or form of address) a change of direction.[*][7]" Amplification was considered at different times in history "a subset of both inventio and dispositio.[*][7] " Aristotle mentions in The Poetics "maximizing and minimizing" as important elements in relation to amplification.[*][7] This is similar to the way we commonly think of amplification; that is going from something smaller

165

and being enlarged. In *The Rhetoric*, Aristotle contrasts amplification with depreciation and admits "they both derive from an enthymeme which serves to show how a thing is great or small.*[7]" The Princeton Encyclopedia of Poetry and Poetics also tells us that Cicero in *De Oratore* "introduced the confusion between amplification and attenuation by saying that the highest distinction of eloquence consists in amplification by means of ornament, which can be used to make one's speech not only increase the importance of a subject and raise it to a higher level, but also to diminish and disparage it *[7] ". The relationship between the words 'conciseness' and 'amplification' is heavy. Nevin Laib, author of Conciseness and Amplification explains that, "We need to encourage profuseness as well as concision, to teach not just brevity but also loquacity, the ability to extend, vary, and expatiate upon one's subject at length to shape, build, augment, or alter the force and effect of communication, and to repeat oneself inventively.*[8] In classical rhetoric, this was the art of amplification.*[8] It included elaboration, emphasis, and copiousness of style.*[8]" The message and understanding of amplification seems blurry to many students.*[8] Laib says, "The stylistic values implicit in our theories, pedagogy, and culture, so overwhelmingly favor consciousness, that elaboration gets lost in the learning process" .*[8] Silva Rhetoricae provided by Dr. Gideon Burton of Brigham Young University understands amplification as something that can be used as a basic notion of imitation: to change the content of a model while retaining its form, or to change its form while retaining the content. Varying a sentence. Double Translation. Metaphrasis. Paraphrasis. Epitome.*[9]

32.1 See also

- Auxesis

- Rhetorical reason

32.2 References

[1] Burton, Gideon O. "Figures of Amplification (Auxesis)." *Silva Rhetoricae*. Brigham Young University, 2007. Web. 28 Sept. 2014.

[2] "Amplification." Merriam-Webster. Merriam-Webster: An Encyclopædia Britannica Company, 2013. Web. 21 Oct. 2013. <http://www.merriam-webster.com/dictionary/amplification>.

[3] "Amplification." *Literary Devices*. N.p., 2010. Web. 25 Sept. 2014.

[4] Nordquist, Richard. "What is the Rhetorical Strategy of Amplification?" *About*. Np., N.d. Web. 25 Sept. 2014.

[5] Silva Rhetoricae

[6] Harris, Robert A. A Handbook of Rhetorical Devices. Virtual Salt, 1997, 2002, 2008. Web. 21 Oct. 2013. <http://www.virtualsalt.com/rhetoric3.htm#Amplification>.

[7] Brogan, T.V.F; Halsall (2012). "Amplification" . *The Princeton Encyclopedia of Poetry and Poetics*. Retrieved 5 March 2014.

[8] Laib, Nevin (December 1990). "Conciseness and Amplification" . *College Composition and Communication* **41** (4): 443–459. doi:10.2307/357934. Retrieved 5 March 2014.

[9] Burton, Gideon. "The Forest of Rhetoric" . Creative Commons Attribution 3.0 License. Retrieved 5 March 2014.

Chapter 33

Anagram

This article is about words that are remade by rearranging their letters. For the game, see Anagrams. For the band, see Anagram (band).

An **anagram** is a type of word play, the result of rearranging the letters of a word or phrase to produce a new word or phrase, using all the original letters exactly once; for example, the word anagram can be rearranged into nag-a-ram. Someone who creates anagrams may be called an "anagrammatist".[1] The original word or phrase is known as the *subject* of the anagram. Anagrams are often used as a form of mnemonic device as well.

Any word or phrase that exactly reproduces the letters in another order is an anagram. However, the goal of serious or skilled anagrammatists is to produce anagrams that in some way reflect or comment on the subject. Such an anagram may be a synonym or antonym of its subject, a parody, a criticism, or praise; e.g. *William Shakespeare = I am a weakish speller*

Another example is "silent" which can be rearranged to "listen".

33.1 Assumptions

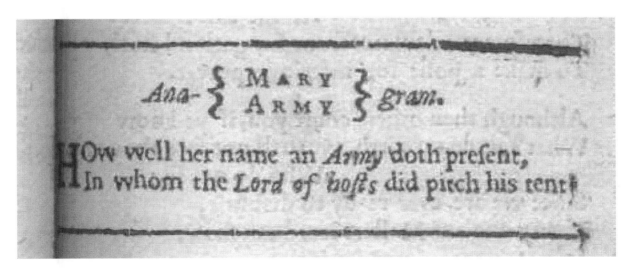

Illustration of an anagram by George Herbert

The creation of anagrams assumes an alphabet, the symbols which are to be permuted. In a perfect anagram, every letter must be used, with exactly the same number of occurrences as in the anagrammed word or phrase. Diacritics are usually disregarded (this is usually not relevant for English anagrams), and standard orthography is to be used.

33.2   History

Anagrams can be traced back to the time of Moses, as "Themuru" or changing, which was to find the hidden and mystical meaning in names.*[2] They were popular throughout Europe during the Middle Ages, for example with the poet and composer Guillaume de Machaut.*[3] They are said to go back at least to the Greek poet Lycophron, in the third century BCE; but this relies on an account of Lycophron given by John Tzetzes in the 12th century.*[4]

Anagrams in Latin were considered witty over many centuries. "Est vir qui adest" , explained below, was cited as the example in Samuel Johnson's *A Dictionary of the English Language*.

Any historical material on anagrams must always be interpreted in terms of the assumptions and spellings that were current for the language in question. In particular spelling in English only slowly became fixed. There were attempts to regulate anagram formation, an important one in English being that of George Puttenham's *Of the Anagram or Posy Transposed* in *The Art of English Poesie* (1589).

33.2.1   Influence of Latin

As a literary game when Latin was the common property of the literate, Latin anagrams were prominent: two examples are the change of "Ave Maria, gratia plena, Dominus tecum" (*Hail Mary, full of grace, the Lord [is] with you*) into "Virgo serena, pia, munda et immaculata" (*Serene virgin, pious, clean and spotless*), and the anagrammatic answer to Pilate's question, "Quid est veritas?" (*What is truth?*), namely, "Est vir qui adest" (*It is the man who is here*). The origins of these are not documented.

Latin continued to influence letter values (such as I = J, U = V and W = VV). There was an ongoing tradition of allowing anagrams to be "perfect" if the letters were all used once, but allowing for these interchanges. This can be seen in a popular Latin anagram against the Jesuits: "Societas Jesu" turned into "Vitiosa seces" , or "cut off the wicked things" . Puttenham, in the time of Elizabeth I of England, wished to start from *Elissabet Anglorum Regina* (Elizabeth Queen of the English), to obtain *Multa regnabis ense gloria* (By thy sword shalt thou reign in great renown); he explains carefully that H is "a note of aspiration only and no letter" , and that Z in Greek or Hebrew is a mere SS. The rules were not completely fixed in the 17th century. William Camden in his *Remains* commented, singling out some letters—Æ, K, W, Z—not found in the classical Roman alphabet:*[5]

> The precise in this practice strictly observing all the parts of the definition, are only bold with H either in omitting or retaining it, for that it cannot challenge the right of a letter. But the Licentiats somewhat licentiously, lest they should prejudice poetical liberty, will pardon themselves for doubling or rejecting a letter, if the sence fall aptly, and think it no injury to use E for Æ; V for W; S for Z, and C for K, and contrariwise.
> —William Camden, *Remains*

33.2.2   Early modern period

When it comes to the 17th century and anagrams in English or other languages, there is a great deal of documented evidence of learned interest. The lawyer Thomas Egerton was praised through the anagram *gestat honorem*; the physician George Ent took the anagrammatic motto *genio surget*, which requires his first name as "Georgius".*[6] James I's courtiers discovered in "James Stuart" "a just master" , and converted "Charles James Stuart" into "Claims Arthur's seat" (even at that point in time, the letters I and J were more-or-less interchangeable). Walter Quin, tutor to the future Charles I, worked hard on multilingual anagrams on the name of father James.*[7] A notorious murder scandal, the Overbury case, threw up two imperfect anagrams that were aided by typically loose spelling and were recorded by Simonds D'Ewes: 'Francis Howard' (for Frances Carr, Countess of Somerset, her maiden name spelled in a variant) became *Car findes a whore*, with the letters E hardly counted, and the victim Thomas Overbury, as 'Thomas Overburie', was written as *O! O! a busie murther*, with a V counted as U.*[8]*[9]

William Drummond of Hawthornden, in an essay *On the Character of a Perfect Anagram,* tried to lay down permissible rules (such as S standing for Z), and possible letter omissions.[10] William Camden[11] provided a definition of "Anagrammatisme" as "a dissolution of a name truly written into his letters, as his elements, and a new connection of it by artificial transposition, without addition, subtraction or change of any letter, into different words, making some perfect sense applyable (i.e., *applicable*) to the person named." Dryden in *MacFlecknoe* disdainfully called the pastime the "torturing of one poor word ten thousand ways" .[12]

"Eleanor Audeley" , wife of Sir John Davies, is said to have been brought before the High Commission in 1634 for extravagances, stimulated by the discovery that her name could be transposed to "Reveale, O Daniel" , and to have been laughed out of court by another anagram submitted by Sir John Lambe, the dean of the Arches, "Dame Eleanor Davies" , "Never soe mad a ladie" .[13][14]

An example from France was a flattering anagram for Cardinal Richelieu, comparing him to Hercules or at least one of his hands (Hercules being a kingly symbol), where "Armand de Richelieu" became "Ardue main d'Hercule" .[15]

33.2.3 Modern period

Examples from the nineteenth century are the transposition of "Horatio Nelson" into "Honor est a Nilo" (Latin = *Honor is from the Nile*); and of "Florence Nightingale" into "Flit on, cheering angel" .[16] The Victorian love of anagramming as recreation is alluded to by Augustus De Morgan[17] using his own name as example; "Great Gun, do us a sum!" is attributed to his son William De Morgan, but a family friend John Thomas Graves was prolific, and a manuscript with over 2,800 has been preserved.[18][19][20]

With the advent of surrealism as a poetic movement, anagrams regained the artistic respect they had had in the Baroque period. The German poet Unica Zürn, who made extensive use of anagram techniques, came to regard obsession with anagrams as a "dangerous fever" , because it created isolation of the author.[21] The surrealist leader André Breton coined the anagram *Avida Dollars* for Salvador Dalí, to tarnish his reputation by the implication of commercialism.

33.3 Applications

While anagramming is certainly a recreation first, there are ways in which anagrams are put to use, and these can be more serious, or at least not quite frivolous and formless. For example, psychologists use anagram-oriented tests, often called "anagram solution tasks" , to assess the implicit memory of young adults and adults alike.[22]

33.3.1 Establishment of priority

Natural philosophers (astronomers and others) of the 17th century transposed their discoveries into Latin anagrams, to establish their priority. In this way they laid claim to new discoveries, before their results were ready for publication.

Galileo used *smaismrmilmepoetaleumibunenugttauiras* for *Altissimum planetam tergeminum observavi* ("I have observed the most distant planet to have a triple form") for discovering the rings of Saturn in 1610.[23][24] Galileo announced his discovery that Venus had phases like the Moon in the form "Haec immatura a me iam frustra leguntur -oy" (Latin: *These immature ones have already been read in vain by me -oy*), that is, when rearranged, "Cynthiae figuras aemulatur Mater Amorum" (Latin: *The Mother of Loves [= Venus] imitates the figures of Cynthia [= the moon]*).

When Robert Hooke discovered Hooke's law in 1660, he first published it in anagram form, *ceiiinosssttuv*, for *ut tensio, sic vis* (Latin: *as the tension, so the force*).[25]

In a related use, from 1975, British naturalist Sir Peter Scott coined the scientific term "Nessiteras rhombopteryx" (Greek for "The monster (or wonder) of Ness with the diamond-shaped fin") for the apocryphal Loch Ness Monster. Shortly afterwards, several London newspapers pointed out that "Nessiteras rhombopteryx" anagrams into "Monster hoax by Sir Peter S" . However, Robert Rines, who previously made two underwater photographs allegedly showing the monster, countered with the fact that they can also be arranged into "Yes, both pix are monsters, R."

33.3.2 Pseudonyms

Anagrams are connected to pseudonyms, by the fact that they may conceal or reveal, or operate somewhere in between like a mask that can establish identity. For example, Jim Morrison used an anagram of his name in The Doors song *L.A. Woman*, calling himself "Mr. Mojo Risin' ". The use of anagrams and fabricated personal names may be to circumvent restrictions on the use of real names, as happened in the 18th century when Edward Cave wanted to get around restrictions imposed on the reporting of the House of Commons.*[26] In a genre such as farce or parody, anagrams as names may be used for pointed and satiric effect.

Pseudonyms adopted by authors are sometimes transposed forms of their names; thus "Calvinus" becomes "Alcuinus" (here V = U) or "François Rabelais" = "Alcofribas Nasier". The name "Voltaire" of François Marie Arouet fits this pattern, and is allowed to be an anagram of "Arouet, l[e] j[eune]" (U = V, J = I) that is, "Arouet the younger". Other examples include

- "Arrigo Boito" = "Tobia Gorrio"

- "Edward Gorey" = "Ogdred Weary", = "Regera Dowdy" or = "E. G. Deadworry" (and others)

- "Vladimir Nabokov" = "Vivian Darkbloom", = "Vivian Bloodmark", = "Blavdak Vinomori" or = "*Dorian Vivalcomb*", "Dorian Vivalkomb"

- "Ted Morgan" = "(Sanche) de Gramont"

- "Dave Barry" = "Ray Adverb"

- "Glen Duncan" = "Declan Gunn" *[27]

- "Damon Albarn" = "Dan Abnormal"

- "Tom Cruise" = "So I'm cuter"

- "Tom Marvolo Riddle" = "I am Lord Voldemort"

- "Buckethead" = "Death Cube K"

- "Daniel Clowes" = "Enid Coleslaw"

- "Siobhan Donaghy" = "Shanghai Nobody"

Several of these are "imperfect anagrams", letters having been left out in some cases for the sake of easy pronunciation.

33.3.3 Titles

Anagrams used for titles afford scope for some types of wit. Examples:

- Shakespeare's *Hamlet* is an anagram for the Danish Prince Amleth.*[28]

- Homer Hickam, Jr.'s book *Rocket Boys* was adapted into the 1999 film *October Sky*.*[28]

- The tapes for the revival of the BBC show Doctor Who were labeled with the anagram Torchwood, which later went on to be used as the name for a spin-off show.

- The New Wave band Missing Persons' best-selling album was called *Spring Session M.*

- Hip-hop artist MF DOOM recorded a 2004 album called *MM..FOOD.*

- Brian Eno's album *Before and After Science* includes a song entitled "King's Lead Hat", an anagram of "Talking Heads", a band Eno has worked with.

- Juan Maria Solare's piano ballad "Jura ser anomalía" (literally "he/she swears to be an anomaly") is an anagram of the composer's full name. His composition for English horn titled "A Dot in Time" is an anagram of "Meditation", which describes the piece. The title of his piano piece that is an homage to Claude Debussy is "Seduce Us Badly".

- Bill Evans's overdubbed piano elegy for fellow jazz pianist Sonny Clark is titled "N.Y.C.'s No Lark," and another composition, "Re: Person I Knew" is a tribute to his producer, Orrin Keepnews.

- The title of Imogen Heap's album *iMegaphone* is an anagram of her name.

- Progressive rock group Rush published a song off their 1989 album *Presto* titled "Anagram (for Mongo)" that makes use of anagrams in every line of their song.

- The title of the fifth album by American rock band Interpol, *El Pintor*, is an anagram of the band's name and also Spanish for "the painter".

33.3.4 Games and puzzles

Anagrams are in themselves a recreational activity, but they also make up part of many other games, puzzles and game shows. The Jumble is a puzzle found in many newspapers in the United States requiring the unscrambling of letters to find the solution. Cryptic crossword puzzles frequently use anagrammatic clues, usually indicating that they are anagrams by the inclusion of a descriptive term like "confused" or "in disarray". An example would be *Businessman burst into tears (9 letters)*. The solution, *stationer*, is an anagram of *into tears*, the letters of which have *burst* out of their original arrangement to form the name of a type of *businessman*.

Numerous other games and contests involve some element of anagram formation as a basic skill. Some examples:

- In Anagrams, players flip tiles over one at a time and race to take words. They can "steal" each other's words by rearranging the letters and extending the words.

- In a version of Scrabble called Clabbers, the name itself being an anagram of Scrabble, tiles may be placed in any order on the board as long as they anagram to a valid word.

- On the British game show *Countdown*, contestants are given 30 seconds to make the longest word from nine random letters.

- In Boggle, players make constrained words from a grid of sixteen random letters, by joining adjacent cubes.

- On the British game show *BrainTeaser*, contestants are shown a word broken into randomly arranged segments and must announce the whole word. At the end of the game there is a "Pyramid" which starts with a three-letter word. A letter appears in the line below to which the player must add the existing letters to find a solution. The pattern continues until the player reaches the final eight-letter anagram. The player wins the game by solving all the anagrams within the allotted time.

- In Bananagrams, players place tiles from a pool into crossword-style word arrangements in a race to see who can finish the pool of tiles first.

33.3.5 Ciphers

Multiple anagramming is a technique used to solve some kinds of cryptograms, such as a permutation cipher, a transposition cipher, and the Jefferson disk.*[29]

33.4   Methods of construction

Sometimes it is possible to "see" anagrams in words, unaided by tools, though the more letters involved the more difficult this becomes. Anagram dictionaries could also be used. Computer programs, known as "anagram servers", "anagram solvers" or "anagrammers", offer a much faster route to creating anagrams, and a large number of these programs are available on the Internet. The program or server carries out an exhaustive search of a database of words, to produce a list containing every possible combination of words or phrases from the input word or phrase. Some programs (such as *Lexpert*) restrict to one-word answers. Many anagram servers (for example, the Internet Anagram Server) can control the search results, by excluding or including certain words, limiting the number or length of words in each anagram, or limiting the number of results. Anagram solvers are often banned from online anagram games. The disadvantage of computer anagram solvers, especially when applied to multi-word anagrams, is their poor understanding of the meaning of the words they are manipulating. They usually cannot filter out meaningful or appropriate anagrams from large numbers of nonsensical word combinations. Some servers attempt to improve on this using statistical techniques that try to combine only words that appear together often. This approach provides only limited success since it fails to recognize ironic and humorous combinations.

Some anagrammatists indicate the method they used. Anagrams constructed without aid of a computer are noted as having been done "manually" or "by hand"; those made by utilizing a computer may be noted "by machine" or "by computer", or may indicate the name of the computer program (using *Anagram Genius*).

There are also a few "natural" instances: English words unconsciously created by switching letters around. The French *chaise longue* ("long chair") became the American "chaise lounge" by metathesis (transposition of letters and/or sounds). It has also been speculated that the English "curd" comes from the Latin *crudus* ("raw"). Similarly, the ancient English word for bird was "brid".

33.5   See also

- Alphagram

- Ambigram

- Anagrammatic poem

- Anagrams, a board game

- Blanagram

- Constrained writing

- Isogram

- Letter bank

- Lipogram

- London Underground anagram map

- Palindrome

- Pangram

- Rebus

- Tautonym

- Word play

33.6 References

[1] Anagrammatist, www.dictionary.com. Retrieved on 2008-08-12.

[2] *Of Anagrams*, By H.B. Wheatley pg. 72, printed 1862 T. & W. Boone, New Bond Street, London

[3] HOASM

[4] The LoveToKnow Free Online Encyclopedia

[5] Cited in Henry Benjamin Wheatley, *Of anagrams: a monograph treating of their history* (1862); online text.

[6] Articles from the *Dictionary of National Biography*.

[7] *Dictionary of National Biography.*

[8] Early Stuart Libels

[9] Early Stuart Libels

[10] Henry Benjamin Wheatley, *On Anagrams* (1862), p. 58.

[11] *Remains,* 7th ed., 1674.

[12] Thy genius calls thee not to purchase fame
In keen iambics, but mild anagram:
Leave writing plays, and choose for thy command
Some peaceful province in acrostic land.
There thou may'st wings display and altars raise,
And torture one poor word ten thousand ways.

[13] *Oxford Book of Word Games*

[14] Hugh Trevor-Roper, *Archbishop Laud* (2000), p. 146.

[15] H. W. van Helsdingen, *Notes on Two Sheets of Sketches by Nicolas Poussin for the Long Gallery of the Louvre*, Simiolus: Netherlands Quarterly for the History of Art, Vol. 5, No. 3/4 (1971), pp. 172–184.

[16] 1911 Britannica article "anagram".

[17] In his *A Budget of Paradoxes*, p. 82.

[18] Robert Edoward Moritz, *On Mathematics and Mathematicians* (2007), p. 151.

[19] Anna Stirling, *William De Morgan and His Wife* (1922) p. 64.

[20] AIM25 home page

[21] Friederike Ursula Eigler, Susanne Kord, The Feminist Encyclopedia of German Literature (1997), pp. 14–5.

[22] Java, Rosalind I. "Priming and Aging: Evidence of Preserved Memory Function in an Anagram Solution Task." *The American Journal of Psychology*, Vol. 105, No. 4. (Winter, 1992), pp. 541–548.

[23] Miner, Ellis D.; Wessen, Randii R.; Cuzzi, Jeffrey N. (2007). "The scientific significance of planetary ring systems". *Planetary Ring Systems*. Springer Praxis Books in Space Exploration. Praxis. pp. 1–16. doi:10.1007/978-0-387-73981-6_1. ISBN 978-0-387-34177-4.

[24] "Galileo's Anagrams and the Moons of Mars". *Math Pages: History*. Retrieved 2009-03-16.

[25] Derek Gjertsen, *The Newton Handbook* (1986), p. 16.

[26] Institute of Historical Research (IHR) home page

[27] I, Lucifer (Glen Duncan)

[28] Lundin, Leigh (2009-11-29). "Anagrams". *Word Play*. Criminal Brief.

[29] Bletchley Park Cryptographic Dictionary. Codesandciphers.org.uk. Retrieved on 2014-05-12.

33.7   Further reading

- Henry Benjamin Wheatley. *Of Anagrams: A Monograph Treating of Their History from the Earliest Ages to the Present Time.* Williams & Norgate, 1862.

- *Word Ways: The Journal of Recreational Linguistics.* Greenwood Periodicals et al., 1968–. ISSN 0043-7980.

- Howard W. Bergerson. *Palindromes and Anagrams.* Dover Publications, 1973. ISBN 978-0486206646.

Chapter 34

Asyndeton

Asyndeton (from the Greek: ἀσύνδετον, "unconnected", sometimes called **asyndetism**) is a figure of speech in which one or several conjunctions are omitted from a series of related clauses.[*][1][*][2] Examples are *veni, vidi, vici* and its English translation "I came, I saw, I conquered". Its use can have the effect of speeding up the rhythm of a passage and making a single idea more memorable. Asyndeton may be contrasted with syndeton (syndetic coordination) and polysyndeton, which describe the use of one or multiple coordinating conjunctions, respectively.

More generally, in grammar, an **asyndetic coordination** is a type of coordination in which no coordinating conjunction is present between the conjuncts.

Quickly, resolutely, he strode into the bank.

No coordinator is present here, but the conjoins are still coordinated.

It does not involve omission, but is grouped with its opposite.

34.1 Examples

34.1.1 Omission of conjunction "and"

Aristotle wrote in his *Rhetoric* that this device was more effective in spoken oratory than in written prose:

- "Thus strings of unconnected words, and constant repetitions of words and phrases, are very properly condemned in written speeches: but not in spoken speeches —speakers use them freely, for they have a dramatic effect. In this repetition there must be variety of tone, paving the way, as it were, to dramatic effect; e.g., 'This is the villain among you who deceived you, who cheated you, **who meant to betray you completely'**". Aristotle, *Rhetoric*, Book III, Chapter 12 (trans. W. Rhys Roberts).

Several notable examples can be found in American political speeches: Aristotle also believed that asyndeton can be used effectively in endings of works, and he himself employs the device in the final passage of the *Rhetoric*:

- "For the conclusion, the disconnected style of language is appropriate, and will mark the difference between the oration and the peroration. 'I have done. You have heard me. The facts are before you. **I ask for your judgement'**". Aristotle, *Rhetoric*, Book III, Chapter 19 (trans. W. Rhys Roberts).

- "...and that government of the people, by the people, **for the people** shall not perish from the earth". Abraham Lincoln, Gettysburg Address

- "...that we shall pay any price, bear any burden, meet any hardship, support any friend, **oppose any foe** to assure the survival and the success of liberty." John F. Kennedy *Inaugural Address*, 20 January 1961.

Another frequently used, extended example, is Winston Churchill's address, "We shall fight on the beaches":

- "We shall go on to the end, we shall fight in France, we shall fight on the seas and oceans, we shall fight with growing confidence and growing strength in the air, we shall defend our Island, whatever the cost may be, we shall fight on the beaches, we shall fight on the landing grounds, we shall fight in the fields and in the streets, we shall fight in the hills; **we shall never surrender**. . ."

34.1.2   Omission of conjunction "as"

The US Declaration of Independence includes an example of asyndeton, referring to the British:

- "We must... hold them, as we hold the rest of mankind, **Enemies in War, in Peace Friends**."

This quotation is also an example of chiasmus.

34.2   See also

- Apokoinu construction

- Parataxis (grammar)

- Reduced relative clause, relative clause not marked by an overt complementizer

- Zeugma

34.3   References

[1]   - Corbett, Edward P.J. *Classical Rhetoric for the Modern Student*. Oxford University Press, New York, 1971.

[2] Smyth, Herbert Weir (1920). *Greek Grammar*. Cambridge MA: Harvard University Press. p. 674. ISBN 0-674-36250-0.

34.4   External links

- Asyndetic Coordination @ The Internet Grammar of English

- Audio illustrations of asyndeton

Chapter 35

Bathos

Not to be confused with pathos, a successful arousal of sympathy and pity.

Bathos (/'beɪθɒs/ *BAY-thoss*;[1] Greek: βάθος, lit. "depth") is a literary term first coined by Alexander Pope's 1727 essay "Peri Bathous"[1] to describe amusingly failed attempts at sublimity (i.e., pathos). In particular, bathos is associated with anticlimax, an abrupt transition from a lofty style or grand topic to a common or vulgar one. This may be either accidental (through artistic ineptitude) or intentional (for comic effect).[2][3] Intentional bathos appears in satiric genres such as burlesque and mock epic. "Bathos" or "bathetic" is also used for similar effects in other branches of the arts, such as musical passages marked *ridicolosamente*. In film, bathos may appear in a contrast cut intended for comic relief or be produced by an accidental jump cut.

35.1 Examples

35.1.1 Traditional

Alfred Lord Tennyson's narrative poem, Enoch Arden, ends with the following lines:

> So past the strong heroic soul away.
> And when they buried him the little port
> Had seldom seen a costlier funeral.

After stanzas of heightened poetic language, the poet, in three short lines, wraps up a pathos-laden story with mundane and practical details. The effect yanks the reader out of the poetic world, simultaneously offering commentary on the finality of death and the transience of heroics.

A musical representation is found in composer Igor Stravinsky's 1923 Octet for wind instruments. The first two movements and the majority of the third movement follow traditional classical structures, albeit employing modern and innovative harmonies. The last fifteen seconds of the 25 minute work, however, abruptly and whimsically turn to popular harmony, rhythm, and style found in contemporary dance hall music.

35.1.2 Modern

"Moviemakers talk about "bad laughs." That's when the audience laughs when it's not supposed to. This is conceivably the first movie which is in its entirety a bad laugh." [4]
—*Roger Ebert, The Hindenburg (1975)*[4]

Contemporary examples often take the form of analogies, written to seem unintentionally funny:

- Week 310: It's Like This of The Style Invitational humor contest column in the *Washington Post* (14 March 1999), on humorous analogies, many exhibiting bathos, such as:

  The ballerina rose gracefully en pointe and extended one slender leg behind her, like a dog at a fire hydrant.*[5]

The Bulwer-Lytton Fiction Contest features purple prose, at times exhibiting bathos:

  They had but one last remaining night together, so they embraced each other as tightly as that two-flavor entwined string cheese that is orange and yellowish-white, the orange probably being a bland Cheddar and the white . . . Mozzarella, although it could possibly be Provolone or just plain American, as it really doesn't taste distinctly dissimilar from the orange, yet they would have you believe it does by coloring it differently.

  Mariann Simms, Wetumpka, AL (2003 Winner)

Legendary Darts commentator Sid Waddell was famed for his one-liners, including this fine example of bathos

  "When Alexander of Macedonia was 33, he cried salt tears because there were no more worlds to conquer..... Bristow's only 27."

35.2   See also

- Anti-climax
- Gallows humor

35.3   References

[1] *Oxford English Dictionary*, 1st ed.   "bathos, *n.* Oxford University Press (Oxford), 1885.

[2] Fiske, Robert Hartwell (1 November 2011). *Robert Hartwell Fiske's Dictionary of Unendurable English: A Compendium of Mistakes in Grammar, Usage, and Spelling with commentary on lexicographers and linguists.* Scribner. p. 71. ISBN 978-1-4516-5134-8.

[3] Abrams, Meyer Howard; Harpham, Geoffrey Galt (2009). *A Glossary of Literary Terms.* Cengage Learning. p. 24. ISBN 978-1-4130-3390-8.

[4] Ebert, Roger. Missing or empty |title= (help)

[5] "Week 310: It's Like This". *The Washington Post.* March 14, 1999. Retrieved 1 June 2014.

35.4   Bibliography

- Pope, Alexander (2006) [1727]. "Peri Bathous". In Pat Rogers. *The Major Works.* Oxford: Oxford University Press. pp. 195–238. ISBN 978-0-19-920361-1. OCLC 317742832.

Chapter 36

Caesura

For the Helios album, see Caesura (album).

In meter, a *caesura* (/siːˈʒʊərə/ or /sɪˈʒʊərə/ ((Latin: *caedere* /ˈkaɪ̯.de.re/); alternative spellings are **cæsura** and **cesura**)

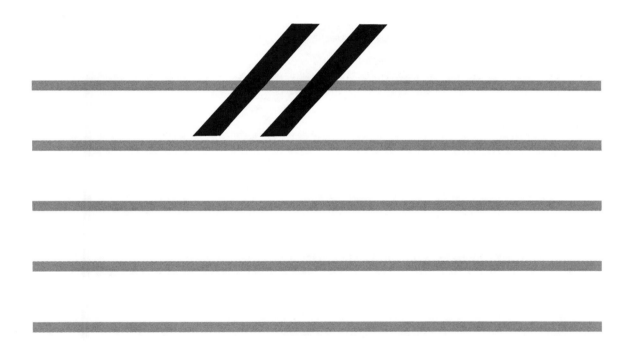

An example of a caesura in modern western music notation.

is a complete pause in a line of poetry and/or in a musical composition. This can also be referred as a quarter rest with a fermata over it.[*][1] The plural form of *caesura* is *caesurae*. In poetry, a *masculine* caesura follows a stressed syllable while a *feminine* caesura follows an unstressed syllable. A caesura is also described by its position in a line of poetry. A caesura close to the beginning of a line is called an *initial* caesura, one in the middle of a line is *medial*, and one near the end of a line is *terminal*. Initial and terminal caesurae are rare in formal, Romance, and Neoclassical verse, which prefer medial caesurae. In scansion, poetry written with signs to indicate the length and stress of syllables, the "double pipe" sign ("‖") is used to denote the position of a caesura.

In musical notation, a caesura denotes a brief, silent pause, during which metrical time is not counted. Similar to a silent

Brief caesura used in choral works.

fermata, caesurae are located between notes or measures (before or over bar lines), rather than on notes or rests (as with a fermata). A fermata may be placed over a caesura to indicate a longer pause.

In musical notation, the symbol for a caesura is a pair of parallel lines set at an angle, rather like a pair of forward slashes: //. The symbol is popularly called "tram-lines" in the U.K. and "railroad tracks" in the U.S.

36.1   Examples

In the following examples, the symbol for the caesura in scanning poetry, the "double pipes" ("||"), are inserted into the text of the poem to indicate the position of the audible pause.

36.1.1   Homer

Caesurae were widely used in Greek poetry, for example, in the opening line of the *Iliad*:

μῆνιν ἄειδε θεὰ ‖ Πηληϊάδεω Ἀχιλῆος

("Sing, o goddess, the rage ‖ of Achilles, the son of Peleus.")

This line includes a masculine caesura after θεὰ, a natural break that separates the line into two logical parts. Unlike later writers, Homeric lines more commonly employ feminine caesurae.

36.1.2   Latin

Caesurae were widely used in Latin poetry, for example, in the opening line of Virgil's *Aeneid*:

Arma virumque cano ‖ Troiae qui primus ab oris

(Of arms and the man, I sing. ‖ Who first from the shores of Troy...)

This line uses caesura in the medial position. In dactylic hexameter, a caesura occurs any time the ending of a word does not coincide with the beginning or the end of a metrical foot; in modern prosody, however, it is only called one when the ending also coincides with an audible pause in the line.

The ancient elegiac couplet form of the Greeks and Romans contained a line of dactylic hexameter followed by a line of pentameter. The pentameter often displayed a clearer caesura, as in this example from Propertius:

> Cynthia prima fuit; ‖ Cynthia finis erit.

> (Cynthia was the first; Cynthia will be the last)

36.1.3 Old English

The caesura was even more important to Old English verse than it was to Latin or Greek poetry. In Latin or Greek poetry, the caesura could be suppressed for effect in any line. In the alliterative verse that is shared by most of the oldest Germanic languages, the caesura is an ever-present and necessary part of the verse form itself. The opening line of *Beowulf* reads:

> Hwæt! We Gardena ‖ in gear-dagum,
>
> þeodcyninga, ‖ þrym gefrunon,
>
> hu ða æþelingas ‖ ellen fremedon.

> (So! The Spear-Danes in days gone by)
>
> (and the kings who ruled them had courage and greatness.)
>
> (We have heard of these princes' heroic campaigns.)

The basic form is accentual verse, with four stresses per line separated by a caesura. Old English poetry added alliteration and other devices to this basic pattern.

36.1.4 Middle English

William Langland's *Piers Ploughman*:

> I loked on my left half ‖ as þe lady me taughte
>
> And was war of a woman ‖ worþeli ycloþed.

> (I looked on my left side / as the lady me taught)
>
> (and was aware of a woman / worthily clothed.)

36.1.5 Other examples

Caesurae can occur in later forms of verse, where they are usually optional. The so-called ballad meter, or the common meter of the hymnodists (see also hymn), is usually thought of as a line of iambic tetrameter followed by a line of trimeter, but it can also be considered a line of heptameter with a fixed caesura at the fourth foot.

Considering the break as a caesura in these verse forms, rather than a beginning of a new line, explains how sometimes multiple caesurae can be found in this verse form (from the ballad Tom o' Bedlam):

> From the hag and hungry goblin ‖ that into rags would rend ye,
>
> And the spirits that stand ‖ by the naked man ‖ in the Book of Moons, defend ye!

In later and freer verse forms, the caesura is optional. It can, however, be used for rhetorical effect, as in Alexander Pope's line:

> To err is human; ‖ to forgive, divine.

36.2   See also

- Haiku
- Meter (poetry)
- Old English poetry
- Prosody (Latin)
- Regulated verse
- Saturnian (poetry)

36.3   References

[1]   "caesura". *Encyclopædia Britannica Online*. Encyclopædia Britannica, Inc. Retrieved 20 December 2013.

Chapter 37

Distancing effect

The **distancing effect**, more commonly known (earlier) by John Willett's 1964 translation the **alienation effect** or (more recently) as the **estrangement effect** (German: *Verfremdungseffekt*), is a performing arts concept coined by playwright Bertolt Brecht. Brecht first used the term in an essay on "Alienation Effects in Chinese Acting" published in 1936, in which he described it as "playing in such a way that the audience was hindered from simply identifying itself with the characters in the play. Acceptance or rejection of their actions and utterances was meant to take place on a conscious plane, instead of, as hitherto, in the audience's subconscious" .*[1]

37.1   Origin

The term *Verfremdungseffekt* is rooted in the Russian Formalist notion of the device of *making strange* (Russian: приём отстранения *priyom otstraneniya*), which literary critic Viktor Shklovsky claims is the essence of all art.*[2] Lemon and Reis's 1965 English translation*[3] of Shklovsky's 1917 coinage as "defamiliarization", combined with John Willett's 1964 translation of Brecht's 1935 coinage as "alienation effect"—and the canonization of both translations in Anglophone literary theory in the decades since—has served to obscure the close connections between the two terms. Not only is the root of both terms "strange" (*stran-* in Russian, *fremd* in German), but both terms are unusual in their respective languages: *ostranenie* is a neologism in Russian, while *Verfremdung* is a resuscitation of a long-obsolete term in German. In addition, according to some accounts Shklovsky's Russian friend playwright Sergei Tretyakov *taught* Brecht Shklovsky's term during Brecht's visit to Moscow in the spring of 1935.*[4] For this reason, many scholars have recently taken to using *estrangement* to translate both terms: "the estrangement device" in Shklovsky, "the estrangement effect" in Brecht.

It was in any case not long after returning in the spring of 1935 from Moscow, where he saw a command performance of Beijing Opera techniques by Mei Lanfang, that Brecht first used the German term in print*[5] to label an approach to theater that discouraged involving the audience in an illusory narrative world and in the emotions of the characters. Brecht thought the audience required an emotional distance to reflect on what was being presented in critical and objective ways, rather than being *taken out of themselves* as conventional entertainment attempts to do.

The proper English translation of *Verfremdungseffekt* is a matter of controversy. The word is sometimes rendered as *defamiliarization effect, estrangement effect, distantiation, alienation effect,* or *distancing effect*. In *Brecht and Method,*[6] Fredric Jameson abbreviates *Verfremdungseffekt* as "the V-effekt"; many scholars similarly leave the word untranslated.

In German, *Verfremdungseffekt* signifies both alienation and distancing in a theatrical context; thus, "theatrical alienation" and "theatrical distancing" . Brecht wanted to "distance" or to "alienate" his audience from the characters and the action and, by dint of that, render them observers who would not become involved in or to sympathize emotionally or to empathize by identifying individually with the characters psychologically; rather, he wanted the audience to understand intellectually the characters' dilemmas and the wrongdoing producing these dilemmas exposed in his dramatic plots. By being thus "distanced" emotionally from the characters and the action on stage, the audience could be able to reach such an intellectual level of understanding (or intellectual empathy); in theory, while alienated emotionally from the action and the characters, they would be empowered on an intellectual level both to analyze and perhaps even to try to change the world, which was Brecht's social and political goal as a playwright and the driving force behind his dramaturgy.

37.2   Techniques

The distancing effect is achieved by the way the "artist never acts as if there were a fourth wall besides the three surrounding him [...] The audience can no longer have the illusion of being the unseen spectator at an event which is really taking place" (Willett 91). The use of direct audience-address is one way of disrupting stage illusion and generating the distancing effect. In performance, as the performer "observes himself", his objective is "to appear strange and even surprising to the audience. He achieves this by looking strangely at himself and his work" (Willett 92). Whether Brecht intended the distancing effect to refer to the audience or to the actor or to both audience and actor is still controversial among teachers and scholars of "Epic Acting" and Brechtian theatre.

By disclosing and making obvious the manipulative contrivances and "fictive" qualities of the medium, the actors alienate the viewer from any passive acceptance and enjoyment of the play as mere "entertainment". Instead, the viewer is forced into a critical, analytical frame of mind that serves to disabuse him or her of the notion that what he is watching is necessarily an inviolable, self-contained narrative. This effect of making the familiar strange serves a didactic function insofar as it teaches the viewer not to take the style and content for granted, since the medium itself is highly constructed and contingent upon many cultural and economic conditions.

It may be noted that Brecht's use of distancing effects in order to prevent audience members from *bathing* themselves in empathetic emotions and to draw them into an attitude of critical judgment may lead to other reactions than intellectual coolness. Brecht's popularization of the *V-Effekt* has come to dominate our understanding of its dynamics. But the particulars of a spectator's psyche and of the tension aroused by a specific alienating device may actually *increase* emotional impact.*[7] Audience reactions are rarely uniform, and there are many diverse, sometimes unpredictable, responses that may be achieved through distancing.

Actors, directors, and playwrights may draw on alienating effects in creating a production. The playwright may describe them in the script's stage directions, in effect requiring them in the staging of the work. A director may take a script that has not been written to alienate and introduce certain techniques, such as playing dialogue forward to remind the audience that there is no fourth wall, or guiding the cast to act "in quotation marks". The actor (usually with the director's permission) may play scenes with an ironic subtext. These techniques and many more are available for artists in different aspects of the show. For the playwright, reference to vaudeville or musical revues, will often allow rapid segues from empathy to a judgmental attitude through comic distancing. A very effective use of such estrangement in an English language script can be found in Brendan Behan's *The Hostage*.

37.3   See also

- Defamiliarization

- Epic Theatre

- Metafiction

- Bertolt Brecht

- Harun Farocki

- Rainer Werner Fassbinder

- Jean-Luc Godard

- Hal Hartley

- Toshiki Okada

- Nagisa Oshima

- Lars von Trier

37.4 References

[1] John Willett, ed. and trans., *Brecht on Theatre* (New York: Hill and Wang, 1964), 91.

[2] "Art as Device", translated by Benjamin Sher in Shklovsky, *The Theory of Prose* (Bloomington, IL: Dalkey Archive Press, 1991).

[3] Lee T. Lemon and Marion J. Reis, eds. and trans., *Russian Formalist Criticism* (Lincoln: University of Nebraska Press).

[4] For discussion, see Douglas Robinson, *Estrangement and the Somatics of Literature: Tolstoy, Shklovsky, Brecht* (Baltimore and London: Johns Hopkins University Press, 2008).

[5] "Alienation Effects in Chinese Acting", in Willett 99.

[6] London: Verso, 1998.

[7] Frau Weigel's famous Gestus of the *stummer Schrei* or "silent scream," following the death of Courage's son Swiss Cheese, moved some to experience deep empathy—based on a vicarious feeling of what it is to so restrain oneself that the full expression of grief is prevented.

37.5 Further reading

- Brecht, Bertolt. "On Chinese Acting", translated by Eric Bentley. *The Tulane Drama Review* 6.1 (1961): 130–136.

- Jameson, Fredric. *Brecht and Method.* London and New York: Verso, 1998. ISBN 1-85984-809-5 (10). ISBN 978-1-85984-809-8 (13).

- Min Tian, *The Poetics of Difference and Displacement: Twentieth-Century Chinese-Western Intercultural Theatre.* Hong Kong: Hong Kong University Press, 2008.

- Robinson, Douglas. *Estrangement and the Somatics of Literature: Tolstoy, Shklovsky, Brecht.* Baltimore and London: Johns Hopkins University Press, 2008.

- Willett, John, ed. and trans. *Brecht on Theatre: The Development of an Aesthetic.* London: Methuen, 1964. ISBN 0-413-38800-X. New York: Hill and Wang, 1964. ISBN 0-8090-3100-0.

Chapter 38

Euphuism

Not to be confused with Euphemism.

Euphuism is a peculiar mannered style of English prose. It takes its name from a prose romance by John Lyly. It consists of a preciously ornate and sophisticated style, employing in deliberate excess a wide range of literary devices such as antitheses, alliterations, repetitions and rhetorical questions. Classical learning and remote knowledge of all kinds are displayed. Euphuism was fashionable in the 1580s, especially in the Elizabethan court, but never previously or subsequently.

38.1 *Euphues* (1580)

"Euphues" is the Greek for "graceful, witty". John Lyly published the works *Euphues: The Anatomy of Wit* (1578) and *Euphues and his England* (1580). Both works illustrated the intellectual fashions and favourite themes of Renaissance society —in a highly artificial and mannered style. The plots are unimportant, existing merely as structural elements on which to display conversations, discourses and letters mostly concerning the subject of love. Its essential features had already appeared in such works as George Pettie's "A Petite Pallace of Pettie his pleasure" (1576), in sermon literature, and Latin tracts. Lyly perfected the distinctive rhetorical devices on which the style was based.

38.2 Principles of the style

The euphuistic sentence followed principles of balance and antithesis to their extremes, purposely using the latter regardless of sense. John Lyly set up three basic structural principles:

1. phrases of equal length that appear in succession;

2. the balance of key verbal elements in successive sentences;

3. the correspondence of sounds and syllables, especially between words that are already balanced against each other.

38.3 Examples

"It is virtue, yea virtue, gentlemen, that maketh gentlemen; that maketh the poor rich, the base-born noble, the subject a sovereign, the deformed beautiful, the sick whole, the weak strong, the most miserable most happy. There are two principal and peculiar gifts in the nature of man, knowledge and reason; the one commandeth, and the other obeyeth: these things neither the whirling wheel of fortune can change, neither the deceitful cavillings of worldlings separate, neither sickness abate, neither age abolish" . (*Euphues, the Anatomy of Wit*)

"Is it not far better to abhor sins by the remembrance of others' faults, than by repentance of thine own follies?" (*Euphues, 1, lecture by the wise Neapolitan*)

"Can any treasure in this transitory pilgrimmage be of more value than a friend? In whose bosom thou mayest sleep secure without fear, whom thou mayest make partner of all thy secrets without suspicion of fraud, and partaker of all thy misfortune without mistrust of fleeting. Who will account thy bale his bane, thy mishap his misery, the pricking of thy finger the piercing of his heart" (Euphues)

"How frantic are those lovers which are carried away with the gay glistering of the fine face? The beauty whereof is parched with the summer's blaze and chipped with the winter's blast: which is of so short continuance, that it fadeth before one perceive it flourish" . (Euphues' after-dinner speech to the 'coy' Neapolitan ladies on whether the qualities of the mind or the composition of the man are more worthy).

"Time hath weaned me from my mother's teat, and age rid me from my father's correction" . (Lucilla, considering her father's reaction in abandoning her fiance Philanthus for Euphues).

"A sharp sore hath a short cure" (Euphues)

"As they be hard to be won without trial of great faith, so are they hard to be lost without great cause of fickleness" . (Euphues to Lucilla on the quality of 'fervency' in women).

"But alas Euphues, what truth can there be found in a traveller? What stay in a stranger? Whose words and bodies both watch but for a wind, whose feet are ever fleeting, whose faith plighted on the shore, is turned to perjury when they hoist sail" . (Lucilla to Euphues).

38.4 Legacy

Lyly's style influenced Shakespeare, who satirises it in speeches by Polonius in *Hamlet* and the florid language of the courtly lovers in *Love's Labour's Lost*; Beatrice and Benedick in *Much Ado About Nothing* also make use of it, as do Richard and Lady Anne in *Richard III*. Many critics did not appreciate Lyly's deliberate excesses. Philip Sidney and Gabriel Harvey castigated his style. Euphuism was, however, taken up by the Elizabethan writers Robert Greene, Thomas Lodge and Barnabe Rich. Walter Scott satirised Euphuism in the character of Sir Piercie Shafton in *The Monastery*, and Charles Kingsley defended *Euphues* in *Westward Ho!*.

38.5 Contemporary equivalents in other languages

Euphuism was not particular to Britain, a manifestation of some social structure and artistic opportunity unique to that country. There were equivalents in other major European languages, each of which was called by a different name: Culteranismo in Spain, Marinismo in Italy, and Préciosité in France, for example.

38.6 See also

- Periodic sentence

38.7 Source

- *Concise Oxford Dictionary of English Literature*, Oxford, 1957. pp. 166/7.

38.8 Further reading

- Child, Clarence Griffin (1894). *John Lyly and Euphuism*. Leipzig: A. Deichert.

- Hunt, T.W. (1889). "Euphuism in Literature and Style," *New Englander and Yale Review,* Vol. L, No. 228, pp. 189–200.

- Pater, Walter (1885). "Euphuism." In: *Marius the Epicurean*. London: Macmillan & Co., pp. 94–111.

38.9 External links

- litencyc.com

- britannica.com

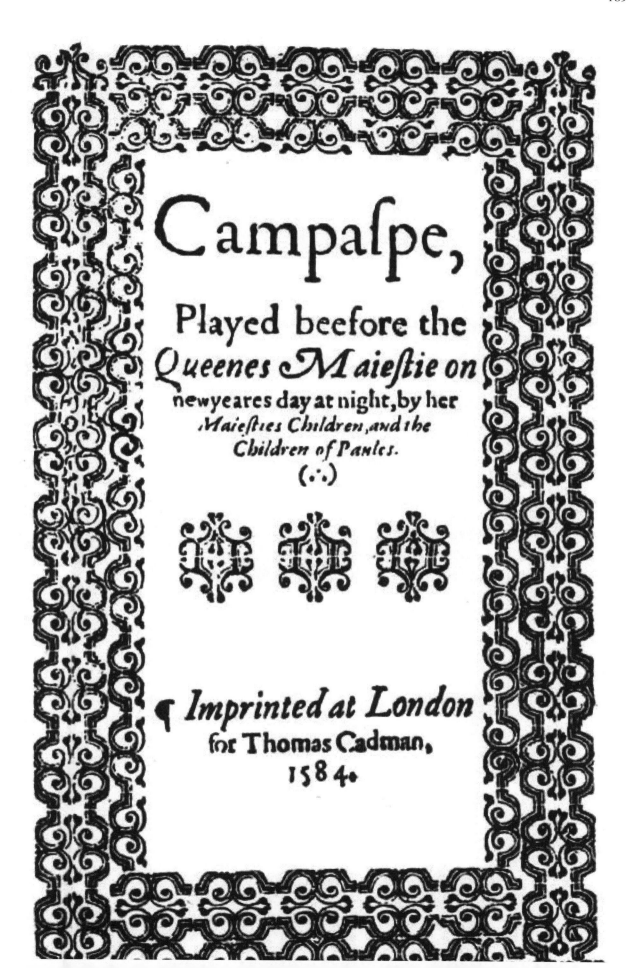

Chapter 39

Hyperbole

This article is about the term used in rhetoric. For the mathematical term, see Hyperbola.

Hyperbole (/haɪˈpɜrbəliː/ *hy-PUR-bə-lee*;[1] Greek: ὑπερβολή, *hyperbolē*, lit. "exaggeration") is the use of exaggeration as a rhetorical device or figure of speech. In rhetoric, it is also sometimes known as **auxesis** (lit. "growth"). In poetry and oratory, it emphasizes, evokes strong feelings, and creates strong impressions. As a figure of speech, it is usually not meant to be taken literally.[2][3]

39.1 Usage

Hyperbole may also be used for instances of such exaggerations for emphasis or effect. Hyperboles are often used in casual speech as intensifiers,[4][5] such as saying "the bag weighed a ton".[6] Hyperbole makes the point that the speaker found the bag to be extremely heavy, although it was nothing like a literal ton.[7] Understanding hyperboles and their use in context can further one's ability to understand the messages being sent from the speaker. It has been established that use of hyperboles relays emotions. They can be used in a form of humour, excitement, distress, and many other emotions, all depending on the context in which the speaker uses it.[8]

39.2 Examples

- Referring to a scratch as a *wound*.

- Referring to a game won by a wide margin as a *slaughter*.

- Referring to a failure as a *trainwreck*.

39.3 See also

- Litotes & meiosis, deliberate understatement

39.4 References

[1] "Hyperbole". Oxford Advanced Learner's Dictionary. Retrieved February 15, 2012.

[2] "Hyperbole". Dictionary.com. Retrieved February 15, 2012.

[3] "Hyperbole". Utk.edu. Retrieved 10 January 2014.

[4] "Definition of Hyperbole". Retrieved 10 January 2014.

[5] http://www.merriam-webster.com/dictionary/hyperbole

[6] Mahony, David (2003). *Literacy Tests Year 7*. Pascal Press. p. 82. ISBN 978-1-877-08536-9.

[7] "Hyperbole". Byu.edu. Retrieved 10 January 2014.

[8] Johnson, Christopher. "The Rhetoric of Excess in Baroque Literature and Thought" (PDF). *Scholar.havard.edu*. Harvard.

39.5 External links

- Examples of hyperbole in poetry

- Definition and Examples of Hyperbole

- Johnson, Christopher. "The Rhetoric of Excess in Baroque Literature and Thought" (PDF). *Scholar.havard.edu*. Harvard.

- Ritter, Joshua. "Recovering Hyperbole: Re-Imagining the Limits of Rhetoric for an age of Excess". *scholarworks.gsu.edu*. Georgia State University.

Chapter 40

Imagery

This article is about imagery in literary texts. For imagery in cognitive psychology, see mental image. For various senses of the word imaging, see Imaging (disambiguation).

Imagery, in a literary text, is an author's use of vivid and descriptive language to add depth to his or her work. It appeals to human senses to deepen the reader's understanding of the work. Powerful forms of imagery engage all of the senses pro lenses.

40.1 Forms of imagery

There are seven types of imagery, each corresponding to a sense, feeling, or action:

- **Visual imagery** pertains to graphics, visual scenes, pictures, or the sense of sight.

- **Auditory imagery** pertains to sounds, noises, music, or the sense of hearing. (This kind of imagery may come in the form of onomatopoeia).

- **Olfactory imagery** pertains to odors, scents, or the sense of smell.

- **Gustatory imagery** pertains to flavors or the sense of taste.

- **Tactile imagery** pertains to physical textures or the sense of touch.

40.2 Less Used

- **Kinesthetic imagery** pertains to movements or the sense of bodily motion.

- **Organic imagery** or **subjective imagery**, pertains to personal experiences of a character's body, including emotion and the senses of hunger, thirst, fatigue, and pain.[1]

40.3 References

[1] "Poetics of Robert Frost: Examples". Friends of Robert Frost. Retrieved 12 March 2013.

40.4 External links

- Imagery and Imagination entry in the *Internet Encyclopedia of Philosophy*

- Thomas, Nigel J.T (Winter 2011), Zalta, Edward N., ed., "Mental Imagery", *The Stanford Encyclopedia of Philosophy* (Stanford University), retrieved February 16, 2012

Chapter 41

Theme (narrative)

In contemporary literary studies, a **theme** is the central topic a text treats.[*][1] Themes can be divided into two categories: a work's *thematic concept* is what readers "think the work is about" and its *thematic statement* being "what the work says about the subject".[*][2]

The most common contemporary understanding of theme is an idea or point that is central to a story, which can often be summed in a single word (e.g. love, death, betrayal). Typical examples of themes of this type are conflict between the individual and society; coming of age; humans in conflict with technology; nostalgia; and the dangers of unchecked ambition.[*][3] A theme may be exemplified by the actions, utterances, or thoughts of a character in a novel. An example of this would be the theme loneliness in John Steinbeck's *Of Mice and Men*, wherein many of the characters seem to be lonely. It may differ from the thesis—the text's or author's implied worldview.[*][4]

A story may have several themes. Themes often explore historically common or cross-culturally recognizable ideas, such as ethical questions, and are usually implied rather than stated explicitly. An example of this would be whether one should live a seemingly better life, at the price of giving up parts of one's humanity, which is a theme in Aldous Huxley's *Brave New World*. Along with plot, character, setting, and style, theme is considered one of the components of fiction.[*][5]

41.1 Techniques

Various techniques may be used to express many more themes.

41.1.1 Leitwortstil

Leitwortstil is the repetition of a wording, often with a theme, in a narrative to make sure it catches the reader's attention.[*][6] An example of a leitwortstil is the recurring phrase, "So it goes", in Kurt Vonnegut's novel *Slaughterhouse-Five*. Its seeming message is that the world is deterministic: that things only could have happened in one way, and that the future already is predetermined. But given the anti-war tone of the story, the message perhaps is on the contrary, that *things could have been different*. A non-fictional example of leitwortstil is in the book *Too Soon Old, Too Late Smart: Thirty True Things You Need to Know Now* written by Gordon Livingston, which is an anthology of personal anecdotes multiple times interjected by the phrases "Don't do the same thing and expect different results", "It is a bad idea to lie to yourself", and "No one likes to be told what to do".

41.1.2 Thematic patterning

Thematic patterning means the insertion of a recurring motif in a narrative.[*][7] For example, various scenes in John Steinbeck's *Of Mice and Men* are about loneliness.[*][8] Thematic patterning is evident in *One Thousand and One Nights*,[*][9] an example being the story of "The City of Brass". According to David Pinault, the overarching theme of that tale, in which a group of travellers roam the desert in search of ancient brass artifacts, is that "riches and pomp tempt one away from God".*[10] The narrative is interrupted several times by stories within the story. These include a tale recorded in an inscription found in the palace of Kush ibn Shaddad; a story told by a prisoner about Solomon; and an episode involving Queen Tadmur's corpse. According to Pinault, "each of these minor narratives introduces a character who confesses that he once proudly enjoyed worldly prosperity: subsequently, we learn, the given character has been brought low by God ... These minor tales ultimately reinforce the theme of the major narrative".*[10]

41.2   See also

- Literary element

- Moral

- Motif (narrative)

41.3   References

[1] *Oxford English Dictionary*, retrieved January 26, 2012

[2] Griffith, Kelley (2010), *Writing Essays about Literature* (8 ed.), Cengage Learning, p. 40, ISBN 1428290419, retrieved February 10, 2013

[3] Kirszner, Laura G.; Mandell, Stephen R. (1994), *Fiction: Reading, Reacting, Writing*, Paulinas, pp. 3–4, ISBN 015501014X, retrieved February 11, 2013

[4] Weitz, Morris (2002), "Literature Without Philosophy: "Antony and Cleopatra"", *Shakespeare Survey* **28**, Cambridge University Press, p. 30, ISBN 0521523656, retrieved February 10, 2013

[5] Obstfeld, 2002, p. 1, 65, 115, 171.

[6] Pinault, David (1992), *Story Telling Techniques in the "Arabian Nights"*, Studies in Arabic Literature **15**, Brill, p. 18, ISBN 9004095306, retrieved February 10, 2013

[7] Pinault, David. 1992. *Story-telling techniques in the Arabian nights*. Leiden: Brill. p. 22. ISBN 9004095306

[8] Scalia, Joseph E.; Shamblin, Lena T. & Research and Education Association (2001), *John Steinbeck's Of mice and men*, Piscataway, N.J: Research & Education Association, p. 13, ISBN 087891997X, retrieved February 11, 2013

[9] Heath, Peter (May 1994), "Reviewed work(s) *Story-Telling Techniques in the Arabian Nights* by David Pinault", *International Journal of Middle East Studies* (Cambridge University Press) **26** (2): 358–360 [359–60], doi:10.1017/s0020743800060633

[10] Pinault, David. 1992. *Story-telling techniques in the Arabian nights*. Leiden: Brill. p. 23. ISBN 9004095306

- Obstfeld, Raymond (2002), *Fiction First Aid: Instant Remedies for Novels, Stories and Scripts*, Cincinnati, OH: Writer's Digest Books, ISBN 1-58297-117-X

41.4   External links

- The dictionary definition of theme at Wiktionary

Chapter 42

Metonymy

Not to be confused with meronymy or meronomy.

Metonymy (/mi'tɒnimi/ *mi-TONN-ə-mee*)*[1] is a figure of speech in which a thing or concept is called not by its own name but rather by the name of something associated in meaning with that thing or concept.*[2] The words "metonymy" and "metonym" come from the Greek: μετωνυμία, *metōnymía*, "a change of name", from μετά, *metá*, "after, beyond" and -ωνυμία, *-ōnymía*, a suffix used to name figures of speech, from ὄνυμα, *ónyma* or ὄνομα, *ónoma*, "name".*[3]

For instance, "Wall Street" is often used metonymously to describe the U.S. financial and corporate sector, while "Hollywood" is used as a metonym for the U.S. film industry because of the fame and cultural identity of Hollywood, a district of the city of Los Angeles, California, as the historical center of film studios and film stars.*[4] The national capital is often used to represent the government or monarchy of a country, such as "Washington" for United States government.

Metonymy and related figures of speech are common in everyday talk and writing. Synecdoche and metalepsis are considered specific types of metonymy. Polysemy, multiple meanings of a single word or phrase, sometimes results from relations of metonymy. Both metonymy and metaphor involve the substitution of one term for another.*[5] In metaphor, this substitution is based on some specific analogy between two things, whereas in metonymy the substitution is based on some understood association or contiguity.*[6]*[7]

American literary theorist Kenneth Burke described metonymy as one of four "master tropes": metaphor, a substitute for perspective; metonymy, a substitute for reduction; synecdoche, a substitute for representation; and irony, a substitute for dialectic. He described these tropes and the way they overlap in *A Grammar of Motives*.*[8]

In addition to its use in everyday speech, metonymy is a figure of speech in some poetry and in much rhetoric. Greek and Latin scholars of rhetoric made significant contributions to the study of metonymy.

42.1 Meaning relationships

Synecdoche, wherein a specific part of something is used to refer to the whole, or the whole to a specific part, usually is understood as a specific kind of metonymy. However, sometimes people make an absolute distinction between a metonymy and a synecdoche, treating metonymy as different from, rather than inclusive of, synecdoche. There is a similar problem with the use of simile and metaphor.

When the distinction is made, it is the following: when "A" is used to refer to "B", it is a synecdoche if A is a component of B or if B is a component of A, and a metonym if A is commonly associated with B but not part of its whole or a whole of its part. Thus, "20,000 hungry mouths to feed" is a synecdoche because mouths (A) are a part of the people (B) referred to. "Australia votes" is also a synecdoche because Australia is a whole of which the people who voted are a part. On the other hand, "The White House said" is metonymy, but not synecdoche, for the president and his staff, because, although the White House is associated with the president and his staff, the building is not a part of the people.

Metalepsis is also closely related to metonymy. Much as synecdoche, it is sometimes understood as a specific kind of metonymy. Metalepsis is a figure of speech in which a word or a phrase from figurative speech is used in a new context. The new figure of speech refers to an existing one.*[9] For example, in the idiom *lead foot*, meaning someone who drives fast, lead is a heavy substance, and a heavy foot on the accelerator pedal would cause a vehicle to go quickly. The use of "lead foot" to describe a person follows the intermediate substitution of "lead" for "heavy".*[10] The figure of speech is a "metonymy of a metonymy".*[9]

The concept of metonymy also informs the nature of polysemy, i.e., how the same phonological form (word) has different semantic mappings (meanings). If the two meanings are unrelated, as in the word *pen* meaning both *writing instrument* and *enclosure*, they are considered homonyms.

Within logical polysemies, a large class of mappings may be considered to be a case of metonymic transfer (e.g., *chicken* for the animal, as well as its meat; *crown* for the object, as well as the institution). Other cases wherein the meaning is polysemous, however, may turn out to be more metaphorical, e.g., *eye* as in the *eye of the needle*.

42.1.1   Metaphor and metonymy

Main article: Metaphor and metonymy

Metonymy works by the contiguity (association) between two concepts, whereas the term *metaphor* is based upon their analogous similarity. When people use metonymy, they do not typically wish to transfer qualities from one referent to another as they do with metaphor.*[11] There is nothing press-like about reporters or crown-like about a monarch, but "the press" and "the crown" are both common metonyms. Some uses of figurative language may be understood as both metonymy and metaphor; for example, the relationship between "a crown" and a "king" could be interpreted metaphorically (i.e., the king, like his gold crown, could be seemingly stiff yet ultimately malleable, over-ornate, and consistently immobile).

Two examples using the term "fishing" help clarify the distinction.*[12] The phrase "to fish pearls" uses *metonymy*, drawing from "fishing" the idea of taking things from the ocean. What is carried across from "fishing fish" to "fishing pearls" is the domain of *metonymy*.

In contrast, the metaphorical phrase "fishing for information" transfers the concept of fishing into a new domain. If someone is "fishing" for information, we do not imagine that the person is anywhere near the ocean; rather, we transpose elements of the action of fishing (waiting, hoping to catch something that cannot be seen, probing) into a new domain (a conversation). Thus, metaphor works by presenting a target set of meanings and using them to suggest a similarity between items, actions, or events in two domains, whereas metonymy calls up or references a specific domain (here, removing items from the sea).

42.1.2   Examples

Main article: List of metonyms

Here are some broad kinds of relationships where metonymy is frequently used:

- Containment: When one thing contains another, it can frequently be used metonymically, as when "dish" is used to refer not to a plate but to the food it contains, or as when the name of a building is used to refer to the entity it contains, as when "the White House" or "the Pentagon" are used to refer to the U.S. presidential staff or the military leadership, respectively.

- Tools/Instruments: Often a tool is used to signify the job it does or the person who does the job, as in the phrase "the press" (referring to the printing press), or as in the proverb, "The pen is mightier than the sword."

- Product for Process: This is a type of metonymy where the product of the activity stands for the activity itself. For example, in "The book is moving right along," *the book* refers to the process of writing or publishing.*[13]

- Punctuation marks often stand metonymically for a meaning expressed by the punctuation mark. For example, "He's a big *question mark* to me" indicates that something is unknown.*[14]

- Synecdoche: A part of something is often used for the whole, as when people refer to "head" of cattle or assistants are referred to as "hands." An example of this is the Canadian dollar, referred to as the loonie for the image of a bird on the one-dollar coin. Also, the whole of something is used for a part, as when people refer to a municipal employee as "the council" or police officers as "the law".

- Toponyms: A country's capital city is frequently used as a metonym for the country's government, such as Washington, D.C., in the United States. Similarly, other important places, such as Wall Street, Madison Avenue, Silicon Valley, Hollywood, and Detroit are commonly used to refer to the industries that are located there (finance, advertising, high technology, entertainment, and motor vehicles, respectively). Such usage may persist even when the industries in question have moved elsewhere - for example, *Fleet Street* continues to be used as a metonym for the British national press, though it is no longer located in the physical street of that name.

Sometimes, metaphor and metonymy may both be at work in the same figure of speech, or one could interpret a phrase metaphorically or metonymically. For example, the phrase "lend me your ear" could be analyzed in a number of ways. One could imagine the following interpretations:

- Analyze "ear" metonymically first – "ear" means "attention" (because we use ears to pay attention to someone's speech). Now, when we hear the phrase "lending an ear (attention)", we stretch the base meaning of "lend" (to let someone borrow an object) to include the "lending" of non-material things (attention), but, beyond this slight extension of the verb, no metaphor is at work.

- Imagine the whole phrase literally – imagine that the speaker literally borrows the listener's ear as a physical object (and the person's head with it). Then the speaker has temporary possession of the listener's ear, so the listener has granted the speaker temporary control over what the listener hears. We then interpret the phrase "lend me your ear" metaphorically to mean that the speaker wants the listener to grant the speaker temporary control over what the listener hears.

- First, analyze the verb phrase "lend me your ear" metaphorically to mean "turn your ear in my direction", since we know that, literally, lending a body part is nonsensical. Then, analyze the motion of ears metonymically – we associate "turning ears" with "paying attention", which is what the speaker wants the listeners to do.

It is difficult to say which of the above analyses most closely represents the way a listener interprets the expression, and it is possible that the phrase is analysed in different ways by different listeners, or even in different ways by the same listener at different times. Regardless, all three analyses yield the same interpretation; thus, metaphor and metonymy, though quite different in their mechanism, may work together seamlessly.*[15]

42.2   Rhetoric in ancient history

Western culture studied poetic language and deemed it to be rhetoric. A. Al-Sharafi supports this concept in his book *Textual Metonymy*, "Greek rhetorical scholarship at one time became entirely poetic scholarship." *[16] Philosophers and rhetoricians thought that metaphors were the primary figurative language used in rhetoric. Metaphors served as a better means to attract the audience's attention because the audience had to read between the lines in order to get an understanding of what the speaker was trying to say. Others did not think of metonymy as a good rhetorical method because metonymy did not involve symbolism. Al-Sharafi explains, "This is why they undermined practical and purely referential discourse because it was seen as banal and not containing anything new, strange or shocking." *[16]

Greek scholars contributed to the definition of metonymy. For example, Isocrates worked to define the difference between poetic language and non-poetic language by saying that "prose writers are handicapped in this regard because their discourse has to conform to the forms and terms used by the citizens and to those arguments which are precise and relevant to the subject-matter. In other words, Isocrates proposes here that metaphor is a distinctive feature of poetic language because it conveys the experience of the world afresh and provides a kind of defamiliarisation in the way the citizens perceive the world." *[16] Democritus described metonymy by saying, "Metonymy, that is the fact that words and meaning change." *[16] Aristotle discussed different definitions of metaphor, regarding one type as what we know to be metonymy today.

Latin scholars also had an influence on metonymy. Auctor's treatise *Rhetorica ad Herennium* states metonymy as, "the figure which draws from an object closely akin or associated an expression suggesting the object meant, but not called by its own name".[16] Auctor describes the process of metonymy to us saying that we first figure out what a word means. We then figure out that word's relationship with other words. We understand and then call the word by a name that it is associated with. "Perceived as such then metonymy will be a figure of speech in which there is a process of abstracting a relation of proximity between two words to the extent that one will be used in place of another."[16] Cicero viewed metonymy as more of a stylish rhetorical method and described it as being based on words, but motivated by style.

42.3 See also

- -onym

- Antonomasia

- Deferred reference

- Eggcorn

- Eponym

- Enthymeme

- Euphemism by comparison

- Generic trademark

- Kenning

- Meronymy

- Newspeak

- Pars pro toto

- Pun

- Sobriquet

- Social stereotype

- Totum pro parte

42.4 References

42.4.1 Notes

[1] "Metonymy | Define Metonymy at Dictionary.com". Dictionary.reference.com. Retrieved 2013-01-17.

[2] "Metonymy - Definition and More from the Free Merriam-Webster Dictionary". Merriam-webster.com. 2012-08-31. Retrieved 2013-08-13.

[3] Welsh, Alfred Hux; James Mickleborough Greenwood (1893). *Studies in English Grammar: A Comprehensive Course for Grammar Schools, High Schools, and Academies*. New York City: Silver Burdett. p. 222.

[4] Gibbs, Jr., Raymond W. (1999). *"Speaking and Thinking with Metyonymy"*, in *Pattern and process: a Whiteheadina perspective on linguistics, ed. Klaus-Uwe Panther and Günter Radden*. Amsterdam: John Benjamins Publishing. pp. 61–76. ISBN 9027223564.

[5] Dirven, René; Pörings, Ralf (2002). *Metaphor and Metonymy in Comparison and Contrast*. Walter de Gruyter. ISBN 978-3-11-017373-4.

[6] Wilber, Ken (2000). *Sex, Ecology, Spirituality*. Shambhala Publications. ISBN 978-0-8348-2108-8.

[7] Tompkins, Penny; James Lawley. "Metonymy and Part-Whole Relationships". www.cleanlanguage.co.uk. Retrieved 19 December 2012.

[8] Burke, Kenneth. (1945) *A Grammar of Motives*. New York: Prentice Hall Inc. pp 503-509.

[9] Bloom, Harold (2003). *A Map of Misreading*. Oxford University Press. ISBN 978-0-19-516221-9.

[10] "metalepsis". *Silva Rhetoricae*. Retrieved 2013-12-05.

[11] Chandler, Daniel. "Rhetorical Tropes". *Semiotics for Beginners*. Aberystwyth University. Retrieved 19 December 2012.

[12] example drawn from Dirven, 1996

[13] Lakoff and Johnson 1999, p. 203

[14] Lakoff and Johnson 1999, p. 245

[15] Geeraerts, Dirk (2002). "The interaction of metaphor and metonymy in composite expressions". In R. Dirven and R. Pörings. *Metaphor and Metonymy in Comparison and Contrast* (PDF). Walter de Gruyter. pp. 435–465. ISBN 978-3-11-017373-4. Retrieved 30 November 2013.

[16] Al-Sharafi, Abdul Gabbar (2004). *Textual Metonymy: A Semiotic Approach*.

42.4.2 Bibliography

- Blank, Andreas (1997). *Prinzipien des lexikalischen Bedeutungswandels am Beispiel der romanischen Sprachen*. Walter de Gruyter. ISBN 978-3-11-093160-0.

- Corbett, Edward P.J. (1998) [1971]. *Classical Rhetoric for the Modern Student* (4th ed.). New York: Oxford University Press. ISBN 978-0-19-511542-0.

- Dirven, René (1999). "Conversion as a Conceptual Metonymy of Event Schemata". In K.U. Panther and G. Radden. *Metonymy in Language and Thought*. John Benjamins Publishing. pp. 275–288. ISBN 978-90-272-2356-2.

- Fass, Dan (1997). *Processing Metonymy and Metaphor*. Ablex. ISBN 978-1-56750-231-2.

- Grzega, Joachim (2004). *Bezeichnungswandel: Wie, Warum, Wozu? Ein Beitrag zur englischen und allgemeinen Onomasiologie*. Heidelberg: Universitätsverlag Winter. ISBN 978-3-8253-5016-1.

- Lakoff, George; Johnson, mark (1999). *Philosophy in the Flesh: The Embodied Mind and Its Challenge to Western Thought*. Basic Books. ISBN 978-0-465-05674-3.

- Somov, Georgij Yu. (2009). "Metonymy and its manifestation in visual artworks: Case study of late paintings by Bruegel the Elder". *Semiotica* **2009** (174): 309–66. doi:10.1515/semi.2009.037.

- Smyth, Herbert Weir (1920). *Greek Grammar*. Cambridge MA: Harvard University Press. p. 680. ISBN 0-674-36250-0.

- Warren, Beatrice (2006). *Referential Metonymy*. Publications of the Royal Society of Letters at Lund. Lund, Sweden: Almqvist & Wiksell International. ISBN 978-91-22-02148-3.

42.5   Further reading

- Fass, Dan (1988). "Metonymy and metaphor: what's the difference?". *Proceedings of the 12th conference on Computational linguistics* **1**. pp. 177–81. doi:10.3115/991635.991671. ISBN 963-8431-56-3.

- Gaines, Charles (2003). "Reconsidering Metaphor/Metonymy: Art and the Suppression of Thought" (64).

- Jakobson, Roman (1995) [1956]. "Two Aspects of Language and Two Types of Disturbances". In Linda Waugh and Monique Monville-Burston. *On Language.* Cambridge, MA: Harvard University Press. ISBN 0-674-63536-1.

- Lakoff, George (1980). *Metaphors We Live By.* Chicago, IL: The University of Chicago Press. ISBN 0-226-46801-1.

- Low, Graham. "An Essay Is a Person". In Cameron, Lynne; Low, Graham. *Researching and Applying Metaphor.* Cambridge: Cambridge University Press. pp. 221–48. ISBN 978-0-521-64964-3.

- Pérez-Sobrino, Paula (2014). "Meaning construction in verbomusical environments: Conceptual disintegration and metonymy" (PDF). *Journal of Pragmatics* (Elsevier) **70**: 130–151. doi:10.1016/j.pragma.2014.06.008.

- Peters, Wim (2003). "Metonymy as a cross-lingual phenomenon" (PDF). *Proceedings of the ACL 2003 Workshop on Lexicon and Figurative Language* **14**: 1–9. doi:10.3115/1118975.1118976.

42.6   External links

- The dictionary definition of metonymy at Wiktionary

Chapter 43

Onomatopoeia

This article is about a category of words. It is not to be confused with the comic character, called Onomatopoeia.

An **onomatopoeia** (🔊i/ˌɒnəmaːtəˈpiːə/,*[1]*[2] or chiefly NZ /-ˈpeɪə/; from the Greek ὀνοματοποιία;*[3] ὄνομα for

A sign in a shop window in Italy proclaims "No Tic Tac", in imitation of the sound of a clock.

"name" *[4] and ποιέω for "I make" ,*[5] adjectival form: "onomatopoeic" or "onomatopoetic") is a word that phonetically imitates, resembles or suggests the source of the sound that it describes. **Onomatopoeia** (as an uncountable noun) refers to the property of such words. Common occurrences of onomatopoeias include animal noises such as "oink" , "miaow" (or "meow"), "roar" or "chirp" . Onomatopoeias are not the same across all languages; they conform to some extent to the broader linguistic system they are part of;[6][7] hence the sound of a clock may be *tick tock* in English, *dī dā* in Mandarin, or *katchin katchin* in Japanese, or "tik-tik" (टिक-टिक) in Hindi.

Although in the English language the term onomatopoeia means the imitation of a sound, in the Greek language the compound word onomatopoeia (ονοματοποιία) means "making or creating names". For words that imitate sounds, the term Ηχομμημτικό (echomimetico or echomimetic) is used. Ηχομμημτικό (echomimetico) derives from Ηχώ, meaning "echo or sound" and μμημτικό, meaning "mimetic or imitation".

43.1   Uses of onomatopoeia

In the case of a frog croaking, the spelling may vary because different frog species around the world make different sounds: Ancient Greek *brekekekex koax koax* (only in Aristophanes' comic play *The Frogs*) for probably *marsh frogs*; English *ribbit* for species of frog found in North America; English verb *croak* for the *common frog*.[8]

Some other very common English-language examples include *hiccup, zoom, bang, beep, moo,* and *splash*. Machines and their sounds are also often described with onomatopoeia, as in *honk* or *beep-beep* for the horn of an automobile, and *vroom* or *brum* for the engine. When someone speaks of a mishap involving an audible arcing of electricity, the word "zap" is often used (and has subsequently been expanded and used to describe non-auditory effects generally connoting the same sort of localized but thorough interference or destruction similar to that produced in short-circuit sparking).

For animal sounds, words like *quack* (duck), *moo* (cow), *bark* or *woof* (dog), *roar* (lion), *meow/miaow* or *purr* (cat), *cluck* (chicken) and *baa* (sheep) are typically used in English. Some of these words are used both as nouns and as verbs.

Some languages flexibly integrate onomatopoeic words into their structure. This may evolve into a new word, up to the point that it is no longer recognized as onomatopoeia. One example is English "bleat" for the sheep noise: in medieval times it was pronounced approximately as "blairt" (but without an R-component), or "blet" with the vowel drawled, which is much more accurate as onomatopoeia than the modern pronunciation.

An example of the opposite case is "cuckoo", which, due to continuous familiarity with the bird noise down the centuries, has kept approximately the same pronunciation as in Anglo-Saxon times and its vowels have not changed as they have in the word "furrow".

Verba dicendi are a method of integrating onomatopoeia and ideophones into grammar.

Sometimes things are named from the sounds they make. In English, for example, there is the universal fastener which is named for the onomatopoeic of the sound it makes: the zip (in the UK) or zipper (in the U.S.). Many birds are named after their calls, such as the bobwhite quail, the weero, the morepork, the killdeer, chickadee, the cuckoo, the chiffchaff, the whooping crane and the whip-poor-will. In Tamil and Malayalam, the word for crow is *kaakaa*. This practice is especially common in certain languages such as Māori and, therefore, in names of animals borrowed from these languages.

43.1.1   Cross-cultural differences

Although a particular sound is heard similarly by people of different cultures, it is often expressed through the use of different consonant strings in different languages. For example, the "*snip*" of a pair of scissors is *su-su* in Chinese, *cri-cri* in Italian, *riqui-riqui* in Spanish, *terre-terre* or *treque-treque* in Portuguese, *krits-krits* in modern Greek and *katr-katr* in Hindi.[9] Similarly, the "honk" of a car's horn is *ba-ba* in Chinese, *tut-tut* in French, *pu-pu* in Japanese, *bbang-bbang* in Korean, *bært-bært* in Norwegian, *fom-fom* in Portuguese and *bim-bim* in Vietnamese.

43.1.2   Onomatopoeic effect without onomatopoeia words

Onomatopoeic effect can also be produced in a phrase or word string with the help of alliteration and consonance alone, without using any onomatopoeic words. The most famous example is the phrase "*furrow followed free*" in Samuel Taylor Coleridge's *The Rime of the Ancient Mariner*. It may be noted that the words "followed" and "free" are not onomatopoeic in themselves, but in conjunction with "forrow", they reproduce the sound of ripples following in the wake of a speeding ship. Similarly, alliteration has been used in the line *"as the surf surged up the sun swept shore..."* , to recreate the sound of breaking waves, in the poem *"I, She and the Sea"* .

43.2 Comics and advertising

Comic strips and comic books made extensive use of onomatopoeia. Popular culture historian Tim DeForest noted the impact of writer-artist Roy Crane (1901–1977), the creator of *Captain Easy* and *Buz Sawyer*:

> It was Crane who pioneered the use of onomatopoeic sound effects in comics, adding "bam," "pow" and "wham" to what had previously been an almost entirely visual vocabulary. Crane had fun with this, tossing in an occasional "ker-splash" or "lickety-wop" along with what would become the more standard effects. Words as well as images became vehicles for carrying along his increasingly fast-paced storylines.[10]

In 2002, DC Comics introduced a villain named Onomatopoeia, an athlete, martial artist and weapons expert who often speaks sounds.

Advertising uses onomatopoeia as a mnemonic, so consumers will remember their products, as in Alka-Seltzer's "Plop, plop, fizz, fizz. Oh, what a relief it is!" jingle, recorded in two different versions (big band and rock) by Sammy Davis, Jr.

Rice Krispies (US and UK) and Rice Bubbles (AU) make a "snap, crackle, pop" when one pours on milk. During the 1930s, the illustrator Vernon Grant developed Snap, Crackle and Pop as gnome-like mascots for the Kellogg Company.

Sounds surface in road safety advertisements: "clunk click, every trip" (click the seatbelt on after clunking the car door closed; UK campaign) or "click, clack, front and back" (click, clack of connecting the seatbelts; AU campaign) or "click it or ticket" (click of the connecting seatbelt; US DOT campaign).

43.2.1 Manner imitation

Main article: Ideophone

In many of the world's languages, onomatopoeia-like words are used to describe phenomena apart from the purely auditive. Japanese often utilizes such words to describe feelings or figurative expressions about objects or concepts. For instance, Japanese *barabara* is used to reflect an object's state of disarray or separation, and *shiin* is the onomatopoetic form of absolute silence (used at the time an English speaker might expect to hear the sound of crickets chirping or a pin dropping in a silent room, or someone coughing). It is used in English as well with terms like *bling*, which describes the glinting of light on things like gold, chrome or precious stones. In Japanese, *kirakira* is used for glittery things.

43.3 Examples in media

- James Joyce in *Ulysses* (1922) coined the onomatopoeic *tattarrattat* for a knock on the door.[11] It is listed as the longest palindromic word in *The Oxford English Dictionary*.[12]

- *Whaam!* (1963) by Roy Lichtenstein is an early example of pop art, featuring a reproduction of comic book art that depicts a fighter aircraft striking another with rockets with dazzling red and yellow explosions.

- In the 1960s TV series *Batman*, comic book style onomatopoeias such as *wham!*, *pow!*, *biff!*, *crunch!* and *zounds!* appear onscreen during fight scenes.

- Ubisoft's *XIII* employed the use of comic book onomatopoeias such as *bam!*, *boom!* and *noooo!* during gameplay for gunshots, explosions and kills, respectively. The comic-book style is apparent throughout the game and is a core theme, and the game is an adaptation of a comic book of the same name.

- The chorus of American popular song writer John Prine's song "Onomatopoeia" cleverly incorporates onomatopoeic words (though as discussed, 'ouch!' is not the sound of pain): "Bang! went the pistol. | Crash! went the window. | Ouch! went the son of a gun. | Onomatopoeia | I don't wanna see ya | Speaking in a foreign tongue."

- The marble game KerPlunk is an onomatopoeia for the sound of the marbles dropping when one too many sticks has been removed.

- The Nickelodeon cartoon *Kablam* is implied to be onomotapoeic to a crash.

- Each episode of the TV series *Harper's Island* is given an onomatopoeic name which imitates the sound made in that episode when a character dies. For example, in the episode titled "*Bang*" a character is shot and fatally wounded, with the "Bang" mimicking the sound of the gunshot.

43.4 Cross-linguistic examples

Main article: Cross-linguistic onomatopoeias

43.5 See also

- Anguish Languish

- List of animal sounds

- List of onomatopoeias

- Sound symbolism
  - Japanese sound symbolism

- Vocal learning

- Sound mimesis in various cultures

43.6 References

43.6.1 Notes

[1] Wells, John C. (2008), *Longman Pronunciation Dictionary* (3rd ed.), Longman, ISBN 9781405881180

[2] Roach, Peter (2011), *Cambridge English Pronouncing Dictionary* (18th ed.), Cambridge: Cambridge University Press, ISBN 9780521152532

[3] ὀνοματοποιία, Henry George Liddell, Robert Scott, *A Greek-English Lexicon*, on Perseus

[4] ὄνομα, Henry George Liddell, Robert Scott, *A Greek-English Lexicon*, on Perseus

[5] ποιέω, Henry George Liddell, Robert Scott, *A Greek-English Lexicon*, on Perseus

[6] Onomatopoeia as a Figure and a Linguistic Principle, Hugh Bredin, The Johns Hopkins University, Retrieved November 14, 2013

[7] Definition of Onomatopoeia, Retrieved November 14, 2013

[8] *Basic Reading of Sound Words-Onomatopoeia*, Yale University, retrieved October 11, 2013

[9] Earl Anderson, *A Grammar of Iconism*, Fairleigh Dickinson, 1999

[10] DeForest, Tim (2004). *Storytelling in the Pulps, Comics, and Radio: How Technology Changed Popular Fiction in America.* McFarland.

[11] James Joyce (1982). *Ulysses.* Editions Artisan Devereaux. pp. 434–. ISBN 978-1-936694-38-9. ...I was just beginning to yawn with nerves thinking he was trying to make a fool of me when I knew his tattarrattat at the door he must ...

[12] O.A. Booty (1 January 2002). *Funny Side of English.* Pustak Mahal. pp. 203–. ISBN 978-81-223-0799-3. The longest palindromic word in English has 12 letters: tattarrattat. This word, appearing in the Oxford English Dictionary, was invented by James Joyce and used in his book Ulysses (1922), and is an imitation of the sound of someone ...

43.6.2 General references

• Crystal, David (1997). *The Cambridge Encyclopedia of Language* (2nd ed.). Cambridge University Press. ISBN 0-521-55967-7.

• Smyth, Herbert Weir (1920). *Greek Grammar.* Cambridge MA: Harvard University Press. p. 680. ISBN 0-674-36250-0.

43.7 External links

• Derek Abbott's Animal Noise Page

• Over 300 Examples of Onomatopoeia

• BBC Radio 4 show discussing animal noises

• Tutorial on Drawing Onomatopoeia for Comics and Cartoons (using fonts)

• WrittenSound, onomatopoeic word list

• Examples of Onomatopeia

Chapter 44

Oxymoron

This article is about the contradiction in terms. For the punk band, see Oxymoron (band). For the album by rapper Schoolboy Q, see Oxymoron (album).

An **oxymoron** (plural **oxymora** or **oxymorons**) is a figure of speech that juxtaposes elements that appear to be contradictory. Oxymora appear in a variety of contexts, including inadvertent errors (such as "ground pilot") and literary oxymorons crafted to reveal a paradox.

44.1 Types

The most common form of oxymoron involves an adjective–noun combination of two words. For example, the following line from Tennyson's *Idylls of the King* contains two oxymora:

> And faith unfaithful kept him falsely true.

Other examples of oxymora of this kind include:

- Dark light

- Living dead *(but has been used for a type of supernatural being)*

- Guest host (also: Permanent guest host)

- Crazy wisdom

- Mournful optimist

- Violent relaxation *(but has been used as a technical term in development of galaxies)*

Less often seen are noun–verb combinations of two words, such as the line "The silence whistles" from Nathan Alterman's "Summer Night", or in a song title like Simon & Garfunkel's "The Sound of Silence".

Oxymora are not always a pair of words; they can also be devised in the meaning of sentences or phrases.

44.2 Etymology

Oxymoron is derived from the 5th century Latin *oxymoron*, which is derived from the Ancient Greek: ὀξύς *oxus* "sharp, keen" and μωρός *mōros* "dull, stupid", making the word itself an oxymoron.[1] However, the combined Greek form ὀξύμωρον (*oxumōron*) does not in fact appear in the extant Greek sources.[2]

44.3   Taxonomy

Richard Lederer assembled a taxonomy of oxymora in an article in *Word Ways* in 1990,*[3] running from single-word oxymora such as "pianoforte" (literally, "soft-loud") through "doublespeak oxymora" (deliberately intended to confuse) and "opinion oxymora" (editorial opinions designed to provoke a laugh). In general, oxymora can be divided into expressions that were deliberately crafted to be contradictory and those phrases that inadvertently or incidentally contain a contradiction, often as a result of a punning use of one or both words.

44.4   Apparent oxymora

Many oxymora have been popularised in vernacular speech. Examples include "controlled chaos", "an honourable death", "open secret", "organized mess", "alone in a crowd", and "accidentally on purpose".

There are also examples in which terms that are superficially contradictory are juxtaposed in such a way that there is no contradiction. Examples include "same difference", "jumbo shrimp", and "hot ice" (where "hot" means "stolen" and "ice" means "diamonds", in criminal argot).

44.5   Oxymora as paradoxes

Writers often use an oxymoron to call attention to an apparent contradiction. For example, Wilfred Owen's poem "The Send-off" refers to soldiers leaving for the front line, who "lined the train with faces grimly gay." The oxymoron "grimly gay" highlights the contradiction between how the soldiers feel and how they act: though they put on a brave face and act cheerfully, they feel grim.

Similarly, in Henry James' novella *The Lesson of the Master*, a character is described as dressed in a manner "conventionally unconventional, suggesting a tortuous spontaneity." In this way James highlights the contradiction between the character's desire to appear spontaneous, and the efforts she makes to appear so.

One case where many oxymora are strung together can be found in Shakespeare's *Romeo and Juliet*, where Romeo declares:

> O heavy lightness! Serious vanity!
> Mis-shapen chaos of well-seeming forms!
> Feather of lead, bright smoke, cold fire, sick health!

Some paradoxical oxymora become clichés:

- Deafening silence

- Dry drunk

- Forward retreat

- Irregular pattern

- Serious joke

- Sweet sorrow

- Lead from behind

44.6   Terms falsely called oxymora for rhetorical effect

Although a true oxymoron is "something that is surprisingly true, a paradox", Garry Wills has argued that modern usage has brought a common misunderstanding*[4] that "oxymoron" is nearly synonymous with "contradiction". The introduction of this misuse, the opposite of its true meaning, has been credited to William F. Buckley.*[5]

Sometimes a pair of terms is claimed to be an oxymoron by those who hold the opinion that the two are mutually exclusive. That is, although there is no *inherent* contradiction between the terms, the speaker expresses the opinion that the two terms imply properties or characteristics that cannot occur together. Such claims may be made purely for humorous effect. Comedian George Carlin popularized many examples, such as "military intelligence", "freedom fighters", and "business ethics". Another example is the term "civil war", which is not an oxymoron, but can be claimed to be so for humorous effect, if "civil" is construed as meaning "polite" rather than "between citizens of the same state". Alternatively, such claims may reflect a genuinely held opinion or ideological position. Well-known examples include claims made against "government worker", "honest broker", "educational television", "Microsoft Works", and "working from home".

44.7   Visual and physical oxymora

In his book *More on Oxymoron*, the artist Patrick Hughes discusses and gives examples of visual oxymorons. He writes:

In the visual version of oxymoron, the material of which a thing is made (or appears to be made) takes the place of the adjective, and the thing itself (or thing represented) takes the place of the noun.*[6]

Examples include waves in the sand, a fossil tree, and topiary representing something solid like an ocean liner. Hughes lists further examples of oxymoronic objects, including:*[7]

- Artificial grass
- Bricked-up windows
- Ceramic eggs to persuade hens to lay
- Electric candles
- Floating soap
- Invisible ink
- Joke rubber coat hooks
- Plastic glass (for drinking)
- Plastic lemons
- Rubber bones for dogs
- Solid water (ice)
- Solid wooden bottle moulds
- Wax fruit
- Ironwood

44.8   Other languages

Oxymora, in the sense of "single-word oxymora" such as "pianoforte", are very common in Chinese and neighboring languages such as Japanese, and consist of two opposing Chinese characters. Archetypal examples include 男女 (man and woman, male and female, gender), 陰陽 (yin and yang), 善悪 (good and evil, morality), and are used to indicate couples, ranges, or the trait that these are extremes of.

44.9   See also

- Auto-antonym
- Colorless green ideas sleep furiously
- Contradictio in terminis
- Irony
- Paradox
- Performative contradiction
- Pleonasm (redundant phrases)
- Retronym (some retronyms form oxymorons).
- Sarcasm
- Self refuting idea
- Tautology
- Wooden iron

44.10   References

[1] ὀξύμωρος in Liddell, Henry George; Scott, Robert (1940) *A Greek–English Lexicon*, revised and augmented throughout by Jones, Sir Henry Stuart, with the assistance of McKenzie, Roderick. Oxford: Clarendon Press. In the Perseus Digital Library, Tufts University. Retrieved 2013-02-26.

[2] "oxymoron laccessdate 26 February 2013". Oxford English Dictionary.

[3] Richard Lederer, "Oxymoronology" *Word Ways: The Journal of Recreational Linguistics*, 1990, reprinted on fun-with-words.com

[4] "Wills watching by Michael McDonald". The New Criterion. Retrieved 2012-03-27.

[5] "*Daredevil* - Garry Wills". *The Atlantic.* 2009-07-01. Retrieved 2012-03-27.

[6] Hughes, Patrick (1984). *More on Oxymoron* (PDF). Jonathan Cape Ltd. p. 47. ISBN 0-224-02246-6. (This work is licensed under a Creative Commons License.) According to Hughes' website "Books authored or co-authored by Patrick Hughes". Retrieved 7 October 2010.

[7] Hughes, Patrick (1984). *More on Oxymoron*. Jonathan Cape Ltd. p. 72. ISBN 0-224-02246-6.

44.11   Further reading

- Shen, Yeshayahu (1987). "On the structure and understanding of poetic oxymoron". *Poetics Today* **8** (1): 105–122. doi:10.2307/1773004. JSTOR 1773004.

Oxymoron *by Acke Hydén, Landskrona konsthall*

Chapter 45

Paradox (literature)

This article is about the figure of speech. For other uses, see Paradox (disambiguation).

In literature, the **paradox** is an anomalous juxtaposition of incongruous ideas for the sake of striking exposition or unexpected insight. It functions as a method of literary composition - and analysis - which involves examining apparently contradictory statements and drawing conclusions either to reconcile them or to explain their presence.[1]

Literary or rhetorical paradoxes abound in the works of Oscar Wilde and G. K. Chesterton. Most literature deals with paradox of situation; Rabelais, Cervantes, Sterne, Borges, and Chesterton are recognized as masters of situation as well as verbal paradox. Statements such as Wilde's "I can resist anything except temptation" and Chesterton's "spies do not look like spies"[2] are examples of rhetorical paradox. Further back, Polonius' observation that "though this be madness, yet there is method in't" is a memorable third.[2] Also, statements that are illogical and metaphoric may be called "paradoxes", for example "the pike flew to the tree to sing". The literal meaning is illogical, but there are many interpretations for this metaphor.

45.1 Cleanth Brooks' "Language of Paradox"

Cleanth Brooks, an active member of the New Critical movement, outlines the use of reading poems through paradox as a method of critical interpretation. Paradox in poetry means that tension at the surface of a verse can lead to apparent contradictions and hypocrisies. Brooks' seminal essay, "The Language of Paradox", lays out his argument for the centrality of paradox by demonstrating that paradox is "the language appropriate and inevitable to poetry".[3] The argument is based on the contention that referential language is too vague for the specific message a poet expresses; he must "make up his language as he goes". This, Brooks argues, is because words are mutable and meaning shifts when words are placed in relation to one another.[4]

In the writing of poems, paradox is used as a method by which unlikely comparisons can be drawn and meaning can be extracted from poems both straightforward and enigmatic.

Brooks points to William Wordsworth's poem "It is a beauteous evening, calm and free".[5] He begins by outlining the initial and surface conflict, which is that the speaker is filled with worship, while his female companion does not seem to be. The paradox, discovered by the poem's end, is that the girl is more full of worship than the speaker precisely because she is always consumed with sympathy for nature and not - as is the speaker - in tune with nature while immersed in it.

In his reading of Wordsworth's poem, "Composed upon Westminster Bridge", Brooks contends that the poem offers paradox not in its details, but in the situation which the speaker creates. Though London is a man-made marvel, and in many respects in opposition to nature, the speaker does not view London as a mechanical and artificial landscape but as a landscape composed entirely of nature. Since London was created by man, and man is a part of nature, London is thus too a part of nature. It is this reason that gives the speaker the opportunity to remark upon the beauty of London as he would a natural phenomenon, and, as Brooks points out, can call the houses "sleeping" rather than "dead", because they too are vivified with the natural spark of life, granted to them by the men that built them.

Brooks ends his essay with a reading of John Donne's poem "The Canonization", which uses a paradox as its underlying metaphor. Using a charged religious term to describe the speaker's physical love as saintly, Donne effectively argues that in rejecting the material world and withdrawing to a world of each other, the two lovers are appropriate candidates for canonization. This seems to parody both love and religion, but in fact it combines them, pairing unlikely circumstances and demonstrating their resulting complex meaning. Brooks points also to secondary paradoxes in the poem: the simultaneous duality and singleness of love, and the double and contradictory meanings of "die" in Metaphysical poetry (used here as both sexual union and literal death). He contends that these several meanings are impossible to convey at the right depth and emotion in any language but that of paradox. A similar paradox is used in Shakespeare's "Romeo and Juliet", when Juliet says "For saints have hands that pilgrims' hands do touch and palm to palm is holy palmer's kiss."

Brooks' contemporaries in the sciences were, in the 40's and 50's, reorganizing university science curricula into codified disciplines. The study of English, however, remained less defined and it became a goal of the New Critical movement to justify literature in an age of science by separating the work from its author and critic (see Wimsatt and Beardsley's Intentional fallacy and Affective fallacy) and by examining it as a self-sufficient artifact. In Brooks's use of the paradox as a tool for analysis, however, he develops a logical case as a literary technique with strong emotional effect. His reading of "The Canonization" in "The Language of Paradox", where paradox becomes central to expressing complicated ideas of sacred and secular love, provides an example of this development.[4]

45.2   Paradox and irony

Although paradox and irony as New Critical tools for reading poetry are often conflated, they are independent poetical devices. Irony for Brooks is "the obvious warping of a statement by the context" [6] whereas paradox is later glossed as "a special kind of qualification which involves the resolution of opposites." [7]

Irony functions as a presence in the text – the overriding context of the surrounding words that make up the poem. Only sentences such as 2 + 2 = 4 are free from irony; most other statements are prey to their immediate context and are altered by it (take, as an example, the following joke. "A woman walks into a bar and asks for a *double entendre*. The bartender gives it to her." This last statement, perfectly acceptable elsewhere, is transformed by its context in the joke to an innuendo). Irony is the key to validating the poem because a test of any statement grows from the context – validating a statement demands examining the statement in the context of the poem and determining whether it is appropriate to that context.[6]

Paradox, however, is essential to the structure and being of the poem. In *The Well Wrought Urn* Brooks shows that paradox was so essential to poetic meaning that paradox was almost identical to poetry. According to literary theorist Leroy Searle, Brooks' use of paradox emphasized the indeterminate lines between form and content. "The form of the poem uniquely embodies its meaning" and the language of the poem "affects the reconciliation of opposites or contraries." While irony functions within the poem, paradox often refers to the meaning and structure of the poem and is thus inclusive of irony.[8] This existence of opposites or contraries and the reconciliation thereof is poetry and the meaning of the poem.

45.3   Criticism

R.S. Crane, in his essay "The Critical Monism of Cleanth Brooks," argues strongly against Brooks' centrality of paradox. For one, Brooks believes that the very structure of poetry is paradox, and ignores the other subtleties of imagination and power that poets bring to their poems. Brooks simply believed that "'imagination' reveals itself in the balance or reconciliation of opposite or discordant qualities." [7] Brooks, in leaning on the crutch of paradox, only discusses the truth which poetry can reveal, and speaks nothing about the pleasure it can give. (231) Also, by defining poetry as uniquely having a structure of paradox, Brooks ignores the power of paradox in everyday conversation and discourse, including scientific discourse, which Brooks claimed was opposed to poetry. Crane claims that, using Brooks' definition of poetry, the most powerful paradoxical poem in modern history is Einstein's formula $E = mc^2$, which is a profound paradox in that matter and energy are the same thing. The argument for the centrality of paradox (and irony) becomes a *reductio ad absurdum* and is therefore void (or at least ineffective) for literary analysis.

45.4   References

[1] Rescher, Nicholas. *Paradoxes: Their Roots, Range, and Resolution.* Open Court: Chicago, 2001.

[2] From "A Tall Story" in *The Paradoxes of Mr. Pond.*

[3] *Literary Theory: An Anthology*, 2nd Ed., Eds. Julie Rivkin and Michael Ryan.

[4] Brooks, Cleanth. *The Well Wrought Urn: Studies in the Structure of Poetry.* New York: Reynal & Hitchcock, 1947.

[5] William Wordsworth (1802). "It is a beauteous evening, calm and free". Bartelby dot org. Retrieved 2011-11-16.

[6] Brooks, Cleanth. "Irony as a Principle of Structure." In *Critical Theory Since Plato*, edited by Hazard Adams. New York: Harcourt Brace Jovanovich, Inc., 1971.

[7] Crane, R.S. "Cleanth Brooks; Or, The Bankruptcy of Critical Monism." In *Modern Philology*, Vol. 45, No. 4 (May 1948) pp 226-245.

[8] Searle, Leroy. "New Criticism." In *The Johns Hopkins Guide to Literary Theory and Criticism*, 2nd edition. Edited by Michael Groden, Martin Kreiswirth, and Imre Szeman. Baltimore: Johns Hopkins University Press, 2005.

Chapter 46

Parody

For the Colombian politician, see Gina Parody.
A **parody** (/ˈpærədi/; also called **spoof**, **send-up** or **lampoon**), in use, is a work created to imitate, make fun of, or

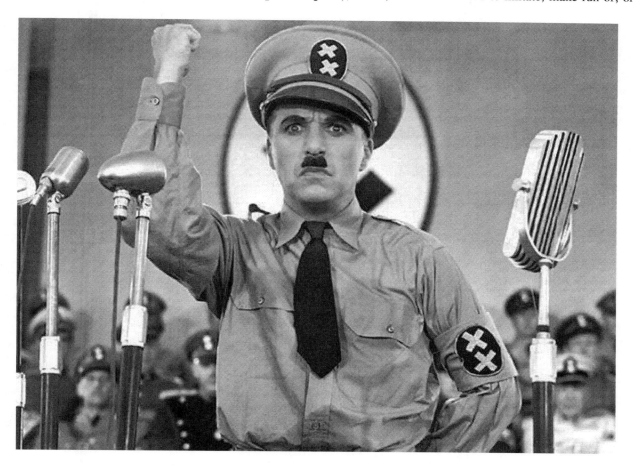

Comedian Charlie Chaplin impersonating Hitler for comic effect in the satirical film The Great Dictator *(1940)*

comment on an original work, its subject, author, style, or some other target, by means of satiric or ironic imitation. As the literary theorist Linda Hutcheon puts it, "parody ···is imitation, not always at the expense of the parodied text." Another critic, Simon Dentith, defines parody as "any cultural practice which provides a relatively polemical allusive imitation of another cultural production or practice." [1] Parody may be found in art or culture, including literature, music (although "parody" in music has an earlier, somewhat different meaning than for other art forms), animation, gaming and film.

The writer and critic John Gross observes in his *Oxford Book of Parodies*, that parody seems to flourish on territory somewhere between pastiche ("a composition in another artist's manner, without satirical intent") and burlesque (which "fools around with the material of high literature and adapts it to low ends").*[2] Meanwhile, the *Encyclopédie* of Denis Diderot distinguishes between the parody and the burlesque, "A good parody is a fine amusement, capable of amusing and instructing the most sensible and polished minds; the burlesque is a miserable buffoonery which can only please the populace." *[3] Historically, when a formula grows tired, as in the case of the moralistic melodramas in the 1910s, it retains value only as a parody, as demonstrated by the Buster Keaton shorts that mocked that genre.*[4]

In his 1960 anthology of parody from the 14th through 20th centuries, critic Dwight Macdonald offered the general definition "Parody is making a new wine that tastes like the old but has a slightly lethal effect." *[5]

46.1   Origins

According to Aristotle (*Poetics*, ii. 5), Hegemon of Thasos was the inventor of a kind of parody; by slightly altering the wording in well-known poems he transformed the sublime into the ridiculous. In ancient Greek literature, a *parodia* was a narrative poem imitating the style and prosody of epics "but treating light, satirical or mock-heroic subjects". *[6] Indeed, the components the Greek word are παρά *para* "beside, counter, against" and ᾠδή *oide* "song". Thus, the original Greek word παρῳδία *parodia* has sometimes been taken to mean "counter-song", an imitation that is set against the original. The *Oxford English Dictionary*, for example, defines parody as imitation "turned as to produce a ridiculous effect". *[7] Because *par-* also has the non-antagonistic meaning of *beside*, "there is nothing in *parodia* to necessitate the inclusion of a concept of ridickule". *[8] Old Comedy contained parody, even the gods could be made fun of. *The Frogs* portrays the hero-turned-god Heracles as a Glutton and the God of Drama Dionysus as cowardly and unintelligent. The traditional trip to the Underworld story is parodied as Dionysus dresses as Heracles to go to the Underworld, in an attempt to bring back a Poet to save Athens.

Roman writers explained parody as an imitation of one poet by another for humorous effect. In French Neoclassical literature, *parody* was also a type of poem where one work imitates the style of another to produce a humorous effect. The Ancient Greeks created satyr plays which parodied tragic plays, often with performers dressed like satyrs.

46.2   Music

Main article: Parody music

In classical music, as a technical term, *parody* refers to a reworking of one kind of composition into another (for example, a motet into a keyboard work as Girolamo Cavazzoni, Antonio de Cabezón, and Alonso Mudarra all did to Josquin des Prez motets).*[9] More commonly, a parody mass (*missa parodia*) or an oratorio used extensive quotation from other vocal works such as motets or cantatas; Victoria, Palestrina, Lassus, and other notable composers of the 16th century used this technique. The term is also sometimes applied to procedures common in the Baroque period, such as when Bach reworks music from cantatas in his *Christmas Oratorio*.

The musicological definition of the term *parody* has now generally been supplanted by a more general meaning of the word. In its more contemporary usage, musical parody usually has humorous, even satirical intent, in which familiar musical ideas or lyrics are lifted into a different, often incongruous, context.*[10] Musical parodies may imitate or refer to the peculiar style of a composer or artist, or even a general style of music. For example, *The Ritz Roll and Rock*, a song and dance number performed by Fred Astaire in the movie *Silk Stockings*, parodies the Rock and Roll genre. Similarly, some YouTube parodies, such as those of The Key of Awesome or The Lonely Island, are based on an artist's style rather than any particular tune.

46.3 English term

The first usage of the word *parody* in English cited in the *Oxford English Dictionary* is in Ben Jonson, in *Every Man in His Humour* in 1598: "A Parodie, a parodie! to make it absurder than it was." The next notable citation comes from John Dryden in 1693, who also appended an explanation, suggesting that the word was in common use, meaning to make fun of or re-create what you are doing. A parody (pronounced /'pærədiː/; also called send-up or spoof), in contemporary usage, is a work created to mock, comment on, or poke fun at an original work, its subject, author, style, or some other target, by means of humorous, satiric or ironic imitation.

46.4 Modernist and post-modernist parody

In the 20th century, parody has been heightened as the central and most representative artistic device, the catalysing agent of artistic creation and innovation.[11][12] This most prominently happened in the second half of the century with postmodernism, but earlier modernism and Russian formalism had anticipated this perspective.[11][13] For the Russian formalists, parody was a way of liberation from the background text that enables to produce new and autonomous artistic forms.[14][15]

Jorge Luis Borges's (1939) short story "Pierre Menard, Author of the Quixote", is often regarded as predicting postmodernism and conceiving the ideal of the ultimate parody.[16][17] In the broader sense of Greek *parodia*, parody can occur when whole elements of one work are lifted out of their context and reused, not necessarily to be ridiculed.[18] Traditional definitions of parody usually only discuss parody in the stricter sense of something intended to ridicule the text it parodies. There is also a broader, extended sense of parody that may not include ridicule, and may be based on many other uses and intentions.[18][19] The broader sense of parody, parody done with intent other than ridicule, has become prevalent in the modern parody of the 20th century.[19] In the extended sense, the modern parody does not target the parodied text, but instead uses it as a weapon to target something else.[20][21] The reason for the prevalence of the extended, recontextualizing type of parody in the 20th century is that artists have sought to connect with the past while registering differences brought by modernity.[22] Major modernist examples of this recontextualizing parody include James Joyce's *Ulysses*, which incorporates elements of Homer's *Odyssey* in a 20th-century Irish context, and T. S. Eliot's *The Waste Land*,[20] which incorporates and recontextualizes elements of a vast range of prior texts, including Dante's *The Inferno*. The work of Andy Warhol is another prominent example of the modern "recontextualizing" parody.[20] According to French literary theorist Gérard Genette, the most rigorous and elegant form of parody is also the most economical, that is a *minimal parody*, the one that literally reprises a known text and gives it a new meaning.[23][24]

Blank parody, in which an artist takes the skeletal form of an art work and places it in a new context without ridiculing it, is common. Pastiche is a closely related genre, and parody can also occur when characters or settings belonging to one work are used in a humorous or ironic way in another, such as the transformation of minor characters Rosencrantz and Guildenstern from Shakespeare's drama Hamlet into the principal characters in a comedic perspective on the same events in the play (and film) *Rosencrantz and Guildenstern Are Dead*. In Flann O'Brien's novel *At Swim-Two-Birds*, for example, mad King Sweeney, Finn MacCool, a pookah, and an assortment of cowboys all assemble in an inn in Dublin: the mixture of mythic characters, characters from genre fiction, and a quotidian setting combine for a humor that is not directed at any of the characters or their authors. This combination of established and identifiable characters in a new setting is not the same as the post-modernist habit of using historical characters in fiction out of context to provide a metaphoric element.

46.5 Reputation

Sometimes the reputation of a parody outlasts the reputation of what is being parodied. For example, *Don Quixote*, which mocks the traditional knight errant tales, is much better known than the novel that inspired it, *Amadis de Gaula* (although Amadis is mentioned in the book). Another notable case is the novel *Shamela* by Henry Fielding (1742), which was a parody of the gloomy epistolary novel *Pamela, or Virtue Rewarded* (1740) by Samuel Richardson. Many of Lewis Carroll's parodies of Victorian didactic verse for children, such as "You Are Old, Father William", are much better known than the (largely forgotten) originals. Stella Gibbons's comic novel *Cold Comfort Farm* has eclipsed the pastoral novels of Mary Webb which largely inspired it.

In more recent times, the television sitcom *'Allo 'Allo!* is perhaps better known than the drama *Secret Army* which it parodies.

Some artists carve out careers by making parodies. One of the best-known examples is that of "Weird Al" Yankovic. His career of parodying other musical acts and their songs has outlasted many of the artists or bands he has parodied. Yankovic is not required under law to get permission to parody; as a personal rule, however, he does seek permission to parody a person's song before recording it. Several artists, such as rapper Chamillionaire and Seattle-based grunge band Nirvana stated that Yankovic's parodies of their respective songs were excellent, and many artists have considered being parodied by him to be a badge of honor.

In the US legal system the point that in most cases a parody of a work constitutes fair use was upheld in the case of Rick Dees, who decided to use 29 seconds of the music from the song *When Sonny Gets Blue* to parody Johnny Mathis' singing style even after being refused permission. An appeals court upheld the trial court's decision that this type of parody represents fair use. *Fisher v. Dees* 794 F.2d 432 (9th Cir. 1986)

46.6   Film parodies

Screenshot of a scene in Jurassic Park *(1993) featuring a* Tyrannosaurus rex *(left), parodied by Rex the Dinosaur in* Toy Story 2 *(1999).*

Some genre theorists, following Bakhtin, see parody as a natural development in the life cycle of any genre; this idea has proven especially fruitful for genre film theorists. Such theorists note that Western movies, for example, after the classic stage defined the conventions of the genre, underwent a parody stage, in which those same conventions were ridiculed and critiqued. Because audiences had seen these classic Westerns, they had expectations for any new Westerns, and when these expectations were inverted, the audience laughed.

Perhaps the earliest parody was the 1922 *Mud and Sand*, a Stan Laurel film that made fun of Rudolph Valentino's film *Blood and Sand*. Laurel specialized in parodies in the mid-1920s, writing and acting in a number of them. Some were send-ups of popular films, such as *Dr. Jekyll and Mr. Hyde*—parodied in the comic *Dr. Pyckle and Mr. Pryde* (1926). Others were spoofs of Broadway plays, such as *No, No, Nanette* (1925), parodied as *Yes, Yes, Nanette* (1925). In 1940 Charlie Chaplin created a satirical comedy about Adolf Hitler with the film *The Great Dictator*, following the first-ever Hollywood parody of the Nazis, the Three Stooges' short subject *You Nazty Spy!*.

About 20 years later Mel Brooks started his career with a Hitler parody as well. After *The Producers* (1968), Brooks became one of the most famous film parodists and did spoofs on any kind of film genre. *Blazing Saddles* (1974) is a parody of western films, *Spaceballs* (1987) is a Star Wars spoof, and *Robin Hood Men in Tights* (1993) Mel's take on the classic Robin Hood tale.

The British comedy group Monty Python is also famous for its parodies, for example, the King Arthur spoof *Monty Python and the Holy Grail* (1974), and the Jesus satire *Life of Brian* (1979). In the 1980s there came another team of parodists including David Zucker, Jim Abrahams and Jerry Zucker. Their most popular films are the *Airplane!*, *Hot Shots!* and *Naked Gun* series. There is a 1989 film parody from Spain of the TV series *The A-Team* called *El equipo Aahhgg* directed by José Truchado.

More recently, parodies have taken on whole film genres at once. One of the first was the *Scary Movie* franchise. Other recent genre parodies include *Not Another Teen Movie*, *Date Movie*, *Epic Movie*, *Meet the Spartans*, *Disaster Movie*, and *Vampires Suck*, all of which have been critically panned.

46.7 Self-parody

Main article: Self-parody

A subset of parody is *self-parody* in which artists parody their own work (as in Ricky Gervais's *Extras*) or notable distinctions of their work (such as Antonio Banderas's Puss in Boots in the *Shrek* sequels) or an artist or genre repeats elements of earlier works to the point that originality is lost.

46.8 Copyright issues

See also: Plagiarism

46.8.1 United States

Although a parody can be considered a derivative work under United States Copyright Law, it can be protected from claims by the copyright owner of the original work under the fair use doctrine, which is codified in 17 U.S.C. § 107. The Supreme Court of the United States stated that parody "is the use of some elements of a prior author's composition to create a new one that, at least in part, comments on that author's works". That commentary function provides some justification for use of the older work. See *Campbell v. Acuff-Rose Music, Inc.*

In 2001, the United States Court of Appeals, 11th Circuit, in *Suntrust v. Houghton Mifflin*, upheld the right of Alice Randall to publish a parody of *Gone with the Wind* called *The Wind Done Gone*, which told the same story from the point of view of Scarlett O'Hara's slaves, who were glad to be rid of her.

In 2007, the 9th Circuit Court of Appeals denied a fair use defense in the *Dr. Seuss Enterprises v. Penguin Books* case. Citing the *Campbell v. Acuff-Rose* decision, they found that a satire of the O.J. Simpson murder trial and parody of *The Cat in the Hat* had infringed upon the children's book because it did not provide a commentary function upon that work.[25][26]

46.8.2 Canada

Under Canadian law, although there is protection for Fair Dealing, there is no explicit protection for parody and satire. In *Canwest v. Horizon*, the publisher of the Vancouver Sun launched a lawsuit against a group which had published a pro-Palestinian parody of the paper. Alan Donaldson, the judge in the case, ruled that parody is not a defence to a copyright claim.[27]

46.8.3   United Kingdom

In 2006 the *Gowers Review of Intellectual Property* recommended that the UK should "create an exception to copyright for the purpose of caricature, parody or pastiche by 2008".*[28] Following the first stage of a two-part public consultation, the Intellectual Property Office reported that the information received "was not sufficient to persuade us that the advantages of a new parody exception were sufficient to override the disadvantages to the creators and owners of the underlying work. There is therefore no proposal to change the current approach to parody, caricature and pastiche in the UK." *[29]

However, following the Hargreaves Review in May 2011 (which made similar proposals to the Gowers Review) the Government broadly accepted these proposals. The current law (effective from 1 October 2014), namely Section 30A*[30] of the Copyright, Designs and Patents Act 1988, now provides an exception to infringement where there is fair dealing of the original work for the purpose of parody (or alternatively for the purpose of caricature or pastiche). The legislation does not define what is meant by "parody", but the UK IPO - the Intellectual Property Office (United Kingdom) - suggests*[31] that a "parody" is something that imitates a work for humorous or satirical effect. See also Fair dealing in United Kingdom law.

46.9   Social and political uses

Parody is a frequent ingredient in satire and is often used to make social and political points. Examples include Swift's "A Modest Proposal", which satirized English neglect of Ireland by parodying emotionally disengaged political tracts; and, recently, *The Daily Show* and *The Colbert Report*, which parody a news broadcast and a talk show to satirize political and social trends and events.

On the other hand, the writer and frequent parodist Vladimir Nabokov made a distinction: "Satire is a lesson, parody is a game." *[32]

Some events, such as a national tragedy, can be difficult to handle. Chet Clem, Editorial Manager of the news parody publication *The Onion*, told *Wikinews* in an interview the questions that are raised when addressing difficult topics:

Parody is by no means necessarily satirical, and may sometimes be done with respect and appreciation of the subject involved, without being a heedless sarcastic attack.

Parody has also been used to facilitate dialogue between cultures or subcultures. Sociolinguist Mary Louise Pratt identifies parody as one of the "arts of the contact zone", through which marginalized or oppressed groups "selectively appropriate", or imitate and take over, aspects of more empowered cultures.*[34]

Shakespeare often uses a series of parodies to convey his meaning. In the social context of his era, an example can be seen in *King Lear* where the fool is introduced with his coxcomb to be a parody of the king.

46.10   Examples

46.10.1   Historic examples

- *Sir Thopas* in *Canterbury Tales*, by Geoffrey Chaucer

- *Don Quixote* by Miguel Cervantes

- *Beware the Cat* by William Baldwin

- *The Knight of the Burning Pestle* by Francis Beaumont and John Fletcher

- *Dragon of Wantley*, an anonymous 17th century ballad

- *Hudibras* by Samuel Butler

- "MacFlecknoe", by John Dryden

- *A Tale of a Tub* by Jonathan Swift
- *The Rape of the Lock* by Alexander Pope
- *Namby Pamby* by Henry Carey
- *Northanger Abbey* by Jane Austen
- *Gulliver's Travels* by Jonathan Swift
- *The Dunciad* by Alexander Pope
- *Memoirs of Martinus Scriblerus* by John Gay, Alexander Pope, John Arbuthnot, *et al.*
- Mozart's *A Musical Joke* (*Ein musikalischer Spaß*), K.522 (1787) - parody of incompetent contemporaries of Mozart, as assumed by some theorists
- *Sartor Resartus* by Thomas Carlyle
- *Ways and Means*, or *The aged, aged man*, by Lewis Carroll. Much of *Alice in Wonderland* and *Through the Looking-Glass* is parodic of Victorian schooling.
- *Batrachomyomachia* (battle between frogs and mice), an *Iliad* parody by an unknown ancient Greek author
- *Britannia Sitting On An Egg*, a machine-printed illustrated envelope published by the stationer W.R. Hume of Leith, Scotland, parodying the machine-printed illustrated envelope (commissioned by Rowland Hill and designed by the artist William Mulready) used to launch the British postal service reforms of 1840.

46.10.2 Modern television examples

- *Saturday Night Live* parodies of Hillary Clinton
- *Saturday Night Live* parodies of Sarah Palin

46.11 See also

- Abridgement
- Détournement
- Internet meme
- Intertextuality
- Joke
- Literary technique
- Metaparody
- Parody advertisement
- Parody music
- Parody religion
- Parody science
- P. D. Q. Bach
- Subvertising
- Tom Lehrer
- "Weird Al" Yankovic

46.12   Notes

[1] Dentith (2000) p.9

[2] J.M.W. Thompson (May 2010). "Close to the Bone". Standpoint magazine.

[3] "Parody." The Encyclopedia of Diderot & d'Alembert Collaborative Translation Project. Translated by Colt Brazill Segrest. Ann Arbor: Michigan Publishing, University of Michigan Library, 2007. Web. [1 Apr. 2015]. <http://hdl.handle.net/2027/ spo.did2222.0000.811>. Trans. of "Parodie," Encyclopédie ou Dictionnaire raisonné des sciences, des arts et des métiers, vol. 12. Paris, 1765.

[4] Balducci, Anthony (2011) *The Funny Parts: A History of Film Comedy Routines and Gags* p.231

[5] Macdonald, Dwight, Parodies, Random House, 1960, pg. 559

[6] (Denith, 10)

[7] Quoted in Hutcheon, 32.

[8] (Hutcheon, 32)

[9] Tilmouth, Michael and Richard Sherr. "Parody (i)"' Grove Music Online, Oxford Music Online, accessed 19 February 2012 (subscription required)

[10] Burkholder, J. Peter. "Borrowing", Grove Music Online, Oxford Music Online, accessed 19 February. 2012 (subscription required)

[11] Sheinberg (2000) pp.141, 150

[12] Stavans (1997) p.37

[13] Bradbury, Malcolm *No, not Bloomsbury* p.53, quoting Boris Eikhenbaum:

> Nearly all periods of artistic innovation have had a strong parodic impulse, advancing generic change. As the Russian formalist Boris Eichenbaum once put it: "In the evolution of each genre, there are times when its use for entirely serious or elevated objectives degenerates aand produces a comic or parodic form....And thus is produced the regeneration of the genre: it finds new possibilities and new forms."

[14] Hutcheon (1985) pp.28, 35

[15] Boris Eikhenbaum *Theory of the "Formal Method"* (1925) and *O. Henry and the Theory of the Short Story* (1925)

[16] Stavans (1997) p.31

[17] Elizabeth Bellalouna, Michael L. LaBlanc, Ira Mark Milne (2000) *Literature of Developing Nations for Students: L-Z* p.50

[18] Elices (2004) p.90 quotation:

> From these words, it can be inferred that Genette's conceptualisation does not diverge from Hutcheon's, in the sense that he does not mention the component of ridicule that is suggested by the prefix *paros*. Genette alludes to the re-interpretative capacity of parodists in order to confer an artistic autonomy to their works.

[19] Hutcheon (1985) p.50

[20] Hutcheon (1985) p.52

[21] Yunck 1963

[22] Hutcheon (1985)

[23] Gérard Genette (1982) *Palimpsests: literature in the second degree* p.16

[24] Sangsue (2006) p.72 quotation:

Genette individua la forma "piú rigorosa" di parodia nella "parodia minimale", consistente nella ripresa letterale di un testo conosciuto e nella sua applicazione a un nuovo contesto, come nella citazione deviata dal suo senso

[25] Richard Stim. "Summaries of Fair Use Cases". *Stanford Copyright and Fair Use Center.*

[26] "Google Scholar". *google.com.*

[27] "The Tyee – Canwest Suit May Test Limits of Free Speech". *The Tyee.* 11 December 2008.

[28] The Stationery Office. (2006) Gowers Review of Intellectual Property. [Online]. Available at official-documents.gov.uk (Accessed: 22 February 2011).

[29] UK Intellectual Property Office. (2009) Taking Forward the Gowers Review of Intellectual Property: Second Stage Consultation on Copyright Exceptions. [Online]. Available at ipo.gov.uk (Accessed: 22 February 2011).

[30] http://www.legislation.gov.uk/uksi/2014/2356/regulation/5/made

[31] https://www.gov.uk/government/uploads/system/uploads/attachment_data/file/359250/Exceptions_to_copyright_-_Guidance_for_creators_and_copyright_owners.pdf

[32] Appel, Alfred, Jr.; Nabokov, Vladimir (1967). "An Interview with Vladimir Nabokov". *Wisconsin Studies in Contemporary Literature* **VIII** (2): 127–152. Retrieved 28 Dec 2013.

[33] An interview with The Onion, David Shankbone, *Wikinews*, November 25, 2007.

[34] Pratt (1991)

46.13   References

- Dentith, Simon (2000). *Parody (The New Critical Idiom).* Routledge. ISBN 0-415-18221-2.

- Elices Agudo, Juan Francisco (2004) *Historical and theoretical approaches to English satire*

- Hutcheon, Linda (1985). "3. The Pragmatic Range of Parody". *A Theory of Parody: The Teachings of Twentieth-Century Art Forms.* New York: Methuen. ISBN 0-252-06938-2.

- Mary Louise Pratt (1991). "Arts of the Contact Zone". *Profession* (New York: MLA) **91**: 33–40. Archived from the original (pdf) on 2008-10-26. archived at University of Idaho, English 506, Rhetoric and Composition: History, Theory, and Research. From Ways of Reading, 5th edition, ed. David Bartholomae and Anthony Petroksky (New York: Bedford/St. Martin's, 1999

- Sangsue, Daniel (2006) *La parodia*

- Sheinberg, Esti (2000) *Irony, Satire, Parody and the Grotesque in the Music of Shostakovich*

- Stavans, Ilan and Jesse H. Lytle, Jennifer A. Mattson (1997) *Antiheroes: Mexico and its detective novel*

- Ore, Johnathan (2014) Youtuber Shane Dawsons fans revolt after Sony pulls his Taylor Wwift parody video

46.14   Further reading

- Bakhtin, Mikhail; Ed. Michael Holquist. Trans. Caryl Emerson and Michael Holquist (1981). *The Dialogic Imagination: Four Essays.* Austin and London: University of Texas Press. ISBN 0-292-71527-7.

- Gates, Henry Louis, Jr. (1988). *The Signifying Monkey: A Theory of Afro-American Literary Criticism.* Oxford University Press. ISBN 0-19-503463-5.

- Petrosky, Anthony; ed. David Bartholomae and Anthony Petroksky (1999). *Ways of Reading* (5th ed.). New York: Bedford/St. Martin's. ISBN 978-0-312-45413-5. An anthology including *Arts of the Contact Zone*

- Rose, Margaret (1993). *Parody: Ancient, Modern and Post-Modern*. Cambridge: Cambridge University Press. ISBN 0-521-41860-7.

- Caponi, Gena Dagel (1999). *Signifyin(g), Sanctifyin', & Slam Dunking: A Reader in African American Expressive Culture*. University of Massachusetts Press. ISBN 1-55849-183-X.

- Harries, Dan (2000). *Film Parody*. London: BFI. ISBN 0-85170-802-1.

- Pueo, Juan Carlos (2002). *Los reflejos en juego (Una teoría de la parodia)*. Valencia (Spain): Tirant lo Blanch. ISBN 84-8442-559-2.

- Gray, Jonathan (2006). *Watching with The Simpsons: Television, Parody, and Intertextuality*. New York: Routledge. ISBN 0-415-36202-4.

- John Gross, ed. (2010). *The Oxford Book of Parodies*. Oxford: Oxford University Press. ISBN 978-0-19-954882-8.

46.15   External links

The dictionary definition of parody at Wiktionary

Satirical political cartoon that appeared in Puck *magazine, October 9, 1915. Caption "I did not raise my girl to be a voter" parodies the anti-World War I song "I Didn't Raise My Boy To Be A Soldier". A chorus of disreputable men support a lone anti-suffrage woman.*

Reggie Brown, a voice actor and Barack Obama impersonator

Chapter 47

Pastiche

For other uses, see Pastiche (disambiguation).

A **pastiche** is a work of visual art, literature, theatre, or music that imitates the style or character of the work of one or more other artists.[1] Unlike parody, pastiche celebrates, rather than mocks, the work it imitates.[2]

The word *pastiche* is a French cognate of the Italian noun *pasticcio*, which is a pâté or pie-filling mixed from diverse ingredients.[1][3] Metaphorically, *pastiche* and *pasticcio* describe works that are either composed by several authors, or that incorporate stylistic elements of other artists' work. Pastiche is an example of eclecticism in art.

Allusion is not pastiche. A literary allusion may refer to another work, but it does not reiterate it. Moreover, allusion requires the audience to share in the author's cultural knowledge.[4] Both allusion and pastiche are mechanisms of intertextuality.

47.1 By art

47.1.1 Literature

See also: Dionysian imitatio

In literature usage, the term denotes a literary technique employing a generally light-hearted tongue-in-cheek imitation of another's style; although jocular, it is usually respectful.

For example, many stories featuring Sherlock Holmes, originally created by Arthur Conan Doyle, have been written as pastiches since the author's time.[5][6] Ellery Queen and Nero Wolfe are other popular subjects of mystery parodies and pastiches.[7][8]

A similar example of pastiche is the posthumous continuations of the Robert E. Howard stories, written by other writers without Howard's authorization. This includes the Conan stories of L. Sprague de Camp and Lin Carter. David Lodge's novel *The British Museum Is Falling Down* (1965) is a pastiche of works by Joyce, Kafka, and Virginia Woolf. In 1991, Alexandra Ripley wrote the novel *Scarlett*, a pastiche of *Gone with the Wind*, in an unsuccessful attempt to have it recognized as a canonical sequel.

47.1.2 Music

For instance, Charles Rosen has characterized Mozart's various works in imitation of Baroque style as pastiche, and Edvard Grieg's Holberg Suite was written as a conscious homage to the music of an earlier age. Some of Pyotr Ilyich Tchaikovsky's works, such as his Variations on a Rococo Theme and Serenade for Strings, employ a poised "Classical" form reminiscent of 18th-century composers such as Mozart (the composer whose work was his favorite).[9] Perhaps

A pastiche combining elements of two PD-art files (original 1 and original 2), in Photoshop

one of the best examples of pastiche in modern music is the that of George Rochberg, who used the technique in his String Quartet No. 3 of 1972 and Music for the Magic Theater. Rochberg turned to pastiche from serialism after the death of his son in 1963.

"Bohemian Rhapsody" by Queen is unusual as it is a pastiche in both senses of the word, as there are many distinct styles imitated in the song, all 'hodge-podged' together to create one piece of music.*[10] A similar earlier example is "Happiness is a Warm Gun" by The Beatles.

A *pastiche Mass* is a Mass where the constituent movements are from different Mass settings. Most often this convention has been chosen for concert performances, particularly by early music ensembles. Masses are composed of movements: Kyrie, Gloria, Credo, Sanctus, Agnus Dei; for example, the *Missa Solemnis* by Beethoven and the *Messe de Nostre Dame* by Guillaume de Machaut. In a pastiche Mass, the performers may choose a Kyrie from one composer, and a Gloria from another, or, choose a Kyrie from one setting of an individual composer, and a Gloria from another.

47.1.3 Musical theater

In musical theater pastiche is often an indispensable tool for evoking the sounds of a particular era for which a show is set. For his 1971 musical Follies, a show about a reunion of performers from a musical revue set between the World Wars, Stephen Sondheim wrote over a dozen songs in the style of Broadway songwriters of the 1920s and 1930s. Sondheim imitates not only the music of composers such as Cole Porter, Irving Berlin, Jerome Kern, and George Gershwin but also the lyrics of writers such as Ira Gershwin, Dorothy Fields, Otto Harbach, and Oscar Hammerstein II. For example, Sondheim notes that the torch song "Losing My Mind" sung in the show contains "near-stenciled rhythms and harmonies" from the Gershwins' "The Man I Love" and lyrics written in the style of Dorothy Fields.*[11] Examples of musical pastiche can also be found in other Sondheim shows including Gypsy, Saturday Night, and Anyone Can Whistle.*[12]

47.1.4 Film

Pastiche can also be a cinematic device wherein the creator of the film pays homage to another filmmaker's style and use of cinematography, including camera angles, lighting, and mise en scène. A film's writer may also offer a pastiche based on the works of other writers (this is especially evident in historical films and documentaries but can be found in non-fiction drama, comedy and horror films as well). A major filmmaker, Quentin Tarantino often uses various plots, characteristics and themes from many lesser-known films to create his films. He has even openly stated that he "steals from everyone".

In cinema, the influence of George Lucas' Star Wars films (spawning their own pastiches – see the 1983 3D film *Metalstorm: The Destruction of Jared-Syn*) can be regarded as a function of postmodernity.*[13]*[14]

47.1.5 Architecture

In urban planning, "pastiche" is used to describe developments as imitations of the building styles created by major architects: the implication is that the work is unoriginal and of little merit, and the term is generally attributed without reference to its urban context. Many post-war European developments can in this way be described as pastiches of the work of architects and planners such as Le Corbusier or Ebenezer Howard. Alain de Botton describes pastiche as "an unconvincing reproduction of the styles of the past".*[15]

However the term 'pastiche' in the architectural and urban context is problematic due to the historical reliance on evolving design traditions in architecture and urban design. Therefore work that shows an evolution of an existing design tradition may embody elements typical of that style. For instance classical architecture recurred and evolved over several millennia without being referred to as pastiche, though basic compositional elements recurred. Similarly, in historic centres where the coherence of the urban environment is paramount, infill buildings have over time adopted the design traditions of the setting and in that sense might be seen as imitative. The term 'pastiche' in architectural criticism should therefore be more precisely associated with an idea from the modernism, that design characteristics of the modernist style would fully supersede and replace earlier design traditions, which were seen as regressive. The use of the word 'pastiche' was developed by proponents of modernism to dismiss contemporary work that sought to adopt and evolve pre-modernist design traditions.

47.2 See also

- Appropriation (art)
- Appropriation (music)
- Archetype
- Bricolage
- Burlesque
- Doujinshi
- Eclecticism in music
- Fan fiction
- Homage
- Mode (literature)
- Postmodernism
- Simulacrum
- Swipe (comics)

47.3 References

[1] Roland Greene, Stephen Cushman, Clare Cavanagh, Jahan Ramazani, Paul F. Rouzer, Harris Feinsod, David Marno, Alexandra Slessarev, ed. (2012). *The Princeton Encyclopedia of Poetry and Poetics*. p. 1005. ISBN 0-691-15491-0.

[2] Hoestery, Ingeborg (2001). *Pastiche: Cultural Memory in Art, Film, Literature*. Bloomington: Indiana University Press. p. 1. ISBN 978-0-253-33880-8. OCLC 44812124. Retrieved 2 August 2013.

[3] Harper, Douglas. "pastiche". *Online Etymology Dictionary*. Retrieved 2013-08-02.

[4] Abrams, Meyer Howard; Harpham, Geoffrey (2009). *A Glossary of Literary Terms*. ISBN 1-4130-3390-3.

[5] Lopresti, Rob (2009-08-12). "Pastiche Nuts". *Tune It Or Die!*. Criminal Brief. Retrieved 2010-01-10.

[6] Lundin, Leigh (2007-07-15). "When Good Characters Go Bad". *ADD Detective*. Criminal Brief. Retrieved 2010-01-10.

[7] Andrews, Dale (2008-10-28). "The Pastiche". *Mystery Masterclass*. Criminal Brief. Retrieved 2010-01-10.

[8] Ritchie, James; Tog; Gleason, Bill; Lopresti, Rob; Andrews, Dale; Baker, Jeff (2009-12-29). "Pastiche vs. fan fiction. Dividing line?". *The Mystery Place*. New York: Ellery Queen, Alfred Hitchock, Dell Magazines. Retrieved 2010-01-10.

[9]   • Brown, David, "Tchaikovsky, Pyotr Ilyich." In *The New Grove Encyclopedia of Music and Musicians* (London: MacMillan, 1980), 20 vols., ed. Sadie, Stanley. ISBN 0-333-23111-2. 18:628

[10] Baker, Roy Thomas (October 1995). "AN INVITATION TO THE OPERA". Sound on Sound. Retrieved 2010-09-29.

[11] Stephen Sondheim, "Follies" Finishing the Hat (New York: Alfred A. Knopf, 2010), p. 235.

[12] Stephen Sondheim, "Follies", Finishing the Hat (New York: Alfred A. Knopf, 2010), p.200.

[13] (Jameson, 1991)

[14] (Sandoval, Chela. Methodology of the Oppressed. Minneapolis,MN: University of Minnesota Press, 2000)

[15] Alain de Botton on architecture

47.4 Further reading

- Jameson, Fredric (1989). "Postmodernism and Consumer Society". In Foster, Hal. *The Anti-Aesthetic: Essays on Post-Modern Culture*. Seattle: Bay Press. pp. 111–125.

- Jameson, Fredric (1991). *Postmodernism, or, the Cultural Logic of Late Capitalism*. Durham: Duke University Press. ISBN 978-0-8223-1090-7. OCLC 21330492.

- Christensen, Jørgen Riber (2004). "Diplopia, or Ontological Intertextuality in Pastiche". In Dorfman, Ben. *Culture, Media, Theory, Practice: Perspectives*. Aalborg: Aalborg University Press. pp. 234–246. ISBN 978-87-7307-729-0. OCLC 57730275.

- Dyer, Richard (2007). *Pastiche*. New York: Routledge. ISBN 978-0-415-34009-0. OCLC 64486475.

Chapter 48

Pathos

Not to be confused with Pothos or Bathos.

Pathos (/ˈpeɪθɒs/, US /ˈpeɪθoʊs/; plural: *pathea*; Greek: πάθος, for "suffering" or "experience;" adjectival form: 'pathetic' from παθητικός) represents an appeal to the emotions of the audience.[*][1] Pathos is a communication technique used most often in rhetoric (where it is considered one of the three modes of persuasion, alongside ethos and logos), and in literature, film and other narrative art.

Emotional appeal can be accomplished in a multitude of ways:

- by a metaphor or storytelling, common as a hook,

- by passion in the delivery of the speech or writing, as determined by the audience.

48.1 Relation to *logos*

The mode of *pathos* is, more often than not, construed as fundamentally emotive, by extension leaving *logos* unemotive.

Another interpretation is that *logos* invokes emotions relevant to the issue at hand, logic and fact based, whereas *pathos* invokes emotions that have no bearing on the issue, in that the *pathē* they stimulate lack, or at any rate are not shown to possess, any intrinsic connection with the point at issue.[*][2]

48.2 Aristotle's text on *pathos*

In Aristotle's *Rhetoric*, he identifies three artistic modes of persuasion, one of which was "awakening emotion (*pathos*) in the audience so as to induce them to make the judgment desired." [*][3] In the first chapter he includes the way in which "men change their opinion in regard to their judgment. As such emotions have specific causes and effects" (Book 2.1.2–3).[*][3] Aristotle identifies *pathos* as one of the three essential modes of proof by his statement that "to understand the emotions---that is, to name them and describe them, to know their causes and the way in which they are excited (1356a24-1356a25).[*][3] Aristotle posits that, alongside *pathos*, the speaker must deploy good ethos in order to establish credibility (Book 2.1.5–9).[*][3] Aristotle details what individual emotions are useful to a speaker (Book 2.2.27).[*][3] In doing so, Aristotle focused on whom, toward whom, and why stating that "It is not enough to know one or even two of these points; unless we know all three, we shall be unable to arouse anger in anyone. The same is true of the other emotions." He also arranges the emotions with one another so that they may counteract one another. For example, one would pair sadness with happiness (Book 2.1.9).[*][3] With this understanding, Aristotle argues for the rhetor to understand the entire situation of goals and audiences to decide which specific emotion the speaker would exhibit or call upon in order to persuade the audience. Aristotle's theory of pathos has three main foci: the frame of mind the audience is in, the variation of emotion between people, and the influence the rhetor has on the emotions of the audience. Aristotle classifies the third of this trio as the ultimate goal of pathos.<ref*[4] Similarly, Aristotle outlines the individual importance of persuasive emotions, as well as the combined effectiveness of these emotions on the audience. Moreover, Aristotle pointedly discusses pleasure and pain in relation to the reactions these two emotions cause in an audience member.<ref*[4] According to Aristotle, emotions vary from person to person, therefore he stresses the importance of understanding specific social situations in order to successfully utilize pathos as a mode of persuasion.<ref*[4] Here, pathos becomes a mode of persuasion and it is from this point of view that Aristotle defines all that is related to pathos, such as the emotions that are appealed tothrough speech making, as persuasive technique.*[5] To further his theory, Aristotle identifies the introduction and the conclusion as the two most important places for an emotional appeal in any persuasive argument.*[5]

48.3   Alternative views on *pathos*

Scholars have discussed the different interpretations of Aristotle's views of rhetoric and his philosophy. Some believe that it is actually a myth, that Aristotle invented it entirely. In the second chapter of *Rhetoric*, Aristotle's view on *pathos* changes from the use in discourse to the understanding of emotions and their effects. William Fortenbaugh pointed out that for the Sophist Gorgias, "Being overcome with emotion is analogous to rape." *[6] Aristotle opposed this view and created a systematic approach to *pathos*. Fortenbaugh argues that Aristotle's systematic approach to emotional appeals "depends upon correctly understanding the nature of individual emotions, upon knowing the conditions favorable to, the objects of, and the grounds for individual emotions" .*[6] Modern philosophers were typically more skeptical of the use of emotions in communication, with political theorists such as John Locke hoping to extract emotion from reasoned communication entirely. George Campbell presents another view unlike the common systematic approach of Aristotle. Campbell explored whether appeals to emotion or passions would be "an unfair method of persuasion," identifying seven circumstances to judge emotions: probability, plausibility, importance, proximity in time, connection of place, relations to the persons concerned, and interest in the consequences.*[7] In 84 BC *Rhetorica ad Herrenium* of an unknown author theorizes that the conclusion is most important place in a persuasive argument to consider emotions such as mercy or hatred, depending on the nature of the persuasion.*[8] The Appeal to Pity, as it is classified in Rheotica ad Herrenium, is a means to conclude by reiterating the major premise of the work and tying while incorporating an emotional sentiment. The author suggests ways in which to appeal to the pity of the audience: "We shall stir pity in our hearers by recalling vicissitudes of future; by comparing the prosperity we once enjoyed with our present adversity; by entreating those whose pity we seek to win, and by submitting ourselves to their mercy." *[8] Additionally, the text impresses the importance of invoking kindness, humanity and sympathy upon the hearer. Finally, the author suggests that The Appeal to Pity be brief for "nothing dries more quickly than a tear." *[8]

48.4   Pathos before Aristotle

The concept of emotional appeal existed in rhetoric long before Aristotle's *Rhetoric*. George A. Kennedy, a well-respected, modern-day scholar, identifies the appeal to emotions in the newly formed democratic court system before 400 BC in his book The Art of Persuasion in Greece.*[9] Gorgias, a Sophist who preceded Aristotle, was interested in the orator's emotional appeal as well. Gorgias believed the orator was able to capture and lead the audience in any direction they pleased through the use of emotional appeal.*[9] In the Enconium of Helen, Gorgias states that a soul can feel a particular sentiment on account of words such as sorrow and pity. Certain words act as "bringers-on of pleasure and takers-off of pain." *[10] Furthermore, Gorgias equates emotional persuasion to the sensation of being overtaken by a drug, "[F]or just as different drug draw off different humors from the body, and some put an end to disease and other to life, so too of discourses: some give pain, others delight, others terrify, others rouse the hearers to courage, and yet others by a certain vile persuasion drug and trick to soul." *[10]

Another philosopher to discuss emotion appeal in rhetoric was Plato. Plato preceded Aristotle and therefore laid the groundwork, as did other sophists, for Aristotle to theorize the concept of pathos. In Gorgias, Plato discusses pleasure versus pain in the realm of pathos though in a fictional conversation between Gorgias and Socrates. The dialogue between several ancient rhetors that Plato created centers around the value of rhetoric, however, the men do incorporate aspects of pathos in their responses. Gorigas, discredits pathos and instead promotes the use of ethos in persuasion.*[11] In another of Plato's texts, Phaedrus, his discussion of emotions is more pointed, however still he does not outline exactly how emotions manipulate an audience.*[12] Plato discusses the danger of emotions in oratory. He argues that emotional appeal in rhetoric should be used as the means to an end and not the point of the discussion.*[12]

48.5 Contemporary pathos

George Campbell, a contributor to the Scottish Enlightenment, was one of the first rhetoricians to incorporate scientific evidence into his theory of emotional appeal.*[13] Campbell relied heavily on a book written by physician David Hartley, entitled *Observations on Man*. The book synthesized emotions and neurology and introduced the concept that action is a result of impression. Hartley determined that emotions drive people to react to appeals based on circumstance, but also passions made up of cognitive impulses.*[13] Campbell argues that belief and persuasion depend heavily on the force of an emotional appeal.*[14] Furthermore, Campbell introduced the importance of the audience's imagination on and will on emotional persuasion that is equally as important as basic understanding of an argument.*[14] Campbell, by drawing on the theories of rhetoricians before him, drew up a contemporary view of Pathos that incorporates the psychological aspect of emotional appeal. An orator's reliance on emotional appeal is evident in modern-day speechmaking, but this technique is no longer referred to as emotional appeal; it is instead psychological.*[13]

48.6 See also

- Appeal to emotion
- Pathetic fallacy
- Pathology
- Rhetoric

48.7 References

[1] Robyn Walker. *Strategic Business Communication: For Leaders.* Google Books.

[2] Robert Wardy, "Mighty Is the Truth and It Shall Prevail?", in *Essays on Aristotle's Rhetoric*, Amélie Rorty (ed), University of California Press, 1996, ISBN 0-520-20228-7, p. 64.

[3] Aristotle, and George Alexander Kennedy. Aristotle On Rhetoric: A Theory of Civic Discourse. New York: Oxford UP, 1991. Print. p.119

[4] Aristotle; Bizzell, Patricia; Herzberg, Bruce (2001). *On Rhetoric* (Second ed.). New York: Bedford/ St. Martin's.

[5] Lee, Irving (12/6/1939). "Some Conceptions on Emotional Appeal in Rhetorical Theory". *Speech Monographs* **6** (1): 66–86. Check date values in: |date= (help)

[6] Fortenbaugh, W. W. Aristotle's Rhetoric on Emotions. Metuchen, NJ: Scarecrow, 1974. Print. p.232.

[7] Campbell, George, and Lloyd F. Bitzer. The Philosophy of Rhetoric. Carbondale: Southern Illinois UP, 1963. Print.p.81-89.

[8] Anonymous; Bizzell, Patricia; Herzberg, Bruce (2001). *Rhetorica ad Herennium.* Bedford/ St.Martins.

[9] Kennedy, George (1963). *The Art of Persuasion in Greece.* Princeton University Press.

[10] Gorgias; Bizzell, Patricia; Bruce, Herzberg. *The Rhetorical Tradition (Second Edition). Encomium of Helen.*

[11] Plato; Bizzell, Patricia; Herzberg, Bruce. *The Rhetorical Tradition Second Edition). Gorgias.* Bedford/ St. Martin's.

[12] Plato; Bizzell, Patricia; Herzberg, Bruce (2001). *The Rhetorical Tradition (Second Edition). Phaedrus.* New York: Bedford/ St. Martin's.

[13] Gardiner, Norman (1937). *Feeling and Emotion: A History of Theories.* New York: American Book Co.

[14] Golden, James; Corbett, Edward (1990). *The Rhetoric of Blair, Campbell, and Whately.* SIU Press.

48.8 External links

- The dictionary definition of pathos at Wiktionary

Chapter 49

Polyptoton

Polyptoton /ˌpɒlɪpˈtoʊtɒn/ is the stylistic scheme in which words derived from the same root are repeated (such as "strong" and "strength"). A related stylistic device is antanaclasis, in which the same word is repeated, but each time with a different sense. Another related term is figura etymologica.

In inflected languages polyptoton is the same word being repeated but appearing each time in a different case. (for example, "Iuppiter," "Iovis," "Iovi," "Iovem," "Iove" [in Latin being the nominative, genitive, dative, accusative, and ablative forms of Iuppiter, respectively]).

The form is relatively common in Latin Christian poetry and prose in a construction called the superlative genitive, in phrases such as sanctum sanctorum ("holy of holies"), and found its way into languages such as Old English, which naturally favored the alliteration that is part and parcel of polyptoton—in fact, polyptoton is "much more prevalent in Old English verse than in Latin verse." The specific superlative genitive in Old English, however, occurs only in Latinate Christian poems, not in secular poetry.*[1]

It is also used in public speaking, and several cases of use can be found in Churchill' speeches. Chesterton frequently resorted to this rhetorical device to create paradoxes:

> [T]hough deserted by the **un-English** government of **England**, they asserted their own ancient charac-
> ter...
> —G.K. Chesterton, speech in the trial of Jean Fertier (1803)*[2]

In combination with verbal active and passive voices, it points out the idea of a latent reciprocity:

> **Judge** not, that ye **be** not **judged**
> —Matthew 7:1*[3]

An alternative way to utilize the stylistic device is to develop polyptoton over the course of an entire novel, which is done in Mary Shelley's Frankenstein. Shelley combines polyptoton with periphrastic naming, which is the technique of referring to someone using several indirect names. The creature in Frankenstein is referred to by many names, such as "fiend", "devil", "being", and "ogre". However, the first name that Shelley uses in reference to the creature is "wretch". Throughout the novel, various forms of the term are used, such as "wretchedly" and "wretchedness", which is indicative of polyptoton. According to Duyfhuizen, the gradual development of polyptoton in *Frankenstein* is significant because it symbolizes the intricacies of one's own identity. *[4]

49.1 Examples

- "The Greeks are **strong**, and **skillful** to their **strength**, **Fierce** to their **skill**, and to their **fierceness** valiant;" William Shakespeare, *Troilus and Cressida* I, i, 7-8

- "With eager **feeding food** doth choke the **feeder**." William Shakespeare *Richard II* II,i,37

- "Not as a call to **battle**, though **embattled** we are." John F. Kennedy, *Inaugural Address*, January 20, 1961.

- "Thou art of **blood**, joy not to make things **bleed**." Sir Philip Sidney

- "**Absolute** power corrupts **absolutely**." Lord Acton

- "Who shall **watch** the **watchmen** themselves (*Quis custodiet ipsos custodes?*)?" Juvenal

- "**Diamond** me no **diamonds**, **prize** me no **prizes**..." Alfred, Lord Tennyson, *Lancelot and Elaine*

49.2 See also

- Antanaclasis

- Figura etymologica

- Cognate object

- Figure of speech

- Rhetoric

49.3 References

[1] Fleming, Damian (2012). "*Rex regum et cyninga cyning*: 'Speaking Hebrew' in Cynewulf's *Elene*". In Michael Fox, Manish Sharma. *Old English Literature and the Old Testament*. Toronto: U of Toronto P. pp. 229–52. ISBN 9780802098542.

[2] (Farnsworth 2011, p. 72).

[3] (Farnsworth 2011, p. 63).

[4] Duyfhuizen, Bernard. "Periphrastic Naming In Mary Shelley's Frankenstein." Studies In The Novel 27.4 (1995): 477. Academic Search Premier. Web. 15 Feb. 2014.

49.4 Sources

- Corbett, Edward P.J. *Classical Rhetoric for the Modern Student*. Oxford University Press, New York, 1971.

- Ward Farnsworth (2011). *Farnsworth's Classical English Rhetoric*. David R. Godine Publisher. pp. 63–73. ISBN 978-1-56792-385-8.

Chapter 50

Polysyndeton

Polysyndeton is the use of several conjunctions in close succession, especially where some could otherwise be omitted (as in "he ran and jumped and laughed for joy"). The word *polysyndeton* comes from the Greek "poly-", meaning "many," and "syndeton", meaning "bound together with".*[1] It is a stylistic scheme used to achieve a variety of effects: it can increase the rhythm of prose, speed or slow its pace, convey solemnity or even ecstasy and childlike exuberance. Another common use of polysyndeton is to create a sense of being overwhelmed, or in fact directly overwhelm the audience by using conjunctions, rather than commas, leaving little room for a reader to breathe.*[2]*[3]

In grammar, a **polysyndetic coordination** is a coordination in which all conjuncts are linked by coordinating conjunctions (usually *and*, *but*, *or*, *nor* in English).

50.1 In the King James' Bible

Polysyndeton is used extensively in the King James Version of the Bible. For example:

- And every living substance was destroyed which was upon the face of the ground, both man, and cattle, and the creeping things, and the fowl of the heaven; and they were destroyed from the earth: and Noah only remained alive, and they that were with him in the ark. Genesis 7:22–24

- Or if a soul touch any unclean thing, whether it be a carcass of an unclean beast, or a carcass of unclean cattle, or the carcass of unclean creeping things, and if it be hidden from him; he also shall be unclean, and guilty. Leviticus 5:2.

- And Joshua, and all of Israel with him, took Achan the son of Zerah, and the silver, and the garment, and the wedge of gold, and his sons, and his daughters, and his oxen, and his asses, and his sheep, and his tent, and all that he had. Joshua 7.24.

50.2 In Shakespeare

Shakespeare is known for using various rhetorical devices in his works, including polysyndeton.

- "When thou dost ask me blessing I'll kneel down and ask of thee forgiveness. So we'll live and pray, and sing, and tell old tales, and laugh at gilded butterflies, and hear poor rogues talk of court news, and we'll talk with them too" *King Lear* (5.3.11–5).

- "Why, this is not a boon! 'Tis as I should entreat you to wear your gloves, or feed on nourishing dishes, or keep you warm, or sue you to do a peculiar profit to your person" *Othello* (3.3.85–9).

- "If there be cords, or knives, or poison, or fire, or suffocating streams, I'll not endure it" *Othello* (3.3.443–5).

- "Though his face be better than any man's, yet his leg excels all men's, and for a hand and a foot and a body, though they be not to be talked on, yet they are past compare" *Romeo and Juliet* (2.5.42–5).

- "Your love says, like an honest gentleman, and a courteous, and a kind, and a handsome, and, I warrant, a virtuous- where is your mother?" *Romeo and Juliet* (2.5.59–61)

50.3 Modern usage

Writers of modern times have also used the scheme:

- "There were frowzy fields, and cow-houses, and dunghills, and dustheaps, and ditches, and gardens, and summer-houses, and carpet-beating grounds, at the very door of the Railway. Little tumuli of oyster shells in the oyster season, and of lobster shells in the lobster season, and of broken crockery and faded cabbage leaves in all seasons, encroached upon its high places." Charles Dickens, *Dombey and Son*, 1848*[4]

- "I said, 'Who killed him?' and he said 'I don't know who killed him, but he's dead all right,' and it was dark and there was water standing in the street and no lights or windows broke and boats all up in the town and trees blown down and everything all blown and I got a skiff and went out and found my boat where I had her inside Mango Key and she was right only she was full of water." Ernest Hemingway, *After the Storm*, 1933

- "Tender as my years may be," said Caspian, "I believe I understand the slave trade from within quite as well as your Sufficiency. And I do not see that it brings into the islands meat or bread or beer or wine or timber or cabbages or books or instruments of music or horses or armour or anything else worth having." C. S. Lewis, *The Voyage of the Dawn Treader*, 1952 (Book 5 in *The Chronicles of Narnia*)

- "Let the whitefolks have their money and power and segregation and sarcasm and big houses and schools and lawns like carpets, and books, and mostly—mostly—let them have their whiteness." Maya Angelou, *I Know Why the Caged Bird Sings*, 1969*[5]

Throughout The Border Trilogy by Cormac McCarthy, for example:

- The mouths of the cans were lensed with tinted cellophane and they cast upon the sheeting a shadowplay in the lights and smoke of antic demon players and a pair of goathawks arced chittering through the partial darkness overhead. Cormac McCarthy, *All the Pretty Horses*, 1992.*[6]

50.4 In film

- "And the Germans will not be able to help themselves from imagining the cruelty their brothers endured at our hands, and our boot heels, and the edge of our knives. And the Germans will be sickened by us. And the Germans will talk about us. And the Germans will fear us. And when the Germans close their eyes at night, and their subconscious tortures them for the evil they've done, it will be with thoughts of us that it tortures them with." Lieutenant Aldo Raine (Brad Pitt), *Inglourious Basterds*

- "But all you have to do is knock on any door and say, 'If you let me in, I'll live the way you want me to live, and I'll think the way you want me to think,' and all the blinds'll go up and all the windows will open, and you'll never be lonely, ever again." Henry Drummond (Spencer Tracy), *Inherit the Wind*

- "And St. Attila raised his hand grenade up on high saying 'O Lord bless this thy hand grenade that with it thou mayest blow thine enemies to tiny bits, in thy mercy. 'and the Lord did grin and people did feast upon the lambs and sloths and carp and anchovies and orangutans and breakfast cereals and fruit bats and...'" *Monty Python and the Holy Grail*, 1975

50.5   Antonym

It can be contrasted with asyndeton, which is a coordination containing no conjunctions often manipulating the rhythm of a passage in the attempt to make a thought more memorable, and syndeton, which is a coordination with one conjunction.

Asyndeton examples include:

- "Veni, vidi, vici" (Julius Caesar)*[7]

- "We shall pay any price, bear any burden, meet any hardships, support any friend, oppose any foe to assure the survival and the success of liberty." (J. F. Kennedy, Inaugural)*[7]

Syndeton examples include:

- "I crawled back under the cover of the boat and huddled there, wet, cold and sobbing." Sam McKinney, *Sailing Uphill*. Touchwood, 2010

- "You are talking to a man who has laughed in the face of death, sneered at doom, and chuckled at catastrophe". The Wizard in *The Wizard of Oz, 1939*.

50.6   References

[1] Burton, Gideon. "Polysyndeton". *Rhetoric.byu.edu*. Silva Rhetoricae. Retrieved 17 September 2013.

[2] Corbett, Edward P.J., *Classical Rhetoric for the Modern Student*. Oxford University, New York, 1971

[3] Smyth, Herbert Weir (1920). *Greek Grammar*. Cambridge MA: Harvard University Press. p. 682. ISBN 0-674-36250-0.

[4] Bryant, Kenzie. "Polysyndeton". Prezi. Retrieved 17 September 2013.

[5] Gabriel, Jacob. "Asyndeton and Polysyndeton". Prezi. Retrieved 17 September 2013.

[6] Cormac McCarthy, *All the Pretty Horses*. New York: Vintage Books/Random House, 1993, p 122.

[7] "A Glossary of Rhetorical Terms with Examples". *Modern & Classical Languages, Literatures & Culture*. University of Kentucky. Retrieved 17 September 2013.

50.7   External links

- Audio illustrations of polysyndeton

Chapter 51

Satire

Not to be confused with satyr.
"Satires" redirects here. For other uses, see Satires (disambiguation).

Satire is a genre of literature, and sometimes graphic and performing arts, in which vices, follies, abuses, and short-comings are held up to ridicule, ideally with the intent of shaming individuals, corporations, government or society itself, into improvement.[1] Although satire is usually meant to be humorous, its greater purpose is often constructive social criticism, using wit to draw attention to both particular and wider issues in society.

A feature of satire is strong irony or sarcasm—"in satire, irony is militant" [2]—but parody, burlesque, exaggeration,[3] juxtaposition, comparison, analogy, and double entendre are all frequently used in satirical speech and writing. This "militant" irony or sarcasm often professes to approve of (or at least accept as natural) the very things the satirist wishes to attack.

Satire is nowadays found in many artistic forms of expression, including literature, plays, commentary, television shows, and media such as lyrics.

51.1 Etymology and roots

The word satire comes from the Latin word *satur* and the subsequent phrase *lanx satura*. *Satur* meant "full" but the juxtaposition with *lanx* shifted the meaning to "miscellany or medley": the expression *lanx satura* literally means "a full dish of various kinds of fruits." [4]

The word *satura* as used by Quintilian, however, was used to denote only Roman verse satire, a strict genre that imposed hexameter form, a narrower genre than what would be later intended as *satire*.[4][5] Quintilian famously said that *satura*, that is a satire in hexameter verses, was a literary genre of wholly Roman origin (*satura tota nostra est*). He was aware of and commented on Greek satire, but at the time did not label it as such, although today the origin of satire is considered to be Aristophanes' Old Comedy. The first critic to use satire in the modern broader sense was Apuleius.[4]

To Quintilian, the satire was a strict literary form, but the term soon escaped from the original narrow definition. Robert Elliott writes:

> As soon as a noun enters the domain of metaphor, as one modern scholar has pointed out, it clamours for extension; and satura (which had had no verbal, adverbial, or adjectival forms) was immediately broadened by appropriation from the Greek word for "satyr" (satyros) and its derivatives. The odd result is that the English "satire" comes from the Latin satura; but "satirize", "satiric", etc., are of Greek origin. By about the 4th century AD the writer of satires came to be known as satyricus; St. Jerome, for example, was called by one of his enemies 'a satirist in prose' ('satyricus scriptor in prosa'). Subsequent orthographic modifications obscured the Latin origin of the word satire: satura becomes satyra, and in England, by the 16th century, it was written 'satyre.'[1]

The word *satire* derives from *satura*, and its origin was not influenced by the Greek mythological figure of the *satyr*.[6] In the 17th century, philologist Isaac Casaubon was the first to dispute the etymology of satire from satyr, contrary to the belief up to that time.[7]

51.2 Satire and humor

Laughter is not an essential component of satire;[8] in fact there are types of satire that are not meant to be "funny" at all. Conversely, not all humour, even on such topics as politics, religion or art is necessarily "satirical", even when it uses the satirical tools of irony, parody, and burlesque.

Even light-hearted satire has a serious "after-taste": the organizers of the Ig Nobel Prize describe this as "first make people laugh, and then make them think".[9]

51.3 Social and psychological functions

Satire and irony in some cases have been regarded as the most effective source to understand a society, the oldest form of social study.[10] They provide the keenest insights into a group's collective psyche, reveal its deepest values and tastes, and the society's structures of power.[11][12] Some authors have regarded satire as superior to non-comic and non-artistic disciplines like history or anthropology.[10][13][14] In a prominent example from Ancient Greece, philosopher Plato, when asked by a friend for a book to understand Athenian society, referred him to the plays of Aristophanes.[15][16]

Historically, satire has satisfied the popular need to debunk and ridicule the leading figures in politics, economy, religion and other prominent realms of power.[17] Satire confronts public discourse and the collective imaginary, playing as a public opinion counterweight to power (be it political, economic, religious, symbolic, or otherwise), by challenging leaders and authorities. For instance, it forces administrations to clarify, amend or establish their policies. Satire's job is to expose problems and contradictions, and it's not obligated to solve them.[18] Karl Kraus set in the history of satire a prominent example of a satirist role as confronting public discourse.[19]

For its nature and social role, satire has enjoyed in many societies a special freedom license to mock prominent individuals and institutions.[20] The satiric impulse, and its ritualized expressions, carry out the function of resolving social tension.[21] Institutions like the ritual clowns, by giving expression to the antisocial tendencies, represent a safety valve which reestablishes equilibrium and health in the collective imaginary, which are jeopardized by the repressive aspects of society.[22][23]

The state of political satire in a given society reflects the tolerance or intolerance that characterizes it,[17] and the state of civil liberties and human rights. Under totalitarian regimes any criticism of a political system, and especially satire, is suppressed. A typical example is the Soviet Union where the dissidents, such as Aleksandr Solzhenitsyn and Andrei Sakharov were under strong pressure from the government. While satire of everyday life in the USSR was allowed, the most prominent satirist being Arkady Raikin, political satire existed in the form of anecdotes[24] that made fun of Soviet political leaders, especially Brezhnev, famous for his narrow-mindness and love for awards and decorations.

51.4 Classifications of satire

Satire is a diverse genre which is complex to classify and define, with a wide range of satiric "modes".[25][26]

51.4.1 Horatian, Juvenalian, Menippean

Satirical literature can commonly be categorized as either Horatian, Juvenalian, or Menippean.[27]

Horatian

Horatian satire, named for the Roman satirist Horace (65–8 BCE), playfully criticizes some social vice through gentle, mild, and light-hearted humour. Horace (Quintus Horatius Flaccus) wrote Satires to gently ridicule the dominant opinions and "philosophical beliefs of ancient Rome and Greece" (Rankin).*[28] Rather than writing in harsh or accusing tones, he addressed issues with humor and clever mockery. Horatian satire follows this same pattern of "gently [ridiculing] the absurdities and follies of human beings" (Drury).*[29]

It directs wit, exaggeration, and self-deprecating humour toward what it identifies as folly, rather than evil. Horatian satire's sympathetic tone is common in modern society.*[30]

A Horatian satirist's goal is to heal the situation with smiles, rather than by anger. A Horatian satirist makes fun of general human folly rather than pointing to any specific follier. Shamekia Thomas suggests, "In a work using Horatian satire, readers often laugh at the characters in the story who are the subject of mockery as well as themselves and society for behaving in those ways." Alexander Pope has been established as an author whose satire "heals with morals what it hurts with wit" (Green).*[31] Alexander Pope—and Horatian satire—attempt to teach.

Examples:

- The Ig Nobel Prizes.

- Bierce, Ambrose, *The Devil's Dictionary*.

- Defoe, Daniel, *The True-Born Englishman*.

- The Savoy Operas of Gilbert and Sullivan.

- Gogol, Nikolai, *Dead Souls*.

- Groening, Matthew 'Matt', *The Simpsons*.

- Kubrick, Stanley, *Dr. Strangelove*.

- Lewis, Clive Staples, *The Screwtape Letters*.

- Mercer, Richard 'Rick', *The Rick Mercer Report*.

- Pope, Alexander, *The Rape of the Lock*.

- Reiner, Rob, *This Is Spinal Tap*.

- Twain, Mark, *Adventures of Huckleberry Finn*.

Juvenalian

Juvenalian satire, named after the Roman satirist Juvenal (late 1st century – early 2nd century AD), is more contemptuous and abrasive than the Horatian. Juvenal disagreed with the opinions of the public figures and institutions of the Republic and actively attacked them through his literature. "He utilized the satirical tools of exaggeration and parody to make his targets appear monstrous and incompetent" (Podzemny).*[32] Juvenal satire follows this same pattern of abrasively ridiculing societal structures.

Juvenalian satire addresses social evil through scorn, outrage, and savage ridicule. This form is often pessimistic, characterized by irony, sarcasm, moral indignation and personal invective, with less emphasis on humor. Strongly polarized political satire is often Juvenalian. See also: *Satires* of Juvenal.

A Juvenal satirist's goal is to provoke some sort of change because he sees his opponent as evil or harmful. A Juvenal satirist mocks "societal structure, power, and civilization" (Thomas).*[33] He will do this by exaggerating the words or position of his opponent in order to jeopardize his opponent's reputation and/or power. Jonathan Swift has been established as an author who "borrowed heavily from Juvenal's techniques in [his critique] of contemporary English society" (Podzemny).*[32] Jonathan Swift—and Juvenalian satire—attempt to punish.

Examples:

- Barnes, Julian, *England, England.*

- Bradbury, Ray, *Fahrenheit 451.*

- Bulgakov, Mikhail, *Heart of a Dog.*

- Burgess, Anthony, *A Clockwork Orange.*

- Burroughs, William, *Naked Lunch.*

- Cooke, Ebenezer, *The Sot-Weed Factor; or, A Voyage to Maryland,—a satire, in which is described the laws, government, courts, and constitutions of the country, and also the buildings, feasts, frolics, entertainments, and drunken humors of the inhabitants in that part of America.*

- Ellis, Bret Easton, *American Psycho.*

- Golding, William, *Lord of the Flies.*

- Hall, Joseph, *Virgidemiarum.*

- Heller, Joseph, *Catch-22.*

- Huxley, Aldous, *Brave New World.*

- Johnson, Samuel, *London*, an adaptation of Juvenal, *Third Satire.*

- Mencken, HL, *Libido for the Ugly.*

- Morris, Chris, *Brasseye.*

- ——, *The Day Today.*

- Orwell, George, *Nineteen Eighty-Four.*

- Orwell, George, *Animal Farm.*

- Swift, Jonathan, *A Modest Proposal.*

- Zamyatin, Yevgeny, *We.*

- Voltaire, *Candide.*

51.4.2   Satire versus teasing

In the history of theatre there has always been a conflict between engagement and disengagement on politics and relevant issue, between satire and grotesque on one side, and jest with teasing on the other.[*][34] Max Eastman defined the spectrum of satire in terms of "degrees of biting", as ranging from satire proper at the hot-end, and "kidding" at the violet-end; Eastman adopted the term kidding to denote what is just satirical in form, but is not really firing at the target.[*][35] Nobel laureate satirical playwright Dario Fo pointed out the difference between satire and teasing (*sfottò*).[*][36] Teasing is the reactionary side of the comic; it limits itself to a shallow parody of physical appearance. The side-effect of teasing is that it humanizes and draws sympathy for the powerful individual towards which it is directed. Satire instead uses the comic to go against power and its oppressions, has a subversive character, and a moral dimension which draws judgement against its targets.[*][37][*][38][*][39][*][40] Fo formulated an operational criteria to tell real satire from *sfottò*, saying that real satire arouses an outraged and violent reaction, and that the more they try to stop you, the better is the job you are doing.[*][41] Fo contends that, historically, people in positions of power have welcomed and encouraged good-humoured buffoonery, while modern day people in positions of power have tried to censor, ostracize and repress satire.[*][34][*][37]

Teasing (*sfottò*) is an ancient form of simple buffoonery, a form of comedy without satire's subversive edge. Teasing includes light and affectionate parody, good-humoured mockery, simple one-dimensional poking fun, and benign spoofs. Teasing typically consists of an impersonation of someone monkeying around with his exterior attributes, tics, physical blemishes, voice and mannerisms, quirks, way of dressing and walking, and/or the phrases he typically repeats. By contrast, teasing never touches on the core issue, never makes a serious criticism judging the target with irony; it never harms the target's conduct, ideology and position of power; it never undermines the perception of his morality and cultural dimension.[37][39] *Sfottò* directed towards a powerful individual makes him appear more human and draws sympathy towards him.[42] Hermann Göring propagated jests and jokes against himself, with the aim of humanizing his image.[43][44]

51.4.3 Classifications by topics

Types of satire can also be classified according to the topics it deals with. From the earliest times, at least since the plays of Aristophanes, the primary topics of literary satire have been politics, religion and sex.[45][46][47][48] This is partly because these are the most pressing problems that affect anybody living in a society, and partly because these topics are usually taboo.[45][49] Among these, politics in the broader sense is considered the pre-eminent topic of satire.[49] Satire which targets the clergy is a type of political satire, while religious satire is that which targets religious beliefs.[50] Satire on sex may overlap with blue comedy, off-color humor and dick jokes.

Scatology has a long literary association with satire,[45][51][52] as it is a classical mode of the grotesque, the grotesque body and the satiric grotesque.[45][53] Shit plays a fundamental role in satire because it symbolizes death, the turd being "the ultimate dead object".[51][52] The satirical comparison of individuals or institutions with human excrement, exposes their "inherent inertness, corruption and dead-likeness".[51][54][55] The ritual clowns of clown societies, like among the Pueblo Indians, have ceremonies with filth-eating.[56][57] In other cultures, sin-eating is an apotropaic rite in which the sin-eater (also called filth-eater),[58][59] by ingesting the food provided, takes "upon himself the sins of the departed".[60] Satire about death overlaps with black humor and gallows humor.

Another classification by topics is the distinction between political satire, religious satire and satire of manners.[61] Political satire is sometimes called topical satire, satire of manners is sometimes called satire of everyday life, and religious satire is sometimes called philosophical satire. Comedy of manners, sometimes also called satire of manners, criticizes mode of life of common people; political satire aims at behavior, manners of politicians, and vices of political systems. Historically, comedy of manners, which first appeared in British theater in 1620, has uncritically accepted the social code of the upper classes.[62] Comedy in general accepts the rules of the social game, while satire subverts them.[63]

Another analysis of satire is the spectrum of his possible tones: wit, ridicule, irony, sarcasm, cynicism, the sardonic and invective.[64][65]

51.4.4 Classifications by medium

Satire is found not only in written literary forms. In preliterate cultures it manifests itself in ritual and folk forms, as well as in trickster tales and oral poetry.[21]

It appears also in graphic arts, music, sculpture, dance, cartoon strips, and graffiti. Examples are Dada sculptures, Pop Art works, music of Gilbert and Sullivan and Erik Satie, punk and rock music.[21] In modern media culture, stand-up comedy is an enclave in which satire can be introduced into mass media, challenging mainstream discourse.[21] Comedy roasts, mock festivals, and stand-up comedians in nightclubs and concerts are the modern forms of ancient satiric rituals.[21]

51.5 Development

51.5.1 Ancient Egypt

One of the earliest examples of what we might call satire, The Satire of the Trades,[66] is in Egyptian writing from the beginning of the 2nd millennium BC. The text's apparent readers are students, tired of studying. It argues that their lot as scribes is useful, and their lot far superior to that of the ordinary man. Scholars such as Helck[67] think that the context was meant to be serious.

The Papyrus Anastasi I[68] (late 2nd millennium BC) contains a satirical letter which first praises the virtues of its recipient, but then mocks the reader's meagre knowledge and achievements.

51.5.2   Ancient Greece

The Greeks had no word for what later would be called "satire", although the terms cynicism and parody were used. Modern critics call the Greek playwright Aristophanes one of the best known early satirists: his plays are known for their critical political and societal commentary,[69] particularly for the political satire by which he criticized the powerful Cleon (as in *The Knights*). He is also notable for the persecution he underwent.[69][70][71][72] Aristophanes' plays turned upon images of filth and disease.[73] His bawdy style was adopted by Greek dramatist-comedian Menander. His early play *Drunkenness* contains an attack on the politician Callimedon.

The oldest form of satire still in use is the Menippean satire by Menippus of Gadara. His own writings are lost. Examples from his admirers and imitators mix seriousness and mockery in dialogues and present parodies before a background of diatribe. As in the case of Aristophanes plays, menippean satire turned upon images of filth and disease.[73]

51.5.3   Roman world

The first Roman to discuss satire critically was Quintilian, who invented the term to describe the writings of Lucilius. The two most prominent and influential ancient Roman satirists are Horace and Juvenal, who wrote during the early days of the Roman Empire. Other important satirists in ancient Latin are Lucilius and Persius. *Satire* in their work is much wider than in the modern sense of the word, including fantastic and highly coloured humorous writing with little or no real mocking intent. When Horace criticized Augustus, he used veiled ironic terms. In contrast, Pliny reports that the 6th century BC poet Hipponax wrote *satirae* that were so cruel that the offended hanged themselves.[74]

51.5.4   Medieval Islamic world

Main articles: Arabic satire and Persian satire

Medieval Arabic poetry included the satiric genre *hija*. Satire was introduced into Arabic prose literature by the Afro-Arab author Al-Jahiz in the 9th century. While dealing with serious topics in what are now known as anthropology, sociology and psychology, he introduced a satirical approach, "based on the premise that, however serious the subject under review, it could be made more interesting and thus achieve greater effect, if only one leavened the lump of solemnity by the insertion of a few amusing anecdotes or by the throwing out of some witty or paradoxical observations. He was well aware that, in treating of new themes in his prose works, he would have to employ a vocabulary of a nature more familiar in *hija*, satirical poetry." [75] For example, in one of his zoological works, he satirized the preference for longer human penis size, writing: "If the length of the penis were a sign of honor, then the mule would belong to the (honorable tribe of) Quraysh". Another satirical story based on this preference was an *Arabian Nights* tale called "Ali with the Large Member".[76]

In the 10th century, the writer Tha'alibi recorded satirical poetry written by the Arabic poets As-Salami and Abu Dulaf, with As-Salami praising Abu Dulaf's wide breadth of knowledge and then mocking his ability in all these subjects, and with Abu Dulaf responding back and satirizing As-Salami in return.[77] An example of Arabic political satire included another 10th-century poet Jarir satirizing Farazdaq as "a transgressor of the Sharia" and later Arabic poets in turn using the term "Farazdaq-like" as a form of political satire.[78]

The terms "comedy" and "satire" became synonymous after Aristotle's *Poetics* was translated into Arabic in the medieval Islamic world, where it was elaborated upon by Islamic philosophers and writers, such as Abu Bischr, his pupil Al-Farabi, Avicenna, and Averroes. Due to cultural differences, they disassociated comedy from Greek dramatic representation and instead identified it with Arabic poetic themes and forms, such as *hija* (satirical poetry). They viewed comedy as simply the "art of reprehension", and made no reference to light and cheerful events, or troubled beginnings and happy endings, associated with classical Greek comedy. After the Latin translations of the 12th century, the term "comedy" thus gained a new semantic meaning in Medieval literature.[79]

Ubayd Zakani introduced satire in Persian literature during the 14th century. His work is noted for its satire and obscene verses, often political or bawdy, and often cited in debates involving homosexual practices. He wrote the *Resaleh-ye Delgosha*, as well as *Akhlaq al-Ashraf* ("Ethics of the Aristocracy") and the famous humorous fable *Masnavi Mush-O-Gorbeh* (Mouse and Cat), which was a political satire. His non-satirical serious classical verses have also been regarded as very well written, in league with the other great works of Persian literature. Between 1905 and 1911, Bibi Khatoon Astarabadi and other Iranian writers wrote notable satires.

51.5.5   Medieval Europe

In the Early Middle Ages, examples of satire were the songs by Goliards or vagants now best known as an anthology called Carmina Burana and made famous as texts of a composition by the 20th-century composer Carl Orff. Satirical poetry is believed to have been popular, although little has survived. With the advent of the High Middle Ages and the birth of modern vernacular literature in the 12th century, it began to be used again, most notably by Chaucer. The disrespectful manner was considered "Unchristian" and ignored but for the **moral satire**, which mocked misbehaviour in Christian terms. Examples are *Livre des Manières* by Étienne de Fougères (~1178), and some of Chaucer's *Canterbury Tales*. The epos was mocked, and even the feudal society, but there was hardly a general interest in the genre.

Two major satirists of Europe in the Renaissance were Giovanni Boccaccio and François Rabelais. Other examples of Renaissance satire include *Till Eulenspiegel, Reynard the Fox*, Sebastian Brant's *Narrenschiff* (1494), Erasmus' *Moriae Encomium* (1509) and Thomas More's *Utopia* (1516).

51.5.6   Early modern western satire

Direct social commentary via satire returned with a vengeance in the 16th century, when farcical texts such as the works of François Rabelais tackled more serious issues (and incurred the wrath of the crown as a result).

The Elizabethan (i.e. 16th-century English) writers thought of satire as related to the notoriously rude, coarse and sharp satyr play. Elizabethan "satire" (typically in pamphlet form) therefore contains more straightforward abuse than subtle irony. The French Huguenot Isaac Casaubon pointed out in 1605 that satire in the Roman fashion was something altogether more civilised. Casaubon discovered and published Quintilian's writing and presented the original meaning of the term (satira, not satyr), and the sense of wittiness (reflecting the "dishfull of fruits") became more important again. 17th-century English satire once again aimed at the "amendment of vices" (Dryden).

In the 1590s a new wave of verse satire broke with the publication of Hall's *Virgidemiarum*, six books of verse satires targeting everything from literary fads to corrupt noblemen. Although Donne had already circulated satires in manuscript, Hall's was the first real attempt in English at verse satire on the Juvenalian model.*[80] The success of his work combined with a national mood of disillusion in the last years of Elizabeth's reign triggered an avalanche of satire – much of it less conscious of classical models than Hall's —until the fashion was brought to an abrupt stop by censorship.*[lower-alpha 1]

51.5.7   Age of Enlightenment

The Age of Enlightenment, an intellectual movement in the 17th and 18th century advocating rationality, produced a great revival of satire in Britain. This was fuelled by the rise of partisan politics, with the formalisation of the Tory and Whig parties —and also, in 1714, by the formation of the Scriblerus Club, which included Alexander Pope, Jonathan Swift, John Gay, John Arbuthnot, Robert Harley, Thomas Parnell, and Henry St John, 1st Viscount Bolingbroke. This club included several of the notable satirists of early 18th century Britain. They focused their attention on Martinus Scriblerus, "an invented learned fool... whose work they attributed all that was tedious, narrow-minded, and pedantic in contemporary scholarship" .*[82] In their hands astute and biting satire of institutions and individuals became a popular weapon. The turn to the 18th century was characterized by a switch from Horatian, soft, pseudo-satire, to biting "juvenal" satire.*[83]

Jonathan Swift was one of the greatest of Anglo-Irish satirists, and one of the first to practise modern journalistic satire. For instance, In his *A Modest Proposal* Swift suggests that Irish peasants be encouraged to sell their own children as food for the rich, as a solution to the "problem" of poverty. His purpose is of course to attack indifference to the plight of the desperately poor. In his book *Gulliver's Travels* he writes about the flaws in human society in general and English society in particular. John Dryden wrote an influential essay entitled "A Discourse Concerning the Original and Progress of Satire" *[84] that helped fix the definition of satire in the literary world. His satirical *Mac Flecknoe* was written in response to a rivalry with Thomas Shadwell and eventually inspired Alexander Pope to write his satirical *The Rape of the Lock*. Other satirical works by Pope include the *Epistle to Dr Arbuthnot*.

Daniel Defoe pursued a more journalistic type of satire, being famous for his *The True-Born Englishman* which mocks xenophobic patriotism, and *The Shortest-Way with the Dissenters* - advocating religious toleration by means of an ironical exaggeration of the highly intolerant attitudes of his time.

The pictorial satire of William Hogarth is a precursor to the development of political cartoons in 18th century England.*[85] The medium developed under the direction of its greatest exponent, James Gillray from London.*[86] With his satirical works calling the king (George III), prime ministers and generals (especially Napoleon) to account, Gillray's wit and keen sense of the ridiculous made him the pre-eminent cartoonist of the era.*[86]

Ebenezer Cooke (1665-1732), author of "The Sot-Weed Factor" (1708), was among the first American colonialists to write literary satire. Benjamin Franklin (1706-1790) and others followed, using satire to shape an emerging nation's culture through its sense of the ridiculous.

51.5.8   Satire in Victorian England

Several satiric papers competed for the public's attention in the Victorian era (1837-1901) and Edwardian period, such as *Punch* (1841) and *Fun* (1861).

Perhaps the most enduring examples of Victorian satire, however, are to be found in the Savoy Operas of Gilbert and Sullivan. In fact, in *The Yeomen of the Guard*, a jester is given lines that paint a very neat picture of the method and purpose of the satirist, and might almost be taken as a statement of Gilbert's own intent:

> *"I can set a braggart quailing with a quip,*
>
> *The upstart I can wither with a whim;*
>
> *He may wear a merry laugh upon his lip,*
>
> *But his laughter has an echo that is grim!"*

Novelists such as Charles Dickens often used passages of satiric writing in their treatment of social issues.

In the same period, in the United States, Mark Twain (1835-1910) was a great American satirist: his novel *Huckleberry Finn* (1884) is set in the antebellum South, where the moral values Twain wishes to promote are completely turned on their heads. His hero, Huck, is a rather simple but goodhearted lad who is ashamed of the "sinful temptation" that leads him to help a runaway slave. In fact his conscience, warped by the distorted moral world he has grown up in, often bothers him most when he is at his best. Ironically, he is prepared to do good, believing it to be wrong.

Twain's younger contemporary Ambrose Bierce (1842-1913) gained notoriety as a cynic, pessimist and black humorist with his dark, bitterly ironic stories, many set during the American Civil War, which satirized the limitations of human perception and reason. Bierce's most famous work of satire is probably *The Devil's Dictionary* (1906), in which the definitions mock cant, hypocrisy and received wisdom.

51.5.9   20th century satire

Karl Kraus is considered the first major European satirist since Jonathan Swift.*[19] In 20th century literature, satire was used by authors such as Aldous Huxley (1930s) and George Orwell (1940s), which under the inspiration of Zamyatin's Russian 1921 novel *We*, made serious and even frightening commentaries on the dangers of the sweeping social changes taking place throughout Europe. Many social critics of this same time in the United States, such as Dorothy Parker and H. L. Mencken, used satire as their main weapon, and Mencken in particular is noted for having said that "one horse-laugh is worth ten thousand syllogisms" in the persuasion of the public to accept a criticism. Novelist Sinclair Lewis was known for his satirical stories such as *Main Street* (1920), *Babbitt* (1922), *Elmer Gantry* (1927; dedicated by Lewis to H.L. Menchen), and *It Can't Happen Here* (1935), and his books often explored and satirized contemporary American values. The film *The Great Dictator* (1940) by Charlie Chaplin is itself a parody of Adolf Hitler; Chaplin later declared that he would have not made the film if he had known about the concentration camps.*[87]

In the United States 1950s, satire was introduced into American stand-up comedy most prominently by Lenny Bruce and Mort Sahl.*[21] As they challenged the taboos and conventional wisdom of the time, were ostracized by the mass media establishment as *sick comedians*. In the same period, Paul Krassner's magazine *The Realist* began publication, to become immensely popular during the 1960s and early 1970s among people in the counterculture; it had articles and cartoons that were savage, biting satires of politicians such as Lyndon Johnson and Richard Nixon, the Vietnam War, the Cold War and the War on Drugs. Prominent satiric stand-up comedian George Carlin acknowledged the influence *The Realist* had in his 1970s conversion to a satiric comedian.[88][89]

A more humorous brand of satire enjoyed a renaissance in the UK in the early 1960s with the satire boom, led by such luminaries as Peter Cook, Alan Bennett, Jonathan Miller, and Dudley Moore, whose stage show *Beyond the Fringe* was a hit not only in Britain, but also in the United States. Other significant influences in 1960s British satire include David Frost, Eleanor Bron and the television program *That Was The Week That Was*.[90]

Joseph Heller's most famous work, *Catch-22* (1961), satirizes bureaucracy and the military, and is frequently cited as one of the greatest literary works of the twentieth century.[91] The film *Dr. Strangelove* from 1964 was a popular satire on the Cold War.

51.5.10 Contemporary satire

Contemporary popular usage of the term "satire" is often very imprecise. While satire often uses caricature and parody, by no means are all uses of these or other humorous devices, satiric. Refer to the careful definition of satire that heads this article.

Satire is used on many UK television programmes, particularly popular panel shows and quiz shows such as *Mock the Week* (2005) and *Have I Got News for You* (1990-ongoing). Similarly it is found on radio quiz shows such as *The News Quiz* (1977-ongoing) and *The Now Show* (1998-ongoing). One of the most-watched UK television shows of the 1980s and early 1990s, the puppet show *Spitting Image* was a satire of the royal family, politics, entertainment, sport and British culture of the era.[92]

The television program *South Park* (1997-ongoing) relies almost exclusively on satire to address issues in American culture, with episodes addressing anti-Semitism, militant atheism, homophobia, environmentalism, corporate culture, political correctness and anti-Catholicism, among many other issues.

Australian Chris Lilley produces comedy art in the style of mockumentaries (*We Can Be Heroes*, *Summer Heights High*, *Angry Boys*) and his work is often described as complex social satire.

Stephen Colbert's television program, *The Colbert Report* (2005-2014), is instructive in the methods of contemporary American satire. Colbert's character is an opinionated and self-righteous commentator who, in his TV interviews, interrupts people, points and wags his finger at them, and "unwittingly" uses a number of logical fallacies. In doing so, he demonstrates the principle of modern American political satire: the ridicule of the actions of politicians and other public figures by taking all their statements and purported beliefs to their furthest (supposedly) logical conclusion, thus revealing their perceived hypocrisy or absurdity.

The American sketch comedy television show *Saturday Night Live* is also known for its satirical impressions and parodies of prominent persons and politicians, among some of the most notable, their parodies of U.S. political figures Hillary Clinton[93] and of Sarah Palin.[94]

Other political satire includes various political causes in the past, including the relatively successful Polish Beer-Lovers' Party and the joke political candidates Molly the Dog[95] and Brian Miner.[96]

In the United Kingdom, a popular modern satirist is Sir Terry Pratchett, author of the internationally best-selling *Discworld* book series. One of the most well-known and controversial British satirists is Sir Chris Morris, co-writer and director of *Four Lions*.

In Canada, satire has become an important part of the comedy scene. Stephen Leacock was one of the best known early Canadian satirists, and in the early 20th century, he achieved fame by targeting the attitudes of small town life. In more recent years, Canada has had several prominent satirical television series and radio shows. Some, including *CODCO*, *The Royal Canadian Air Farce*, *This Is That*, and *This Hour Has 22 Minutes* deal directly with current news stories and political figures, while others, like *History Bites* present contemporary social satire in the context of events and figures in history. The Canadian organization *Canada News Network* provides commentary on contemporary news events that are primarily Canadian in nature. Canadian songwriter Nancy White uses music as the vehicle for her satire, and her comic folk songs are regularly played on CBC Radio.

Cartoonists often use satire as well as straight humour. Al Capp's satirical comic strip *Li'l Abner* was censored in September 1947. The controversy, as reported in *Time*, centred on Capp's portrayal of the US Senate. Said Edward Leech of Scripps-Howard, "We don't think it is good editing or sound citizenship to picture the Senate as an assemblage of freaks and crooks... boobs and undesirables." *[97] Walt Kelly's *Pogo* was likewise censored in 1952 over his overt satire of Senator Joe McCarthy, caricatured in his comic strip as "Simple J. Malarky". Garry Trudeau, whose comic strip *Doonesbury* focuses on satire of the political system, and provides a trademark cynical view on national events. Trudeau exemplifies humour mixed with criticism. For example, the character Mark Slackmeyer lamented that because he was not legally married to his partner, he was deprived of the "exquisite agony" of experiencing a nasty and painful divorce like heterosexuals. This, of course, satirized the claim that gay unions would denigrate the sanctity of heterosexual marriage.

Like some literary predecessors, many recent television satires contain strong elements of parody and caricature; for instance, the popular animated series *The Simpsons* and *South Park* both parody modern family and social life by taking their assumptions to the extreme; both have led to the creation of similar series. As well as the purely humorous effect of this sort of thing, they often strongly criticise various phenomena in politics, economic life, religion and many other aspects of society, and thus qualify as satirical. Due to their animated nature, these shows can easily use images of public figures and generally have greater freedom to do so than conventional shows using live actors.

Fake News is also a very popular form of contemporary satire, appearing in as wide an array of formats as the news media itself: print (e.g. *The Onion, Canada News Network, Private Eye*), "Not Your Homepage,*[98]" radio (e.g. *On the Hour*), television (e.g. *The Day Today, The Daily Show, Brass Eye*) and the web (e.g. Mindry.in, The Fruit Dish, Scunt News,*[99] Faking News, El Koshary Today, The Giant Napkin,*[100] Unconfirmed Sources*[101] and The *Onion's* website). Other satires are on the list of satirists and satires. Another internet-driven form of satire is to lampoon bad internet performers. An example of this is the Internet meme character Miranda Sings.*[102]*[103]

In an interview with *Wikinews*, Sean Mills, President of *The Onion*, said angry letters about their news parody always carried the same message. "It's whatever affects that person", said Mills. "So it's like, 'I love it when you make a joke about murder or rape, but if you talk about cancer, well my brother has cancer and that's not funny to me.' Or someone else can say, 'Cancer's *hilarious*, but don't talk about rape because my cousin got raped.' Those are rather extreme examples, but if it affects somebody personally, they tend to be more sensitive about it." *[104]

Zhou Libo, a comedian from Shanghai, is the most popular satirist in China. His humour has interests middle-class people and has sold out shows ever since his rise to fame. Primarily a theater performer, Zhou said his work is never scripted, allowing him to improvise jokes about recent events. He often mocks political figures he supports.

51.6   Techniques

Literary satire is usually written out of earlier satiric works, reprising previous conventions, commonplaces, stance, situations and tones of voice.*[105] Exaggeration is one of the most common satirical techniques.*[3]

51.7   Legal status

For its nature and social role, satire has enjoyed in many societies a special freedom license to mock prominent individuals and institutions.*[20] In Germany,*[106] and Italy*[17]*[107] satire is protected by the constitution.

Since satire belongs to the realm of art and artistic expression, it benefits from broader lawfulness limits than mere freedom of information of journalistic kind.*[107] In some countries a specific "right to satire" is recognized and its limits go beyond the "right to report" of journalism and even the "right to criticize." *[107] Satire benefits not only of the protection to freedom of speech, but also to that to culture, and that to scientific and artistic production.*[17]*[107]

51.8 Censorship and criticism of satire

Descriptions of satire's biting effect on its target include 'venomous', 'cutting', 'stinging',[108] vitriol. Because satire often combines anger and humor, as well as the fact that it addresses and calls into question many controversial issues, it can be profoundly disturbing.

51.8.1 Typical arguments

Because it is essentially ironic or sarcastic, satire is often misunderstood. A typical misunderstanding is to confuse the satirist with his persona.[109]

Bad taste

Common uncomprehending responses to satire include revulsion (accusations of poor taste, or that "it's just not funny" for instance), to the idea that the satirist actually does support the ideas, policies, or people he is attacking. For instance, at the time of its publication, many people misunderstood Swift's purpose in *A Modest Proposal*, assuming it to be a serious recommendation of economically motivated cannibalism.

Targeting the victim

Some critics of Mark Twain see *Huckleberry Finn* as racist and offensive, missing the point that its author clearly intended it to be satire (racism being in fact only one of a number of Mark Twain's known concerns attacked in *Huckleberry Finn*).[110][111] This same misconception was suffered by the main character of the 1960s British television comedy satire *Till Death Us Do Part*. The character of Alf Garnett (played by Warren Mitchell) was created to poke fun at the kind of narrow-minded, racist, little Englander that Garnett represented. Instead, his character became a sort of anti-hero to people who actually agreed with his views. The same thing happened in regard to the main character in the American TV Show *All in the Family*, Archie Bunker.

The Australian satirical television comedy show *The Chaser's War on Everything* has suffered repeated attacks based on various perceived interpretations of the "target" of its attacks. The "Make a Realistic Wish Foundation" sketch (June 2009), which attacked in classical satiric fashion the heartlessness of people who are reluctant to donate to charities, was widely interpreted as an attack on the Make a Wish Foundation, or even the terminally ill children helped by that organisation. Prime Minister of the time Kevin Rudd stated that The Chaser team "should hang their heads in shame". He went on to say that "I didn't see that but it's been described to me. ...But having a go at kids with a terminal illness is really beyond the pale, absolutely beyond the pale." [112] Television station management suspended the show for two weeks and reduced the third season to eight episodes.

Romantic prejudice

The romantic prejudice against satire is the belief spread by the romantic movement that satire is something unworthy of serious attention; this prejudice has held considerable influence to this day.[113] Such prejudice extends to humor and everything that arouses laughter, which are often underestimated as frivolous and unworthy of serious study.[114] For instance, humor is generally neglected as a topic of anthropological research and teaching.[115]

51.8.2 History of opposition toward notable satires

Because satire criticises in an ironic, essentially indirect way, it frequently escapes censorship in a way more direct criticism might not. Periodically, however, it runs into serious opposition, and people in power who perceive themselves as attacked attempt to censor it or prosecute its practitioners. In a classic example, Aristophanes was persecuted by the demagogue Cleon.

1599 book ban

In 1599, the Archbishop of Canterbury John Whitgift and the Bishop of London Richard Bancroft, whose offices had the function of licensing books for publication in England, issued a decree banning verse satire. The decree, now known as the Bishops' Ban of 1599, ordered the burning of certain volumes of satire by John Marston, Thomas Middleton, Joseph Hall, and others; it also required histories and plays to be specially approved by a member of the Queen's Privy Council, and it prohibited the future printing of satire in verse.*[116]

The motives for the ban are obscure, particularly since some of the books banned had been licensed by the same authorities less than a year earlier. Various scholars have argued that the target was obscenity, libel, or sedition. It seems likely that lingering anxiety about the Martin Marprelate controversy, in which the bishops themselves had employed satirists, played a role; both Thomas Nashe and Gabriel Harvey, two of the key figures in that controversy, suffered a complete ban on all their works. In the event, though, the ban was little enforced, even by the licensing authority itself.

21st century polemics

In 2005, the Jyllands-Posten Muhammad cartoons controversy caused global protests by offended Muslims and violent attacks with many fatalities in the Near East. It was not the first case of Muslim protests against criticism in the form of satire, but the Western world was surprised by the hostility of the reaction: Any country's flag in which a newspaper chose to publish the parodies was being burnt in a Near East country, then embassies were attacked, killing 139 people in mainly four countries; politicians throughout Europe agreed that satire was an aspect of the freedom of speech, and therefore to be a protected means of dialogue. Iran threatened to start an International Holocaust Cartoon Competition, which was immediately responded to by Jews with an Israeli Anti-Semitic Cartoons Contest.

In 2006 British comedian Sacha Baron Cohen released *Borat: Cultural Learnings of America for Make Benefit Glorious Nation of Kazakhstan*, a "mockumentary" that satirized everyone, from high society to frat boys. The film was criticized by many. Although Baron Cohen is Jewish, some complained that it was antisemitic, and the government of Kazakhstan boycotted the film. The film itself had been a reaction to a longer quarrel between the government and the comedian.

In 2008, popular South African cartoonist and satirist Jonathan Shapiro (who is published under the pen name Zapiro) came under fire for depicting then-president of the ANC Jacob Zuma in the act of undressing in preparation for the implied rape of 'Lady Justice' which is held down by Zuma loyalists.*[117] The cartoon was drawn in response to Zuma's efforts to duck corruption charges, and the controversy was heightened by the fact that Zuma was himself acquitted of rape in May 2006. In February 2009, the South African Broadcasting Corporation, viewed by some opposition parties as the mouthpiece of the governing ANC,*[118] shelved a satirical TV show created by Shapiro,*[119] and in May 2009 the broadcaster pulled a documentary about political satire (featuring Shapiro among others) for the second time, hours before scheduled broadcast.*[120] Apartheid South Africa also had a long history of censorship.

On December 29, 2009, Samsung sued Mike Breen, and the *Korea Times* for $1 million, claiming criminal defamation over a satirical column published on Christmas Day, 2009.*[121]*[122]

On April 29, 2015, the UK Independence Party (UKIP) requested Kent Police investigate the BBC, claiming that comments made about Party leader Nigel Farage by a panelist on the comedy show *Have I Got News For You* might hinder his chances of success in the general election (which would take place a week later), and claimed the BBC breached the Representation of the People Act.*[123] Kent Police rebuffed the request to open an investigation, and the BBC released a statement, "Britain has a proud tradition of satire, and everyone knows that the contributors on *Have I Got News for You* regularly make jokes at the expense of politicians of all parties." *[123]

51.9   Satirical prophecy

Satire is occasionally prophetic: the jokes precede actual events.*[124]*[125] Among the eminent examples are:

- The 1784 presaging of modern daylight saving time, later actually proposed in 1907. While an American envoy to France, Benjamin Franklin anonymously published a letter in 1784 suggesting that Parisians economise on candles by arising earlier to use morning sunlight.*[126]

- In the 1920s an English cartoonist imagined a laughable thing for the time: a hotel for cars. He drew a multi-story car park.*[125]

- The second episode of *Monty Python's Flying Circus*, which debuted in 1969, featured a *skit* entitled "The Mouse Problem" (meant to satirize contemporary media exposés on homosexuality), which depicted a cultural phenomenon eerily similar to modern furry fandom (which did not become widespread until the 1980s, over a decade after the skit was first aired)

- The comedy film *Americathon*, released in 1979 and set in the United States of 1998, predicted a number of trends and events that would eventually unfold in the near future, including an American debt crisis, Chinese capitalism, the fall of the Soviet Union, terrorism aimed at the civilian population, a presidential sex scandal, and the popularity of reality shows.

- In January 2001, a satirical news article in *The Onion*, entitled "Our Long National Nightmare of Peace and Prosperity Is Finally Over" *[127] had newly elected President George Bush vowing to "develop new and expensive weapons technologies" and to "engage in at least one Gulf War-level armed conflict in the next four years." Furthermore, he would "bring back economic stagnation by implementing substantial tax cuts, which would lead to a recession." This prophesies the Iraq War and to the Bush tax cuts.

- In 1975, the first episode of *Saturday Night Live* included an ad for a triple blade razor called the Triple-Trac; in 2001, Gillette introduced the Mach3. In 2004, *The Onion* satirized Schick and Gillette's marketing of ever-increasingly multi-blade razors with a mock article proclaiming Gillette will now introduce a five-blade razor.*[128] In 2006, Gillette released the Gillette Fusion, a five-blade razor.

51.10   See also

- Cringe comedy
- Culture jamming
- Freedom of the press
- List of satirists and satires
- News satire
- Onomasti komodein
- Parody religion
- Stupidedia

*[129]==Notes==

[1] The Archbishop of Canterbury and the Bishop of London, the censors of the press, issued Orders to the Stationers' Company on June 1 and 4, 1599, prohibiting the further printing of satires —the so-called 'Bishop's Ban'.*[81]

51.11   References

[1] Elliott 2004.

[2] Frye, Northrop, *quote*[1] (literary critic).

[3] Claridge, Claudia (2010) *Hyperbole in English: A Corpus-based Study of Exaggeration* p.257

[4] Kharpertian, Theodore D, "Thomas Pynchon and Postmodern American Satire", in Kharpertian, *A hand to turn the time: the Menippean satires of Thomas Pynchon*, pp. 25–7

[5] Branham 1997, p. xxiv.

[6] Ullman, BL (1913), "Satura and Satire", *Classical Philology* **8** (2), The Renaissance confusion of the two origins encouraged a satire more aggressive than that of its Roman forebearers

[7] Antonia Szabari (2009) *Less Rightly Said: Scandals and Readers in Sixteenth-Century France* p.2

[8] Corum 2002, p. 175.

[9] "Ig", *Improbable*

[10] Rosenberg, Harold (1960), "Community, Values, Comedy", *Commentary* (The American Jewish Committee) **30**: 155, the oldest form of social study is comedy... If the comedian, from Aristophanes to Joyce, does not solve sociology's problem of "the participant observer", he does demonstrate his objectivity by capturing behavior in its most intimate aspects yet in its widest typicality. Comic irony sets whole cultures side by side in a multiple exposure (e.g., *Don Quixote, Ulysses*), causing valuation to spring out of the recital of facts alone, in contrast to the hidden editorializing of tongue-in-cheek ideologists.

[11] Deloria, Vine (1969), "Indian humor", *Custer Died For Your Sins: An Indian Manifesto*, p. 146, Irony and satire provide much keener insights into a group's collective psyche and values than do years of [conventional] research as quoted in Ryan, Allan J, *The trickster shift: humour and irony in contemporary native art*, p. 9

[12] Nash, Roderick Frazier (1970), "21. The New Humor", *The Call of the Wild: 1900–1916*, p. 203, Humor is one of the best indicators of popular thought. To ask what strikes a period as funny is to probe its deepest values and tastes.

[13] Babcock, Barbara A (1984), "Arrange Me Into Disorder: Fragments and Reflections on Ritual Clowning", in MacAloon, *Rite, Drama, Festival, Spectacle*. Also collected as Babcock, Barbara A Grimes (1996), Ronald, L, ed., *Readings in ritual studies*, p. 5, Harold Rosenberg has asserted that sociology needs to bring comedy into the foreground, including "an awareness of the comedy of sociology with its disguises", and, like Burke and Duncan, he has argued that comedy provides "the radical effect of self-knowledge which the anthropological bias excludes.

[14] Coppola, Jo (1958), *The Realist* (1), Good comedy is social criticism—although you might find that hard to believe if all you ever saw were some of the so-called clowns of videoland.... Comedy is dying today because criticism is on its deathbed... because telecasters, frightened by the threats and pressure of sponsors, blacklists and viewers, helped introduce conformity to this age... In such a climate, comedy cannot flourish. For comedy is, after all, a look at ourselves, not as we pretend to be when we look in the mirror of our imagination, but as we really are. Look at the comedy of any age and you will know volumes about that period and its people which neither historian nor anthropologist can tell you. Missing or empty |title= (help)

[15] Willi, Andreas (2003), *The Languages of Aristophanes: Aspects of Linguistic Variation in Classical Attic Greek*, Oxford University Press, pp. 1–2

[16] Ehrenberg, Victor (1962), *The people of Aristophanes: a sociology of old Attic comedy*, p. 39

[17] Bevere, Antonio and Cerri, Augusto (2006) *Il Diritto di informazione e i diritti della persona* pp.265-6 quotation:

nella storia della nostra cultura, la satira ha realizzato il bisogno popolare di irridere e dissacrare il *gotha* politico ed economico, le cui reazioni punitive non sono certo state condizionate da critiche estetiche, ma dalla tolleranza o intolleranza caratterizzanti in quel momento storico la società e i suoi governanti. (...) la reale esistenza della satira in una società deriva, (...) dal margine di tolleranza espresso dai poteri punitivi dello Stato.

[18] Amy Wiese Forbes (2010) The Satiric Decade: Satire and the Rise of Republicanism in France, 1830-1840 p.xv, quotation:

a critical public discourse (...) Satire rose the daunting question of what role public opinion would play in government. (...) satirists criticized government activities, exposed ambiguities, and forced administrators to clarify or establish policies. Not surprisingly, heated public controversy surrounded satiric commentary, resulting in an outright ban on political satire in 1835 (...) Government officials cracked down on their humorous public criticism that challenged state authority through both its form and content. Satire had been a political resource in France for a long time, but the anxious political context of the July Monarchy had unlocked its political power. Satire also taught lessons in democracy. It fit into the July Monarchy's tense political context as a voice in favor of public political debate. Satiric expression took place in the public sphere and spoke from a position of public opinion-that is, from a position of the nations expressing a political voice and making claims on its government representatives and leadership. Beyond mere entertainment, satire's humor appealed to and exercised public opinion, drawing audiences into new practices of representative government.

[19] Knight, Charles A. (2004) *Literature of Satire* p.254

[20] Test (1991) p.9 quotation:

> A surprising variety of societies have allowed certain persons the freedom to mock other individuals and social institutions in rituals. From the earliest times the same freedom has been claimed by and granted to social groups at certain times of the year, as can be seen in such festivals as the Saturnalia, the Feast of Fools, Carnival, and similar folk festivals in India, nineteenth-century Newfoundland, and the ancient Mediterranean world.

[21] Test (1991) pp.8-9

[22] Cazeneuve (1957) p.244-5 quotation:

> Ils constituent donc pour la tribu un moyen de donner une satisfaction symbolique aux tendances anti-sociales. Les Zunis, précisément parce qu'ils sont un peuple apollinien [où la règle prédomine], avaient besoin de cette soupape de sûreté. Les Koyemshis représentent ce que M. Caillois nomme le « Sacré de transgression ».

[23] Durand (1984) p.106 quotation:

> Déjà Cazeneuve (2) [*Les dieux dansent à Cibola*] avait mis auparavant en relief, dans la Société « apollinienne » des Zuñi, l'institution et le symbolisme saturnal des clowns Koyemshis, véritable soupape de sûreté « dionysienne ».

[24] Yatsko, V, *Russian folk funny stories*

[25] Corum (2002) p.163

[26] David Worcester (1968) *The Art of Satire* p.16

[27] Müller, Rolf Arnold (1973). *Komik und Satire* (in German). Zürich: Juris-Verlag. p. 92. ISBN 978-3-260-03570-8.

[28] "What Is Horatian Satire?". *wiseGEEK*.

[29] "Satire Terms" . *nku.edu*.

[30] Sharma, Raja, "Comedy" in New Ligt-Literary Studies

[31] http://www.uh.edu/honors/Programs-Minors/honors-and-the-schools/houston-teachers-institute/curriculum-units/pdfs/2008/comedy/green-08-comedy.pdf

[32] "What Is Juvenalian Satire?". *wiseGEEK*.

[33] "Satire in Literature: Definition, Types & Examples" . *Education Portal*.

[34] Fo (1990) p.9 quotation:

> Nella storia del teatro si ritrova sempre questo conflitto in cui si scontrano impegno e disimpegno ... grottesco, satirico e lazzo con sfottò. E spesso vince lo sfotto. tanto amato dal potere. Quando si dice che il potere ama la satira

[35] Eastman, Max (1936), "IV. Degrees of Biting" , *Enjoyment of Laughter*, pp. 236–43

[36] Fo, Dario; Lorch, Jennifer, *Dario Fo*, p. 128, In other writings Fo makes an important distinction between *sfottò* and satire.

[37] Fo (1990) pp.2-3

> ... Una caricatura che, è ovvio, risulta del tutto bonaria, del tutto epidermica, che indica, come dicevo prima, soltanto la parte più esteriore del loro carattere, i tic la cui messa in risalto non lede assolutamente l'operato, l'ideologia, la morale e la dimensione culturale di questi personaggi. ... ricordando che i politici provano un enorme piacere nel sentirsi presi in giro; è quasi un premio che si elargisce loro, nel momento stesso in cui li si sceglie per essere sottoposti alla caricatura, a quella caricatura. ... Di fatto questa è una forma di comicità che non si può chiamare satira, ma solo sfottò. ... Pensa quanti pretesti satirici si offrirebbero se solo quei comici del "Biberon" volessero prendere in esame il modo in cui questi personaggi gestiscono il potere e lo mantengono, o si decidessero a gettare l'occhio sulle vere magagne di questa gente, le loro violenze più o meno mascherate, le loro arroganze

e soprattutto le loro ipocrisie. ...un teatro cabaret capostipite: il Bagaglino, un teatro romano che, già vent'anni fa, si metteva in una bella chiave politica dichiaratamente di estrema destra, destra spudoratamente reazionaria, scopertamente fascista. Nelle pieghe del gruppo del Bagaglino e del suo lavoro c'era sempre la caricatura feroce dell'operaio, del sindacalista, del comunista, dell'uomo di sinistra, e una caricatura bonacciona invece, e ammiccante, accattivante, degli uomini e della cultura al potere

[38] Fo (1990) quotation:

> L'ironia fatta sui tic, sulla caricatura dei connotati più o meno grotteschi dei politici presi di mira, dei loro eventuali difetti fisici, della loro particolare pronuncia, dei loro vezzi, del loro modo di vestire, del loro modo di camminare, delle frasi tipiche che vanno ripetendo. ...[lo sfottò è] una chiave buffonesca molto antica, che viene di lontano, quella di giocherellare con gli attributi esteriori e non toccare mai il problema di fondo di una critica seria che è l'analisi messa in grottesco del comportamento, la valutazione ironica della posizione, dell'ideologia del personaggio.

[39] Arroyo, José Luís Blas; Casanova, Mónica Velando, *Discurso y sociedad: contribuciones al estudio de la lengua en...* **1**, pp. 303–4

[40] Morson, Gary Saul (1988), *Boundaries of Genre*, p. 114, second, that parodies can be, as Bakhtin observes, "shallow" as well as "deep" (*Problems of Dostoevsky's Poetics*, 160), which is to say, directed at superficial as well as fundamental faults of the original. [...] the distinction between shallow and deep [...] [is] helpful in understanding the complex ways in which parodies are used. For instance, shallow parody is sometimes used to pay an author an indirect compliment. The opposite of damning with faint praise, this parody with faint criticism may be designed to show that no more fundamental criticism *could* be made.

[41] Luttazzi, Daniele (2005), *Matrix*, IT, archived from the original on December 25, 2005, Dario Fo disse a Satyricon: —La satira vera si vede dalla reazione che suscita.

[42] Luttazzi, Daniele (October 2003), Fracassi, Federica; Guerriero, Jacopo, eds., "State a casa a fare i compiti" (interview), *Nazione Indiana* (in Italian), Lo sfottò è reazionario. Non cambia le carte in tavola, anzi, rende simpatica la persona presa di mira. La Russa, oggi, è quel personaggio simpatico, con la voce cavernosa, il doppiatore dei Simpson di cui Fiorello fa l' imitazione. Nessuno ricorda più il La Russa picchiatore fascista. Nessuno ricorda gli atti fascisti e reazionari di questo governo in televisione.

[43] Kremer, S Lillian (2003), *Holocaust Literature: Agosín to Lentin*, p. 100

[44] Lipman, Stephen 'Steve' (1991), *Laughter in hell: the use of humour during the Holocaust*, Northvale, NJ: J Aronson, p. 40

[45] Clark (1991) pp.116-8 quotation:

> ...religion, politics, and sexuality are the primary stuff of literary satire. Among these sacret targets, matters costive and defecatory play an important part. ... from the earliest times, satirists have utilized scatological and bathroom humor. Aristophanes, always livid and nearly scandalous in his religious, political, and sexual references...

[46] Clark, John R; Motto, Anna Lydia (1973), *Satire–that blasted art*, p. 20

[47] Clark, John R; Motto, Anna Lydia (1980), "Menippeans & Their Satire: Concerning Monstrous Learned Old Dogs and Hippocentaurs", *Scholia satyrica* **6** (3/4): 45, [Chapple's book *Soviet satire of the twenties*]... classifying the very *topics* his satirists satirized: housing, food, and fuel supplies, poverty, inflation, "hooliganism", public services, religion, stereotypes of nationals (the Englishman, German, &c), &c. Yet the truth of the matter is that no satirist worth his salt (Petronius, Chaucer, Rabelais, Swift, Leskov, Grass) ever avoids man's habits and living standards, or scants those delicate desiderata: religion, politics, and sex.

[48] Ferdie Addis (2012) *Qual è il tuo "tallone da killer"?* p.20

[49] Hodgart (2009) ch 2 *The topics of satire: politics* p.33

The most pressing of the problems that face us when we close the book or leave the theatre are ultimately political ones; and so politics is the pre-eminent topic of satire. ...to some defree public affairs vex every man, if he pays taxes, does military service or even objects to the way his neighbour is behaving. There is no escape from politics where more than a dozen people are living together.
There is an essential connection between satire and politics in the widest sense: satire is not only the commonest form of political literature, but, insofar as it tries to influence public behavious, it is the most political part of all literature.

[50] Hodgart (2009) p.39

[51] Wilson (2002) pp. 14–5, 20 and notes 25 (p. 308), 32 (p. 309)

[52] Anspaugh, Kelly (1994) *'Bung Goes the Enemay': Wyndham Lewis and the Uses of Disgust.* in *Mattoid* (ISSN 0314-5913) issue 48.3, pp.21-29. As quoted in Wilson (2002):

> The turd is the ultimate dead object.

[53] Lise Andries *Etat des recherche. Présentation* in *Dix-Huitième Siècle* n.32, 2000, special on *Rire* p.10, as quoted in Jean-Michel Racault (2005) *Voyages badins, burlesques et parodiques du XVIIIe siècle*, p.7, quotation: "Le corps grotesque dans ses modalités clasiques - la scatologie notamment - ..."

[54] Klein, Cecelia F. (1993) *Teocuitlatl, 'Divine Excrement': The Significance of 'Holy Shit' in Ancient Mexico*, in *Art Journal (CAA)*, Vol.52, n.3, Fall 1993, pp.20-7

[55] Duprat, Annie (1982) *La dégradation de l'image royale dans la caricature révolutionnaire* p.178 quotation:

> Le corps grotesque est una realite populaire detournee au profit d'une representation du corps a but politique, plaquege du corps scatologique sur le corps de ceux qu'il covient de denoncer. Denonciation scatologique projetee sur le corps aristocratique pour lui signifier sa degenerescence.

[56] Parsons, Elsie Clews; Ralph L. Beals (October–December 1934). "The Sacred Clowns of the Pueblo and Mayo-Yaqui Indians" . *American Anthropologist* **36** (4): 491–514. doi:10.1525/aa.1934.36.4.02a00020. JSTOR 661824.

[57] Hyers, M. Conrad (1996) [1996]. *The Spirituality of Comedy: comic heroism in a tragic world*. Transaction Publishers. p. 145. ISBN 1-56000-218-2.

[58] Donald Alexander Mackenzie (1923) *Myths of Pre-Columbian America* p.229

[59] Patrick Marnham (2000) *Dreaming with His Eyes Open: A Life of Diego Rivera* p.297

[60] Hilda Ellis Davidson (1993) *Boundaries & Thresholds* p.85 quotation:

> It is this fear of what the dead in their uncontrollable power might cause which has brought forth apotropaic rites, protective rites against the dead. (...) One of these popular rites was the funeral rite of sin-eating, performed by a sin-eater, a man or woman. Through accepting the food and drink provided, he took upon himself the sins of the departed.

[61] Bloom, Edward Alan; Bloom, Lillian D (1979), *Satire's persuasive voice.*

[62] Nicoll, Allardyce (1951), *British drama: an historical survey from the beginnings to the present time*, p. 179

[63] Hodgart (2009) p.189

[64] Pollard, Arthur (1970), "4. Tones" , *Satire*, p. 66

[65] Clark, Arthur Melville (1946), "The Art of Satire and the Satiric Spectrum" , *Studies in literary modes*, p. 32

[66] Lichtheim, M (1973), *Ancient Egyptian Literature* **I**, pp. 184–93

[67] Helck, W (1970), *Die Lehre des DwA-xtjj*, Wiesbaden

[68] Gardiner, Alan H (1911), *Egyptian Hieratic Texts*, I: Literary Texts of the New Kingdom **I**, Leipzig

[69] Sutton, DF (1993), *Ancient Comedy: The War of the Generations*, New York, p. 56

[70] Bates, Alfred, ed. (1906), "Political and social satires of Aristophanes", *The Drama, Its History, Literature and Influence on Civilization* **2**, London: Historical Publishing, pp. 55–59

[71] Atkinson, JE (1992), "Curbing the Comedians: Cleon versus Aristophanes and Syracosius' Decree", *The Classical Quarterly*, New **42** (1): 56–64, doi:10.1017/s0009838800042580

[72] Anderson, John Louis, *Aristophanes: the Michael Moore of his Day*

[73] Wilson 2002, p. 17.

[74] Cuddon (1998), "Satire", *Dictionary of Literary Terms*, Oxford

[75] Bosworth 1976, p. 32.

[76] Marzolph, Ulrich; van Leeuwen, Richard; Wassouf, Hassan (2004). *The Arabian Nights Encyclopedia*. ABC-CLIO. pp. 97–8. ISBN 1-57607-204-5.

[77] Bosworth 1976, pp. 77–8.

[78] Bosworth 1976, p. 70.

[79] Webber, Edwin J (January 1958). "Comedy as Satire in Hispano-Arabic Spain". *Hispanic Review* (University of Pennsylvania Press) **26** (1): 1–11. doi:10.2307/470561. JSTOR 470561.

[80] Hall 1969: 'Hall's *Virgidemiae* was a new departure in that the true Juvenalian mode of satire was being attempted for the first time, and successfully, in English.'

[81] Davenport 1969.

[82] *The Broadview Anthology of British Literature: The Restoration and the Eighteenth Century* **3**, p. 435

[83] Weinbrot, Howard D. (2007) *Eighteenth-Century Satire: Essays on Text and Context from Dryden to Peter...* p.136

[84] Dryden, John, Lynch, Jack, ed., *Discourse* (2), Rutgers

[85] Charles Press (1981). *The Political Cartoon*. Fairleigh Dickinson University Press. p. 34.

[86] "Satire, sewers and statesmen: why James Gillray was king of the cartoon". The Guardian. 18 June 2015.

[87] Chaplin (1964) *My Autobiography*, p.392, quotation:

> Had I known of the actual horrors of the German concentration camps, I could not have made *The Great Dictator*, I could not have made fun of the homicidal insanity of the Nazis.

[88] Sullivan, James (2010) *Seven Dirty Words: The Life and Crimes of George Carlin* p.94

[89] George Carlin (2002) *Introduction* to *Murder At the Conspiracy Convention*

[90] "David Frost's Q&A on how to be a satirist". *The Guardian* (London). Retrieved February 2, 2015

[91] "What is Catch-22? And why does the book matter?". BBC. March 12, 2002.

[92] Van Norris (2014). British Television Animation 1997-2010: Drawing Comic Tradition". p. 153. Palgrave Macmillan,

[93] Liz Raftery - "Who Did the Best Hillary Clinton Impression on SNL?", *TV Guide*, April 30, 2015. (Video) Retrieved 2015-08-15

[94] "You betcha —Tina Fey wins Emmy as Sarah Palin on 'SNL'". *Los Angeles Times*. 2009-09-13. Retrieved 2009-09-13.

[95] *Molly the Dog*, 2008

[96] *Brian Miner*, 2008

[97] "Tain't Funny - "Time"". Time.com. September 29, 1947. Retrieved August 29, 2009.

[98] "Not Your Homepage - Check Your Morals At The Door, Come See the Internet Lore!". *notyourhomepage.com.*

[99] "FRONT PAGE - Satirical News, Review, Comment & Analysis". Scunt.co.uk. Retrieved August 17, 2013.

[100] "The Giant Napkin". Thegiantnapkin.com. Retrieved August 17, 2013.

[101] "Unconfirmedsources.com". Unconfirmedsources.com. Retrieved August 17, 2013.

[102] Ng, David (May 11, 2009), "YouTube sensation Miranda seduces Broadway", *Los Angeles Times*

[103] "This Week", *San Francisco Chronicle*, October 4, 2009

[104] An interview with The Onion, David Shankbone, *Wikinews*, November 25, 2007.

[105] Griffin, Dustin H. (1994) *Satire: A Critical Reintroduction* p.136

[106] Geisler, Michael E. (2005) *National Symbols, Fractured Identities: Contesting the National Narrative* p.73

[107] Pezzella, Vincenzo (2009) *La diffamazione: responsabilità penale e civile* pp.566-7 quotation:

> Il diritto di satira trova il suo fondamento negli artt. 21 e 33 della Costituzione che tutelano, rispettivamente, la libertà di manifestazione del pensiero e quella di elaborazione artistica e scientifica. (...) la satira, in quanto operante nell'ambito di ciò che è arte, non è strettamente correlata ad esigenze informative, dal che deriva che i suoi limiti di liceità siano ben più ammpi di quelli propri del diritto di cronaca

[108] Kinservik, Matthew J. (2002) *Disciplining Satire: The Censorship of Satiric Comedy on the Eighteenth...* p.21

[109] Test (1991) p.10

[110] Leonard, James S; Tenney, Thomas A; Davis, Thadious M (December 1992). *Satire or Evasion?: Black Perspectives on Huckleberry Finn*. Duke University Press. p. 224. ISBN 978-0-8223-1174-4.

[111] Fishin, Shelley Fisher (1997), *Lighting out for the Territory: Reflections on Mark Twain and American Culture*, New York: Oxford University Press

[112] "'Hang your heads' Rudd tells Chaser boys". Australian Broadcasting Corporation. June 4, 2009. Retrieved June 5, 2009.

[113] Sutherland, James (1958), *English Satire*

[114] Martin, Rod A (2007), *The Psychology of Humor: An Integrative Approach*, pp. 27–8

[115] Apte, Mahadev L (1985), "Introduction", *Humor and laughter: an anthropological approach*, p. 23, The general neglect of humor as a topic of anthropological research is reflected in teaching practice. Most introductory textbooks do not even list humor as a significant characteristic of cultural systems together with kinship, social roles, behavioral patterns, religion, language, economic transactions, political institutions, values, and material culture.

[116] Arber, Edward, ed. (1875–94), *A Transcript of the Registers of the Company of Stationers of London, 1554–1640* **III**, London, p. 677

[117] "Zuma claims R7m over Zapiro cartoon". *Mail and Guardian*. ZA. December 18, 2008.

[118] "Democratic Alliance spokesperson Helen Zille" (interview). *Mail and Guardian*. ZA. Retrieved August 2005.

[119] "ZNews: Zapiro's puppet show". *Dispatch*. ZA. Archived from the original on August 18, 2014.

[120] "SABC pulls Zapiro doccie, again". *Mail and Guardian*. ZA. September 26, 2009.

[121] "Samsung Sues Satirist, Claiming Criminal Defamation, Over Satirical Column Poking Fun At Samsung". Techdirt. May 11, 2010. Retrieved June 9, 2012.

[122] Glionna, John M (May 10, 2010). "Samsung doesn't find satirical spoof amusing". *Los Angeles Times*.

[123] "Ukip asks police to investigate the BBC over Have I Got News for You". BBC. Retrieved June 18, 2015

[124] Krassner, Paul (August 26, 2003), "Terminal velocity television is here", *New York Press* **16** (35)

[125] Luttazzi, Daniele (2007), *Lepidezze postribolari* (in Italian), Feltrinelli, p. 275

[126] Franklin, Benjamin (April 26, 1784). "Aux auteurs du Journal". *Journal de Paris* (in French) (117). Wrote anonymously. Its first publication was in the journal's "Économie" section. *An Economical Project* (revised English version ed.), retrieved May 26, 2007 has a title that is not Franklin's; see A.O. Aldridge (1956). "Franklin's essay on daylight saving". *American Literature* (American Literature) **28** (1): 23–29. doi:10.2307/2922719. JSTOR 2922719.

[127] "Bush: 'Our Long National Nightmare of Peace And Prosperity Is Finally Over'". The Onion. Retrieved June 9, 2012.

[128] "Fuck Everything, We're Doing Five Blades". The Onion. Retrieved June 9, 2012.

[129] https://books.google.com/books?id=5CL1ONLMCCQC&pg=PA72&lpg=PA72&dq=the+poems+1969+davenport&source= bl&ots=f4ZpBNtXUF&sig=IYhu74VnRzyYFU_dqbDknNzRFd4&hl=en&sa=X&ved=0CD4Q6AEwBmoVChMIgL6-z6PUxwIVgcG. v=snippet&q=bishop&f=false. Missing or empty |title= (help)

51.12   Bibliography

- Bosworth, Clifford Edmund (1976), *The Mediaeval Islamic Underworld: The Banu Sasan in Arabic Society and Literature*, Brill Publishers, ISBN 90-04-04392-6.

- Branham, R Bracht; Kinney, Daniel (1997), *Introduction* to Petronius, *Satyrica*, p. xxiv.

- Clark, John R (1991), *The Modern Satiric Grotesque and its traditions*, Lexington: U of Kentucky P.

- Corum, Robert T (2002), "The rhetoric of disgust and contempt in Boileau", in Birberick, Anne Lynn; Ganim, Russell, *The Shape of Change: Essays in Early Modern Literature and La Fontaine in Honor of David Lee Rubin*.

- Elliott, Robert C (2004), "The nature of satire", *Encyclopædia Britannica*.

- Fo, Dario (1990), "Satira e sfottò", in Allegri, Luigi, *Dialogo provocatorio sul comico, il tragico, la follia e la ragione* (interview) (in Italian), pp. 2, 9.

    - Fo, Dario (1993), *Provocative Dialogue on the Comic, the Tragic, Folly and Reason*, London: Methuen Publishing (transl.).

- Frye, Northrop (1957), *Anatomy of Criticism* (in particular the discussion of the 4 "myths").

- Hall, Joseph (1969), Davenport, A, ed., *The Poems*, Liverpool University Press.

- Hodgart, Matthew; Connery, Brian (2009) [1969], *Satire: Origins and Principles*.

- Pietrasik, Vanessa (2011), *La satire en jeu. Critique et scepticisme en Allemagne à la fin du XVIIIe siècle* (in French), Tusson: Du Lérot éditeur, Charente.

- Test, George Austin (1991), *Elliott's Bind; or, What Is Satire, Anyway?* in *Satire: Spirit & Art*

- Wilson, R Rawdon (2002), *The hydra's tale: imagining disgust*.

51.13   Further reading

- Bloom, Edward A (1972), "Sacramentum Militiae: The Dynamics of Religious Satire", *Studies in the Literary Imagination* **5**: 119–42.

- Bronowski, Jacob; Mazlish, Bruce (1993), *The Western Intellectual Tradition From Leonardo to Hegel*, Barnes & Noble, p. 252 .

- Connery, Brian A, *Theorizing Satire: A Bibliography*, Oakland University.

- Dooley, David Joseph (1972), *Contemporary satire*.

- Feinberg, Leonard, *The satirist*.

- Lee, Jae Num (1971), *Scatology in Continental Satirical Writings from Aristophanes to Rabelais and English Scatological Writings from Skelton to Pope, 1,2,3 maldita madre. Swift and Scatological Satire*, Albuquerque: U of New Mexico P, pp. 7–22; 23–53.

Theories/critical approaches to satire as a genre

- Connery, Brian; Combe, Kirk, eds. (1995). *Theorizing Satire: Essays in Literary Criticism*. New York: St. Martin's Press. p. 212. ISBN 0-312-12302-7.

- Draitser, Emil (1994), *Techniques of Satire: The Case of Saltykov-Shchedrin*, Berlin-New York: Mouton de Gruyter, ISBN 3-11-012624-9.

- Hammer, Stephanie, *Satirizing the Satirist*.

- Highet, Gilbert, *Satire*.

- Kernan, Alvin, *The Cankered Muse*.

- Kindermann, Udo (1978), *Satyra. Die Theorie der Satire im Mittellateinischen*, Vorstudie zu einer Gattungsgeschichte (in German), Nürnberg.

The plot of satire

- Seidel, Michael, *Satiric Inheritance*.

- Zdero, Rad (2008), *Entopia: Revolution of the Ants*.

51.14 External links

- The dictionary definition of satire at Wiktionary

- Media related to Satire at Wikimedia Commons

1867 edition of Punch, *a ground-breaking British magazine of popular humour, including a great deal of satire of the contemporary, social, and political scene.*

12

SATIRA III.

A' musici è comun qnesto difetto,
Che pregati a cantare infra gli amici,
Mai non fan grazia; se nessun gli cerca,
Costor non danno mai più fine al canto.
Tal fu Tigellio il Sardo. A lui potea
Fare Augusto medesmo istanze e preghi
Del suo gran padre e di se stesso in grazia,
Tutto era van; se gli saltava il grillo,
Dal suo primo cenar sino alle frutta
Trillava, evviva Bacco, ora in soprano,
Or nel più basso tuono. Ei non fu mai
A sè medesmo ugual. Correa sovente
Qual chi fugge il nemico, e spesso andava
Lento come chi porta in giro i sacri
Cesti di Giuno. Or ei dugento servi,
Or n' avea dieci a pena. A bocca gonfia
Parlamentava di tetrarchi e regi;
Poi detto avria, d' un qualsivoglia desco,
D' un salin puro, d' una grossa vesta,
Che dal freddo mi pari, io son contento.
Ma se a quest' uom sì moderato e parco
Donavi un milion, tra cinque giorni

The Satirical papyrus at the British museum

Satirical Ostraca showing a Cat guarding geese c1120 BC, Egypt.

Figured Ostracon Showing a Cat Waiting on a Mouse, Egypt

Pieter Bruegel's 1568 satirical painting The Blind Leading the Blind.

Benzino Napaloni and Adenoid Hynkel in The Great Dictator *(1940). Chaplin later declared that he would have not made the film if he had known about the* concentration camps.*[87]*

Peter Sellers in famous satire Dr. Strangelove *(1964).*

Stephen Colbert satirically impersonated an opinionated and self-righteous television commentator on his Comedy Central program in the United States.

Tina Fey as Sarah Palin (left) and Amy Poehler as Hillary Clinton (right) on the American comedy television show Saturday Night Live.

'Remember, Putin - It's me who won the gold!'

Political satire by Ranan Lurie

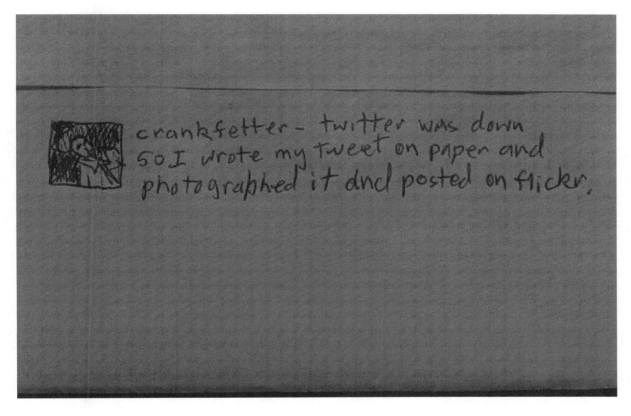

Satire on internet culture

Chapter 52

Mental image

"Mental images" redirects here. For the computer graphics software company, see Mental Images.

A **mental image** or **mental picture** is the representation in a person's mind of the physical world outside of that person.[*1] It is an experience that, on most occasions, significantly resembles the experience of perceiving some object, event, or scene, but occurs when the relevant object, event, or scene is not actually present to the senses.[*2][*3][*4][*5] There are sometimes episodes, particularly on falling asleep (hypnagogic imagery) and waking up (hypnopompic), when the mental imagery, being of a rapid, phantasmagoric and involuntary character, defies perception, presenting a kaleidoscopic field, in which no distinct object can be discerned.[*6]

The nature of these experiences, what makes them possible, and their function (if any) have long been subjects of research and controversy in philosophy, psychology, cognitive science, and, more recently, neuroscience. As contemporary researchers use the expression, mental images or imagery can comprise information from any source of sensory input; one may experience auditory images,[*7] olfactory images,[*8] and so forth. However, the majority of philosophical and scientific investigations of the topic focus upon *visual* mental imagery. It has sometimes been assumed that, like humans, some types of animals are capable of experiencing mental images.[*9] Due to the fundamentally introspective nature of the phenomenon, there is little to no evidence either for or against this view.

Philosophers such as George Berkeley and David Hume, and early experimental psychologists such as Wilhelm Wundt and William James, understood ideas in general to be mental images. Today it is very widely believed that much imagery functions as mental representations (or mental models,) playing an important role in memory and thinking.[*10][*11][*12][*13] William Brant (2013, p. 12) traces the scientific use of the phrase "mental images" back to the John Tyndall's 1870 speech called the "Scientific Use of the Imagination." Some have gone so far as to suggest that images are best understood to be, by definition, a form of inner, mental or neural representation;[*14][*15] in the case of hypnagogic and hypnapompic imagery, it is not representational at all. Others reject the view that the image experience may be identical with (or directly caused by) any such representation in the mind or the brain,[*16][*17][*18][*19][*20][*21] but do not take account of the non-representational forms of imagery.

In 2010, IBM applied for a patent on a method to extract mental images of human faces from the human brain. It uses a feedback loop based on brain measurements of the fusiform face area in the brain that activates proportionate with degree of facial recognition.[*22] It was issued in 2015.[*23]

52.1 How mental images form in the brain

Common examples of mental images include daydreaming and the mental visualization that occurs while reading a book. Another is of the pictures summoned by athletes during training or before a competition, outlining each step they will take to accomplish their goal.[*24] When a musician hears a song, he or she can sometimes "see" the song notes in their head, as well as hear them with all their tonal qualities.[*25] This is considered different from an after-effect, such as an after-image. Calling up an image in our minds can be a voluntary act, so it can be characterized as being under various degrees of conscious control.

According to psychologist and cognitive scientist Steven Pinker,*[26] our experiences of the world are represented in our minds as mental images. These mental images can then be associated and compared with others, and can be used to synthesize completely new images. In this view, mental images allow us to form useful theories of how the world works by formulating likely sequences of mental images in our heads without having to directly experience that outcome. Whether other creatures have this capability is debatable.

There are several theories as to how mental images are formed in the mind. These include the Dual-Code Theory, the Propositional Theory, and the Functional-Equivalency Hypothesis. The Dual-Code Theory, created by Allan Paivio in 1971, is the theory that we use two separate codes to represent information in our brains: image codes and verbal codes. Image codes are things like thinking of a picture of a dog when you are thinking of a dog, whereas a verbal code would be to think of the word "dog" .*[27] Another example is the difference between thinking of abstract words such as *justice* or *love* and thinking of concrete words like *elephant* or *chair*. When abstract words are thought of, it is easier to think of them in terms of verbal codes- finding words that define them or describe them. With concrete words, it is often easier to use image codes and bring up a picture of a *human* or *chair* in your mind rather than words associated or descriptive of them.

The Propositional Theory involves storing images in the form of a generic propositional code that stores the meaning of the concept not the image itself. The propositional codes can either be descriptive of the image or symbolic. They are then transferred back into verbal and visual code to form the mental image.*[28]

The Functional-Equivalency Hypothesis is that mental images are "internal representations" that work in the same way as the actual perception of physical objects.*[29] In other words, the picture of a dog brought to mind when the word *dog* is read is interpreted in the same way as if the person looking at an actual dog before them.

52.2 Philosophical ideas

Main article: Mental representation

Mental images are an important topic in classical and modern philosophy, as they are central to the study of knowledge. In the *Republic*, Book VII, Plato has Socrates present the Allegory of the Cave: a prisoner, bound and unable to move, sits with his back to a fire watching the shadows cast on the cave wall in front of him by people carrying objects behind his back. These people and the objects they carry are representations of real things in the world. Unenlightened man is like the prisoner, explains Socrates, a human being making mental images from the sense data that he experiences.

The eighteenth-century philosopher Bishop George Berkeley proposed similar ideas in his theory of idealism. Berkeley stated that reality is equivalent to mental images —our mental images are not a copy of another material reality but that reality itself. Berkeley, however, sharply distinguished between the images that he considered to constitute the external world, and the images of individual imagination. According to Berkeley, only the latter are considered "mental imagery" in the contemporary sense of the term.

The eighteenth century British writer, Dr. Samuel Johnson, criticized idealism. When asked what he thought about idealism, he is alleged to have replied "I refute it thus!" as he kicked a large rock and his leg rebounded. His point was that the idea that the rock is just another mental image and has no material existence of its own is a poor explanation of the painful sense data he had just experienced.

David Deutsch addresses Johnson's objection to idealism in *The Fabric of Reality* when he states that, if we judge the value of our mental images of the world by the quality and quantity of the sense data that they can explain, then the most valuable mental image —or theory —that we currently have is that the world has a real independent existence and that humans have successfully evolved by building up and adapting patterns of mental images to explain it. This is an important idea in scientific thought.

Critics of scientific realism ask how the inner perception of mental images actually occurs. This is sometimes called the "homunculus problem" (see also the mind's eye). The problem is similar to asking how the images you see on a computer screen exist in the memory of the computer. To scientific materialism, mental images and the perception of them must be brain-states. According to critics, scientific realists cannot explain where the images and their perceiver exist in the brain. To use the analogy of the computer screen, these critics argue that cognitive science and psychology have been unsuccessful in identifying either the component in the brain (i.e., "hardware") or the mental processes that store these images (i.e. "software").

52.3 Mental imagery in experimental psychology

Cognitive psychologists and (later) cognitive neuroscientists have empirically tested some of the philosophical questions related to whether and how the human brain uses mental imagery in cognition.

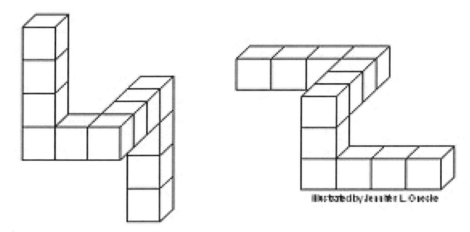

Figure 1: Based on Shepard & Metzlar's 'Mental Rotation Task'

Figure 2: Mental Rotation Task Based on Canonical Orientations

One theory of the mind that was examined in these experiments was the "brain as serial computer" philosophical metaphor of the 1970s. Psychologist Zenon Pylyshyn theorized that the human mind processes mental images by decomposing them into an underlying mathematical proposition. Roger Shepard and Jacqueline Metzler challenged that view by presenting subjects with 2D line drawings of groups of 3D block "objects" and asking them to determine whether that "object" is the same as a second figure, some of which rotations of the first "object".*[30] Shepard and Metzler proposed that if we decomposed and then mentally re-imaged the objects into basic mathematical propositions, as the then-dominant view of cognition "as a serial digital computer" *[31] assumed, then it would be expected that the time it took to determine whether the object is the same or not would be independent of how much the object had been rotated. Shepard and Metzler found the opposite: a linear relationship between the degree of rotation in the mental imagery task and the time it took participants to reach their answer.

This mental rotation finding implied that the human mind —and the human brain —maintains and manipulates mental images as topographic and topological wholes, an implication that was quickly put to test by psychologists. Stephen

Kosslyn and colleagues[32] showed in a series of neuroimaging experiments that the mental image of objects like the letter "F" are mapped, maintained and rotated as an image-like whole in areas of the human visual cortex. Moreover, Kosslyn's work showed that there are considerable similarities between the neural mappings for imagined stimuli and perceived stimuli. The authors of these studies concluded that, while the neural processes they studied rely on mathematical and computational underpinnings, the brain also seems optimized to handle the sort of mathematics that constantly computes a series of topologically-based images rather than calculating a mathematical model of an object.

Recent studies in neurology and neuropsychology on mental imagery have further questioned the "mind as serial computer" theory, arguing instead that human mental imagery manifests both visually and kinesthetically. For example, several studies have provided evidence that people are slower at rotating line drawings of objects such as hands in directions incompatible with the joints of the human body,[33] and that patients with painful, injured arms are slower at mentally rotating line drawings of the hand from the side of the injured arm.[34]

Some psychologists, including Kosslyn, have argued that such results occur because of interference in the brain between distinct systems in the brain that process the visual and motor mental imagery. Subsequent neuroimaging studies[35] showed that the interference between the motor and visual imagery system could be induced by having participants physically handle actual 3D blocks glued together to form objects similar to those depicted in the line-drawings. Amorim et al. have recently shown that, when a cylindrical "head" was added to Shepard and Metzler's line drawings of 3D block figures, participants were quicker and more accurate at solving mental rotation problems.[36] They argue that motoric embodiment is not just "interference" that inhibits visual mental imagery but is capable of facilitating mental imagery.

These and numerous related studies have led to a relative consensus within cognitive science, psychology, neuroscience, and philosophy on the neural status of mental images. In general, researchers agree that, while there is no homunculus inside the head viewing these mental images, our brains do form and maintain mental images as image-like wholes.[37] The problem of exactly how these images are stored and manipulated within the human brain, in particular within language and communication, remains a fertile area of study.

One of the longest-running research topics on the mental image has basis on the fact that people report large individual differences in the vividness of their images. Special questionnaires have been developed to assess such differences, including the Vividness of Visual Imagery Questionnaire (VVIQ) developed by David Marks. Laboratory studies have suggested that the subjectively reported variations in imagery vividness are associated with different neural states within the brain and also different cognitive competences such as the ability to accurately recall information presented in pictures[38] Rodway, Gillies and Schepman used a novel long-term change detection task to determine whether participants with low and high vividness scores on the VVIQ2 showed any performance differences.[39] Rodway et al. found that high vividness participants were significantly more accurate at detecting salient changes to pictures compared to low-vividness participants.[40] This replicated an earlier study.[41]

Recent studies have found that individual differences in VVIQ scores can be used to predict changes in a person's brain while visualizing different activities.[42] Functional magnetic resonance imaging (fMRI) was used to study the association between early visual cortex activity relative to the whole brain while participants visualized themselves or another person bench pressing or stair climbing. Reported image vividness correlates significantly with the relative fMRI signal in the visual cortex. Thus, individual differences in the vividness of visual imagery can be measured objectively.

Logie, Pernet, Buonocore and Della Sala (2011) used behavioural and fMRI data for mental rotation from individuals reporting vivid and poor imagery on the VVIQ. Groups differed in brain activation patterns suggesting that the groups performed the same tasks in different ways. These findings help to explain the lack of association previously reported between VVIQ scores and mental rotation performance.

52.4 Training and learning styles

Some educational theorists have drawn from the idea of mental imagery in their studies of learning styles. Proponents of these theories state that people often have learning processes that emphasize visual, auditory, and kinesthetic systems of experience. According to these theorists, teaching in multiple overlapping sensory systems benefits learning, and they encourage teachers to use content and media that integrates well with the visual, auditory, and kinesthetic systems whenever possible.

Educational researchers have examined whether the experience of mental imagery affects the degree of learning. For example, imagining playing a 5-finger piano exercise (mental practice) resulted in a significant improvement in performance over no mental practice —though not as significant as that produced by physical practice. The authors of the study stated that "mental practice alone seems to be sufficient to promote the modulation of neural circuits involved in the early stages of motor skill learning." *[43]

52.5   Visualization and the Himalayan traditions

In general, Vajrayana Buddhism, Bön, and Tantra utilize sophisticated visualization or *imaginal* (in the language of Jean Houston of Transpersonal Psychology) processes in the thoughtform construction of the yidam sadhana, kye-rim, and dzog-rim modes of meditation and in the yantra, thangka, and mandala traditions, where holding the fully realized form in the mind is a prerequisite prior to creating an 'authentic' new art work that will provide a sacred support or foundation for deity.*[44]*[45]

52.6   See also

- Animal cognition
- Cognition
- Creative visualization
- Fantasy (psychology)
- Fantasy prone personality
- Guided imagery
- Imagination
- Mental event
- Mental rotation
- Mind
- Motor imagery
- Visual space

52.7   References

[1] Eysenck, M. W. (2012). Fundamentals of cognition, 2nd ed. New York, NY: Psychology Press.

[2] McKellar, 1957

[3] Richardson, 1969

[4] Finke, 1989

[5] Thomas, 2003

[6] Wright, Edmond (1983). "Inspecting images". *Philosophy* **58** (223): 57–72 (see pp. 68–72). doi:10.1017/s0031819100056266.

[7] Reisberg, 1992

[8] Bensafi et al., 2003

[9] Aristotle: *On the Soul* III.3 428a

[10] Pavio, 1986

[11] Egan, 1992

[12] Barsalou, 1999

[13] Prinz, 2002

[14] Block, 1983

[15] Kosslyn, 1983

[16] Sartre, 1940

[17] Ryle, 1949

[18] Skinner, 1974

[19] Thomas, 1999

[20] Bartolomeo, 2002

[21] Bennett & Hacker, 2003

[22] IBM Patent Application: Retrieving mental images of faces from the human brain

[23] Business Machines : Patent Issued for Retrieving Mental Images of Faces from the Human Brain

[24] Plessinger, Annie. *The Effects of Mental Imagery on Athletic Performance.* The Mental Edge. 12/20/13. Web. http://www.vanderbilt.edu

[25] Sachs, Oliver (2007). *Musicophilia: Tales of Music and the Brain.* London: Picador. pp. 30–40.

[26] Pinker, S. (1999). *How the Mind Works.* New York: Oxford University Press.

[27] Paivio, Allan. 1941. *Dual Coding Theory. Theories of Learning in Educational Psychology.* (2013). Web. http://www.lifecircles-inc.com/Learningtheories/IP/paivio.html

[28] Mental Imaging Theories. 2013. Web. http://faculty.mercer.edu

[29] Eysenck, M. W. (2012). *Fundamentals of Cognition*, 2nd ed. New York, NY: Psychology Press.

[30] Shepard and Metzler 1971

[31] Gardner 1987

[32] Kosslyn 1995; see also 1994

[33] Parsons 1987; 2003

[34] Schwoebel et al. 2001

[35] Kosslyn et al. 2001

[36] Amorim et al. 2006

[37] Rohrer 2006

[38] Marks, 1973

[39] Rodway, Gillies and Schepman 2006

[40] Rodway et al. 2006

[41] Gur and Hilgard 1975

[42] Cui et al. 2007

[43] Pascual-Leone et al. 1995

[44] The Dalai Lama at MIT (2006)

[45] Mental Imagery

52.8   Further reading

- Amorim, Michel-Ange, Brice Isableu and Mohammed Jarraya (2006) Embodied Spatial Transformations: "Body Analogy" for the Mental Rotation. Journal of Experimental Psychology: General.

- Barsalou, L.W. (1999). Perceptual Symbol Systems. *Behavioral and Brain Sciences* 22: 577-660.

- Bartolomeo, P. (2002). The Relationship Between Visual perception and Visual Mental Imagery: A Reappraisal of the Neuropsychological Evidence. *Cortex* 38: 357-378. Cortex open access archive

- Bennett, M.R. & Hacker, P.M.S. (2003). *Philosophical Foundations of Neuroscience.* Oxford: Blackwell.

- Bensafi, M., Porter, J., Pouliot, S., Mainland, J., Johnson, B., Zelano, C., Young, N., Bremner, E., Aframian, D., Kahn, R., & Sobel, N. (2003). Olfactomotor Activity During Imagery Mimics that During Perception. *Nature Neuroscience* 6: 1142-1144.

- Block, N. (1983). Mental Pictures and Cognitive Science. *Philosophical Review* 92: 499-539.

- Brant, W. (2013). Mental Imagery and Creativity: Cognition, Observation and Realization. Akademikerverlag. pp. 227. Saarbrücken, Germany. ISBN 978-3-639-46288-3

- Cui, X., Jeter, C.B., Yang, D., Montague, P.R.,& Eagleman, D.M. (2007). "Vividness of mental imagery: Individual variability can be measured objectively". Vision Research, 47, 474-478.

- Deutsch, David. *The Fabric of Reality.* ISBN 0-14-014690-3.

- Egan, Kieran (1992). *Imagination in Teaching and Learning.* Chicago: University of Chicago Press.

- Fichter, C. & Jonas, K. (2008). Image Effects of Newspapers. How Brand Images Change Consumers' Product Ratings. *Zeitschrift für Psychologie / Journal of Psychology, 216,* 226-234.

- Finke, R.A. (1989). *Principles of Mental Imagery.* Cambridge, MA: MIT Press.

- Garnder, Howard. (1987) *The Mind's New Science: A History of the Cognitive Revolution* New York: Basic Books.

- Gur, R.C. & Hilgard, E.R. (1975). "Visual imagery and discrimination of differences between altered pictures simultaneously and successively presented". British Journal of Psychology, 66, 341-345.

- Kosslyn, Stephen M. (1983). *Ghosts in the Mind's Machine: Creating and Using Images in the Brain.* New York: Norton.

- Kosslyn, Stephen (1994) *Image and Brain: The Resolution of the Imagery Debate.* Cambridge, MA: MIT Press.

- Kosslyn, Stephen M., William L. Thompson, Irene J. Kim and Nathaniel M. Alpert (1995) Topographic representations of mental images in primary visual cortex. *Nature* 378: 496-8.

- Kosslyn, Stephen M., William L. Thompson, Mary J. Wraga and Nathaniel M. Alpert (2001) Imagining rotation by endogenous versus exogenous forces: Distinct neural mechanisms. *NeuroReport* 12, 2519–2525.

- Logie, R.H., Pernet, C.R., Buonocore, A., & Della Sala, S. (2011). "Low and high imagers activate networks differentially in mental rotation". Neuropsychologia, 49, 3071-3077.

- Marks, D.F. (1973). Visual imagery differences in the recall of pictures. *British Journal of Psychology,* 64, 17-24.

- Marks, D.F. (1995). New directions for mental imagery research. Journal of Mental Imagery, 19, 153-167.

- McGabhann. R, Squires. B, 2003, 'Releasing The Beast Within —A path to Mental Toughness', Granite Publishing, Australia.

- McKellar, Peter (1957). *Imagination and Thinking.* London: Cohen & West.

- Norman, Donald. *The Design of Everyday Things.* ISBN 0-465-06710-7.

- Paivio, Allan (1986). *Mental Representations: A Dual Coding Approach.* New York: Oxford University Press.

- Parsons, Lawrence M. (1987) Imagined spatial transformations of one's hands and feet. *Cognitive Psychology* 19: 178-241.

- Parsons, Lawrence M. (2003) Superior parietal cortices and varieties of mental rotation. *Trends in Cognitive Science* 7: 515-551.

- Pascual-Leone, Alvaro, Nguyet Dang, Leonardo G. Cohen, Joaquim P. Brasil-Neto, Angel Cammarota, and Mark Hallett (1995). Modulation of Muscle Responses Evoked by Transcranial Magnetic Stimulation During the Acquisition of New Fine Motor Skills. *Journal of Neuroscience*

- Plato. *The Republic (New CUP translation into English).* ISBN 0-521-48443-X.

- Plato. *Respublica (New CUP edition of Greek text).* ISBN 0-19-924849-4.

- Prinz, J.J. (2002). *Furnishing the Mind: Concepts and their Perceptual Basis.* Boston, MA: MIT Press.

- Pylyshyn, Zenon W. (1973). What the mind's eye tells the mind's brain: a critique of mental imagery. *Psychological Bulletin* 80: 1-24

- Reisberg, Daniel (Ed.) (1992). *Auditory Imagery.* Hillsdale, NJ: Erlbaum.

- Richardson, A. (1969). *Mental Imagery.* London: Routledge & Kegan Paul.

- Rodway, P., Gillies, K. & Schepman, A. (2006). "Vivid imagers are better at detecting salient changes". *Journal of Individual Differences* 27: 218-228.

- Rohrer, T. (2006). The Body in Space: Dimensions of embodiment The Body in Space: Embodiment, Experientialism and Linguistic Conceptualization]. In *Body, Language and Mind, vol. 2.* Zlatev, Jordan; Ziemke, Tom; Frank, Roz; Dirven, René (eds.). Berlin: Mouton de Gruyter, forthcoming 2006.

- Ryle, G. (1949). *The Concept of Mind.* London: Hutchinson.

- Sartre, J.-P. (1940). *The Psychology of Imagination.* (Translated from the French by B. Frechtman, New York: Philosophical Library, 1948.)

- Schwoebel, John, Robert Friedman, Nanci Duda and H. Branch Coslett (2001). Pain and the body schema evidence for peripheral effects on mental representations of movement. *Brain* 124: 2098-2104.

- Skinner, B.F. (1974). *About Behaviorism.* New York: Knopf.

- Shepard, Roger N. and Jacqueline Metzler (1971) Mental rotation of three-dimensional objects. *Science* 171: 701-703.

- Thomas, Nigel J.T. (1999). Are Theories of Imagery Theories of Imagination? An Active Perception Approach to Conscious Mental Content. *Cognitive Science* 23: 207-245.

- Thomas, N.J.T. (2003). Mental Imagery, Philosophical Issues About. In L. Nadel (Ed.), *Encyclopedia of Cognitive Science* (Volume 2, pp. 1147–1153). London: Nature Publishing/Macmillan.

- Traill, R.R. (2015). Concurrent Roles for the Eye *Concurrent Roles for the Eye (Passive 'Camera' plus Active Decoder) —Hence Separate Mechanisms?,* Melbourne: Ondwelle Publications.

52.9 External links

- Mental Imagery in the *Stanford Encyclopedia of Philosophy*

- Imagination, Mental Imagery, Consciousness, and Cognition: Scientific, Philosophical and Historical Approaches.

- Roadmind University The Roerich Psychodynamic Inventory (RPI) provides statistical data to determine the validity of mental imagery for cognition of the minds raw emotional state. (Dr. Robert Roerich MD.)

- Mental Imagery in Mathematics

- The Human Brain, Really Amazing!

Chapter 53

Understatement

Understatement is a form of speech or disclosure which contains an expression of less strength than would be expected. Understatement may be employed for emphasis,[1] for humour, or ironically. This is not to be confused with euphemism, where a polite phrase is used in place of a harsher or more offensive expression, though understatement too can be used to moderate something that might seem harsh.[2]

The figure of speech used in understatement, litotes, is always deliberate.[1]

53.1 In English culture

Main article: English understatement

Understatement is often associated with traditional English culture,[3] where it may be used for comic effect,[4][5] or may refer to the verbally calm English way of dealing with extreme situations.[6][7]

53.2 See also

- Hyperbole
- Meiosis (figure of speech)
- Minimisation (psychology)
- Overstatement

53.3 References

[1] Smyth, Herbert Weir (1920). *Greek Grammar*. Cambridge MA: Harvard University Press. p. 680. ISBN 0-674-36250-0.

[2] "*litotes*". *Dictionary.com*. Retrieved 7 June 2015.

[3] Hübler, Axel (1983). *Understatements and Hedges in English*. John Benjamins Publishing. ISBN 978-9027225313.

[4] "Monty Python's Meaning of Life Script Part 1". MontyPython.net. Retrieved 5 June 2015.

[5] The Oxford Dictionary of Quotations, rev. 4th ed., Anonymous, 14:12, which notes that the quote is "probably apocryphal".

[6] "The day 650 Glosters faced 10,000 Chinese". *The Daily Telegraph*. 20 April 2001.

[7] Job, Macarthur (1994). *Air Disaster Volume 2*. Aerospace Publications. pp. 96–107. ISBN 1-875671-19-6.

Chapter 54

Irony

"Ironic" redirects here. For the song, see Ironic (song). For other uses, see Irony (disambiguation).

Irony (from Ancient Greek εἰρωνεία *(eirōneía)*, meaning "dissimulation, feigned ignorance" *[1]), in its broadest sense, is a rhetorical device, literary technique, or event in which what appears, on the surface, to be the case, differs radically from what is actually the case. Irony may be divided into categories such as **verbal**, **dramatic**, and **situational**.

Verbal, dramatic, and situational irony are often used for emphasis in the assertion of a truth. The ironic form of simile, used in sarcasm, and some forms of litotes can emphasize one's meaning by the deliberate use of language which states the opposite of the truth, denies the contrary of the truth, or drastically and obviously understates a factual connection.*[2]

Other forms, as identified by historian Connop Thirlwall, include dialectic and practical irony.*[3]

54.1 Definitions

Henry Watson Fowler, in *The King's English*, says "any definition of irony—though hundreds might be given, and very few of them would be accepted—must include this, that the surface meaning and the underlying meaning of what is said are not the same." Also, Eric Partridge, in *Usage and Abusage*, writes that "Irony consists in stating the contrary of what is meant."

The use of irony may require the concept of a *double audience*. Fowler's *A Dictionary of Modern English Usage* says:

> Irony is a form of utterance that postulates a double audience, consisting of one party that hearing shall hear & shall not understand, & another party that, when more is meant than meets the ear, is aware both of that more & of the outsiders' incomprehension.*[4]

The term is sometimes used as a synonym for *incongruous* and applied to "every trivial oddity" in situations where there is no double audience.*[4] An example of such usage is:

> Sullivan, whose real interest was, ironically, serious music, which he composed with varying degrees of success, achieved fame for his comic opera scores rather than for his more earnest efforts.*[5]

The *American Heritage Dictionary*'s secondary meaning for *irony*: "incongruity between what might be expected and what actually occurs" .*[6] This sense, however, is not synonymous with "incongruous" but merely a definition of dramatic or situational irony. It is often included in definitions of irony *not only* that incongruity is present *but also* that the incongruity must reveal some aspect of human vanity or folly. Thus the majority of *American Heritage Dictionary*'s usage panel found it unacceptable to use the word *ironic* to describe mere unfortunate coincidences or surprising disappointments that "suggest no particular lessons about human vanity or folly." *[7]

On this aspect, the Oxford English Dictionary (OED) has also:

> A condition of affairs or events of a character opposite to what was, or might naturally be, expected; a contradictory outcome of events as if in mockery of the promise and fitness of things. (In French *ironie du sort.*)[8]

54.2 Origin of the term

According to the *Encyclopædia Britannica*,

> The term irony has its roots in the Greek comic character Eiron, a clever underdog who by his wit repeatedly triumphs over the boastful character Alazon. The Socratic irony of the Platonic dialogues derives from this comic origin.[9]

According to Richard Whately:

> Aristotle mentions *Eironeia*, which in his time was commonly employed to signify, not according to the modern use of 'Irony, saying the contrary to what is meant', but, what later writers usually express by Litotes, i.e. 'saying less than is meant'.[10]

The word came into English as a figure of speech in the 16th century as similar to the French *ironie*. It derives from the Latin *ironia* and ultimately from the Greek εἰρωνεία eirōneía, meaning *dissimulation, ignorance purposely affected.*[11]

54.3 Types

The New Princeton Encyclopedia of Poetry and Poetics distinguishes between the following types of irony:[3]

- **Classical** irony: referring to the origins of irony in Ancient Greek comedy, and the way classical and medieval rhetoricians delineated the term.

- **Romantic** irony: The Encyclopedia states that "The most significant change in meaning took place in 1797, when Schlegel observed in his Fragments: 'there are ancient and modern poems which breathe throughout, in their entirety and in every detail, the divine breath of [irony].'" It is seen as "a consistent alternation of affirmation and negation, of exuberant emergence from oneself and self-critical retreat into oneself, of enthusiasm and skepticism."

- **Tragic** irony: The Encyclopedia says this term: "was introduced by Connop Thirlwall in 1833, who based it on a distinction among three basic types of [irony]: verbal, dialectic, and practical."

- **Cosmic** irony: "[Irony] took on a new and more comprehensive dimension with Hegel, who strongly opposed romantic [irony] because of its "annihilating" tendency, seeing in it nothing but poetic caprice."

  > In The History of Philosophy, Hegel sensed in the "crowding of world historical affairs," in the trampling down of the "happiness of peoples, wisdom of states, and virtue of individuals," in short, in his comprehensive view of history, an ironic contrast between the absolute and the relative, the general and the individual, which he expressed by the phrase, "general [irony] of the world." [3]

- **Verbal** irony: The Encyclopedia states that, in this:

  > one meaning is stated and a different, usually antithetical, meaning is intended. The [irony] of a statement often depends on context. If one looks out of his window at a rain storm and remarks to a friend, "Wonderful day, isn't it?" the contradiction between the facts and the implied description of them establishes the [irony].[3]

- **Dramatic** irony:

> a plot device according to which (a) the spectators know more than the protagonist; (b) the character reacts in a way contrary to that which is appropriate or wise; (c) characters or situations are compared or contrasted for ironic effects, such as parody; or (d) there is a marked contrast between what the character understands about his acts and what the play demonstrates about them.[3]

A disparity of awareness between actor and observer: when words and actions possess significance that the listener or audience understands, but the speaker or character does not; for example when a character says to another "I'll see you tomorrow!" when the audience (but not the character) knows that the character will die before morning. It is most often used when the author causes a character to speak or act erroneously, out of ignorance of some portion of the truth of which the audience is aware. In tragic irony, the audience knows the character is making a mistake, even as the character is making it.

- **Poetic** irony. The Encyclopedia says that: "during the modern period [especially], beginning with romanticism, [irony] has become inseparable from literary and poetic expression itself.[3]"

Lars Elleström would add:

- **Situational** irony: The disparity of intention and result; when the result of an action is contrary to the desired or expected effect.

54.3.1   Verbal irony

According to *A glossary of literary terms* by Abrams and Hartman,

> **Verbal irony** is a statement in which the meaning that a speaker employs is sharply different from the meaning that is ostensibly expressed. The ironic statement usually involves the explicit expression of one attitude or evaluation, but with indications in the overall speech-situation that the speaker intends a very different, and often opposite, attitude or evaluation.[12]

Verbal irony is distinguished from situational irony and dramatic irony in that it is produced *intentionally* by speakers. For instance, if a man exclaims, "I'm not upset!" but reveals an upset emotional state through his voice while truly trying to claim he's not upset, it would not be verbal irony by virtue of its verbal manifestation (it would, however, be situational irony). But if the same speaker said the same words and intended to communicate that he was upset by claiming he was not, the utterance would be verbal irony. This distinction illustrates an important aspect of verbal irony—speakers communicate implied propositions that are intentionally contradictory to the propositions contained in the words themselves. There are, however, examples of verbal irony that do not rely on saying the opposite of what one means, and there are cases where all the traditional criteria of irony exist and the utterance is not ironic.

In a clear example from literature, in Shakespeare's *Julius Caesar*, Mark Antony's speech after the assassination of Caesar appears to praise the assassins, particularly Brutus ("But Brutus says he was ambitious; / And Brutus is an honourable man"), while actually condemning them. "We're left in no doubt as to who's ambitious and who's honourable. The literal truth of what's written clashes with the perceived truth of what's meant to revealing effect, which is irony in a nutshell" . [13]

Ironic similes are a form of verbal irony where a speaker intends to communicate the opposite of what they mean. For instance, the following explicit similes begin with the deceptive formation of a statement that means *A* but that eventually conveys the meaning *not A*:

- as soft as concrete

- as clear as mud

- as pleasant as a root canal

- "as pleasant and relaxed as a coiled rattlesnake" (Kurt Vonnegut from *Breakfast of Champions*)

The irony is recognizable in each case only by using knowledge of the source concepts (e.g., that mud is opaque, that root canal surgery is painful) to detect an incongruity.

Verbal irony and sarcasm

A fair amount of confusion has surrounded the issue regarding the relationship between verbal irony and sarcasm.

Fowler's *A Dictionary of Modern English Usage* states:

> Sarcasm does not necessarily involve irony and irony has often no touch of sarcasm.

This suggests that the two concepts are linked but may be considered separately. The OED entry for sarcasm does not mention irony, but the irony entry reads:

> A figure of speech in which the intended meaning is the opposite of that expressed by the words used; usually taking the form of sarcasm or ridicule in which laudatory expressions are used to imply condemnation or contempt.

The *Encyclopædia Britannica* has "Non-literary irony is often called sarcasm"; while the Webster's Dictionary entry is:

> Sarcasm: 1 : a sharp and often satirical or ironic utterance designed to cut or give pain. 2 a : a mode of satirical wit depending for its effect on bitter, caustic, and often ironic language that is usually directed against an individual.

Partridge in *Usage and Abusage* would separate the two forms of speech completely:

> Irony must not be confused with sarcasm, which is direct: sarcasm means precisely what it says, but in a sharp, caustic, ... manner.

The psychologist Martin, in *The psychology of humour*, is quite clear that irony is where "the literal meaning is opposite to the intended"; and sarcasm is "aggressive humor that pokes fun" .*[14] He has the following examples: For irony he uses the statement "What a nice day" when it is raining. For sarcasm, he cites Winston Churchill, who is supposed to have said, when told by Bessie Braddock that he was drunk, "But I shall be sober in the morning, and you will still be ugly" , as being sarcastic, while not saying the opposite of what is intended.

Psychology researchers Lee and Katz (1998) have addressed the issue directly. They found that ridicule is an important aspect of sarcasm, but not of verbal irony in general. By this account, sarcasm is a particular kind of personal criticism leveled against a person or group of persons that incorporates verbal irony. For example, a woman reports to her friend that rather than going to a medical doctor to treat her cancer, she has decided to see a spiritual healer instead. In response her friend says sarcastically, "Oh, brilliant, what an ingenious idea, that's really going to cure you." The friend could have also replied with any number of ironic expressions that should not be labeled as sarcasm exactly, but still have many shared elements with sarcasm.

Most instances of verbal irony are labeled by research subjects as sarcastic, suggesting that the term *sarcasm* is more widely used than its technical definition suggests it should be (Bryant & Fox Tree, 2002; Gibbs, 2000). Some psycholinguistic theorists (e.g., Gibbs, 2000) suggest that sarcasm ("Great idea!", "I hear they do fine work."), hyperbole ("That's the best idea I have heard in years!"), understatement ("Sure, what the hell, it's only cancer..."), rhetorical questions ("What, does your spirit have cancer?"), double entendre ("I'll bet if you do that, you'll be communing with spirits in no time...") and jocularity ("Get them to fix your bad back while you're at it.") should all be considered forms of verbal irony. The differences between these rhetorical devices (tropes) can be quite subtle and relate to typical emotional reactions of listeners, and the rhetorical goals of the speakers. Regardless of the various ways theorists categorize figurative language types, people in conversation who are attempting to interpret speaker intentions and discourse goals do not generally identify, by name, the kinds of tropes used (Leggitt & Gibbs, 2000).

54.3.2   Dramatic irony

This type of irony is the device of giving the spectator an item of information that at least one of the characters in the narrative is unaware of (at least consciously), thus placing the spectator a step ahead of at least one of the characters. The OED defines this as:

> the incongruity created when the (tragic) significance of a character's speech or actions is revealed to the audience but unknown to the character concerned; the literary device so used, orig. in Greek tragedy.[15]

According to Stanton,[16] dramatic irony has three stages—installation, exploitation, and resolution (often also called preparation, suspension, and resolution)—producing dramatic conflict in what one character relies or appears to rely upon, the *contrary* of which is known by observers (especially the audience; sometimes to other characters within the drama) to be true. In summary, it means that the reader/watcher/listener knows something that one or more of the characters in the piece is not aware of.

For example:

- In *City Lights* the audience knows that Charlie Chaplin's character is not a millionaire, but the blind flower girl (Virginia Cherrill) believes him to be rich.[17]

- In *North by Northwest*, the audience knows that Roger Thornhill (Cary Grant) is not Kaplan; Vandamm (James Mason) and his accomplices do not. The audience also knows that Kaplan is a fictitious agent invented by the CIA; Roger (initially) and Vandamm (throughout) do not.[18]

- In *Oedipus the King*, the audience knows that Oedipus himself is the murderer that he is seeking; Oedipus, Creon and Jocasta do not.[19]

- In *Othello*, the audience knows that Desdemona has been faithful to Othello, but Othello does not. The audience also knows that Iago is scheming to bring about Othello's downfall, a fact hidden from Othello, Desdemona, Cassio and Roderigo.[20]

- In *The Cask of Amontillado*, the reader knows that Montresor is planning on murdering Fortunato, while Fortunato believes they are friends.[21]

- In *The Truman Show*, the viewer is aware that Truman is on a television show, but Truman himself only gradually learns this.[22]

- In *Romeo and Juliet*, the audience knows that Juliet is already married to Romeo, but her family does not. Also, in the crypt, most of the other characters in the cast think Juliet is dead, but the audience knows she only took a sleeping potion. Romeo is also under the same misapprehension when he kills himself.[23]

Tragic irony

Tragic irony is a special category of dramatic irony. In tragic irony, the words and actions of the characters contradict the real situation, which the spectators fully realize. The Oxford English Dictionary defines this as:

> the incongruity created when the (tragic) significance of a character's speech or actions is revealed to the audience but unknown to the character concerned, the literary device so used, orig. in Greek tragedy.[15]

Ancient Greek drama was especially characterized by tragic irony because the audiences were so familiar with the legends that most of the plays dramatized. Sophocles' *Oedipus the King* provides a classic example of tragic irony at its fullest. Colebrook writes:

> Tragic irony is exemplified in ancient drama ... The audience watched a drama unfold, already knowing its destined outcome. ... In Sophocles' *Oedipus the King*, for example, 'we' (the audience) can see what Oedipus is blind to. The man he murders is his father, but he does not know it.[24]

Further, Oedipus vows to find the murderer and curses him for the plague that he has caused, not knowing that the murderer he has cursed and vowed to find is himself.

Irony has some of its foundation in the onlooker's perception of paradox that arises from insoluble problems. For example, in the William Shakespeare play *Romeo and Juliet*, when Romeo finds Juliet in a drugged deathlike sleep, he assumes her to be dead and kills himself. Upon awakening to find her dead lover beside her, Juliet stabs herself with a dagger thus killing herself.

54.3.3 Situational irony

This is a relatively modern use of the term, and describes a sharp discrepancy between the expected result and actual results in a certain situation.

Lars Elleström writes:

> *Situational irony,* ... is most broadly defined as a situation where the outcome is incongruous with what was expected, but it is also more generally understood as a situation that includes contradictions or sharp contrasts,[25]

For example:

- When John Hinckley attempted to assassinate Ronald Reagan, all of his shots initially missed the President; however, a bullet ricocheted off the bullet-proof Presidential limousine and struck Reagan in the chest. Thus, a vehicle made to protect the President from gunfire instead directed gunfire to the president.[26][27]

- *The Wonderful Wizard of Oz* is a story whose plot revolves around situational irony. Dorothy travels to a wizard and fulfills his challenging demands to go home, before discovering she had the ability to go back home all the time. The Scarecrow longs for intelligence, only to discover he is already a genius, and the Tin Woodsman longs to be capable of love, only to discover he already has a heart. The Lion, who at first appears to be a whimpering coward, turns out to be bold and fearless. The people in Emerald City believed the Wizard to be a powerful deity, only to discover that he is a bumbling, eccentric old man with no special powers at all.[27][28]

- In O. Henry's story "The Gift of the Magi", a young couple are too poor to buy each other Christmas gifts. The wife cuts off her treasured hair to sell it to a wig-maker for money to buy her husband a chain for his heirloom pocket watch. She's shocked when she learns he had pawned his watch to buy her a set of combs for her long, beautiful, prized hair. "The double irony lies in the particular way their expectations were foiled." [29]

- In the ancient Indian story of Krishna, King Kamsa is told in a prophecy that a child of his sister Devaki would kill him. To prevent this, he imprisons both Devaki and her husband Vasudeva, allowing them to live only if they hand over their children as soon as they are born. He murders nearly all of them, one by one, but the seventh and eighth children, Balarama and Krishna, are saved and raised by a royal couple, Nanda and Yashoda. After the boys grow up, Krishna eventually kills Kamsa as the prophecy foretold. Kamsa's attempt to prevent the prophecy led to it becoming a reality.[30]

- This story is similar to those in Greek mythology. Cronus prevents his wife from raising any children, but the one who ends up defeating him is Zeus, the later King of the Gods.[31] Other similar tales in Greek Mythology include Perseus (who killed his grandfather, Acrisius by accident with a discus despite Acrisius' attempt to avert his fate), and, more famously, Oedipus who killed his father and married his mother not knowing their relationship, due to being left to die by his father to prevent that very prophecy from occurring.

Cosmic irony (irony of fate)

The expression cosmic irony or "irony of fate" stems from the notion that the gods (or the Fates) are amusing themselves by toying with the minds of mortals with deliberate ironic intent. Closely connected with situational irony, it arises from sharp contrasts between reality and human ideals, or between human intentions and actual results. The resulting situation is poignantly contrary to what was expected or intended.

According to Sudhir Dixit, "Cosmic irony is a term that is usually associated with [Thomas] Hardy. ... There is a strong feeling of a hostile deus ex machina in Hardy's novels." In *Tess of the d'Urbervilles* "there are several instances of this type of irony." [32]

> "Justice" was done, and the President of the Immortals (in Æschylean phrase) had ended his sport with Tess.[33]

Historical irony

When history is seen through modern eyes, there often appear sharp contrasts between the way historical figures see their world's future and what actually transpires. For example, during the 1920s *The New York Times* repeatedly scorned crossword puzzles. In 1924, it lamented "the sinful waste in the utterly futile finding of words the letters of which will fit into a prearranged pattern." In 1925 it said "the question of whether the puzzles are beneficial or harmful is in no urgent need of an answer. The craze evidently is dying out fast." Today, no U.S. newspaper is more closely identified with the crossword than *The New York Times*.[34]

In a more tragic example of historical irony, what people now refer to as "The First World War" was called by H.G. Wells "The war that will end war" ,[35] which soon became "The war to end war" and "The War to End All Wars" , and this became a widespread truism, almost a cliché. Historical irony is therefore a subset of cosmic irony, but one in which the element of time is bound to play a role. Another example could be that of the Vietnam War, where in the 1960s the U.S. attempted to stop the Viet Cong (Viet Minh) taking over South Vietnam. However, it is an often ignored fact that, in 1941, the U.S. originally supported the Viet Minh in its fight against Japanese occupation.[36]

In the introduction to *The Irony of American History*, Andrew Bacevich writes:

> After 9/11, the Bush administration announced its intention of bringing freedom and democracy to the people of the Middle East. Ideologues within the Bush administration persuaded themselves that American power, adroitly employed, could transform that region ... The results speak for themselves.[37]

Gunpowder was, according to prevailing academic consensus, discovered in the 9th century by Chinese alchemists searching for an elixir of immortality.[38]

Historical irony also includes inventors killed by their own creations, such as William Bullock—unless, due to the nature of the invention, the risk of death was always known and accepted, as in the case of Otto Lilienthal, who was killed by flying a glider of his own devising.

In certain kinds of situational or historical irony, a factual truth is highlighted by some person's complete ignorance of it or his belief in its opposite. However, this state of affairs does not occur by human design. In some religious contexts, such situations have been seen as the deliberate work of Divine Providence to emphasize truths and to taunt humans for not being aware of them when they could easily have been enlightened (this is similar to human use of irony). Such ironies are often more evident, or more striking, when viewed retrospectively in the light of later developments which make the truth of past situations obvious to all.

Other prominent examples of outcomes now seen as poignantly contrary to expectation include:

- In the *Dred Scott v. Sandford* ruling in 1856, the United States Supreme Court held that the Fifth Amendment barred any law that would deprive a slaveholder of his property, such as his slaves, upon the incidence of migration into free territory. So, in a sense, the Supreme Court used the Bill of Rights to deny rights to slaves. Also, chief justice Taney hoped that the decision would resolve the slavery issue, but instead it helped cause the American Civil War.[39]

- In the Kalgoorlie (Australia) gold rush of the 1890s, large amounts of the little-known mineral calaverite (gold telluride) were ironically identified as fool's gold. These mineral deposits were used as a cheap building material, and for the filling of potholes and ruts. When several years later the mineral was identified, there was a minor gold rush to excavate the streets.[40]

- John F. Kennedy's last conversation was ironic in light of events which followed seconds later. During the motorcade in Dallas, in response to Mrs. Connolly's comment, "Mr. President, you can't say that Dallas doesn't love you," Kennedy replied, "That's very obvious." Immediately after, he was mortally wounded.*[41]

- In 1974, the U.S. Consumer Product Safety Commission had to recall 80,000 of its own lapel buttons promoting "toy safety", because the buttons had sharp edges, used lead paint, and had small clips that could be broken off and subsequently swallowed.*[42]

- Introducing cane toads to Australia to control the cane beetle not only failed to control the pest, but introduced, in the toads themselves, a very much worse pest. This irony is exemplified by the song "There Was an Old Lady Who Swallowed a Fly", in which the lady swallows a fly, and then swallows a spider to catch the fly, and so on with larger and larger animals, until she dies.

54.4 Use

54.4.1 Comic irony

Irony is often used in literature to produce a comic effect. This may also be combined with satire. For instance, an author may facetiously state something as a well-known fact and then demonstrate through the narrative that the fact is untrue.

Jane Austen's *Pride and Prejudice* begins with the proposition "It is a truth universally acknowledged, that a single man in possession of a good fortune, must be in want of a wife." In fact, it soon becomes clear that Austen means the opposite: women (or their mothers) are always in search of, and desperately on the lookout for, a rich single man to make a husband. The irony deepens as the story promotes this romance and ends in a double marriage proposal. "Austen's comic irony emerges out of the disjunction between Elizabeth's overconfidence (or pride) in her perceptions of Darcy and the narrator's indications that her views are in fact partial and prejudicial." *[43]

"*The Third Man* is a film that features any number of eccentricities, each of which contributes to the film's perspective of comic irony as well as its overall cinematic self-consciousness." *[44]

Writing about performances of Shakespeare's *Othello* in apartheid South Africa, Robert Gordon suggests: "Could it be that black people in the audience ... may have viewed as a comic irony his audacity and naïvety in thinking he could pass for white." *[45]

54.4.2 Romantic irony and metafiction

Romantic irony is "an attitude of detached scepticism adopted by an author towards his or her work, typically manifesting in literary self-consciousness and self-reflection". This conception of irony originated with the German Romantic writer and critic Karl Wilhelm Friedrich Schlegel.*[46]

Joseph Dane writes "From a twentieth-century perspective, the most crucial area in the history of irony is that described by the term romantic irony." He discusses the difficulty of defining romantic irony: "But what is romantic irony? A universal type of irony? The irony used by romantics? or an irony envisioned by the romantics and romanticists?" He also describes the arguments for and against its use.*[47]

Referring to earlier self-conscious works such as Don Quixote and Tristram Shandy, Douglas Muecke points particularly to Peter Weiss's 1964 play, "Marat/Sade". This work is a play within a play set in a lunatic asylum, in which it is difficult to tell whether the players are speaking only to other players or also directly to the audience. When The Herald says, "The regrettable incident you've just seen was unavoidable indeed foreseen by our playwright", there is confusion as to who is being addressed, the "audience" on the stage or the audience in the theatre. Also, since the play within the play is performed by the inmates of a lunatic asylum, the theatre audience cannot tell whether the paranoia displayed before them is that of the players, or the people they are portraying. Muecke notes that, "in America, Romantic irony has had a bad press", while "in England ... [it] is almost unknown." *[48]

However, in a book entitled *English Romantic Irony*, Anne Mellor, referring to Byron, Keats, Carlyle, Coleridge and Lewis Carroll, writes, "Romantic irony is both a philosophical conception of the universe and an artistic program. Ontologically, it sees the world as fundamentally chaotic. No order, no far goal of time, ordained by God or right reason, determines the progression of human or natural events." Furthermore,

> Of course, romantic irony itself has more than one mode. The style of romantic irony varies from writer to writer. ... But however distinctive the voice, a writer is a romantic ironist if and when his or her work commits itself enthusiastically both in content and form to a hovering or unresolved debate between a world of merely man-made being and a world of ontological becoming.*[49]

Similarly, metafiction is "Fiction in which the author self-consciously alludes to the artificiality or literariness of a work by parodying or departing from novelistic conventions (esp. naturalism) and narrative techniques." *[50] It is a type of fiction that self-consciously addresses the devices of fiction, thereby exposing the fictional illusion.

Gesa Giesing writes that "the most common form of metafiction is particularly frequent in Romantic literature. The phenomenon is then referred to as Romantic Irony." Giesing notes that "There has obviously been an increased interest in metafiction again after World War II." *[51]

For examples, Patricia Waugh quotes from several works at the top of her chapter headed "What is metafiction?". These include:

"The thing is this./ That of all the several ways of beginning a book ... I am confident my own way of doing it is best" - *Tristram Shandy*

"Fuck all this lying look what I am trying to write about is writing" - *Albert Angelo*

"Since I've started this story, I've gotten boils ..." - *The death of the novel and other stories* by Ronald Sukenick*[52]

Additionally, *The Cambridge Introduction to Postmodern Fiction* refers to John Fowles's *The French Lieutenant's Woman*:*[53]

> For the first twelve chapters ... the reader has been able to immerse him or herself in the story, enjoying the kind of 'suspension of disbelief ' required of realist novels ... what follows is a remarkable act of metafictional 'frame-breaking'. Chapter 13 notoriously begins:

> I do not know. This story I am telling is all imagination. These characters I create never existed outside my own mind. ... if this is a novel, it cannot be a novel in the modern sense.

54.4.3 Socratic irony

Main article: Socratic method

This is "The dissimulation of ignorance practised by Socrates as a means of confuting an adversary" .*[54] Socrates would pretend to be ignorant of the topic under discussion, to draw out the inherent nonsense in the arguments of his interlocutors. *The Chambers Dictionary* defines it as "a means by which a questioner pretends to know less than a respondent, when actually he knows more" .

Zoe Williams of *The Guardian* wrote: "The technique [of Socratic irony], demonstrated in the Platonic dialogues, was to pretend ignorance and, more sneakily, to feign credence in your opponent's power of thought, in order to tie him in knots." *[55]

A more modern example of Socratic irony can be seen on the American crime fiction television film series, *Columbo*. The character Lt. Columbo is seemingly naïve and incompetent. His untidy appearance adds to this fumbling illusion. As a result, he is underestimated by the suspects in murder cases he is investigating. With their guard down and their false sense of confidence, Lt. Columbo is able to solve the cases leaving the murderers feeling duped and outwitted.*[56]

54.4.4 Irony as infinite, absolute negativity

Danish philosopher Søren Kierkegaard, and others, see irony, such as that used by Socrates, as a disruptive force with the power to undo texts and readers alike.*[57] The phrase itself is taken from Hegel's *Lectures on Aesthetics*, and is applied by

Kierkegaard to the irony of Socrates. This tradition includes 19th-century German critic and novelist Friedrich Schlegel ("On Incomprehensibility"), Charles Baudelaire, Stendhal, and the 20th century deconstructionist Paul de Man ("The Concept of Irony"). In Kierkegaard's words, from On the Concept of Irony with Continual Reference to Socrates:

> [Socratic] irony [is] the infinite absolute negativity. It is negativity, because it only negates; it is infinite, because it does not negate this or that phenomenon; it is absolute, because that by virtue of which it negates is a higher something that still is not. The irony established nothing, because that which is to be established lies behind it...*[58]

Where much of philosophy attempts to reconcile opposites into a larger positive project, Kierkegaard and others insist that irony—whether expressed in complex games of authorship or simple litotes—must, in Kierkegaard's words, "swallow its own stomach" . Irony entails endless reflection and violent reversals, and ensures incomprehensibility at the moment it compels speech. Similarly, among other literary critics, writer David Foster Wallace viewed the pervasiveness of ironic and other postmodern tropes as the cause of "great despair and stasis in U.S. culture, and that for aspiring fictionists [ironies] pose terrifically vexing problems." *[59]

54.4.5 Irony and awkwardness

The '90s saw an expansion of the definition of irony from "saying what one doesn't mean" into a "general stance of detachment from life in general" *[60] This detachment served as a shield against the awkwardness of everyday life. Humor from that era (most notably *Seinfeld*) relies on the audience watching the show with some detachment from the show's typical signature awkward situations.

The generation of people in the United States who grew up in the 90s (Millennials) are seen as having this same sort of detachment from serious or awkward situations in life as well. Hipsters are thought of as using irony as a shield against those same serious or genuine confrontations.*[61]

54.5 Misuse

Some speakers of English complain that the words *irony* and *ironic* are often misused,*[62] though the more general casual usage of a tragic coincidence or "contradiction between circumstance and expectation" originates in the 1640s.*[63]

Dan Shaughnessy wrote:

> We were always kidding about the use of irony. I maintained that it was best never to use the word because it was too often substituted for coincidence. (Alanis Morissette's song "Isn't it Ironic?" cites multiple examples of things that are patently not ironic)*[64]

Tim Conley cites the following: "Philip Howard assembled a list of seven implied meanings for the word "ironically" , as it opens a sentence:

- By a tragic coincidence

- By an exceptional coincidence

- By a coincidence of no importance

- You and I know, of course, though other less intelligent mortals walk benighted under the midday sun

- Oddly enough, or it's a rum thing that

- Oh hell! I've run out of words to start a sentence with." *[65]

54.6   Punctuation

Main article: Irony punctuation

No agreed method for indicating irony exists, though many ideas have been suggested. For instance, an irony punctuation mark was proposed in the 1580s, when Henry Denham introduced a rhetorical question mark or percontation point which resembles a reversed question mark. This mark was also advocated by the French poet Marcel Bernhardt at the end of the 19th century to indicate irony or sarcasm. French writer Hervé Bazin suggested another *pointe d'ironie*: the Greek letter *psi* Ψ with a dot below it, while Tom Driberg recommended that ironic statements should be printed in italics that lean the other way to conventional italics.*[66]

54.7   See also

- Accismus

- Apophasis

- Auto-antonym

- Contradiction

- Double standard

- Hypocrisy

- Ironism

- Irony punctuation

- Oxymoron

- Paradox

- Post-irony

- Sarcasm

- Satire

54.8   Notes

[1] Liddell & Scott, *A Greek-English Lexicon*, v. sub εἰρωνεία.

[2] Muecke, DC., *The Compass of Irony*, Routledge, 1969. p. 80

[3] Preminger, A. & Brogan, T. V. F. Brogan, *The New Princeton Encyclopedia of Poetry and Poetics*, MJF Books, 1993, ISBN 9780691032719, pp. 633–635.

[4] Fowler, H. W., A dictionary of modern English usage, 1926.

[5] Gassner, J., Quinn, E., *The Reader's Encyclopedia of World Drama*, Courier Dover Publications, 2002, p. 358.

[6] ""irony" at dictionary.com" . Dictionary.reference.com. Retrieved 2010-12-23.

[7] Quoted in *The Free Dictionary* under *ironic*: http://www.thefreedictionary.com/ironic.

[8] Oxford English Dictionary, second entry for *irony*

[9] *Encyclopædia Britannica*

[10] Whately, R. *Rhet. in Encycl. Metrop.* (1845) I. 265/1 (cited in the OED entry)

[11] *Oxford English Dictionary*

[12] Abrams, M. H., & Harpham, G. G., *A glossary of literary terms*, 9th Ed., Wadsworth Cengage Learning, 2009.

[13] Horberry, R., *Sounds Good on Paper: How to Bring Business Language to Life*, A&C Black, 2010. p. 135.

[14] Martin, R. A., *The psychology of humor: an integrative approach*, Elsevier Academic Press, 2007. p. 13.

[15] Oxford English Dictionary entry for *irony*

[16] Stanton, R., Dramatic Irony in Hawthorne's Romances, *Modern Language Notes*, Vol. 71, No. 6 (Jun., 1956), pp. 420–426, The Johns Hopkins University Press.

[17] Clausius, C., *The gentleman is a tramp: Charlie Chaplin's comedy*, P. Lang, 1989, p. 104.

[18] Gulino, P., *Screenwriting: The Sequence Approach*, Continuum, 2004, pp. 9–10.

[19] Storey, I. C. and Allan, A., *A Guide to Ancient Greek Drama*, John Wiley & Sons, 2008, p. 125.

[20] Booth, W. C., *A Rhetoric of Irony*, University of Chicago Press, 1974, p. 63.

[21] Poe, E. A., *The Cask of Amontillado*, The Creative Company, 2008, pp. 22–23.

[22] Adams, A., *Parallel Lives of Jesus: A Guide to the Four Gospels*, Presbyterian Publishing Corp, 2011, p. 30.

[23] William, J., *Cliffs Complete Romeo and Juliet*, Houghton Mifflin Harcourt, 2009, pp. 135, 169, 181.

[24] Colebrook, Claire. *Irony*. London and New York: Routledge, 2004, p. 14.

[25] Elleström, L., *Divine Madness: On Interpreting Literature, Music and the Visual Arts*, Bucknell University Press, 2002, p. 51.

[26] The Trial of John W. Hinckley, Jr. by Doug Linder. 2001 Retrieved 9 September 2008.

[27] Horberry, R., *Sounds Good on Paper: How to Bring Business Language to Life*, A&C Black, 2010. p. 138.

[28] Lenguazco, CD., *English through movies. The wizard of Oz*, Librería-Editorial Dykinson, 2005, p. 27.

[29] Gibbs, W. G., & Colston, H. L., *Irony in Language and Thought: A Cognitive Science Reader*, Routledge, 2007, p. 59.

[30] Shanta Rameshwar Rao, *The Krishna*, Orient Blackswan, 2005, p. 69

[31] Hesiod, *Theogony Works and Days Testimonia*, Harvard University Press, 2006, p. xxxii.

[32] Dixit, S., *Hardy's Tess Of The D'urbervilles*, Atlantic Publishers & Dist, 2001, p. 182.

[33] Hardy, T., *Tess of the d'Urbervilles*, Oxford World's Classics, p. 420.

[34] Wordplay

[35] Wells, H.G., *The war that will end war*, 1914.

[36] Neale, Jonathan *The American War*, p. 17, ISBN 1-898876-67-3.

[37] Bacevich, A., in Niebuhr, R., *The Irony of American History*, University of Chicago Press, 2010, p. xiv.

[38] Jack Kelly *Gunpowder: Alchemy, Bombards, and Pyrotechnics: The History of the Explosive that Changed the World*, Perseus Books Group: 2005, ISBN 0465037224, 9780465037223: pp. 2–5

[39] Fehrenbacher, D. E., *Slavery, Law, and Politics : The Dred Scott Case in Historical Perspective*, Oxford University Press, 1981, p. 90.

[40] Kean, S., *The Disappearing Spoon: And Other True Tales of Madness, Love and the History of the World from the Periodic Table of the Elements*, Random House, 2011, pp. 226–228.

[41] Last words of presidents

[42] *Wall Street Journal*, December 3, 2007, Page B1: It Dawned on Adults After WWII: 'You'll Shoot Your Eye Out!'. Retrieved October 29, 2009.

[43] Ferriss, S. & Young, M., *Chick Lit: The New Woman's Fiction*, Routledge, 2006, p. 77.

[44] Jones, W. E. & Vice, S., *Ethics at the Cinema*, Oxford University Press, 2010, p. 295.

[45] Gordon, R., in *The Shakespearean International Yearbook: Special Section, South African Shakespeare in the Twentieth Century*, Volume 9, Ashgate Publishing, Ltd., 2009. p. 147.

[46] OED, entry under *Romantic irony*.

[47] Dane, J. A., *The Critical Mythology of Irony*, University of Georgia Press, 2011, Ch. 5

[48] Muecke, DC., *The Compass of Irony*, Routledge, 1969. pp. 178–180

[49] Mellor, A. K., *English romantic irony*, Harvard University Press, 1980, pp. 4, 187.

[50] OED, entry for metafiction.

[51] Giesing, G., *Metafictional Aspects in Novels by Muriel Spark*, GRIN Verlag, 2004, p. 6.

[52] Waugh, P., *Metafiction: The Theory and Practice of Self-Conscious Fiction*, Routledge, 2002, p. 1.

[53] Nicol, B., *The Cambridge Introduction to Postmodern Fiction*, Cambridge University Press, 2009, pp. 108–109.

[54] Oxford English Dictionary under *irony*.

[55] "Online: The Final Irony". London: Guardian. 28 June 2003. Retrieved 2010-12-23.

[56] Cox, G. *How to Be a Philosopher: Or How to Be Almost Certain That Almost Nothing Is Certain,* Continuum International Publishing Group, 2010, p. 23.

[57] Kierkegaard, S, *The concept of irony with continuous reference to Socrates* (1841), Harper & Row, 1966, p. 278.

[58] Quoted in

[59] Wallace, David Foster. "E Unibus Pluram: Television and U.S. Fiction". *Review of Contemporary Fiction* **13** (2): 151–194.

[60] Kotsko, Adam, *Awkwardness.*, O-Books, 2010, pp. 21

[61] How to Live Without Irony

[62] http://www.bostonglobe.com/ideas/2015/06/05/how-learned-love-alanis-morissette-irony/Em8dl58iYReUmXrYElJOPN/story.html

[63] http://en.wiktionary.org/wiki/irony#Etymology_1

[64] Shaughnessy, D., *Senior Year: A Father, A Son, and High School Baseball*, Houghton Mifflin Harcourt, 2008, pp. 91-92.

[65] Conley, T., *Joyces Mistakes: Problems of Intention, Irony, and Interpretation*, University of Toronto Press, 2011, p. 81.

[66] Houston, K., *Shady Characters: The Secret Life of Punctuation, Symbols, and Other Typographical Marks*, W. W. Norton & Company, 2013, pp. 211-244.

54.9 Bibliography

- Bogel, Fredric V. "Irony, Inference, and Critical Understanding." Yale Review, 503–19.

- Booth, Wayne C. *A Rhetoric of Irony*. Chicago: University of Chicago Press, 1975.

- Bryant, G. A., & Fox Tree, J. E. (2002). Recognizing verbal irony in spontaneous speech. *Metaphor and Symbol, 17*, 99–115.

- Colebrook, Claire. *Irony*. London and New York: Routledge, 2004.

- Gibbs, R. W. (2000). Irony in talk among friends. *Metaphor and Symbol, 15*, 5–27.

- Hutcheon, Linda. *Irony's Edge: The Theory and Politics of Irony*. London: Routledge, 1994.

- Kierkegaard, Søren. *On the Concept of Irony with Continual Reference to Socrates*. 1841; Princeton: Princeton University Press, 1992.

- Lavandier, Yves. *Writing Drama*, pages 263–315.

- Lee, C. J., & Katz, A. N. (1998). The differential role of ridicule in sarcasm and irony. *Metaphor and Symbol, 13*, 1–15.

- Leggitt, J., & Gibbs, R. W. (2000). Emotional reactions to verbal irony. *Discourse Processes, 29*(1), 1–24.

- Muecke, D. C. *The Compass of Irony*. London: Methuen, 1969.

- Star, William T. "Irony and Satire: A Bibliography." Irony and Satire in French Literature. Ed. University of South Carolina Department of Foreign Languages and Literatures. Columbia, SC: University of South Carolina College of Humanities and Social Sciences, 1987. 183–209.

54.10 External links

- "The final irony"—a *Guardian* article about irony, use and misuse of the term

- Article on the etymology of Irony

- "Irony", by Norman D. Knox, in *Dictionary of the History of Ideas* (1973)

- "Sardonicus"—a web-resource that provides access to similes, ironic and otherwise, harvested from the web.

- Excerpt on dramatic irony from Yves Lavandier's Writing Drama *Writing Drama* has a 52-page chapter on dramatic irony (with insights on the three phases (installation-exploitation-resolution), surprise, mystery, suspense, diffuse dramatic irony, etc.)

- "American Irony" compared with British irony, quoting Stephen Fry

- American and British irony compared by Simon Pegg

- Modern example of ironic writing

- Irony definition by Baldrick (BlackAdder)

A "No smoking" sign surrounded by images of a smoking Sherlock Holmes at Baker Street tube station.

Chapter 55

Metaphor

This article is about the figure of speech. For other uses, see Metaphor (disambiguation).

A **metaphor** is a figure of speech that identifies something as being the same as some unrelated thing for rhetorical effect, thus highlighting the similarities between the two. While a simile compares two items, a metaphor directly equates them, and so does not necessarily apply any distancing words of comparison, such as "like" or "as" . A metaphor is a type of analogy and is closely related to other rhetorical figures of speech which achieve their effects via association, comparison or resemblance - including allegory, hyperbole, and simile.

One of the most commonly cited examples of a metaphor in English literature is the "All the world's a stage" monologue from *As You Like It*:

> All the world's a stage,
> And all the men and women merely players;
> They have their exits and their entrances[...]
> —William Shakespeare, *As You Like It*, 2/7*[1]

> 1. ^ "As You Like It: Entire Play" . Shakespeare.mit.edu. Retrieved 4 March 2012.

This quotation expresses a metaphor because the world is not literally a stage. By figuratively asserting that the world is a stage, Shakespeare uses the points of comparison between the world and a stage to convey an understanding about the mechanics of the world and the behavior of the people within it.

The Philosophy of Rhetoric (1937) by I. A. Richards describes a metaphor as having two parts: the **tenor** and the **vehicle.** The tenor is the subject to which attributes are ascribed. The vehicle is the object whose attributes are borrowed. In the previous example, "the world" is compared to a stage, describing it with the attributes of "the stage"; "the world" is the **tenor,** and "a stage" is the **vehicle**; "men and women" is the secondary tenor, and "players" is the secondary vehicle.

Other writers employ the general terms **ground** and **figure** to denote the tenor and the vehicle. Cognitive linguistics uses the terms **target** and **source** respectively.

55.1 Etymology

The English *metaphor* derived from the 16th-century Old French word *métaphore*, which comes from the Latin *metaphora*, "carrying over" , in turn from the Greek μεταφορά (*metaphorá*), "transfer" ,*[1] from μεταφέρω (*metapherō*), "to carry over" , "to transfer" *[2] and that from μετά (*meta*), "after, with, across" *[3] + φέρω (*pherō*), "to bear" , "to carry" .*[4]

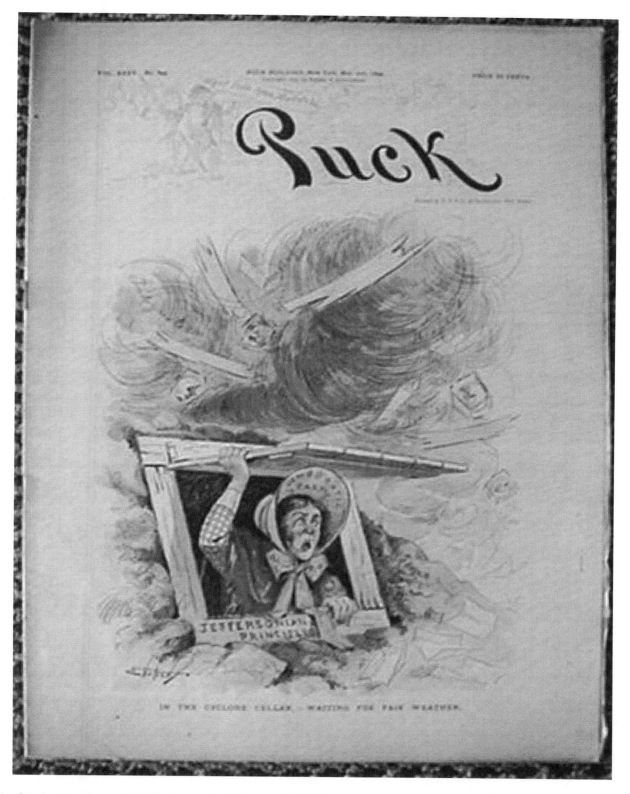

A political cartoon from an 1894 Puck *magazine by illustrator S.D. Ehrhart, shows a farm woman labeled "Democratic Party" sheltering from a tornado of political change.*

55.2   Comparison with other types of analogy

Metaphors are most frequently compared with similes. The Columbia Encyclopedia (6th edition) explains the difference as:

> a simile states that A is like B, a metaphor states that A is B or substitutes B for A.

Where a metaphor asserts the two objects in the comparison are identical on the point of comparison, a simile merely asserts a similarity. For this reason a metaphor is generally considered more forceful than a simile.

The metaphor category also contains these specialised types:

- Allegory: An extended metaphor wherein a story illustrates an important attribute of the subject.

- Catachresis: A mixed metaphor used by design and accident (a rhetorical fault).

- Parable: An extended metaphor narrated as an anecdote illustrating and teaching such as in Aesop's fables, or Jesus' teaching method as told in the Bible.

- Pun: Similar to a metaphor, a pun alludes to another term. However the main difference is that a pun is a frivolous allusion between two different things whereas a metaphor is a purposeful allusion between two different things.[5]

Metaphor, like other types of analogy, can usefully be distinguished from metonymy as one of two fundamental modes of thought. Metaphor and analogy both work by bringing together two concepts from different conceptual domains, whereas metonymy works by using one element from a given domain to refer to another closely related element. Thus, a metaphor creates new links between otherwise distinct conceptual domains, whereas a metonymy relies on the existing links within them.

55.3   Common types

A **dead metaphor** is one in which the sense of a transferred image is absent. Examples: "to grasp a concept" and "to gather what you've understood" use physical action as a metaphor for understanding. The audience does not need to visualize the action; dead metaphors normally go unnoticed. Some people distinguish between a dead metaphor and a cliché. Others use "dead metaphor" to denote both.

A **mixed metaphor** is one that leaps from one identification to a second identification inconsistent with the first, e.g.:

> I smell a rat [...] but I'll nip him in the bud"
> —Irish politician Boyle Roche

This form is often used as a parody of metaphor itself:

> If we can hit that bull's-eye then the rest of the dominoes will fall like a house of cards... Checkmate.
> —*Futurama* character Zapp Brannigan.[6]

55.4   Aristotle on Rhetoric

- Aristotle said in his work, The Rhetoric, that metaphors make learning pleasant; "To learn easily is naturally pleasant to all people, and words signify something, so whatever words create knowledge in us are the pleasantest." [7] When discussing The Rhetoric, Jan Garret quoted how "Metaphor most brings about learning; for when

[Homer] calls old age "stubble," he creates understanding and knowledge through the genus, since both old age and stubble are [species of the genus of] things that have lost their bloom." *[8] Metaphors, according to Aristotle, have "qualities of the exotic and the fascinating; but at the same time we recognize that strangers do not have the same rights as our fellow citizens." *[9]

55.5 Larger applications of metaphor

A metaphorical visualization of the word anger.

The term metaphor is also used to describe more basic or general aspects of experience and cognition:

- A **cognitive metaphor** is the association of object to an experience outside the object's environment

- A **conceptual metaphor** is an underlying association that is systematic in both language and thought

- A **root metaphor** is the underlying worldview that shapes an individual's understanding of a situation

- A **nonlinguistic metaphor** is an association between two nonlinguistic realms of experience

- A visual metaphor uses an image to create the link between different ideas

Metaphors can also be implied and extended throughout pieces of literature.

55.5.1   Conceptual metaphors

Main article: Conceptual metaphor

Some theorists have suggested that metaphors are not merely stylistic, but that they are cognitively important as well. In *Metaphors We Live By*, George Lakoff and Mark Johnson argue that metaphors are pervasive in everyday life, not just in language, but also in thought and action. A common definition of a metaphor can be described as a comparison that shows how two things that are not alike in most ways are similar in another important way. They explain how a metaphor is simply understanding and experiencing one kind of thing in terms of another. The authors call this concept a "conduit metaphor". By this they meant that a speaker can put ideas or objects into words or containers, and then send them along a channel, or conduit, to a listener who takes that idea or object out of the container and makes meaning of it. In other words, communication is something that ideas go into. The container is separate from the ideas themselves. Lakoff and Johnson give several examples of daily metaphors we use, such as "argument is war" and "time is money". Metaphors are widely used in context to describe personal meaning. The authors also suggest that communication can be viewed as a machine: "Communication is not what one does with the machine, but is the machine itself." (Johnson, Lakoff, 1980).*[10]

55.5.2   Nonlinguistic metaphors

Metaphors can also map experience between two nonlinguistic realms. In *The Dream Frontier*, Mark Blechner describes musical metaphors, in which a piece of music can "map" to the personality and emotional life of a person.*[11] Musicologist Leonard Meyer demonstrated how purely rhythmic and harmonic events can express human emotions.*[12]

Art theorist Robert Vischer argued that when we look at a painting, we "feel ourselves into it" by imagining our body in the posture of a nonhuman or inanimate object in the painting. For example, the painting "The Solitary Tree" by Caspar David Friedrich shows a tree with contorted, barren limbs.*[13]*[14] In looking at that painting, we imagine our limbs in a similarly contorted and barren shape, and that creates a feeling in us of strain and distress. Nonlinguistic metaphors may be the foundation of our experience of visual, musical,*[15] dance,*[16] and other art forms.

55.6   In historical linguistics

In historical onomasiology or in historical linguistics, a metaphor is defined as a semantic change based on a similarity in form or function between the original concept named by a word and the target concept named by this word.*[17]

For example, **mouse**: *small, gray rodent* → *small, gray, mouse-shaped computer device*.

Some recent linguistic theories view language as by its nature all metaphorical; or that language in essence is metaphorical.*[18]

55.7   Historical theories of metaphor

Friedrich Nietzsche's *On Truth and Lies in the Non-Moral Sense**[19] makes metaphor the conceptual centre of his early theory of society. Some sociologists have found this an essay useful for thinking about metaphors at use in society, as well as for reflecting on their own use of metaphor. Sociologists of religion, for example, note the importance of metaphor in religious worldviews, but also that it is impossible to think sociologically about religion without metaphor*[20]

55.7.1   Metaphor as style in speech and writing

Viewed as an aspect of speech and writing, metaphor qualifies as style, in particular, style characterized by a type of analogy. An expression (word, phrase) that by implication suggests the likeness of one entity to another entity gives style to an item of speech or writing, whether the entities consist of objects, events, ideas, activities, attributes, or almost

Tombstone of a Jewish woman depicting broken candles, a visual metaphor of the end of life.

anything expressible in language. For example, in the first sentence of this paragraph, the word "viewed" serves as a metaphor for "thought of", implying analogy of the process of seeing and the thought process. The phrase, "viewed as an aspect of", projects the properties of seeing (vision) something from a particular perspective onto thinking about something from a particular perspective, that "something" in this case referring to "metaphor" and that "perspective" in this case referring to the characteristics of speech and writing.

As a characteristic of speech and writing, metaphors can serve the poetic imagination, allowing Sylvia Plath, in her poem "Cut", to compare the blood issuing from her cut thumb to the running of a million soldiers, "redcoats, every one";[21][22] and enabling Robert Frost, in "The Road Not Taken", to compare a life to a journey.[23]

Viewed also as an aspect of speech, metaphor can serve as a device for persuading the listener or reader of the speaker or writer's argument or thesis, the so-called rhetorical metaphor.

55.7.2 Metaphor as foundational to our conceptual system

Cognitive linguists emphasize that metaphors serve to facilitate the understanding of one conceptual domain, typically an abstract one like "life" or "theories" or "ideas", through expressions that relate to another, more familiar conceptual domain, typically a more concrete one like "journey" or "buildings" or "food".[24][25] *Food for thought*: we *devour* a book of *raw* facts, try to *digest* them, *stew* over them, let them *simmer on the back-burner*, *regurgitate* them in discussions, *cook* up explanations, hoping they do not seem *half-baked*. Theories as buildings: we establish a *foundation* for them, a *framework*, *support* them with *strong* arguments, *buttressing* them with facts, hoping they will *stand*. Life as journey: some of us *travel* hopefully, others seem to have no *direction*, many *lose their way*.

A convenient short-hand way of capturing this view of metaphor is the following: CONCEPTUAL DO-MAIN (A) IS CONCEPTUAL DOMAIN (B), which is what is called a **conceptual metaphor**. A conceptual metaphor consists of two conceptual domains, in which one domain is understood in terms of another. A conceptual domain is any coherent organization of experience. Thus, for example, we have coherently organized knowledge about journeys that we rely on in understanding life.*[25]

Lakoff and Johnson (1980, 1999) greatly contributed to establishing the importance of conceptual metaphor as a framework for thinking in language. In recent years many scholars have investigated the original ways in which writers use novel metaphors and question the fundamental frameworks of thinking implicit in conceptual metaphors.

When considering the role conceptual metaphor plays in the worldview of the community, the problem becomes twofold. From a sociological,*[26] cultural, or philosophical perspective, the question becomes, to what extent ideologies maintain and impose conceptual patterns of thought by introducing, supporting, and adapting fundamental patterns of thinking metaphorically. To what extent does the ideology fashion and refashion the idea of the nation as a container with borders? How are enemies and outsiders represented? As diseases? As attackers? How are the metaphoric paths of fate, destiny, history, and progress represented? As the opening of an eternal monumental moment (German fascism)? Or as the path to communism (in Russian or Czech for example)?

Though cognitive scholars have made some attempts to take on board the idea that different languages have evolved radically different concepts and conceptual metaphors, they have on the whole remained tied up in the somewhat reductive concept of worldview which derives from the Sapir-Whorf hypothesis. The true source of ethnolinguistics and the thinker who contributed most to the debate on the relationship between culture, language, and linguistic communities was the German philologist Wilhelm von Humboldt (1767–1835). Humboldt remains, however, little known in English-speaking nations. Andrew Goatly, in "Washing the Brain" (John Benjamins 2007) does take on board the dual problem of conceptual metaphor as a framework implicit in the language as a system, and the way individuals and ideologies negotiate conceptual metaphors.

James W. Underhill, in *Creating Worldviews: Ideology, Metaphor & Language* (Edinburgh UP), considers the way individual speech adopts and reinforces certain metaphoric paradigms. This involves a critique of both communist and fascist discourse. But Underhill's studies are situated in Czech and German, which allows him to demonstrate the ways individuals are both thinking "within", and resisting the modes by which ideologies seek to appropriate key concepts such as "the people", "the state", "history", and "struggle".

Though metaphors can be considered to be "in" language, Underhill's chapter on French, English and ethnolinguistics demonstrates that we cannot conceive of language or languages in anything other than metaphoric terms. French is a treasure, for example. English is a "tool" for liberating minorities engaging in debate in the global world. Underhill continues his investigation of the relationship between worldview and language in *Ethnolinguistics and Cultural Concepts: Truth, Love, Hate & War* (Cambridge UP 2012).

55.8   See also

- Alliteration
- Camel's nose
- Colemanballs
- Conceptual blending
- Description
- Hypocatastasis
- Ideasthesia
- List of English-language metaphors
- Metaphor in philosophy

- Origin of language

- Origin of speech

- Pataphor

- Personification

- Reification (fallacy)

- Simile

- Tertium comparationis

- World Hypotheses

55.9 Notes

[1] μεταφορά, Henry George Liddell, Robert Scott, *A Greek-English Lexicon*, on Perseus

[2] cdasc3D%2367010 μεταφέρω, Henry George Liddell, Robert Scott, *A Greek-English Lexicon*, on Perseus

[3] μετά, Henry George Liddell, Robert Scott, *A Greek-English Lexicon*, on Perseus

[4] φέρω, Henry George Liddell, Robert Scott, *A Greek-English Lexicon*, on Perseus

[5] Herscberger, Ruth (Summer 1943). "The Structure of Metaphor". *The Kenyan Review* **5** (3): 433–443. Retrieved 11 October 2013.

[6] "Zapp Brannigan (Character)". *IMDb*. Retrieved 21 September 2014.

[7] Aristotle, W. Rhys Roberts, Ingram Bywater, and Friedrich Solmsen. Rhetoric. New York: Modern Library, 1954. Print.

[8] Garret, Jan. "Aristotle on Metaphor.", Excerpts from Poetics and Rhetoric. N.p., 28 Mar. 2007. Web. 29 Sept. 2014.

[9] Moran, Richard. 1996. Artifice and persuasion: The work of metaphor in the rhetoric. In Essays on Aristotle's rhetoric, ed. Amelie Oksenberg Rorty, 385-398. Berkeley: University of California Press.

[10] Lakoff, G. & Johnson, M. Metaphors We Live By (IL: University of Chicago Press, 1980), Chapters 1–3. (pp. 3–13).

[11] Blechner, M. (2001) The Dream Frontier, NJ: The Analytic Press, p. 28

[12] Meyer, L. (1956) Emotion and Meaning in Music. Chicago: University of Chicago Press

[13] Blechner, M. (1988) Differentiating empathy from therapeutic action. Contemporary Psychoanalysis, 24:301–310.

[14] Vischer, R. (1873) Über das optische Formgefühl: Ein Beitrag zur Aesthetik. Leipzig: Hermann Credner. For an English translation of selections, see Wind, E. (1963) Art and Anarchy. London: Faber and Faber.

[15] Johnson, M. & Larson, S. (2003) "Something in the way she moves" – Metaphors of musical motion. Metaphor and Symbol, 18:63–84

[16] Whittock, T. (1992) The role of metaphor in dance. British Journal of Aesthetics, 32:242–249.

[17] Cf. Joachim Grzega (2004), *Bezeichnungswandel: Wie, Warum, Wozu? Ein Beitrag zur englischen und allgemeinen Onomasiologie*, Heidelberg: Winter, and Blank, Andreas (1997), *Prinzipien des lexikalischen Bedeutungswandels am Beispiel der romanischen Sprachen*, Tübingen: Niemeyer.

[18] "Radio 4 – Reith Lectures 2003 – The Emerging Mind". BBC. Retrieved 4 March 2012.

[19] "T he Nietzsche Channel: On Truth and Lie in an Extra-Moral Sense". *oregonstate.edu*.

[20] McKinnon, A. M. (2012). "Metaphors in and for the Sociology of Religion: Towards a Theory after Nietzsche" (PDF). *Journal of Contemporary Religion*. 27, no. 2. pp. 203–216.

[21] "Cut". Sylvia Plath Forum. Retrieved 4 March 2012.

[22] Archived 12 September 2010 at the Wayback Machine

[23] "1. The Road Not Taken. Frost, Robert. 1920. Mountain Interval". Bartleby.com. Retrieved 4 March 2012.

[24] Lakoff G., Johnson M. (2003) [1980]. *Metaphors We Live By*. Chicago: University of Chicago Press. ISBN 0-226-46801-1.

[25] Zoltán Kövecses. (2002) Metaphor: a practical introduction. Oxford University Press US. ISBN 978-0-19-514511-3.

[26] McKinnon, AM. (2013). 'Ideology and the Market Metaphor in Rational Choice Theory of Religion: A Rhetorical Critique of "Religious Economies" '. Critical Sociology, vol 39, no. 4, pp. 529-543.

55.10   References

- *This article incorporates material from the Citizendium article "Metaphor", which is licensed under the Creative Commons Attribution-ShareAlike 3.0 Unported License but not under the GFDL.*

- Stefano Arduini (2007). (ed.) *Metaphors*, Roma, Edizioni di Storia e Letteratura.

- Aristotle. *Poetics*. Trans. I. Bywater. In *The Complete Works of Aristotle: The Revised Oxford Translation*. (1984). 2 Vols. Ed. Jonathan Barnes. Princeton, Princeton University Press.

- Max Black (1954). *Metaphor*, Proceedings of the Aristotelian Society, 55, pp. 273–294.

- Max Black (1962). *Models and metaphors: Studies in language and philosophy*, Ithaca: Cornell University Press.

- Max Black (1979). *More about Metaphor*, in A. Ortony (ed) Metaphor & Thought.

- Clive Cazeaux (2007). *Metaphor and Continental Philosophy: From Kant to Derrida*. New York: Routledge.

- L. J. Cohen (1979). *The Semantics of Metaphor*, in A. Ortony (ed), *Metaphor & Thought*

- Donald Davidson. (1978). "What Metaphors Mean." Reprinted in *Inquiries Into Truth and Interpretation*. (1984), Oxford, Oxford University Press.

- Jacques Derrida (1982). "White Mythology: Metaphor in the Text of Philosophy." In *Margins of Philosophy*. Trans. Alan Bass. Chicago, University of Chicago Press.

- René Dirvens & Ralf Pörings, ed. (2002). *Metaphor and Metonymy in Contrast*. Berlin.: Mouton de Gruyter.

- Fass, Dan (1988). "Metonymy and metaphor: what's the difference?". *Proceedings of the 12th conference on Computational linguistics* **1**. pp. 177–81. doi:10.3115/991635.991671. ISBN 963-8431-56-3.

- Jakobson, Roman (1990). "Two Aspects of Language and Two Types of Aphasic Disturbances". In Linda Waugh and Monique Monville-Burston (ed.). *On Language*. Cambridge, MA: Harvard University Press. pp. 115–133. ISBN 0-674-63536-1.

- Lakoff, G. & Johnson, M. *Metaphors We Live By* (IL: University of Chicago Press, 1980), Chapters 1–3. (pp. 3–13).

- Lakoff, George (1980). *Metaphors We Live By*. Chicago, IL: The University of Chicago Press. ISBN 0-226-46801-1..

- Low, Graham. "An Essay is a Person". In Cameron, Lynne; Low, Graham. *Researching and Applying Metaphor*. Cambridge: Cambridge University Press. pp. 221–48. ISBN 978-0-521-64964-3.

- Peters, Wim (2003). "Proceedings of the ACL 2003 workshop on Lexicon and figurative language" **14**. pp. 1–9. doi:10.3115/1118975.1118976. |chapter= ignored (help)

- McKinnon, AM. (2012). 'Metaphors in and for the Sociology of Religion: Towards a Theory after Nietzsche'. Journal of Contemporary Religion, vol 27, no. 2, pp. 203–216.

- David Punter (2007). *Metaphor*, London, Routledge.

- Paul Ricoeur (1975). *The Rule of Metaphor: Multi-Disciplinary Studies in the Creation of Meaning in Language*, trans. Robert Czerny with Kathleen McLaughlin and John Costello, S. J., London: Routledge and Kegan Paul 1978. (Toronto: University of Toronto Press 1977)

- I. A. Richards. (1936). *The Philosophy of Rhetoric*. Oxford, Oxford University Press.

- John Searle (1979). "Metaphor," in A. Ortony (ed.) *Metaphor and Thought*, Cambridge University Press.

- Underhill, James W., Creating Worldviews: Metaphor, Ideology & Language, Edinburgh UP, 2011.

- Herscberger, Ruth (Summer 1943). "The Structure of Metaphor". *The Kenyan Review* **5** (3): 433–443. Retrieved 11 October 2013.

- Rudmin, Floyd W. (1991). "Having: A Brief History of Metaphor and Meaning". *Syracuse Law Review* **42**: 163. Retrieved 11 October 2013.

- Somov, Georgij Yu. (2013). "The interrelation of metaphors and metonymies in sign systems of visual art: An example analysis of works by V. I. Surikov". *Semiotica* **193**: 31–66.

55.11 External links

-

- History of metaphor on *In Our Time* at the BBC. (listen now)

- *A short history of metaphor*

- Audio illustrations of metaphor as figure of speech

- Top Ten Metaphors of 2008

- Shakespeare's Metaphors

- Metaphor Examples (categorized)

- List of ancient Greek words starting with $\mu\varepsilon\tau\alpha$-, on Perseus

- Metaphor and Phenomenology article in the *Internet Encyclopedia of Philosophy*

- Metaphors algebra

- Pérez-Sobrino, Paula (2014). "Meaning construction in verbomusical environments: Conceptual disintegration and metonymy" (PDF). *Journal of Pragmatics* (Elsevier) **70**: 130–151. doi:10.1016/j.pragma.2014.06.008.

Chapter 56

Anthropomorphism

Anthropomorphism is the attribution of human form or other characteristics to beings other than humans, particularly deities and animals. **Personification** is the related attribution of human form and characteristics to abstract concepts such as nations and natural forces likes seasons and the weather. Both have ancient roots as storytelling and artistic devices. Most cultures have traditional fables with anthropomorphized animals as characters.

56.1 Name

Anthropomorphism derives from its verb form *anthropomorphize*,[*][n 1] itself derived from the Greek *ánthrōpos* (ἄνθρωπος, lit. "human") and *morphē* (μορφή, "form"). It is first attested in 1753, originally in reference to the heresy of applying a human form to the Christian God.[*][n 2][*][1]

56.2 Pre-history

From the beginnings of human behavioural modernity in the Upper Paleolithic, about 40,000 years ago, examples of zoomorphic (animal-shaped) works of art occur that may represent the earliest evidence we have of anthropomorphism. One of the oldest known is an ivory sculpture, the Löwenmensch figurine, Germany, a human-shaped figurine with the head of a lioness or lion, determined to be about 32,000 years old.[*][3][*][4]

It is not possible to say what these prehistoric artworks represent. A more recent example is The Sorcerer, an enigmatic cave painting from the Trois-Frères Cave, Ariège, France: the figure's significance is unknown, but it is usually interpreted as some kind of great spirit or master of the animals. In either case there is an element of anthropomorphism.

This anthropomorphic art has been linked by archaeologist Steven Mithen with the emergence of more systematic hunting practices in the Upper Palaeolithic (Mithen 1998). He proposes that these are the product of a change in the architecture of the human mind, an increasing fluidity between the natural history and social intelligences, where anthropomorphism allowed hunters to identify empathetically with hunted animals and better predict their movements.[*][n 3]

56.3 In religion and mythology

Main article: Anthropotheism

In religion and mythology, anthropomorphism refers to the perception of a divine being or beings in human form, or the recognition of human qualities in these beings.

In this illustration by Milo Winter of Aesop's fable, "The North Wind and the Sun", an anthropomorphic North Wind tries to strip the cloak off of a traveler

Ancient mythologies frequently represented the divine as deities with human forms and qualities. They resemble human beings not only in appearance and personality; they exhibited many human behaviors that were used to explain natural phenomena, creation, and historical events. The deities fell in love, married, had children, fought battles, wielded weapons, and rode horses and chariots. They feasted on special foods, and sometimes required sacrifices of food, beverage, and sacred objects to be made by human beings. Some anthropomorphic deities represented specific human concepts, such as love, war, fertility, beauty, or the seasons. Anthropomorphic deities exhibited human qualities such as beauty, wisdom, and power, and sometimes human weaknesses such as greed, hatred, jealousy, and uncontrollable anger. Greek deities such as Zeus and Apollo often were depicted in human form exhibiting both commendable and despicable human traits.

Anthropomorphism in this case is referred to as anthropotheism.*[6]

From the perspective of adherents to religions in which humans were created in the form of the divine, the phenomenon may be considered theomorphism, or the giving of divine qualities to humans.

Anthropomorphism has cropped up as a Christian heresy, particularly prominently with the Audians in third century Syria, but also in fourth century Egypt and tenth century Italy.*[7] This often was based on a literal interpretation of Genesis 1:27: "So God created man in His own image, in the image of God created He him; male and female created He them".*[8]

56.3.1 Criticism

Some religions, scholars, and philosophers objected to anthropomorphic deities. The Greek philosopher Xenophanes (570–480 BCE) argued against the conception of deities as fundamentally anthropomorphic:

> But if cattle and horses and lions had hands
> or could paint with their hands and create works such as men do,
> horses like horses and cattle like cattle
> also would depict the gods' shapes and make their bodies
> of such a sort as the form they themselves have.
> ...
> Ethiopians say that their gods are snub–nosed [σιμούς] and black
> Thracians that they are pale and red-haired.*[9]*[n 4]

He said that "the greatest god" resembles man "neither in form nor in mind".*[10]

Both Judaism and Islam reject an anthropomorphic deity, believing that God is beyond human comprehension. Judaism's rejection of an anthropomorphic deity grew during the Hasmonean period (circa 300 BCE), when Jewish belief incorporated some Greek philosophy.* Judaism's rejection grew further after the Islamic Golden Age in the tenth century, which Maimonides codified in the twelfth century, in his thirteen principles of Jewish faith.*[n 5]

Hindus do not reject the concept of a deity in the abstract unmanifested, but note practical problems. Lord Krishna said in the Bhagavad Gita, Chapter 12, Verse 5, that it is much more difficult for people to focus on a deity as the unmanifested than one with form, using anthropomorphic icons (murtis), because people need to perceive with their senses.*[12]*[13]

In *Faces in the Clouds*, anthropologist Stewart Guthrie proposes that all religions are anthropomorphisms that originate in the brain's tendency to detect the presence or vestiges of other humans in natural phenomena.*[14]

56.4 In literature

56.4.1 Religious texts

There are various examples of personification as a literary device in both Hebrew Bible and Christian New Testament and also in the texts of some other religions.

56.4.2 Fables

Anthropomorphism, sometimes referred to as personification, is a well established literary device from ancient times. The story of "The Hawk and the Nightengale" in Hesiod's *Works and Days* preceded Aesop's fables by centuries.*[15] Collections of linked fables from India, the *Jataka Tales* and *Panchatantra*, also employ anthropomorphized animals to illustrate principles of life. Many of the stereotypes of animals that are recognized today, such as the wiley fox and the proud lion, can be found in these collections. Aesop's anthropomorphisms were so familiar by the first century CE that they colored the thinking of at least one philosopher:

> And there is another charm about him, namely, that he puts animals in a pleasing light and makes them interesting to mankind. For after being brought up from childhood with these stories, and after being as it were nursed by them from babyhood, we acquire certain opinions of the several animals and think of some of them as royal animals, of others as silly, of others as witty, and others as innocent.
> —Apollonius of Tyana*[16]

Apollonius noted that the fable was created to teach wisdom through fictions that are meant to be taken as fictions, contrasting them favorably with the poets' stories of the deities that are sometimes taken literally. Aesop, "by announcing a story which everyone knows not to be true, told the truth by the very fact that he did not claim to be relating real events" .*[16] The same consciousness of the fable as fiction is to be found in other examples across the world, one example being a traditional Ashanti way of beginning tales of the anthropomorphic trickster-spider Anansi: "We do not really mean, we do not really mean that what we are about to say is true. A story, a story; let it come, let it go." *[17]

56.4.3   Fairy tales

Anthropomorphic motifs have been common in fairy tales from the earliest ancient examples set in a mythological context to the great collections of the Brothers Grimm and Perrault. The *Tale of Two Brothers* (Egypt, 13th century BCE) features several talking cows and in *Cupid and Psyche* (Rome, 2nd century CE) Zephyrus, the west wind, carries Psyche away. Later an ant feels sorry for her and helps her in her quest.

56.4.4   Modern literature

Building on the popularity of fables and fairy tales, specifically *children's* literature began to emerge in the nineteenth century with works such as *Alice's Adventures in Wonderland* (1865) by Lewis Carroll, *The Adventures of Pinocchio* (1883) by Carlo Collodi and *The Jungle Book* (1894) by Rudyard Kipling, all employing anthropomorphic elements. This continued in the twentieth century with many of the most popular titles having anthropomorphic characters,*[18] examples being *The Tales of Beatrix Potter* (1901 onwards),*[n 6] *The Wind in the Willows* (1908) by Kenneth Grahame, *The Lion, the Witch, and the Wardrobe* by C. S. Lewis and *Winnie-the-Pooh* (1926) by A. A. Milne. In many of these stories the animals can be seen as representing facets of human personality and character.*[20] As John Rowe Townsend remarks, discussing *The Jungle Book* in which the boy Mowgli must rely on his new friends the bear Baloo and the black panther Bagheera, "The world of the jungle is in fact both itself and our world as well" .*[20] A notable work aimed at an adult audience is George Orwell's *Animal Farm*, in which all the main characters are anthropomorphic animals. Non-animal examples include Rev.W Awdry's children's stories of *Thomas the Tank Engine* and other anthropomorphic locomotives.

The fantasy genre developed from mythological, fairy tale, and Romance motifs*[21] and characters, sometimes with anthropomorphic animals. The best-selling examples of the genre are *The Hobbit*[22] (1937) and *The Lord of the Rings*[n 7] (1954–1955), both by J. R. R. Tolkien, books peopled with talking creatures such as ravens, spiders, and the dragon Smaug and a multitude of anthropomorphic goblins and elves. John D. Rateliff calls this the "Doctor Dolittle Theme" in his book *The History of the Hobbit*[24] and Tolkien saw this anthropomorphism as closely linked to the emergence of human language and myth: "...The first men to talk of 'trees and stars' saw things very differently. To them, the world was alive with mythological beings... To them the whole of creation was "myth-woven and elf-patterned" .*[25]

By the 21st century, the children's picture book market had expanded massively.*[n 8] Perhaps a majority of picture books have some kind of anthropomorphism,*[18]*[27] with popular examples being *The Very Hungry Caterpillar* (1969) by Eric Carle and *The Gruffalo* (1999) by Julia Donaldson.

Anthropomorphism in literature and other media led to a sub-culture known as furry fandom, which promotes and creates stories and artwork involving anthropomorphic animals, and the examination and interpretation of humanity through anthropomorphism.*[28]

Various Japanese manga have used anthropomorphism as the basis of their story. Examples include *Squid Girl* (anthropomorphized squid), *Hetalia: Axis Powers* (personified countries), *Upotte!!* (personified guns), and *Arpeggio of Blue Steel* (personified ships).

56.5   In film, television, and video games

56.5.1   Film

Some of the most notable examples are the Walt Disney characters the Magic Carpet from Disney's Aladdin franchise, Mickey Mouse, Donald Duck, Goofy, and Oswald the Lucky Rabbit; the Looney Tunes characters Bugs Bunny, Daffy Duck, and Porky Pig; and an array of others from the 1920s to present day.

In the films *Cars* (2006), *Cars 2* (2011), *Planes* (2013) and *Planes: Fire & Rescue* (2014), all the characters are anthropomorphic vehicles.*[29] Discussing *Madagascar, Escape 2 Africa* (2008), and *Europe's Most Wanted* (2012), Laurie suggests that "social differences based on conflict and contradiction are naturalized and made less 'contestable' through the classificatory matrix of human and nonhuman relations".*[29]

In the motion picture *Fantastic Mr. Fox* (2009), most of the characters are anthropomorphic animals very similar to the style seen in the Furry Fandom. They are given especially human characteristics such as body shape, hands, and clothing among other things.

Most of film director Mark Dindal's projects, *Cats Don't Dance, The Emperor's New Groove, Chicken Little*, and *The Emperor's New School*, feature anthropomorphic animals. *Cats Don't Dance's* cast includes talking animals, *New Groove* had an Incan turned into a llama, *Chicken Little* had an all animal cast, and *New School* feature the main characters getting turned into various animals throughout the entire show, almost every episode.

56.5.2   Television

Since the 1960s, anthropomorphism has also been represented in various animated television shows such as *Biker Mice From Mars* (1993–1996) and *SWAT Kats: The Radical Squadron* (1993–1995). *Teenage Mutant Ninja Turtles*, first aired in 1987, features four pizza-loving anthropomorphic turtles with a great knowledge of ninjutsu, led by their anthropomorphic rat sensei, Master Splinter.

TUGS (1988) is a British children's series, set in the 1920s, featuring anthropomorphic tugboats. They moved like real boats but would sometimes perform certain actions without the aid of humans although not seen. Like real boats they obeyed maritime laws but would sometimes perform actions of their own will.

In the American animated TV series *Family Guy*, one of the show's main characters, Brian, is a dog. Brian shows many human characteristics – he walks upright, talks, smokes, and drinks Martinis – but also acts like a normal dog in other ways; for example he cannot resist chasing a ball and barks at the mailman, believing him to be a threat.

A Canadian–New Zealand-American animated TV show called *Turbo Dogs* (2008) starred anthropomorphized dog characters. In 2010, a French-American animated TV show *The Mysteries of Alfred Hedgehog* was mostly consisted of woodland anthropomorphic characters.

A British TV series, *Thomas and Friends*, features anthropomorphized trains, airplanes, helicopters, and cars.

Both the YouTube series *The Annoying Orange* and its American television adaptation *The High Fructose Adventures of Annoying Orange* feature anthropomorphized fruits and vegetables.

An American–Canadian series, *Johnny Test*, features a talking dog named Dukey, who is genetically engineered by the title character's sisters, which they all try to keep a secret from anyone else (except in a couple of episodes).

56.5.3   Video games

Sonic the Hedgehog, a game released in 1991, features a speedy blue hedgehog as the protagonist. This series' characters are almost all anthropomorphic animals such as foxes, cats, and other hedgehogs who are able to speak and walk on their hind legs like normal humans. As with most anthropomorphisms of animals, clothing is of little or no importance, where some characters may be fully clothed while some wear only shoes and gloves.

Another example in video games is *Super Mario Bros.*, which was released in 1985. Some of the characters include Yoshi, a dinosaur who is able to talk, run and jump, and Bowser, a "Koopa" that is able to perform most human characteristics, with some exceptions, as he can breathe fire.

56.5.4 Radio programs

The Signature Series is a radio program based in Canada that explores the personality traits of the 24 keys of western music by personifying them and giving each key a gender, a story and specific character traits.

56.6 Art history

56.6.1 Claes Oldenburg

Claes Oldenburg's soft sculptures are commonly described as anthropomorphic. Depicting common household objects, Oldenburg's sculptures were considered Pop Art. Reproducing these objects, often at a greater size than the original, Oldenburg created his sculptures out of soft materials. The anthropomorphic qualities of the sculptures were mainly in their sagging and malleable exterior which mirrored the not so idealistic forms of the human body. In "Soft Light Switches" Oldenburg creates a household light switch out of Vinyl. The two identical switches, in a dulled orange, insinuate nipples. The soft vinyl references the aging process as the sculpture wrinkles and sinks with time.

56.6.2 Minimalism

In the essay "Art and Objecthood", Michael Fried makes the case that "Literalist art" (Minimalism) becomes theatrical by means of anthropomorphism. The viewer engages the minimalist work, not as an autonomous art object, but as a theatrical interaction. Fried references a conversation in which Tony Smith answers questions about his "six-foot cube, Die."

Q: Why didn't you make it larger so that it would loom over the observer? A: I was not making a monument. Q: then why didn't you make it smaller so that the observer could see over the top? A: I was not making an object.

Fried implies an anthropomorphic connection by means of "a surrogate person-that is, a kind of statue."

The minimalist decision of "hollowness" in much of their work, was also considered by Fried, to be "blatantly anthropomorphic." This "hollowness" contributes to the idea of a separate inside; an idea mirrored in the human form. Fried considers the Literalist art's "hollowness" to be "biomorphic" as it references a living organism.*[30]

56.6.3 Post Minimalism

Curator Lucy Lippard's Eccentric Abstraction show, in 1966, sets up Briony Fer's writing of a post minimalist anthropomorphism. Reacting to Fried's interpretation of minimalist art's "looming presence of objects which appear as actors might on a stage", Fer interprets the artists in Eccentric Abstraction to a new form of anthropomorphism. She puts forth the thoughts of Surrealist writer Roger Caillous, who speaks of the "spacial lure of the subject, the way in which the subject could inhabit their surroundings." Caillous uses the example of an insect who "through camouflage does so in order to become invisible... and loses its distinctness." For Fer, the anthropomorphic qualities of imitation found in the erotic, organic sculptures of artists Eva Hesse and Louise Bourgeois, are not necessarily for strictly "mimetic" purposes. Instead, like the insect, the work must come into being in the "scopic field... which we cannot view from outside." *[31]

56.7   In science

In the scientific community, the use of anthropomorphic language that suggests animals have intentions and emotions has traditionally been deprecated as indicating a lack of objectivity. Biologists have been warned to avoid assumptions that animals share any of the same mental, social, and emotional capacities of humans, and to rely instead on strictly observable evidence.[32] In 1927 Ivan Pavlov wrote that animals should be considered "without any need to resort to fantastic speculations as to the existence of any possible subjective states".[33] More recently, *The Oxford companion to animal behaviour* (1987) advised that "one is well advised to study the behaviour rather than attempting to get at any underlying emotion".[34] Some scientists, like William M Wheeler (writing apologetically of his use of anthropomorphism in 1911), have used anthropomorphic language in metaphor to make subjects more humanly comprehensible or memorable.[n 9]

Despite the impact of Charles Darwin's ideas in *The Expression of the Emotions in Man and Animals* (Konrad Lorenz in 1965 called him a "patron saint" of ethology)[36] ethology has generally focused on behavior, not on emotion in animals.[36] Though in other ways Darwin was and is the epitome of science, his acceptance of anecdote and anthropomorphism stands out in sharp contrast to the lengths to which later scientists would go to overlook apparent mindedness, selfhood, individuality, and agency:

The study of great apes in their own environment and in captivity[n 10] has changed attitudes to anthropomorphism. In the 1960s the three so-called "Leakey's Angels", Jane Goodall studying chimpanzees, Dian Fossey studying gorillas and Biruté Galdikas studying orangutans, were all accused of "that worst of ethological sins – anthropomorphism".[39] The charge was brought about by their descriptions of the great apes in the field; it is now more widely accepted that empathy has an important part to play in research.

De Waal has written: "To endow animals with human emotions has long been a scientific taboo. But if we do not, we risk missing something fundamental, about both animals and us."[40] Alongside this has come increasing awareness of the linguistic abilities of the great apes and the recognition that they are tool-makers and have individuality and culture.

Writing of cats in 1992, veterinarian Bruce Fogle points to the fact that "both humans and cats have identical neurochemicals and regions in the brain responsible for emotion" as proof that "it is not anthropomorphic to credit cats with emotions such as jealousy".[41]

56.7.1   Antonym

In the context of the sciences, the term *anthropomorphism* has been deprecated to the point that, when applied to a scientist, the term functions as a pejorative (see above). There is also a risk of straying off the path of objectivity, however, when scientists choose to assume that only humans possess any degree of certain traits.[42] This assumption is called anthropocentrism, practitioners of which either believe in or unintentionally form an outlook of human exceptionalism. Darwin —to the chagrin of many religious philosophers —dismissed these ideas of human exceptionalism in his book *The Descent of Man* by saying that our differences are "only in degree and not in kind".[43]

56.8   Mascots

Main articles: Mascot and List of mascots

For branding, merchandizing, and representation, figures known as mascots are now often employed to personify sports teams, corporations, and major events such as the World's Fair and the Olympics. These personifications may be simple human or animal figures, such as Ronald McDonald or the ass that represents America's Democratic Party. Other times, they are anthropomorphic items, such as "Clippy" or the "Michelin Man". Most often, they are anthropomorphic animals such as the Energizer Bunny or the San Diego Chicken.

The practice is particularly widespread in Japan, where cities, regions, and companies all have mascots, collectively known as *yuru-chara*. Two of the most popular are Kumamon (a bear who represents Kumamoto Prefecture)[44] and Funassyi (a pear who represents Funabashi, a suburb of Tokyo).[45]

56.9 Gallery

- A glass door in the Chatham House

- Almada tram in smiley livery

- Pareidolia of an Indian face in a rock

- Seymore D. Fair 1st-ever World Expo Mascot

56.10 See also

- Aniconism: antithetic concept

- Animism

- Anthropic principle

- Anthropocentrism

- Anthropology

- Anthropomorphic maps

- Anthropopathism

- Great Chain of Being

- Humanoid

- Moe anthropomorphism

- National personification

- Pareidolia: seeing faces in everyday objects

- Pathetic Fallacy

- Prosopopoeia

- Speciesism

- Anthropomorphic animals

    - Human-animal hybrid

    - Funny animal

    - Furry fandom

    - Talking animals in fiction

    - Zoomorphism

56.11   Notes

[1] Possibly via French *anthropomorphisme.*[1]

[2] Anthropomorphism, among divines, the error of those who ascribe a human figure to the deity.[2]

[3] In the *New York Review of Books*, Gardner opined that "I find most convincing Mithen's claim that human intelligence lies in the capacity to make connections: through using metaphors".[5]

[4] Many other translations of this passage have Xenophanes state that the Thracians were "blond".

[5] Moses Maimonides quoted Rabbi Abraham Ben David: "It is stated in the Torah and books of the prophets that God has no body, as stated 'Since G-d your God is the god (lit. *gods*) in the heavens above and in the earth below" and a body cannot be in both places. And it was said 'Since you have not seen any image' and it was said 'To who would you compare me, and I would be equal to them?' and if he was a body, he would be like the other bodies." *[11]

[6] The Victoria and Albert Museum wrote: "Beatrix Potter is still one of the world's best-selling and best-loved children's authors. Potter wrote and illustrated a total of 28 books, including the 23 Tales, the 'little books' that have been translated into more than 35 languages and sold over 100 million copies." *[19]

[7] 150 million sold, a 2007 estimate of copies of the full story sold, whether published as one volume, three, or some other configuration.[23]

[8] It is estimated that the UK market for children's books was worth £672m in 2004.[26]

[9] In 1911, Wheeler wrote: "The larval insect is, if I may be permitted to lapse for a moment into anthropomorphism, a sluggish, greedy, self-centred creature, while the adult is industrious, abstemious and highly altruistic..." *[35]

[10] In 1946, Hebb wrote: "A thoroughgoing attempt to avoid anthropomorphic description in the study of temperament was made over a two-year period at the Yerkes laboratories. All that resulted was an almost endless series of specific acts in which no order or meaning could be found. On the other hand, by the use of frankly anthropomorphic concepts of emotion and attitude one could quickly and easily describe the peculiarities of individual animals... Whatever the anthropomorphic terminology may seem to imply about conscious states in chimpanzee, it provides an intelligible and practical guide to behavior." *[38]

56.12   References

56.12.1   Citations

[1] *Oxford English Dictionary*, 1st ed. "anthropomorphism, *n.*" Oxford University Press (Oxford), 1885.

[2] *Chambers's Cyclopædia, Supplement*, 1753.

[3] "Lionheaded Figurine".

[4] Dalton (1 January 2004). "Löwenmensch Oldest Statue". VNN World.

[5] Gardner, Howard (9 October 1997), "Thinking About Thinking", *New York Review of Books*, archived from the original on 29 March 2010, retrieved 8 May 2010.

[6] "anthropotheism". *Ologies & -Isms*. The Gale Group, Inc. 2008.

[7] Fox, James Joseph (1907). "Anthropomorphism". *Catholic Encyclopedia* **1**. New York: Robert Appleton Company.

[8] Chambers, Ephraim, ed. (1728). "Anthropomorphite". *Cyclopædia, or an Universal Dictionary of Arts and Sciences* (first ed.). James and John Knapton, *et al.*

[9] Diels-Kranz, *Die Fragmente der Vorsokratiker*, Xenophanes frr. 15-16.

[10] Clement of Alexandria, *Miscellanies* V xiv 109.1–3

[11] Maimonides, Moses, "Fundamentals of Torah, Ch. 1, § 8", *Book of Science*.

[12] Fowler, Jeanne D. (1997). *Hinduism: Beliefs and Practices*. Sussex Academic Press. pp. 42–43. ISBN 1898723605.

[13] Narayan, M. K. V. (2007). *Flipside of Hindu Symbolism*. Fultus. pp. 84–85. ISBN 1596821175.

[14] Guthrie, Stewart E. (1995). *Faces in the Clouds: A New Theory of Religion*. Oxford University Press. p. 7. ISBN 0-19-509891-9.

[15] *EB* (1911).

[16] Philostratus, Flavius (c.210 CE). *The Life of Apollonius*, 5.14. Translated by F.C. Conybeare. the Loeb Classical Library (1912)

[17] Kwesi Yankah (1983). "The Akan Trickster Cycle: Myth or Folktale?" (PDF). Trinidad University of the West Indes.

[18] "The top 50 children's books". *The Telegraph*. 22 Feb 2008. and Sophie Borland (22 Feb 2008). "Narnia triumphs over Harry Potter". *The Telegraph*.

[19] "Beatrix Potter", Official website, Victoria and Albert Museum.

[20] Gamble, Nikki; Yates, Sally (2008). *Exploring Children's Literature*. Sage Publications Ltd;. ISBN 978-1-4129-3013-0.

[21] John Grant and John Clute, *The Encyclopedia of Fantasy*, p 621, ISBN 0-312-19869-8

[22] 100 million copies sold: BBC: Tolkien's memorabilia go on sale. 18 March 2008

[23] *The Toronto Star*, 16 April 2007.

[24] Rateliff, John D. (2007). *The History of the Hobbit: Return to Bag-end*. London: HarperCollins. p. 654. ISBN 978-0-00-723555-1.

[25] Carpenter, Humphrey (1979). *The Inklings: C. S. Lewis, J. R. R. Tolkien, Charles Williams and Their Friends*. Boston: Houghton Mifflin. p. 43. ISBN 0-395-27628-4.

[26] "The Value of the Children's Picture Book Market".

[27] Ben Myers (10 June 2008). "Why we're all animal lovers". *The Guardian*.

[28] Patten, Fred (2006). *Furry! The World's Best Anthropomorphic Fiction*. ibooks. pp. 427–436. ISBN 1-59687-319-1.

[29] Laurie, Timothy (2015), "Becoming-Animal Is A Trap For Humans", *Deleuze and the Non-Human* eds. Hannah Stark and Jon Roffe.

[30] Fried, Michael (1998). *Art and Objecthood*. Chicago: University of Chicago Press. ISBN 0-226-26319-3.

[31] Fer, Briony (1999). "Objects Beyond Objecthood". *Oxford Art Journal* **22**: 25–36. doi:10.1093/oxartj/22.2.25.

[32] Introduction to Flynn, Cliff (2008). *Social Creatures: A Human and Animal Studies Reader*. Lantern Books. ISBN 1-59056-123-6.

[33] Ryder, Richard. *Animal Revolution: Changing Attitudes Towards Speciesism*. Berg, 2000, p. 6.

[34] Masson and McCarthy 1996, xviii

[35] Wheeler, William Morton (November 1911), "Insect parasitism and its peculiarities", *Popular Science,* Vol. 79, p. 443.

[36] Black, J (Jun 2002). "Darwin in the world of emotions" (Free full text). *Journal of the Royal Society of Medicine* **95** (6): 311–3. doi:10.1258/jrsm.95.6.311. ISSN 0141-0768. PMC 1279921. PMID 12042386.

[37] Darwin, Charles (1871). *The Descent of Man* (1st ed.). p. 39.

[38] Hebb, Donald O. (1946), "Emotion in man and animal: An analysis of the intuitive processes of recognition", *Psychological Review,* Vol. 53, No. 2, pp. 88–106, doi:10.1037/h0063033, PMID 21023321.

[39] cited in Masson and McCarthy 1996, p9 Google books

[40] Frans de Waal (1997-07). "Are We in Anthropodenial?". *Discover*. pp. 50–53.

[41] Fogle, Bruce (1992). *If Your Cat Could Talk*. London: Dorling Kindersley. p. 11. ISBN 9781405319867.

[42]   "Merriam Webster – Anthropocentrism.".

[43]   "The Descent Of Man".

[44]   Official website. (Japanese)

[45]   Official website. (Japanese)

56.12.2   Bibliography

- "Anthropomorphism", *Encyclopædia Britannica*, 9th ed., Vol. II, New York: Charles Scribner's Sons, 1878, pp. 123–124.

- "Anthropomorphism", *Encyclopædia Britannica*, 11th ed., Vol. II, Cambridge: Cambridge University Press, 1911, p. 120.

- Masson, Jeffrey Moussaieff; Susan McCarthy (1996). *When Elephants Weep: Emotional Lives of Animals.* Vintage. p. 272. ISBN 0-09-947891-9.

- Mithen, Steven (1998). *The Prehistory Of The Mind: A Search for the Origins of Art, Religion and Science.* Phoenix. p. 480. ISBN 978-0-7538-0204-5.

56.13   External links

- "Anthropomorphism" entry in the Encyclopedia of Human-Animal Relationships (Horowitz A., 2007)

- "Anthropomorphism" entry in the Encyclopedia of Astrobiology, Astronomy, and Spaceflight

- "Anthropomorphism" in mid-century American print advertising. Collection at The Gallery of Graphic Design.

From the Panchatantra: Rabbit fools Elephant by showing the reflection of the moon

John Tenniel's depiction of this anthropomorphic rabbit was featured in the first chapter of Lewis Carroll's Alice's Adventures in Wonderland

Anthropomorphic pareidolia by Giuseppe Arcimboldo

Fatso the Fat-Arsed Wombat, a popular symbol of the Sydney 2000 Summer Olympics created as a parody of the blandly commercial official mascots.

Chapter 57

Hamartia

This article is about classical Greek term. For medical term, see Hamartia (medical term).

The term **hamartia** derives from the Greek ἁμαρτία, from ἁμαρτάνειν *hamartánein*, which means "to miss the mark" or "to err".[1][2] It is most often associated with Greek tragedy, although it is also used in Christian theology.[3] *Hamartia* as it pertains to dramatic literature was first used by Aristotle in his Poetics. In tragedy, hamartia is commonly understood to refer to the protagonist's error or flaw that leads to a chain of plot actions culminating in a reversal from their good fortune to bad. What qualifies as the error or flaw can include an error resulting from ignorance, an error of judgement, a flaw in character, or sin. The spectrum of meanings has invited debate among critics and scholars, and different interpretations among dramatists.

57.1 *Hamartia* in Aristotle's Poetics

Hamartia is first described in the subject of literary criticism by Aristotle in his Poetics. The source of *hamartia* is at the juncture between Character and the character's actions or behaviors as outlined by Aristotle.

"Character in a play is that which reveals the moral purpose of the agents, i.e. the sort of thing they seek or avoid." [4]

In his introduction to the S. H. Butcher translation of "Poetics", Francis Fergusson describes hamartia as the inner quality that initiates, in Dante's words, a "movement of spirit" within the protagonist to commit actions which drive the plot towards its tragic end, inspiring in the audience a build of pity and fear that leads to a purgation of those emotions, or Catharsis.[5][6]

Jules Brody, however, argues that "it is the height of irony that the idea of the tragic flaw should have had its origin in the Aristotelian notion of *hamartia*. Whatever this problematic word may be taken to mean, it has nothing to do with such ideas as fault, vice, guilt, moral deficiency, or the like. *Hamartia* is a morally neutral non-normative term, derived from the verb *hamartano*, meaning 'to miss the mark,' 'to fall short of an objective.' And by extension: to reach one destination rather than the intended one; to make a mistake, not in the sense of a moral failure, but in the nonjudgmental sense of taking one thing for another, taking something for its opposite. *Hamartia* may betoken an error of discernment due to ignorance, to the lack of an essential piece of information. Finally, *hamartia* may be viewed simply as an act which, for whatever reason, ends in failure rather than success." [7]

In Greek Tragedy, for a story to be "of adequate magnitude" it involves characters of high rank, prestige, or good fortune. If the protagonist is too worthy of esteem, or too wicked, his/her change of fortune will not evoke the ideal proportion of pity and fear necessary for catharsis. Here Aristotle describes hamartia as the quality of a tragic hero that generates that optimal balance.

"...the character between these two extremes - that of a man who is not eminently good and just, yet whose misfortune is brought about not by vice or depravity, but by some error or frailty." [8]

57.2   *Hamartia* in Christian theology

Hamartia is also used in Christian theology because of its use in the Septuagint and New Testament. The Hebrew (*chatá*) and its Greek equivalent (*àµαρτία/hamartia*) both mean "missing the mark" or "off the mark".*[9] There are four basic usages for *hamartia*.

1. *Hamartia* is sometimes employed to mean acts of sin "by omission or commission in thought and feeling or in speech and actions" as in Romans 5:12, "all have sinned".*[10]

2. *Hamartia* is sometimes applied to the fall of man from original righteousness that resulted in humanity's innate propensity for sin, that is original sin.*[11] For example, as in Romans 3:9, everyone is "under the power of sin".*[12]

3. A third application concerns the "weakness of the flesh" and the free will to resist sinful acts. "The original inclination to sin in mankind comes from *the weakness of the flesh*." *[13]

4. *Hamartia* is sometimes "personified".*[14] For example, Romans 6:20 speaks of being enslaved to *hamartia* (sin).

57.3   Tragic flaw, tragic error, and divine intervention

Aristotle mentions hamartia in *Poetics*. He argues that is a powerful device to have a story begin with a rich and powerful hero, neither exceptionally virtuous nor villainous, who then falls into misfortune by a mistake or error (harmartia). Discussion among scholars centers mainly on the degree to which hamartia is defined as *tragic flaw* or *tragic error*.

57.3.1   Critical Argument for flaw

Poetic justice describes the obligation of the dramatic poet, along with philosophers and priests, to see that their work promotes moral behavior.*[15] 18th century French dramatic style honored that obligation with the use of hamartia as a vice to be punished*[16]*[17] *Phèdre*, Racine's adaptation of Euripides' Hippolytus, is an example of French Neoclassical use of hamartia as a means of punishing vice.*[18]*[19]Jean Racine says in his Preface to *Phèdre*, as translated by R.C. Knight:

"The failings of love are treated as real failings. The passions are offered to view only to show all the ravage they create. And vice is everywhere painted in such hues, that its hideous face may be recognized and loathed." *[20]

The play is a tragic story about a royal family. The main characters respective vices; rage, lust and envy lead them to their tragic downfall.*[21]

57.3.2   Critical argument for error

In her 1963 Modern Language Review article, *The Tragic Flaw: Is it a Tragic Error?*, Isabel Hyde traces the twentieth century history of hamartia as tragic flaw, which she argues is an incorrect interpretation. Ms. Hyde draws upon the language in Butcher's interpretation of Poetics regarding hamartia as both error and "defect in character." Hyde points out a footnote in which Butcher qualifies his second definition by saying it is not a "natural" expression to describe a flaw in behavior.*[22] Hyde calls upon another description from A.C. Bradley's *Shakespearean Tragedy* of 1904 which she contends is misleading:

"...the comparatively innocent hero still shows some marked imperfection or defect, irresolution, precipitancy, pride, credulousness, excessive simplicity, excessive susceptibility to sexual emotion and the like...his weakness or defect is so intertwined with everything that is admirable in him..." *[23]

Hyde goes on to elucidate interpretive pitfalls of treating hamartia as tragic flaw by tracing the tragic flaw argument through several examples from well-known tragedies including *Hamlet* and *Oedipus the King*. Hyde observes that students often cite "thinking too much" as Hamlet's tragic flaw upon which his demise in the story depends. That citation does not, however, offer explanation for the moments when Hamlet does act impulsively and violently. It also embarks down a trail of logic that suggests he ought to have murdered Claudius right away to avoid tragedy, which Hyde asserts is problematic. In *Oedipus the King,* she observes that regard of Oedipus' hasty behavior at the crossroads, or his trust in his intellect as the qualities upon which the change of fortune relies, is incomplete. Instead, to regard his ignorance of the true identity of his parents as the keystone to his downfall takes into account all of his decisions that lead to the tragic end. Rather than a flaw in character, error, in Oedipus' case based upon lack of information, is the more complete interpretation.

In his 1978 Classical World (journal) article *Hamartia, Ate, and Oedipus*, Leon Golden compares scholarship that examines where to place hamartia's definition along a spectrum connecting the moral, flaw, and the intellectual, error. His goal is to revisit the role, if any, Ate, or divine intervention, plays in hamartia. The Butcher translation of "Poetics" references hamartia as both a "single great error", and "a single great defect in character", prompting critics to raise arguments. Mid-twentieth century scholar Phillip W. Harsh sees hamartia as tragic flaw, observing that Oedipus assumes some moral ownership of his demise when he reacts excessively with rage and murder to the encounter at the crossroads.*[24] Van Braam, on the other hand, notes of Oedipus' hamartia, "no specific sin attaching to him as an individual, but the universally human one of blindly following the light of one's own intellect."*[25] He adds that a defining feature of tragedy is that the sufferer must be the agent of his own suffering by no conscious moral failing on his part in order to create a tragic irony. O. Hey's observations fall into this camp as well. He notes that the term refers to an action that is carried out in good moral faith by the protagonist, but as he has been deprived of key pieces of information, the action brings disastrous results.*[26] J.M. Bremer then conducted a thorough study of hamartia in Greek thought, focusing on its usage in Aristotle and Homer. His findings lead him, like Hyde, to cite hamartia as an intellectual error rather than a moral failing.*[27]

57.3.3   Critical arguments on divine intervention

J.M. Bremer and Dawe both conclude that the will of the gods may factor into Aristotelian hamartia. Golden disagrees.*[28] Bremer observes that the Messenger in Oedipus Rex says, "He was raging - one of the dark powers pointing the way, ...someone, something leading him on - he hurled at the twin doors and bending the bolts back out of their sockets, crashed through the chamber,".*[29] Bremer cites Sophocles' mention of Oedipus being possessed by "dark powers" as evidence of guidance from either divine or daemonic force. Dawe's argument centers around tragic dramatists' four areas from which a protagonist's demise can originate. The first is fate, the second is wrath of an angry god, the third comes from a human enemy, and the last is the protagonist's frailty or error. Dawe contends that the tragic dénouement can be the result of a divine plan as long as plot action begets plot action in accordance with Aristotle. Golden cites Van Braam's notion of Oedipus committing a tragic error by trusting his own intellect in spite of Tiresias' warning as the argument for human error over divine manipulation. Golden concludes that hamartia principally refers to a matter of intellect, although it may include elements of morality. What his study asserts is separate from hamartia, in a view that conflicts with Dawe's and Bremer's, is the concept of divine retribution.*[30]

57.4   Examples of *hamartia* in literature

57.5   See also

- Catharsis

- Tragic hero

- Victory disease

- Hamartiology

- anagnorisis

- peripeteia

57.6 Notes

[1] "Hamartia" . *Merriam-Webster.com*. Merriam-Webster, n.d. Web. 28 September 2014.

[2] Hamartia: (Ancient Greek: ἁμαρτία) Error of Judgement or Tragic Flaw. "Hamartia". *Encyclopædia Britannica Online*. Encyclopædia Britannica Inc., 2014. Web. 28 September 2014.

[3] Cooper, Eugene J. "Sarx and Sin in Pauline Theology" *Laval théologique et philosophique*. 29.3 (1973) 243–255. Web. Érudit. 1 Nov 2014.

[4] Aristotle. "Poetics" . Trans. Ingram Bywater. The Project Gutenberg EBook. Oxford: Clarendon P, 2 May 2009. Web. 26 Oct. 2014.

[5] Fergusson 8

[6] The Internet Classics Archive by Daniel C. Stevenson, Web Atomics. Web. 11 Dec. 2014. http://classics.mit.edu/Aristotle/poetics.html

[7] Jules Brody, "Fate, Philology, Freud," *Philosophy and Literature* 38.1 (April 2014): 23.

[8] Aristotle. "Poetics" . Trans. Ingram Bywater. The Project Gutenberg EBook. Oxford: Clarendon P, 2 May 2009. Web. 26 Oct. 2014.

[9] http://www.blbclassic.org/lang/lexicon/lexicon.cfm?Strongs=H2398&t=KJV, http://www.blueletterbible.org/lang/lexicon/lexicon.cfm?strongs=G266, and http://legal-dictionary.thefreedictionary.com/miss+the+mark

[10] Thayer, J. H. *Greek-English Lexicon of the New Testament* (Harper, 1887), s.v. ?μα?t?a online at https://books.google.com/books?id=1E4VAAAAYAAJ&printsec=frontcover&dq=Thayer++Greek-English&hl=en&sa=X&ei=EsAdVdiLBM6uogSsn4LADw&ved=0CDEQ6AEwAA#v=onepage&q=Thayer%20%20Greek-English&f=false.

[11] Cooper, Eugene "Sarx and Sin in Pauline Theology" in *Laval théologique et philosophique*. 29.3 (1973) 243-255. Web. Érudit. 1 Nov 2014 and
Thayer, J. H. *Greek-English Lexicon of the New Testament* (Harper, 1887), s.v. ?μα?t?a online at https://books.google.com/books?id=1E4VAAAAYAAJ&printsec=frontcover&dq=Thayer++Greek-English&hl=en&sa=X&ei=EsAdVdiLBM6uogSsn4LADw&ved=0CDEQ6AEwAA#v=onepage&q=Thayer%20%20Greek-English&f=false.

[12] http://biblehub.com/romans/3-9.htm

[13] Edward Stillingfleet, *Fifty Sermons Preached upon Several Occasions* (J. Heptinstall for Henry Mortlock, 1707), 525. Online at https://books.google.com/books?id=kSVWAAAAYAAJ&dq=%22weakness+of+the+flesh%22&source=gbs_navlinks_s

[14] Geoffrey W. Bromiley, *Theological Dictionary of the New Testament: Abridged in One Volume* (Eerdmans, 1985), 48.

[15] Burnley Jones and Nicol, 125

[16] Burnley Jones and Nicol,12,125

[17] Thomas Rymer. (2014). In Encyclopædia Britannica. Retrieved from http://www.britannica.com/EBchecked/topic/514581/Thomas-Rymer

[18] Worthen, B. *The Wadsworth Anthology of Drama* 5th ed. 444-463. Boston: Thomspon Wadsworth. 2007. Print.

[19] Racine, Jean. *Phédre*, Harvard Classics, Vol. 26, Part 3. Web. 11 Dec. 2014. http://www.bartleby.com/26/3/

[20] Worthen,446

[21] Euripedes. *Hippolytus*, Harvard Classics, 8.7. Web. 8 Dec. 2014. http://www.bartleby.com/8/7/

[22] Butcher, Samuel H., Aristotle's Theory of Poetry and Fine Art, New York 41911

[23] Bradley, A. C. 1851-1935. Shakespearean Tragedy: Lectures On Hamlet, Othello, King Lear, Macbeth. London: Macmillan and co., limited, 1904. Web, 13 Dec. 2014. http://babel.hathitrust.org/cgi/pt?id=uva.x000240890;view=1up;seq=1

[24] Golden, Leon. "Hamartia, Ate, and Oedipus". *The Classical World*, 72.1 (Sep., 1978), 3-12. Baltimore: Johns Hopkins UP. Web. 7 Dec. 2014. http://www.jstor.org/stable/4348969

[25] P. van Braam, "Aristotle's Use of Ἁμαρτία" *The Classical Quarterly*, 6.4 (Oct., 1912), 266-272. London: Cambridge UP. Web. 7 Dec. 2014. http://www.jstor.org/stable/635946

[26] Hey, O. "ἁμαρτία Zur Bedeutungsgeschichte des Wortes" *Philologus* 83 1-15, (1928). Web. 7 Dec. 2014.

[27] Bremer, J.M. "Hamartia." Tragic Error in the Poetics of Aristotle and in Greek Tragedy. Amsterdam, Adolf M. Hakkert, 1969.

[28] Golden, 6

[29] Worthen, 85

[30] Golden, 10

[31] Sophocles. "Antigone" The Internet Classics Archive by Daniel C. Stevenson, Web Atomics. Web. 13 Dec. 2014. http://classics.mit.edu/Sophocles/antigone.html

[32] Sophocles. "Tragedy And Archaic Greek Thought" Introduction, D.L. Cairns, 2013. cf. Ant. 332-84, 582-630, 1347-53

[33] Worthen 282

[34] "Julius Caesar: Entire Play" . *shakespeare.mit.edu*. Retrieved 2015-05-15.

[35] O'Neill, Eugene. "Long Day's Journey Into Night," New Haven: Yale UP. 2002. Web 13 Dec. 2014. http://yalepress.yale.edu/yupbooks/excerpts/oneill_journey.pdf

[36] Shakespeare. "Macbeth." The Complete Works of William Shakespeare. Boston: MIT online database. Web. 13 Dec. 2014. http://shakespeare.mit.edu/macbeth/full.html

[37] Worthen 69

[38] Racine, Jean. "Phédre," Harvard Classics, Vol. 26, Part 3. Web. 11 Dec. 2014. http://www.bartleby.com/26/3/

57.7 References

- Bremer, J.M. "Hamartia." *Tragic Error in the Poetics of Aristotle and in Greek Tragedy*. Amsterdam, Adolf M. Hakkert, 1969.

- Cairns, D. L. *Tragedy and Archaic Greek Thought*. Swansea, The Classical Press of Wales, 2013.

- Dawe, R D. "Some Reflections on Ate and Hamartia." *Harvard Studies in Classical Philology* 72 (1968): 89-123. JSTOR. St. Louis University Library, St. Louis. 29 Apr. 2008.

- Hyde, Isabel. "The Tragic Flaw: is It a Tragic Error?" *The Modern Language Review* 58.3 (1963): 321-325. JSTOR. St. Louis University Library, St. Louis. 29 Apr. 2008.

- Moles, J L. "Aristotle and Dido's 'Hamartia'" *Greece & Rome*, Second Series 31.1 (1984): 48-54. JSTOR. St. Louis University Library, St. Louis. 29 Apr. 2008.

- Stinton, T. C. W. "Hamartia in Aristotle and Greek Tragedy" *The Classical Quarterly*, New Series, Vol. 25, No. 2 (Dec., 1975): 221 - 254. JSTOR. St. Louis University, St. Louis. 29 Apr. 2008.

- Golden, Leon, "Hamartia, Ate, and Oedipus", Classical World, Vol. 72, No. 1 (Sep., 1978), pp. 3–12.

- Hugh Lloyd-Jones, *The Justice of Zeus*, University of California Press, 1971, p. 212.

ΑΡΙΣΤΟΤΕΛΟΥΣ

ΠΕΡΙ

ΠΟΙΗΤΙΚΗΣ.

ARISTOTELIS

DE

POETICA

LIBER

EX VERSIONE

THEODORI GOULSTONI.

LECTIONIS VARIETATEM E CODD. IV. BIBLIO-
THECÆ MEDICEÆ, VERBORUM INDICEM ET
OBSERVATIONES SUAS ADJUNXIT

T. WINSTANLEY, A. M.

COLL. HERT. SOC.

OXONII,

TYPOGRAPHEO CLARENDONIANO.

MDCCLXXX.

Six Parts of Aristotle's Ideal Greek Tragedy

1. **Plot (Fable)**

2. **Character**

3. **Diction**

4. **Thought**

5. **Spectacle**

6. **Melody**

6 Parts of Aristotle's Greek Tragedy

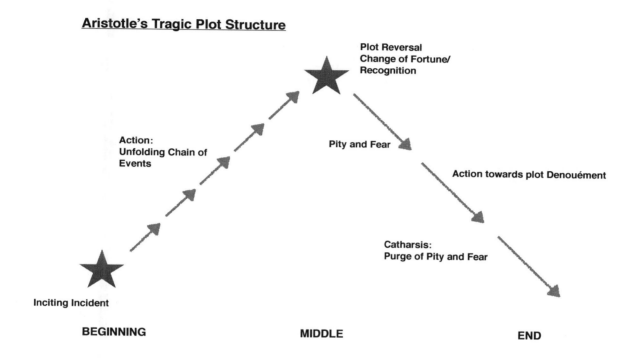

Aristotle's Tragic Plot Structure

Chapter 58

Pathetic fallacy

The phrase **pathetic fallacy** is a literary term for the attributing of human emotion and conduct to all aspects within nature.[*][1] It is a kind of personification that is found in poetic writing when, for example, clouds seem sullen, when leaves dance, or when rocks seem indifferent.[*][1][*][2][*][3][*][4][*][5]

The British cultural critic, John Ruskin, coined the term in his book, *Modern Painters* (1843–60).[*][6]

58.1 History of the phrase

Ruskin coined the term "pathetic fallacy" to attack the sentimentality that was common to the poetry of the late 18th century, and which was was rampant among poets including Burns, Blake, Wordsworth, Shelley and Keats. Wordsworth supported this use of personification based on emotion by claiming that "objects ···derive their influence not from properties inherent in them ···but from such as are bestowed upon them by the minds of those who are conversant with or affected by these objects." [*][8] However Tennyson, in his own poetry, began to refine and diminish such expressions, and introduced an emphasis on what might be called a more scientific comparison of objects in terms of sense perception. The old order was beginning to be replaced by the new just as Ruskin addressed the matter, and the use of the pathetic fallacy markedly began to disappear. As a critic, Ruskin proved influential and is credited with having helped to refine poetic expression.[*][5]

The meaning of the term has changed significantly from the idea Ruskin had in mind.[*][9] Ruskin's original definition is "emotional falseness", or the falseness that occurs to one's perceptions when influenced by violent or heightened emotion. For example, when a person is unhinged by grief, the clouds might seem darker than they are, or perhaps mournful or perhaps even uncaring.[*][2][*][10]

There have been other changes to Ruskin's phrase since he coined it: The particular definition that Ruskin used for the word "fallacy" has since become obsolete. The word "fallacy" nowadays is defined as an example of a flawed logic, but for Ruskin and writers of the 19th century and earlier, "fallacy" could be used to mean simply a "falseness".[*][11] In the same way, the word "pathetic" simply meant for Ruskin "emotional" or "pertaining to emotion".[*][12]

Setting aside Ruskin's original intentions, and despite this linguistic 'rocky road', the two-word phrase has survived, though with a significantly altered meaning.

58.2 Examples of Ruskin's original meaning

In his essay, Ruskin demonstrates his original meaning by offering lines of a poem:

> They rowed her in across the rolling foam—
> The cruel, crawling foam···

John Ruskin *at Glenfinlas, Scotland (1853–54), by John Everett Millais.*[7]

Ruskin then points out that "the foam is not cruel, neither does it crawl. The state of mind which attributes to it these characters of a living creature is one in which the reason is unhinged by grief"—yet, Ruskin did not disapprove of this use of the pathetic fallacy:

> Now, so long as we see that the feeling is true, we pardon, or are even pleased by, the confessed fallacy of sight, which it induces: we are pleased, for instance, with those lines ... above quoted, not because they fallaciously describe foam, but because they faithfully describe sorrow.[13]

Ruskin intended that pathetic fallacy may also refer to any "untrue" quality: as in the description of a crocus as "gold", when the flower is, according to Ruskin, saffron in color.[2]

The following, a stanza from the poem "Maud" (1855) by Alfred Lord Tennyson, demonstrates what John Ruskin, in *Modern Painters*, said was an "exquisite" instance of the use of the pathetic fallacy:[13]

MAUD
There has fallen a splendid tear
From the passion-flower at the gate.
She is coming, my dove, my dear;
She is coming, my life, my fate.
The red rose cries, "She is near, she is near;"
And the white rose weeps, "She is late;"
The larkspur listens, "I hear, I hear;"
And the lily whispers, "I wait." (Part 1, *XXII*, 10)

58.3 Science

In science, the term "pathetic fallacy" is used in a pejorative way in order to discourage the kind of figurative speech in descriptions that might not be strictly accurate and clear, and that might communicate a false impression of a natural phenomenon. An example is the metaphorical phrase "Nature abhors a vacuum", which contains the suggestion that nature is capable of abhorring something. There are more accurate and scientific ways to describe nature and vacuums.

Another example of a pathetic fallacy is the expression, "Air hates to be crowded, and, when compressed, it will try to escape to an area of lower pressure." It is not accurate to suggest that air "hates" anything or "tries" to do anything. One way to express the ideas that underlie that phrase in a more scientific manner can be found and described in the kinetic theory of gases: effusion or movement towards lower pressure occurs because unobstructed gas molecules will become more evenly distributed between high- and low-pressure zones, by a flow from the former to the latter.[14][15][16]

58.4 See also

- Anthropomorphism
- Figure of speech
- Literary technique
- Morgan's Canon

58.5 References

[1] pathetic fallacy (figure of speech) - Encyclopedia Britannica

[2] Ruskin, John (1856). "Of the Pathetic Fallacy". *Modern Painters,*. volume iii. pt. 4.

[3] *The Penguin Dictionary of Philosophy* Second Edition (2005). Thomas Mautner, Editor. p. 455.

[4] Abrams, M.H.; Harpham, G.G. (2011) [1971]. *A Glossary of Literary Terms*. Wadsworth, Cengage Learning. p. 269. ISBN 9780495898023. LCCN 2010941195.

[5] *Princeton Encyclopedia of Poetry and Poetics*, Alex Preminger, Ed., Princeton University Press, 1974 ISBN 0-691-01317-9

[6] *The New Encyclopædia Britannica*, 15th Edition (1988), volume 9, p. 197.

[7] Ruskin and Millais at Glenfinlas, *The Burlington Magazine*, Vol. 138, No. 1117, pp. 228–234, April 1996. (Accessed via JSTOR, UK.)

[8] Wordsworth, William. Knight, William Angus, editor. *The Poetical Works of William Wordsworth, Volume 4*. W Paterson (1883) page 199

[9] Fowler, H.W. (1994) [1926]. *A Dictionary of Modern English Usage*. Wordsworth Collection. Wordsworth Editions. p. 425. ISBN 9781853263187.

[10] Hurwit, Jeffrey M. (1982). "Palm Trees and the Pathetic Fallacy in Archaic Greek Poetry and Art". *The Classical Journal* (The Classical Association of the Middle West and South) **77** (3): 193–199. JSTOR 3296969.

[11] "Fallacy". *The Oxford English Dictionary*. Oxford University Press. 1st ed. 1909.

[12] "Pathetic". *The Oxford English Dictionary*. Oxford University Press. 1st ed. 1909.

[13] Ruskin, J., "Of the Pathetic Fallacy", Modern Painters vol. III part 4. (1856)

[14] Bronowski, Jacob. *The Common Sense of Science*. Faber & Faber. 2011.

[15] Biltoft, Benapfl, and Swain. *Vacuum Technology 60A & 60B, Chapter 3: Review of Basic Vacuum Calculations*. Las Positas College. Fall 2002.

[16] Encyclopedia Britannica online.

58.6 Further reading

- Ruskin, J., "Of the Pathetic Fallacy", Modern Painters III (1856) http://www.ourcivilisation.com/smartboard/shop/ruskinj/

- Abrams, M.H. *A Glossary of Literary Terms*, 7th edition. Fort Worth, Texas: Harcourt Brace College Publishers, 1999. ISBN 0-15-505452-X.

- Groden, Michael, and Martin Kreiswirth (eds.). *The Johns Hopkins Guide to Literary Theory and Criticism*. Baltimore: Johns Hopkins University Press, 1994. ISBN 0-8018-4560-2.

58.7 Text and image sources, contributors, and licenses

58.7.1 Text

- **List of narrative techniques** *Source:* https://en.wikipedia.org/wiki/List_of_narrative_techniques?oldid=678680179 *Contributors:* -- April, Deb, Ortolan88, Camembert, Modemac, Michael Hardy, Jahsonic, Muriel Gottrop~enwiki, CatherineMunro, Rossami, DJ Clayworth, HappyDog, Imc, Robbot, SecretAgent, Chris Roy, Flauto Dolce, Kpflude, Jhi, GreatWhiteNortherner, DocWatson42, DavidCary, Xeresblue, Naufana, Jason Quinn, Christopherlin, Beland, Tothebarricades.tk, Bodnotbod, CesarFelipe, Gary D, Discospinster, EliasAlucard, Goochelaar, Bender235, El C, Prsephone1674, Bobo192, Billymac00, La goutte de pluie, Ral315, Benbread, Peter Shearan, Arthena, Velella, AFox2, Sketchee, LFaraone, Bsadowski1, Zntrip, Woohookitty, RHaworth, Twobitsprite, JFG, Tabletop, Stefanomione, Mandarax, BD2412, Brolin Empey, Rjwilmsi, Mayumashu, Quale, XP1, MitchellTF, Tomtheman5, Gurp13, Stilanas, Ewlyahoocom, CJLL Wright, Mattgenne, TimNelson, Gaius Cornelius, Shanel, NawlinWiki, Wiki alf, Dialectric, Chick Bowen, Number 57, Moe Epsilon, Tonyfuchs1019, Sixten8, Salmanazar, Thespian, Paul Erik, AndrewWTaylor, SmackBot, Reedy, Jagged 85, Nscheffey, IstvanWolf, TantalumTelluride, Amatulic, Mazeface, Persian Poet Gal, Jprg1966, Miquonranger03, Airmcnair8643, Parent5446, Huon, TenPoundHammer, The undertow, Henebry, Nrrinard, Cielomobile, Prosopopeia, JHunterJ, Caiaffa, Phuzion, B7T, Saltlakejohn, Tofoo, The71, Antemeridian, Tawkerbot2, Fvasconcellos, Wolfdog, S ried, CmdrObot, SamSandy, NickW557, Talamus, JBDRanger, Yaris678, Cydebot, Danrok, Inkington, Thijs!bot, LazyManJackson, Epbr123, 0dd1, RxK MsC, Leon7, Dfrg.msc, AgentPeppermint, Nick Number, AntiVandalBot, Luna Santin, Mk*, Chill doubt, Oddity-, JAnDbot, Rheez, The Transhumanist, Jfetteroll, Magioladitis, Unitedcraig, ***Ria777, Johnwoods, Upholder, Laura1822, Gwern, Flowanda, MartinBot, CliffC, R'n'B, Yessopie, J.delanoy, Rlsheehan, Silverxxx, Extransit, Shawn in Montreal, McSly, Steventity, NewEnglandYankee, Heero Kirashami, Mirage GSM, CatoftheNight, Idioma-bot, Soliloquial, Myurtoglu, Wolfnix, Cloudbreath9, Lerdthenerd, TravelingCat, Lcarlson27, MikeRumex, KaizenNk, Euryalus, DavisGL, Flyer22, Gryphon044, Oxymoron83, Dposte46, Denisarona, Henry Merrivale, Mr. Granger, Opsuty, ClueBot, SummerWithMorons, Marcinjeske, The Thing That Should Not Be, DionysosProteus, Keraunoscopia, Mike Klaassen, Mjflanagan0, VandalCruncher, Rockfang, Zack wadghiri, EAKugler, Spain11201, Ngebendi, Razorflame, Antediluvian67, Emehri~enwiki, Zombie Hunter Smurf, Jed 20012, Zoey101fan, Stickee, Avoided, Addbot, Rdrgz93, Willking1979, Jafeluv, Ronhjones, TutterMouse, Vishnava, CanadianLinuxUser, Cst17, Redheylin, Tide rolls, Lightbot, Yobot, KamikazeBot, Samisue421, Kookyunii, AnomieBOT, DemocraticLuntz, Jim1138, IRP, D barranco, Violetwhispers, LilHelpa, Obersachsebot, ChildofMidnight, YPchicken, Stepcool, Ruy Pugliesi, J04n, FrescoBot, Vinceouca, RoyGoldsmith, JIK1975, Jomanted, Robo Cop, Gordonwoodbine, Johammer, Minimac, Slaytor1, Difu Wu, Jin Fright, DASHBot, EmausBot, Energy Dome, Aedail, DoubleRT, Dewritech, Dem1995, CC.Carnes, Tommy2010, Thecheesykid, Lobsterthermidor, Illegitimate Barrister, Gonfishin, Anir1uph, Quilpower1, Ipabrams, IGeMiNix, ChuispastonBot, Anita5192, ClueBot NG, Nildram, Katiker, Laj315, Spannerjam, Helpful Pixie Bot, HMSSolent, Barbara Bess, Moradmandali, ItMustBeKate, Smallerjim, Lkmrg, Bigdon128, Awagner1, Kenneyspace, Glacialfox, Benjitheijneb, Pythasis, Teammm, Mrssife, Jklolomglmfao, Jadzia626, Andrew Eugene, Hmainsbot1, Jp426, Paul daniel gomes7, Saehry, Riverstogo, Isarra (HG), AldezD, Frosty, Mb58rich, JamesDLankin, JamesMoose, Shae00, Chris24Sahadeo, Wharg53, Andude2, Crutixex, ANicoleE and Anonymous: 410

- **Backstory** *Source:* https://en.wikipedia.org/wiki/Backstory?oldid=666312396 *Contributors:* Comte0, Someone else, JohnOwens, DopefishJustin, Eric119, Tregoweth, Lee M, Jay, TowerDragon, Jerzy, Merovingian, Jhi, Sheridan, Dmmaus, Matt Crypto, TonyW, Gary D, Triona, Merenta, Anthony Appleyard, Stack, Bacteria, Josh Parris, Master Justin, Jonny2x4, Koveras, Fabartus, DragonHawk, Garion96, Robertd, SmackBot, Jagged 85, Hmains, Tamfang, Moulton, Goodnightmush, TravKoolBreeze, Redeagle688, Cyrusc, Matthew Auger, Cydebot, Goldfritha, Ameliorate!, Nabokov, Noneofyourbusiness, Alientraveller, Aericanwizard, AgentPeppermint, Tocharianne, Fluffyd13, Dekimasu, The Original Threepwood, Ling.Nut, Hifrommike65, Fconaway, Clariosophic, WRK, Necoplay, Mike Klaassen, SchreiberBike, Berean Hunter, Koro Neil, Addbot, Ronhjones, Favonian, Pointer1, Yobot, Granpuff, MihalOrela, AnomieBOT, Shadowmaster13, Thehelpfulbot, Mean as custard, Winner 42, Princess Lirin, Savh, BackfireBotII, ClueBot NG, Spannerjam, Flax5, AmericanDad86, YiFeiBot, Your local kfc and Anonymous: 44

- **Cliffhanger** *Source:* https://en.wikipedia.org/wiki/Cliffhanger?oldid=668300987 *Contributors:* Eclecticology, Novalis, Xoder, Ixfd64, DropDead-Gorgias, Lee M, Charles Matthews, DJ Clayworth, Furrykef, VeryVerily, Slawojarek, Robbot, Moriori, Fredrik, Masao, Academic Challenger, Flauto Dolce, Meelar, Ungvichian, Mushroom, Xanzzibar, Mattflaschen, David Gerard, Jrquinlisk, Karn, AlistairMcMillan, Taak, Fys, Melonhead, Bodnotbod, Darksun, WpZurp, Gary D, Neutrality, Cab88, TheCustomOfLife, Lacrimosus, Night Gyr, Violetriga, Ylee, Sockatume, CanisRufus, FirstPrinciples, JustPhil, El C, TMC1982, Bobo192, StoatBringer, 3mta3, Q0, Anthony Appleyard, Atlant, Jtalledo, Fritz Saalfeld, Idont Havaname, Rick Sidwell, Cburnett, RJFJR, Dippit, Nintendo Maximus, Ianblair23, SteinbDJ, Czolgolz, Berserker79, Firsfron, Veemonkamiya, Woohookitty, Jannex, Jsawczuk, Jackel, MattGiuca, Falameufilho, Lkjhgfdsa, Alfakim, Chris Buckey, Scm83x, Skyman8081, OCNative, Stefanomione, Josiah Rowe, ComputerBox, The wub, MarnetteD, Fred Bradstadt, MinorEdit, FlaBot, Allycat, Ian Pitchford, SchuminWeb, LeeWilson, Ground Zero, CR85747, GrayFox92, CarolGray, Celestianpower, DevastatorIIC, Antilived, Igordebraga, ColdFeet, YurikBot, Koveras, Michial, RussBot, ChrisP2K5, Witan, LordThomas~enwiki, Stefan@freimark.de~enwiki, Rick Norwood, Robertvan1, Thiseye, Gooberliberation, Caerwine, Fallout boy, Getcrunk, Igglybuff, Nikkimaria, Zeppocity, Sitenl, Smurrayinchester, Giant89, Katieh5584, Philip Stevens, Dr. R.K.Z, UltimatePyro, Yvwv, User24, SmackBot, RDBury, Asa01, AdamDobay, Jagged 85, Timbo 1985, Goldkin, Liamgibbs, Master Deusoma, Viewtiful Zoidberg, Bluebot, Joseph Q Publique, DStoykov, Raymondluxuryacht, EmperorBrandon, Nedlum, Toughpigs, Olympis41, Rocks~enwiki, DeaconTaylor, Can't sleep, clown will eat me, Teemeah, Mr Snrub, Silent Tom, Dmoon1, Krsont, Jedi of redwall, COMPFUNK2, Fuhghettaboutit, Swainstonation, Шизомби, Inuyasha20985, Drake Clawfang, Dvorak729, Ultraexactzz, Knuckles sonic8, BrotherFlounder, BryanEkers, Synthe, Snowgrouse, BrownHairedGirl, SilverWoodchuck47, Zerath13, Lampman, Grandpafootsoldier, Doczilla, E-Kartoffel, Sonic Shadow, Animedude360, Keith-264, TheFarix, ISD, Bronzethumb, JoeBot, Regf798, Dto, Rorshacma, Azure, Jehfes, Cydebot, SiR GadaBout, Rifleman 82, Goldfritha, Gogo Dodo, Lugnuts, Peptuck, Zomic13, Shirulashem, Paddles, Bryan Seecrets, DaBears34, Damon207, Thijs!bot, Runch, Xaurtmj, Zatronus, Marek69, Brian Night, HelenKMarks, JustAGal, Davidhorman, AgentPeppermint, The Legendary Ranger, Format, HMC, AdamDeanHall, Blu3d, Cyckath, Tempest115, Yensed, Aranho, Waddelldj, Areaseven, MegX, Breuben, ZPM, Xtremeblur, H.sanat, Swordcut, Superx, MikkoMan, Jack turnip, Pax:Vobiscum, Erpbridge, Oren0, SuperMarioMan, Anaxial, VirtualDelight, Wikitiki89, Didgeman, Zipzipzip, McSly, DigitalLeonardo, Richard D. LeCour, Dr Von, Cometstyles, S, Ultraflame, Iconoclast09, 28bytes, Derekbd, Speedy3702, Abigailgem, Refsworldlee, Martinevans123, Andreas Kaganov, Cyberwriter, Freak104, Gridironrb, Sesshomaru, AlleborgoBot, Wraithdart, SieBot, Soxin07, Fredler Brave, Anedit, ThegirlwhotalksXXX, JohnnyMrNinja, Twinsday, Martarius, ClueBot, SummerWithMorons, Sundeuce98, The Thing That Should Not Be, Mike Klaassen, Addisonstrack, Bde1982, Five-toed-sloth, Muro Bot, BOTarate, Thingg, Tuzapicabit, Addbot, Blanche of King's Lynn, SoSaysChappy, Tassedethe, Lightbot, LuK3, Luckas-bot, Yobot, Legobot II, AnomieBOT, ArthurBot, Lamppis, Xqbot, Addihockey10, Connor5612, Green Cardamom, Prari, FrescoBot, Kkj11210, I dream of horses, RedBot, Piandcompany, Aardvarkzz, Brother Valencio, Onel5969, Atreklin, Samuel Rosenbaum, RjwilmsiBot, EmausBot, John of Reading, Klantry01, Poiuyt5rewq, ZéroBot, NathanielTheBold, Erianna, ClueBot NG, Spannerjam, Eliskuya2, Futuremoviewriter, Altaïr, PatTag2659, Dexbot, Mymis, Jc86035, Coolbeans443, Corn cheese, Melonkelon, DmC169, Andrewmhhs, UneCanardNoire, Evonyvac, ProprioMe OW and Anonymous: 309

- **Deus ex machina** *Source:* https://en.wikipedia.org/wiki/Deus_ex_machina?oldid=674251012 *Contributors:* AxelBoldt, Mav, Bryan Derksen, Stephen Gilbert, Koyaanis Qatsi, Manning Bartlett, Malcolm Farmer, Gritchka, Chuq, Frecklefoot, Edward, Kchishol1970, Dante Alighieri, Taras, Wwwwolf, Wapcaplet, Paul A, Tregoweth, Ellywa, Cyp, Alexander, Angela, Marco Krohn, Rossami, Vzbs34, Kwekubo, Evercat, Wooster, Ec5618, Charles Matthews, Nohat, Tedius Zanarukando, The Anomebot, Muerte, WhisperToMe, DJ Clayworth, Mephistopheles, Hyacinth, Stormie, EldKatt, Slawojarek, Shantavira, Bearcat, Robbot, Fredrik, Calmypal, Geogre, Premeditated Chaos, Auric, JB82, Hippietrail, Robinoke, Wlievens, Sheridan, TexasDex, Jrash, Seaeagle04, AviDrissman, Philwelch, Lefty, NeoJustin, Gilgamesh~enwiki, AlistairMcMillan, Hiphats, Luigi30, Nathan Hamblen, Cjensen, Junkyardprince, Wmahan, Neilc, Fishal, Mackeriv, Utcursch, Toytoy, R. fiend, Eloj, DaveJB, OverlordQ, ClockworkLunch, Setokaiba, Kit Foxtrot, Cylauj, Rdsmith4, Ellsworth, Rogerzilla, Heirpixel, Histrion, RobertBradbury, WpZurp, Gary D, Mschlindwein, Fabrício Kury, Picapica, Kasreyn, Mwsealey, Jtmendes, Lacrimosus, Kingal86, PhennPhawcks, Caswin, The demiurge, DanielCD, Alsadius, Pixel8, Smyth, Max Terry, Bibble, Notinasnaid, Mani1, Paul August, Rubicon, Iamtheari, CanisRufus, Gnrlotto, MBisanz, El C, Kwamikagami, Gilgamesh he, DarkSoldier, Jpceayene, Flxmghvgvk, Mikemsd, The KZA, Pikawil, Pschemp, 4v4l0n42, Jumbuck, Alansohn, Gary, Anthony Appleyard, Quatermass, Philip Cross, Jezmck, D prime, TZOTZIOY, Metron4, Snowolf, Ross Burgess, Melaen, Earpol, Tony Sidaway, RainbowOfLight, Pixelfire, MIT Trekkie, Ringbang, LukeSurl, Kazvorpal, Cristan, Kenyon, Dismas, BadLeprechaun, Bacteria, Velho, DavidK93, Lochaber, LeonWhite, Falameufilho, Tabletop, Htetrasme, Scm83x, DCT, Dlinga, Marskell, WBardwin, Kbdank71, RxS, Pmj, Search4Lancer, Rjwilmsi, Nightscream, Cactuar12, Plourdm, Josiah Rowe, Bruce1ee, MZMcBride, Joeymartin64, Wwjdd, Datapharmer, ABot, SeanMack, Prizm, Cfortunato, Olessi, Purple Rose, Matt Deres, FireCrack, FlaBot, SchuminWeb, New299, Fragglet, AJR, Gurch, Str1977, BitterMan, Jonny2x4, TheSiGuy, Lemuel Gulliver, Hibana, CJLL Wright, Rikoshi, Willeraab, Igordebraga, VolatileChemical, Agamemnon2, Jpfagerback, ColdFeet, EamonnPKeane, Satanael, YurikBot, Reverendgraham, Koveras, Sceptre, Rtkat3, Huw Powell, Jimp, Pterantula, RussBot, Fabartus, Hede2000, Gaius Cornelius, The Hokkaido Crow, Gram123, Eddie.willers, Nahallac Silverwinds, Icthyos, Sinisterscrawl, KissL, Dialectric, Cryptoid, Exir Kamalabadi, Rock DJ, Gront, Toya, Inhighspeed, Saudigamer, StriderSubzero, Haoie, Tranquil demon, Scs, Bozoid, Khonsali, Antoshi, Polpo, Kapoing, Kander, FiggyBee, Siyavash, Pegship, Crisco 1492, Jcrook1987, Squidward2602, KristoferM, Nikkimaria, Closedmouth, Clayhalliwell, Bluesykillerhorn~enwiki, Nae'blis, Stx, Warreed, Jonathan.s.kt, Thomas Blomberg, Guppy313, Rehevkor, CrniBombarder!!!, SmackBot, Dweller, Mangoe, Thelukeeffect, Africanpoet, Lestrade, Estoy Aquí, Postbagboy, Destron Commander, McGeddon, Akmenon, Hobbes747, Silverfoxx, Tjtryon, Bomac, Jagged 85, Chairman S., Alksub, ProveIt, ZS, BiT, Mauls, Gilliam, Ghosts&empties, Richfife, ERcheck, Chris the speller, Bluebot, MagnusW, TimBentley, Khamel83, PrimeHunter, Kashami, Greatgavini, SchfiftyThree, Basalisk, HubHikari, Clconway, Mladifilozof, Can't sleep, clown will eat me, MadameArsenic, Jonthecheet, Writtenright, Aumakua, PlatformerMastah, Pboyd04, Mitrius, Alphabeter, Evilrhino, SwitChar, Cybercobra, Charles Merriam, Bowlhover, Regulus Tera, Geetarawker, Drake Clawfang, LoveMonkey, Dief88, Silentblade, Eynar, Jklin, ShadowUltra, ILike2BeAnonymous, Pilotguy, Fyver528, Ceoil, SashatoBot, Serein (renamed because of SUL), Microchip08, Hawjam, Treyt021, Xalpharis, Loodog, G33K, Btg2290, JorisvS, YdoUask, Majorclanger, Itharu, Jbonneau, Sailko, Rataube, Comicist, TheHYPO, Noah Salzman, Grandpafootsoldier, LainOfIICHAN, Luvtheheaven, Youradhere, Dr.K., Peyre, Hectorian, Blue eyed writer, Lucid, PaulGS, Seb Patrick, TheFarix, JoeBot, StephenBuxton, Kanangra, Rnb, Marysunshine, Olir, Phantasy Phanatik, Sikkapox, Traitorfish, Wolfdog, CmdrObot, Jlbarron, TheEditrix, Legolasegb, Morganfitzp, Kmoffatt, Krb3141, Bernie Wadelheim, Chmee2, FlyingToaster, Daigo Kazama III, Toabaltabeta, Alaska Jack, Tim1988, Liu Bei, Addude, Cydebot, Ryzellon, Ionix, ChrisKennedy, Rpogge, Goldfritha, Padde, ST47, UberMan5000, Superbowlbound, Acoryst, Jamesjiao, Brown Bomber, Epbr123, Glocks Out, Daniel, Vidor, Nalvage, ClosedEyesSeeing, Furiso, Luigifan, Pacific PanDeist, Aric de Lioncourt, Java13690, Alphius, Kisai, Noclevername, WikiSlasher, Luna Santin, R.A Huston, Cheesegunner, Yeshalkno, Darrenhusted, Vokalist, DOSGuy, Deflective, Husond, Pipedreamergrey, Reallybored999, NE2, Mcorazao, SuperBrickDude, Supertheman, Naugahyde, Andylindsay, TheEditrix2, Nunki~enwiki, Magioladitis, Yurei-eggtart, 75pickup, VoABot II, QuizzicalBee, Hullaballoo Wolfowitz, JuhadJones, Animum, IkonicDeath, ForestAngel, Bluesqueak, DerHexer, Interrobamf, Pax:Vobiscum, Renetus, TPG~enwiki, Marshmallow1304, Hdt83, MartinBot, Revenge of Bulish.org, SuperMarioMan, Anaxial, CommonsDelinker, Lilac Soul, Bogey97, Ginsengbomb, Lincstrunk, Reedy Bot, Ncmvocalist, NewEnglandYankee, Molly-in-md, Chris Croy, Dubhe.sk, Juliancolton, JtMinahan, Equazcion, Titus Yorick, WarFox, Zzzronnyzzz, JavierMC, The Behnam, HxG, VolkovBot, ABF, Drussaxe, Breed3011, Khutuck, Link, Z.E.R.O., Anonymous Dissident, GcSwRhIc, PatrickWaters, Killjoy966, Clarince63, Beyond silence, Mannafredo, Sforzanda~enwiki, Cnyh, Jcchurch, Petero9, Dirkbb, Haseo9999, Jumble Jumble, Ubiquitousnewt, The Last Melon, LuigiManiac, The Realms of Gold, S8333631, Jonah22, Babystar69, SieBot, ALLbeing, Dreamafter, Phe-bot, Bobfinger, 5150pacer, Omhseoj, Lfbates, Darth Chyrsaor, Chridd, Doctorfluffy, Snookerfran, SilverbackNet, Tonybaize, Oniscoid, Triberocker, Harry the Dirty Dog, Twistedoriginal, OKBot, UB65, Wonchop, Unhappybuffalo, Gorguz greek gal, Martarius, ClueBot, FoxDiamond, Kissyfurb, Theseven7, Gamerdonkey, DionysosProteus, Mike Klaassen, LUUSAP, Gates3353, Ifnkovhg, Samayl6, Niceguyedc, Blanchardb, Trivialist, Jaydd, Kitsunegami, 842U, Editor510, Yoman82, Shawis, Lstutchman, DumZiBoT, Asianfilmguy, Aardila, Sir Adrian Fayan, Zombie Hunter Smurf, XLinkBot, Will-B, Carritotito, WikHead, Ougner, NellieBly, Artaxerxes, ZooFari, Osarius, Darth Payn, Briareos89, Addbot, Ocrasaroon, Rockstar25, SunDragon34, Daedalus733, Unclesquirt, Svernon19, SpartaGeek23, Farmercarlos, Raisininthesun, Erutuon, OlEnglish, Kelbydole, Qwertyytrewqqwerty, LightningNinja2, Windward1, Luckas-bot, Yobot, Tohd8BohaithuGh1, Deusexmachina123, Freikorp, Maringaense, Jhpmatt, Ladililn, AnomieBOT, Rubinbot, NathanoNL, Mr.Grave, Piano non troppo, Clarinetguy097, LlywelynII, Spelari2012, Big papi001, Bob Burkhardt, LilHelpa, Xqbot, Twentysixpurple, HMCJ, PsuedoName, Hi878, Omnipaedista, Mark Schierbecker, RibotBOT, Green Cardamom, Elcochan, Nagualdesign, FrescoBot, Surv1v4l1st, MTSUGoRaidersGo, Kalidiscope, Student Anselmus~enwiki, Wifione, Noobtoober, Citation bot 1, DrilBot, Symplectic Map, Backwardsd4, Fsyemogushi, BigDwiki, SongOfTheWeave, MastiBot, DMBradbury, Aardvarkzz, Dutchmonkey9000, Lone F, McHildinger, Hiationi, DTRHStudios, Aoidh, Pianomaneli, Independent70000, RjwilmsiBot, Ripchip Bot, EmausBot, BLGM5, Nataly8, Nakada~enwiki, Lithistman, PBS-AWB, Casperhightower, Pringl123, Kaleb904, Fred Gandt, K kisses, Unreal7, Kilopi, MarinaMichaels, Erianna, Abiohazard, Donner60, Triviamaster9, The Big F, Hecate Dreadnought, ClueBot NG, Magpieram, Joefromrandb, Ryuye, Widr, BLGM7, WikiMedicAidan, Helpful Pixie Bot, DBigXray, Island Monkey, MusikAnimal, Davidiad, BenGliterate, Futuremoviewriter, Doomfish01, Actualghosts, Slashstriker, Daturtle, Carliitaeliza, Paleozone, Jakemaster64, Hridith Sudev Nambiar, Hennez4250, Jollysunbro, CryogenicTFN, CaiusRagnarok, Mogism, Kbog, Ranze, SFK2, Locobiscuits, Jdmccright, Altion33, Mahosian, BreakfastJr, SevenWarriors1, Tyler Summers, Kovl, Nrcowles, Pokebub22, DJ Doena, GreyWinterOwl,

Computer Science Scientist, Guintee, Rhalferty, Litātiō, SkeletorFarnsworth, LeoHalliwell, Melcous, Stenskjaer, OnePointSystem, Nuri20024, Thomas Petra, Irvingswiftj, Bammie73, Leolaurindo, Jsattler07, Jonathan Markoff and Anonymous: 1046

- **Eucatastrophe** *Source:* https://en.wikipedia.org/wiki/Eucatastrophe?oldid=665220431 *Contributors:* The Anome, William Avery, Vanieter, Furrykef, Finlay McWalter, Andycjp, Rich Farmbrough, Dbachmann, Barfooz, Thu, BDD, Carcharoth, Before My Ken, Nightscream, Satanael, Jlittlet, Peter S., FunkyJazzMonkey, Tree&Leaf, Yamara, Kimchi.sg, PTSE, Allium, SmackBot, Mangoe, Chris the speller, Kingdon, ShakingSpirit, Judgesurreal777, Phoenixrod, JimMiller, BCSWowbagger, Thijs!bot, HomerNet, I do not exist, Helianthi, GimliDotNet, Pepe26, KazakhPol, Bear-fry, Vranak, Deor, Coffee, Canislupusarctos, De728631, Niceguyedc, Headshep, Addbot, Legobot, AnomieBOT, WikiBCman, BenzolBot, RjwilmsiBot, ZéroBot, Spannerjam, Helpful Pixie Bot, 5176shutt, Ranze, Mpov, Blindwithstars, Edledhron, Gódhellim and Anonymous: 39

- **Flashback (narrative)** *Source:* https://en.wikipedia.org/wiki/Flashback_(narrative)?oldid=675569326 *Contributors:* Mjb, Patrick, David Shay, AnonMoos, Robbot, Andrew Levine, Christopherlin, Manuel Anastácio, Ukexpat, JustPhil, Prsephone1674, Bobo192, TomStar81, Alansohn, Anthony Appleyard, Tony Sidaway, Mikeo, Geraldshields11, Bsadowski1, Linas, TLG, BillC, BD2412, Josh Parris, Quale, MarSch, FlaBot, Roboto de Ajvol, YurikBot, Kateweb, Welsh, Robert McClenon, Tough Little Ship, Eugrus, Tony1, Dissolve, Tachs, Square87~enwiki, Reader781, Garion96, Stevouk, Trolleymusic, SmackBot, RDBury, Felicity4711, Proudhug, Jagged 85, Eskimbot, Gilliam, The monkeyhate, Bluebot, Colonies Chris, Wirkman, Lenin and McCarthy, Tamfang, Chlewbot, Flyguy649, Cybercobra, Johnlumgair, Bob Castle, Kc12286, SashatoBot, Lambiam, Robofish, Physis, Muadd, Iridescent, Bifgis, New User, AlbertSM, Rawling, Cydebot, Gogo Dodo, Mathew5000, Raistlin Majere, Thijs!bot, Wikidenizen, Rjmail, AntiVandalBot, SummerPhD, Mcdreamy, Hopiakuta, Darrenhusted, JAnDbot, PhilKnight, Magioladitis, Lord antares, VoABot II, MartinDK, Convoy of Conwy, DerHexer, Edward321, SuperMarioMan, Anonymous 57, Hugo Bogarov, J.delanoy, Didgeman, Cop 663, Skier Dude, Squids and Chips, VolkovBot, CWii, Thisisborin9, TXiKiBoT, Teh06001, Qxz, Persiana, Pinknoise, Cw6165, Cnilep, Dreamafter, WereSpielChequers, Pwojdacz, Radon210, Mygerardromance, Escape Orbit, Twinsday, Martarius, ClueBot, DeadMansShoes, Mike Klaassen, Aitias, Apparition11, FlamesInDarkness, XLinkBot, Addbot, Ronhjones, Weatherbed, Tassedethe, Lightbot, Quantumobserver, Luckas-bot, Yobot, Granpuff, TaBOT-zerem, Anypodetos, Raviaka Ruslan, Gunnar Hendrich, Kookyunii, Slipknotfreakk90, Orion11M87, AnomieBOT, Mzselinakyle, Cocolala, RibotBOT, Locobot, Ddpattison, Thehelpfulbot, IceAgeWanderer4000, FrescoBot, LucienBOT, RoyGoldsmith, Spidey104, Saimcheeda, Reconsider the static, Timk70, Niri.M, Regineibcalen, Brunoais, Ohemgeeeeeee, Hmmwhatsthisdo, Alph Bot, Justpoppingintosayhi, EmausBot, Wwejamal09, Sonicyouth86, ClueBot NG, Spannerjam, MerlIwBot, Helpful Pixie Bot, Ering01, Zeus pogi, Tony Mach, Melonkelon, Eyesnore, Cinerama Comment, Doctorwily, RockStarrMusicLover95, Mickey 420 and Anonymous: 145

- **Flashforward** *Source:* https://en.wikipedia.org/wiki/Flashforward?oldid=670822233 *Contributors:* Kidburla, Shoaler, Mxn, AnonMoos, DocWatson42, Saaga, Hazzamon, Girolamo Savonarola, Eep², Triona, Richard Arthur Norton (1958-), Woohookitty, SqueakBox, Graham87, FlaBot, TheSun, EamonnPKeane, Koveras, Cliffb, GunnarRene, Bill shannon, SMcCandlish, SmackBot, Jagged 85, Jrockley, Eskimbot, Lonelymiesarchie, Sdalmonte, Schmiteye, Radagast83, Sherrard912, Trick man01, Lambiam, Smartyllama, JHunterJ, Toptucker, Im.a.lumberjack, ShelfSkewed, Cydebot, Rekameohs, Yelocab, MitchDoner, Mathew5000, Thijs!bot, JAF1970, Robsinden, Hopiakuta, AdamDeanHall, Davewho2, Albany NY, Yaoming7511, Boffob, Chris G, JaGa, DocNox, General Jazza, Anonymous 57, WTRiker, Jerrying, Ronningt, Vchimpanzee, AlleborgoBot, StAnselm, Brenont, Oxymoron83, My-dog-is-shep, Martarius, ClueBot, Poisonous-pastry, The Thing That Should Not Be, Jaro7788, Vancouver 2008, Maniago, Xme, JasonAQuest, BOTarate, Matthew Desjardins, DerBorg, Will-B, Bdiu2008, Tustin2121, Addbot, Corvus Fox, Ronhjones, TutterMouse, Simps1234, Glane23, Doniago, Tassedethe, Lightbot, ماني, Czar Brodie, Mind abuse, Ptbotgourou, Simonsaysabc123, Raviaka Ruslan, Kookyunii, Cameron Scott, Munin75, Xqbot, LostHavoc, Fortdj33, Val Killpack, LinDrug, Zainkhan05, Justpoppingintosayhi, Daniel Kemp, ClueBot NG, Lemuellio, Spannerjam, Demon Hill, Bubbathemonkey, Webclient101, Tony Mach and Anonymous: 101

- **Foreshadowing** *Source:* https://en.wikipedia.org/wiki/Foreshadowing?oldid=675726175 *Contributors:* R Lowry, Mrwojo, Karada, Mw66, DJ Clayworth, Flockmeal, Kizor, R3m0t, Sheridan, TexasDex, Matthew Stannard, Everyking, OverlordQ, Mamizou, Jossi, Gary D, Mike Rosoft, Brother Dysk~enwiki, Discospinster, Rich Farmbrough, Matthewfallshaw, ESkog, Harryfdoherty, Bobo192, Viriditas, Urthogie, Stephen Bain, Alansohn, Diego Moya, Snowolf, Velella, Woohookitty, WadeSimMiser, GregorB, Macaddct1984, AnmaFinotera, Stefanomione, Magister Mathematicae, BD2412, VF, FlaBot, Tysto, Koveras, Jlittlet, Stephenb, Tanzeel, GunnarRene, NawlinWiki, Borbrav, Catamorphism, JHCaufield, Tonywalton, Pegship, Sandstein, CWenger, SmackBot, Teh Pogo, Unschool, McGeddon, Jagged 85, Delldot, SchfiftyThree, Sbharris, Yanksox, Gsp8181, MinuteHand, AndyBQ, Wikipedical, Ser Amantio di Nicolao, Kuru, Accurizer, IronGargoyle, Slakr, דניאל צבי, Keith-264, Tawkerbot2, Signinstranger, Gregbard, Ryan, Goldfritha, Michael C Price, Shirulashem, DumbBOT, Alaibot, Joshua1995, Epbr123, N5iln, Marek69, A3RO, Dark Observer, AntiVandalBot, QuiteUnusual, Jj137, Skomorokh, GurchBot, Y2kcrazyjoker4, VoABot II, MartinDK, Kevinmon, Deliriousandlost, Damuna, Matan Hemli, Tgeairn, MrBell, Rob Burbidge, Bobbyi, Jofafrazze, Extransit, Jesper Jurcenoks, Katalaveno, Biglovinb, Juliancolton, STBotD, Lights, Deor, King Lopez, Dogsgomoo, Philip Trueman, Martin451, JhsBot, LeaveSleaves, Seresin, StAnselm, Accounting4Taste, GrooveDog, Flyer22, Oda Mari, Allmightyduck, Oxymoron83, GGGold, StaticGull, Catalina 123, Martarius, Sfan00 IMG, ClueBot, The Thing That Should Not Be, Mike Klaassen, Uncle Milty, Cirt, Passargea, Stevengfeldman, Blueshadow9, Vivio Testarossa, DamageW, Razorflame, Egmontaz, Laceycece, PseudoOne, ZooFari, Osarius, Addbot, Some jerk on the Internet, Ronhjones, Favonian, Idiottom, Peridon, Tide rolls, Zorrobot, Luckas-bot, Yobot, 2D, Tempodivalse, AnomieBOT, Masoncc, Jim1138, Kingpin13, 90 Auto, E2eamon, Frogulis, Mononomic, The Evil IP address, Shadowjams, Chaheel Riens, Thehelpfulbot, FrescoBot, Moloch09, Pinethicket, Saayiit, Tofutwitch11, Miracle Pen, Reaper Eternal, Jamietw, Derild4921, RjwilmsiBot, Pqn0308, Bento00, NameIsRon, Ripchip Bot, Justpoppingintosayhi, Salvio giuliano, Immunize, Japi-chan, Wikipelli, MikeyMouse10, Roflkitten6, Brock4, L Kensington, Donner60, Heyyou45, ChuispastonBot, EdoBot, DASHBotAV, Xanchester, ClueBot NG, This lousy T-shirt, Hiperfelix, Marechal Ney, Johny Bob 111, Spannerjam, Reaganfox01, Helpful Pixie Bot, Poopsupbra, Hallows AG, Mark Arsten, Benzband, Noremray22, Fylbecatulous, Mrt3366, Anonnymos, Frosty, RandomLittleHelper, Reatlas, Epicgenius, Isaac Mayne, A.sky245, Edito83, Luluckp, Parabolooidal, Juliandunn, CamelCase, Fred1234580, Chaskelrevs, Enzokarate and Anonymous: 358

- **Frame story** *Source:* https://en.wikipedia.org/wiki/Frame_story?oldid=678321084 *Contributors:* Sjc, Eclecticology, Ortolan88, Dws, Michael Hardy, Erall, Furrykef, Wetman, Mordomo, Owen, Vespristiano, L3prador, Jmabel, Romanm, Securiger, Nateji77, LGagnon, Acegikmo1, David Edgar, Haeleth, Vfp15, Herbee, Chinasaur, Daniel Brockman, Gdr, IYY, Drant, Kuralyov, Gary D, Shadypalm88, Rich Farmbrough, MeltBanana, LindsayH, Dbachmann, Stbalbach, Bender235, Leif, Kotuku33, Edwards ic, Alpheus, Mrzaius, Anthony Appleyard, Velella, Bsadowski1, Mahanga, Megan1967, Sandover, Awostrack, StradivariusTV, Stefanomione, Fieari, OrphicPedant, Flowerparty, Chobot, Bgwhite, Kollision, Hornplease, RL0919, Philip Stevens, Robertd, SmackBot, OrientalHero, Leki, Jagged 85, Vanished user 3dk2049pot4,

Hbackman, Clampton, Chris the speller, Colonies Chris, Nerrolken, JesseRafe, Radagast83, Шизомби, Stevenkrauss, Minaker, Teancum, TheHYPO, Blakegripling ph, CapitalR, ChrisCork, Wolfdog, Agemegos, Cassmus, Cydebot, Goldfritha, M a s, Ruaraidh-dobson, JamesAM, Barticus88, Mentifisto, Alphachimpbot, Davewho2, MegX, VictorLaszlo, Coughinink, STBot, Alro, J.delanoy, Tlim7882, Nothingofwater, McSly, JayJasper, Westfalr3, Bovineboy2008, Paulburnett, Soundofmusicals, Eggishorn, Pitoutom, Darrell Wheeler, Dreamafter, JohnnyMrN-inja, Phil wink, Fost219, ClueBot, Mike Klaassen, CharlieRCD, Jumbolino, Xme, Aurigas, Evilninja123, Addbot, Ronhjones, HerculeBot, Goregore~enwiki, Amirobot, Colossalcalamari, KamikazeBot, AbigailAbernathy, Prunesqualer, RibotBOT, Tetraedycal, HamburgerRadio, Calmer Waters, Booksrule9, Lotje, Jeffrd10, Fitoschido, DASHBot, EmausBot, Noaddedsugarr, Ὁ οἶστρος, Erianna, L Kensington, Usb10, ClueBot NG, Exterion, Shadowcamel, Rezabot, Spannerjam, BendelacBOT, Plaischaque, AtomGuy, MusikAnimal, Creilly14, Jionpedia, EagerToddler39, Jamesx12345, Reatlas, Yu369576, DavidLeighEllis, Azure Anteater, DangerousJXD, BioApple and Anonymous: 100

- **MacGuffin** *Source:* https://en.wikipedia.org/wiki/MacGuffin?oldid=676733311 *Contributors:* The Epopt, Tarquin, Koyaanis Qatsi, Yooden, Heron, Modemac, JohnOwens, Ettlz, Axlrosen, Karada, Skysmith, Paul A, Card~enwiki, Ihcoyc, Nerd~enwiki, Milkfish, ZachsMind, Ghewgill, Dcoetzee, WhisperToMe, DJ Clayworth, Furrykef, Hyacinth, K1Bond007, Tempshill, Marc omorain, Rbellin, Kev, Rossumcapek, Bshort, Dale Arnett, Postdlf, Rfc1394, Rhombus, Sheridan, Dodger~enwiki, Ungvichian, Ruakh, Decrypt3, DocWatson42, Gtrmp, Nifboy, Geeoharee, Tom harrison, Karn, DO'Neil, Beardo, Hiphats, Macrakis, Iceberg3k, Matt Crypto, Edcolins, Wpjonathan, Alexf, Antandrus, Msahutty, FC, Saucepan, Chuuumus, Khaosworks, MacGyverMagic, Rlquall, Cubelodyte, SimonLyall, Rlcantwell, Nickptar, Gary D, Sam, Neale Monks, Grm wnr, Ghilz, The stuart, Lacrimosus, Mike Rosoft, David Sneek, Eyrian, Mindspillage, Oliyoung, Rich Farmbrough, KillerChihuahua, Rhobite, IKato, Hcs, Narsil, Daydream believer2, Rorschach567, Notinasnaid, Edgarde, Kaisershatner, Mr. Billion, Viriditas, Giraffedata, Sriram sh, Rje, Douglasr007, Sebastian Goll, Polylerus, Zellin, Grutness, Mithent, Anthony Appleyard, Gargaj, CyberSkull, Geo Swan, Alex-Fitzpatrick, PatrickFisher, Dachannien, Ricky81682, Fuzlogic, Cibumamo, Elchupachipmunk, Sobolewski, Dhartung, Cgmusselman, Shad-owolf, Zxcvbnm, Ianblair23, Alai, Ghirlandajo, Zosodada, Dryman, Sidney Gould, Dismas, Hijiri88, Havu, Ap0ught, Preaky, Joriki, The JPS, Lemi4, Woohookitty, MagicBez, Percy Snoodle, Aaron McDaid, Before My Ken, Thebogusman, Staatenloser~enwiki, Mandarax, Josh Parris, Rjwilmsi, Seidenstud, Coemgenus, Fieari, Rogerd, Adjusting, Urbane Legend, Josiah Rowe, Gunslinger, Carbonite, Wahkeenah, David Matchen, Yar Kramer, Platypus222, Reedbeta, FlaBot, Jeepo~enwiki, McPhail, Smajie, Elmer Clark, RMS Oceanic, Quuxplusone, A. Manley Lush, Tysto, WhyBeNormal, Schrodingers catsup, VolatileChemical, Manscher, Samwaltz, Sophitus, EamonnPKeane, Sus scrofa, YurikBot, Koveras, Hairy Dude, Kafziel, SPKx, Andyroid, Nintendorulez, Fabartus, Toquinha, Chuck Carroll, Hydrargyrum, Tenebrae, Dmlandfair, Anomalocaris, Purodha, Lemon-s, DragonHawk, Brace, Chariset, ONEder Boy, Thesloth, Awa64, Splitter8, Dfgarcia, RL0919, Lomn, Dan-ger Poodle, Beanyk, BL Lacertae, JdwNYC, Superluser, Pegship, Jfilcik, Plkrtn, Deville, Nikkimaria, SMcCandlish, Canley, Bryn666, Red Jay, Opiaterein, Fram, Mais oui!, Mrblondnyc, Abu Dhabi, Isoxyl, Winick88, SmackBot, EvilCouch, Michaelcox, Lestrade, Gorast, SCSI Com-mando, McGeddon, Rrius, KocjoBot~enwiki, Redmess, Gregory j, Fitch, Bwithh, Alksub, Antrophica, Eskimbot, CapitalSasha, Wakuran, Lumines, GraemeMcRae, Wittylama, Alana Smithy, Master Deusoma, Kudzu1, Hanna144, Ohnoitsjamie, Durova, Stuart P. Bentley, Tyciol, Bluebot, Wubb, Quinsareth, Jyroberson, Deadlyvices, Coffin, The Rogue Penguin, Samanathon, Krallja, Scix, Esprix, Ishmayl, Garydave, Tamfang, Jonthecheet, Zagrebo, Skribb, Yorick8080, The dez, Metageek, Airogos, Шизомби, Decltype, UK-Logician-2006, Coolbho3000, Jackr, Artihcus, TCorp, BinaryTed, Joseph blue, Threegee, ILike2BeAnonymous, Zadignose, RustStorm, Fosibodu, Twigge, Dmh~enwiki, Ser Amantio di Nicolao, BrownHairedGirl, EpicFantasyStory, Potosino, Perfectblue97, Shadowlynk, JoshuaZ, Jaywubba1887, 041744, Boy-liciousDarian, Walrus125, SQGibbon, Mets501, Simonscott, Wrlee~enwiki, IceHunter, Dr.K., Jimpoz, Aren't I Obscure?, Zepheus, Bolt Vanderhuge, The Drainpipe, Lee Carre, Mbelrose, ILovePlankton, Simon12, Kencf0618, Clarityfiend, Shadoman, JoeBot, StephenBuxton, Sabrewing, 'Ff'lo, LearningKnight, Taram, Exo2000, Randroide, Signinstranger, Zotdragon, TORR, Wolfdog, CmdrObot, W guice, K00bine, Dogman15, Cydebot, Nayeryouakim, Goldfritha, Llort, Tfgbd, Lugnuts, Erluti, Georgehwilliams, Soetermans, Rand21althor, Codingmasters, Tparisi, UberMan5000, DumbBOT, After Midnight, Ken41, Krylonblue83, Jmac27@aol.com, Bagheadinc, Thijs!bot, Edman274, Dubc0724, MatheMezzaMorphis163, Ace ofgabriel, Mrogilvie, Nalvage, Markdarb, Floridasand, TRiG, Vafthrudnir, SummerPhD, Bladestorm, Matariel, Dr who1975, Jtwiss, Marquess, Tgwizard, Klow, Knotwork, Darrenhusted, Xzamuel, AniRaptor2001, Dd 8630, Janejellyroll, Valdean, MegX, TheEditrix2, Rothorpe, Papa Lima Whiskey, Siddharth Mehrotra, BonnySwan, Geniac, Magioladitis, Robbui, TheEnigma411, JNW, Ad-Murray, Froid, D-Gen, Aplardi, Silentaria, DerHexer, Schaedenfreud82, R Flavell, LoganTheGeshrat, MartinBot, Leobot~enwiki, Hm313, Ryan murphy, Richiekim, Itzcuauhtli, Hamiltonap, JVTruman, Vbatz, Thomas Larsen, SongMonk, Samtheboy, Milkyface, AdamBMorgan, Cognita, Floaterfluss, Steveran, SCOCSOOCSOSC, Nwbeeson, SporkWieldingFerret, Malerin, Mlcrowne, GEWilker, BrettAllen, Kidlittle, Seishino, Equazcion, Diloretojazz, Mangraa, Rekrdskratcher, Thoroughbred Phoenix, VolkovBot, Neverwake, Thedjatclubrock, Moviefreake, Javance, Jmrowland, Myurtoglu, Begeun, SunZoomSpark, Salvar, Brunton, ^demonBot2, RSHerrero, Mpfreivald, Moonblight, JCSBimp, Metadat, Mars11, AlleborgoBot, Thatother1dude, Atlantabravz, Matt.bateman, Pontin007, Ghostwords, Tiddly Tom, Lakester10, JabbaThe-Bot, Exemplar sententia, Colfer2, Umrguy42, The Clawed One, Aruton, Jack1956, Benea, GMBFly98, Gyrorobo, Marksman 91, KColagio, Mad Hlaine Larkin, Teapot37, Mr. Granger, Faithlessthewonderboy, Wikievil666, MMetro, Mike Klaassen, Eddroid, Ccutting, Dlabtot, Triv-ialist, LoneKnightProductions, Chimesmonster, Andrewbernst, Mctmike, PixelBot, Jammy0002, Ngebendi, Thefishnamedcarl, Holothurion, Quizzing, Pherdy~enwiki, Mnlg, Vanished user uih38riiw4hjlsd, DumZiBoT, Life of Riley, Zombie Hunter Smurf, Will-B, Fastily, DrOx-acropheles, TRTX, Shadowmask, ErgoSum88, Kasper2006, WikHead, Sophie996, Nukebros, Darth Payn, NFLPatriot, Addbot, Wakablog-ger2, Smiddly, Queenmomcat, Ronhjones, Leszek Jańczuk, Download, PranksterTurtle, Rawsushy, Absurdtrousers, Mosedschurte, Bigzteve, Shpyda, AbleDangerTheMovie, RitzWolf, Meisam, Luckas-bot, Yobot, Ptbotgourou, Xanasbarro, AnomieBOT, NotHugo, Hughesdavidw, Pi-ano non troppo, Daviessimo, GismoZ312, Citation bot, LiteraryMaven, Onedaylemurswillruletheworld, A dullard, Xuz, RibotBOT, Mrjotz, Green Cardamom, DarkHeroEncore, FrescoBot, Neo79189, Seductionist, 99ant99, Anonymouth, Kalmbach, Pristino, SW3 5DL, Dont slip on the muesli, Reaper Eternal, Levague, Robert Kohen, Tbhotch, RjwilmsiBot, S2theb, Acather96, WikitanvirBot, Illdisposed, GoingBatty, Drekmorin, Lithistman, Wytzox1, The badgers nadgers, Cloud212, Shigoroku, Jacobisq, Tír na nÓg 1982, TheRoon, NTox, PatrickGuadalupe, Brauden, JohnsonL623, Cchanak, Spannerjam, Reify-tech, FunkyStyle63, Nylar4000, BattyBot, Kephir, Cerabot~enwiki, Love Chocolate 123, Pincrete, MatthewHoobin, Termah71, Meteor sandwich yum, Tentantoes, RubyJewelHeart, TheRealGaryPrivate, Logorc Beaumont 11, Majestic2016 and Anonymous: 790

- **In medias res** *Source:* https://en.wikipedia.org/wiki/In_medias_res?oldid=672589965 *Contributors:* Jni, Sanders muc, Cholling, Wereon, Varlaam, Macrakis, Mu, Klemen Kocjancic, Picapica, Jiy, Haruo, Discospinster, Rich Farmbrough, YUL89YYZ, Bobo192, Viriditas, Kbir1, Aan, Keenan Pepper, Mhazard9, Angr, Woohookitty, Gerbrant, Marudubshinki, Mandarax, Nightscream, The jt, Ademkader, Brighterorange, FlaBot, Petruchi41, VolatileChemical, EamonnPKeane, Bhny, D. F. Schmidt, Ruhrfisch, Haoie, Kermitmorningstar, Dissolve, Closedmouth, Nae'blis, Jeff Silvers, SmackBot, Jagged 85, Kintetsubuffalo, BiT, Chris the speller, Thumperward, Sct72, Schwallex, Derek R Bullamore,

TCHJ3K, Marcus Brute, Andrew Dalby, Byelf2007, Rklawton, TheStripèdOne, Fijo Dena~enwiki, Grandpafootsoldier, Dimos87, Taram, MoistTowelette, Wolfdog, Prlsmith, Neelix, Cydebot, Future Perfect at Sunrise, Treybien, DustinFreeman, Thijs!bot, TonyTheTiger, Al Lemos, Undomiel, ResurgamII, TheEditrix2, TheGreenKnight, Anarchemitis, Jenniferjwchang, Earlobe, Reflector88, MistyMorn, Shobhit102, AdamBMorgan, NhuyBURDETTE, NewEnglandYankee, Nikki311, Donmike10, Wikimandia, Wikipeterproject, CardinalDan, Wikiedi-tor06, VolkovBot, Lexein, RyanB88, Eldaran~enwiki, Broadbot, Cacaoatl, K. Hiippari, Fratrep, Sindala, Denisarona, WickerGuy, ClueBot, Quackiv, Unbuttered Parsnip, Drmies, Ajhodd, MJDTed, SchreiberBike, Mlaffs, Ex penumbrae, SoxBot III, XLinkBot, Addbot, Dunhere, Ronhjones, Ccacsmss, Erutuon, Tide rolls, Goregore~enwiki, Cote d'Azur, Luckas-bot, Yobot, AnomieBOT, Piano non troppo, LeftClicker, Citation bot, Xqbot, Annmey87, Omnipaedista, Cercopithecidae, Paine Ellsworth, Hirpex, Citation bot 1, HowardJWilk, ScottMHoward, Meconomou89, QuipQuotch, Andyman1125, DASHBotAV, ClueBot NG, Widr, Spannerjam, Helpful Pixie Bot, Myrmecophagavir, Guitar-Dudeness, Edward Roussac, BG19bot, PiusImpavidus, CitationCleanerBot, Sebastianne13, Laodah, Arttechlaw, Cwobeel, OcelotHod, Per-mafrost46, Monkbot, Catobonus, Miraclexix and Anonymous: 163

- **Narrative hook** *Source:* https://en.wikipedia.org/wiki/Narrative_hook?oldid=653773037 *Contributors:* DJ Clayworth, Sunray, Macrakis, Mathx314, BrokenSegue, Ekem, Bhny, SmackBot, Jagged 85, Ale jrb, Hga, Cydebot, Goldfritha, Majoria, AntiVandalBot, SummerPhD, Al-bany NY, Hbent, Bufh, STBot, Swinquest, Lear's Fool, IAmTheCoinMan, Lradrama, WatermelonPotion, Pittsburghmuggle, Mike Klaassen, Alexbot, La Pianista, XLinkBot, Vsm01, Richard-of-Earth, Addbot, Jojhutton, Ronhjones, Mpruh, LilHelpa, Loving-kindness, I dream of horses, RjwilmsiBot, EmausBot, Sagaciousphil, A930913, Antidisestablishmentarian, ClueBot NG, Spannerjam, Helpful Pixie Bot, Chave-neau, Melonkelon, Ntomlin1996 and Anonymous: 34

- **Rakugo** *Source:* https://en.wikipedia.org/wiki/Rakugo?oldid=672863171 *Contributors:* The Anome, Leandrod, DopefishJustin, Nanshu, Max-imus Rex, Furrykef, Lumos3, Davide Mana, DocWatson42, TY~enwiki, Andycjp, Sam Hocevar, Fg2, JeroenHoek, Circeus, Pearle, Kentin, Pa-leorthid, Isnow, Shikai shaw, BD2412, FlaBot, DannyWilde, Pinkville, Benlisquare, Yahya Abdal-Aziz, Freshgavin, Mkill, KnightRider~enwiki, SmackBot, Nihonjoe, Kintetsubuffalo, Hmains, Quartermaster, Ser Amantio di Nicolao, Tadakuni, Ryulong, DDD DDD~enwiki, Nekohakase, Destro, Vickerman625, Thijs!bot, I do not exist, RobotG, WinBot, Giggy, D.h, EdBever, Skumarlabot, VolkovBot, TXiKiBoT, Azukimonaka, Der Rabe Ralf, EmanWilm, Kyoww, CRobClark, Deerstop, GFHandel, Lx 121, XLinkBot, Good Olfactory, Addbot, Japwn, Lightbot, Mari-marina, Luckas-bot, MarioS, KamikazeBot, Ciphers, ImizuCIR, GrouchoBot, Ionutzmovie, RedBot, Haaninjo, EmausBot, WikitanvirBot, Gray eyes, Haylden, PJZEN, Dentalplanlisa, Vegtan, KasparBot and Anonymous: 34

- **Plot twist** *Source:* https://en.wikipedia.org/wiki/Plot_twist?oldid=678642543 *Contributors:* D, Steinsky, DJ Clayworth, Dale Arnett, Choco-lateboy, Tobias Bergemann, Neuro, The Land, Bumphoney, Violetriga, Sketchee, Runtime, Grenavitar, SteinbDJ, Dejvid, Exeunt, Volatile-Chemical, TexasAndroid, RussBot, Michael Slone, ONEder Boy, CLW, SmackBot, McGeddon, Jagged 85, Aleksmot, Raymondluxuryacht, Clconway, Gildir, Robofish, 09bmarcu, Antonielly, A.Z., P199, TheFarix, BeekeeperGOP, Schwenkstar, Wolfdog, ShelfSkewed, Cydebot, StevenNemes, Gogo Dodo, Luigifan, Gondomwing, SummerPhD, JIGZ, Albany NY, Mal32, J Greb, MartinDK, Blotsfan, GammaShade, Pikasneez27, Zerokitsune, Mufka, Bluecatcinema, Ttias, FeralDruid, Signalhead, Bacchus87, Paulturtle, King Womp, Bentley4, TravelingCat, Dca5347, Flyer22, Dancemotron, Martarius, ClueBot, Mike Klaassen, Niceguyedc, DarthVado210, Stampede1961, NellieBly, Addbot, Jafeluv, Yobmod, 5 albert square, Trachtemacht, Krano, Jarble, Angrysockhop, Yobot, Amirobot, Kookyunii, AnomieBOT, Jeff Muscato, Citation bot, Khajidha, Mario777Zelda, TheSameGuy, Green Cardamom, FrescoBot, LittleWink, MikeAllen, TheLastDeusExMachina, RjwilmsiBot, John of Reading, ZéroBot, Bamyers99, Unreal7, Erianna, AbsoluteGleek92, ClueBot NG, Satellizer, Widr, Spannerjam, JordoCo, Helpful Pixie Bot, Simpsonguy1987, Jetwhale, JohnChrysostom, MusikAnimal, Robert the Devil, Meatsgains, Dinnooo444, MEH boi 616, Helsabott, Mrt3366, Cpt.a.haddock, Akmrcleg, AldezD, TwistEndings, BoxOfficeWeekend, Newnightmare, Melonkelon, Molekularbiologe, Smeagol-Bergman, Fathomd and Anonymous: 124

- **Poetic justice** *Source:* https://en.wikipedia.org/wiki/Poetic_justice?oldid=672064991 *Contributors:* The Anome, Jahsonic, Furrykef, Geogre, UtherSRG, Snowdog, Ratwod, Andycjp, Bender235, Espoo, Thorfinn~enwiki, Sizzlingsteaks, Samaritan, Bacteria, Manwe, Fbv65edel, Table-top, Bluemoose, Toussaint, Graham87, BD2412, MZMcBride, FuriousFreddy, Ground Zero, YurikBot, Sceptre, Goofy14, Nirvana2013, Grafen, Sixten8, Urger48400, Squib, Katieh5584, Leon2323, SmackBot, Peterven, Jagged 85, Gilliam, Iskunk, Scwlong, Neo139, Morio, Robofish, Slakr, Grandpafootsoldier, Skinsmoke, Mackan, Slippyd, Eastlaw, Cyrusc, ShelfSkewed, Playtime, Gogo Dodo, NorthernThunder, Nietzscheswife, Oryanw~enwiki, CharlotteWebb, Nick Number, AxiomShell, MegX, Y2kcrazyjoker4, JaGa, Smartings, Francis Tyers, Don Cuan, Bernard S. Jansen, Osaboramirez, Group29, BrettAllen, CA387, Langrel, Philip Trueman, Technopat, Mathaytace, Saturn star, Rjakew, Flyer22, Taggard, Jum-bot, Martarius, Excirial, Versus22, Baron von HoopleDoople, Dthomsen8, MystBot, Basua, Addbot, Yousou, Decibert, Tassedethe, Luckas-bot, AnomieBOT, DemocraticLuntz, Materialscientist, Abolibibelot, LitrainianKnight, Andrewowen2000, Pinethicket, Tamariki, Dr Demagor, Skakkle, Serendipitynow, Deadlyops, SecretAgentMan0079, GoingBatty, Edlitz36, Tommy2010, LaSirèneÉnigma-tique, Imgx64, Manytexts, ClueBot NG, MelbourneStar, Spannerjam, Lnsoccerchick6, Benzband, IsaacBTTF, KeleosKarli, Khazar2, Isaid-noway, BDE1982, TinaCFLE, Hempopottamus, Gigityman676, Sarah Joy Jones, Eric Corbett, Tmuchiri, Bdanno24, Team eesh and Anony-mous: 112

- **Causal loop** *Source:* https://en.wikipedia.org/wiki/Causal_loop?oldid=675644499 *Contributors:* Angela, Cnilep, IsaacAA, Trevithj, Going-Batty, Orange Suede Sofa and Anonymous: 1

- **Quibble (plot device)** *Source:* https://en.wikipedia.org/wiki/Quibble_(plot_device)?oldid=678596840 *Contributors:* Zundark, DJ Clayworth, Altenmann, David Gerard, Karn, Goochelaar, Thu, Bobo192, Army1987, Diego Moya, Jess Cully, Feezo, Xover, Ashmoo, Nightscream, Urbane Legend, Hairy Dude, Chuck Carroll, Beanyk, Lockesdonkey, D'Agosta, Plactus, SmackBot, Hmains, OldSkoolGeek, Kendrick7, Am-niarix, CmdrObot, Jayunderscorezero, Nautilator, ChristineD, Cydebot, Goldfritha, TonyTheTiger, Jj137, Mdotley, Rhinoracer, Darklilac, Kcowolf, BranER, Lady Mondegreen, DoctorWorm, Fluffybun, Natg 19, Dreamafter, Mike Klaassen, The Moyster, Qwertyytrewqqwerty, Yobot, GateKeeper, AnomieBOT, LilHelpa, Remotelysensed, RobertMfromLI, Fitoschido, Mcc1789, Kentaru Z, Spannerjam, Evolvedmi-crobe, The Illusive Man, Marksteinhardt and Anonymous: 60

- **Red herring** *Source:* https://en.wikipedia.org/wiki/Red_herring?oldid=674753922 *Contributors:* Yves Junqueira, Theresa knott, DJ Clay-worth, Joy, LGagnon, David Gerard, Gtrmp, Lee J Haywood, Bfinn, Chowbok, Mineminemine, Tooki, Huffers, Bender235, Mr2001, Espoo, Alansohn, Gary, Stillnotelf, BRW, Skyring, BDD, WadeSimMiser, Stefanomione, Matilda, Graham87, Vegaswikian, Raider Duck, DVdm, Sus scrofa, Koveras, Thane, Seegoon, Yzb, LaraCroft NYC, Ron Stoppable, TDogg310, Epipelagic, Bill shannon, Emc2, Luna Whistler, SmackBot, McGeddon, C.Fred, Jagged 85, J.J.Sagnella, Janneman, Janey Dowerstruffel, MikeRM, Ikiroid, GRuban, Luigi III, Mwtoews,

Ivysaur12, Kevinbsmith, Saile, Robofish, JoshuaZ, Rekstout, Hiiiiiiiiiiiiiiiiiiiii, UKER, RichardF, RLamb, IvanDíaz, George100, Signin-stranger, Jayunderscorezero, Centurion Ry, Cydebot, Future Perfect at Sunrise, Quibik, Awakeandalive1, Smgunasekara, Aericanwizard, Seaphoto, Foxhill, Myofilus, Jedermann, Barek, JadamR15, Adjwilley, Albany NY, Max Hyre, TAnthony, Rothorpe, Bongwarrior, Toomai Glittershine, Mindgames11, Tedclaymore, Maurice Carbonaro, Cpiral, Acalamari, Funguy06, Johnbod, Zojj, Nowai0, MishaPan, Sgeureka, Kelapstick, PopsWomic, Aymatth2, Falcon8765, Cwmacdougall, Michael Frind, Sakkura, Matthew Yeager, SouthLake, Doctorfluffy, Light-mouse, IdreamofJeanie, Henry Merrivale, Mr. Granger, Twinsday, ClueBot, TableManners, Mike Klaassen, Thudworthy, Kitsunegami, Ktr101, PixelBot, 7&6=thirteen, CowboySpartan, Wycked, DumZiBoT, Michael gimson, SilvonenBot, Addbot, Cst17, Jarble, Fryed-peach, Luckas-bot, Yobot, Legobot II, Windowmaker525, Adam Hauner, AnomieBOT, Citation bot, Green Cardamom, FrescoBot, Paine Ellsworth, Haeinous, Machine Elf 1735, Cannolis, Citation bot 1, Jonesey95, Full-date unlinking bot, FoxBot, ConcernedVancouverite, Lotje, Bratface11, The Stick Man, Stevengfowler, Olof nord, Solomonfromfinland, Shuipzv3, H3llBot, Staszek Lem, KarasuGamma, Doug Shaver, Donner60, Tijfo098, EdoBot, TYelliot, Ahhuggs, ClueBot NG, Rich Smith, Galilsnap, Rlbfruhstuck, JohnsonL623, Widr, Spannerjam, M0rphzone, Northamerica1000, Merrelltom, B1naryatr0phy, Ajaxfiore, Aron7913, ChrisGualtieri, Timelezz, Ranze, Lugia2453, Cd247, Froglich, Harkan-war, AJBarcs, Staplerguy211, BlueRidgeRider, IProbl3m, Coconutporkpie, Maxtheslayer, Homesculptor and Anonymous: 185

- **Self-fulfilling prophecy** *Source:* https://en.wikipedia.org/wiki/Self-fulfilling_prophecy?oldid=671865107 *Contributors:* The Anome, Jim McKeeth, Michael Hardy, Mahjongg, Cyp, Docu, Slusk, Evercat, Conti, Nikola Smolenski, Magnus.de, Imc, Dogface, Bloodshedder, Raul654, Wetman, Slawojarek, Denelson83, Twang, Altenmann, Clngre, Rrjanbiah, David Gerard, Sethoeph, Smjg, Snowdog, Mboverload, Taak, Christofurio, Antandrus, Beland, Piotrus, SAMAS, Qui1che, Kingal86, Oskar Sigvardsson, Dbachmann, Bender235, JustPhil, El C, DS1953, Thu, Johnkarp, La goutte de pluie, Ranveig, Arthena, SHIMONSHA, Mailer diablo, Richard Arthur Norton (1958-), Madmardigan53, Dandv, GlaucusAtlanticus, Ekem, Pol098, Goodgerster, BD2412, Rjwilmsi, MZMcBride, 25~enwiki, Vegaswikian, Volty, Da Stressor, Andy85719, RexNL, RMS Oceanic, Jeremygbyrne, Lirelyn, YurikBot, Mukkakukaku, Enviroknot, Red Slash, Ksyrie, Ritchy, Anomalocaris, Chrisbrl88, BBnet3000, JeremyStein, Felsir, Leotohill, Typer 525, Closedmouth, CWenger, Shimonnyman, Nsevs, Saikiri, Entheta, SmackBot, Lehla, Cubs Fan, KnowledgeOfSelf, C.Fred, Jagged 85, Keakealani, UrsaFoot, Evanreyes, Portillo, Algont, Chris the speller, Bluebot, Gonzalo84, Nbarth, Colonies Chris, KingAlanI, Verrai, Frap, ThreeAnswers, Captain Zyrain, Nakon, Qmwne235, Tesseran, Byelf2007, Kuzaar, Euchias-mus, Sophie-Lou, Mgiganteus1, Gnevin, Hotblaster, Boomshadow, Noah Salzman, Puffy Treat, Iridescent, I'mMe!!, JForget, ŠJů, Penbat, Ford-madoxfraud, Enigmatical, Cydebot, Athiran, Matrix61312, Goldfritha, Myscrnnm, Pascal.Tesson, Lindsay658, Mr Gronk, Letranova, N5iln, Hylas Chung, Philippe, MechaEmperor, DrowningInRoyalty, Operator link, Luna Santin, Seaphoto, Julia Rossi, Mahousu, Joe Schmedley, Blackwater009, Alphachimpbot, Darrenhusted, JAnDbot, Ikanreed, RainbowCrane, MegX, TekNOSX, MartinBot, Meatbites, R'n'B, Com-monsDelinker, AstroHurricane001, Mathglot, Roman V. Odaisky, Ajfweb, Pancasila~enwiki, EmerySean, Midasminus, VolkovBot, Door-sAjar, TXiKiBoT, Sroc, Tomsega, Nenohrok, JhsBot, FourteenDays, FironDraak, Noamerez, Madhero88, Eubulides, Lova Falk, CryptWiz-ard, TravelingCat, Cnilep, Chicogringosegundo, Daveh4h, Paul Breeuwsma, RufioUniverse, Tehjustice, Dreamafter, Winchelsea, BloodDoll, Yerpo, Rinconsoleao, KingFanel, Twinsday, ClueBot, Statalyzer, MikeVitale, Elmao, Supertouch, Mike Klaassen, Drmies, Ifnkovhg, Brain seltzer, Sun Creator, NoriMori, Levent, Ilikecameras, XLinkBot, Gnowor, Rror, Dthomsen8, Addbot, Some jerk on the Internet, LaaknorBot, Ccacsmss, Ayoopdog, Lazyteen542, Lightbot, AtiwH, Czar Brodie, Jarble, Legobot, Yobot, Ann Firebird, AnomieBOT, Pricebank, Resarcio, Alivine, Citation bot, ArthurBot, LilHelpa, J04n, Frosted14, Wikieditor1988, FrescoBot, Malibusunny, QuéSéYo2, Citation bot 1, DrilBot, Skyerise, Taravatli, RedBot, Trappist the monk, Lotje, DARTH SIDIOUS 2, RjwilmsiBot, MMS2013, Tesseract2, Neshantsharma, Goin-temm, GoingBatty, Geetha nitc, AvicBot, Biglulu, Klavierspieler, Ὁ οἶστρος, Jacobisq, Wikiloop, Mcc1789, ClueBot NG, Jack Greenmaven, Benjamin9832, MerllwBot, Helpful Pixie Bot, Jeraphine Gryphon, MusikAnimal, Davidiad, Rtrammel, Meclee, Bluebird29, Darylgolden, Lhu720, Mediran, MotivationLPBH, Lean n mean, BLGX26, Nennes, JimmyMcWilliams, Epicgenius, Abiramy1, Ginsuloft, Abilhomme C, Monkbot, Asdklf; and Anonymous: 314

- **Story within a story** *Source:* https://en.wikipedia.org/wiki/Story_within_a_story?oldid=675983244 *Contributors:* -- April, Eclecticology, Paul A, Timwi, Jogloran, Wetman, Mezaco, Bearcat, Gentgeen, Rfc1394, Smjg, Everyking, Brequinda, Marqoz, Perey, Rich Farmbrough, MeltBanana, Bender235, CanisRufus, Sietse Snel, Longhair, Viriditas, Giraffedata, Homerjay, Anthony Appleyard, Logologist, Dabbler, Dave.Dunford, Kusma, Stemonitis, Sandover, Woohookitty, Camw, Awostrack, Robert K S, WJE, Stefanomione, Zpb52, Mandarax, BD2412, Rjwilmsi, Drpaule, Old Moonraker, Banazir, Russavia, DaGizza, Rob T Firefly, Cliffb, Shawn81, Friedfish, Anomalocaris, Korny O'Near, ONEder Boy, Nick, Tony1, BobGreenwade, Nikkimaria, Mike Selinker, Philip Stevens, SmackBot, Leki, Jagged 85, Sebesta, Gilliam, Chris the speller, Sadads, Tartan, AMK152, Paroxysm, Hl, Jklin, Marcus Brute, Vina-iwbot~enwiki, Drumnbach, Axem Titanium, Kransky, Syr-catbot, Yyyyyyyyyyy, Childzy, Imagine Wizard, Neddyseagoon, Jc37, Sky Captain, AshcroftIleum, Wolfdog, CmdrObot, Aherunar, Cyde-bot, Henrymrx, Thijs!bot, Octoberdan, DanTD, JustAGal, Nick Number, WinBot, Lemonv1, Saxophobia, Robina Fox, Tobycek, Albmont, JMyrleFuller, Gwern, Ronyu02, Keith D, J.delanoy, TheAlmanac, Uncle Dick, MKohut, McSly, The Quidam, Sean McHugh, BowToChris, TXiKiBoT, Gune, Lots42, Vipinhari, Someguy1221, AtaruMoroboshi, Optigan13, Gridironrb, Synthebot, Logan, Wjl2, Tpb, Dreamafter, SpecialAgentUncleTito, Dravecky, Lord Opeth, Drunkenpeter99, ClueBot, Lynnburn15, DionysosProteus, The Drama Llama, Mike Klaassen, Cirt, Nike787, Trixi72, Brewcrewer, Xme, XLinkBot, Dthomsen8, Ost316, Aucassin, Addbot, Vjmorton, Ronhjones, Tassedethe, Bigzteve, Lightbot, Skarjo, Yobot, AnomieBOT, Citation bot, LilHelpa, Jyusin, J04n, Ten-pint, NOLA504ever, FrescoBot, ⊠ ⊠ ⊠ ⊠, Notsincecar-rie, Citation bot 1, JIK1975, Motorizedlamb, Foobarnix, Rabiddog51sb, Cnwilliams, Goldenmelody722, Idiotchalk, Abie the Fish Peddler, Adamsargant, Unreal7, Erianna, BornonJune8, John of Wood Green, CookieMattster, ClueBot NG, Azurengar, Spannerjam, Darthpineap-ple401, Helpful Pixie Bot, BG19bot, Princetoniac, MusikAnimal, Ntspringer, Viadelcorso, TBrandley, Irockz, Dexbot, ThatFilmGuy92, Hel-lojebediah, Monkbot, Vijayyamgar and Anonymous: 155

- **Ticking time bomb scenario** *Source:* https://en.wikipedia.org/wiki/Ticking_time_bomb_scenario?oldid=669651946 *Contributors:* Edward, Greenrd, Katana0182, PBS, Ich, Neutrality, Lacrimosus, Rama, Vapour, Gronky, RoyBoy, Longhair, Smalljim, Geo Swan, Andrew Gray, Bat-manand, Caywood, Scriberius, Apokrif, GregorB, Carl Logan, Copperchair, Uvaduck, RussBot, Nescio, D'Agosta, SmackBot, Jokl, InverseHy-percube, Ck4829, Federal Street, Betacommand, Nedlum, Zvar, Calbaer, Bigturtle, Nakon, Tomtom9041, Loodog, Tktktk, Legi, Nobunaga24, Macellarius, Bobamnertiopsis, Gregbard, Dunx, Hervegirod, RR, Fredhamann, VoABot II, Terjen, Allstarecho, VonKorf, KTo288, Comp25, Olegwiki, WLRoss, Mattdpollard, Eyob Tesfaye, Hilts99, Moonriddengirl, Soz101, ClueBot, Father Inire, Mild Bill Hiccup, Bonewah, In-troductory adverb clause, DumZiBoT, XLinkBot, JGDross, Ost316, Addbot, Lightbot, חובבשירה, Luckas-bot, AnomieBOT, LilHelpa, Full-date unlinking bot, Wikipelli, Wayne Slam, Accotink2, -xwingsx-, Mcc1789, Blatteroon, ClueBot NG, Parjlarsson, BG19bot, Mifter Public, BenGliterate, XXzoonamiXX, Jarrheadd0 and Anonymous: 69

- **Unreliable narrator** *Source:* https://en.wikipedia.org/wiki/Unreliable_narrator?oldid=677579905 *Contributors:* Bryan Derksen, The Anome,

don, Deathlibrarian, Wehwalt, MJMyers2~enwiki, Jagged 85, Eskimbot, JAStewart, RobertCMWV1974, Doc Strange, Nerd42, IstvanWolf, Xaosflux, Insomniduck, Skizzik, Valley2city, OrangeDog, Roscelese, Keith Paynter, Knightryderrwn, Jxm, Hotwire132002, Htra0497, Sangajin, Kindall, Sommers, Wagimawr, Bardsandwarriors, COMPFUNK2, Johaen, Nakon, Minasbeede, Luigi III, Derek R Bullamore, BullRangifer, BayBoy, DMacks, Kimpire, Dlangsam, Salamurai, Marcus Brute, Mightyfastpig, Midkay, Vasilycus, Kuru, Jidanni, Disavian, Moabdave, Teancum, Mr. Lefty, Stratadrake, Heksterb, 16@r, Across.The.Synapse, Loadmaster, Flamerule, Snake712, Meco, Daviddaniel37, Fredwerner, Alseeger, The Real Walrus, Blue eyed writer, TJ Spyke, Iridescent, Vocaro, Cls14, Brianoneil, Alegoo92, Billastro, Dantai Amakiir, DKqwerty, Bstepp99, Amniarix, ShakespeareFan00, Wolfdog, Anton-2492, CmdrObot, AlbertSM, The Cake is a Lie, Kris Schnee, Neoyamaneko, Green caterpillar, Tenn9fan, El aprendelenguas, ShelfSkewed, Lentower, Angelsfreeek, Qrc2006, Icarus of old, Matt. P, Trimp, Bur, Estolyj, Lugnuts, UberMan5000, Dumaka, Bronzey214, Malleus Fatuorum, Chris CII, Thijs!bot, D4g0thur, 0dd1, Pampas Cat, Dachande, Conqueror Hibernensis, Merkhant, Brianmarx, Captain Crawdad, Ryan123004, Vcg3rd, Xionication, AntiVandalBot, Dekkanar, Pgoldenberg, Kitty Davis, Das654, Danger, PunyaBiswal, Jhsounds, Ingolfson, QuantumEngineer, OhanaUnited, Xeno, MegX, Lawilkin, Geniac, Steve Bob, Magioladitis, VoABot II, GoorooV, Sebras, Decembermouse, CTF83!, Enternickname, Superx, Boffob, Cailil, JMyrleFuller, THobern, Xoxi, Cocytus, Nietzscheanlie, Flameninja311, Schmloof, Kiore, Juansidious, Swizzie024, Kostisl, Senthryl, EdiTor, RockMFR, J.delanoy, Hu Totya, Richiekim, Captain Infinity, Kenshinflyer, It Is Me Here, Shawn in Montreal, Zedmelon, Chiswick Chap, SCOCSOOCSOSC, Molly-in-md, Harani66, Glenntwiddle, Iceanimal2, Furiosity06, Phpgeek~enwiki, Burzmali, JazzyGroove, OsirisV, Feasoron, Potaco99, Dorftrottel, Xiahou, Sir0709, Junglar, Lights, Vranak, Gothbag, YmerejO42, Ai4ijoel, Rogerborn, Paulburnett, Dantastic202, Anonymous Dissident, Jmac0585, Brian Eisley, ^demonBot2, HawkeAnyone, Slips, Icecold.trashcan, Jedi32738, DCico, SheffieldSteel, Tapalmer99, Falcon8765, Cw6165, Stracner, Regnevakrad, MrChupon, Anthony Gooch, YumeMei, XXShigaXX, Superbabymario, SalaComMander, SieBot, Saturation2, Moonriddengirl, WereSpielChequers, Chad Gerson, JoshEdgar, Ultim87, Fabullus, 5150pacer, Drumski89, WRK, Jryfle, Toddst1, Nagosgerg, Nuttycoconut, Baseball Bugs, SaniOKh, SimonTrew, Wanderer32, Oilfieldtiger, Brontoraptor, Watch Rider, Backin5minutes, Adragon111, Anchor Link Bot, Aureliadalziel, Halflife4life, Loismustdie231, Zeng8r, Eljayess, ImageRemovalBot, Jessejaksin, SWJS, Ironman1104, Martarius, Dave T Hobbit, $tink0man, Nobody Specialx, Song of the Dragon, Mriya, Spxmet, DionysosProteus, Da gr8 1, Super pokemon bros, Keraunoscopia, Agustinaldo, Bob31415, Toad of Steel, Razor Rozar7, Enobeno, GENERALZERO, Keithbowden, Combineownage, Elecmahm, Arjayay, Ferky123, JasonAQuest, ADBandicoot, Silverscaledsalmon, Thingg, Aitias, Lord Cornwallis, Samurai Cerberus, Vespagirl, Stoned philosophaster, Lilhottieemo, DumZiBoT, Flojo22, MichaelQSchmidt, XLinkBot, Bilsonius, RebirthThom, Rror, HappyJake, Stitchill, Manyanswer, Colliric, The Rationalist, Stevierayknopfler, Adanarama, Palindrome, Addbot, Barsoomian, Steve Durnin, Queenmomcat, Jamesj09, Ronhjones, SiegfriedZ, Precis-chan, Glane23, Spittlespat, AnnaFrance, Kyle1278, Doniago, TheVitalRed, Launcher2000, Leekspinner93, Spaced35, Luckas-bot, Amirobot, Space Mountain Mike, Vegitausa, Macmooreno, Jenna12381, AnomieBOT, Pokeronskis, Jim1138, Valeriaha, Materialscientist, Danno uk, Ianjs, ArthurBot, TomB123, Sparkstriff, CelticCymru, Supensa, 94knux, Jeffhardyred, Selfish Gene 2009, MikeR613, RibotBOT, Wikieditor1988, Jal11497, HsiehLi, Classica1607, Ophilye, Xander Fury, NPending, Ausimeman21, Intelligentsium, MaxPhd, XxTimberlakexx, Pinethicket, Vicenarian, Ar558, That guy from 3A3, StevenMario, Threewords,eightletters..., Jackhipgrave94, Giomarques, Beyond My Ken, Talbut, Damiwh2, EmausBot, WikitanvirBot, 142 and 99, RenamedUser01302013, Slightsmile, Naru14358, ZéroBot, John Cline, Cinefilou, Cobaltcigs, Wayne Slam, Nateguimondart, Mister Dragon, AbsoluteGleek92, ClueBot NG, Gareth Griffith-Jones, Frietjes, Fossil1961, Jhaupt, Wikifan1836, Kevlarsen, Anonpony, BG19bot, Halokid12, Adamlarke, Waffle6271, Holyjoe722, Newvally, DeMicheal, Tomska62, Filamena, Aidesinu, Lingon of the Dark, Bon do ro, Josephpatrickobrien, Vampirestingray, GuyInTheHat, Ryan115, Yzd323, Joeleoj123, Gcc333, ToBk, Occults, Phaasch, OptimusMagnus, SOBpublishing, Katherinego, Mylittlebirdies, DirtyFlame95, TheCorduroyEffect, Knife-in-the-drawer, Gabelisabeth and Anonymous: 1144

- **Defamiliarization** *Source:* https://en.wikipedia.org/wiki/Defamiliarization?oldid=663968800 *Contributors:* The Cunctator, Jahsonic, Chinju, Sethmahoney, Phthoggos, Ruakh, Sonjaaa, DaveGorman, Lmviterbo, Taylortbb, Bjones, Stefanomione, Sparkit, Literaphile, Korg, Wavelength, RussBot, Jkelly, Validusername, Jeremy Butler, Argrig~enwiki, Kintetsubuffalo, Bluebot, Mladifilozof, Jonig4, ZachPruckowski, Outriggr, Goldenrowley, Actio, Obsessiveatbest, Froid, Wehpudicabok, Mrathel, InnocuousPseudonym, DRATSAL, Vertumn, SlipperyHippo, Cnilep, Tomas e, Savvierthanu, Addbot, Fryed-peach, Pink!Teen, TaBOT-zerem, AnomieBOT, Mx96, Skakkle, صوفی حامد, Piscator47, NathanAdams, Spannerjam, MerlIwBot, DefamAlex, Yamaha5, Fixture and Anonymous: 28

- **First-person narrative** *Source:* https://en.wikipedia.org/wiki/First-person_narrative?oldid=676388967 *Contributors:* Derek Ross, Tarquin, Rmhermen, Ortolan88, Robert Foley, R Lowry, Someone else, Paul A, RickK, Melody, Aron1, Phil Boswell, Nurg, Elysdir, Rockwood3, Chinasaur, Adam McMaster, Alteripse, Rdsmith4, Gary D, Simonides, Ckelsh, Bendono, Arthena, Jeltz, Mattbrundage, Falcorian, Megan1967, Woohookitty, Asterism, Flowerparty, Ewlyahoocom, Hibana, CJLL Wright, Sus scrofa, RussBot, Robertvan1, Antoshi, Jogers, SmackBot, Hydrogen Iodide, Billy Lovelady, Eskimbot, Yamaguchi 先生, Chris the speller, Bluebot, Erika Altek, Colonies Chris, Doh286, Kevlar67, Marcus Brute, Curly Turkey, Lambiam, Harryboyles, Childzy, White Ash, Tawkerbot2, Gnosbush, Wolfdog, FilipeS, UberMan5000, Iempleh, Ruscular, Epbr123, D4g0thur, Marek69, Nick Number, Pfranson, Scottandrewhutchins, Escarbot, Mentifisto, Just Chilling, Phosphaenus, Stagehand, VoABot II, McAngeOK, Rich257, Jdheyerman, WLU, J.delanoy, FJPB, Potatoswatter, Parable1991, Jevansen, Squids and Chips, ABF, Butwhatdoiknow, Brianga, AlleborgoBot, SieBot, Ttony21, Mraceebb, Stillwaterising, Animeronin, ClueBot, NickCT, Gigacephalus, Unbuttered Parsnip, Mike Klaassen, Excirial, TheRedPenOfDoom, Aitias, Somewhere123, Camboxer, Bearsona, Vegas949, MystBot, HexaChord, Addbot, Some jerk on the Internet, Fyrael, West.andrew.g, Tassedethe, Leptogenesis, Albeiror24, Luckas-bot, Yobot, Majestic-chimp, THEN WHO WAS PHONE?, AnimalExtender, Jaucourt, Synchronism, Roh72, LilHelpa, S h i v a (Visnu), FrescoBot, RedBot, Beyond My Ken, John of Reading, WikitanvirBot, K6ka, JediActor1998, SporkBot, Wayne Slam, Président, Donner60, DASHBotAV, ClueBot NG, ThaddeusSholto, Dr. Zombieman, Helpful Pixie Bot, MusikAnimal, Solomon7968, Aranea Mortem, BattyBot, LieutenantLatvia, Quenhitran, Juleis23, RationalBlasphemist, Charlotte1531, Kc4602$, Maplestrip and Anonymous: 187

- **Magic realism** *Source:* https://en.wikipedia.org/wiki/Magic_realism?oldid=678325574 *Contributors:* Brion VIBBER, Tarquin, Atorpen, Ortolan88, Edward, Jahsonic, Eric119, Minesweeper, Ellywa, BigFatBuddha, Sethmahoney, Jonik, Norwikian, Wik, Topbanana, Wetman, Frazzydee, Slawojarek, Twang, Robbot, Postdlf, Robinoke, JerryFriedman, GreatWhiteNortherner, Dina, Stirling Newberry, DocWatson42, Cobra libre, Lupin, Anville, Cantus, Hob, Andycjp, Toytoy, Gdm, Rdsmith4, DragonflySixtyseven, Gary D, D6, Discospinster, Rich Farmbrough, Leyanese, Wadewitz, Stbalbach, Ascorbic, Kross, DanielNuyu, Uncertaintimes, Robotje, Nk, Rje, Alansohn, Mo0, Rgclegg, Splat, Macl, Mac Davis, DreamGuy, Tycho, AFox2, Cough, Dtcdthingy, Evil Monkey, Nrtzhu, Recury, Woohookitty, Miaow Miaow, Zubro, GeorgeTSLC, Waldir, Sideris, Mandarax, Sparkit, BD2412, Dvyost, ZeframCochrane, Rjwilmsi, Allenc28, Georgelazenby, AceTracer, AySz88, Leisaie, TheMidnighters, RexNL, Revolving Bugbear, Gheorghe Zamfir, Le Anh-Huy, Chobot, Evilphoenix, Sharkface217, Jared Preston, YurikBot, Koveras, Splamo, RussBot, Geoffharriman, Maw, SluggoOne, CambridgeBayWeather, Philopedia, Nicke L, NawlinWiki, Chick

Lorenagoldsmith, VictorianMutant, DASHBotAV, ClueBot NG, Gareth Griffith-Jones, Katiker, Danisidhe, Vacation9, Echobox1, Snotbot, Braincricket, Widr, Spannerjam, Meniv, Oddbodz, Helpful Pixie Bot, Vt1947, 0zero9nine, BG19bot, Mark Arsten, Suziebeezie, Stirmysoultogigglemode, Harrison 1979, John from Idegon, Ducknish, Ssonnier, Codename Lisa, Mysterious Whisper, JoeCampbell666, Frosty, Gabby Merger, Ieneach fan 'e Esk, Melonkelon, PhantomTech, Dalesideas, Wikkichiky, Penitence, Rockrunnerthecard, Heraclites, Suisuitsu, Reradford, Lemonyhams, Crossleague, Bestofthebest165 and Anonymous: 738

- **Stream of consciousness (narrative mode)** *Source:* https://en.wikipedia.org/wiki/Stream_of_consciousness_(narrative_mode)?oldid=662771787 *Contributors:* Derek Ross, Koyaanis Qatsi, Ortolan88, Mintguy, KF, JDG, Thomas Mills Hinkle, Jahsonic, Ixfd64, IZAK, Pweemeeuw, BigFatBuddha, Ineuw, Gofreddo63, Norwikian, Charles Matthews, Wik, Kaare, Morwen, Saltine, Topbanana, Robbot, Kzhr, Ruakh, Mandel, Wayland, Amir Dekel, Motown Junkie, Advance, Jason Quinn, Christofurio, Neilc, Andycjp, R. fiend, LiDaobing, Karol Langner, Gary D, StewartMine, Tordek ar, Discospinster, Rich Farmbrough, YUL89YYZ, Gronky, Project2501a, Harryfdoherty, Kjayant, Mrbicrevise, Kx1186, GChriss, Jigen III, Gary, D32, Valiantis, WikiParker, Gautam3, Chicopac, Ankur Banerjee, Firsfron, Shreevatsa, Derktar, Stefanomione, Graham87, Buxtehude, Rjwilmsi, Seidenstud, Kinu, Golden Eternity, Bruce1ee, Mahlum~enwiki, RobertG, Flowerparty, Ewlyahoocom, Emiao, David H Braun (1964), CJLL Wright, VolatileChemical, Thodin, Monicasdude, YurikBot, BuddyJesus, Koveras, RussBot, Bhny, Leopold Bloom, ONEder Boy, Rallette, Nlu, Pegship, Closedmouth, Reyk, Jogers, Sugar Bear, Mrblondnyc, SmackBot, Moeron, KnowledgeOfSelf, DCDuring, Unyoyega, Hackinosa, Eskimbot, HalfShadow, Balazs, Buck Mulligan, Ng iman@USA, Urukagina, Chris the speller, LinguistAtLarge, CSWarren, CartoonChess, Davemo, Marcus Brute, Wikipedical, RiseRover, Rory096, Dr. Sunglasses, Loodog, Bohemian tosspot, EdK, RichardF, Samael775~enwiki, TheLostProphet, Uirp, Foxylibrarian, Dreftymac, Dnheff, BrOnXbOmBr21, Malickfan86, TORR, Wolfdog, Stephenjh, W guice, Picaroon, Im.a.lumberjack, Arturobandini, ShelfSkewed, Non lo so., Leviathan09~enwiki, The Amazing Pudding, Omicronpersei8, Thijs!bot, Ante Aikio, Aurelien Langlois, Ryusenshi, K7jetto, Freewilly2009, JAnDbot, Fhqwgads, F. Simon Grant, Magioladitis, Bfx12a9, Jpcohen, Froid, MartinBot, XCrunner1422, JustASimpleMonk, AgarwalSumeet, Pomte, Wiki Raja, Tgeairn, RatSkrew, Numbo3, Agadant, Degelh, Farquad92, Trumpet marietta 45750, Smellycow123, Hubacelgrand, Jevansen, Bothhooks, GrahamHardy, Thedoggedtruth, VolkovBot, A Bourne, Omegastar, Bamadude, TwentySixMots, JoeSachmo, Finlayramsay, Wyseman101, MC Bucky, Hashaw, MachiavellianHorse, GoddersUK, Romuald Wróblewski, SieBot, StAnselm, InfantInquisitor, Dreamafter, Yintan, Mazdakabedi, Polymath618, J steinhaus, Pundit8086, TheBoyWhoBlockdHisOwnShot, LarRan, Raquebarshad, ClueBot, The Thing That Should Not Be, T3hmyth, Mike Klaassen, AmishSexy, Niceguyedc, Trivialist, Passargea, M.A.Kampman, Ngebendi, Cashed1612, Taranet, Marine7, DumZiBoT, MaximillianRiese, Bearsona, Silentecho84, Stitchill, Boreras, Carlotheblue, Anticipation of a New Lover's Arrival, The, Addbot, Experimental Hobo Infiltration Droid, Asfreeas, Tassedethe, Tide rolls, Jojocool117, Jarble, Ben Ben, Yobot, Flabiator, DORC, AnomieBOT, John Holmes II, Ciphers, Sonia, Jim1138, Piano non troppo, S34nc0, Minnecologies, Materialscientist, Wandering Courier, Pdxtwin, Liloumace, Gba030, WalkingFiasco, Omnipaedista, Richard BB, Haritada, Eguygabe, Irbian, FrescoBot, Artimaean, SpacemanSpiff, 5Celcious, Jauhienij, WincakeSpag, Doc2234, Oracleofottawa, LilyKitty, CobraBot, Fayedizard, Onel5969, Rocco9, Rwood128, Diogotorres, Corndog890, AndrewOne, Cosman246, Spobin, Spr3sso, ClueBot NG, Yihaa, Whistleauthor, Snotbot, MerlIwBot, Helpful Pixie Bot, Engranaje, PhnomPencil, CitationCleanerBot, Glacialfox, Eduardofeld, Timothy Gu, Khazar2, Penwatchdog, Mogism, Gibran20133, Fourpassos, Robevans123, WowSuchAuthority, Johnsoniensis, DavidXBarron, Xsophia3x and Anonymous: 322

- **Allegory** *Source:* https://en.wikipedia.org/wiki/Allegory?oldid=672092660 *Contributors:* Mav, Bryan Derksen, The Anome, Tarquin, Malcolm Farmer, Sjc, Toby Bartels, Heron, DennisDaniels, D, Jahsonic, Dcljr, Ihcoyc, Muriel Gottrop~enwiki, Jacquerie27, Conti, Pladask, Colipon, Wetman, Phil Boswell, Robbot, Elonen, Naddy, Wikibot, Aetheling, JerryFriedman, Matt Gies, Halda, Macrakis, Antandrus, CesarFelipe, Histrion, Gary D, Neutrality, Joyous!, Chmod007, Mike Rosoft, Discospinster, Kdammers, Stbalbach, Syp, Mattisgoo, Gershwinrb, Thu, Abroeck, Renice, Bsktcase, Smalljim, Orbst, SpeedyGonsales, Rje, Lysdexia, Jumbuck, Alansohn, Wiki-uk, ExpatEgghead, Jnothman, Lectonar, Garfield226, Wtmitchell, Crablogger, Yuckfoo, Pwqn, Ghirlandajo, Kenyon, Daranz, Mindmatrix, LOL, Rocastelo, Squiddhartha, Stefanomione, Graham87, Ash211, Rjwilmsi, Kinu, Lockley, Bensin, Scartol, Yamamoto Ichiro, FlaBot, SchuminWeb, Ground Zero, Margosbot~enwiki, Nihiltres, Flowerparty, RexNL, Aethralis, Bgwhite, YurikBot, Koveras, I need a name, Hairy Dude, Briaboru, Pigman, Aburad, Bachrach44, Snek01, BlackAndy, Mass147, PhilipC, FlyingPenguins, Bota47, Wknight94, Ms2ger, Crisco 1492, FF2010, Zzuuzz, Imaninjapirate, Closedmouth, ArielGold, Slinberg, Allens, Mr. ATOZ, SmackBot, KnowledgeOfSelf, Unyoyega, KocjoBot~enwiki, Verne Equinox, Lsommerer, Taxee, Gilliam, Hmains, Chris the speller, Bluebot, Enkyklios, Greatgavini, Jfsamper, Nbarth, DHN-bot~enwiki, Colonies Chris, A. B., TrackZero, SenSo, Doh286, Wanjuscha, RandomP, Wybot, DMacks, Sayden, The Fwanksta, SashatoBot, HollywoodHawk, Kuru, John, Buchanan-Hermit, Gobonobo, JoshuaZ, Jimmydare, Fernando S. Aldado~enwiki, Doctor Bumble Bee, Interlingua, Pieguy48, SubSeven, Focomoso, Iridescent, Aeternus, Beno1000, Blehfu, Coffeezombie, Tawkerbot2, JForget, Peter1c, Artemis Kuiper, Rwflammang, Jherm, 3Speed, ShelfSkewed, Neelix, Nilfanion, Cydebot, A876, Goldfritha, Zgystardst, Sam Staton, ST47, JohnnE, DumbBOT, Fourthhorseman, Thijs!bot, Epbr123, Daniel Newman, D4g0thur, Ucanlookitup, Marek69, JustAGal, Qp10qp, AntiVandalBot, Seaphoto, StringRay, Mr Grim Reaper, Modernist, Afaz, MER-C, Ringsjöodjuren, Midnightdreary, Hut 8.5, KEKPΩΨ, Magioladitis, Bongwarrior, VoABot II, Kutu su~enwiki, Cgingold, Allstarecho, Cpl Syx, DerHexer, Philg88, Ntang, Pikazilla, MartinBot, Jay Litman, R'n'B, J.delanoy, Rgoodermote, Extransit, Adasarathy, Johnbod, McSly, Janus Shadowsong, AntiSpamBot, SJP, StoptheDatabaseState, Ossido, Idioma-bot, Deor, 28bytes, VolkovBot, Westfalr3, Johan1298~enwiki, A Ramachandran, Macedonian, Jeff G., Kakoui, Ryan032, Philip Trueman, TXiKiBoT, Sroc, Obenkirane~enwiki, Seraphim, Broadbot, Abdullais4u, LeaveSleaves, Seb az86556, Petero9, Synthebot, Cnilep, EmxBot, Radagast3, SieBot, StAnselm, DavisGL, Caltas, Poikax, Yintan, Oobleshmerfadarkle, Marcercam, Jack Hare, Benea, Hooty88888, Magic9mushroom, OKBot, Reginmund, Firefly322, Wahrmund, Smkstoll, Denisarona, JL-Bot, Martarius, ClueBot, SummerWithMorons, NickCT, The Thing That Should Not Be, Der Golem, Hafspajen, Niceguyedc, MrMetalFLower, HeWasCalledYClept, Arjayay, Tnxman307, Bensoncr, Versus22, Miami33139, GKantaris, Micmachete, Fastily, MrBunko, Jed 20012, Forderip, Grapito123, Tksxpookx20, AVand, Fieldday-sunday, Clementkuehn, AndersBot, Woland1234, Tsange, Tassedethe, Ehrenkater, Alain08, Jarble, DrFO.Tn.Bot, Legobot, Luckas-bot, Yobot, Fraggle81, Mattthefunkyone, Necronaut, Kookyunii, AnomieBOT, KDS4444, Floquenbeam, Rubinbot, ImperatorExercitus, E235, LJHALL, Alexander.xii, LilHelpa, Xqbot, Zad68, Kasimir Katowitsch, Capricorn42, Trap The Drum Wonder, Samiperk, Kithira, GrouchoBot, Armbrust, Omnipaedista, SUBUTAI 314, Zefr, SassoBot, The Interior, Amaury, A70463548, Thehelpfulbot, FrescoBot, Anna Roy, LucienBOT, Sckum555, Pinethicket, Adlerbot, Alpaydin, RedBot, Secret Saturdays, RandomStringOfCharacters, Dude1818, FoxBot, Huckfin0, Lotje, DARTH SIDIOUS 2, Bm9898, Lilhenry77, Rwood128, The Stick Man, J36miles, EmausBot, Cehrabehra, Mk5384, GoingBatty, SofiePedersen, Marish Glides, Rhone, Tommy2010, Wikipelli, Lildawg, Yeepsi, Thecheesykid, Malcolm77, Evanh2008, 1990Jessica, 15turnsm, Prayerfortheworld, Rjmains, MithrandirAgain, Sagaciousphil, AndrewOne, Crochet, Δ, Forteana, Julius f, Sunshine4921, EdoBot, Ghazzard, LM2000, ClueBot NG, Artvoyt, Conmann18, Widr, MaxKen, MerlIwBot, Jorgenev, HMSSolent, Lowercase sigmabot, M00dyb00y, Saetow, Lewis Jackson333, Blueplasticring, YodaRULZ, Snow Blizzard, ChemicalCorpse, Analpoop89, Artsyman, ChrisGualtieri, Sermadison, Khazar2, Manar al Zraiy, Cekempainen, Hendrik.knoche, Mr. Guye, Hmainsbot1, Etjean0905, Joe4522, Snicketts, Graphium, Nirenosnilmot, TheCaptainsPi, Apaukovitz, JustAMuggle, Myconix, Sarah Joy Jones, Sol1, Puthoni, AKiwiDeerPin, Sid 3000, Igel457, Perillus, Rubunny, Earnest worthing, KasparBot and Anonymous: 493

- **Alliteration** *Source:* https://en.wikipedia.org/wiki/Alliteration?oldid=678840719 *Contributors:* Mav, Tarquin, Sjc, Ortolan88, SimonP, Davitf, Robert Foley, Heron, Kchishol1970, Michael Hardy, Ixfd64, Ihcoyc, Ellywa, TUF-KAT, Feedmecereal, Emperorbma, Charles Matthews, Maximus Rex, Jusjih, Ldo, MD87, Gromlakh, Robbot, Psmith, Kristof vt, Texture, Hadal, Wikibot, JackofOz, Wereon, Crculver, Nmg20, Meursault2004, Henry Flower, HellAlex~enwiki, Jorge Stolfi, Andycjp, R. fiend, Jizz, Antandrus, Jossi, JHCC, Thorwald, Mike Rosoft, Discospinster, Solitude, Bishonen, Pavel Vozenilek, Flapdragon, Kjoonlee, Czrisher, Syp, Project2501a, El C, Bobo192, Smalljim, Elipongo, Nk, Kunzite, Sam Korn, Nsaa, Lysdexia, Ranveig, Jumbuck, Ice-Soft-Eng, Brianboru, Alansohn, Eixo, Anthony Appleyard, Wtmitchell, Velella, Keepsleeping, RainbowOfLight, Nibblus, Bsadowski1, Freyr, SteinbDJ, Japanese Searobin, Edwardkerlin, Angr, Anilocra, Camw, Rocastelo, WadeSimMiser, Vekron, Pictureuploader, Prashanthns, Stefanomione, Dpaking, Graham87, Yurik, Mendaliv, Caudron, Wahkeenah, Brighterorange, Joti~enwiki, Yamamoto Ichiro, EvanSeeds, Michaelschmatz, Vsion, RexNL, Gurch, Graeme Hefner, Volunteer Marek, Korg, EamonnPKeane, Kummi, YurikBot, Wavelength, Jimp, Petiatil, Splash, Raquel Baranow, Rsrikanth05, Pseudomonas, Draeco, Finbarr Saunders, Bloodofox, Jaxl, Shultz, Musiclover, JPMcGrath, EEMIV, Daltonls, Zythe, Jhinman, Cmcfarland, Wknight94, Johndrinkwater, Orioane, Johndburger, Thnidu, Theda, Josh3580, H Hog, Spliffy, Curpsbot-unicodify, Allens, Katieh5584, SDS, NeilN, DVD R W, Weiteck, SmackBot, Hangingonastar, Griot~enwiki, KnowledgeOfSelf, CSZero, Unyoyega, Pgk, Naveenrox, Jab843, Monz, Wakuran, Gilliam, Skizzik, E20Ci, ERcheck, Computer Guru, JordeeBec, Ejg930, Aquila9, Klichka, J. Spencer, JavaJake, Kungming2, Baa, Darth Panda, Lazylizards8, Gracenotes, Can't sleep, clown will eat me, Addshore, Amazins490, Gohst, Flyguy649, Valenciano, "alyosha", Mini-Geek, Kuronue, Mtelewicz, DMacks, Zahid Abdassabur, John, Jodamn, Goodnightmush, Hackwrth, Mr. Lefty, Narlee, Ckatz, The Man in Question, 16@r, Stupid Corn, Stwalkerster, SQGibbon, Nwwaew, Ryulong, Abog, PratzStrike, Wjejskenewr, Igoldste, Shultz III, Regal Atrocity, Courcelles, Nkayesmith, Tawkerbot2, JForget, Wolfdog, Hyphen5, RedRollerskate, Dgw, Green caterpillar, ShelfSkewed, Lazulilasher, Anil1956, Penbat, Cydebot, Clownboat, SyntaxError55, Gogo Dodo, Anonymi, Chasingsol, Jim Raynor~enwiki, Bushido Brown, Tkynerd, Julian Mendez, DumbBOT, After Midnight, Daven200520, Thijs!bot, JAF1970, Epbr123, Pajz, Frozenport, Pampas Cat, Mojo Hand, Dalahäst, John254, AgentPeppermint, Natalie Erin, PrescitedEntity, Mentifisto, AntiVandalBot, Luna Santin, Quintote, KP Botany, Nithin-Bekal, Jj137, BigThunderMtn, Dthurston, Ozgod, CraigNKeys, Res2216firestar, Kcowolf, Sluzzelin, JAnDbot, MER-C, M@RIX, RicardoFachada, Ty580, Freedom usually cares, kindly, Greendot1, Canjth, Bongwarrior, VoABot II, Avjoska, TheIsland'sEye, Transcendence, Fusionmix, CattleGirl, Iainsona, Duggy 1138, KConWiki, Scraimer, Styrofoam1994, DerHexer, InvertRect, TheRanger, Mynameisntbob1, Mrathel, MartinBot, Kjhf, Comme le Lapin, Bissinger, Dbc334, Burnedthru, Mschel, LedgendGamer, Paranomia, J.delanoy, Uncle Dick, ZydecoRogue, Extransit, BrokenSphere, Katalaveno, Darkspots, McSly, Mikhail Dvorkin, JayJasper, Rocket71048576, Carvedstars, Tomas-Bat, NewEnglandYankee, Hennessey, Patrick, MKoltnow, Pundit, Kozka, Jc4p, Xiahou, Idioma-bot, VolkovBot, CWii, ABF, Science4sail, Nburden, Chango369w, KitsuneCybe, VasilievVV, Soliloquial, Philip Trueman, Spurius Furius Fusus, DrSlony, Joemommasllama, JayC, Qxz, Cootiequits, Broadbot, Antsam, Abdullais4u, LeaveSleaves, Farmors111, B. Jennings Perry, Vanos13, Madhero88, Rhopkins8, Insanity Incarnate, Tas96, AlleborgoBot, Symane, Quantpole, Angelastic, Logan, PGWG, MrChupon, GarudaZuke, NHRHS2010, Deconstructhis, StAnselm, K. Annoyomous, Jauerback, GerryPerry01, Caltas, Yintan, Archambe, Keilana, Toddst1, Flyer22, Tiptoety, Oxymoron83, Faradayplank, Gangsterls, Tnabtaf, Dancermansi, Dear Reader, Anakin101, Tesi1700, Troy 07, Marciano guerrero, Martarius, ClueBot, John P Hartley, The Thing That Should Not Be, Elzb, FCivish, TheOldJacobite, Uncle Milty, Jaddi27, Zacefron52, Yenemus, PÆon, BlueAmethyst, Zack wadghiri, Excirial, GrogMcGee, Jusdafax, Simonmckenzie, Choubaka, Latoven, 7&6=thirteen, Holothurion, Razorflame, Saebjorn, BOTarate, Kazfernandes, Thingg, Aitias, Versus22, Tigeron, SoxBot III, Life of Riley, XLinkBot, ChyranandChloe, Stickee, Rror, Little Mountain 5, DR4G0NM4N, Anturiaethwr, Skarebo, NellieBly, Noctibus, Gggh, Metodicar, Addbot, Elefant132, Some jerk on the Internet, Guoguo12, Landon1980, Nortonius, Friginator, Tom Ketchum, D0762, NjardarBot, Cst17, Morning277, West.andrew.g, 5 albert square, Doriethurston, Sharpie5982, LarryJeff, Erutuon, Tide rolls, Jan eissfeldt, Luckas-bot, Yobot, 2D, Ptbotgourou, Fraggle81, Cflm001, HieronymousCrowley, Yngvadottir, Wikipedian Penguin, NERVUN, Gongshow, Joshua.ewer, AnomieBOT, Piano non troppo, Kingpin13, English-Patterns, Materialscientist, 90 Auto, ArthurBot, Xqbot, Capricorn42, Maddie!, AbigailAbernathy, Txmy, Derekwashere, Ashershow1, Dangerman200k, RibotBOT, Amaury, 2008saints44, Sophus Bie, D.e.kwan, Nickbeland, Erik9, SD5, Josemanimala, FrescoBot, Ivashchuk303, LucienBOT, Marvel164131, Ugadeee, D'ohBot, Udubjoe, Finalius, Kwiki, Fatedbreath, Citation bot 1, Nevershoutnever36, Pinethicket, I dream of horses, Elockid, Jonesey95, RobinHoudt, Rushbugled13, Hamtechperson, A8UDI, SpaceFlight89, OrlandoMatthews, RandomStringOfCharacters, Diabelli23, Dude1818, Jauhienij, Tim1357, PiRSquared17, Guymontague, Lotje, Vrenator, Weedwhacker128, Satdeep Gill, Caractecus, DARTH SIDIOUS 2, Whisky drinker, Ccrazymann, DarknessShines2, Vinnyzz, EmausBot, John of Reading, Orphan Wiki, Candid145, Tommy2010, ZéroBot, Fæ, MJS1996, K kisses, Water14, Donner60, Damirgraffiti, Orange Suede Sofa, Tara969, ChuispastonBot, DASHBotAV, Ysaimanoj, Xanchester, ClueBot NG, Gareth Griffith-Jones, Joclown, Satellizer, Tricolor Truce, JohnsonL623, MarcoSchuffelen, O.Koslowski, Widr, Spannerjam, Exceedingly Rare, Serene150, Jkneel, Wilstar53, Oddbodz, Helpful Pixie Bot, Poiwaterwater, HMSSolent, DBigXray, BG19bot, Alessadri, Bilal mazhar 88, Teachingarcher, Northamerica1000, ISTB351, Kyrmyzy gul, PhnomPencil, JohnElizabethGray, MusikAnimal, Chris the Paleontologist, Ricordisamoa, Miss Bono, Glacialfox, Klilidiplomus, Mihir26, Sgtlemonpepper, GoShow, AlexJarrell82899, 22dragon22burn, Soulbust, Experty of experties, Mogism, Etjean0905, Ranze, Lugia2453, Telfordbuck, MeadOfPoetry, Pincrete, Γαλαδριήλ, Lfdder, Tentinator, Bumblekapera, Sarah Joy Jones, Pizzagreen, Efabrication, Vincenzo Bacon Quandorf, Ireneshih, Meander78, Lakun.patra, ERL52pitt, Whisham, Imconfusednow, JohnSHicks, Monkbot, Neiyah123, ChamithN, Loraof, Emipef, SoccerQueen2014, Brubarrett, ThePagedChanger123, KasparBot, Bradso0554, Glacialfrost, Ashor46 and Anonymous: 1096

- **Amplification (rhetoric)** *Source:* https://en.wikipedia.org/wiki/Amplification_(rhetoric)?oldid=665709953 *Contributors:* Discospinster, Daniel Case, Roboto de Ajvol, Unyoyega, Gobonobo, Anne97432, Ridernyc, SieBot, Wahrmund, 1ForTheMoney, Addbot, HerculeBot, Goregore~enwiki, Luckas-bot, Yobot, KamikazeBot, Bility, Rubinbot, PigFlu Oink, Trappist the monk, GoingBatty, Spannerjam, Frze, ALT88, BethNaught, Nmg47, Pitpenguins8718 and Anonymous: 9

- **Anagram** *Source:* https://en.wikipedia.org/wiki/Anagram?oldid=678879552 *Contributors:* Derek Ross, Brion VIBBER, Mav, Bryan Derksen, The Anome, Tarquin, AstroNomer~enwiki, Andre Engels, Arvindn, Fritzlein, Christian List, PierreAbbat, Ortolan88, SimonP, FvdP, Richhill, Mintguy, DW, Montrealais, Fransvannes, Steverapaport, JohnOwens, Michael Hardy, JakeVortex, Dante Alighieri, Liftarn, Chuck SMITH, Yann, Delirium, Geoffrey~enwiki, Paul A, Shimmin, Ahoerstemeier, Den fjättrade ankan~enwiki, Jfitzg, Cimon Avaro, Grin, Dod1, Palfrey, Eralos, Lee M, Complex Analysis, Iseeaboar, Ideyal, Charles Matthews, Andy G, Stismail, Dysprosia, KRS, Maximus Rex, Hyacinth, Topbanana, Wiwaxia, Shantavira, Phil Boswell, Robbot, Paul Klenk, Psychonaut, Paul G, Wikibot, JackofOz, Wereon, Raeky, Wayland, Mattflaschen, Radagast, David Gerard, Matthew Stannard, Barbara Shack, Tadpole, Itay2222~enwiki, Jgritz, Frencheigh, LarryGilbert, Yekrats, Mboverload, Joshuapaquin, Macrakis, Jrdioko, ChicXulub, John Foley, Bodnotbod, Icairns, Keresaspa, Publunch, Abdull, Chepry, Freakofnurture, Spiffy sperry, Davidbod, Pyrop, Rich Farmbrough, Guanabot, Andros 1337, Kzzl, Mani1, Pavel Vozenilek, Andrejj, Kbh3rd, Petersam, Elwikipedista~enwiki, Brian0918, Frenchgeek, Bennylin, Walden, Tom, Razor X, Bobo192, Utopianfiat, Stesmo, Marblespire, LuoShengli, Polylerus, Mareino, HasharBot~enwiki, Faulenzer, Alansohn, Anthony Appleyard, Arthena, Borisblue, Andrewpmk, M7, JoaoRicardo, Saga City, Max Naylor, Papovik, Woohookitty, Swamp Ig, Orz, Pufferfish101, Pictureuploader, Ashmoo, Graham87, Paulpan, JIP, BorgHunter, Coemgenus, Koavf, Rillian, Sdornan, Bubba73, Sango123, Fish and karate, FlaBot, Ground Zero, RMc, Otets, Riki, Gareth E Kegg, Chobot, DVdm, Dzzl, Timothykhoo, Gdrbot, YurikBot, Kiscica, Aminto, Jtkiefer, Stephenb, Archelon, Gaius Cornelius, Sandpiper, Ff4eva, Astral, Grafen, Cooker, Rmky87, Moe Epsilon, Jgoard, Tony1, Deckiller, MicroFeet, Action potential, Asarelah, DRosenbach, Thnidu, Mike Selinker, SMcCandlish, GraemeL, JLaTondre, Tyrhinis, Aewold, Schizobullet, Coquigamer, Yakudza, SmackBot, KnowledgeOfSelf, McGeddon, Jfurr1981, Rastapopoulos, Lukas.S, Siradia, Gilliam, Hmains, Chris the speller, Ciacchi, H2ppyme, Thaimodz, Jprg1966, Octahedron80, JGXenite, H Bruthzoo, Huji, Salmar, NYKevin, Can't sleep, clown will eat me, Shalom Yechiel, JonHarder, Rrburke, MDCollins, JesseRafe, Tlusťa, Ziyingjiang, MichaelBillington, Dreadstar, Jowston, Hgilbert, ShadowUltra, Vriullop, JzG, Pliny, Joshua Scott, JHunterJ, BillFlis, Slakr, Balabinba, Ace Class Shadow, Novangelis, MTSbot~enwiki, Jona2112, Norm mit, J Di, Igoldste, CapitalR, Phoenixrod, Unidyne, Galo1969X, The Font, Kalliope~enwiki, Ckuzyk, ShelfSkewed, Kalaong, WeggeBot, Fordmadoxfraud, Polyorchid, Besieged, Tom mai78101, Suzannah Subrosa, Optimist on the run, UberScienceNerd, Sigmund1989, Eubulide, Mglovesfun, Thijs!bot, Epbr123, Vertium, SGGH, Aericanwizard, Adri K., Nick Number, Escarbot, Luna Santin, Emeraldcityserendipity, Teamphysicks, Dane 1981, Jezzerk, Daytona2, Sluzzelin, JAnDbot, Gedeyenite, TheBooRadley, Adjwilley, Sophie means wisdom, Andonic, TAnthony, Y2kcrazyjoker4, .anacondabot, Frankly speaking, Magioladitis, VoABot II, Ballyhooha, Wrightaway, ClovisPt, Huseyx2, Allstarecho, Mwvandersteen, Philg88, Ericster08, CliffC, Bballoakie, Mschel, J.delanoy, The dark lord trombonator, Trusilver, Bogey97, Rob Burbidge, 88888, Thaurisil, Funguy06, QuasiAbstract, Pyrospirit, Shadowfox98, NewEnglandYankee, Botx, Brogine, Ajfweb, WinterSpw, Disco hat, CardinalDan, DraxusD, UnicornTapestry, VolkovBot, LouisWins, Ryan032, TXiKiBoT, D4S, Erik the Red 2, Oconnor663, Rei-bot, Dendodge, Slysplace, Mannafredo, Dragana666, Sandman1701, StuartDD, January2007, Ar-wiki, Vadimn, Mknoll1, Ziphon, Turgan, HiDrNick, Kktor, GirasoleDE, Ceanne, DesertEagle73, Guthriewinters, Munkelin, Portalian, Dprice99, Mickalicious711, BotMultichill, Ravid0520, Skootles, Yintan, Bubbulubbaloo, Greenhound, Crowstar, BenoniBot~enwiki, Mad Hlaine Larkin, D4tis, Beemer69, Explicit, Goldenliquid, Faithlessthewonderboy, ClueBot, HujiBot, The Thing That Should Not Be, Newzild, Cygnis insignis, Polyamorph, CounterVandalismBot, Shawnallen, Trivialist, Hmpxrii, Andrei Iosifovich, Excirial, Jusdafax, Jefflayman, Jgp123, Lartoven, Lumpy27, Promethean, Sugarfreak 07, Cexycy, Morel, 7, Ybisaabb, Montaced, ConradTF3, Magellan545, Fastily, WildMIKE123, Helloperson212, Valvin, HexaChord, Narayansg, TheNeutroniumAlchemist, Hartfelt, Ronhjones, Martín Cerón, Download, Morning277, Glane23, Bassbonerocks, AnnaFrance, Tassedethe, Numbo3-bot, Theking17825, Lightbot, InbredScorpion, Legobot, Luckas-bot, Yobot, Cyanoa Crylate, Plazmatyk, DemocraticLuntz, GGsYoyo, JackieBot, Piano non troppo, Materialscientist, Citation bot, Blankname123, Artgan, Parthian Scribe, Janet Davis, SJkoDo, Capricorn42, TracyMcClark, Nasnema, Mononomic, DSisyphBot, GrouchoBot, Brandon5485, Auréola, Aaron Kauppi, Henry25, HamburgerRadio, Jacobmenkus, Cardiacparade, HRoestBot, Onthegogo, Gourisgupta, Rathrobynrye, Lars Washington, Erector Euphonious, Dinamik-bot, Miracle Pen, Stephenshero, Tbhotch, RobertMfromLI, RjwilmsiBot, In ictu oculi, EmausBot, WikitanvirBot, RA0808, Senor Reparar, Lanceallenhall, Wikipelli, Werieth, ZéroBot, John Cline, Ichthyoid, Hodgdon's secret garden, Unreal7, AndrewOne, Molod, PowerToast, Pooja Radhakrishnan, EdoBot, ClueBot NG, Riya Sharma Pune, NathanaelTaylor, Elcrixan, Szszszsj, Compfreak7, Dainomite, Don of Cherry, Grouches101, ChrisGualtieri, GoShow, Cbielich, தமிழ்க்கணிசில், AlneltheGreat, MisterTrollMan123, OcelotHod, Dara Allarah, Darth Sitges, Biggiemike, A catnap comic, KevinHebbeler, DudeWithAFeud, Qwertyxp2000, TranquilHope, Pankaj.editor, AychAych, Quantumofthought, Childlovertommy, The Drarry Fangirl, MoonPlaysAll, KasparBot and Anonymous: 559

- **Asyndeton** *Source:* https://en.wikipedia.org/wiki/Asyndeton?oldid=663008635 *Contributors:* Michael Hardy, Ihcoyc, Ellywa, Kingturtle, Altenmann, JerryFriedman, Wmahan, Manuel Anastácio, Thorwald, Bill Thayer, NetBot, Immanuel Giel, Rocastelo, Stefanomione, Dpaking, Wragge, FlaBot, YurikBot, Anomalocaris, Nolanus, SmackBot, SashatoBot, IvanLanin, WillowW, John254, KEKPΩΨ, CapnPrep, Gwern, Андрей Романенко, VolkovBot, TXiKiBoT, Tpb, K. Annoyomous, Oxymoron83, Keinstein, ComputerGeezer, Addbot, Goregore~enwiki, Luckas-bot, Anypodetos, AnomieBOT, Citation bot, Achillestendon69, Petropoxy (Lithoderm Proxy), ApusChin, FoxBot, AXRL, EmausBot, ZéroBot, ClueBot NG, Spannerjam, Dan653, ColonelHenry, Aphillipsmusique and Anonymous: 24

- **Bathos** *Source:* https://en.wikipedia.org/wiki/Bathos?oldid=676024375 *Contributors:* SimonP, Edward, Michael Hardy, Angela, Hyacinth, Wetman, Rfc1394, Geogre, Bfinn, Bkonrad, Kpalion, Eckhart Wörner~enwiki, Huwr, Cyopardi, Rich Farmbrough, Bishonen, Mrbicrevise, Jaredfaulkner, Pearle, Oolong, Hektor, !!, Ghirlandajo, Woohookitty, DavidFarmbrough, Kesla, Biederman, Quiddity, Miserlou, DVdm, Chris Capoccia, Tenebrae, Tony1, Nlu, Joysofpi, SmackBot, Chris the speller, Nbarth, HisSpaceResearch, Melampus, MatthewPetty, GDallimore, Wolfdog, W guice, Neelix, Cydebot, Travelbird, Alaibot, Folantin, Ctashian, Scottandrewhutchins, Colin MacLaurin, Albany NY, Zouavman Le Zouave, Bennelliott, SabreWolfy, Insanity Incarnate, Logan, Flyer22, SummerWithMorons, Bobman108, Badmachine, Addbot, Xp54321, Totorotroll, Goregore~enwiki, AnomieBOT, Apollo1758, Лудольф, LlywelynII, AbigailAbernathy, Ubcule, J04n, Omnipaedista, FrescoBot, SoloUnEditor, Merlion444, Hbrakhage, Jeffrd10, Curlyyklr, Richard1962, Woederze, ClueBot NG, Spannerjam, BattyBot, KidA424, Bjhodge8, BenStein69 and Anonymous: 56

- **Caesura** *Source:* https://en.wikipedia.org/wiki/Caesura?oldid=675953599 *Contributors:* Ihcoyc, Emperorbma, Vincent Ramos, Hyacinth, Hajor, Ianhowlett, Brockert, Chameleon, SarekOfVulcan, Fredcondo, ArthurDenture, Klemen Kocjancic, Adashiel, Skal, Silence, Nicke Lilltroll~enwiki, Alansohn, Caesura, Ringbang, Kevin Hayes, Jwanders, Tabletop, Jacob Finn, Remurmur, FlaBot, Great Deku Tree, EamonnPKeane, Darsie, RussBot, Welsh, Zwobot, S. Neuman, 21655, Closedmouth, LeonardoRob0t, Stumps, Dfloren1, SmackBot, Eaglizard, Edgar181, Wall-Lyneaux, Bluebot, Persian Poet Gal, Fresma~enwiki, MalafayaBot, Nbarth, Williamlear, Criacow, Ryan Roos, Attys, OrbiliusMagister, Ourai, Backstabb, Tominator~enwiki, Lfbayer, Xcentaur, Rambam rashi, AVIosad, Lo2u, Huddahbuddah, Thijs!bot, YK Times, George the Rhino, A4, Feeeshboy, Gwern, Riccardobot, R'n'B, Smartguy0, Deor, VolkovBot, Tavix, FinnWiki, Dpsaves, VVVBot, Saxstudio, Dcattell, Neznanec, Martarius, ClueBot, PipepBot, Kafka Liz, Cenarium, El bot de la dieta, Addbot, Wakablogger2, NjardarBot, Redheylin, Legobot, IDangerMouse, RibotBOT, FrescoBot, RicHard-59, RQPS, Bmclaughlin9, Dauthier, Jfmantis, Georgewquinn, Marish Glides, Άρτεμις, Solarra, ZéroBot, Vanished user kweiru239aqwijur3, L Kensington, Mentibot, Wilbysuffolk, ClueBot NG, Ethg242, Gilderien, Davidiad, Eyeless in Gaza, Metalello, Hmainsbot1, Lugia2453, Inanygivenhole, DtheZombie and Anonymous: 75

- **Distancing effect** *Source:* https://en.wikipedia.org/wiki/Distancing_effect?oldid=668924649 *Contributors:* Michael Hardy, Jahsonic, Tregoweth, Editor B, Rbellin, DHN, Wayland, DocWatson42, Matthead, Hob, Joyous!, LeeHunter, Alansohn, Nightstallion, CWH, 25or6to4, Stefanomione, Urbane Legend, The wub, FayssalF, Hairy Dude, NYScholar, Seanver~enwiki, Stijndon, Arthur Rubin, Davidals, Jeremy Butler, SmackBot, Thumperward, Neo-Jay, Dumpendebat, Keith Lehwald, VMS Mosaic, Bardsandwarriors, UK-Logician-2006, LeoNomis, Khait, Cody5, Wolfdog, Morganfitzp, Cydebot, Dancter, In Defense of the Artist, Thijs!bot, AntiVandalBot, Darklilac, Pixelface, JAnDbot, Freshacconci, Girdi, Froid, Coughinink, StarX, Shawn in Montreal, Redmagic, Hypermusic~enwiki, STBotD, Philip Trueman, Tantalizing Posey, Spkfilm, Flyer22, XDanielx, ClueBot, DionysosProteus, Namcurrienguyen, Nipper1500m, RyanCross, Addbot, Yobot, Bsimmons666, Jim1138, Omnipaedista, Kahoun, Jiří Janíček, Rushbugled13, Mx96, LilyKitty, TjBot, John of Reading, Orphan Wiki, ClueBot NG, Badgerstick, Helpful Pixie Bot, Pblchkn, Susiesongling, KFFOWLER, Hong12kong, Fixuture, Bnyantuka, Bstouttt, Pinklaine and Anonymous: 66

- **Euphuism** *Source:* https://en.wikipedia.org/wiki/Euphuism?oldid=661520021 *Contributors:* Paul Barlow, Ihcoyc, Charles Matthews, Burschik, Robert K S, FlaBot, Jlittlet, Rolf-Peter Wille, JLaTondre, SmackBot, AlexTornado~enwiki, Mitrius, Cybercobra, The Font, Neelix, Cydebot, Thijs!bot, .anacondabot, Magioladitis, Chiswick Chap, Cnilep, Wrightcj01, Icarusgeek, Xme, Addbot, Yobot, KamikazeBot, Jim1138, Erud, Capricorn42, Erik9bot, I dream of horses, Lotje, Lobsterthermidor, Crosslegged, ClueBot NG, Pamplifier, Julian Felsenburgh and Anonymous: 20

- **Hyperbole** *Source:* https://en.wikipedia.org/wiki/Hyperbole?oldid=674115222 *Contributors:* Mav, Tarquin, Ed Poor, Andre Engels, Mjb, Patrick, Michael Hardy, Bewildebeast, Karada, Ellywa, BevRowe, Docu, DropDeadGorgias, Aimaz, AugPi, Rossami, Vzbs34, Nikai, Hashar, Mbstone, Dcoetzee, David Latapie, Haukurth, Furrykef, Paul-L~enwiki, Italo Svevo, Ldo, Aleph4, Robbot, Burn the asylum, Rfc1394, Academic Challenger, LGagnon, Hadal, Mattflaschen, Ancheta Wis, DJSupreme23, JimD, Macrakis, Jackol, Andycjp, Antandrus, Jh51681, Thorwald, Mormegil, Perey, Poccil, Discospinster, Kooo, Goochelaar, Indil, Kwamikagami, MPS, Bobo192, Meggar, Matt Britt, Toh, Shlomital, Sam Korn, Alansohn, Anthony Appleyard, GenkiNeko, Corwin8, Fritzpoll, Jaw959, Melaen, Simer190, Computerjoe, Marasmusine, WadeSimMiser, Firien, Macaddct1984, Toussaint, Stefanomione, Palica, Ashmoo, Graham87, Ryajinor, Offtherails, Afterwriting, Matt Deres, Tumble, RexNL, Xollob, TruthInEvidence, Alfadog, Vanished user psdfiwnef3niurunfiuh234ruhfwdb7, DVdm, KwisatzDan, YurikBot, RobotE, Sceptre, RussBot, Lincolnite, Aree, TeeEmCee, Kyorosuke, Rsrikanth05, Wimt, Aeusoes1, Worldruler20, Apokryltaros, Brandon, Wknight94, Ms2ger, Jimblackler, Raistlin8r, Deville, Zzuuzz, Vicarious, Spliffy, Sugar Bear, Kungfuadam, NeilN, Tyomitch, タチコマ robot, Winick88, SmackBot, MattieTK, Unschool, Royalguard11, Hydrogen Iodide, C.Fred, D C McJonathan, Eskimbot, The Ronin, Canthusus, Yamaguchi 先生, Gilliam, Ohnoitsjamie, Skizzik, Durova, Bodil~enwiki, CrookedAsterisk, MalafayaBot, Tsca.bot, Can't sleep, clown will eat me, Winston-Smith, RedHillian, Mosca, Dreadstar, Only, Mwtoews, Where, Vina-iwbot~enwiki, Andrei Stroe, SashatoBot, Just.enough.luck, Kreuzfeld, Javit, Majorclanger, Stwalkerster, Noah Salzman, Martinp23, Takintadayyon, Iridescent, IvanLanin, Ewulp, Balldontlie, George100, FatalError, SkyWalker, JForget, Wolfdog, Ale jrb, Wafulz, Ventifax, Addict 2006, Alexbuirds, KyraVixen, Jom~enwiki, CWY2190, Jamu, Fungible, 1sjohnlee, .mdk., DShantz, Penbat, Mike 7, Nauticashades, Cydebot, Fukutu, MC10, Gogo Dodo, Flowerpotman, Christian75, Chrislk02, Mattisse, Rpassero, Thijs!bot, Epbr123, SkonesMickLoud, Mojo Hand, Marek69, Grayshi, Mentifisto, AntiVandalBot, Seaphoto, Cacahuate, DarkAudit, LibLord, Jhsounds, Spencer, Codem01, Myanw, Serpent's Choice, Deflective, Leuko, Dar book, LittleOldMe, Bakilas, Cokert, Bongwarrior, VoABot II, AtticusX, CattleGirl, Becksguy, Midgrid, Ihafez, Animum, Mlsquad, IvoShandor, Wikifan0101, Rettetast, Mostly water, DBlomgren, Aeeiou, J.delanoy, Pharaoh of the Wizards, Zoara, Numbo3, Sp3000, Uncle Dick, Extransit, Darth Mike, Zabrak, Gurchzilla, NewEnglandYankee, Dhaluza, Fltchr, LaughingVulcan, CardinalDan, Idioma-bot, X!, Kirby1103, VolkovBot, Macedonian, Dark-Archer, Cguuiperikdfikf, Philip Trueman, TXiKiBoT, A4bot, NPrice, Helgers7, Nekonome, Leafyplant, Sanfranman59, Eubulides, Joseph A. Spadaro, MDfoo, Falcon8765, Enviroboy, ATG77401, Logan, Celestial.sticker, SieBot, Tealeuph, Meltonkt, K. Annoyomous, Hertz1888, Yintan, Flyer22, Oxymoron83, Harry~enwiki, Csloomis, Techman224, Manway, OKBot, Nancy, Nn123645, Canglesea, Explicit, Atif.t2, Clue-Bot, Shruti14, The Thing That Should Not Be, Rjd0060, Abhinav, CowmanII, RashersTierney, Uncle Milty, CounterVandalismBot, Alexbot, Jusdafax, Dasheepslaya, Estirabot, Ember of Light, Razorflame, Ulmedas, Versus22, Vanished user uih38riiw4hjlsd, DumZiBoT, Vibrato5, Pengolodh, Duncan, WikiHead, WikiDao, Vianello, Rush242, Addbot, Percivl, Otisjimmy1, Nz26, Ronhjones, Vishnava, Tills, Download, Glane23, Chzz, Kyle1278, 5 albert square, Aleex3, Thewonderidiot, Mbinebri, Tide rolls, Krano, Mjquinn id, HerculeBot, Goregore~enwiki, Artichoke-Boy, Luckas-bot, Yobot, Ptbotgourou, Fraggle81, KamikazeBot, Wiki Roxor, Jim1138, Cptnono, Piano non troppo, LlywelynII, Are you ready for IPv6?, 90 Auto, Obersachsebot, Capricorn42, Wperdue, Fol de rol troll, RibotBOT, Bellerophon, Shateraftermath1, Sophus Bie, Koala33, David McDonald, عبد المؤمن, Michael93555, Connoiseur, Not done enough work really, Bouott, Javert, StriderTol, Pinethicket, Wmp13, Tinton5, Pikiwyn, NarSakSasLee, SkyMachine, Dinamik-bot, Vrenator, Luver Bunny, Tbhotch, DARTH SIDIOUS 2, AXRL, Beyond My Ken, Navyman9013, Skamecrazy123, Polly12323, EmausBot, Catoman4000, Super48paul, Amish leader, Tommy2010, K6ka, Anirudh Emani, Erpert, Thecheesykid, Mz7, AvicBot, White Trillium, Fæ, GreenNintendo, Unreal7, Zap Rowsdower, FinalRapture, Wayne Slam, Wagino 20100516, Calliostoma, Siparuna, L Kensington, Donner60, SemanticMantis, HandsomeFella, GrayFullbuster, 28bot, Rocketrod1960, Petrb, ClueBot NG, Ozhamada, Caute AF, MelbourneStar, This lousy T-shirt, Lord Roem, Cntras, Primergrey, Rezabot, Widr, Rockhayb, 16benedictj, Theopolisme, Jk2q3jrklse, Helpful Pixie Bot, Alistr woitkowiak, Calidum, Calabe1992, DBigXray, Iluvatlantis, Roberticus, Northamerica1000, Hza a 9, MusikAnimal, Davidiad, Samokhin13, Assassinburrito, HMman, Glacialfox, Morning Sunshine, HumanNaturOriginal, Lukriscamirobgnr, WikiGuider, SupernovaExplosion, Mrt3366, Mediran, Bob12341234, MadGuy7023, JYBot, Qwertytrains, Spray787, Lugia2453, Rfassbind, Theo's Little Bot, Lfdder, Pwnage-619, Glaisher, Jsanders0705, Esteph18, Gabe.Jon, Library Guy, Applause52, Itsalleasy, Local4554, Garrrick, Danglemuffin, TranquilHope, GeorgeB15, Squinge, Gamingforfun365, Faithd1991 and Anonymous: 783

- **Imagery** *Source:* https://en.wikipedia.org/wiki/Imagery?oldid=678671114 *Contributors:* Michael Hardy, Daggerbox, Niteowlneils, Saaga, Andycjp, Freakofnurture, Paul August, Bobo192, Reprah, Snowolf, Ish ishwar, RainbowOfLight, Sciurinæ, Angr, Lochaber, Camw, Encyclopedist, Jeff3000, Dysepsion, RxS, MarnetteD, Yamamoto Ichiro, RexNL, Gurch, CJLL Wright, The Rambling Man, Sceptre, Anomalocaris, Welsh, Catamorphism, Moe Epsilon, Dv82matt, Crisco 1492, 21655, Junglecat, TLSuda, DVD R W, SmackBot, Canthusus, Mike McGregor (Can), Gilliam, Chris the speller, Bob the ducq, Can't sleep, clown will eat me, Andy120290, Nodnarb125, Chwech, Atzbacher2, Kuru, John, 16@r, JHunterJ, Werdan7, Stwalkerster, Optakeover, RichardF, BranStark, Iridescent, Vivaelnorte07, Tawkerbot2, JForget, Wolfdog, Dgw, Cydebot, Stopmenow100, Asenine, Alaibot, Vanished User jdksfajlasd, Epbr123, Marek69, RFerreira, Dfrg.msc, Sturm55, Spencer, Zidane tribal, Mathmagus37, CosineKitty, T L Miles, Kerotan, Connormah, Bongwarrior, VoABot II, CTF83!, Animum, 28421u2232nfenfcenc, JaGa, FisherQueen, MartinBot, Ortensia, Krushdiva, Juansidious, Xcitfan, Bus stop, J.delanoy, Uncle Dick, Kpmiyapuram, Darkspots, NewEnglandYankee, K hallenb, Heshy613, Wikieditor06, CWii, Philip Trueman, Oshwah, Zidonuke, Technopat, Lradrama, Waycool27, Tfrey54, Shanata, Enigmaman, Enviroboy, Coffee, TJRC, Tiddly Tom, Docta247, Oxymoron83, Aflumpire, Dcattell, Pinkadelica, Escape Orbit,

Smashville, Atif.t2, ClueBot, Treharne, NicoBattersby, Alexzhander, Mike Klaassen, Truco, 05waltersb, Orderspoke~enwiki, Vivio Testarossa, 032gavmal, SchreiberBike, LobStoR, La Pianista, Tofu-chan, Thingg, Aitias, Kryon562, Cyberdalek, Versus22, Zachroth, Vanished user uih38riiw4hjlsd, XLinkBot, SwirlBoy39, Swimmingchic345, NAL400, Junior6756, Skarebo, Dsanderson14, Addbot, Friginator, Ihatefindingausername, Random1ofmany, Fieldday-sunday, McGillis117, Cst17, Bassbonerocks, 5 albert square, Tohd8BohaithuGh1, II MusLiM HyBRiD II, Washburnmav, AmeliorationBot, Eric-Wester, AnomieBOT, Kingpin13, Materialscientist, Limideen, Rtyq2, Teddks, FrescoBot, Koc61, Miracle Pen, Kookaburra17, Mean as custard, Locks13, Zaixionito, K6ka, ZéroBot, Thine Antique Pen, ClueBot NG, Jack Greenmaven, MelbourneStar, O.Koslowski, Calabe1992, DBigXray, Atsamp, Mdann52, ProjectTermina, JSR11, Lugia2453, 069952497a, Katherineissexy, Daydreamers, Jakec, DavidLeighEllis, Michael.bez, Ugog Nizdast, Aubreybardo, Harivarshan, Kukicolo, Ridhwan786, AlphonseW, Olibob123, Nicole200004, Evannerraw, Woahimagirk and Anonymous: 401

- **Theme (narrative)** *Source:* https://en.wikipedia.org/wiki/Theme_(narrative)?oldid=677549790 *Contributors:* Jahsonic, Silvonen, Haukurth, Robbot, Bradenm, Wereon, Mattflaschen, Xeresblue, Andycjp, Roachgod, WpZurp, Neutrality, Ukexpat, Mike Rosoft, Discospinster, Eel, Lovelac7, Dbachmann, Paul August, Shanes, C1k3, Triona, Icundell, Bobo192, Longhair, Hintha, Alansohn, Arthena, Creedrapso, Logologist, Valiantis, Velella, ClockworkSoul, Bsadowski1, Deror avi, WadeSimMiser, Stefanomione, Dysepsion, Artailraven, Deafgeek, Enzo Aquarius, Rjwilmsi, Lars T., Donn Smith, Gurch, Bgwhite, Borgx, Dnik, Wiki alf, Moe Epsilon, Wknight94, Shepard, Resolute, SmackBot, 1dragon, Prodego, InverseHypercube, Hydrogen Iodide, Jagged 85, Jab843, Nathan.tang, Gilliam, Hmains, Mazeface, Keegan, Jprg1966, Greatgavini, DHN-bot~enwiki, Darth Panda, A. B., VirtualSteve, Can't sleep, clown will eat me, Maksim-bot, Addshore, RedHillian, Zuby555, Snapping-Turtle, Salamurai, Wikipedical, Will Beback, Michael miceli, Scetoaux, Mr. Lefty, Applejuicefool, Alethiophile, A Clown in the Dark, Snezzy, Iridescent, Ewulp, Tawkerbot2, JForget, Tjkiesel, Bardiak, Goldfritha, Zginder, Synergy, DumbBOT, Alaibot, UberScienceNerd, JamesAM, Thijs!bot, Epbr123, Earth KING, Möchtegern, A3RO, Escarbot, Mentifisto, Bi11yjo3lou5, AntiVandalBot, Pizzazzle, Leuko, Robina Fox, Maryfrancesfahey, TheEditrix2, Bongwarrior, VoABot II, Wtstar, Shablog, WikkiedDemon, Cat-five, Catgut, CheetahMan1, Schumi555, Der-Hexer, Ángel Luis Alfaro, MartinBot, EyeSerene, Anaxial, Tgeairn, J.delanoy, Trusilver, Amitakanekar, Cem59, Katalaveno, Vanished user g454XxNpUVWvxzlr, Sd31415, Heero Kirashami, Cometstyles, Vanished user 39948282, Pdcook, Useight, Wikipedian1234, Piemaster89, Deor, MDTeacher, Mrh30, Hersfold, Philip Trueman, TXiKiBoT, Cremepuff222, Billinghurst, Michaeldsuarez, Eve Teschlemacher, Skarz, Spitfire8520, AlleborgoBot, SieBot, Mikemoral, Nubiatech, Scarian, Malcolmxl5, RJaguar3, Keilana, Bentogoa, Flyer22, Grimey109, Arknascar44, Faradayplank, Steven Crossin, Alex.muller, StaticGull, Mygerardromance, Soyseñorsnibbles, Explicit, Atif.t2, ClueBot, GorillaWarfare, TransporterMan, The Thing That Should Not Be, Vespertineflora, Jtchap05, Mike Klaassen, Drmies, LionsPhil, Uncle Milty, Yummyboy1, CounterVandalismBot, Blanchardb, LizardJr8, Dylan620, Auntof6, Robert Skyhawk, Excirial, Sisterdetestai, Vanisheduser12345, Lartoven, Beartone, Huntthetroll, Frozen4322, Thingg, Aitias, SoxBot III, Egmontaz, Vanished user uih38riiw4hjlsd, Runefrost, XLinkBot, Fastily, Sammy32, Smithck0, Gelzo, Jovianeye, Little Mountain 5, Avoided, WikHead, SilvonenBot, Noctibus, Thatguyflint, Addbot, Vorpal192, Some jerk on the Internet, Tcncv, Meowmix4jo, Fieldday-sunday, Fluffernutter, Download, Glane23, Bassbonerocks, Nickin, AndersBot, Favonian, Myheartinchile, Tide rolls, Cuprum, Math Champion, Fraggle81, Amirobot, THEN WHO WAS PHONE?, QueenCake, Tempodivalse, Juliancolton Alternative, AnomieBOT, Andrewrp, Kristen Eriksen, Rjanag, Killiondude, Jim1138, Neptune5000, Piano non troppo, Kingpin13, Materialscientist, RobertEves92, ImperatorExercitus, Maxis ftw, Kgraves001, LilHelpa, Estlandia~enwiki, Puert0ricanman4, Voksen, AbigailAbernathy, Amaury, Doulos Christos, CnkALTDS, 69 editor, Editor182, Sarwicked, Sesu Prime, Dreampsy, Tangent747, Tobby72, Vinceouca, Michael93555, Chinokitty08, QuintusQuill, Profsjg, DivineAlpha, HamburgerRadio, Citation bot 1, I dream of horses, Trijnstel, Dude1818, Reconsider the static, Vrenator, Horrorjuice, FrankDev, Diannaa, Weedwhacker128, Tbhotch, Reach Out to the Truth, Keegscee, DARTH SIDIOUS 2, Jordankent, RjwilmsiBot, Luosa Schwartz, EmausBot, GeneralCheese, Davejohnsan, Acather96, Az29, Marish Glides, NotAnonymous0, Challisrussia, Wikipelli, Jargoness, Traxs7, Kevinzaft, 1234r00t, Wayne Slam, Rcsprinter123, Barrrower, Sailsbystars, ClamDip, VictorianMutant, 28bot, Frozen Wind, Petrb, ClueBot NG, Skoot13, Widr, Spannerjam, Theopolisme, Helpful Pixie Bot, Txrazy, Extflowex, Strike Eagle, DBigXray, F. Armstrong Green, Cilix1329, Elanimador200, Wiki13, Metricopolus, Layali.elkhameesi, Peskybuckwater, Anbu121, BattyBot, Tpu778, Riley Huntley, Teammm, SergeantHippyZombie, ChrisGualtieri, Webclient101, Lugia2453, Frosty, Jamesx12345, Wywin, Kevin12xd, Taliptako, SnarkyShark, 1234google1234, Dragonister, JamesMoose, EvergreenFir, Ginsuloft, Thewikiguru1, Omgreally1010101010101010101, BluePhantom321, JaconaFrere, Leflerz, Vieque, TheQ Editor, Noahthesmartguy, TranquilHope, Alejandrox88, Jackson76239052307u0976487456, MCBC6421 and Anonymous: 748

- **Metonymy** *Source:* https://en.wikipedia.org/wiki/Metonymy?oldid=675415345 *Contributors:* Vicki Rosenzweig, XJaM, Vaganyik, Ortolan88, Thomas Mills Hinkle, Bdesham, Michael Hardy, GTBacchus, SebastianHelm, BevRowe, TUF-KAT, Andres, Haukurth, Furrykef, Spikey, Mackensen, Dale Arnett, Altenmann, Dduck, Ashley Y, Rfc1394, SchmuckyTheCat, Hadal, Pko, Gerv, Pengo, Ancheta Wis, Matt Gies, Centrx, Smjg, DocWatson42, Jhf, Dratman, Requiem18th, Macrakis, Golbez, Christopherlin, Rheun, Noe, Doops, Mukerjee, Roisterer, Karl-Henner, MRSC, Neutrality, Sonett72, Kaustuv, Zondor, Flex, Eyrian, Discospinster, Rich Farmbrough, Ericamick, Kwamikagami, Kyz, Shanes, RoyBoy, Mike Schwartz, ZayZayEM, JW1805, Red Winged Duck, Alansohn, Anthony Appleyard, PatrickFisher, Mysdaao, Avenue, Simon Dodd, Cosmodematteo, BDD, Sleigh, Walshga, Bobrayner, DrDaveHPP, Alvis, Woohookitty, Kokoriko, Thruston, Dionyziz, Alan Canon, Stefanomione, Dpaking, Deltabeignet, BD2412, CheshireKatz, Rjwilmsi, Koavf, Syndicate, Neuron132, FlaBot, Sinatra, SamAMac, Scottinglis, GreyCat, Srleffler, BMF81, Benlisquare, Flcelloguy, YurikBot, Ste1n, RussBot, Chris Capoccia, RadioFan, Anomalocaris, Mhartl, Voidxor, Denihilonihil, EEMIV, Eleusinian, Eurosong, Getcrunk, Cbogart2, Imgroup, Tvarnoe~enwiki, A Doon, Kungfuadam, C mon, IslandHopper973, SmackBot, NickyMcLean, Hydrogen Iodide, McGeddon, Kilo-Lima, Persian Poet Gal, Pillforyourills, Thumperward, Breadandcheese, Kostmo, DHN-bot~enwiki, Margavriel, Praveens, Krsont, Addshore, Elendil's Heir, TedE, Drphilharmonic, Dvorak729, Deepred6502, JLogan, Spiritia, Michael J, Eliyak, Khazar, Loodog, Barabum, JorisvS, Minna Sora no Shita, Tehcarp, 16@r, Hvn0413, Korovioff, Tyrrell McAllister, Ehheh, Thoscsii, Eridani, Peter Horn, OnBeyondZebrax, Iridescent, Darth Narutorious, Gregory Benoit, R~enwiki, Hokeman, Tawkerbot2, Tubbyspencer, JForget, Wolfdog, Blue-Haired Lawyer, The Font, Birdhurst, Bardiak, Cydebot, WillowW, Arthurtran, Junglehungry, Mr Gronk, Thijs!bot, Biruitorul, Gtbob12, Widefox, Hamaryns, JAnDbot, Deflective, The Transhumanist, Mcorazao, Hypnometal, Giler, Albany NY, Greensburger, Rothorpe, KEKPΩΨ, Passingtramp, Mileage, GearedBull, Voloshinov, Lošmi, Soonersfan168, Hveziris, Lrgjr72, Dapang~enwiki, KarBOT, Ulkomaalainen, Londubh, J.delanoy, RoyBatty42, Arronax50, Tarotcards, Fullmetal2887, 83d40m, Ontarioboy, Joshua Issac, Cavebutter, WizardDuck, JohnDoe0007, WolkvBot, Macedonian, Jcmitch96, Johnny Au, Philip Trueman, TXiKiBoT, Technopat, Knock-kneed, Pwnage8, Wikidemon, HaItsNotOver, Una Smith, Spandox, BubbleDine, Broadbot, Abdullais4u, Eliotistic, Michelle192837, Cnilep, Symane, Enkyo2, Markdraper, SieBot, Roberto85, Dawn Bard, Caltas, MrBoire, Hamish Harvey, Mizushui, Umrguy42, Chrisdonovan356, Mrxinu, Oxymoron83, Khanzhinvlad, Mstachowsky, Niraba, Yoda2000, Stfg, Mumble45, EmanWilm, ClueBot, SummerWithMorons, Flyingdics, Highpointer, Wanderer57, Hierowritarohseht, Mpd1989, Bay Area Native, Three-quarter-ten, Megiddo1013,

Bracton, Razorflame, SchreiberBike, Pifreak94, XLinkBot, Vanished user k3rmwkdmn4tjna3d, Mitch Ames, Dr sign, SilvonenBot, Addbot, Blanche of King's Lynn, Willking1979, Ederiel, Mfo321, AndersBot, Quercus solaris, Blaylockjam10, Numbo3-bot, Megaman en m, Legobot, Luckas-bot, Bunnyhop11, Denispir, ThinkingTwice, Bathysphere, AnomieBOT, AdjustShift, Hunnjazal, Roadnote, Citation bot, JohnnyB256, Xqbot, Jburlinson, Tomwsulcer, Magicxcian, Riotrocket8676, Omnipaedista, Headhitter, Trafford09, Aidas, Sushiflinger, FrescoBot, D'ohBot, Haeinous, DrilBot, MastiBot, Alnawah, Jonkerz, Lotje, Vrenator, TjBot, Acsian88, Beyond My Ken, EmausBot, John of Reading, ZéroBot, بهار نیشنمہ, Illegitimate Barrister, Ὁ οἶστρος, Michaelenandry, SporkBot, ErratumMan, AlasdairShaw, ClueBot NG, Minas anor, Clarinda Romain, Castncoot, Spannerjam, MerlIwBot, Helpful Pixie Bot, LMMaidens, CTF83! Alt, Metricopolus, Davidiad, Cyberdave03, BattyBot, ChrisGualtieri, Sonarclawz, Corinne, JustAMuggle, Blythwood, Jafarli21, JamesieGod at Hotmail Dot Com, Lucy1982, JaconaFrere, Chb99, Heraclites, Monkbot, KBB24, Quezerque and Anonymous: 307

- **Onomatopoeia** *Source:* https://en.wikipedia.org/wiki/Onomatopoeia?oldid=677815631 *Contributors:* Damian Yerrick, Eloquence, Tarquin, Sjc, Enchanter, William Avery, Karl Palmen, Hephaestos, Stevertigo, PhilipMW, Michael Hardy, Vera Cruz, Ixfd64, Shoaler, GTBacchus, Logotu, Gbleem, Minesweeper, Ahoerstemeier, DavidWBrooks, Mac, Jimfbleak, DropDeadGorgias, Netsnipe, Rl, Robertkeller, Raven in Orbit, Conti, Nohat, Magnus.de, WhisperToMe, Wik, Selket, Furrykef, Hyacinth, Saltine, Itai, Jgm, Fibonacci, Olathe, Ldo, Onebyone, Robbot, Pigsonthewing, ChrisO~enwiki, Fredrik, Tomchiukc, P0lyglut, Rursus, Auric, Paul G, Mushroom, EvanED, Adam78, Nagelfar, Matt Gies, Exploding Boy, DocWatson42, Brouhaha, Elf, Ferkelparade, Average Earthman, Everyking, Henry Flower, Mboverload, Gracefool, Eequor, Solipsist, WorldsApart, Mooquackwooftweetmeow, Quite, Andycjp, Gdm, Antandrus, Kusunose, Mitaphane, Ganymead, Jeremykemp, SatyrEyes, Gscshoyru, Robin klein, Jh51681, Kevyn, MementoVivere, M1ss1ontomars2k4, Zondor, Aponar Kestrel, Thorwald, Eep², MichaelMcGuffin, Imroy, Rich Farmbrough, Cacycle, FiP, Adam850, Dbachmann, Mani1, Kjoonlee, Evice, CanisRufus, El C, Sietse Snel, Krystine, Bobo192, Arlewis, AtomicDragon, Wisdom89, Pikawil, Kappa, Audrey, Nsaa, Luffy, Bladeswin, Danski14, Cma, Gary, Anthony Appleyard, Mark Dingemanse, V2Blast, Arthena, Cctoide, Typhlosion, Ricky81682, Abe Lincoln, Iothiania, Sade, Fuzzygerdes, Jpenix, Apoc2400, Redfarmer, Snowolf, Evil Monkey, Amorymeltzer, Sumergocognito, Vuo, ThomasWinwood, Alai, Netkinetic, New Age Retro Hippie, Japanese Searobin, Hojimachong, Simetrical, Woohookitty, Mindmatrix, Camw, LOL, Twobitsprite, Bonus Onus, Pixeltoo, -Ril-, Jraregris, Al E., Thebogusman, Goystein~enwiki, Karmosin, Umofomia, Plrk, Tokek, Abd, Stefanomione, Gerbrant, Dysepsion, Emerson7, Dpaking, Dirknachbar, Graham87, BD2412, SamuraiClinton, Jclemens, Zoz, Vary, Bob A, Marasama, Bruce1ee, Boccobrock, FlaBot, Dvortygirl, Bettaa, Ewlyahoocom, Gurch, Tijuana Brass, Joedeshon, Kmanoj, Phoenix2~enwiki, Hansonc, King of Hearts, Gwernol, Billpg, Gumby701, YurikBot, PiMemoryTuna, Sceptre, Jimp, Retodon8, Kafziel, Wolfmankurd, Boldymumbles, RussBot, FrenchIsAwesome, DanMS, Casey J. Morris, Matt Fitzpatrick, Akamad, Ksyrie, Natovr, PaulGarner, NawlinWiki, Aeusoes1, Deskana, Ashwinr, Thiseye, Irishguy, Aaron Brenneman, Ngorongoro, Davilla~enwiki, Brandon, Daniel Mietchen, InvaderJim42, Nick C, SameerKhan, M3taphysical, Uzyn, Ckamaeleon, Peter Knutsen, Wknight94, Eurosong, 21655, Deville, The-, ChrisGriswold, Theda, Closedmouth, Cauzilo, SMcCandlish, Dspradau, Sean Whitton, Vicarious, Fram, JLaTondre, Seadog1611, Rcharman, Kookykman, Carlosguitar, Mabisa, KNHaw, Llauren, NetRolller 3D, Pasi, Torgo, Poisonouslizzie, SmackBot, Jasy jatere, SteveTraylen, Amatire, Unyoyega, Matveims, RedSpruce, Eskimbot, The Ronin, Wakuran, Spongtastic, BiT, Nil Einne, HeartofaDog, HalfShadow, Sebesta, Gaff, Xaosflux, Peter Isotalo, Gilliam, Ohnoitsjamie, Ghosts&empties, Zuiko, Nmmm, Anastasios~enwiki, Valley2city, Dahn, H2ppyme, Punxunite, Dr bab, Master of Puppets, Elagatis, EncMstr, MalafayaBot, Bazonka, H Bruthzoo, WikiPedant, Can't sleep, clown will eat me, Size J Battery, Bonecrusher, Mhym, XQ fan, Adamantios, Cameron Nedland, Lanhikari, Jmlk17, BesselDekker, Nibuod, Decltype, Nakon, T-borg, Obina, Dreadstar, Weregerbil, Jon Awbrey, Tactik, AnonymousBroccoli, RyGuy17, Kennedye, Acdx, Kukini, Clicketyclack, Nasz, Куиксилвър, Oneilius, Michael J, Saccerzd, BurnDownBabylon, Robofish, Slogby, James.S, Wickethewok, Bjankuloski06en~enwiki, Andres.Velasquez, Svippong, The Man in Question, MarkSutton, Slakr, Thunk00, Lukis100, JimHxn, Bw b dub, Dicklyon, Dragon Sand, Typetive~enwiki, Jonaslind, Redeagle688, AudioWorks, Jakhay, Avant Guard, ScreaminEagle, Isaac Crumm, BranStark, Tjeerdnet, Dexterdud860, Bluemike, Impy4ever, CzarB, Davin Flite, Shoeofdeath, Evildoctorbluetooth, Chris53516, Falkflyer, Senis, Tawkerbot2, Kbarends, Bearingbreaker92, J Milburn, Wolfdog, Avg, CmdrObot, Neoyamaneko, Basawala, Thursday Postal, DanielRigal, Lazulilasher, Karenjc, King Hildebrand, Oo7565, Cydebot, WillowW, Arthurian Legend, Supreme Bananas, Ben414, Tkynerd, Julian Mendez, Thaddius, Clovis Sangrail, Shirulashem, NukeMTV, DumbBOT, FastLizard4, White Mage Cid, UberScienceNerd, Click23, Hairmare, Epbr123, SonicBlue, Jedibob5, Teh tennisman, Mojo Hand, Dalahäst, Missvain, Basement12, SomeStranger, Picus viridis, Tellyaddict, Natalie Erin, Escarbot, AntiVandalBot, Majorly, Luna Santin, AnemoneProjectors, Bigtimepeace, Quintote, DarkAudit, Nemobius, Fayenatic london, LibLord, Farosdaughter, AjaaniSherisu, Sluzzelin, Toshotosho, Winndm31, MER-C, Instinct, Andonic, Roleplayer, Jimmy, Ny156uk, Bongwarrior, VoABot II, Dekimasu, JNW, CattleGirl, Brewhaha@edmc.net, Veeliam, Nyttend, Aflaksp, Catgut, Eiyuu Kou, Animum, Miss Mondegreen, 28421u2232nfenfcenc, Glen, DerHexer, Plutochaun, Goldenrod111, Oroso, Rickterp, Jerem43, Hdt83, MartinBot, Ebizur, Dorvaq, MaraNeo127, R'n'B, AlexiusHoratius, Wikista~enwiki, SplinterCell37, Wiki Raja, Tgeairn, Hasanisawi, J.delanoy, Elysonius, Consci, Peter Chastain, RedPoptarts, Mike.lifeguard, Jerry, Jeffro29325, Elite gym, Katalaveno, Ersaloz, M4yh3m, DarkFalls, FUNKIEFAIRY, Supuhstar, Richard D. LeCour, Neueregel, DemiLemon, LeighvsOptimvsMaximvs, KCinDC, Aronarien, STBotD, Jc4p, Hc5duke, Aretnap, Zornoxx, Nawulf, Greg-si, CardinalDan, Lights, Caribbean H.Q., ChrisBlueStone, Deor, VolkovBot, Johan1298~enwiki, Macedonian, Kriplozoik~enwiki, Wouter89, ROxBo, Aesopos, Philip Trueman, TXiKiBoT, EvanCarroll, Riffraffselbow, Marskuzz, Deleet, Psyclet, Ann Stouter, Soundofmusicals, Z.E.R.O., Midlandstoday, Sean D Martin, Srikipedia, Lradrama, Marvel52, LeaveSleaves, Billinghurst, Kinkijui KNK, Synthebot, Andrimahos, AjitPD, Kusyadi, Cnilep, Newsaholic, Insanity Incarnate, Agüeybaná, Nagy, PGWG, Antoncampos, Tsv, Ham27, Munci, Dark3rbol, Shesammy, RC93, Felix ahlner, Mmarulla, SieBot, Zenlax, Dpsaves, Weeliljimmy, King of Corsairs, Triwbe, Tedgxke, Holiday56, Danielgrad, Tiptoety, Rrvnd, Oxymoron83, Avnjay, Pepso2, Aether22, Nabilft, JohnnyMrNinja, The2belo, Puus, AllHailZeppelin, Pirate mafia, Denisarona, Wee Curry Monster, Mr. Granger, Martarius, ClueBot, Ersomn, Sskim, Kyoww, PipepBot, Fyyer, The Thing That Should Not Be, Snowmew, Monkeytheboy, Rjd0060, Astrological Mayhem, Mild Bill Hiccup, Anapazapa, DanielDeibler, Blanchardb, RafaAzevedo, Puchiko, PlagueBearer666, DragonBot, Alexbot, Draconis57, Kanguole, Susw, Wasserstoff~enwiki, Prietoquilmes, Jak91, Nobody117711, Arjayay, Thecoshman, Ember of Light, Basketball110, Morel, Frozen4322, SchreiberBike, Smashyofacefaceface, El bot de la dieta, La Pianista, Thingg, Aitias, Kikos, Versus22, Htmlcoderexe, Templarion, Wjk90125, Anonymous10001, Oldekop, Ffsimrob, Laser brain, Ost316, Nepenthes, Badgernet, WikiDao, Lovaananda, KingFerg, Poignantlecture, Addbot, Xp54321, Paper Luigi, Otisjimmy1, Theleftorium, KizuKid, Pavlen666, Older and ... well older, Fieldday-sunday, Cuaxdon, Vishnava, CanadianLinuxUser, Leszek Jańczuk, Justin kanouse, Mentisock, Rickardspaghetti~enwiki, Sqib, Rogierland, Henkt, Laqlaq, AnnaFrance, Ascanio11, Mandanali, Beala, Tassedethe, 84user, Peridon, Puffofmagic, Tide rolls, Lightbot, Zorrobot, Stratford490, David0811, Wikilover98, Jarble, Cottonrabbit, Legobot, Luckas-bot, Yobot, Tohd8BohaithuGh1, TaBOT-zerem, Hohenloh, Daqo89, KamikazeBot, AmeliaIsland, Hener8, Speciallynx, Hairhorn, A user, Choij, Rjanag, Killiondude, IRP, Piano non troppo, K50 Dude, Aditya, Henry Godric, Kingpin13, Dinesh smita, Ambaryer, Azhay, Rtyq2, Wispre, Citation bot, Scruberjacob, LovesMacs, Jchthys, Marlah æ, Capricorn42, 28ajay, Burzumko, Neurotard, Bobisbobbob, J04n, GrouchoBot, Michaelfol0, Omnipaedista, RibotBOT, Lunow3, FrescoBot, Surv1v4l1st, Krj373, Jansay, Jaramee fan, Recognizance, Naty451, Tlork Thunderhead, Redletternight, Ranchysurf, Pinethicket, Jarshabff, Poloonamat, Spidey104, Smuckola, Ttweed, Jikybebna, La Grande Reverteur, Slytrrek, GossamerBliss, Wicked.fable, Diannaa, EmausBot, Milkunderwood, Ἄρτεμις, Mz7, ChipmunkRaccoon, The Nut, Hodgdon's secret garden, Tot12, Senator2029, Gwen-chan, Klock101, ClueBot NG, Gilderien, Ewp2cool, -sche, OxygenBlue, Spannerjam, Helpful Pixie Bot, Electriccatfish2, DBigXray, Lowercase sigmabot, Kyoakoa, Wiki13, Ducksfordollars, Gautehuus, Argento Surfer, Tea and a lump o' cake, X-179, Aks23121990, Wthannah, The Illusive Man, Kupiakos, Electricmuffin11, Notesfrommynest, CurryTime7-24, Sarah Joy Jones, Srtª PiriLimPomPom, Inanygivenhole, Sam Sailor, Ireneshih, Itsalleasy, Ryk72, Meemo16, Qwertyxp2000, Peter238, SoSivr and Anonymous: 1011

- **Oxymoron** *Source:* https://en.wikipedia.org/wiki/Oxymoron?oldid=676088204 *Contributors:* The Epopt, Sjc, Ortolan88, Jaknouse, DevilRaysFan, Michael Hardy, IZAK, Pagingmrherman, KAMiKAZOW, Ffx, Nikai, Netsnipe, Cadr, Andres, Smack, Nohat, Dandrake, Mendor, Haukurth, Maximus Rex, Furrykef, Bloodshedder, Bcorr, Pakaran, Donarreiskoffer, Robbot, Kizor, ZimZalaBim, Psychonaut, Rorro, Premeditated Chaos, Meelar, Auric, Caknuck, Wereon, Seth Ilys, Vuara, GreatWhiteNortherner, Alan Liefting, Kenny sh, Tom harrison, Lupin, Everyking, Lefty, Micru, Saaga, Djegan, Macrakis, Edcolins, Rheun, Mike R, Antandrus, Dinero, Joyous!, Xoddf2, Sonett72, Kadambarid, Cun, Mike Rosoft, Alkivar, Spiffy sperry, Slady, Discospinster, FrickFrack, Bishonen, Quiensabe, Dbachmann, Paul August, ESkog, JoeSmack, El C, Shanes, Triona, Bobo192, Spalding, Marblespire, Duk, .:Ajvol:., Angie Y., Richi, Sriram sh, TACD, Hesperian, Helix84, Sam Korn, Alansohn, Gary, Anthony Appleyard, Yamla, Albino Fox, Snowolf, Ombudsman, Krazykillaz, Bsadowski1, Shimeru, Gosgood, Sam Vimes, Newnoise~enwiki, Vanished User 3388458, ScottDavis, Camw, TomTheHand, Ekem, BlankVerse, Sdgjake, Tabletop, Htetrasme, PhattyFatt, Waldir, Stefanomione, PhilippWeissenbacher, Mandarax, Dpaking, Graham87, BD2412, Kbdank71, FreplySpang, Wahkeenah, Netan'el, Afterwriting, The wub, DoubleBlue, Matt Deres, MapsMan, Fred Bradstadt, Yamamoto Ichiro, Berserk798, Saksham, FlaBot, Doc glasgow, Jak123, Aligator Man, Margosbot~enwiki, AndriuZ, Brendan Moody, Rare, Joedeshon, Theshibboleth, Vanished user psdfiwnef3niurunfiuh234ruhfwdb7, Chobot, DaGizza, DVdm, Random user 39849958, FrankTobia, Loco830, Ben Tibbetts, The Rambling Man, YurikBot, Pigman, SluggoOne, Rick Norwood, Dysmorodrepanis~enwiki, Leutha, Janke, Arichnad, Jaxl, SigPig, Mccready, Aaron Brenneman, Brian Crawford, Jpbowen, Panscient, Falcon9x5, Kkarcher, Zephalis, Vlad, Nescio, DuffDudeX1, Black Falcon, Alpha 4615, Wknight94, Raistlin8r, FF2010, Lt-wiki-bot, Closedmouth, SMcCandlish, BorgQueen, Geoffrey.landis, Jaranda, Katieh5584, Thomas Blomberg, Airconswitch, SkerHawx, David Wahler, Luk, Phinnaeus, SmackBot, Lestrade, RBrackstone, Prodego, Unyoyega, Ifnord, WookieInHeat, Delldot, Firstrock, Sansvoix, Imzadi1979, Gaff, Gilliam, Betacommand, Trebor, Donbas, Thumperward, Poetryarchive, Greatgavini, Nbarth, Hgrosser, Can't sleep, clown will eat me, Cheezwzl, LukasPietsch, Avb, Bisected8, Alice.haugen, DrDnar, Pevarnj, Nakon, Richard001, Eran of Arcadia, BullRangifer, Jon Awbrey, Wybot, Michalchik, Doownyl32, Terrasidius, J.smith, Saippuakauppias, ArglebargleIV, AThing, John, Gobonobo, JorisvS, Minna Sora no Shita, Ckatz, Hvn0413, Jeez19, Renrenren, Sara123abc, Tasoskessaris, Achorn316, MTSbot~enwiki, Peyre, KJS77, Nox13last, Dysprod1975, Asclepias, IvanLanin, Late Leo, Cls14, Mrguyguy226, Ewulp, Tawkerbot2, The Letter J, Powerslide, Nicd, Will Pittenger, INkubusse, Wolfdog, Picaroon, Baiji, Searles2sels, KnightLago, Dgw, Gregbard, Cydebot, Anurooparora, WillowW, Peterdjones, Michaelas10, Corpx, Daniel J. Leivick, Odie5533, DumbBOT, Profundity06, EqualRights, JodyB, Thijs!bot, Qwyrxian, N5iln, Mojo Hand, Jojan, Marek69, Dmws, Bethpage89, Pkapitola, Deipnosophista, Dark Serge, Natalie Erin, Heraldofilipino, AntiVandalBot, Seaphoto, Paul from Michigan, Ozzieboy, Clamster5, Danger, Mutt Lunker, Wl219, JAnDbot, Petecarney, The Transhumanist, Instinct, MelanieN, Jonemerson, VoABot II, JamesBWatson, Twsx, Mapetite526, KConWiki, Cgingold, Spanchangam, Dirac66, Allstarecho, Styrofoam1994, Casachs, Dontdoit, Cliff smith, MartinBot, Mmoneypenny, Kiore, Mschel, R'n'B, CommonsDelinker, EdiTor, AlphaEta, J.delanoy, Pharaoh of the Wizards, Carre, AstroHurricane001, Bogey97, Silverxxx, Uncle Dick, Dogwag25, Maurice Carbonaro, Jerry, Barts1a, Marcsin, Johnbod, Forsaken Morningstar, Coppertwig, SJP, Threegunvash, Hanacy, Catman6000, Uber Cuber, Putturvenkatesh, Ja 62, BOBRLY, JohnDoe0007, Rennagata92, Bennerhingl, Lights, Naznomarn, Adolf Hitler IV, Ryan032, Philip Trueman, JayEsJay, RevSavitar, TXiKiBoT, Jispoobell, Tumblingsky, Carlangas, Targuman, Emigdioofmiami, Anna Lincoln, Megadeth186, Italian beauty, Leobrien, ChozoBoy, Malick78, Napoleon1815, Tamilmani, Synthebot, Pinknoise, Rhopkins8, Falcon8765, Enviroboy, Turgan, Mallerd, Brianga, Benlicia, Twooars, Nagy, Adient, Tvinh, Chuck Sirloin, 23richardsonthomas, SieBot, Rusty7, Yoda317, Nubiatech, Gerakibot, Dawn Bard, X-Fi6, Quest for Truth, HermanHiddema, Green-eyed girl, Doctorfluffy, Oxymoron83, Mastr hook, MrDebaker, Steven Crossin, Ccbgabc, Mezmerizer, Doinovertime, RouterIncident, Caaaggf, NamelessMoron, Oatmealisforlovers, Escape Orbit, EricPaynter, Stillwaterising, Tej68, Tomdobb, Twinsday, ClueBot, Binksternet, Wikievil666, The Thing That Should Not Be, Elphiedude135, NotnventedHere, Gregcaletta, CliffordWest, Mild Bill Hiccup, Matt 118118, Liempt, Thepack1138, SlavaP, Excirial, Alexbot, Pnaren786, SpikeToronto, Ksmalls8610, Solargreg, Computer97, Thehelpfulone, Light show, 7, Mattissa, Seabiscuit uk, His Manliness, Ericbrocolli, SoxBot III, Mwatson27, XLinkBot, Morrowgamer, Dthomsen8, WikiDao, Torchflame, Tooanthonese, CalumH93, Metodicar, Addbot, Xp54321, Ckriebel, Spanks2010, Beamathan, Non-dropframe, Shadowhead123, Annielogue, Fgnievinski, Older and ... well older, Fieldday-sunday, T.bolyda, Cognatus, Bush shep, Download, Protonk, Glane23, Sateros, Ayabellaya, 5 albert square, Herr Gruber, ChannyX, Tide rolls, Agrophobe, Zorrobot, KUSSOMAK, Math Champion, Luckas-bot, Yobot, JohnnyCalifornia, Tohd8BohaithuGh1, Senator Palpatine, Rsquire3, NERVUN, Bananarse, Mmxx, THEN WHO WAS PHONE?, Mskydragons908, Tempodivalse, AndrooUK, Piano non troppo, Ipatrol, Grolltech, Lizindarozo, Crecy99, JakeBB, RobertEves92, Branabus, Citation bot, Uber Badger, Boxstaa, Xqbot, ManningBartlett, Cooper21, Capricorn42, Anonymouscadet, Sellyme, Jmundo, JohnPaul69, H34th3rr1, VanHelsing23, Omnipaedista, Anime Addict AA, Fiskehaps, RibotBOT, James Pain, Brutaldeluxe, Sophus Bie, Handuo99, Shadowjams, B767-500, Sky Attacker, Iheartme1996, Uzumaki42, BTRchik, Goodbye Galaxy, Arbenzz, Ssssuuuuccccckkk, POMAH 6EKKEP, Enoch exe inc, Robo37, HamburgerRadio, Citation bot 1, Intelligentsium, Pinethicket, Elockid, Adlerbot, Minsofla, LittleWink, Calmer Waters, Eastcostbiased, A8UDI, Conorz100lulz, Hessamnia, White Shadows, Logical Gentleman, Lotje, Pilot850, Fastilysock, Passcod, Minimac, TjBot, Youarenotfat, Noommos, DASHBot, Treesforourchildren, Mistercontributer, EmausBot, STATicVapor, MrRandomPerson, JJWest56, NotAnonymous0, Hohho56oy, Tommy2010, Wikipelli, Hrld11, JamesMohr, Nitin.i.azam, Solomonfromfinland, Susfele, Ida Shaw, Studly2, Shuipzv3, AlexWolfx, Ratheron, Hazard-SJ, EXIT=IHateMyLife, Christina Silverman, Erianna, LewisLong, Daviddrew30, Anglais1, L Kensington, Kasplatermix, Forever Dusk, Petrb, ClueBot NG, Scotnielson616, Gigilian, Vashi18, Diliptr, Mookmerkin, Dr. Fixated, BG19bot, TyFitzgerald, Kyoakoa, Zollo9999, Tatchell, Gonnym, TejasDiscipulus2, Justincheng12345-bot, Laodah, StarryGrandma, Dennisoosterwaal, Majilis, FiverFan65, Hair, BreakfastJr, Epic Failure, SoonerOrLaterJohn, Highway 231, Marcrower, KasparBot, Billatict, Aristotles, RounakGupta and Anonymous: 1116

- **Paradox (literature)** *Source:* https://en.wikipedia.org/wiki/Paradox_(literature)?oldid=651339502 *Contributors:* Ruakh, R. S. Shaw, Giraffedata, Vuo, Rjwilmsi, Koavf, Nikkimaria, INkubusse, Outriggr, TheBigA, Wayiran, Bongwarrior, J.delanoy, Mrlydian, SieBot, StAnselm, Paradoctor, WRK, Oneidman, AproposLesser, WikHead, Firebat08, Addbot, DreamHaze, Doulos Christos, Paine Ellsworth, DivineAlpha,

Vrenator, Yamaha5, David Kaminski and Anonymous: 23

- **Parody** *Source:* https://en.wikipedia.org/wiki/Parody?oldid=678789086 *Contributors:* Koyaanis Qatsi, Sjc, Ed Poor, Deb, Ortolan88, Road-runner, SimonP, Shii, Ellmist, Heron, Camembert, Mintguy, Mrwojo, DennisDaniels, Steverapaport, Tubby, Ixfd64, Lquilter, TakuyaMurata, Paul A, Eric119, Ahoerstemeier, Jebba, Ireneshusband, Glenn, Alex756, Lee M, Conti, Charles Matthews, Zoicon5, Lee Cremeans, Fur-rykef, Saltine, Nv8200pa, Jgm, K1Bond007, Paul-L~enwiki, Opus33, PuzzletChung, Dimadick, Joyojeet, Gromlakh, Robbot, Dale Arnett, Kristof vt, RedWolf, Rfc1394, Texture, Geogre, Wereon, Alba, JerryFriedman, Diberri, Cutler, Decrypt3, Crculver, Christopher Parham, Andries, Cobra libre, Geeoharee, Bradeos Graphon, Anville, Revth, Maroux, BigHaz, Kpalion, Gracefool, Eequor, JillandJack, ALargeElk, 159753, Slowking Man, Antandrus, Lesgles, Rdsmith4, OwenBlacker, B.d.mills, Joyous!, Picapica, Adashiel, Chowchow, Imroy, Rich Farm-brough, Cacycle, Bishonen, MeltBanana, Dagonet, Notinasnaid, Android79, Evice, Soilguy8, CanisRufus, Mr. Billion, Livajo, Kwamikagami, Longhair, Pikawil, Jonathunder, Jjron, Ranveig, Alansohn, Arthena, Tabor, Andrewpmk, Craigy144, Riana, Differentgravy, Crablogger, Ird-epesca572, Dave.Dunford, Ianblair23, Angr, The JPS, Robwingfield, Lkjhgfdsa, Tabletop, Iisryan, Stefanomione, BD2412, L-Zwei, RxS, Kotukunui, Mayumashu, Seidenstud, Wahoofive, Amire80, Trekkiemonster, Bensin, Mark272, FlaBot, Rarosalion, Maximus7, Nihiltres, RexNL, Ellehcor, Tequendamia, Str1977, Joonasl, Topazbutterfly, Mrschimpf, Chobot, Gwernol, Kralahome, Ben Tibbetts, YurikBot, Dk-kicks, RobotE, Hairy Dude, Kafziel, RussBot, Pigman, Cswrye, Stalmannen, Epolk, Ytgy111, Jasonglchu, NawlinWiki, ONEder Boy, Irishguy, Anetode, Croatoan1, Brandon, Bob569, Haoie, Lomn, Lipothymia, EEMIV, Bota47, CLW, Pooryorick~enwiki, Takethemud, Pegship, Zzu-uzz, Closedmouth, Ratagonia, JoanneB, Pavone~enwiki, MagneticFlux, Thomas Blomberg, GLmathgrant, Nick Michael, Veinor, Sintonak.X, Krabs502, SmackBot, FClef, Nick Dillinger, David Kernow, KnowledgeOfSelf, Potatoes345, Unyoyega, Pgk, Gwax, Mikecraig, Lifebaka, Jagged 85, Snowmobile, Eskimbot, Jab843, HornetMike, Hbackman, Yamaguchi 先生, Hmains, Skizzik, Carl.bunderson, Durova, Ciacchi, WikiFlier, Kaid100, Jeff5102, The1exile, Trekphiler, Shuttlebug, Can't sleep, clown will eat me, Zordrac, JoelWhy, Djido, OrphanBot, Left-ism, Michael.Pohoreski, VMS Mosaic, GeorgeMoney, Addshore, Kcordina, FelineFanatic13, Jwy, Viewdrix, T-borg, Mtmelendez, Demm, Ryan Roos, Hgilbert, The PIPE, Longshot1980, Vina-iwbot~enwiki, Spiritia, SashatoBot, Petr Kopač, NapoleonicMedicalHistoryWhiz, Jin-nai, Jszack, Rigadoun, Neuromantrice, Cheekywee~enwiki, Michael Bednarek, ReZips, Special-T, Werdan7, Stwalkerster, JimHxn, Andy-roo316, Galadh, Jc37, Japoniano, Iridescent, Father Time89, Judgesurreal777, Basicdesign, King kong92, Signor, Blehfu, TheEasterBunny, Ewulp, Woodshed, Tawkerbot2, George100, Tinlobster, J Milburn, JForget, CmdrObot, Scohoust, Joncnunn, Jaldridge86, Neelix, Orca1 9904, Keithh, Flammingo, Banjokangaroo, Fluence, Samuell, Warhorus, Reywas92, Steel, Crossmr, SyntaxError55, Handtrembler, Flowerpotman, Corpx, Ssilvers, KirchnerE07, In Defense of the Artist, Gnfnrf, NorthernThunder, After Midnight, Nuwewsco, Atomsmasher86, Thijs!bot, Btball, Bonchanz, Tyx, 0dd1, Marek69, Dark Rain, Fez2005, Reynaert-ad, Reswobslc, Nick Number, Ju66l3r, Yuanchosaan, Just Chilling, Dr. Blofeld, Jordan199311, David Shankbone, Djackmanson, Wahabijaz, JackSparrow Ninja, Deflective, Kaobear, Barek, Chaucer1387, Smiddle, Greensburger, MegX, Cynwolfe, Bongwarrior, VoABot II, No substitute for you, Elcapitane, Galactus5000, Hickoryhillster, Catgut, Jodi1234, DerHexer, Esanchez7587, ChazBeckett, Lady Mondegreen, Hdt83, Pmac135, Ombudswiki, Chrishy man, J.delanoy, Lriley47, Tiki-wont, MistyMorn, BigZeeff, TomS TDotO, JoefromRML, BrokenSphere, Athene cunicularia, M-le-mot-dit, Rev. John, ULC, SJP, Toon05, Shoessss, Cometstyles, Lord Jubjub, Mmoople, Worthtowns~enwiki, Straw Cat, Teddierx, Sgeureka, GrandpaDoc, VolkovBot, Sporti, Camster, Temporarily Insane, Indubitably, Al.locke, Philip Trueman, A4bot, Rei-bot, Amergirlchels, Soundofmusicals, Zurishaddai, RaZoRb0iz, Terp-sichoreus, Mrhotsurferguy, Rarmin, Wenli, Corrupt one, Vladsinger, Enigmaman, Nagy, Sssprkrao~enwiki, Onondagan opossum, Daveh4h, Firefoxobsession, GPigeon, Magiccrab, GreaterWikiholic, SieBot, JS13JeFF, Theace524, Moonriddengirl, Paradoctor, Lampooon, JoeyETS, Calusarul, Nummer29, Artist Formerly Known As Whocares, Interchange88, Bentogoa, Toddst1, Joe Egan, Danielgrad, Flyer22, Nate Speed, Natenate6733, Captain Jay, Smaug123, Lyltry, Altzinn, ImageRemovalBot, Invertzoo, John Doe42, ClueBot, SummerWithMorons, Go-rillaWarfare, WurmWoode, The Thing That Should Not Be, Blackangel25, Drmies, Razimantv, Uncle Milty, MyMii, Metaxcentric~enwiki, Passargea, Andrei Iosifovich, Bbb2007, Ottre, Estirabot, Alpha Ralpha Boulevard, Surfdarthvader, Arjayay, Lurexus3rd, Ngebendi, Mr Alex, Another Believer, Stinky Cheese 1, MikeCp76, Skulcouncilor08, XLinkBot, Cresent sit, Stickee, WikHead, MrN9000, Shoemaker's Holiday, Mrgehnahri, MatthewVanitas, Tinkerbell567, Addbot, Otterathome, Betterusername, Luis2134, EjsBot, C3r4, Manaphy.NZ, Bfroud, D0762, MrOllie, LaaknorBot, Glane23, Tassedethe, Dayewalker, Tide rolls, Lightbot, OlEnglish, Krano, Fireattack, The Mummy, Luckas-bot, Yobot, SpontaneousCombusken, Passandid, Gongshow, Herwest, Sishmers, ParodyLV, Kookyunii, AnomieBOT, Rjanag, Wise Raven, Materialscien-tist, Eumolpo, Maxis ftw, MacintoshWriter, Synaptophysin, Xqbot, Samoboow, Masterius, Damienivan, Abce2, Epileptic Mushroom, Profes-sorfree, PMDX, Omnipaedista, Mark Schierbecker, Shadowjams, Schekinov Alexey Victorovich, Tweak2020, Poppy1955, FrescoBot, Tan-gent747, Captain Fishy, Tobby72, Recognizance, SayWhatRollerCoasterUhUhUh, Irfan2009, Hamlet, Prince of Trollmark, RockfangSemi, Hellknowz, Impala2009, RavenRawr, Che Querido, Barras, Quoz, Tygr11, Gerda Arendt, Sierrabonitaguy, 11nniuq, TobeBot, Ticklewick-leukulele, Lotje, Vrenator, Jim6pearson, Weedwhacker128, Tbhotch, DARTH SIDIOUS 2, RjwilmsiBot, VernoWhitney, John of Reading, IGG8998, Azkm, ZéroBot, Dolovis, Doddy Wuid, Suslindisambiguator, Unreal7, Gz33, L Kensington, Exequielhandig, 04joshuac, Peter Karlsen, Txsling, 28bot, ClueBot NG, Wilde Jagd, FlowFan2300, Jcgoble3, Clearlyfakeusername, Reify-tech, Helpful Pixie Bot, Krial, Funny-lady64, Cdrysdale, MasterMind5991, Puramyun31, AdventurousSquirrel, Curlyw42, Morning Sunshine, Parody Master, BattyBot, Dr Brain-Lock, Eryat, Marxlives, The Anonymouse, Katherine.mason, Eyesnore, PhantomTech, Gorlabot, The Herald, Mobarbush, Guillaume.blanchet, Chicken262920, Eagurin, Rasheedagardner, Dubeyn, KasparBot, Professor JR and Anonymous: 523

- **Pastiche** *Source:* https://en.wikipedia.org/wiki/Pastiche?oldid=674329670 *Contributors:* Ortolan88, Mintguy, KF, Someone else, Michael Hardy, Cprompt, Jahsonic, Choster, Hyacinth, Itai, Opus33, Wetman, Dale Arnett, Pigsonthewing, RedWolf, Ajd, Geogre, Litefantastic, Wereon, Ruakh, Eran, Beardo, Pgan002, Beland, Thomas Veil, Pacian, GeoGreg, Gary D, Acedian, Discospinster, Piewalker, Zaslav, Sole Soul, Bobo192, Boredzo, Diego Moya, Elchupachipmunk, Avenue, DreamGuy, Tony Sidaway, Ianblair23, Ringbang, Kenyon, Mjpotter, NeoChaosX, Fraterm, Stefanomione, BD2412, Miq, Dwaipayanc, Lockley, FlaBot, RobertG, Margosbot~enwiki, Ewlyahoocom, Revolv-ing Bugbear, Hairy Dude, FlareNUKE, RussBot, Spiralout987, Pigman, The Final Dream, Simon Lieschke, Msikma, Aeusoes1, Jpbowen, MollyTheCat, PhilipC, Zwobot, Quentin mcalmott, OutRider2003, SmackBot, DCGeist, Gigs, Ghosts&empties, Jprg1966, Thumperward, Kleinzach, Thomas Gebhardt, Andrewdt85, Hstarr, Bob Castle, BlackTerror, Henebry, Ser Amantio di Nicolao, Yms, Mr Stephen, Gheuf, JForget, Adam Keller, Amalas, Jedzz, NisseSthlm, Jac16888, Cydebot, A876, Gogo Dodo, Ssilvers, Marina T., Thijs!bot, Esemono, Stosh-master, Captain Crawdad, Deipnosophista, Turbotape, MegX, Yahel Guhan, Magioladitis, Duggy 1138, Ludvikus, Edward321, Évangéline, R'n'B, WFinch, Prhartcom, STBotD, UnicornTapestry, ViccoLizcano, TXiKiBoT, Jonyungk, Vanished user ikijeirw34iuaeolaseriffic, Broad-bot, 1-555-confide, Bporopat, Mcgma709, Coastside, Caltas, DigitalShepherd, Moonraker12, Anchor Link Bot, Sindala, SummerWithMorons, Jersey emt, No such user, Nymf, Crywalt, Jumbolino, Arjayay, Xme, Ukrazy, Olirp, Mabalu, Addbot, Melab-1, Fothergill Volkensniff IV, Jdvil-lalobos, Tassedethe, OlEnglish, Luckas-bot, Yobot, Amirobot, NaidNdeso, AnomieBOT, Citation bot, Quebec99, LilHelpa, CrushSoda, Lele giannoni, Mario777Zelda, FrescoBot, Riberriber, MastiBot, SJJM4EVER, FadulJA, Lotje, QuentinUK, Ida Shaw, Donner60, ShedCorner, WIERDGREENMAN, Spannerjam, BG19bot, Marcocapelle, BattyBot, Khazar2, Hotcheetos06, Donfbreed2, Jeromedina~enwiki, Dsprc, WikiOriginal-9, NightMusic34 and Anonymous: 95

- **Pathos** *Source:* https://en.wikipedia.org/wiki/Pathos?oldid=677656865 *Contributors:* Glenn, Evercat, Nohat, Wileycoyote707, Rfc1394, OldakQuill, Andycjp, OwenBlacker, Mike Rosoft, Pie4all88, EliasAlucard, Kwamikagami, Shanes, Bobo192, Nectarflowed, Alansohn, Velella, VivaEmilyDavies, Ur Wurst Enema, Bookandcoffee, Angr, Camw, Parallelstripes, FreplySpang, Vary, GregAsche, FlaBot, Pathoschild, Gurch, Lemuel Gulliver, Aethralis, EamonnPKeane, YurikBot, Koveras, RussBot, Deskana, Tomisti, HereToHelp, SmackBot, Eaglizard, Gaff, DarkAdonis255, DStoykov, Egsan Bacon, Onorem, Cybercobra, Nakon, Ceoil, Lunarbunny, Runa27, William conway bcc, IronGargoyle, Flying*seal, Larrymcp, Iridescent, SkyWalker, Wolfdog, Avg, Ale jrb, Juhachi, Karenjc, Gregbard, Cydebot, Tkircher, Hebrides, Thijs!bot, Robsinden, Peace01234, RichardVeryard, Narssarssuaq, Deflective, Barek, ElComandanteChe, Turnadreunit, .anacondabot, Penubag, Monowiki, Levarris, Patstuart, MartinBot, Kguirnela, J.delanoy, (jarbarf), CraZyBryan, Idioma-bot, ACSE, DoorsAjar, IAmTheCoinMan, Tricky Wiki44, Maxim, Matthew Yeager, Cyfal, Bubbathebut, ClueBot, TierNiel, Piledhigheranddeeper, DragonBot, Excirial, Alexbot, Kved, Onyxchuck, HumphreyW, DumZiBoT, Darkicebot, MatthewVanitas, Addbot, CanadianLinuxUser, Omnipedian, RanZag, Yobot, Julia W, SwisterTwister, Killiondude, Jim1138, Danno uk, Eumolpo, ArthurBot, LovesMacs, JimVC3, Arubirurei, J04n, Omnipaedista, Erik9bot, FrescoBot, Paine Ellsworth, Logomachy, Phantasmagorias, Pollinosisss, UNIT A4B1, NerdyScienceDude, ArchaicTruth, Eekerz, ZéroBot, Virbonusdicendiperitus, Monterey Bay, Donner60, ClueBot NG, Joefromrandb, Spannerjam, DBigXray, MusikAnimal, Phillipberkowitz, Chow11, Khazar2, Vanished user sdij4rtltkjasdk3, Mr. Guye, Makecat-bot, Ekips39, Boomerme, Rybec, KillzoneCH, Gwilkins35, Eileen.penny, KasparBot and Anonymous: 176

- **Polyptoton** *Source:* https://en.wikipedia.org/wiki/Polyptoton?oldid=675151766 *Contributors:* Michael Hardy, Ruakh, Jyril, Jorge Stolfi, TheObtuseAngleOfDoom, Flapdragon, Kwamikagami, Dpaking, Graham87, Gdrbot, RobotE, RussBot, D'Agosta, Incnis Mrsi, Cydebot, Deflective, Ryangibsonstewart, Vinograd19, Wherewillyoube, Ve4ernik, Drmies, Mild Bill Hiccup, Vegetator, Addbot, SamatBot, Goregore~enwiki, Cote d'Azur, Omnipaedista, Ripchip Bot, EmausBot, WikitanvirBot, Spannerjam, Ekh25, La femme de menage and Anonymous: 30

- **Polysyndeton** *Source:* https://en.wikipedia.org/wiki/Polysyndeton?oldid=660862340 *Contributors:* Michael Hardy, Ellywa, Merriam~enwiki, Altenmann, Jason Quinn, Wmahan, Manuel Anastácio, Andycjp, Beland, Bill Thayer, NetBot, Dpaking, BD2412, Wragge, FlaBot, VolatileChemical, YurikBot, SmackBot, Nbarth, Spiritia, SashatoBot, Ledmonkey, CmdrObot, WillowW, Thijs!bot, Pixor, Albany NY, CapnPrep, Gwern, J.delanoy, Idioma-bot, VolkovBot, Philip Trueman, Andreas Carter, BenoniBot~enwiki, Niceguyedc, Deineka, Addbot, Goregore~enwiki, Awersowy, AnomieBOT, Citation bot, Xqbot, Michael93555, Longliveemomusic, EmausBot, WikitanvirBot, Jara001, Ralphbacchus, ZéroBot, Bugmenot10, Spannerjam, Helpful Pixie Bot, HMSSolent, Faizan, Page264, Ead61, Vieque, Smseium and Anonymous: 40

- **Satire** *Source:* https://en.wikipedia.org/wiki/Satire?oldid=678839361 *Contributors:* The Anome, Koyaanis Qatsi, Malcolm Farmer, Sjc, --April, Ortolan88, SimonP, Ellmist, Heron, Mintguy, R Lowry, Modemac, KF, Stevertigo, Kchishol1970, D, Jahsonic, Liftarn, Ixfd64, Karl Stas, Karada, Delirium, Dori, Mdebets, Александър, Julesd, Glenn, Marteau, Poor Yorick, Jeandré du Toit, Evercat, Astudent, Marknew, Silverfish, Charles Matthews, Wik, Dtgm, Zoicon5, Peregrine981, Tpbradbury, Furrykef, Morwen, Wellington, Mksmith, David.Monniaux, Joyojeet, Bearcat, Gentgeen, Nufy8, Robbot, Dale Arnett, Kizor, Jredmond, RedWolf, Moondyne, Vexes, Altenmann, Chris Roy, Spike, Auric, LGagnon, Leumi, Davodd, Mervyn, Hadal, Resisobilus, Mushroom, Philwiki, Jacoplane, Gtrmp, Cobra libre, ShaneKing, BenFrantzDale, Geeoharee, Fosse8, Sashal, Karn, Everyking, KevinAllen, Beta m, Eequor, Foobar, VampWillow, Matt Crypto, Gadfium, Andycjp, Alexf, Antandrus, Elembis, Rdsmith4, DragonflySixtyseven, Tothebarricades.tk, Bodnotbod, WpZurp, Tomwalden, Jh51681, GreenReaper, Grstain, Jayjg, Righthere, Discospinster, Rich Farmbrough, Leibniz, Peak Freak, Notinasnaid, Bender235, Flapdragon, Kbh3rd, Geoking66, CanisRufus, Kyz, Shanes, RoyBoy, Bookofjude, Bobo192, Infocidal, Evolauxia, Viriditas, Of~enwiki, Man vyi, Kx1186, Krellis, Merenta, Alansohn, Duffman~enwiki, Arthena, Atlant, Philip Cross, Tabor, CheeseDreams, Thesatirist, Bart133, DreamGuy, Mswer, ClockworkSoul, Super-Magician, RainbowOfLight, Moshplant, Axeman89, RyanGerbil10, Abanima, Gmaxwell, OleMaster, Angr, Woohookitty, Garylhewitt, Maprovonsha172, A.K.A.47, Marc K, Gherald, BillC, Kasuga~enwiki, Xyz-321, WadeSimMiser, Jeff3000, Acerperi, Steinbach, Isnow, Wayward, Rilstix, Prashanthns, Bold Italic, Stefanomione, Sin-man, Deltabeignet, Magister Mathematicae, BD2412, RadioActive~enwiki, Rjwilmsi, Vary, Feydey, Darguz Parsilvan, Benzamin, Jdowland, Kazrak, Equinox137, CQJ, Kalogeropoulos, The wub, Ian Dunster, MarnetteD, Jajasoon, Matt Deres, Sango123, SNIyer12, Mikecron, FlaBot, SchuminWeb, Eldamorie, Windchaser, Jeff Fries, Margosbot~enwiki, SouthernNights, Nivix, MosheZadka, RexNL, Maustrauser, Alphachimp, Thiefinni, Moriane, BMF81, Nsteinberg, King of Hearts, Benlisquare, Mhking, Bgwhite, Hall Monitor, Mysekurity, Ben Tibbetts, YurikBot, ThunderPeel2001, Schmancy47, Err0neous, Wild one, Hairy Dude, NTBot~enwiki, Fearwig, Jlittlet, RussBot, Epolk, Sophroniscus, Yllosubmarine, Stephenb, Grubber, Mbellavia, Cryptic, Guiltyspark343, NawlinWiki, Yserarau, 0001, Beno1990, Wiki alf, Welsh, ONEder Boy, Introgressive, Lexicon, Irishguy, PhilipO, PhilipC, Davemck, Ezeu, Lockesdonkey, New Era Outlaw, Bota47, MDubrac, Brisvegas, Philip Arthur, Mugunth Kumar, Newagelink, Tanet, Deville, Theodolite, Gtdp, Teiladnam, ChrisGriswold, Spondoolicks, Fang Aili, KGasso, SMcCandlish, CapitalLetterBeginning, GraemeL, JoanneB, Croat Canuck, Tyrenius, Allens, Larsbars, RG2, Asterion, Jeff Silvers, DVD R W, Dandelions, Jenn xD, Fernandobouregard, SmackBot, PoloShot, Sagie, Moeron, KnowledgeOfSelf, Jimbow25, McGeddon, Jagged 85, Eidako, Verne Equinox, KelleyCook, The Ronin, ZS, Yamaguchi 先生, Gilliam, Ohnoitsjamie, Malatesta, Grey.Label, Durova, Bluebot, Thumperward, MalafayaBot, Roscelese, Neo-Jay, Darth Panda, Gracenotes, GodKirkHimself, Jane of baden, Famspear, Can't sleep, clown will eat me, Themusicinmyhead, Naturezak, Chlewbot, Avb, Jjjsixsix, Todd unt, Jmnbatista, Jlneedham, Cybercobra, Llafeht, EVula, Seattleraptor, Mtmelendez, Chrylis, Brainyiscool, BullRangifer, Andrew c, Fatla00, LeoNomis, Mion, Luke C, Pilotguy, Js2081, OneTopJob6, Formicula, SashatoBot, Lambiam, Visium, 01bemounce, Sophia, Hkrieger, Vanished user 9i39j3, Kuru, Khazar, Ronald11, T g7, Richardbates2002, ShadowPuppet, Jaffer, Tsaetre, IanF, Nolte, This user has left wikipedia, Woer$, Deathbygimppy, IronGargoyle, Ckatz, A. Parrot, MarkSutton, BillFlis, Stwalkerster, CHEWBACAJC, Makyen, SQGibbon, Feureau, Moszczynski, Plattler01, Neddyseagoon, Dhp1080, SmokeyJoe, SewerRanger, -Dense-, Zepheus, Ashwincashwin, Ginkgo100, Levineps, MaggieT, Nehrams2020, Iridescent, RLamb, Joseph Solis in Australia, Shoeofdeath, Beno1000, MottyGlix, Marysunshine, Redtitan, FairuseBot, Tawkerbot2, J Milburn, Wolfdog, CmdrObot, Mattbr, Wafulz, Artiste-extraordinaire, Alex Shih, SupaStarGirl, BeenAroundAWhile, Bernie Wadelheim, Photozone, Timothylord, Leujohn, Neelix, Twilight Elk, Penbat, Gregbard, Flammingo, Sebastian789, Cydebot, Karimarie, MantaRay, POLLUX, ChristTrekker, Gogo Dodo, Bellerophon5685, Travelbird, Red Director, Anthonyhcole, Llort, Islander, Myscrnnm, Clovis Sangrail, Drstrnglv64, Ssilvers, Kozuch, NorthernThunder, Brian.Burnell, TheJC, Mcmillancaleb, Christopherherbert01, Alexanderbest, Thijs!bot, Qwyrxian, Wilson556, Keraunos, Al Lemos, Magnate, Anupam, Marek69, NorwegianBlue, HelenKMarks, Dr Ofaha, CharlotteWebb, Pmacfar, Santaj, Uncle J, Pfranson, NotoriousNick500, Mentifisto, Hmrox, AntiVandalBot, Yuanchosaan, Dancingwaters, Just Chilling, KP Botany, Kbthompson, Prof.Thamm, Jj137, Isilanes, Modernist, Azaghal of Belegost, David

Shankbone, Zidane tribal, Caecilius, Gökhan, Denkefriede, Husond, Tanyushka, Mr Jiggy Fly, Snowolfd4, Repku, Jukke, NintendoFB, Sangak, Magioladitis, Connor Kelley5, Bongwarrior, VoABot II, EOBeav, Hickoryhillster, Eros888, Twsx, KConWiki, Eqdoktor, Andi d, Professor chaos, Frotz, Cpl Syx, DerHexer, Weird Sam Ramone, Warchef, Gphoto, Patstuart, AngelicaZ, Selachophile, Budapest8786, MartinBot, Arjun01, Smilingsuzy, Juansidious, Cholga, Clearlyhidden19, Thisiswill, R'n'B, Kateshortforbob, Wikitiki89, Artawiki, GrWikiMan, J.delanoy, Eusebius12, Brenda maverick, Century0, Taruru, Satire2006, Mahewa, Neonrev, NewEnglandYankee, Egress13, ThinkBlue, MondoJeff, Rumpelstiltskin223, Cornpop~enwiki, Sigmundur, KylieTastic, Lord Jubjub, Mike V, Kvdveer, Dotnetman, Jarry1250, Toddalbers, MonocleSalesman, M. Frederick, Cartiod, Kamalsajja, CardinalDan, Spellcast, Xnuala, Anomie Schmidt, X!, Deor, Penduindylan, Jamminjames, ABF, The800lbgorilla, AdamSommerton, Barneca, Philip Trueman, TXiKiBoT, Sroc, Dcallier, Davehi1, Thejoegriffin, Rei-bot, Soundofmusicals, Finwailin, Morinohtar, Seraphim, Martin451, Leafyplant, Amog, George7777777, Thryth, New Rave?, Cremepuff222, AzureAzul, CO, Madhero88, Mwilso24, Kurowoofwoof111, Greswik, The Vortext, Literarywanderer, Wassamatta, Doushe, Falcon8765, Cnilep, WatermelonPotion, The Devil's Advocate, Lobby Closer, AlleborgoBot, Tumadoireacht, Boat123, EmxBot, D. Recorder, MikeRumex, SieBot, Portalian, Jinf22, Gerakibot, Juru, Dawn Bard, Phaethon 0130, Flyer22, Tiptoety, Phil Bridger, Inferus, Lightmouse, Hobartimus, Akarkera, Behtis, Mygerardromance, Tradereddy, Escape Orbit, Bee Cliff River Slob, Kinkyturnip, Martarius, Sfan00 IMG, ClueBot, SummerWithMorons, Tom H12, Artichoker, PoisonedPigeon, Libraryg, Editsalot, String-bean, Czarkoff, Drmies, AlphaArry, LizardJr8, Singinglemon~enwiki, RAWRMASTER, Tuxedobob, Ashashyou, Pittsburgh Poet, Bendersky, Jusdafax, TRAUMA the Kid, Walkerlax, Dynamiter, Lartoven, Gahks, 0XQ, NoriMori, Redthoreau, Railfence, SchreiberBike, Another Believer, TEHB, Samjammer, Thingg, Lambtron, Ffalotico, Longm8, DumZiBoT, FenwayFrank, XLinkBot, Silent.reprobate, Piratejosh, Stbassett, Nothing2do, Jbeans, Grapito123, Addbot, Xp54321, Proofreader77, Otterathome, C6541, DOI bot, Kazytc, Tcncv, Betterusername, Rustyspell, Mynameispritch, Fieldday-sunday, Zarcadia, CanadianLinuxUser, Fluffernutter, London prophet, Riarox, Cst17, Mentisock, CarsracBot, LAAFan, LinkFA-Bot, Tassedethe, MUDKIPZPLS, Tide rolls, Alan16, Gail, Zorrobot, Legobot, Luckas-bot, Yobot, Tohd8BohaithuGh1, Alertnik, Locusfocus13, AnomieBOT, AaRH, Ehh Mon Ehh, Marauder40, Saginaw-hitchhiker, Piano non troppo, AdjustShift, Ulric1313, Materialscientist, Citation bot, BlurTento, ArthurBot, Clark89, Markworthen, Veryoldandverydead, Xqbot, Melmann, Mibalaev, Gilo1969, J04n, Wiki Initio, Omnipaedista, Cpt tragedy, Vamink, The Interior, Georgeorwell9, Bjs17, Mindry.in, FrescoBot, Emma-emz 15, Tobby72, Recognizance, Inscription, Drew R. Smith, Citation bot 1, AstaBOTh15, Pinethicket, I dream of horses, LittleWink, Lyricallysatirical, Zachary Klaas, Kalmbach, Lineslarge, Quoz, IVAN3MAN, Gerda Arendt, Trappist the monk, BreezyBee719, Sweet xx, Dz4n, Lotje, TrinitasXVII, Vrenator, LilyKitty, Adonovan0, Tbhotch, Keegscee, Whisky drinker, RjwilmsiBot, Beyond My Ken, EmausBot, John of Reading, Orphan Wiki, Gfoley4, DomDozeDoze, Kurr, Dewritech, GoingBatty, Ben10Joshua, Wingdude88, Wikipelli, K6ka, John Cline, CormanoWild, Balrogi, Unreal7, GrindtXX, Zap Rowsdower, May Cause Dizziness, Erianna, Thine Antique Pen, Yatsko, L Kensington, Donner60, Boogaboo2521, Matthewrbowker, Authorharb, Plumitife, Allaboutimages, Arunregi007, ClueBot NG, Gratte-papier, Emilyl86, Snakepit93, Lemuellio, Bennydigital, HazelAB, Theinactivist, Kasirbot, Rezabot, Jessvj, Sirkh1, Widr, JordoCo, Markhickey, Pluma, LucreziaSmith, Helpful Pixie Bot, BrendaFearon, Simpsonguy1987, ProfessorKilroy, Calabe1992, BG19bot, Kirk combe, MusikAnimal, AvocatoBot, AdventurousSquirrel, Joydeep, North911, HMman, Zujua, Neotarf, Shaun, Mehmehmagnus, Fodorized, BattyBot, StarryGrandma, Spainluv112, Cyberbot II, Chie one, ChrisGualtieri, Khazar2, Faberglas, Linkman22, Dexbot, Mr. Guye, Mogism, Cerabot~enwiki, Tehblooguy, Queyh, Sidelight12, York in progress, NoMatterTryAgain, Lgfcd, Naesala21, Ananner, Jodosma, Tentinator, RUSALKA 99, Isaian97, BlueRidiculous, Ginsuloft, Loomspicker, George8211, Kind Tennis Fan, Johnpaulteti, Meowcatzmeow, Carlos Rojas77, Monkbot, CourtCelts1988, Johanhilge, Mhanski, Alfredsamuels25, Halfhat, Allycatjones365, PoliticalSatire, RyanTQuinn, Adg7z, Acarrotonastick, Reindeer9, Squinge, Christofray, Qweerbait Joe, Arielwall, Jtrain98, Fearnow21, GeneralizationsAreBad, KasparBot, Crabbyfour, Professor JR, Lejlaismir and Anonymous: 1175

- **Mental image** *Source:* https://en.wikipedia.org/wiki/Mental_image?oldid=674082644 *Contributors:* Rbrwr, Pnm, Kku, Goethean, Andycjp, Sam Hocevar, Pgreenfinch, Guppyfinsoup, Chris Howard, Perey, Rich Farmbrough, Jaberwocky6669, Bobo192, Mdd, Annexia, Grutness, Logologist, Ringbang, Thruston, Rjwilmsi, Bubba73, Fred Bradstadt, FlaBot, Roboto de Ajvol, YurikBot, Katsuya, Stephenb, Matthew0028, Action potential, Tomisti, Trickstar, That Guy, From That Show!, SmackBot, GregA, Mgreenbe, Chris the speller, Thanissaro, MalafayaBot, Antonrojo, Mion, BrownHairedGirl, Mgiganteus1, DoItAgain, Doczilla, Nbhatla, George100, CmdrObot, Juhachi, Penbat, Gregbard, Scott Coleman, TicketMan, Julian Mendez, Mattisse, Al Lemos, Helgus, Edhubbard, Mentifisto, Scepia, JAnDbot, Skalchemist, VoABot II, MichaelSHoffman, Torchiest, Wikivangelist, B9 hummingbird hovering, Shapeev, Nothingdefinesme, CommonsDelinker, Tgeairn, MrBell, Master shepherd, Imiranda9, Glenyshanson, Petrus hispanus, Andrewaskew, Synthebot, StAnselm, Brenont, Phe-bot, Flyer22, Pylyshyn, Panslabrinth, TheConstantGardner, SummerWithMorons, Treharne, DanielDeibler, Jumbolino, MATRIX, Qwfp, Tegiap, Addbot, Nate Wessel, Jarble, Yobot, Tempodivalse, AnomieBOT, SunekaeGod, EryZ, Materialscientist, Citation bot, Xqbot, Fichter, The Evil IP address, GrouchoBot, Doctor Dodge, Edmond Wright, Paine Ellsworth, RandomDSdevel, Baboshed, Msasscts, Lotje, Vrenator, Diannaa, DARTH SIDIOUS 2, Kookaburra17, RjwilmsiBot, John of Reading, ChuispastonBot, ClueBot NG, TwoTwoHello, OcelotHod, Guevera2013, Brainiacal, Xifoid and Anonymous: 66

- **Understatement** *Source:* https://en.wikipedia.org/wiki/Understatement?oldid=665865120 *Contributors:* William Avery, Patrick, IZAK, Error, Robbot, Chealer, JackofOz, Wereon, Orpheus, Atemperman, Poccil, Rich Farmbrough, Dbachmann, Szyslak, RoyBoy, Jjron, Captain Seafort, Omphaloscope, Zawersh, Drbreznjev, Novacatz, Queerudite, Stefanomione, Betsythedevine, Marudubshinki, Graham87, Riki, TeaDrinker, YurikBot, Koveras, RussBot, Closedmouth, Tssha, SmackBot, Jrockley, Pedrose, UK-Logician-2006, Pwjb, Captainbeefart, Tlesher, Iridescent, Wolfdog, Mattbr, Penbat, Dmtipper, StringRay, Jj137, Narssarssuaq, ExplicitImplicity, Maurice Carbonaro, Chiswick Chap, VolkovBot, Philip Trueman, Andrewaskew, Insanity Incarnate, 2Rocks, Flyer22, CutOffTies, Oxymoron83, Galacticmule, Djadvance, ClueBot, Wikievil666, Arunsingh16, Jimbomonkey, Read20red, Rhododendrites, Luau dude, DumZiBoT, WikHead, Alansplodge, Addbot, Luckas-bot, Scy1192, AnomieBOT, IRP, Zangar, Erik9bot, Aldy, RjwilmsiBot, Wikipelli, Ccalliafas, ClueBot NG, Helpful Pixie Bot, Ramaksoud2000, Zvd and Anonymous: 74

- **Irony** *Source:* https://en.wikipedia.org/wiki/Irony?oldid=678756665 *Contributors:* Eloquence, Bryan Derksen, The Anome, Grouse, Rmhermen, SimonP, Heron, Mintguy, Montrealais, R Lowry, Rbrwr, DennisDaniels, Frecklefoot, Bdesham, Patrick, Nixdorf, GUllman, Liftarn, MartinHarper, Collabi, Ixfd64, GTBacchus, Paul A, Tregoweth, Egil, Mkweise, Ellywa, Ahoerstemeier, TUF-KAT, TUF-KAT, Kingturtle, Darkwind, Glenn, Bogdangiusca, AugPi, Poor Yorick, Vzbs34, Scott, Kaihsu, Evercat, Atob, Conti, Timwi, Kbk, AudioPervert, Will, Hao2lian, Haukurth, Markhurd, Pedant17, Tpbradbury, RayKiddy, Populus, Dpbsmith, Wetman, Ldo, Sewing, Jni, Robbot, Chealer, Kizor, Chris 73, RedWolf, Donreed, Chocolateboy, Kowey, Nurg, Merovingian, Pingveno, Geogre, Dodger~enwiki, Hadal, Wereon, Benc, Mushroom, Ruakh, Anthony, TexasDex, Cyrius, Wayland, Pablo-flores, Dave6, Matthew Stannard, Gwalla, Christopher Parham, Xeresblue, Philwelch, Nadavspi, Seabhcan, Kenny sh, Tom harrison, Meursault2004, Angmering, Ausir, Risk one, Bradeos Graphon, Everyking, Lefty, Anville, Dratman, Henry

Flower, Frencheigh, Luigi30, Khalid hassani, Dainamo, Edcolins, Alexf, Jonel, Quadell, Ran, Antandrus, Beland, Mitaphane, Cornischong, Lucky13pjn, Vasile, Sam Hocevar, Histrion, TonyW, Slidewinder, Joyous!, Neale Monks, Ukexpat, Alperen, M1ss1ontomars2k4, Trevor MacInnis, Lacrimosus, Jayjg, Spiffy sperry, Discospinster, Neep, Adam850, Triskaideka, CODOR, Alistair1978, Dbachmann, GregoryWeir, Bumhoolery, Goochelaar, Neko-chan, PhilHibbs, Wesman83, Sietse Snel, RoyBoy, Plantperson, Bdoserror, Mqduck, Adambro, Bobo192, Circeus, Smalljim, Herzliyya, Teorth, Foobaz, Redquark, Daniel FR, Mr2001, Yonkie, SpeedyGonsales, La goutte de pluie, Pschemp, DCEdwards1966, MPerel, Haham hanuka, Nsaa, Kentin, Wendell, Alansohn, Gary, Eleland, PatrickFisher, Riana, Wikidea, Mac Davis, Phocks, Malo, Metron4, Snowolf, Bucephalus, ElJayDee, Dalillama, Evil Monkey, RainbowOfLight, Sciurinæ, TheAznSensation, Reaverdrop, Axeman89, Red dwarf, Smedley Hirkum, Kenyon, Hq3473, OleMaster, Kelly Martin, Woohookitty, LizardWizard, Gccwang, TigerShark, Camw, LOL, Localh77, StradivariusTV, Bkkbrad, BillC, Unixer, Sysys, MGTom, JeremyA, MONGO, Dzordzm, Male1979, MechBrowman, Christianjb, Stefanomione, Pfalstad, Gallaghp, Dysepsion, Mandarax, G.hartig, MassGalactusUniversum, Ashmoo, Graham87, Deltabeignet, OGRastamon, FreplySpang, Sjö, Rjwilmsi, Markkawika, Zbxgscqf, Jivecat, Voretus, ElKevbo, Jehochman, Bensin, The wub, DoubleBlue, Matt Deres, AySz88, Yamamoto Ichiro, Nam, Baryonic Being, FlaBot, Spencerian, ACodispo, Crazycomputers, Nivix, Chanting Fox, Celestianpower, Ewlyahoocom, Gurch, Quuxplusone, KFP, Semi-awesome, Akhenaten0, BMF81, Theshibboleth, Introvert, Psantora, Michaelritchie200, Benlisquare, DVdm, Citizen Premier, Igordebraga, VolatileChemical, Mysekurity, Gwernol, EamonnPKeane, YurikBot, JoeMystical, Sceptre, Blightsoot, Hairy Dude, Jimp, Flameviper, Boldymumbles, JarrahTree, Logixoul, RussBot, Muchness, Bhny, RJC, Rubber cat, Hgranqvist, Lar, Grubber, Gaius Cornelius, Dns3, Alex Bakharev, Rsrikanth05, Wimt, GeeJo, NawlinWiki, Astral, Dialectric, Clashfrankcastle, Petter Strandmark, Jaxl, Shaun F, Mosquitopsu, JeremyStein, Davemck, Derekg18, Uzairhaq, JGorton, Bmuzal, Alex43223, Bozoid, Syrthiss, Dbfirs, Leotohill, Mrpex, Zephalis, DeadEyeArrow, Superiority, Avraham, FF2010, Scheinwerfermann, Deville, Theda, Closedmouth, Skenmy, Great Cthulhu, Th1rt3en, SMcCandlish, JQF, GriffJon, Ion seal, Digfarenough, CWenger, Smileyface11945, Kevin, HereToHelp, Katieh5584, Teryx, Paul Erik, GrinBot~enwiki, CeeKay, Jeff Silvers, DVD R W, Twilight Realm, Crystallina, JoshuaGarton, Yakudza, SmackBot, NickyMcLean, Twdldee, Felicity4711, Cubs Fan, SSJeskimobob, Lestrade, Slashme, Prodego, InverseHypercube, KnowledgeOfSelf, Hydrogen Iodide, McGeddon, Gnangarra, Pgk, Thorseth, Jagged 85, Gold333, Doc Strange, Nero Kalem, BiT, Not a slave, Jpvinall, Kuzmatt9, Ema Zee, Gilliam, Ohnoitsjamie, Doktor Wilhelm, Skizzik, Rmosler2100, Durova, BenAveling, Jeffro77, Chris the speller, Bluebot, KaragouniS, Davepealing, Jsn4, Jprg1966, Thumperward, Upled, Marbehraglaim, SchfiftyThree, Kaid100, TheFeds, Kungming2, Baa, Sbharris, Colonies Chris, KingAlanI, Rlevse, Yanksox, Scwlong, WDGraham, Schwallex, Can't sleep, clown will eat me, Frap, Onorem, Cabanaguy, Rrburke, BeefJerkyMonster, Addshore, Mr.Z-man, Phaedriel, YankeeDoodle14, Radagast83, BesselDekker, Mystic eye, Nakon, Detruncate, S Roper, PokeTIJeremy, Gregh, Lessthanthree, Drc79, KeithB, N Shar, Sigma 7, Nelamm, Aviron, Kukini, BryanEkers, SashatoBot, Lambiam, Missamo80, BrownHairedGirl, Voytek s, JzG, FreemDeem, Mr415, Potosino, Lapaz, Edwy, Smartyllama, Nichenbach, Arbustoo, SpyMagician, Ckatz, ThePHPSolution.com, A. Parrot, Across.The.Synapse, Hvn0413, Stwalkerster, Interpretivechaos, Ehheh, GilbertoSilvaFan, Stainedglasscurtain, Doczilla, Funnybunny, MTSbot~enwiki, JakeApple, NinjaCharlie, Rory O'Kane, Ginkgo100, Maddog281, Fan-1967, Iridescent, Dekaels~enwiki, Blackmage337, CzarB, Aeternus, Twas Now, Dclayh, Courcelles, Ziusudra, Pjbflynn, Tawkerbot2, George100, Chandra friend, SkyWalker, Vincent31, Cyrusc, JForget, Simba Jones, Hondo1, Wolfdog, CmdrObot, KyraVixen, Neoyamaneko, DeLarge, Cleanr, El aprendelenguas, CKozeluh, Neelix, Penbat, Oden, Equester, Fletcher, AdaronKentano, Funnyfarmofdoom, Muzer, Cydebot, Tendancer, NealIRC, Goonies~enwiki, Crossmr, Gogo Dodo, Corpx, 8bitKronik, ST47, Caparn, Odie5533, Thaddius, UberMan5000, Quibik, Shirulashem, Christian75, Paddles, Pi3832, Nabokov, Lnkprkmusiq92, Ssilvers, Deleriamour, In Defense of the Artist, Ryanbomber, Viridae, NorthernThunder, Archnoble, Andmatt, Omicronpersei8, Identiti crisis, Epbr123, Qwyrxian, N5iln, Chickenflicker, Marek69, Vertium, Tronk, NorwegianBlue, TheTruthiness, Delaluzm, James086, Editorinchimp, Strausszek, Aericanwizard, Miller17CU94, Dfrg.msc, The Fat Man Who Never Came Back, Nick Number, Jcrabb, Doremítzwr, Hmrox, Porqin, Vafthrudnir, AntiVandalBot, Seaphoto, Crabula, AnemoneProjectors, StringRay, AlexTrusk, F McGady, IrishPete, Zappernapper, Cinefusion, LibLord, Danger, Danny lost, Darklilac, Arifex~enwiki, AubreyEllenShomo, Spinningobo, Ophias, Klow, Gökhan, Dreaded Walrus, Ioeth, Serpent's Choice, JAnDbot, Skibum8713, Leuko, Husond, Barek, MER-C, Jonemerson, Midnightdreary, Albany NY, Megafat, Copy Editor, PhilKnight, Doctorhawkes, GoodDamon, Acroterion, Swordmistress, Daydreams21, Sgb235, Zz414, Canjth, Bongwarrior, VoABot II, JNW, JamesBWatson, Madame Choucroute, Khalidkhoso, Think outside the box, CTF83!, Mtiffany71, Asdfg12345, Blackdiamondbay, Twsx, Nevlow, Bubba hotep, KConWiki, Lucinde, Hveziris, Anarcho-capitalism, DerHexer, Bradle, Eastmbr, Smartings, David3001, B. Wolterding, Seba5618, HumanProdigy, 0612, Mrspotter444, Nathanmcginty, Oren0, Gmckenney, Hdt83, MartinBot, HeeroYuiX, Rettetast, Roastytoast, Juansidious, Anaxial, Sneedy, Sleepyjuly, Tbisciglia, AlexiusHoratius, Koobaxion, IceD, Naughty Bob, Tgeairn, Paranomia, J.delanoy, Jamespeterka, Pharaoh of the Wizards, Trusilver, Critical Reader, Bogey97, Ayecee, ChaosSwordsman, Jonpro, Sirtrebuchet, Cocoaguy, Shotime900, Acalamari, Littlebum2002, Billydeeuk, It Is Me Here, Antelope19, McSly, D Marcescu, Trumpet marietta 45750, OAC, IngSoc BigBrother, Gurchzilla, Coppertwig, HiLo48, Daward2, NewEnglandYankee, Ainshi, Tiggerjay, Postofficebox, U.S.A.U.S.A.U.S.A., Bass hound, Ziqidel, Treisijs, Ajfweb, Dorftrottel, Tkgd2007, Richard New Forest, Montchav, Elliot.wolk, Sam Blacketer, Deor, Blankornot, Xanucia, Andyroo g, ABF, Shahid1618, Meaningful Username, DSRH, Enders shadow89, The Duke of Waltham, Ndsg, Jeff G., Jesrapo, Kakoui, CalviNet, Ryan032, Dougie monty, Philip Trueman, Sweetness46, TXiKiBoT, Jyuujin, Mike12489, Shaun22, Uagehry456, Ssri1983, Soundofmusicals, Easel3, Aletheus, Lethal humour, Qxz, Anna Lincoln, Melsaran, Martin451, KatinaW, AndrewJD, Mcclarke, Iggie666, Morgino, Cremepuff222, Marcwiki9, Rumiton, Roadclosed82, CO, Jesin, Butterscotch, Larklight, Dick Kimball, Petero9, Redwalltungro, Clintville, Df747jet, Ryguy1994, Rabid weasels, Falcon8765, Enviroboy, Seresin, ManfrenjenStJohn, HiDrNick, 229guy, AnotherAdjectivePhil, DrewSears, OrangeAipom, AtreemFromVenus, EmxBot, Sgt9004, SMC89, SieBot, TJRC, Brenont, Tresiden, Dreamafter, Scarian, SheepNotGoats, Lemonflash, Dawn Bard, Ezsaias, Keilana, Earl273A, Tiptoety, Radon210, Exert, The Evil Spartan, MinorContributor, Captain Yankee, Le Pied-bot~enwiki, Oxymoron83, Steven Crossin, Crisis, Techman224, Hobartimus, Taskspanic~enwiki, Eouw0o83hf, StaticGull, Mrobfire, Shadowfirebird, Momma1998, Fishnet37222, Wrudebusch, Wahrmund, Denisarona, Escape Orbit, Araveugnitsuga, Rocktheboat111111111, SoLowRockerMan, LucyPinder001, Supermelon928, Myrvin, Atif.t2, Sfan00 IMG, Beeblebrox, Beauty Bird, Elassint, ClueBot, Yamanbaiia, NickCT, Avenged Eightfold, GorillaWarfare, Artichoker, WikiSkeptic, TransporterMan, Fyyer, The Thing That Should Not Be, ArdClose, Rodhullandemu, Keeper76, IceUnshattered, Arkalochori, Chess123mate, Gaia Octavia Agrippa, Mike Klaassen, Rmbjspd, Meekywiki, Shinpah1, Regibox, Xavexgoem, CounterVandalismBot, Slade Barker, DaronDierkes, WikiWrecker, LizardJr8, TheMerricat, Dylan620, JuliaVeitch, Somno, SteveRamone, Excirial, Encyclopedia77, Three-quarter-ten, Erebus Morgaine, Jnate19, PixelBot, John Nevard, Tim0they, Bum cheese pooped ur nose, Neil.dewhurst, NuclearWarfare, Peter.C, Blondeychck7, Xianbataar, 7&6=thirteen, Computer97, Razorflame, Three Dollar Bill, Digimatt20, ChrisHodgesUK, Ankithreya, La Pianista, Matthew Desjardins, Unclemikejb, Dhadams, Agebert, Thingg, Srooke, Aitias, Samurai Cerberus, Ehyeh-Asher-Ehyeh, Versus22, Burner0718, SoxBot III, Wannabe99, Wikidas, Party, DumZiBoT, Like A Rainbow, KingsOfHearts, Skunkboy74, XLinkBot, Neologian, DACS42~enwiki, Toldwrote90, Steven787, Ajcheema, Dr sign, WikHead, Doc9871, Looka-

ture, NewEnglandYankee, Creepzerg3, Alnokta, Tanaats, Cmichael, Entropy, Cometstyles, Geopoet, Lhsonic, Treisijs, Bamsefar75, Pdcook, Useight, CardinalDan, Funandtrvl, Wikieditor06, Kirby1103, VolkovBot, CWii, ABF, Macedonian, MemeGeneScene, Jeff G., Indubitably, DOAer, Spontaneous generation, Soliloquial, Wolfnix, Philip Trueman, TXiKiBoT, Oshwah, Jomasecu, Wasabiroot, Antoni Barau, Wherenow, Aymatth2, Qxz, Sintaku, Ontoraul, Abdullais4u, Bored461, Raymondwinn, Cremepuff222, Cuddlyable3, Wikiisawesome, Majav15, Katimawan2005, Madhero88, Eubulides, Doug, Todwyer, Cooley5758, Lova Falk, Enviroboy, Zuchinni one, Spinningspark, Why Not A Duck, Brianga, Monty845, HiDrNick, Michelleem, Nagy, Symane, Logan, Jehorn, H92, Red, Thohstadt, Bsumpn, SieBot, NATO.Caliber, Dusti, K. Annoyomous, Skipnicholson, Dreamafter, Scarian, Ori, Dimwight, Tbo 157, YourEyesOnly, Jimbobaii, Matthew Yeager, RJaguar3, Vickaul, Keilana, Breawycker, Toddst1, Flyer22, Radon210, Xingzeng, TheThingy, Aruton, Oxymoron83, MattiG69, Techman224, Spartan-James, StaticGull, Anchor Link Bot, Nn123645, Wahrmund, Pinkadelica, TubularWorld, Escape Orbit, LarRan, Matreiya, XDanielx, WikipedianMarlith, Twinsday, Elassint, ClueBot, Zeke8888, GorillaWarfare, The Thing That Should Not Be, TychaBrahe, Supertouch, Mike Klaassen, Mjaballah, Gregcaletta, WDavis1911, Shinpah1, Boing! said Zebedee, Niceguyedc, EconomicsGuy, Comkid20, Neverquick, Seramai, Davidovic, Halo3 man, Aua, Excirial, Canis Lupus, Jusdafax, Erebus Morgaine, PixelBot, Eeekster, Clive Cazeaux, Khorne85, Vivio Testarossa, Ykhwong, Arjayay, 7&6=thirteen, Tnxman307, Morel, Razorflame, Vani chan, Dekisugi, SchreiberBike, O.Duke, Your grey blue eyes, Thingg, Aitias, Versus22, Peacearena, SoxBot III, Riversider2008, Ban Bridges, Vanished user 01, BendersGame, Against the current, XLinkBot, Pichpich, Gotxcho, PseudoOne, Stickee, Jovianeye, Rror, AMRDeuce, Ruiner73, Little Mountain 5, Avoided, Anturiaethwr, Lockal, Dr sign, WikHead, Lincolnoct, Mifter, Noctibus, Subversive.sound, WikiDao, Skata*d, Ryan-McCulloch, Addbot, Cxz111, Lordoliver, Frozen architecture, Some jerk on the Internet, KCFS00, Guoguo12, Tcncv, Captain-tucker, Binary TSO, Haruth, Damatt, DougsTech, Ronhjones, Willy brown, Mr. Wheely Guy, CanadianLinuxUser, Fluffernutter, Cst17, MrOllie, Download, Proxima Centauri, BepBot, Jolygolywog, Chzz, Debresser, Doniago, West.andrew.g, Vysotsky, Ks 7508, Tide rolls, Bfigura's puppy, Nguyễn Thanh Quang, Vrrad, Gail, Luispepe, Bartledan, Legobot, Zaynabasdfghjklpoiuybnm, 14tjoyce, Yobot, Tohd8BohaithuGh1, Ojay123, QueenCake, KamikazeBot, Dzied Bulbash, Swister-Twister, Buffalo Robert, South Bay, Sicaruma, Synchronism, AnomieBOT, DemocraticLuntz, Idle Tears, IRP, Galoubet, Tigerclaw221, Piano non troppo, Kingpin13, Yellow Evan, Bluerasberry, Giants27, Materialscientist, Amacleod03, E2eamon, Carlsotr, Maxis ftw, Nifky?, Usuallylucid, Sionus, Cureden, Beeeee7, Merla25, TATOLPREP, Lozy91, Wailmer1997, ZuilSerip, GrouchoBot, Abce2, Kgncombavato, GorgeCustersSabre, RibotBOT, SassoBot, Mathonius, Notnd, IamAfakeAndrewsBot, Doulos Christos, Acwild, Twiggy17, Shadowjams, Erik9, SD5, Dougofborg, FrescoBot, Altg20April2nd, Ghost9998, Psychlohexane, Alaphent, Kentastic2, Wzf09iwzd, Alxeedo, Dottydotdot, Haeinous, HJ Mitchell, Lilydjwg, Tb149208, Finalius, Bgbblg, DivineAlpha, Javert, Dshfwerkj, Winterst, Pinethicket, ShadowRangerRIT, I dream of horses, Elockid, Chris09j, Calmer Waters, Rushbugled13, Kyledaniels, Mutinus, 09191863GbA, Lars Washington, Bikebikebike72, Yutsi, Jandalhandler, Dude1818, December21st2012Freak, Robvanvee, FoxBot, CityGator, Dark Lord of the Sith, ItsZippy, Lotje, Vrenator, Horrorjuice, Defender of torch, 070time070, Jhenderson777, Dchau503, Bobby122, Jessicamarie1995, MegaSloth, Keegscee, DARTH SIDIOUS 2, 2bluey, OGKingMonkey, Buddy89, Theteloch, Gfeldman999, Beav4life, Enauspeaker, DASHBot, EmausBot, Acather96, WikitanvirBot, Immunize, Jtalise, ExistentialBliss, Racerx11, Britannic124, Razor2988, RA0808, Marish Glides, Pottypat, Slightsmile, Tommy2010, Wikipelli, K6ka, Pseudosection, Kvardek du, Erpert, Mz7, Fæ, Josve05a, Bollyjeff, Érico Júnior Wouters, Antedater, Kiwi128, Azuris, A930913, Git2010, Harperrrrr, Confession0791, Wayne Slam, Tolly4bolly, Zimmermanstein, L Kensington, Donner60, Puffin, Orange Suede Sofa, Matthewrbowker, Herk1955, Sonicyouth86, Petrb, ClueBot NG, Gareth Griffith-Jones, Jack Greenmaven, Joclown, This lousy T-shirt, Qarakesek, SusikMkr, Guyucguy, Sevenone71, Louthecat, Jrathy, Marechal Ney, Edzabomb, Widr, Spannerjam, Gleek13, Helpful Pixie Bot, Mnmx, HMSSolent, BG19bot, Island Monkey, ISTB351, Brustopher, Ciaramcglacken, MusikAnimal, Davidiad, AwamerT, Kalkaii, Dipankan001, Reporter shrimpy, Rhae Ray, Terrencereilly, Snow Blizzard, MrBill3, Insidiae, Glacialfox, Minsbot, Knowledge Permeating Your Cranium, Staglit, BattyBot, W.D., Cyberbot II, KobinMacroy, ChrisGualtieri, 1234567890-=qwertyuiop, Tylerthebuilder, Dbzlabrat, Codename Lisa, Webclient101, TwoTwoHello, Lugia2453, Lavoulte, Dr. Tim Farcopolous, Whitechocolate, 93, Andyhowlett, 069952497a, Cadillac000, Reatlas, Gwooodward, Zjrong, Soccergirly108, Bettyboop330, Vanamonde93, Lsmll, Ggdoc, Benss1111, Shadowblade468, ChaseAm, Babitaarora, Haminoon, Aubreybardo, Kind Tennis Fan, Meteor sandwich yum, JaconaFrere, Skr15081997, Maddconn, Evangruiz, Heraclites, Monkbot, Ddogger, Rmani1234, Bobbytilton, VeeSimmonds, Drewtoofin, Himanshu Kunwar, A random person234, Tee Antone, Rk2k5, Evilkid101, Social Theory, Ryan0224, Jackamac1996, Jdhdvdhx, Magicpotato1234, Yohoona, Fthtsvxgdgd, KasparBot and Anonymous: 1820

- **Anthropomorphism** *Source:* https://en.wikipedia.org/wiki/Anthropomorphism?oldid=677719325 *Contributors:* Derek Ross, Wesley, Bryan Derksen, Sjc, Ed Poor, Aldie, Cayzle, KF, Rbrwr, Patrick, Infrogmation, Michael Hardy, BoNoMoJo (old), MartinHarper, Zanimum, Nine Tail Fox, Baylink, Angela, Kingturtle, DropDeadGorgias, Glenn, Jacquerie27, Kaysov, Conti, JASpencer, Charles Matthews, Timwi, WhisperToMe, Furrykef, Gutsul, Pakaran, Firebird, Jni, PuzzletChung, Robbot, Fredrik, Naddy, Chris Roy, Ashley Y, Henrygb, Clngre, Litefantastic, Premeditated Chaos, Kamakura, Wikibot, TexasDex, Fabiform, Decumanus, Smjg, DocWatson42, Pretzelpaws, Everyking, Gus Polly, Pashute, Daibhid C, Gilgamesh~enwiki, Sundar, Mboverload, Taak, Critto~enwiki, Dainamo, Tagishsimon, Tipiac, Lenehey, Chowbok, Andycjp, Abu badali, Fangz, OverlordQ, Thray, Jossi, Bodnotbod, Zfr, Gary D, Joyous!, Ukexpat, Didactohedron, GreenReaper, Pasd, Lord Bodak, Heegoop, SoM, Rich Farmbrough, Florian Blaschke, Bender235, ESkog, Yamavu, Neko-chan, Violetriga, Brian0918, Kwamikagami, Tgeller, Bobo192, Deathawk, AmosWolfe, Johnkarp, BalooUrsidae, Nicke Lilltroll~enwiki, Basilwhite, Jonathunder, Ekevu, Mdd, Mareino, Jason One, Raj2004, Alansohn, Jeltz, AzaToth, SlimVirgin, Mac Davis, Pwqn, Alai, Ekedolphin, Asuma, Angr, Firsfron, DrMel, Mel Etitis, Woohookitty, Mondhir~enwiki, Trödel, Anthony Dean, Stefanomione, DL5MDA, RuM, Mandarax, Dpaking, Idraeus, Graham87, BD2412, Jcmo, Search4Lancer, Xydexx, Ketiltrout, Sjö, Rjwilmsi, Syndicate, NatusRoma, Jweiss11, Amire80, Lendorien, Fire King, Husky, FlaBot, Hiding, Vanished user sfoi943923kjd94, Valentinian, ManuBhardwaj, VolatileChemical, Kummi, YurikBot, TheTrueSora, Torinir, Zafiroblue05, Pigman, Epolk, RadioFan2 (usurped), Wimt, Artful Dodger, NawlinWiki, Msikma, Journalist, Anetode, RayMetz100, GHcool, Leontes, DeadEyeArrow, Aristotle2600, Gentaur, Igiffin, BooooooooB, Langdell~enwiki, Th1rt3en, Plankhead, Black Kat, LeonardoRob0t, Fram, Curpsbot-unicodify, Cassandraleo, Nimbex, Sugar Bear, GrinBot~enwiki, Miilousuede, Finell, Brentt, Edward Waverley, Sarah, Jbalint, SmackBot, FocalPoint, 1dragon, K1234567890y, C.Fred, Vald, Delldot, Darklock, Proctris, Portillo, Hmains, The Famous Movie Director, BenAveling, Parrothead1983, Chris the speller, Bluebot, Cush, SonicHOG, Slimline, Trebor, Crashmatrix, Miles the Fox, Apeloverage, Victorgrigas, Boris Crépeau, Sadads, Veggies, Kotra, Can't sleep, clown will eat me, Eliezg, Tamfang, Rrburke, Cernen, MrRadioGuy, Underbar dk, Chaos386, Cubbi, Richard001, Weregerbil, Only, Alamagoosa, Tfl, Ohconfucius, Rdavout, Mukadderat, Rory096, Dak, Wavy G, SilkTork, Coyoty, Jaywubba1887, The Man in Question, Filanca, George The Dragon, Ryulong, Cbuckley, Pabobfin, Aefields, Jc37, Olivierd, J Di, MGlosenger, Lenoxus, Octane, Hikui87~enwiki, Anger22, Nydas, Cberman, Wile e2005, Wolfdog, Markhu, ShelfSkewed, MeekMark, Haridan, (chubbstar), Nauticashades, FilipeS, Cydebot, Atticmouse, Lizafreak, ST47, Desmond Hobson, Benjiboi, Amandajm, George dodds, Christian75, Flind, Ameliorate!, Smeazel, Epbr123, Kotengu, Luigifan, Missvain, NorwegianBlue, Astrobiologist, Alientraveller, Siawase, NigelR, Nick Number, TylerRick, Mentifisto, EdJogg, Mr Bungle, Luna Santin, Eruption257, Alexthurleyrat-

58.7.2 Images

58.7.3   Content license

Made in the USA
San Bernardino, CA
16 March 2017